Communications
in Computer and Information Science 1924

Rationale

The CCIS series is devoted to the publication of proceedings of computer science conferences. Its aim is to efficiently disseminate original research results in informatics in printed and electronic form. While the focus is on publication of peer-reviewed full papers presenting mature work, inclusion of reviewed short papers reporting on work in progress is welcome, too. Besides globally relevant meetings with internationally representative program committees guaranteeing a strict peer-reviewing and paper selection process, conferences run by societies or of high regional or national relevance are also considered for publication.

Topics

The topical scope of CCIS spans the entire spectrum of informatics ranging from foundational topics in the theory of computing to information and communications science and technology and a broad variety of interdisciplinary application fields.

Information for Volume Editors and Authors

Publication in CCIS is free of charge. No royalties are paid, however, we offer registered conference participants temporary free access to the online version of the conference proceedings on SpringerLink (http://link.springer.com) by means of an http referrer from the conference website and/or a number of complimentary printed copies, as specified in the official acceptance email of the event.

CCIS proceedings can be published in time for distribution at conferences or as post-proceedings, and delivered in the form of printed books and/or electronically as USBs and/or e-content licenses for accessing proceedings at SpringerLink. Furthermore, CCIS proceedings are included in the CCIS electronic book series hosted in the SpringerLink digital library at http://link.springer.com/bookseries/7899. Conferences publishing in CCIS are allowed to use Online Conference Service (OCS) for managing the whole proceedings lifecycle (from submission and reviewing to preparing for publication) free of charge.

Publication process

The language of publication is exclusively English. Authors publishing in CCIS have to sign the Springer CCIS copyright transfer form, however, they are free to use their material published in CCIS for substantially changed, more elaborate subsequent publications elsewhere. For the preparation of the camera-ready papers/files, authors have to strictly adhere to the Springer CCIS Authors' Instructions and are strongly encouraged to use the CCIS LaTeX style files or templates.

Abstracting/Indexing

CCIS is abstracted/indexed in DBLP, Google Scholar, EI-Compendex, Mathematical Reviews, SCImago, Scopus. CCIS volumes are also submitted for the inclusion in ISI Proceedings.

How to start

To start the evaluation of your proposal for inclusion in the CCIS series, please send an e-mail to ccis@springer.com.

Marta Tabares · Paola Vallejo · Biviana Suarez ·
Marco Suarez · Oscar Ruiz · Jose Aguilar
Editors

Advances in Computing

17th Colombian Conference on Computing, CCC 2023
Medellin, Colombia, August 10–11, 2023
Revised Selected Papers

 Springer

Editors
Marta Tabares 🆔
Universidad EAFIT
Medellín, Colombia

Paola Vallejo 🆔
Universidad EAFIT
Medellín, Colombia

Biviana Suarez 🆔
Universidad EAFIT
Medellín, Colombia

Marco Suarez 🆔
Pedagogical and Technological University
Tunja, Colombia

Oscar Ruiz 🆔
Universidad EAFIT
Medellín, Colombia

Jose Aguilar 🆔
Universidad EAFIT
Medellín, Colombia

ISSN 1865-0929   ISSN 1865-0937 (electronic)
Communications in Computer and Information Science
ISBN 978-3-031-47371-5   ISBN 978-3-031-47372-2 (eBook)
https://doi.org/10.1007/978-3-031-47372-2

This Springer imprint is published by the registered company Springer Nature Switzerland AG
The registered company address is: Gewerbestrasse 11, 6330 Cham, Switzerland

Paper in this product is recyclable.

Preface

Industry 4.0 covers different concepts; one with greater emphasis is the concept of "cyber-physical systems," which makes intelligent automation take on a new meaning in different industry types. At the same time, Digital Transformation is onboarding emerging technologies to transform businesses related to the Internet of Things and digital businesses. This new revolution is becoming the transversal axis of many industrial sectors, fields of knowledge, and technological trends. That is how the agricultural sector can understand its world from cyber-physical systems, artificial intelligence, and sensor data. Besides, it impacts academia and research to face significant challenges and generate solutions that allow access to new knowledge for different types of businesses, industries, and governments.

The 17th edition of the Colombian Congress of Computing (17CCC) was organized by the Universidad EAFIT and took place in Medellín, Colombia at August 10-11, 2023. The event belongs to the Colombian Society of Computing which provided an academics platform for exchanging ideas, techniques, methodologies, and tools. It fostered collaboration among researchers, professionals, students, and companies within the Congress's areas of interest, promoting synergy and knowledge sharing. The conference combined in-person attendance with virtual article presentation, allowing participants to actively engage in paper discussions, attend keynote lectures, and participate in various workshops and poster sessions. This book compiles a diverse selection of papers presented at the conference, covering a wide range of topics within the field of computer science. These topics include Industrial Applications - Industry 4.0 - Precision Agriculture, Artificial Intelligence, Distributed Systems and Large-Scale Computing, Computational Statistics, Digital Learning - E-learning, Software Engineering, Human Machine Interaction, Image Processing and Computer Vision, Robotics in Industry 4.0, and Scientific Applications, among others. The contributions in this book offer valuable insights into the most recent research and advancements in computer science. These findings will undoubtedly pique the interest of researchers, students, and professionals alike. The 17th Colombian Congress of Computing received 68 submissions in response to its call for papers. From this pool of submissions, 22 full papers and 11 short papers have been selected for inclusion in this book. The selection process was conducted by at least three national and international reviewers, guaranteeing the quality of the selected papers. The type of peer review used was double blind.

We thank the members of our Program Committee for their work and contribution to the conference's success. We also thank the authors for their submissions, the organizers, the collaborators, and Springer, our partner over the past years, for facilitating the compilation and publication of the best papers for this book.

September 2023

Marta Tabares
Paola Vallejo
Biviana Suarez
Marco Suarez
Oscar Ruiz
Jose Aguilar

Organization

General Chair

Marta Silvia Tabares-Betancur   Universidad EAFIT, Colombia

Program Committee Chairs

Paola Andrea Vallejo Correa   Universidad EAFIT, Colombia
Biviana Marcela Suarez Sierra   Universidad EAFIT, Colombia
Marco Javier Suarez   Universidad Pedagógica y Tecnológica de
                                Colombia, Colombia
Oscar Ruiz-Salguero   Universidad EAFIT, Colombia
Jose Lisandro Aguilar Castro   Universidad EAFIT, Colombia

Program Committee

Juan David Martinez   Universidad EAFIT, Colombia
Juan Carlos Rivera-Agudelo   Universidad EAFIT, Colombia
Jairo Serrano   Universidad Tecnológica de Bolívar, Colombia
Julián Moreno   Universidad Nacional de Colombia, Colombia
Johany Armando Carreño Gamboa   Católica del Norte Fundación Universitaria,
                                Colombia
Daniel Correa   Universidad EAFIT, Colombia
John William Branch   Universidad Nacional de Colombia, Colombia
Edison Valencia   Universidad EAFIT, Colombia
Edwin Montoya Munera   Universidad EAFIT, Colombia
Cesar Jaramillo   Universidad Tecnológica de Pereira, Colombia
Edilberto Cepeda   Universidad Nacional de Colombia, Colombia
Andrés Sicard-Ramírez   Universidad EAFIT, Colombia
Sergio Ramirez   Universidad EAFIT, Colombia
Liliana Gonzalez   Universidad EAFIT, Colombia
Maria Clara Gómez   Universidad de Medellín, Colombia
Bell Manrique   Universidad de Medellín, Colombia
Francisco Javier Moreno   Universidad Nacional de Colombia, Colombia
Cesar Collazos   Universidad del Cauca, Colombia

Additional Reviewers

Alejandro Marulanda
Alejandro Peña
Alexandra Gonzalez
Andrés Eduardo Castro Ospina
Andrés Felipe Giraldo Forero
Camilo Cortes
Carlos Mera
Carlos Taimal
Christian Abraham Dios Castillo
Daniel Alexis Nieto Mora
Darío José Delgado-Quintero
David Luna
Diana Londoño
Diego Montoya-Zapata
Ernst Leiss
Fredy Humberto Vera-Rivera
Froylan Jimenez Sanchez
Gabriel Mauricio Ramirez Villegas
Hector Cancela
Jorge Iván Cordero
Juan Carlos Arbeláez
Juan Felipe Restrepo-Arias

Juan Francisco Diaz
Juan Sebastian Botero Valencia
L. Leticia Ramírez Ramírez
Leonardo Duque Muñoz
Lina Maria Sepulveda-Cano
Lucia Quintero Montoya
Luis Fernando Londoño
Luis Palacio
Maria C Torres-Madroñero
Maria Isabel Hernández Pérez
Mario C. Velez-Gallego
Mauricio Gonzalez
Monica Arteaga Nestor Duque
Nicolas Moreno
Oscar Franco-Bedoya
Pablo Andres Maya Duque
Paula Andrea Rodríguez Marín
Paula María Almonacid Hurtado
Ricardo López-López
Robinson Andrey Duque
Rodrigo Santos
Tomas Ramirez-Guerrero

Contents

Machine Learning Based Plant Disease Detection Using EfficientNet B7 1
Amit Kumar Bairwa, Sandeep Joshi, and Shikha Chaudhary

Land Cover Classification Using Remote Sensing and Supervised
Convolutional Neural Networks 13
Jheison Perez-Guerra, Veronica Herrera-Ruiz,
Juan Carlos Gonzalez-Velez, Juan David Martinez-Vargas,
and Maria Constanza Torres-Madronero

Fusion of Optical and Radar Data by Aggregation into a Single Feature
Space for LULC Classification 25
Veronica Herrera-Ruiz, Jheison Perez-Guerra,
Juan David Martínez-Vargas, Juan Carlos Gonzalez-Velez,
and Maria Constanza Torres-Madronero

Computer Room Failure Reporting System for a Higher Education
Institution 35
Johan Manuel Alvarez Pinta, Mateo Jesús Cadena Cabrera,
Juan Diego Eraso Muñoz, Miguel Angel Llanten Llanten,
Brayan Fabian Meza, Nicolas Rodriguez Trujillo,
Juan Manuel Quijano, and Marta Cecilia Camacho Ojeda

Recent Advances in Machine Learning for Differential Cryptanalysis 45
Isabella Martínez, Valentina López, Daniel Rambaut, Germán Obando,
Valérie Gauthier-Umaña, and Juan F. Pérez

Addressing the Diet Problem with Constraint Programming Enhanced
with Machine Learning 57
Sara Jazmín Maradiago Calderón, Juan José Dorado Muñoz,
Juan Francisco Díaz Frías, and Robinson Andrey Duque Agudelo

Assessing ChatGPT's Proficiency in CS1-Level Problem Solving 71
Mario Sánchez and Andrea Herrera

Clean Architecture: Impact on Performance and Maintainability of Native
Android Projects 82
Javier Alfonso Santiago-Salazar and Dewar Rico-Bautista

Evaluation of AI Techniques to Implement Proactive Container
Auto-scaling Strategies   91
   Bryan Leonardo Figueredo González and Mariela J. Curiel H.

Teaching Strategy for Enabling Technologies of Industry 4.0 to High
School Students   97
   Duby Castellanos-Cárdenas and María Clara Gómez-Álvarez

Automatic Translation of Text and Audio to Colombian Sign Language 109
   Santiago Fernández Becerra, Fabián Andrés Olarte Vargas,
   Johan Mateo Rosero Quenguan, Andrés Felipe Vásquez Rendón,
   and Andrea Rueda-Olarte

Movement in Video Classification Using Structured Data: Workout Videos
Application 115
   Jonathan Múnera and Marta Silvia Tabares

Planning Navigation Routes in Unknown Environments 128
   Laura Rodriguez, Fernando De la Rosa, and Nicolás Cardozo

Integration of Cyber-Physical System and Digital Twin for Controlling
a Robotic Manipulator: An Industry 4.0 Approach 141
   Oscar Loyola, Benjamín Suarez, César Sandoval, and Eduardo Carrillo

Declarative Visual Programming with Invariant, Pre- and Post-conditions
for Lattice Approximation of 3D Models 153
   Oscar Ruiz-Salguero, Carolina Builes-Roldan, Juan Lalinde-Pulido,
   and Carlos Echeverri-Cartagena

Using Open Data for Training Deep Learning Models: A Waste
Identification Case Study 173
   Juan Carlos Arbeláez, Paola Vallejo, Marta Silvia Tabares,
   Jose Aguilar, David Ríos Zapata, Elizabeth Rendón Vélez,
   and Santiago Ruiz-Arenas

Instructional Strategies for Performance Improvement in Algebra:
A Systematic Mapping 188
   Shirley Tatiana Garcia-Carrascal, Laura Daniela Sepulveda-Vega,
   and Dewar Rico-Bautista

Model for Fruit Tree Classification Through Aerial Images 199
   Valentina Escobar Gómez, Diego Gustavo Guevara Bernal,
   and Javier Francisco López Parra

Change Point Detection for Time Dependent Counts Using Extended
MDL and Genetic Algorithms 215
    Sergio Barajas-Oviedo, Biviana Marcela Suárez-Sierra,
    and Lilia Leticia Ramírez-Ramírez

An Exploration of Genetic Algorithms Operators for the Detection
of Multiple Change-Points of Exceedances Using Non-homogeneous
Poisson Processes and Bayesian Methods 230
    Carlos A. Taimal, Biviana Marcela Suárez-Sierra,
    and Juan Carlos Rivera

Synthetic Hyperspectral Data for Avocado Maturity Classification 259
    Froylan Jimenez Sanchez, Marta Silvia Tabares, and Jose Aguilar

Fuzzy Model for Risk Characterization in Avocado Crops for Index
Insurance Configuration 271
    Juan Pablo Jiménez Benjumea, Laura Isabel López Giraldo,
    Juan Alejandro Peña Palacio, and Tomas Ramirez-Guerrero

Safety Verification of the Raft Leader Election Algorithm Using Athena 285
    Mateo Sanabria, Leonardo Angel, and Nicolás Cardozo

Modeling Detecting Plant Diseases in Precision Agriculture: A NDVI
Analysis for Early and Accurate Diagnosis 297
    Manuela Larrea-Gomez, Alejandro Peña, Juan David Martinez-Vargas,
    Ivan Ochoa, and Tomas Ramirez-Guerrero

Towards the Construction of an Emotion Analysis Model in University
Students Using Images Taken in Classrooms 311
    Jader Daniel Atehortúa Zapata, Santiago Cano Duque,
    Santiago Forero Hincapié, and Emilcy Hernández-Leal

Cloud-Native Architecture for Distributed Systems that Facilitates
Integration with AIOps Platforms 318
    Juan Pablo Ospina Herrera and Diego Botia

Comparing Three Agent-Based Models Implementations of Vector-Borne
Disease Transmission Dynamics 330
    María Sofía Uribe, Mariajose Franco, Luisa F. Londoño,
    Paula Escudero, Susana Álvarez, and Rafael Mateus

Towards a Predictive Model that Supports the Achievement of More
Assertive Commercial KPIs Case: Wood Trading Company 350
    Jhon Walter Tavera Rodríguez

BDI Peasants Model for the WellProdSim Agent-Based Social Simulator 367
  Jairo E. Serrano and Enrique González

Discovering Key Aspects to Reduce Employee Turnover Using a Predictive
Model 380
  Paula Andrea Cárdenas López and Marta Silvia Tabares Betancur

Findby: An Application for Accessibility and Inclusive Exploration 396
  David Madrid Restrepo, Mariana Vasquez Escobar,
  Diego Alejandro Vanegas González, and Liliana González-Palacio

Tracing the Visual Path: Gaze Direction in the 360 Video Experience 406
  Valentina Rozo-Bernal and Pablo Figueroa

Using Virtual Reality to Detect Memory Loss: An Exploratory Study 416
  Melissa Lizeth Contreras Rojas and Pablo Figueroa

Author Index 427

Machine Learning Based Plant Disease Detection Using EfficientNet B7

Amit Kumar Bairwa, Sandeep Joshi$^{(\boxtimes)}$, and Shikha Chaudhary

Manipal University Jaipur, Jaipur, India
sjoshinew@yahoo.com

Abstract. Plant diseases have effects on the growth and production of the plant. Plant diseases can be figured out by using digital image processing, and nowadays, Deep learning has made a lot of progress in digital image processing to identify the disease efficiently. This paper finds the plant diseases using EfficientNet by focusing on three data steps: pre-processing, model selection, and detection network, using a canny edge detection algorithm. The model is trained and tested on plant disease data set. The model provides 97.2% accuracy in detecting the disease than existing CNN-based models.

Keywords: Plant diseases · Deep learning · Machine Learning · Classification · Segmentation · Detection

1 Introduction

Planting is one of the important ways for farmers to make money. Farmers can plant many kinds of crops, but diseases can make it hard for plants to grow. Plant diseases are a big reason agricultural products aren't as helpful or easy to sell as they could be. With the help of new technology, we can make enough food to feed more than 7 billion people. The safety of plants is still a risk because of things like climate change, fewer pollinators, plant diseases, etc. Farmers work hard to choose the best crop for production, but many diseases affect [18]. In agriculture, it's essential to figure out the issues with plants as soon as possible. This lets the reduction in damage to crops, lower production costs, and good quality of crops, which leads to profit for the farmers [11]. From the existing data, it has been analyzed that the disease affects and reduces crop production from 10% to 95%. There are several ways to get rid of plant diseases right now, such as removing infected plants by hand, planting them mechanically, or using pesticides [4].

A simple way to figure out what's wrong with a plant is to ask an expert in agriculture. But figuring out an infection manually takes a long time and is hard to implement. Pesticides can be used as a precaution and recovery from such diseases, but too much use can hurt crop yields, the environment, and people's health. Before using such things, the exact quantity must be calculated and used within a specific time window, and limit [16].

Plants and infectious diseases can be separated using digital imaging and machine learning algorithms for Timely Detection and recovery before spreading

M. Tabares et al. (Eds.): CCC 2023, CCIS 1924, pp. 1–12, 2024.
https://doi.org/10.1007/978-3-031-47372-2_1

the disease. Automatically diagnosing plant diseases is essential because it might be helpful for farmers to figure out and watch over large fields using state-of-the-art techniques using image processing and deep learning. Plants make up more than 80% of what people eat, and in many countries like India, the economy is majorly based upon farming. So, it is essential to find out the cause, detect the disease timely for instant recovery, and ensure that everyone has cheap enough, clean, healthy food to live a long, healthy life [7].

Traditional methods are less effective, necessitating automatic, quick, accurate, and cost-effective ways to identify plant diseases. Numerous agricultural applications utilize digital cameras to capture images of leaves, flowers, and fruits for disease identification. Through image processing and analytical techniques, valuable information is extracted for analysis. Precise farming data aids farmers in making optimal decisions for high agricultural productivity. This research explores various diagnostic approaches for plant diseases, leveraging image analysis and machine intelligence to achieve easy, automatic, and accurate identification of leaf diseases [5]. Early signs of disease detection, such as changes in leaf color and patches, enhance crop yields through automated disease identification.

Machine learning studies algorithms that change and improve on their own as more data is collected and used. Machine learning techniques are used to train the model on collected data (called "training data") so that it can make predictions or decisions on its own without being told what to do [?]. Machine learning algorithms can be used in many fields, such as medicine, email filtering, speech recognition, and computer vision, where it is hard to make a single algorithm that can do all the tasks that need to be done. Machine learning algorithms can be categorized as supervised learning, unsupervised learning, and reinforcement learning [?]. Supervised learning is the process of using labeled data sets to teach models or algorithms predict outcomes. Classification is a well-known model in which the data can predict the label. It expects different kinds of responses, like whether an email is spam or a tumor is cancerous [1]. Support Vector Machine (SVM), Naïve Bayes, Random Forest, K-NN, discriminant analysis, etc. are some of the well-known methods of classification [12]. Regression techniques are trained using labels for what goes in and what comes out. Measures how one variable affects another to determine how they are connected using continuous values [?]. Some examples are predicting how much electricity will be used and trading based on algorithms. Linear regression, Ridge, LASSO, decision trees, neural network regression, KNN, and SVM are some of the well-known algorithms of regression algorithms [9].

2   Literature Review

According to a suggestion by M.P. Vaishnave [10], one of the essential elements that bestow reduced yield is disease assault. The groundnut plant is susceptible to diseases caused by a fungus, viruses, and soil-borne organisms. The software determination to robotically classify and categorize groundnut leaf illnesses is shown to us in this paper. The output of the crops will increase as a result of using this strategy. Image capture, image pre-processing, segmentation, feature extraction, and classifier with K Nearest Neighbor are some of the processes it consists of (KNN). The KNN classification is used instead of the SVM classifier, which improves the present algorithm's performance.

Agriculture is a significant part of the Indian economy, which Debasish Das [?] mentioned in his cite-singh2019comparative article. The primary objective of this research is to determine the various illnesses that can affect leaf tissue. Several feature extraction strategies have been tried and tested to improve the accuracy of the categorization. Statistical methods such as Support Vector Machine (SVM), Random Forest, and Logistic Regression have been utilized to categorize the various leaf diseases. When the outputs of the three classifiers are compared, the support vector machine comes out on top. The findings demonstrate that the model applies to situations that occur in real life.

In this review, Shruti [2] reviewed the comparative study on five different types of machine learning classification algorithms for recognizing plant disease. Compared to other classifiers, the SVM classifier is frequently utilized by writers for disease classification. The findings indicate that the CNN classifier is superior in precisely identifying a more significant number of diseases.

Training a convolutional neural network as a method for disease detection in plants was offered by Prasanna Mohanty [8] in a recent study. The CNN model has been trained to distinguish healthy plants from ill plants across 14 species. The model's accuracy was determined to be 99.35% based on the test set data. When applied to pictures obtained from reliable internet sources, the model achieves an accuracy of 31.4%. While this is superior to the accuracy achieved by a straightforward model based on random selection, the accuracy might be improved by utilizing a more varied training data collection.

Sharada P. Mohanty [2] described crop diseases and the methods for quickly identifying them. The rising prevalence of smartphone users globally and recent developments in computer vision made feasible by deep learning have paved the path for disease diagnosis that may be performed with a smartphone. We train a deep convolutional neural network to recognize 14 crop species and 26 diseases using a public data-set of 54,306 photos of damaged and healthy plant leaves taken under controlled settings (or absence thereof). This strategy is viable when the trained model achieves an accuracy of 99.35% on a held-out test set. Table 1 shows the accuracy comparison among all the reviewed techniques discussed in the section using various classification techniques.

3   Statement of the Problem

Plant disease detection using machine learning approach, applying various techniques/ algorithms, analyzing their efficiency, comparing them, and defining the best out of them.

4   Methodology

We have developed a plant disease detection model using EfficientNets [6], and it has been observed to perform well on the plant disease dataset [3]. The methodology of the model is described here in the subsections below.

Table 1. Accuracy Comparison

Classification Technique	Culture	No. of diseases	Accuracy
SVM	Citrus	2	95%
	Grape	2	88.9%
	Oil Palm	2	97%
	Potato	2	90%
	Tea	3	93%
	Soyabean	3	90%
KNN	Sugarcane	1	95%
	Cotton	1	88.5%
CNN	Peach, Cherry, Pear, Apple and Grapevine	13	96.3%
	14 crops	12	99.35%
	Soyabean	3	99.32%
	25 Plants	58	99.53%

KNN. K-means algorithm is an iterative algorithm that tries to partition the dataset into pre-defined distinct non-overlapping subgroups (clusters) where each data point belongs to only one group. It is a centroid-based algorithm or a distance-based algorithm. In K-Means, each cluster is associated with a centroid.

SVM. Support Vector Machine (SVM) is a supervised machine learning algorithm for classification and regression. Though we say regression problems as well, it's best suited for classification. The objective of the SVM algorithm is to find a hyperplane in an N-dimensional space that distinctly classifies the data points.

4.1 Implemented Algorithms

A Convolutional Neural Network (ConvNet/CNN) is a Deep Learning algorithm that can take in an input image, assign importance (learnable weights and biases) to various aspects/objects in the image, and be able to differentiate one from the other. The pre-processing required in a ConvNet is much lower than in other classification algorithms. While in primitive methods, filters are hand-engineered, with enough training, ConvNets can learn these filters/characteristics.

4.2 Data Pre-processing

Exploratory Data Analysis (EDA) is a process of performing initial investigations on data to discover patterns, spot anomalies, test hypotheses, and check assumptions with the assistance of summary statistics and graphical representations. This is a crucial step in the pre-processing phase. The leaf image is distributed in R-G-B channels separately, the green part or healthy area has shallow blue values, but by contrast, the brown parts have high blue values. This might suggest that the blue channel may be the key to detecting plant diseases.

The red channel values seem to roughly normal distribution, but with a slight rightward (positive skew). This indicates that the red channel tends to be more concentrated at lower values, at around 100 as in figure. There is large variation in average red values across images. The green channel of contains the high contrast region of image due to this Microaneurysms are clearly visible in figure. The blue channel has the most uniform distribution out of the three colour channels, with minimal skew (slight leftward skew). The blue channel shows great variation across images in the dataset as in figure.

4.3   Model Selection

The performance of the base network is heavily dependent on the model's measurements. Therefore, to further enhance performance, we are also developing a new primary network by doing neural architecture searches using the AutoML MNAS framework, which improves accuracy and efficiency. These searches are being done to improve performance (FLOPS) further. The produced structures use mobile inverted bottleneck convolution (MBConv), which is com-Machine, learning-based plant diseases detection, using EfficientNet B7 parable to MobileNetV2 and MnasNet. However, these structures are significantly more significant due to an enhanced FLOP budget. After that, we broaden the scope of the initial network to discover a family of models known as EfficientNets. EfficientNets was tested on eight different databases, too, for transfer learning. EfficientNets attained modern accuracy in five out of eight data sets, such as CIFAR-100 (91.7%) and Flowers (98.8%), with only a few parameter settings (up to 21 times in the parameter reduction), which suggests that EfficientNets also transmits well. We anticipate that EfficientNets will provide considerable gains in model performance and, as a result, will serve as a new foundation for future operations involving computer vision.

The performance of our EfficientNets is compared to that of other CNNs hosted on ImageNet. EfficientNet models can attain higher accuracy and better performance than currently available CNNs. This is accomplished by reducing the parameter size and FLOPS by size system. For instance, in a high-precision system, our EfficientNet-B7 achieves 84.4% with a maximum accuracy of 1/97.1% a maximum of 5 in ImageNet, while at the same time being 8.4 times more compact and 6.1 times in CPU precision than Gpipe was previously. Our EfficientNet-B4 employs the same number of FLOPS as the widely used ResNet-50, but it improves the maximum accuracy of 1 from 76.3% of ResNet-50 to 82.6% (+6.3%).

4.4   Image Processing Using Canny Edge Detection Algorithm

Canny edge detection algorithm is used to detect edges of a leaf and the detected region/ edges will be used to fed in the proposed model. A common edge detection method that recognizes picture edges based on the multistep algorithm.

1. Noise reduction: Edge detection is sensitive to picture noise, it is eliminated using a 5×5 Gaussian filter.

2. Finding Intensity Gradient of the Image: The smoothed picture is then filtered using a Sobel kernel horizontally and vertically to produce the first derivative (Gx, Gy). These two photos show each pixel's gradient and orientation.
3. Rounding: Always perpendicular to edges. It's rounded to a vertical, horizontal, or diagonal angle.
4. Non-maximum suppression: After collecting the gradient magnitude and direction, a thorough scan of the picture is done to eliminate any unnecessary pixels. Every pixel is checked for a local maximum in the gradient's direction.
5. Hysteresis Thresholding: This step determines edges. minVal and maxVal are needed. Any edges with an intensity gradient over maxVal are deemed edges, while those below mineral are removed. Based on their neighborhood, those between these two thresholds are edges or non-edges. They're regarded as edges if they're near "sure-edge" pixels; otherwise, they're ignored. Five stages provide a two-dimensional binary map (0 or 255) of picture edges. Leaves show Canny edge.

5   Results

The model is trained and tested on plant disease dataset [3]. The dataset contains 71.7% unhealthy leaves having multiple diseases, rust, and scab, whereas 28.3% are healthy leaves are available in the dataset. The 80% of data from the dataset is used to train the designed model, and 20% data is used for testing. In the Fig. 1, we can see that the healthy leaves are entirely green and do not have any brown/yellow spots or scars. Healthy leaves do not have scabs or rust.

Fig. 1. Sample of Healthy Dataset (Color figure online)

Fig. 2. Sample of rusty Dataset (Color figure online)

In Fig. 2, leaves with "scab" have significant brown marks and stains across the leaf. Scab is "any of various plant diseases caused by fungi or bacteria resulting in crust like spots on fruits, leaves, or roots". The brown marks across the leaf are a sign of these bacterial/fungal infections. Once diagnosed, scabs can be treated using chemical or non-chemical methods.

In the Fig. 3, we can see that leaves with "rust" have several brownish-yellow spots across the leaf. Rust is "a disease, especially of cereals and other grasses, characterized by rust-colored pustules of spores on the affected leaf blades and sheaths and caused by any of several rust fungi". The yellow spots are a sign of infection by a particular type of fungi called "rust fungi". Rust can also be treated with several chemical and non-chemical methods once diagnosed.

In Fig. 4, we can see that the leaves show symptoms of several diseases, including brown marks and yellow spots. These plants have more than one of the above-described diseases.

Table 2. Accuracy comparison of Proposed model using various classification techniques

Classification Technique	Accuracy(Training Data)	Accuracy(Testing Data)
SVM	88.9%	%
K-Means	85%	%
CNN	96.3%	%
EffiecientNet-B7	97.2%	90%

Fig. 3. Sample with "scab" Dataset (Color figure online)

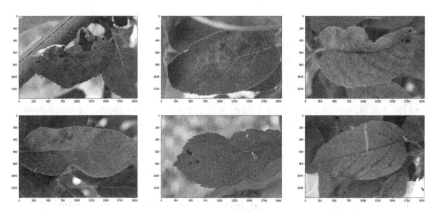

Fig. 4. Sample of Diseased Dataset (Color figure online)

All the models mentioned in the proposed research were implemented with Tensorflow in python. Further, Kaggle was used to train the models mentioned, with the following specs - GPU Tesla P100-PCI-E-16GB computes capability: 6.0 and 16 GB GPU RAM.

EfficientNet predicts leaf diseases with great accuracy as describe in the Fig. 5, 6, 7, 8 and 9. No red bars are seen. The probabilities are very polarized (one very high and the rest shallow), indicating that the model is making these predictions with great confidence. The semi-supervised weights seem to set this model apart from EfficientNet. Once again, the red and blue bars are more

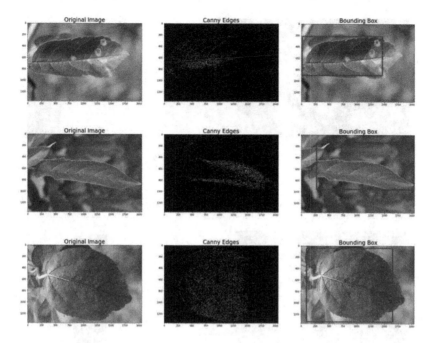

Fig. 5. Canny Edge Detection (Color figure online)

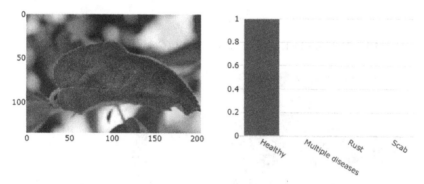

Fig. 6. Result of Healthy leaf (Color figure online) .

prominent in the last (fourth) leaf labeled "multiple_diseases". This is probably because leaves with multiple diseases may also show symptoms of rust and scab, thus slightly confusing the model.

From the Fig. 10, we can see that the accuracy of the model achieved in training data is 97.2% and using the testing data is 90%. The training metrics settle down very fast (after 1 or 2 epochs), whereas the validation metrics have

Fig. 7. Result of Scab Leaf (Color figure online)

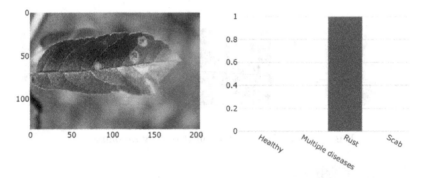

Fig. 8. Scenario 1: Result of Rust Leaf (Color figure online)

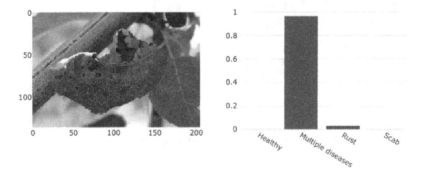

Fig. 9. Scenario 2: Result of Rust Leaf (Color figure online)

much greater volatility and start to settle down only after 12–13 epochs (similar to DenseNet). This is expected because validation data is unseen and more challenging to predict than training data.

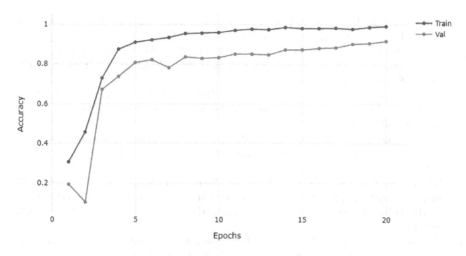

Fig. 10. Performance of EfficientNet-B7 (Color figure online)

6   Future Work

This paper develops a disease detection model using the convolutional neural network EfficientNet-B7 is developed and compared with other models by applying K-means and SVM techniques. The accuracy of the proposed model came out best from cross-validation, given its high scores. The model predicts the diseased plants with high precision so that unnecessary expenses in treatment can be avoided. It has been observed from the investigation that the proposed model provides the accuracy of highest 90% using EfficientNet-B7 on testing data-set and 97.2% accuracy on training dataset to detect the leaves more than other proposed and existing models.

References

1. Ai, Y., Sun, C., Tie, J., Cai, X.: Research on recognition model of crop diseases and insect pests based on deep learning in harsh environments. IEEE Access **8**, 171686–171693 (2020)
2. Alotaibi, F.S.: Implementation of machine learning model to predict heart failure disease. Int. J. Adv. Comput. Sci. Appl. **10**(6), 261–268 (2019)
3. AlSuwaidi, A., Grieve, B., Yin, H.: Feature-ensemble-based novelty detection for analyzing plant hyperspectral datasets. IEEE J. Sel. Top. Appl. Earth Obs. Remote Sens. **11**(4), 1041–1055 (2018)
4. Ashourloo, D., Aghighi, H., Matkan, A.A., Mobasheri, M.R., Rad, A.M.: An investigation into machine learning regression techniques for the leaf rust disease detection using hyperspectral measurement. IEEE J. Sel. Top. Appl. Earth Obs. Remote Sens. **9**(9), 4344–4351 (2016)
5. Azimi, S., Wadhawan, R., Gandhi, T.K.: Intelligent monitoring of stress induced by water deficiency in plants using deep learning. IEEE Trans. Instrum. Meas. **70**, 1–13 (2021)

6. Sunil, C.K., Jaidhar, C.D., Patil, N.: Cardamom plant disease detection approach using EfficientNetV2. IEEE Access **10**, 789–804 (2022)

7. Huang, S., Zhou, G., He, M., Chen, A., Zhang, W., Hu, Y.: Detection of peach disease image based on asymptotic non-local means and PCNN-IPELM. IEEE Access **8**, 136421–136433 (2020)

8. Jadon, S.: SSM-net for plants disease identification in low data regime. In: 2020 IEEE/ITU International Conference on Artificial Intelligence for Good (AI4G), pp. 158–163 (2020)

9. Joshi, P., Das, D., Udutalapally, V., Pradhan, M.K., Misra, S.: Ricebios: identification of biotic stress in rice crops using edge-as-a-service. IEEE Sens. J. **22**(5), 4616–4624 (2022)

10. Khosla, A., Cao, Y., Lin, C.C.-Y., Chiu, H.-K., Hu, J., Lee, H.: An integrated machine learning approach to stroke prediction. In: Proceedings of the 16th ACM SIGKDD International Conference on Knowledge Discovery and Data Mining, pp. 183–192 (2010)

11. Kumar, M., Kumar, A., Palaparthy, V.S.: Soil sensors-based prediction system for plant diseases using exploratory data analysis and machine learning. IEEE Sens. J. **21**(16), 17455–17468 (2021)

12. Liu, L., et al.: Deep learning based automatic multiclass wild pest monitoring approach using hybrid global and local activated features. IEEE Trans. Ind. Inf. **17**(11), 7589–7598 (2021)

Land Cover Classification Using Remote Sensing and Supervised Convolutional Neural Networks

Jheison Perez-Guerra[1]([✉]) [ID], Veronica Herrera-Ruiz[1] [ID],
Juan Carlos Gonzalez-Velez[1] [ID], Juan David Martinez-Vargas[2] [ID],
and Maria Constanza Torres-Madronero[1] [ID]

[1] Department of Engineering, MIRP Research Group, Instituto Tecnológico
Metropolitano ITM, CL 73 No. 76 A 354, Medellín, Colombia
jheisonperez239463@correo.itm.edu.co
[2] EAFIT University, Carrera 49, Cl. 7 Sur No. 50, Medellín, Colombia

Abstract. The rapid and uncontrolled population growth and the development of various industrial sectors have accelerated the rate of changes in land use and land cover (LULC). The quantitative assessment of changes in LULC plays a fundamental role in understanding and managing these changes. Therefore, it is necessary to examine the accuracy of different algorithms for LULC mapping. We compared the performance of three deep learning architectures (PSPNet, U-Net, and U-Net++) with four different backbones, including ResNet-18, ResNet-34, ResNet-50, and ResNext50_32x4d pre-trained on ImageNet. Besides, we compared the model's performance using the same scene but using: 1) a single date, 2) a time series, and 3) data augmentation. For this, we used Sentinel 2 images captured on Antioquia-Colombia and four main categories of the Corine Land Cover as ground truth. The mean Intersection-Over-Union (mIoU) metric and pixel accuracy was used like evaluation metrics. All models showed an increase in performance with data augmentation. The best models were U-Net with ResNet-50 encoder and U-Net with Resnext50-32x4d, with pixel accuracies of 88.6% and 89.2%, respectively, and mIoU 74.6% and 74.8%. Both models had similar computing times (244.07 min and 248.06 min). PSPNet was the lowest-performing architecture, with pixel accuracy between 83.2% and 84.1% and mIoU between 63.3% and 64.6%. In summary, our results show that semantic segmentation models are suitable for classifying the LC of optical images and provide benchmark accuracy for evaluating the integration of new techniques and sensors.

Keywords: Remote Sensing · Deep Learning · Sentinel 2 · Semantic Segmentation · Land Use and Land Cover

M. Tabares et al. (Eds.): CCC 2023, CCIS 1924, pp. 13–24, 2024.
https://doi.org/10.1007/978-3-031-47372-2_2

1   Introduction and Literature Review

Humans and the environment maintain a close interaction; therefore, understanding how different actions, natural phenomena, and ecosystemic changes are related is essential for the efficient management and use of natural resources [1]. The land cover represents physical attributes of the surface, while land use refers to transformations caused by human activity [1]; however, land use (LU) and land cover (LC) are interdependent, i.e., use affects cover, and changes in cover vary use [2]. The study of LULC changes has become essential due to its potential in various real-world applications, such as natural disaster monitoring [3], environmental vulnerability assessment [4], land-use planning [5], climate change study [6], among others. Moreover, quantitative and dynamic assessment of LULC is the most effective means of understanding landscape alterations [7] and modeling impacts of ecosystem change at different scales [8].

Most of the information used for land use and land cover classification is collected by remote sensing, especially with passive sensors [9]. Traditional machine learning techniques generate LULC maps, requiring significant financial resources, personnel, and time [9]. Machine learning models have played a key role in remote sensing classification. Algorithms such as Random Forest (RF), Support Vector Machine (SVM), K-Nearest Neighbor (KNN), and others have shown excellent results in LULC classification [10]. However, these methods have reached their limit in terms of performance and require many exogenous indices to obtain excellent results [11].

The rapid evolution of computing has allowed the development of new techniques for LULC classification, precisely, deep learning techniques (DL) [11]. These algorithms have been applied to image classification and object segmentation, proving their effectiveness in remote sensing applications [12]. DL can learn higher-level and abstract features, which can amplify discrimination and reduce irrelevant variations present in the data [13]. There are studies of encoder/decoder networks that report excellent performances for semantic segmentation problems or scene of scenes classification [9]. Considering the literature, the enhanced segmentation capability with deep learning has the potential to accurately detect and extract the variety and complexity of ground cover features [9]. Therefore, the framework of deep neural networks has improved state of the art in many applications, such as remote sensing [12].

We used transfer learning/based DL approaches to employ an encoder/decoder paradigm as feature extractors in the encoding stage. Additionally, we performed a comprehensive performance analysis of various land cover classification models with different database augmentations.

2   Materials and Methods

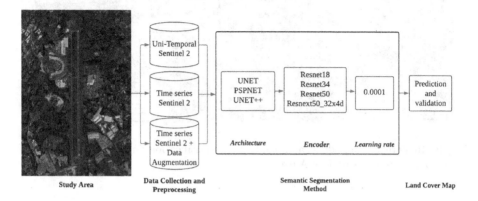

Fig. 1. Flowchart of the methodology proposed land cover classification approach. Source: Created by Authors.

Figure 1 presents the methodology of this research. Initially, training and test samples were generated from optical images captured over a grid section of Antioquia, Colombia. We applied the semantic segmentation models (PSPNet, U-Net, and U-Net++) by combining them with four pre-trained backbones (ResNet-18, ResNet-34, ResNet-50, and ResNext50_32x4) trained on RGB images from ImageNet. The Sentinel 2 (S2) imagery and a land cover dataset consisting of four main classes were used for this purpose. Subsequently, several supervised DL algorithms were employed to classify the image of the study area. Finally, the results of the best models are obtained and discussed.

2.1   Study Area

The study area is located in the eastern subregion of Antioquia, Colombia, including the municipalities of Medellín, Guatapé, and La Unión. The geographic area comprises approximately 189900 ha and altitudes between 377 and 3343 m a.s.l. This region exhibits a complex mosaic of LC classes (Fig. 2): purple corresponds to artificial surfaces, yellow to water surfaces, blue to agricultural areas, and green to forested areas with natural vegetation. The study area was chosen to be vulnerable to transitions from natural to agricultural or artificial zones, primarily due to the construction of greenhouses and plots.

Fig. 2. Remote sensing data and land cover classification in Eastern Antioquia/ Colombia. Source: Created by Authors.

2.2   Data Collection and Preprocessing

We use three Sentinel 2 images on L2A (Orthorectified atmospherically corrected surface reflectance) downloaded from the Google Earth Engine (GEE). The images were taken in January, July, and August 2019. Spectral bands of the S2 satellite imagery used in this research are shown in Table 1. All the bands were resampled to 10m using GEE. GEE automatically takes care of the scaling, ensuring that all bands align perfectly with each other.

The labels were obtained from the Corine Land Cover map (2018) developed by the Instituto de Hidrología, Meteorología y Estudios Ambientales (IDEAM). Corine Land Cover provides a huge labeled dataset on all of Colombia. In the study area, four LULC classes have been identified based on Corine Land Cover's first level: Artificial surfaces (AS) with 1,875,067 pixels, indicating areas characterized by human-made structures and infrastructure. The largest land cover class is the agricultural areas (AA) encompassing 11,794,080 pixels, which indicates extensive regions dedicated to farming and cultivation. Forested areas with natural vegetation (FANV) comprising 4,967,302 pixels, representing significant forested regions in the area, and water surfaces (WF) with 597,712 pixels, representing bodies of water within the region. The Corine Land Cover vector labels were converted to raster at 10m resolution (S2 resolution) and, together with the S2 images, were cropped to the size of the study area employing Python Software.

Table 1. Bands from S2A and S2B. Wavelength and Bandwidth columns have information from S2A/S2B, respectively.

Spectral Band	Wavelength (nm)	Bandwidth (nm)	Spatial Resolution (m)
Band 2 - Blue	492.4/492.1	66/66	10
Band 3 - Green	559.8/559.0	36/36	10
Band 4 - Red	664.6/664.9	31/31	10
Band 5 - VRE	704.1/703.8	15/16	20
Band 6 - VRE	740.5/739.1	15/15	20
Band 7 - VRE	782.8/779.7	20/20	20
Band 8 - NIR	832.8/832.9	106/106	10
Band 8A - N-NIR	864.7/864.0	21/22	20
Band 11 - WIR	1614.0/1610.4	91/94	20
Band 12 - SWIR	2202.0/2185.7	175/185	20

The mask and S2 rasters were divided into patches of size 256×256 pixels ($2.56\,km \times 2.56\,km$). Our dataset X consists of these patches, with each patch containing the S2 image bands as features for each pixel, while dataset Y consists of the corresponding labels. Data augmentation techniques were applied using vertical and horizontal flips to enhance the model efficiency in terms of performance. Table 2 shows the number of patches of the original and different image augmentation datasets.

Table 2. Different sizes of the original and image-augmentation datasets.

Scenario/Dataset	Uni-Temporal	Time Series	Time Series + Aug
Train	148	541	1623
Test	27	61	61
Validation	76	151	151
Total	251	753	1835

2.3 Semantic Segmentation Methods

In this study, we chose to use U-Net, U-Net++, and PSPNet as base architectures given their broad spectrum of use in the semantic segmentation of Land Cover. The models were selected to evaluate a different pool of approaches to semantic segmentation. In the following, we describe the specific architecture for each DL model.

PSPNet. Pyramid Scene Parsing Network (PSPNet) uses a pre-trained classification architecture to extract the feature map [14]. The main module of this network is the pyramid pooling with 4-level. This module can gather more representative information levels, covering the whole, half, and small portions of the image. Pyramid pooling gathers features coarse (first level) whit the features fine (fourth level). PSPNet concatenates the pyramid pooling output with the original feature map [14]. Finally, a convolution layer is used to generate the final prediction map (Fig. 3(c)).

U-Net. The details of the U-Net model architecture are illustrated in Fig. 3(a). The U-Net model is known for its architecture with two main paths, the encoder (left side) and decoder (right side). U-Net concatenates the encoder feature maps with the decoder feature maps at each step [15]. The contracting path follows the typical architecture of a convolutional network. It consists of the repeated application of two 3×3 convolutions, each followed by a ReLU activation function and a 2×2 max pooling operation. In the decoder path, each step contains a 2 by 2 up-convolutional layer and a concatenation layer with its corresponding feature map from the encoder path, two 3 by 3 convolution layers with ReLU activation function, finally layer a 1×1 convolution [16].

U-Net++. It significantly enhances the U-Net architecture used in semantic image segmentation. This hierarchical structure incorporates longer skip connections between network levels, enabling the capture of multi-scale features. In Fig. 3(b), the green and blue colors denote the dense convolution blocks integrated within the skip pathways. Additionally, red signifies the incorporation of deep supervision [17].

DL algorithms must have access to large volumes of data for training [18]. In order to train DL algorithms, access to large volumes of data is essential. However, the presence of frequent and dense cloud cover poses a significant challenge in land cover mapping tasks, causing data sparsity. To overcome this limitation, supervised pre-trained models (Transfer Learning) on ImageNet are employed to acquire specific fundamental parameters. All models were combined with four different backbones, including ResNet-18, ResNet-34, ResNet-50, and Resnext50-32x4d. We decided to use the Jaccard Loss function metric for the backpropagation optimization, a learning rate of 0.001, and a batch size of 32. Python library with Neural Networks for Image Segmentation based on PyTorch was used [19].

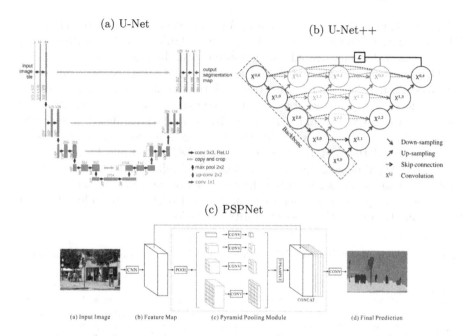

Fig. 3. Architectures of (a) U-Net [16], (b) U-Net++ [17], (c) PSPNet [14]

2.4   Performance Comparison DL Models

Comparing the model classification results, we utilize the following metrics. 1) average pixel-wise intersection over union (mIoU) and 2) pixel accuracy, given that it is one of the most widely used metrics in state of the art [20].

The mIoU is defined by 1.

$$IoU = \frac{Tp}{Tp + Fp + Fn} \rightarrow mIoU = \sum_{i=1}^{m} IoU_i \tag{1}$$

The accuracy is defined by 2.

$$Accuraccy = \frac{Tp + Tn}{Tp + Tn + Fp + Fn} \tag{2}$$

where Tp and Tn denote true positives and true negatives; Fp and Fn represent false positives and false negatives, and m corresponds to the number of testing images.

3   Results

3.1   Experimental Results

The experimental results are presented in Table 3. The training time is calculated in seconds, the blue color represents the highest performance, whereas the red

color represents the lowest performance. For training the model, we used Kaggle's
NVIDIA TESLA P100 GPU. Scenarios 2 and 3 exhibited the best performances,
while Scenario 1 demonstrated low performance at the mIoU level.

The scenario that achieved the highest mIoU and pixel accuracy values was
Scenario 3, using the U-Net architecture with the ResNext50_32x4d and ResNet-
50 encoders. The pixel accuracy for this scenario was 89.27%/88.60% while
the mIoU was 74.81%/74.60%, respectively. Scenario 2 exhibited similar performance to Scenario 3; however, the U-Net++ architecture with the ResNet-50
encoder showed the best pixel accuracy value (87.5%), while U-Net++ with
ResNext50_32x4d demonstrated the highest mIoU value (72.1%). The PSPNET
model with all encoders generally exhibited inferior performance across all scenarios, with pixel accuracy between 83.21% and 84.13%, and mIoU between
63.30% and 65.30% in the most optimistic scenario.

Table 3. Comparisons between DL models, with different backbone and scenarios.

		Uni-Temporal			Time Series			Time Series + Aug		
Method	Backbone	Accuracy	mIoU	Training Time	Accuracy	mIoU	Training Time	Accuracy	mIoU	Training Time
U-Net	ResNet-18	0.766	0.582	19.85	0.836	0.660	64.80	0.873	0.722	180.88
	ResNet-34	0.774	0.560	19.55	0.854	0.641	71.74	0.884	0.744	203.60
	ResNet-50	**0.781**	**0.581**	31.55	0.841	0.615	83.85	0.886	0.746	244.07
	ResNext50_32x4d	0.778	0.582	36.35	0.852	0.632	91.17	**0.892**	**0.748**	258.06
U-Net++	ResNet-18	0.754	0.545	28.64	0.849	0.674	90.42	0.870	0.721	250.22
	ResNet-34	0.759	0.558	31.55	0.855	0.69	98.13	0.883	0.739	272.72
	ResNet-50	0.770	0.573	55.67	**0.875**	0.719	167.79	0.885	0.736	487.05
	ResNext50_32x4d	0.769	0.575	57.48	0.871	**0.721**	175.00	0.884	0.737	511.06
PSPNET	ResNet-18	0.739	0.515	14.99	0.826	0.603	46.60	0.832	0.635	162.01
	ResNet-34	0.746	0.530	17.75	0.831	0.619	49.94	0.835	0.644	171.56
	ResNet-50	0.752	0.518	19.03	0.836	0.631	54.93	0.841	0.653	162.71
	ResNext50_32x4d	0.744	0.526	20.32	0.832	0.626	60.61	0.836	0.646	181.79

3.2   Comparison of Predicted Results

The S2 images, the ground truth, and the prediction images for the best models
in each scenario are displayed in Fig. 4. After evaluating all segmentation models,
it was concluded that all of them can classify and segment S2 images to some
extent once they have been trained. However, the detailed effect in the prediction
results for the classification and segmentation of linear infrastructure (such as
roads and others) is unsatisfactory.

Figure 5 illustrates the confusion matrix; it was used to show the performance of each classified pixel, which allows us to evaluate the segmentation
accuracy against the ground truth in each of the scenarios. The water surface
(WS) exhibits the highest class-wise accuracy, surpassing 93.6% in all scenarios,
followed by agricultural areas (AA) with a precision exceeding 92%. Despite AA
being the most dominant coverage in the area, it demonstrates a precision higher
than 92.5% in all scenarios. Forested areas with natural vegetation (FANV) and
artificial surfaces (AS) displayed the lowest performance across all scenarios,
with misclassifications as agricultural areas.

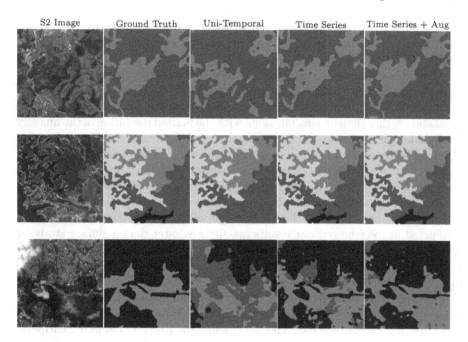

Fig. 4. Segmentation map examples for selected regions of the testing dataset. Uni-Temporal (U-Net ResNet-50). Time Series (U-Net++ ResNet-50). Time Series + AUG (U-NetResNext50 32x4d).

4   Discussion

The evolution of remote sensing devices has led to new platforms that allow the acquisition and processing of large amounts of geographic information [21]. GEE offers a broad S2 time-series image, representing a substantial advance for constantly monitoring land cover. DL approaches using remote sensing images for land cover and land use classification gained popularity. In this paper, we utilize three semantic segmentation approaches. We created three scenarios to counteract the performance, considering: 1) the base architecture, 2) the type of backbone, and 3) data augmentation.

The models can classify and segment the low-resolution RS images, with accuracy and mIoU higher than 73% and 51%, respectively. Using only time series (Scenario 2), U-Net++ showed the best performance; however, U-Net was the most competitive model for low- to medium-resolution satellite RS images. These results corroborate what was stated by [20]. The PSPNetmodel, regardless of encoder selection, exhibited comparatively inferior performance across all scenarios. The best results were obtained using data augmentation techniques, which is to be expected given that data augmentation enhances the size and quality of training datasets and strengthens the model's ability to generalize and capture more complex patterns [22].

The models have poor performance in the detailed classification of artificial surfaces. However, this error may be influenced by the dissimilarity between the actual Corine Land Cover labels and the accurate type of artificial zones. Corine Land Cover tends to misclassify numerous artificial areas as agricultural areas. In addition, the presence of artificial surfaces interspersed between trees and green vegetation throughout the territory can cause them to exhibit signatures close to the plantation rather than urban [23], along with the limited resolution of the imagery used, making it even more difficult to label such areas accurately. The approaches obtained better performances in recognizing the water surfaces, agricultural areas, and forested areas with natural vegetation, while, the urban fabric represented the most challenging class to classify, ratifying what has been evidenced by [23].

Finally, our results show a high degree of accuracy in LC classification, indicating that our approach and methodology are promising. Compared to other studies conducted in the country, our results are slightly lower than a similar study by [24], which achieved 93% accuracy using images at 5 m from the Planet Explorer sensor. However, it is important to note that Planet is not freely available, which may limit its replication in other studies. On the other hand, our study obtained results superior to those reported by [25], who achieved an accuracy of 88.75% by integrating radar and visible-near infrared and SVM data and also surpassed the results of [26], who obtained 62% accuracy using the 10-meter bands of Sentinel 2.

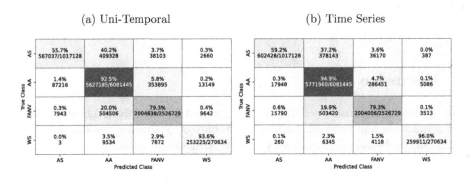

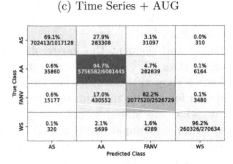

Fig. 5. Confusion matrices for the best models of each scenario. a) Uni-Temporal (U-Net ResNet-50). b) Time Series c) (U-Net++ ResNet-50). Time Series + AUG (U-Net ResNext50 32x4d).

5   Conclusions and Future Works

The classification of LC on S2 imagery using different deep-learning algorithms was implemented, evaluated, and compared. Three different image datasets: unitemporal, time series, and data augmentation implementation-were included in this study. Our results showed good performance for the multiclass segmentation, with an 89% accuracy and 74% mIoU. The presence of clouds can limit the availability of optical data, reducing the amount of usable information for models. This can hurt the performance of data classification and analysis models. It is proposed to consider the integration of data from radars in future research, which offer the ability to penetrate clouds and provide valuable land cover information. Our study provides baseline results that can be used to evaluate newly developed models, including techniques involving semi-supervised learning and the integration of multisensorial data. Finally, this research contributes to assessing the potentiality of S2 data and DL-supervised approach for land cover classification in Colombia.

References

1. Rawat, J.S., Kumar, M.: Monitoring land use/cover change using remote sensing and GIS techniques: a case study of Hawalbagh block, district Almora, Uttarakhand, India. Egypt. J. Remote Sens. Space Sci. **18**(1), 77–84 (2015). https://doi.org/10.1016/j.ejrs.2015.02.002

2. Ritse, V., Basumatary, H., Kulnu, A.S., Dutta, G., Phukan, M.M., Hazarika, N.: Monitoring land use land cover changes in the Eastern Himalayan landscape of Nagaland, Northeast India. Environ. Monit. Assess. **192**(11) (2020). https://doi.org/10.1007/s10661-020-08674-8

3. Talukdar, S., Pal, S.: Effects of damming on the hydrological regime of Punarbhaba river basin wetlands. Ecol. Eng. **135**, 61–74 (2019). https://doi.org/10.1016/j.ecoleng.2019.05.014

4. Nguyen, K.A., Liou, Y.A.: Global mapping of eco-environmental vulnerability from human and nature disturbances. Sci. Total Environ. **664**, 995–1004 (2019). https://doi.org/10.1016/j.scitotenv.2019.01.407

5. Hashem, N., Balakrishnan, P.: Change analysis of land use/land cover and modelling urban growth in Greater Doha, Qatar. Ann. GIS **21**(3), 233–247 (2015). https://doi.org/10.1080/19475683.2014.992369

6. Dutta, D., Rahman, A., Paul, S.K., Kundu, A.: Changing pattern of urban landscape and its effect on land surface temperature in and around Delhi. Environ. Monit. Assess. **191**(9) (2019)

7. Talukdar, S., et al.: Land-use land-cover classification by machine learning classifiers for satellite observations-a review. Remote Sens. **12**(7) (2020)

8. Turner, B.L.: Local faces, global flows: the role of land use and land cover in global environmental change. Land Degrad. Dev. **5**(2) (1994)

9. Boonpook, W., et al.: Deep learning semantic segmentation for land use and land cover types using landsat 8 imagery. ISPRS Int. J. Geo-Inf. **12**(1) (2023). https://www.mdpi.com/2220-9964/12/1/14

10. Qu, L., Chen, Z., Li, M., Zhi, J., Wang, H.: Accuracy improvements to pixel-based and object-based LULC classification with auxiliary datasets from google earth engine. Remote Sens. **13**(3) (2021). https://www.mdpi.com/2072-4292/13/3/453

11. Wenger, R., Puissant, A., Weber, J., Idoumghar, L., Forestier, G.: Multimodal and multitemporal land use/land cover semantic segmentation on sentinel-1 and sentinel-2 imagery: an application on a multisenge dataset. Remote Sens. **15**(1) (2023). https://www.mdpi.com/2072-4292/15/1/151
12. Garg, R., Kumar, A., Bansal, N., Prateek, M., Kumar, S.: Semantic segmentation of PolSAR image data using advanced deep learning model. Sci. Rep. **11**, 15 365, 1–18 (2021)
13. LeCun, Y., Bengio, Y., Hinton, G.: Deep learning. Nature **521**(7553), 436–444 (2015)
14. Zhao, H., Shi, J., Qi, X., Wang, X., Jia, J.: Pyramid scene parsing network. CoRR, vol. abs/1612.01105 (2016). http://arxiv.org/abs/1612.01105
15. Garg, L., Shukla, P., Singh, S., Bajpai, V., Yadav, U.: Land use land cover classification from satellite imagery using mUnet: a modified Unet architecture, pp. 359–365 (2019)
16. Ronneberger, O., Fischer, P., Brox, T.: U-net: convolutional networks for biomedical image segmentation. In: Navab, N., Hornegger, J., Wells, W.M., Frangi, A.F. (eds.) MICCAI 2015. LNCS, vol. 9351, pp. 234–241. Springer, Cham (2015). https://doi.org/10.1007/978-3-319-24574-4_28
17. Zhou, Z., Rahman Siddiquee, M.M., Tajbakhsh, N., Liang, J.: UNet++: a nested U-net architecture for medical image segmentation. In: Stoyanov, D., et al. (eds.) DLMIA/ML-CDS -2018. LNCS, vol. 11045, pp. 3–11. Springer, Cham (2018). https://doi.org/10.1007/978-3-030-00889-5_1
18. Barzekar, H., et al.: Multiclass semantic segmentation mediated neuropathological readout in Parkinson's disease. Neurosci. Inform. 100131 (2023). https://www.sciencedirect.com/science/article/pii/S277252862300016X
19. Iakubovskii, P.: Segmentation models PyTorch (2019). https://github.com/qubvel/segmentatio_models.pytorch
20. Fan, Z., et al.: Land cover classification of resources survey remote sensing images based on segmentation model. IEEE Access **10**, 56 267–56 281 (2022)
21. Carrasco, L., O'Neil, A.W., Daniel Morton, R., Rowland, C.S.: Evaluating combinations of temporally aggregated sentinel-1, sentinel-2 and landsat 8 for land cover mapping with google earth engine. Remote Sens. **11**(3), 288 (2019). https://www.mdpi.com/2072-4292/11/3/288/htm
22. Shorten, C., Khoshgoftaar, T.M.: A survey on image data augmentation for deep learning. J. Big Data **6**(1), 1–48 (2019)
23. Šćepanović, S., Antropov, O., Laurila, P., Rauste, Y., Ignatenko, V., Praks, J.: Wide-area land cover mapping with sentinel-1 imagery using deep learning semantic segmentation models. IEEE J. Sel. Top. Appl. Earth Obs. Remote Sens. **14**, 10 357–10 374 (2021)
24. González-Vélez, J.C., Martinez-Vargas, J.D., Torres-Madronero, M.C.: Land cover classification using CNN and semantic segmentation: a case of study in Antioquia, Colombia. In: Narváez, F.R., Proaño, J., Morillo, P., Vallejo, D., González Montoya, D., Díaz, G.M. (eds.) SmartTech-IC 2021. CCIS, vol. 1532, pp. 306–317. Springer, Cham (2022). https://doi.org/10.1007/978-3-030-99170-8_22
25. Clerici, N., Calderón, C.A.V., Posada, J.M.: Fusion of sentinel-1a and sentinel-2a data for land cover mapping: a case study in the lower Magdalena region, Colombia. J. Maps **13**(2), 718–726 (2017). https://doi.org/10.1080/17445647.2017.1372316
26. Anaya, J., Rodríguez-Buriticá, S., Londoño, M.: ñolClasificación de cobertura vegetal con resolución espacial de 10 metros en bosques del caribe colombiano basado en misiones sentinel 1 y 2. ñolRevista de Teledeteccion, vol. 2023, no. 61, pp. 29–41 (2023)

Fusion of Optical and Radar Data by Aggregation into a Single Feature Space for LULC Classification

Veronica Herrera-Ruiz[1]([✉])[iD], Jheison Perez-Guerra[1][iD],
Juan David Martínez-Vargas[2][iD], Juan Carlos Gonzalez-Velez[1][iD],
and Maria Constanza Torres-Madronero[1][iD]

[1] Department of Engineering, MIRP Research Group, Institución Universitaria ITM,
Medellín, Colombia
veronicaherrera239462@correo.itm.edu.co
[2] Universidad EAFIT, Medellín, Colombia

Abstract. Land use and land cover classification (LULC) is a fundamental input for ecological and socioeconomic models worldwide, generating a large volume of data from space-based platforms, mainly optical technologies. However, these can be affected by atmospheric conditions. Colombia has a high percentage of cloud cover due to its geographical location, which makes it challenging to map LULC changes. Studies have emerged that evaluate the integration of optical and radar images with algorithms that allow for good results despite the information gaps that affect these processes. Therefore, this work compares three supervised machine learning approaches, Support Vector Machines, Random Forest, and XGBoost, to classify land use and land cover from multispectral and radar images, contemplating four scenarios for data fusion. Optical, optical + SAR, optical + SAR ascending, and optical + SAR descending. The result for the Random Forest model using optical + ascending SAR has the best accuracy (76.02%), followed by Random Forest with optical + descending SAR data (75.97%) and with little difference for Random Forest using optical data (75.83%). In future studies, it is of great interest to explore feature extraction on both data sets to improve LULC representation and classification.

Keywords: Land Use Land Cover · Classification · Machine Learning · Remote sensing · Multispectral images · Fusion data

1 Introduction

Natural resources in the world are excessively exploited by human beings to satisfy subsistence needs, such as food, health, economy, and leisure [1]. However, the great tendency of waste and over-exploitation of these resources produces severe consequences for the planet year after year. Some of the human activities that cause these effects are the expansion of the agricultural frontier, livestock,

M. Tabares et al. (Eds.): CCC 2023, CCIS 1924, pp. 25–34, 2024.
https://doi.org/10.1007/978-3-031-47372-2_3

infrastructure, and mining, in addition to other indirect causes associated with social, political, and economic changes [2]. Thus, the care and evolution of natural resources have awakened great interest in generating information and knowledge on land use, land cover, and its changes over time, representing a great need in the scientific community [3].

Large volumes of remote sensing data are produced annually from various systems, also associated with many Earth observation satellites used to monitor activities related to land use and land cover [4]. This increased availability of remotely sensed data has led to a rapid advance and interest in the fusion of optical and radar data. Whereas optical sensors are passive and receive the solar electromagnetic waves reflected from objects to obtain spatial and spectral information, while synthetic aperture radar (SAR) is active, and its images are not affected by weather conditions or sunlight levels [4,5], which together allow obtaining the best of both and complement each other's deficiencies [6]. However, this data fusion has not yet received sufficient attention.

For LULC processing and classification, multiple algorithms have been studied; among these, machine learning (ML) techniques are one of the most relevant [7]. This technique seeks to extract knowledge from the data. Its main objective is to find models that can identify patterns to obtain more secure and reliable classifications [3]. In studies on supervised methods in classification applications, Support Vector Machines (SVM), Random Forest (RF), and Extreme Gradient Boosting (XGBoost) are reported as the most popular ones [8]. Since these generally provide better performance than other traditional classifiers [9]. Furthermore, it is valuable to highlight the potential of machine learning to deal with large historical and current data sets, which are indispensable in applying these algorithms for LULC analysis and classification [10].

Therefore, the purpose of this study is to identify the possibility of increasing the performance of the LULC classification through the fusion of optical and radar data in areas with a high percentage of clouds. It is hoped that this fusion will allow for mitigating the deficiency in data acquisition with optical sensors due to atmospheric conditions in Colombia, a country in which these studies are currently minimal. Initially, the use of 4 of the 5 classes specified in Level 1 of CORINE Land Cover (CLC) is proposed to allow a generic exploration of very common areas in the territory; some examples are artificialized territories (urban areas), agricultural territories (crops), forests and semi-natural areas (pastures), and water surfaces (watercourses).

2   Methods

This research used the main steps of the methodology shown in Fig. 1 to examine land cover classification and analysis from radar and optical data:

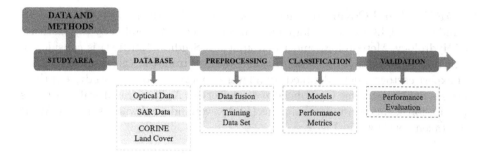

Fig. 1. Data and Methods. Source: Created by Authors.

2.1   Study Area

The study area chosen for this research is located in Antioquia, Colombia. It covers approximately 190,000 hectares of widely diversified territory and is better known as the Oriente Antioqueño sub-region, precisely between the municipalities of Guarne, Guatapé, La Ceja, and Cocorná.

2.2   Data Base

The database comprises optical images from the Sentinel 2 sensor and SAR images from the Sentinel 1 sensor, taken as of August 2019. For Sentinel 2 data, we used the bands with spatial resolution below 20 m and level 2 A (i.e., the orthorectified image with reflectance levels below the atmosphere). While for Sentinel 1, the data were taken from the Ground Range Detected (GRD) collection in vertical transmit and receive (VV) and vertical transmit and horizontal receive (VH) polarization, each in ascending and descending orbit. Resampling was performed for both datasets using the Google Earth Engine tool so that the Sentinel 2 bands were all taken to 20 m, as were the SAR data.

Table 1 details the satellite images and sensors used for the different tasks in this study.

Table 1. Optical and SAR data details

	Sensor	Number of bands	Date	Download Source
Optical	Sentinel 2	10	2019	Google Earth Engine
SAR	Sentinel 1	4	2019	Google Earth Engine

CORINE Land Cover. As reference data to validate the process, the CORINE Land Cover (CLC) methodology map currently led in Colombia by the Institute of Hydrology, Meteorology and Environmental Studies (IDEAM) is considered, which includes land cover classifications obtained from the visual interpretation of expert cartographers, detailed from level 1 to level 6. For this study, 4 of the 5 classes defined at level 1 (artificialized territories (ArT), agricultural territories (AgT), forests and semi-natural areas (FSA), wetlands and water surfaces (WS)) are taken, as shown in Fig. 2.

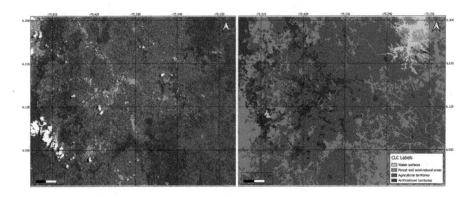

Fig. 2. Study Area & CLC Classes. Source: Created by Authors.

2.3   Preprocessing

The data preparation generally included the construction of the data sets for each image, organizing the matrices of equal length and order according to the bands of each sensor; additionally, all the data were normalized using the Min-MaxScaler function and divided in a relation of 70% training and 30% test using the train_test_split function.

Data Fusion. The pixel values of each image were used for data fusion, considering four scenarios: Optical, Optical + SAR, Optical + ascending SAR, and Optical + descending SAR. The fusions' composition details can be seen in Table 2.

Training Data Set. The information for the training dataset is initially structured using the QGIS Geographic Information System software. Multiple slices of the image are extracted in specific areas so that each class of interest is properly identified, as can be seen in Fig. 3.

Table 2. Composite Images

Composite Images	Bands
Optical	B2, B3, B4, B5, B6, B7, B8, B8A, B11, and B12
SAR	VV ascending, VV descending, VH ascending, and VH descending
Optical + SAR	B2, B3, B4, B5, B6, B7, B8, B8A, B11, B12,
	VV ascending, VH ascending, VV descending, VH descending
Optical + SAR	B2, B3, B4, B5, B6, B7, B8, B8A, B11, B12,
Ascending	VV ascending, VH ascending
Optical + SAR	B2, B3, B4, B5, B6, B7, B8, B8A, B11, B12,
Descending	VV descending, and VH descending

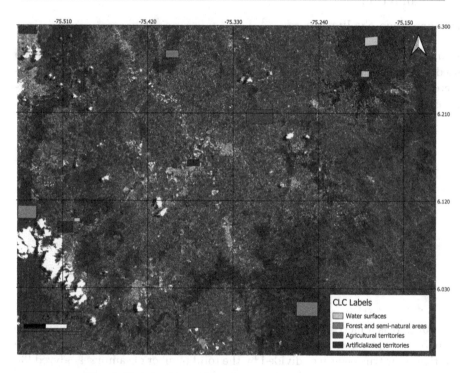

Fig. 3. Training Data Sets. Source: Created by Authors.

2.4   Classification

Models. Three models with supervised machine learning approaches, all set in classification mode, were used for comparison. The first one is SVM which behaves as a tool that maximizes prediction accuracy by automatically avoiding overfitting the data. It seeks to find hyperplanes that determine the decision boundary to classify data points into different classes [11,12]. In addition to supporting multiple continuous and categorical variables and linear and nonlinear samples. The training samples that constrain the margin or hyperplane are the support vectors [7]. The second model is RF which consists of a collection of tree-structured classifiers with identically distributed independent random vectors, where, each tree casts a unitary vote for the most popular class of the input, allowing to obtain a more accurate and stable prediction [6,7]. Finally, XGBoost with a concurrent tree boosting approach provides more accurate large scale problem solving. [8] A classifier is constructed from gradient boosting that predicts a new classification membership after each iteration in an additive manner, making predictions from a weak tree that constantly improves the error of previous classifiers to create a robust classifier [13].

2.5   Validation

Performance Evaluation

Confusion Matrix (CM). A tool for visualizing the performance of an algorithm used in supervised learning, it contains information about the actual and predicted classifications performed by the classification system (See Fig. 4). The performance of these systems is usually evaluated using the matrix data itself [14].

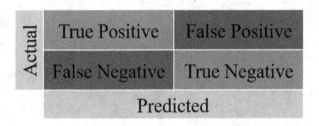

Fig. 4. Confusion matrix. Source: Created by Authors.

Accuracy. It is a metric widely used to evaluate classification models, where the probability that a sample is correctly classified is established: the sum of true positives plus true negatives divided by the total number of samples analyzed [6].

$$Accuracy = \frac{TruePositive + TrueNegative}{AllSamples} \qquad (1)$$

3   Result and Discussion

The results obtained for the database are shown in the Table 3 with the number of records for each class according to the training and validation test respectively. The number of records is equal for each of the 4 data sets.

The classification of optical images, SAR, and the fusion of both was performed using Random Forest, Support Vector Machine, and XGBoost algorithms. The parameters established for the models were the following: SVM with Kernel Radial Basis Function ('rbf'), RF with a maximum depth of the tree at 2 and Random State at 0, and XGBoost was set for multiple classes using the softmax objective and Random State at 42.

The best accuracies obtained were using the Random Forest model, specifically with optical data + ascending SAR (76.02%), followed by optical data + descending SAR (75.97%), and with little difference continued with optical data (75.83%). Table 4 shows the comparison of accuracies according to the data set and each model. Overall over the data sets, the classification using optical imaging + SAR was surprisingly the least accurate, very close to the optical imaging set; however, when considering the difference in data by orbit, the accuracy using optical imaging + ascending SAR increased.

Table 3. Database Size

Class	Train	Test
ArT	12819	460853
AgT	28961	2960360
FSA	20826	1240530
WS	5991	149005
Total	**68597**	**4810748**

Table 4. Comparison of Model Accuracy

Data	Model	Accuracy
Optical	RF	75,83%
Optical	XGB	68,91%
Optical	SVM	75,27%
Optical + SAR	RF	75,59%
Optical + SAR	XGB	69,80%
Optical + SAR	SVM	75,19%
Optical + SAR Ascending	RF	76,02%
Optical + SAR Ascending	XGB	69,19%
Optical + SAR Ascending	SVM	75,17%
Optical + SAR Descending	RF	75,97%
Optical + SAR Descending	XGB	69,47%
Optical + SAR Descending	SVM	75,25%

Figure 5 shows the classification maps obtained using the RF model with the Optical, SAR Ascending, and Descending images, respectively, to allow visual

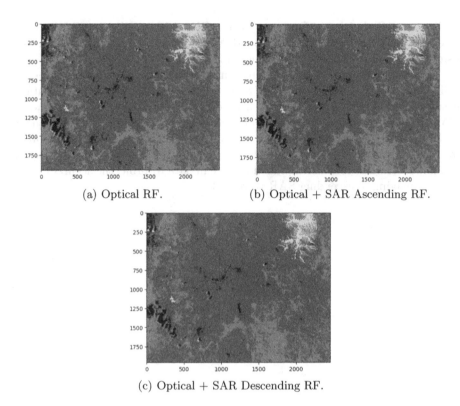

(a) Optical RF.   (b) Optical + SAR Ascending RF.

(c) Optical + SAR Descending RF.

Fig. 5. Images of predictions. Source: Created by Authors.

comparison of the effectiveness of the different dataset approaches that obtained the best accuracy.

With the optical data, it can be identified that the presence of clouds does indeed affect the predictions, and these are classified on the map as artificialized territories; however, the shadows produced by these are also classified, but in this case, as primarily water surfaces. Meanwhile, with the fusion of optical and SAR data, a visually improved land cover map was obtained since the pixels erroneously classified by the phenomenon of cloudiness was reduced.

Figure 6 presents the confusion matrices for the three best results obtained with RF mentioned above. The number of correct classifications is shown in the diagonals in dark green shades. For example, 2537175 optical pixels were correctly classified as AgT, while for the merged data, it increases to around 40000 samples, respectively. It is also identified that this class is the most preponderant in all the classifications obtained, possibly because of the specific properties that differentiate it from the others. In turn, the second best-predicted class is WS, where the class has about 75,4% equivalent to 112395 correctly sorted samples, specifically in optical data.

Table 5. Label abbreviation

ArT	Artificialized territories
AgT	Agricultural territories
FSA	Forests and semi-natural areas
WS	Water surfaces

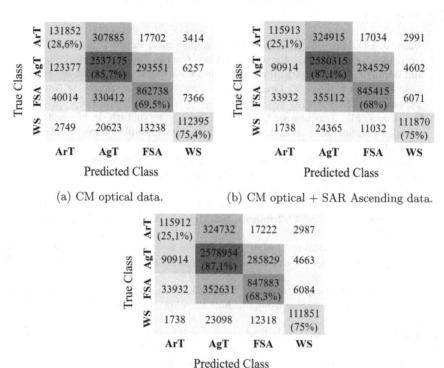

(a) CM optical data.

(b) CM optical + SAR Ascending data.

(c) CM optical + SAR Descending data.

Fig. 6. Confusion matrix of predictions. Source: Created by Authors.

4   Conclusion

This research fused optical and SAR imagery for LULC classification using machine learning algorithms and evaluates the accuracy of maps obtained with optical imagery, SAR, and the combination of both.

The accuracy of the map obtained using optical and SAR imagery was superior to that obtained with optical imagery alone, demonstrating that better land cover classification can be obtained by providing details from both systems that allow them to complement each other. However, there is still an increase in the error of the classifications due to the presence of clouds in the optical data, for which it is necessary to advance in the investigation of techniques to reduce the interference of these clouds in the information provided by the data characteristics.

Finally, this research presents baseline results that can be used to give continuity to the analysis of multisensory data fusion techniques and optimization of supervised models for LULC classification (Table 5).

References

1. Salas, J.A.O., Portilla, T.D.C.L.: Uso e importancia de los recursos naturales y su incidencia en el desarrollo turístico. Caso Cantón Chilla, El Oro, Ecuador Use and importance of the natural resources and their impact on tourism development. Case of Chilla Canton, El Oro, Ecuador. Revista Interamericana de Ambiente y Turismo **14**, 65–79 (2018)
2. Constanza, M., Armenteras, D.: Uso del suelo y estructura de la vegetación en paisajes fragmentados en la amazonia, Colombia. Colombia Forestal **21**(2), 205–223 (2018)
3. Mancera Florez, J.: Evaluación de imágenes de radar Sentinel- 1A e imágenes multiespectrales Sentinel-2A en la clasificación de cobertura del suelo en diferentes niveles de detalle. Ph.D. dissertation (2019)
4. Chen, Y., Bruzzone, L.: Self-supervised SAR-optical data fusion and land-cover mapping using sentinel-1/-2 images, no. Mcl, pp. 1–10 (2021). http://arxiv.org/abs/2103.05543
5. Yuan, Y., et al.: Multi-resolution collaborative fusion of SAR, multispectral and hyperspectral images for coastal wetlands mapping. Remote Sens. **14**(14), 1–27 (2022)
6. Nhemaphuki, D., Thapa Chetri, K., Shrestha, S.: Fusion of radar and optical data for land cover classification using machine learning approach. J. Geoinform. **20**(1), 39–45 (2020)
7. Talukdar, S., et al.: Land-use land-cover classification by machine learning classifiers for satellite observations-a review. Remote Sens. **12**(7) (2020)
8. Shakya, A., Biswas, M., Pal, M.: Fusion and classification of SAR and optical data using multi-image color components with differential gradients. Remote Sens. **15**(1) (2023)
9. Lapini, A., Pettinato, S., Santi, E., Paloscia, S., Fontanelli, G., Garzelli, A.: Comparison of machine learning methods applied to SAR images for forest classification in mediterranean areas. Remote Sens. **12**(3) (2020)
10. Basheer, S., et al.: Comparison of land use land cover classifiers using different satellite imagery and machine learning techniques. Remote Sens. **14**(19), 1–18 (2022)
11. Ouma, Y., et al.: Comparison of machine learning classifiers for multitemporal and multisensor mapping of urban LULC features. Int. Arch. Photogrammetry Remote Sens. Spatial Inf. Sci. - ISPRS Arch. **43**(B3–2022), 681–689 (2022)
12. Thyagharajan, K.K., Vignesh, T.: Soft computing techniques for land use and land cover monitoring with multispectral remote sensing images: a review. Arch. Comput. Methods Eng. **26**(2), 275–301 (2019)
13. Georganos, S., Grippa, T., Vanhuysse, S., Lennert, M., Shimoni, M., Wolff, E.: Very high resolution object-based land use-land cover urban classification using extreme gradient boosting. IEEE Geosci. Remote Sens. Lett. **15**(4), 607–611 (2018)
14. Shultz, T.R., Fahlman, S.E.: Encyclopedia of Machine Learning and Data Mining (2017)

Computer Room Failure Reporting System for a Higher Education Institution

Johan Manuel Alvarez Pinta, Mateo Jesús Cadena Cabrera,
Juan Diego Eraso Muñoz, Miguel Angel Llanten Llanten,
Brayan Fabian Meza, Nicolas Rodriguez Trujillo, Juan Manuel Quijano,
and Marta Cecilia Camacho Ojeda

Institución Universitaria Colegio Mayor del Cauca, Popayán, Colombia
cecamacho@unimayor.edu.co
https://unimayor.edu.co

Abstract. Computer rooms are essential spaces in higher education institutions, they are used for classes, laboratories, and practice sessions related to the various academic programs. In order for students to be able to use computer room equipment without any inconvenience, it must be in perfect working order. Nevertheless, it is very common for computer room equipment to experience malfunctions as a result of excessive or improper use. Therefore, it is essential that these malfunctions are identified and communicated promptly so that they can be resolved by those responsible for equipment maintenance. To address this need, SisReport is proposed as a platform that allows students affected by device failures to make a direct report to the maintenance area. The proposed system will be evaluated from the point of view of user experience. The evaluation of the first version of SisReport involved students, teachers, and the Information and Communications Technology (ICT) team of the Institución Universitaria Colegio Mayor del Cauca. The findings of the evaluation showed that the proposed system is effective for notifying equipment failures in computer rooms compared to the current manual way. The system described in this article can be used by other institutions of higher education to facilitate students' reports of failure of computer equipment in the computer rooms.

Keywords: Web Development · Failure Reporting · User Experience · Computer Rooms

1 Introduction

Higher Education Institutions must comply with the standards established by the Ministry of Education or similar entities in each country in order to provide a quality education service. One of the items to be considered is the technological resources, and it is the obligation of the institutions to guarantee the

Supported by Institución Universitaria Colegio Mayor del Cauca.

M. Tabares et al. (Eds.): CCC 2023, CCIS 1924, pp. 35–44, 2024.
https://doi.org/10.1007/978-3-031-47372-2_4

number and availability of equipment to carry out educational activities such as classes, practices, and laboratories. Ensuring the availability of computer equipment involves preventive and corrective maintenance. Systematization of the maintenance management processes is an existing need in these institutions, in order to facilitate communication and the sending of fault reports between equipment users and the people in charge of their maintenance.

1.1 Problem Description

The computer rooms of a higher education institution are one of the most important tools and spaces to carry out classes, laboratories, and practices of all programs. In most of these institutions, the computer rooms are shared by the different academic programs offered, therefore the use of computer equipment is constant and demanding. It is important that this equipment is in perfect condition in order to guarantee its availability. However, in several of the institutions, the procedure to report failures by teachers or students is not clear, in some cases, it is not known who should address a failure report. Therefore, it happens very often that equipment can remain damaged for weeks, without the people who make up the maintenance team being aware of the damage and therefore it is not being repaired.

Given the importance of the equipment in the computer rooms of higher education institutions, there is a need to implement maintenance actions for the equipment in order to guarantee its availability and permanence over time. This makes it necessary to implement tools to improve administration and management. Several questions arise: Does a web application that allows notification of damaged equipment in computer rooms facilitate the reporting of damages and the attention to them? What is the information needed to make a report? and what is the easiest and most efficient way to report a computer equipment failure?

2   Related Works

A review of the literature on the "Computer Room Fault Reporting System" was conducted using Google Scholar, Springer and IEEE Xplore as sources. Specific keywords related to the topic were used and studies published in the last ten years, related to computer room equipment, were prioritized. The information obtained was organized and analyzed in a synthesis matrix. Keywords: Web Development, Fault Reporting, User Experience, Computer Rooms.

Search string: "Web Development" or "Bug Reporting" and "User Experience" and "Computer Rooms", other string: "User Experience" and "Computer Rooms" or "Web Development" and "Bug Reporting". The results obtained from the search strings were refined, initially by reading the abstract of the papers. As inclusion criteria, articles and papers related to computer rooms or laboratories were considered. Papers related to other types of equipment were excluded.

Table 1. Synthesis matrix results of the literature review.

Paper title	Description
Web control system for requests and failure reporting in the computer equipment of module 4	The objective of this project was to improve the reporting of failures that were done manually and without adequate follow-up. The problem posed is similar to the one presented in this article. They propose an administrative module to obtain a history of requests and reports. This element will be considered in the design of the proposed solution
Development of maintenance management system for computer equipment in the Educational Unit El Triunfo	It proposes to implement a management and maintenance control system for computer equipment, automating processes and improving incident management. An interesting feature of this proposal is that the software product considers the status of the report and which person is responsible for performing the maintenance
Control and management tool for computer classrooms at Universidad Minuto de Dios (CMAC)	This work coincides with the proposal being presented in that the authors identified the need for software to optimize the operation of computer rooms. Similarly, it also uses a web platform to facilitate reporting
Implementation of a failure a reporting system that allows of failure analysis to improve the machine reliability index	This system allows recording failures, classifying them by systems and subsystems, and obtaining monthly reports to analyze the progressive behavior of the machines. In the work presented in this paper, the aim is to make monthly reports on the reports and the maintenance performed
Improved failure reporting through an app	In this project, it detects that one of the drawbacks is the inaccurate information in the report made by the users of the equipment that fails. In this work, we propose as a solution the categorization of the possible failures that an equipment can suffer. The maintenance team will be consulted to see if they use categories for the types of failures

The most important findings are summarized in Table 1. The results found in the literature review evidenced the importance of systematizing the failure-reporting procedure in computer rooms. Applying technologies such as the web, artificial intelligence or the Internet of Things can help to improve the equipment maintenance procedure. The projects have shown that by automating this procedure, problem detection and resolution can be accelerated, downtime can be reduced and user experience can be improved. However, the specific conditions of each institution require the adaptability of the software to different environments and the long-term evaluation of its effectiveness and sustainability.

2.1   Similar Software Products

A non-systematic search was carried out in the Google search engine and in mobile application stores for software products similar to the one that is to be developed in this work. Four web applications similar to the one to be developed were explored. These applications were ServiceNow [6], Spiceworks [7], Asset Panda [8] and GLPI [9]. The Table 2 shows a comparison between the four products explored and eight characteristics identified.

Unlike these applications, the proposed system focuses exclusively on the reporting and tracking of laptops, computers and peripherals in the university environment. This allows for a focused and simplified experience for the users: students and university professors. From this review, it is sought that the report information is complete so that the maintenance team can identify the equipment to be repaired and the failure it presents. The importance of the functionalities for the administrator and for the maintenance team that should be included is evident.

Table 2. Comparison of similar software products.

Characteristics	ServiceNow	Spiceworks	Asset Panda	GLPI
Incident management	Included	Included	not included	Included
Change management	Included	not included	not included	Included
Problem management	Included	not included	not included	Included
Configuration management	Included	not included	not included	Included
Asset management	Included	not included	Included	Included
Code labels	not included	not included	Bars and QR code	not included
Life cycle of assets	not included	not included	Included	Included
Web platform	Included	not included	Included	not included

3   Methodology

The methodology used is based on a five-phase approach, which seeks to integrate different procedures proposed by Viloria [?] for conducting applied research. The phases of preliminary, organization, development/execution, completion and maintenance will be followed, adapting them to the needs of the project. In the preliminary phase, a diagnosis of the problem, characterization of the target audience, and background review were carried out. The second phase, called organization, defined the problem, the objectives and the planning of the project. The development and execution phase involved the definition of the elements of the equipment failure reporting procedure. In this phase the Scrum management framework was followed. A sprint 0 was performed where the requirements were defined and 3 sprints were proposed, each one with an objective and an evaluation focused on the user experience. The last phase called culmination is projected to evaluate the project and its achievements.

4   Results

At the Institución Universitaria Colegio Mayor del Cauca, it was identified that the process of reporting equipment failures in the computer rooms is manual. The problem identified was the lack of knowledge of the failure reporting process and the lack of accurate and complete information on the reports made. These two shortcomings were identified in several of the higher education institutions in the city of Popayán. The equipment failure reporting procedures observed showed long repair times since the failures were not reported and the few reports made did not have the necessary information for the maintenance team. The problem identified can be seen Fig. 2. The elements identified to systematize the process of reporting equipment failures have been included in a web application that allows students and university teachers to make the reports and facilitate the entry of the correct and necessary data. The proposed system has been named SisReport.

4.1   SisReport

This is a software product oriented to students and professors of a higher education institution, who face problems and technical failures in the equipment belonging to the computer rooms of the institution. The SisReport product is a web-based system that facilitates the reporting of failures, which seeks to improve the efficiency and speed in responding to requests for maintenance of computer room equipment. Unlike manual ways of fault reporting such as mail or voice-to-voice notification to the support team, this product is faster to use and does not require travel or search of the personnel in charge, allowing users to quickly notify the support team about any technical problem. In addition, our product provides real-time information on the status of service requests, ensuring efficient communication between users and the support team, adapting them to the needs of the project (Fig. 1).

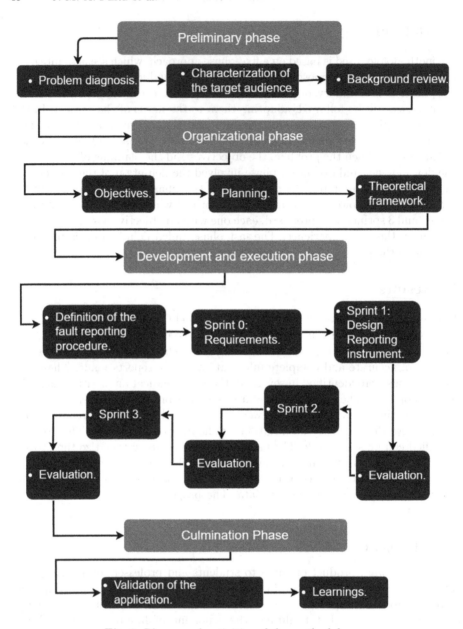

Fig. 1. Phases and activities of the methodology

In the SisReport requirements approach, seven user stories were initially identified, and 2 to 4 acceptance criteria were associated per story, see Table 3. Three iterations were planned with an approximate duration of two months. At the end of each iteration, acceptance tests were carried out with a group of student users and directors of the information and communication technologies management team of a higher education institution in the city of Popayán.

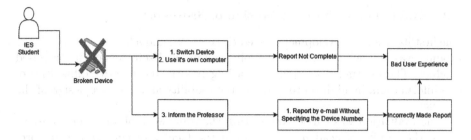

Fig. 2. Problem statement

Table 3. User Stories of the first version of SisReport.

User stories	User	Priority
Report Failure	student or professor	7
Receive Failure Report	Maintenance Team	6
Modify Report Status	Maintenance Team	5
Assignment of reporting responsibility	Maintenance Team	4
Importance Report Rating	Maintenance Team	3
Query report status	student or professor	2
Supplemental Report	student or professor	1

For the first iteration, the test report histories and the visualization of the report by the maintenance team were considered. The user experience is considered to seek ease of use, seeking to meet the needs and expectations of users, reducing the possible difficulties that may arise when reporting a failure of computer equipment. The Fig. 3 shows a basic schematic of the SisReport architecture.

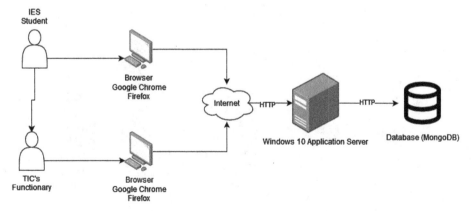

Fig. 3. SisReport Schematic

4.2   Evaluation of the First Version of SisReport

The first iteration of development lasted three weeks, and a first evaluation of the product was planned to estimate the following items: Usefulness of the proposed product, The information required in a bug report, and identify difficulties of this information, in addition to evaluate the usability and interface design of the product.

The evaluation was carried out within the framework of an academic event where the results of academic projects of the faculty of engineering are presented. Eighteen students and professors from the Institución Universitaria Colegio Mayor Del Cauca participated in the evaluation, who were able to get to know and interact with the SisReport prototype and then evaluate it through the application of a survey. The questions asked were: Do you find SisReport useful? Do you like the design of SisReport? Is the reporting process easy to carry out? Did you have difficulties in making the report? What suggestions do you have for SisReport? Would you use SisReport? Would you recommend the use of SisReport for the institution?

Of the eighteen students and university professors surveyed 94%find SisReport useful. 78% like the design, 94%consider that it is not difficult for them to make a report. 100%would use SisReport. Among the suggestions they made was to make it easier to enter the team identifier, since the report asks for the room number and the team number, the latter of which is not always known by the student. One possible solution that the development team is going to consider is to use a QR code to increase the reliability of the information in the report and facilitate the entry of the information, improving the user experience.

A second evaluation was carried out with the participation of three members of the management team. In this evaluation we considered the correctness of

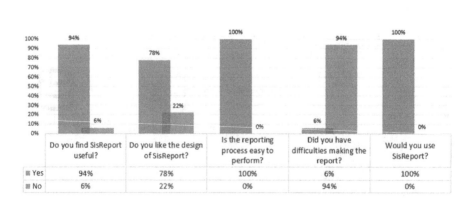

Fig. 4. Results of the SisReport version 1 surveys

the information considered in the report of the failure of a computer equipment and the usefulness of the report to initiate the maintenance required by the equipment to be repaired (Fig. 4).

Regarding the appreciation of the support team members, the surveys revealed that SisReport is considered very useful by the ICT team. In addition, they are satisfied with the design and find it easy to use. They recommend its implementation in the institution. Some difficulties identified include user verification, report validation and status verification. They suggest improving the system with a mobile version, email alerts of report status, and the ability to add observations by the maintenance team. These suggestions will help strengthen the system and meet user needs.

5   Preliminary Conclusions and Future Work

The need for software systems in higher education institutions is constant, especially for systems that support the performance of daily tasks and facilitate communication. The system development process involves requirements identification techniques and technical tasks. It is considered that the evaluation of the quick versions allows improving the quality of the product and refining requirements and validating the data in the reports to achieve a functional product with a good user experience. The evaluation of the first version shows that SisReport would facilitate the correct and prompt notification of damaged equipment, which would allow the maintenance group to attend to requirements more promptly, providing satisfaction to students and teachers when their requests are attended to.

The project will continue to be developed. SisReport will include a form that facilitates reporting, specifically the recognition of each piece of equipment without the need to enter the number or code, thus avoiding errors. The implementation of a QR code to identify the equipment and its location within the institution will be evaluated, as well as the development of a mobile version. In addition, notifications to the student's email facilitating the interaction and solution of the ICT team. Future versions should consider how to validate the student making the report to avoid false reports. These improvements will contribute to optimize the reporting process, ensure efficient communication, and provide users with a more pleasant and satisfactory experience.

Eventually the product is proposed to expand to other entities outside the IES, such as banks, offices, or other institutions that need to strengthen communication with their technical service, for this a user identification system (Login) can be implemented based on the environment where the software is required. When the software is integrated into other environments it is necessary to have a ChatBot, which can give possible quick solutions, depending on the problem that is described, as there are situations where the technical service can not come instantly, these improvements will help ensure the adaptability of the software in new environments where it is very demanding.

Acknowledgements. We are grateful for the support of the research system of the Institución Universitaria Colegio Mayor del Cauca for the realization of this project url: https://unimayor.edu.co/web/.

References

1. Gamino, M.P.: Sistema de control web para peticiones y reporte de fallas en los equipos de cómputo del módulo 4. Facultad de ciencias de la computación. Benemérita Universidad Autonoma de Puebla. Tesina, Octuber 2021. https://repositorio.unemi.edu.ec
2. Mantilla, C.A.: Desarrollo de un sistema de gestión de mantenimiento de equipos de cómputo en la Unidad Educativa el Triunfo. Facultad ciencias e ingeniería, Universidad Estatal de Milagro. Trabajo de integración curricular, February, México (2020). https://repositorioinstitucional.buap.mx/
3. Ortiz Piñeros, J.J., Olaya, J.S., Vivas Gómez, B.J.: Herramienta de control y manejo de las aulas de cómputo en La Universidad Minuto de Dios (CMAC). Facultad de ingeniería. Corporación Universitaria Minuto de Dios. Trabajo de grado. Ecuador (2012). https://repository.uniminuto.edu/handle/10656/2596
4. Lorca Rojas, D.A., Albornoz, A.L.: Implementación de un sistema de reportes de fallas que permita realizar análisis de fallas mejorando el índice de confiabilidad de las máquinas. Escuela de Ingenieria Mecanica. Universidad de Talca, Chile (2005). http://dspace.utalca.cl/handle/1950/2137
5. Uribe Escobar, C.M.: Mejoramiento de los reportes de falla por medio de App. Facultad de ingeniería. Universidad de Antioquia. Trabajo de grado, Colombia (2020). https://hdl.handle.net/10495/16075
6. Aldama, L.: ServiceNow: Flujos de trabajo flexibles e inteligentes (2017). https://blog.softtek.com/es/servicenow. Accessed 4 May 2023
7. Capterra: Spiceworks IT Help Desk (s.f.). https://www.cap-terra.co/software/102709/spiceworks-it-help-desk. Accessed 25 Mar 2023
8. Appvizer: Asset Panda: software de seguimiento de activos (s.f.). https://www.appvizer.es/contabilidad-finanzas/seguimiento-activos/asset-panda. Accessed 22 Apr 2023
9. Beiro, O.: Aprovechando GLPI para su uso como ESM en diversas áreas de negocio. España (2023). https://tic.gal/es/aprovechando-glpi-para-su-uso-como-esm-en-diversas-areas-de-negocio/. Accessed 22 May 2023
10. Viloria Cedeño, N.: Metodología para investigaciones aplicadas con enfoque transdisciplinario: sociales y tecnológicas. Universidad Pedagógica Experimental Libertador, Caracas, Venezuela (2016)

Recent Advances in Machine Learning for Differential Cryptanalysis

Isabella Martínez[1], Valentina López[1], Daniel Rambaut[2], Germán Obando[3], Valérie Gauthier-Umaña[4(✉)] ⓘ, and Juan F. Pěrez[5] ⓘ

[1] Ressolve, Bogotá, Colombia
[2] Opensc, Bogotá, Colombia
[3] Departamento de Ingeniería Electrónica, Universidad de Nariño, Nariño, Colombia
[4] Systems and Computing Engineering Department, Universidad de los Andes, Bogotá, Colombia
ve.gauthier@uniandes.edu.co
[5] Department of Industrial Engineering, Universidad de los Andes, Bogotá, Colombia

Abstract. Differential cryptanalysis has proven to be a powerful tool to identify weaknesses in symmetric-key cryptographic systems such as block ciphers. Recent advances have shown that machine learning methods are able to produce very strong distinguishers for certain cryptographic systems. This has generated a large interest in the topic of machine learning for differential cryptanalysis as evidenced by a growing body of work in the last few years. In this paper we aim to provide a guide to the current state of the art in this topic in the hope that a unified view can better highlight the challenges and opportunities for researchers joining the field.

Keywords: Differential cryptanalysis · Machine learning · Survey

1 Introduction

Since the seminal paper of Rivest [24], a large number of machine learning approaches for cryptanalysis have been proposed. While a steady flow of progress has been sustained since, the recent paper of Gohr [12] has provided a new flurry of excitement as it manages to employ recent deep learning architectures to improve upon known results in differential cryptanalysis.

Given that the space of cryptographic systems is quite large, and that there exist many machine learning techniques, it can be hard to gather a clear picture of the current state of the art in the field of machine learning for cryptanalysis. This paper aims to provide a guide to the current state of the art in this field, especially in regards to *differential* cryptanalysis, where most of the recent work has centered.

M. Tabares et al. (Eds.): CCC 2023, CCIS 1924, pp. 45–56, 2024.
https://doi.org/10.1007/978-3-031-47372-2_5

1.1 Related Work

In spite of the increasing number of works in the field of machine learning for cryptanalysis there are very few surveys on the topic. In [4], the authors provide a detailed analysis of the strengths and weaknesses of various machine learning techniques and their effectiveness in breaking different types of cryptographic systems. However, being over a decade old, it does not consider the recent progress in the field. A more recent survey [1] provides a wider overview of machine learning in cryptography, considering not just cryptanalysis but also image steganalysis, side-channel analysis, power analysis attacks, and encrypted traffic classification. With this wider spectrum of applications, the topic of cryptanalysis receives a corresponding limited attention span, thus focusing on only the most relevant contributions according to the authors. Finally, the most recent survey [33] considers the dichotomy between neural networks and cryptography, and in particular covers the application of neural computing to attack cryptographic systems. The survey considers a number of contributions in this area but misses the proposal of neural distinguishers by Gohr [12] and others, which is a key development in the area. In this survey paper we provide an up-to-date guide to these and other recent advances in the field of machine learning for differential cryptanalysis.

In the following we provide some background definitions to summarize the main concepts in both differential cryptanalysis and machine learning. Next, we survey existing works in the area of machine learning for differential cryptanalysis, with a focus on the most recent results.

2 Foundations

In this section we provide a brief summary of definitions of symmetric cryptography and machine learning necessary for the discussion on how these topics coalesce around cryptanalysis.

2.1 Symmetric Cryptography

Symmetric-key algorithms use the same key for encryption and the decryption. One type of symmetric-key algorithms are stream ciphers, where the bits of the message are XORed with a pseudorandom secret key, which is expensive but fast, such as ARC4. Another type are block ciphers, where the message is divided into blocks of the same size. Block ciphers are typically made of several rounds, which are almost the same, except for some special values (called round constants) and the round key. These round keys are built from the secret key using an algorithm called "key schedule".

There are several families of block ciphers, such as the ones based on substitution-permutation networks (SPN), examples of which include the standard AES, Serpent and PRESENT. In SPNs, each round involves an XOR between the message and the round key followed by a substitution box (S-Box) and a permutation box (P-Box) that is in charge of distributing the outputs of the S-box to many other S-boxes in the next round. Another family is the one constructed using a Feistel structure, such as DES, TEA, Blowfish and Twofish. In this structure, the message is divided in left and right parts. The right part is the input of a so-called F function and its output is XORed with the left part of the message. The F function is made by a non-linear function that has an SPN structure and hides the relation between the ciphertext and the key ensuring Shanon's property of confusion. A simpler set of block ciphers are those in the ARX (Add-Rotate-Xor) family, such as SPECK and SIMON. The symmetric cryptography used in constrained environments (e.g. IoT) is called lightweight. The ARX cipher is considered to be a lightweight, fast, and secure encryption method. It is widely used in applications that require high-performance cryptography, such as embedded systems, mobile devices, and network security protocols. Examples include Salsa20, ChaCha and SPECK, SIMON and SIMECK. Lightweight cryptosystems based on other structures include PRESENT and GIFT64.

Block ciphers structures are often used as the base of Message Authentication Code (MAC) schemes, like Chasky, and for the construction of Hash functions. Also, some permutation primitives can be used to build high-security block ciphers, stream ciphers, ans MAC's, authenticated ciphers, hash functions, etc. with a unified hardware. Examples include Gimli, KNOT and ASCON.

Symmetric ciphers can also be found in different so-called modes, like for example Electronic Codebook (ECB) and Cipher Block Chaining (CBC) modes. In ECB mode, each block is encrypted independently while in CBC mode, each plaintext is XORed with the ciphertext. They have different advantages and some of them can provide more security.

2.2 Symmetric Cryptanalysis

There are a number of different techniques to analyze the security of symmetric cryptosystems, such as brute force attacks, linear and differential cryptanalysis, among others.

On the one hand, linear cryptanalysis looks for linear relationships between the plaintext, ciphertext and the key and by analyzing these relationships, an attacker can deduce information about the secret key. On the other hand, differential cryptanalysis methods depend on identifying high-probability differences between plaintext and ciphertext pairs. These differences, also known as characteristics, are essential for successful attacks. The idea was first introduced in 1990 [6] where it was used to attack DES. Since then, differential cryptanalysis has been considered to attack a wide range of symmetric key cryptosystems, including AES, Blowfish, and Twofish. The goal is to find techniques that are aimed at tracking differences across the transformation network, identifying instances where the cipher deviates from random behavior, and exploiting such properties to recover the secret key. Let $E : \{0,1\}^n \rightarrow \{0,1\}^m$ be a map. A differential transition for E is a pair $(\Delta_{\text{in}}, \Delta_{\text{out}})$ in $\{0,1\}^n \times \{0,1\}^m$. The probability of the differential transition is defined as

$$P\left(\Delta_{\text{in}} \to \Delta_{\text{out}}\right) = \frac{\text{Card}\left(\{x \in \{0,1\}^n : E(x) \oplus E\left(x \oplus \Delta_{\text{in}}\right) = \Delta_{\text{out}}\}\right)}{2^n}.$$

Considerable research has been devoted to improving methods for finding characteristics. In the seminal paper by Wang et al. [30], characteristics of the hash function SHA-0 were manually constructed using knowledge of the hash function's structure. Later advancements were made by De Canniere and Rechberger in [10], and by Leurent in [18] and [19], who enhanced Wang's approach by imposing constraints on the plaintexts. Additionally, Chen et al. introduced a ranking system for discovering differential characteristics and applied it to lightweight block ciphers [7]. Furthermore, novel methods utilizing Mixed-Integer Linear Programming have been proposed to enhance the process of characteristic finding, as demonstrated by Mouha et al. in [22], Sun et al. in [29], and Zhao et al. in [32].

For cryptographic systems built based on the iteration of a cipher block, a differential trail or differential characteristic is a sequence of differential transitions. Thus, these characteristics show how the differences in the input propagate through the internal components of the primitive. The higher the probability of the differential characteristic, the more pairs that can be studied to recover the key, which increases the insecurity of the encryption, since for the basic differential attack, one particular output difference is expected to be more frequent, which means the cipher output can be distinguished from a random one. Any dependence of the differential probability on the key is usually suppressed. Further details can be found in [11,26] and [28].

2.3   Machine Learning

Machine learning (ML) comprises a large number of methods that enable computers to learn patterns from datasets. It has found many applications in computer vision, natural language processing, voice recognition, among others. In cryptography, supervised learning, a type of ML, helps recognize encrypted data patterns and detect malicious activity. In particular, neural networks are ML models composed of a number of nodes linked by weighted connections. Neural networks are trained by adjusting connection weights and biases to minimize a loss function, $L(\theta)$, which can be represented as

$$L(\theta) = \frac{1}{N} \sum_{i=1}^{N} \mathcal{L}(y_i, f(x_i; \theta)),$$

where N denotes the number of samples, y_i represents the observed output, $f(x_i; \theta)$ the predicted output, and $\mathcal{L}(y_i, f(x_i; \theta))$ measure the difference between the observed and the predicted outputs. The objective of training the neural network is to find the optimal parameters θ^* that minimize the loss function, i.e.,

$$\theta^* = \arg \min_{\theta} L(\theta). \tag{1}$$

As discussed in the next section, many of the ML approaches for cryptanalysis rely on neural networks to build so-called neural distinguishers.

3   Machine Learning Approaches for Differential Cryptanalysis

This section presents a number of recent approaches for differential cryptanalysis based on machine learning methods. We classify these approaches in two categories: attacks on SIMON and SPECK, as many methods centered on these, and attacks on other cryptosystems. Table 1 provides a summary of the methods considered, classified by the cryptosystem attacked and the type of neural network employed.

Table 1. Comparative Table for Distinguisher Approach

		Neural network			
		Residual Net	Multilayer Perceptron	Convolutional	LSTM
Cryptosystem	SPECK	[2, 12, 14]	[31]	[8]	
	SIMON	[13, 14, 20]	[31]		
	SIMECK	[20]	[15]		
	GIMLI		[3]	[3]	[3]
	ASCON		[3]	[3]	[3]
	KNOT		[3]	[3]	[3]
	CHASKEY		[3]	[3, 8]	[3]
	TEA		[5]	[5]	
	RAIDEN		[5]	[5]	
	PRESENT		[15]		
	GIFT64		[31]		
	DES			[8]	

3.1   Attacks for SIMON and SPECK

As mentioned before, the recent contribution by Gohr [12] has become a keystone in the area of machine learning for differential cryptanalysis. The paper presents a novel technique to improve attacks on the round-reduced version of the Speck32/64 block cipher using deep learning. The author argues that existing attacks on the cipher are limited by the complexity of the differential and linear approximations used to analyze the cipher. To overcome this limitation, the proposed approach consists of training a deep neural network to predict the cipher output for a given input, considering a specific number of rounds. The author demonstrates the effectiveness of the approach by applying it to up to eight rounds of Speck 32/64 and shows that it can improve the success rate of the attack compared to existing techniques. The author also shows that the approach is robust to noise and can generalize to larger numbers of rounds, although it is limited by the amount of training data needed, which increases with the number of rounds. A number of papers have extended and improved Gohr's work recently, as we describe next.

Next, Hou et. al. [13] use deep residual neural networks to train differential distinguishers for SIMON32 with eight and nine rounds. They investigate how patterns in the input differences affect the model accuracy. Even though the input differences they employ result from differential characteristics with the same probability, they discover that their accuracy is different. Employing this distinguisher, the paper develops an 11-round SIMON32 last subkey recovery attack, extends the 9-round SAT-based distinguisher to an 11-round distinguisher, and subsequently suggests a 13-round SIMON32 attack. They employ a Ghor-inspired architecture and discover that for SIMON32, the input difference has a significant impact on the model's performance. The suggested attacks have a success rate of over 90% and require about 45 s to obtain the last subkey. To locate the key, they employ a Bayesian search technique.

In [2], the authors look for alternatives to the Gohr distinguisher that are either smaller or perform better. They are able to successfully prune to one layer, resulting in a network that performs within 1% of the original network. Convolutional autoencoders, a type of neural network, are trained on the ciphertext pairs in order to test whether preparing the input improves performance. They find out, though, that the network was no longer sufficiently sophisticated to extract pertinent data from the input, and employ LIME [23] to further assess the significance of the characteristics. They use iterative and one-shot trimming techniques and note that at least 90% of the 10-layer network (and even the 1-layer network) may be pruned without degrading average performance, and that some of the resulting networks are superior to the original network. Additionally, they investigated whether all 64 input bits were required using LIME, and discovered that each feature's significance is very limited and no region in the bit space has a significant impact on the ranking.

An improvement to neural distinguishers based on SAT/SMT is proposed in [14], where new distinguishers for SIMON and SPECK are proposed. Specifically, the approach is able to consider large-size block-based ciphers, which leads to key recovery attacks for 13 rounds of SIMON32/64, and 14 rounds of SIMON48/96, as well as an attack on 13 rounds of SIMON64/128 using an 11-round neural distinguisher. Unlike Gohr [12], which uses text and ciphertext pairs as samples, the authors in [14] design the distinguisher by taking several differences, arranged in a matrix, as a sample. The matrix is treated as an image, and each output difference is treated as an objective feature, such that if all output differences of the matrix are from the same input difference, the sample is labeled with one, and zero otherwise. They show experimentally that the improvement in the accuracy of distinguishers is due to learning more features from the relationship between the output differences.

More recently, [20] proposes an improved differential neural distinguisher for the SIMON and SIMECK block ciphers. The proposed method improves upon previous neural distinguishers by incorporating related-key attacks, which can improve the accuracy of the distinguisher when the attacker has access to related keys. On the 8-round SIMON-64 cipher with a *single* key, the proposed neural distinguisher achieved an accuracy of 99.98%, while on the same cipher with related keys, it achieved an accuracy of 94.9%. On the six round SIMECK-64 cipher, the proposed neural distinguisher achieved an accuracy of 99.92% for a single-key attack, and of 91.7% for a related-key attack.

3.2 Attacks on Other Systems

Baksi et. al. [3] propose distinguishers for non-Markov ciphers to replicate "all-in-one" differentials, i.e., differentials that take into account the impact on all output differences under the same input difference. The paper presents distinguishers based on deep learning for eight rounds of Gimli-Hash, Gimli-Cipher, and Gimli-Permutation, three rounds of the Ascon-Permutation, ten rounds each of the Knot-256 and Knot-512 permutations, and four rounds of the Chaskey-Permutation. The paper compares different net architectures and experimentally shows that the multi-layer perceptron (MLP) outperforms both CNN and LSTM networks in terms of precision.

In [15], Jain et. al. propose a distinguisher based on deep neural networks for PRESENT-80 and Simeck64/128, attaining excellent precision for six and seven rounds, respectively. They pick a few input differentials and closely follow the steps in [3]. Additionally, they test four differential distinguisher models, the first of which makes use of the design recommended in [3] while the second makes use of the authors' own architecture, with input differentials selected at random. Models three and four employ the same architectures as models one and two, respectively, but with selected differentials instead of random ones. Their tests show model four outperforms the rest with a validation precision of 0.86, 0.76, 0.39 and 0.27 for three, four, five and six rounds of PRESENT, respectively. For SIMECK, this precision is 1, 1, 0.83, 0.48 and 0.27 for three, four, five, six and seven rounds, respectively.

Yadav and Kumar [31] aim to create a framework for ML-based distinguishers to tackle Feistel, SPN, and ARX block ciphers. They apply it to SPECK, SIMON, and GIFT64, lowering the amount of data complexity needed for 9, 12, and 8 rounds, respectively. The paper proposes the first SIMON 12-round distinguisher with a complexity lower than 2^{32}. They name this approach as hybrid Differential-ML distinguisher, which combines traditional differential distinguishers with ML models to tackle more rounds. They take advantage of Gohr's suggested design [12] and Baksi's improvements [3]. The network is trained using the differences directly rather than ciphertext pairs and employ a multi-layer perceptron architecture. The results show that the hybrid approach is able to increase the number of rounds considered without the need for much more data.

The Tiny Encryption Algorithm (TEA) and its evolution, RAIDEN, are put to the test in [5] using two deep learning-based distinguishers. Compared to Speck32/64, in TEA and RAIDEN the block and key sizes are both doubled. The neural distinguishers proposed are based on a multi-layer perceptron architecture and a convolutional architecture, which are shown to outperform traditional ones based on differential trails and statistical methods. Additionally, the paper shows that the loss can be greatly reduced while keeping the number of training samples constant. This is done by breaking the problem into two phases: first, a time-distributed network that treats each 32-bit chunk individually, and second, a fully connected layer. With this approach, the paper shows that the neural distinguishers are able to improve upon traditional bitflip and differential distinguishers for up to six rounds of TEA, with as little as 10^3 samples. This result holds too for a large number of rounds employing a larger number of samples.

A simplified version of DES (S-DES), SIMON, and SPECK, which are considered lightweight systems, are considered in [27], which proposes a general deep learning-based cryptanalysis algorithm that starts with pairs of known plaintext and ciphertext and attempts to determine the block cipher key. The authors consider two setups: i) a simplified setup where the key is made of 8 characters, each one corresponding to one of 64 ASCII characters; ii) a general setup where the key can be made of any string of bits. The neural network model proposed is able to fully attack S-DES, but it can only break SIMON and SPECK under the simplified setup. Under this setup, the ML-based attack broke the S-DES cipher with a success probability of 0.9 given $2^{8.08}$ known plaintexts. Also, it achieved a 0.99 success probability to find 56 bits of Simon32/64 with $2^{12.34}$ known plaintexts and 56 bits of Speck32/64 with $2^{12.33}$ known plaintexts, both under the simplified setup.

Another approach is presented in [16], which proposes a deep learning-based cryptanalysis technique for S-DES, S-AES, and S-SPECK. The proposed method utilizes a fully-connected neural network to learn the characteristics of plaintexts and their corresponding ciphertexts in order to predict the key used by the encryption algorithm. The paper introduces an improvement to Gohr's deep learning model [12] by incorporating skip connections and gated linear units into the neural network structure, enabling a more stable learning. As a result, an average improvement of 5.3% in accuracy is achieved compared to previous works on S-DES [27], while reducing the number of parameters by 93.16%. Furthermore, when applied on S-AES and S-SPECK, the method is able to successfully recover keys of up to 12 bits for S-AES and 6 bits for S-SPECK.

In [8] the authors propose the Extended Differential-Linear Connectivity Table (EDLCT), a tool that describes a cipher and its features relevant to a ciphertext pair. They build various machine learning-based distinguishers, including the neural distinguisher in [12], using these features. They also develop a Feature Set Sensitivity Test (FSST) to identify influential features and create surrogate models based on these features. Experiments on Speck32/64 and DES confirm that the distinguisher learns features corresponding to the

EDLCT. Additionally, the authors explain phenomena related to the neural distinguishers using the EDLCT and demonstrate how machine learning can be used to search for high-correlation differential-linear propagations in the differential-linear attack. The advantages of machine learning in applications such as Chaskey and DES are also showcased.

Another approach is presented in [25], which proposes an artificial neural network-based cryptanalysis method for a simple 8-bit substitution-permutation cipher. The method utilizes a multi-layer perceptron network with a backpropagation learning algorithm to estimate the cipher's inverse function and recover the plaintext. The authors demonstrate the effectiveness of the proposed method on several test cases and show that it outperforms traditional cryptanalysis methods in terms of speed and accuracy.

Finally, we would like to mention an earlier paper [9], which proposes the application of a neural network to S-DES to seek a relationship between plaintext, cipher text and key bits. The network can map the relation between inputs, keys and outputs and to obtain the correct values for the key bits k_0, k_1 and k_4. They also propose new S-boxes, which are more resistant to the differential attack, such that the neural network was not able to point out bits of the key under these S-boxes.

4   Discussion

Prior to the breakthrough generated by Gohr's proposal [12], machine learning applications to cryptanalysis were too limited to be considered efficient in a real-world context. What highlights Gohr's work is its ability to achieve a clear improvement in accuracy and data complexity in contrast to traditional differential analysis. Soon after the publication of this proposal, a number of works have emerged exploring different approaches, in particular considering changes on the network type [3], tweaks to the input layer [2,5,14] and hybrid approaches [13,31], to mention just a few.

Out of the many recent works in this direction, the work by Baksi [3] deserves particular attention as it performed a comparison between network architectures to find experimentally that the multi-layer perception had the best results. This result led several authors to focus their research on this type of network architecture. However, machine learning is currently a rapidly evolving field and new architectures are regularly proposed in a variety of areas of application, opening the door for new methods to be considered for differential cryptanalysis.

While this paper has focused on machine learning methods for differential cryptanalysis, these methods have been considered in many other areas of cryptography. For instance, [21] examines the use of ML for the identification of encryption algorithms. The objective is to determine the encryption algorithm being used by employing a set of plaintexts and their ciphered versions under several encryption algorithms. Seven encryption methods, each in the EBC and CBC modes, six classification algorithms, and plaintexts in seven distinct languages were employed. Specifically, the paper considers DES, Blowfish, RSA,

ARC4, Rijndael, Serpent, and Twofish as the encryption methods, while the machine learning methods are C4.5, PART, FT, Complement Naive Bayes, Multilayer Perceptron, and WiSARD. The authors find that the classification algorithms are unaffected by the plaintexts' original language, and perform significantly better in ECB than in CBC mode. In ECB mode, the Complement Naive Bayes algorithm displays the best performance with 100% accuracy.

Another prominent application of machine learning in cryptanalysis lies in profiled side-channel analysis [17], where information leaked from a physical cryptosystem is used to break it. Here, convolutional neural networks have shown significant potential, especially by means of adding artificial noise to the input signal, which improves the performance of the neural network and reduces the number of measurements needed to reveal the secret key. These are but a couple of examples of the diverse and promising applications of machine learning in cryptography, from differential cryptanalysis and identification of encryption algorithms to profiled side-channel analysis.

5   Conclusion

This survey has shed light on the remarkable progress of machine learning in the field of cryptography, with a particular focus on differential attacks and the utilization of deep learning for distinguishers. These findings emphasize the dynamic and ever-evolving nature of the machine learning domain. As new architectures and algorithms emerge, there is great potential for significant advancements in the performance and efficiency of these distinguishers. The integration of deep learning techniques is a novel approach in the field of cryptanalysis, empowering researchers to tackle complex cryptographic problems and enhancing the security of modern cryptographic systems. As machine learning continues to mature, we can anticipate further breakthroughs, highlighting the importance for researchers and practitioners to remain vigilant and adapt to the evolving landscape of machine learning to stay ahead of potential security threats and leverage the transformative potential of this technology for the betterment of cryptography.

References

1. Alani, M.M.: Applications of machine learning in cryptography: a survey. In: Proceedings of the 3rd International Conference on Cryptography, Security and Privacy, pp. 23–27 (2019)
2. Băcuieti, N., Batina, L., Picek, S.: Deep neural networks aiding cryptanalysis: a case study of the speck distinguisher. In: Ateniese, G., Venturi, D. (eds.) ACNS 2022. LNCS, pp. 809–829. Springer, Cham (2022). https://doi.org/10.1007/978-3-031-09234-3_40
3. Baksi, A., Breier, J., Chen, Y., Dong, X.: Machine learning assisted differential distinguishers for lightweight ciphers. In: 2021 Design, Automation & Test in Europe Conference & Exhibition (DATE), pp. 176–181 (2021)

4. Baragada, S., Reddy, P.S.: A survey on machine learning approaches to crypt-analysis. Int. J. Emerg. Trends Technol. Comput. Sci. (IJETTCS) **2**(4), 148–153 (2013)
5. Bellini, E., Rossi, M.: Performance comparison between deep learning-based and conventional cryptographic distinguishers. In: Arai, K. (ed.) Intelligent Computing. LNNS, vol. 285, pp. 681–701. Springer, Cham (2021). https://doi.org/10.1007/978-3-030-80129-8_48
6. Biham, E., Shamir, A.: Differential cryptanalysis of DES-like cryptosystems. J. Cryptol. **4**, 3–72 (1991)
7. Chen, J., Miyaji, A., Su, C., Teh, J.: Improved differential characteristic searching methods. In: 2nd International Conference on Cyber Security and Cloud Computing, pp. 500–508. IEEE (2015)
8. Chen, Y., Yu, H.: Bridging machine learning and cryptanalysis via EDLCT. Cryptology ePrint Archive (2021)
9. Danziger, M., Henriques, M.A.A.: Improved cryptanalysis combining differential and artificial neural network schemes. In: 2014 International Telecommunications Symposium (ITS), pp. 1–5 (2014)
10. De Cannière, C., Rechberger, C.: Finding SHA-1 characteristics: general results and applications. In: Lai, X., Chen, K. (eds.) ASIACRYPT 2006. LNCS, vol. 4284, pp. 1–20. Springer, Heidelberg (2006). https://doi.org/10.1007/11935230_1
11. Ferguson, N., Schneier, B.: Practical Cryptography, vol. 141. Wiley, New York (2003)
12. Gohr, A.: Improving attacks on round-reduced speck32/64 using deep learning. In: Boldyreva, A., Micciancio, D. (eds.) CRYPTO 2019. LNCS, vol. 11693, pp. 150–179. Springer, Cham (2019). https://doi.org/10.1007/978-3-030-26951-7_6
13. Hou, Z., Ren, J., Chen, S.: Cryptanalysis of round-reduced simon32 based on deep learning. IACR Cryptology ePrint Archive **2021**, 362 (2021)
14. Hou, Z., Ren, J., Chen, S.: Improve neural distinguisher for cryptanalysis. IACR Cryptology ePrint Archive **2021**, 1017 (2021)
15. Jain, A., Kohli, V., Mishra, G.: Deep learning based differential distinguisher for lightweight cipher present. IACR Cryptology ePrint Archive **2020**, 846 (2020)
16. Kim, H., Lim, S., Kang, Y., Kim, W., Seo, H.: Deep learning based cryptanalysis of lightweight block ciphers, revisited. Cryptology ePrint Archive (2022)
17. Kim, J., Picek, S., Heuser, A., Bhasin, S., Hanjalic, A.: Make some noise. Unleashing the power of convolutional neural networks for profiled side-channel analysis. IACR Trans. Cryptographic Hardw. Embed. Syst. 148–179 (2019)
18. Leurent, G.: Analysis of differential attacks in ARX constructions. In: Wang, X., Sako, K. (eds.) ASIACRYPT 2012. LNCS, vol. 7658, pp. 226–243. Springer, Heidelberg (2012). https://doi.org/10.1007/978-3-642-34961-4_15
19. Leurent, G.: Construction of differential characteristics in ARX designs application to skein. In: Canetti, R., Garay, J.A. (eds.) CRYPTO 2013. LNCS, vol. 8042, pp. 241–258. Springer, Heidelberg (2013). https://doi.org/10.1007/978-3-642-40041-4_14
20. Lu, J., Liu, G., Sun, B., Li, C., Liu, L.: Improved (related-key) differential-based neural distinguishers for SIMON and SIMECK block ciphers. Comput. J. (2023)
21. de Mello, F.L., Xexéo, J.A.M.: Identifying encryption algorithms in ECB and CBC modes using computational intelligence. J. Univers. Comput. Sci. **24**, 25–42 (2018)
22. Mouha, N., Wang, Q., Gu, D., Preneel, B.: Differential and linear cryptanalysis using mixed-integer linear programming. In: Wu, C.-K., Yung, M., Lin, D. (eds.) Inscrypt 2011. LNCS, vol. 7537, pp. 57–76. Springer, Heidelberg (2012). https://doi.org/10.1007/978-3-642-34704-7_5

23. Ribeiro, M.T., Singh, S., Guestrin, C.: "Why should I trust you?": explaining the predictions of any classifier. In: Proceedings of the 22nd ACM SIGKDD International Conference on Knowledge Discovery and Data Mining, pp. 1135–1144. Association for Computing Machinery, New York (2016)

24. Rivest, R.L.: Cryptography and machine learning. In: Imai, H., Rivest, R.L., Matsumoto, T. (eds.) ASIACRYPT 1991. LNCS, vol. 739, pp. 427–439. Springer, Heidelberg (1993). https://doi.org/10.1007/3-540-57332-1_36

25. Ruzhentsev, V., Levchenko, R., Fediushyn, O.: Cryptanalysis of simple substitution-permutation cipher using artificial neural network. In: 2020 IEEE International Conference on Problems of Infocommunications. Science and Technology (PIC S&T), pp. 631–634 (2020)

26. Schneier, B.: Applied Cryptography: Protocols, Algorithms, and Source Code in C. Wiley, Hoboken (2007)

27. So, J.: Deep learning-based cryptanalysis of lightweight block ciphers. Secur. Commun. Netw. **2020**, 1–11 (2020)

28. Stinson, D.R., Paterson, M.: Cryptography: Theory and Practice. CRC Press, Boca Raton (2018)

29. Sun, S., et al.: Towards finding the best characteristics of some bit-oriented block ciphers and automatic enumeration of (related-key) differential and linear characteristics with predefined properties. Cryptology ePrint Archive (2014)

30. Wang, X., Yu, H., Yin, Y.L.: Efficient collision search attacks on SHA-0. In: Shoup, V. (ed.) CRYPTO 2005. LNCS, vol. 3621, pp. 1–16. Springer, Heidelberg (2005). https://doi.org/10.1007/11535218_1

31. Yadav, T., Kumar, M.: Differential-ML distinguisher: machine learning based generic extension for differential cryptanalysis. In: Longa, P., Ràfols, C. (eds.) LATINCRYPT 2021. LNCS, vol. 12912, pp. 191–212. Springer, Cham (2021). https://doi.org/10.1007/978-3-030-88238-9_10

32. Zhao, H., Han, G., Wang, L., Wang, W.: MILP-based differential cryptanalysis on round-reduced midori64. IEEE Access **8**, 95888–95896 (2020)

33. Zolfaghari, B., Koshiba, T.: The dichotomy of neural networks and cryptography: war and peace. Appl. Syst. Innov. **5**(4), 61 (2022)

Addressing the Diet Problem with Constraint Programming Enhanced with Machine Learning

Sara Jazmín Maradiago Calderón, Juan José Dorado Muñoz[✉],
Juan Francisco Díaz Frías, and Robinson Andrey Duque Agudelo

AVISPA Research Group, Escuela de Ingenieria de Sistemas y Computacion, Universidad del
Valle, Cali, Colombia
{sara.maradiago,juan.jose.dorado,juanfco.diaz,
robinson.duque}@correounivalle.edu.co
http://avispa.univalle.edu.co

Abstract. In Colombia there is a problem related to eating habits that has its ori-
gin, mainly, in two causes: the lack of budget that allows access to a wider variety
of food, and the lack of awareness among the population about their nutritional
needs. To tackle this issue, a solution has been proposed using a Constraint Programming (CP) approach enhanced with Machine Learning (ML) for a version
of the Diet Problem (DP).

A CP model was developed to find a shopping list that meets a family's nutritional needs while minimizing costs; and a synthetic dataset was created to test
the model, which was run multiple times to collect results. Since DP is an NP-
complete problem and computational time to find optimal solutions varies from
one solver to another, a ML classifier was used to choose a solver that best performs in small cap time limits based on instance features (i.e., selection from an
Algorithm Portfolio). After carrying out an extensive evaluation of the CP model,
including our approach that implements a Classifier for algorithm selection, the
model correctly selects the best solver over 68.07% of the time, for a sample of
1378 instances.

By analyzing the performance of different solvers on a set of instances, it can
be predicted which solver is likely to achieve the best results on new instances.
This approach could be extended to tuning solver parameters, which would further improve their efficiency and effectiveness. (The dataset used for the creation
of this paper is available on: https://github.com/Git-Fanfo/dataset_CCC)

Keywords: Constraint Programming · Machine Learning · Classifier ·
Algorithm Selection · Diet Problem

1 Introduction

The problem of optimal food distribution dates back to ancient times, from the moment
the first societies were formed. The methods to ensure equitable distribution were limited to dividing portions for different foods based on arbitrary parameters such as size,
age, sex, occupation, and social caste. This arithmetic-based method persisted for most
of human history, aiming to feed armies, institutions, households, and others while minimizing costs.

© The Author(s), under exclusive license to Springer Nature Switzerland AG 2024
M. Tabares et al. (Eds.): CCC 2023, CCIS 1924, pp. 57–70, 2024.
https://doi.org/10.1007/978-3-031-47372-2_6

It was not until the 20th century, as modern computer science took its first great steps, that the Diet Problem emerged. It is an optimization problem model created by George Stigler in 1947 [11], "motivated by the desire of the United States military to ensure nutritional requirements at the lowest cost" [6]. Stigler formulated the problem in terms of Linear Programming, seeking to minimize the function corresponding to the total cost of the food to be purchased while satisfying a set of constraints related to a person's nutritional requirements. The DP is considered a challenging problem, classified as NP-Complete, and has been approached by multiple researchers since the early 1960s in their attempt to computerize it.

This study employs Constraint Programming to address the Diet Problem. Various methods exist for propagating and evaluating constraint problems, and the search for the optimal solution depends on the algorithm (solver) utilized. However, it is known that the chosen solver's performance relies on the specific parameters of the problem, including the problem domain, constraints, problem size, and objective function. To mitigate this issue, the utilization of Machine Learning is proposed to identify patterns that can establish a correlation between the initial parameters and the most suitable solver, leading to the discovery of better solutions.

In the following sections, we start by presenting a detailed explanation of the fundamental subjects for this study, Constraint Programming (Sect. 2.1), Algorithm Portfolio (Sect. 2.2) and Machine Learning (Sect. 2.3). Next, we delve into the details of the Diet Problem Model Formulation (Sect. 3) as a Constraint Programming model; this model defines the parameters, variables, and constraints necessary to optimize a shopping list for meeting nutritional requirements within a given budget with the objective to minimize nutritional deficiencies or excesses and minimize cost using a weighted sum approach. We then present the experimental setup (Sect. 4) and results, showcasing the performance and effectiveness of our proposed method.

Finally, we discuss the conclusions (Sect. 5) drawn from our findings and outline potential directions for future work. Since our Machine Learning approach showcased precise predictions, validating its effectiveness and potential for improvement, we were able to significantly reduce the computational time for solving the computationally intensive NP-Complete Diet Problem. This opens up possibilities for optimizing food distribution in previously infeasible real-world scenarios.

2   Constraint Programming and Machine Learning

2.1   Constraint Programming

Constraint Programming (CP) is a problem-solving methodology that centers on the definition and resolution of problems through the use of constraints. It involves the specification of variables, their possible values, and the necessary conditions that must be met. A key component in the CP approach is the utilization of a solver algorithm, which is a specialized software tool or component responsible for finding solutions to constraint satisfaction problems.

A Constraint Optimization Problem (COP) is a type of problem that involves finding the best possible solution while satisfying a set of constraints. It requires optimizing an objective function by adjusting variables within specified bounds, ensuring that all constraints are satisfied. The goal is either to minimize or maximize the objective function, depending on the problem's requirements.

A "solver" in Constraint Programming applies various algorithms to systematically explore the search space defined by the constraints assigning values to the variables, propagating constraints, and backtracking when necessary. The solver's role is to efficiently navigate through the solution space, considering different combinations and configurations of variable assignments, until a valid solution is found or proven to be impossible [8].

2.2 Algorithm Portfolio

The term "Algorithm Portfolio" was first introduced by Huberman, Lukose, and Hogg in 1997, where they describe a strategy to execute several algorithms in parallel [4]. An algorithm portfolio refers to a collection of different algorithms that are selected and combined strategically to solve a particular problem or class of problems. Instead of relying on a single algorithm, an algorithm portfolio aims to leverage the strengths and weaknesses of multiple algorithms to improve the overall performance and robustness. Each algorithm in the portfolio may excel in specific situations, and by selecting the most suitable algorithm for a given problem instance, better results can be achieved. For this project, the algorithm portfolio consists of a set of Minizinc Solvers that will be evaluated according to their performance.

2.3 Machine Learning

Machine Learning (ML) refers to a collection of techniques designed to automatically identify patterns in data and utilize these patterns to make predictions or informed decisions in uncertain situations [7]. It is commonly divided into two main types: supervised learning and unsupervised learning. In supervised learning, which is the focus of this project, the training dataset includes a set of input features and their corresponding labels, enabling the model to learn the mapping between them and facilitating classification and prediction tasks.

In the context of Machine Learning, a classification problem assigns input data instances to predefined categories based on their features. The objective is to train a classification model that can accurately classify new, unseen instances into the correct categories. The training data for a classification problem consists of labeled examples, where each instance is associated with a known class label. In real-world scenarios, there is often limited knowledge about the relevant features, therefore, many candidate features are typically introduced, resulting in the presence of irrelevant and redundant features that can lead to overfitting in the training model [12]. A relevant feature is one that directly contributes to the target concept, while an irrelevant feature does not have a direct association with it, but still affects the learning process. A redundant feature does not provide any new information about the target concept [1]. Hence, it is crucial to select only the most informative features that provide relevant information for the specific problem at hand. The classification model establishes relationships between the selected features and the labeled examples to define decision boundaries that differentiate between classes, enabling accurate classification of unseen data.

Random Forest is an ensemble learning method that utilizes randomized decision trees. It creates a diverse set of classifiers by introducing randomness during the construction of each tree. The ensemble prediction is obtained by averaging the predictions of individual classifiers. The parameter "n_estimators" represents the number of decision trees included in the ensemble. It determines the size and complexity of the random forest model [9].

k-fold Cross Validation is a technique that addresses the problem of overfitting by splitting the data into subsets. The model is trained on a portion of the data, and its performance is evaluated on the remaining subset. This process is repeated multiple times, using different subsets for training and testing, to obtain a more robust estimation of the model's performance. The parameter "k" represents the number of subsets (folds) into which the data is divided for cross-validation, but each subset is used for both training and testing the model. The model is trained on k-1 subsets (i.e., using k-1 folds) and evaluated on the remaining 1 subset (i.e., using the last fold). This process is repeated k times, each time using a different subset as the evaluation set, until all subsets have been used as the evaluation set exactly once [10].

3   Diet Problem Model

Parameters:

- **n:** total amount of products available to buy ($n \in \mathbb{N}$).
- **budget:** budget available to make the purchase ($budget \in \mathbb{N}$).
- **groceries:** array containing information about each product available for purchase. Each row contains information about a product, where the columns respectively represent: the amount of protein per unit, the amount of carbohydrates per unit, the amount of fat per unit, the amount available in inventory and the price per unit. Then $groceries_{p,d} \in \mathbb{N}$, where $p \in \{1, ..., n\}$ represents the index of each *product*, and $d \in \{1, ..., 5\}$ represents the *columns* mentioned above for each product.
- **requirements:** array containing information on the nutritional requirements of the person or group of people. Each row represents one type of macronutrient: protein, carbohydrates, and fat. The first column represents the minimum quantity required per day and the second represents the maximum quantity required per day. Then $requirements_{m,l} \in \mathbb{N}$, where $m \in \{1, ..., 3\}$ represents each *macronutrient* and $l \in \{1, ..., 2\}$ represents the *columns* mentioned above for each macronutrient.
- **offset:** array containing the values of the maximum deviation allowed for each macronutrient, will be used in the objective function. Then $offset_{m,l} \in \mathbb{N}$, where $m \in \{1, ..., 3\}$ represents the *macronutrient* and $l \in \{1, 2\}$ represents the lower and upper *offset* respectively.
- **variety:** maximum limit of units of the same product that can be purchased ($variety \in \mathbb{N}$).

Variables:

- **grocerylist:** represents the shopping list, stores the number of units to be suggested for each product p ($grocerylist_p \in \mathbb{N}$).

- **acumprice**: represents the accumulated price of the shopping list. It will be used in the objective function ($acumprice \in \mathbb{N}$).
- **protein, carbo and fat**: they represent the amount of total protein, carbohydrate, and fat on the grocery list ($protein, carbo, fat \in \mathbb{N}$).
- **lackPro, lackCar and lackFat**: they represent the missing quantity of proteins, carbohydrates and fats necessary in the diet, for the requirements given according to the shopping list ($lackPro, lackCar, lackFat \in \mathbb{N}$).
- **excessPro, excessCar and excessFat**: they represent the excess quantity of proteins, carbohydrates and fats in the diet, for the requirements given according to the shopping list ($excessPro, excessCar, excessFat \in \mathbb{N}$).

Constraints:

- **Variety:** ensures that the number of units of each product on the shopping list does not exceed the value of *variety* (Eq. 1).

$$grocerylist_p \leqslant variety, \quad 1 \leq p \leq n \tag{1}$$

- **Protein, Carbohydrates and Fats:** constraints that calculate the amount of total protein (Eq. 2), carbohydrate (Eq. 3), and fat (Eq. 4) on the grocery list, respectively.

$$protein = \sum_{p=1}^{n} grocerylist_p * groceries_{p,1} \tag{2}$$

$$carbo = \sum_{p=1}^{n} grocerylist_p * groceries_{p,2} \tag{3}$$

$$fat = \sum_{p=1}^{n} grocerylist_p * groceries_{p,3} \tag{4}$$

- **Range:** these constraints establish the missing or excess amounts of each macronutrient in the diet, comparing the amounts calculated above with the dietary requirements defined in the *requirements* parameter. There are three constraints that measure deficiency (Eq. 5, Eq. 7, Eq. 9) and three that measure the excess (Eq. 6, Eq. 8, Eq. 10).

  • **Protein Limits:**

$$lackPro = \begin{cases} requirements_{1,1} - protein & si\ requirements_{1,1} > protein \\ 0 & if\ not \end{cases}$$
$$\tag{5}$$

$$excessPro = \begin{cases} protein - requirements_{1,2} & si\ protein > requirements_{1,2} \\ 0 & if\ not \end{cases}$$
$$\tag{6}$$

- **Carbohydrates Limits:**

$$lackCar = \begin{cases} requirements_{2,1} - carbo \ si \ requirements_{2,1} > carbo \\ 0 \qquad\qquad\qquad\quad \text{if not} \end{cases} \quad (7)$$

$$excessCar = \begin{cases} carbo - requirements_{2,2} \ si \ carbo > requirements_{2,2} \\ 0 \qquad\qquad\qquad\quad \text{if not} \end{cases}$$

$$(8)$$

- **Fats Limits:**

$$lackFat = \begin{cases} requirements_{3,1} - fat \ si \ requirements_{3,1} > fat \\ 0 \qquad\qquad\qquad\quad \text{if not} \end{cases} \quad (9)$$

$$excessFat = \begin{cases} fat - requirements_{3,2} \ si \ fat > requirements_{3,2} \\ 0 \qquad\qquad\qquad\quad \text{if not} \end{cases} \quad (10)$$

- **Offset:** these constraints ensure that the deficiency and excess values are within the minimum and maximum offset range allowed, with three restrictions for deficiency (Eq. 11, Eq. 13, Eq. 15) and three for excess (Eq. 12, Eq. 14, Eq. 14).

  - **Protein Offset:**

$$lackPro \leq offset_{1,1} \quad\quad (11)$$

$$excessPro \leq offset_{1,2} \quad\quad (12)$$

  - **Carbohydrates Offset:**

$$lackCar \leq offset_{2,1} \quad\quad (13)$$

$$excessCar \leq offset_{3,2} \quad\quad (14)$$

  - **Fats Offset:**

$$lackFat \leq offset_{3,1} \quad\quad (15)$$

$$excessFat \leq offset_{3,2} \quad\quad (16)$$

- **Inventory:** ensures that the number of units of each product on the shopping list does not exceed the value of available units in inventory, which is defined in column 4 of the parameter $groceries_{p,d}$ (Eq. 17).

$$grocerylist_p \leqslant groceries_{p,4}, 1 \leq p \leq n \quad\quad (17)$$

Objective: due to the nature of the problem, it was necessary to implement a multi-target feature. In this case, the weighted sum method was proposed, which has three objectives that must be **minimized**:

- **Lacks:** corresponds to minimum compliance with nutritional requirements. It is the relationship between the deficiencies of each macronutrient and the minimum allowable gap.
- **Excesses:** corresponds to maximum compliance with nutritional requirements. It is the relationship between the excesses of each macronutrient and the maximum allowable gap.
- **Budget:** corresponds to minimizing the accumulated cost of the chosen products. The relationship between the total price of food and the budget.

For the balancing of the weights in the weighted sum, the weights of all the objectives are equalized in an equitable relationship, in this case, the results obtained in each objective were transformed to a percentage scale so that they can be compared with each other.

For the lacks objective the energy consumption of each macronutrient deficiency is calculated, establishing a relationship with the minimum offset percentage allowed for each one, then the average is calculated by summing and dividing by 3, rounding off down since $mnt \in \mathbb{N}$ (Eq. 18).

$$lacks = \left\lfloor \frac{\left\lfloor \frac{lackPro*100}{offset_{1,1}} \right\rfloor + \left\lfloor \frac{lackCar*100}{offset_{2,1}} \right\rfloor + \left\lfloor \frac{lackFat*100}{offset_{3,1}} \right\rfloor}{3} \right\rfloor \tag{18}$$

For the **excesses objective**, a similar procedure is applied. The energy consumption of each macronutrient excess is calculated, establishing a relationship with the percentage of maximum offset allowed for each one, then the average is calculated by adding and dividing by 3, rounding down since $mnt \in \mathbb{N}$ (Eq. 19).

$$excesses = \left\lfloor \frac{\left\lfloor \frac{excessPro*100}{offset_{1,2}} \right\rfloor + \left\lfloor \frac{excessCar*100}{offset_{2,2}} \right\rfloor + \left\lfloor \frac{excessFat*100}{offset_{3,2}} \right\rfloor}{3} \right\rfloor \tag{19}$$

For the budget objective there is the variable $acumprice$, which represents the accumulated price for the purchase of all the products (Eq. 20). As with the previous objective. The percentage value is calculated with the total budget, rounding down since $mnt \in \mathbb{N}$ (Eq. 21).

$$acumprice = \sum_{p=1}^{n} grocerylist_p * groceries_{p,5} \tag{20}$$

$$bud = \left\lfloor \frac{acumprice}{budget} \times 100 \right\rfloor \tag{21}$$

The weight variables W_1, W_2, and W_3 are added as adjustable values to balance the previously established relationships (Eq. 22).

$$\text{mnt} = lacks \times W_1 + excesses \times W_2 + bud \times W_3 \tag{22}$$

Finally, the objective of the problem is defined as minimizing mnt (Eq. 23).

$$\textbf{solve minimize } mnt \tag{23}$$

4   Experiments

For the elaboration of this paper, a computer equipped with an AMD Ryzen™ 7 5800X processor was utilized, accompanied by 16 GB of RAM memory. The experimentation took place within an isolated environment employing Python 3.9.13 and Minizinc 2.7.4 which is a language for specifying constrained optimization and decision problems over integers and real numbers. A MiniZinc model does not dictate how to solve the problem, the MiniZinc compiler can translate it into different forms suitable for a wide range of solvers, such as Constraint Programming (CP), Mixed Integer Linear Programming (MIP) or Boolean Satisfiability (SAT) solvers [2]. Each test was conducted using instances generated by a synthetic instance generator (Sect. 4.1). The evaluation of the model, as described in Sect. 3, was performed using a search annotation provided by Minizinc (variable selection: **largest**, value choice: **indomain_max**) and with some solvers installed on Minizinc (Sect. 4.2).

The objective of this study is to observe the presence of patterns in the synthetic instances received by the Minizinc model, thereby justifying the employment of Machine Learning techniques to select the algorithm that offers the best solution in the shortest time [3].

4.1   Synthetic Instance Generation

Because the base Minizinc model requires data files to work, a synthetic instance generator written in Python was implemented. It provides a synthetic database that can be used to test the model. These files consist of random data that is consistent with nutritional inputs, requirements and budget constraints generated using real-world data from the Instituto Colombiano de Bienestar Familiar (ICBF) [5].

4.2   Algorithm Selection

In order to create the Algorithm Portfolio, a comparison was conducted among five solvers available for Minizinc. An initial set of tests were performed on multiple instances, wherein the value of n (number of products) and related constraints were varied, while maintaining a timeout of 5 s, in order to observe the behavior on five different solvers (i.e., reach the optimal solution within the cap time).

Table 1. Number of solved instances with a timeout of 5 s.

n	HiGHS	COIN-BC	OR-TOOLS	Gecode	Chuffed
5	100	100	87	6	18
20	100	98	17	1	0
50	100	98	11	0	2
100	100	92	10	0	0
500	99	94	3	0	0
1000	79	79	6	0	0
2000	27	85	0	0	0
Total	605	646	134	7	20

Table 1 contains the results of 700 experiments (100 per number of products). The values represent the number of instances an algorithm could solve in the cap time. OR-TOOLS, Gecode and Chuffed decreased their solving rate significantly as n increased, while HiGHS and COIN-BC won on the 86.42% and the 92.28% of the cases, respectively. As a result, the last two were selected as potential contenders for achieving the best solution within the optimal time limit.

alg_portfolio = [HiGHS, COIN-BC]

4.3 Creating the Training Dataset from Synthetic Instances

The chosen algorithms are evaluated within a maximum time limit of 5 s, using 1400 synthetic instances. which range from $10 \leq n \leq 1700$. The algorithm that successfully solves each instance with the best *mnt* solution and in the shortest time is labeled as the winner. Subsequently, a list called *labels* is generated, associating each instance with its respective winning algorithm. Once the labeling process finished, the list had an irregular distribution between both algorithms, where HiGHS won 49.21% of the time and COIN-BC, the 50.78%. Therefore, *undersampling* was applied to COIN-BC, resulting in a balanced dataset with an exact 50/50 distribution (i.e., 689 instances for each).

The *features* matrix was constructed with n rows and 45 columns, where each column represents statistical values of the numeric instances, translating each instance into its corresponding set of features (Appendix. B).

4.4 Exploration of Feature Selection in Machine Learning

For the feature selection, three main tools were used: the correlation matrix (Appendix A), a scatter plot analysis (Fig. 2), and our previous knowledge about the problem. These were employed to compare the interrelationships among all the available features and identify those that may need to be removed to enhance the performance of the model. In a correlation matrix, a value close to 1 means that the compared features are highly directly correlated. That's why features with values greater than 0.7 were removed. The features left were compared into a scatter plot to find for similar patterns between them, discarding the ones with high correlation values.

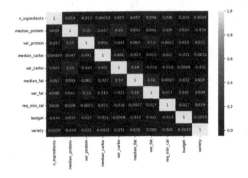

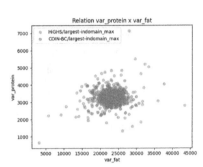

Fig. 1. Correlation matrix with selected features.

Fig. 2. Scatter plot of the relation between var_protein and var_fat.

In Fig. 2, it can be observed that COIN-BC shows a higher concentration in the values of protein and fat variations, while HiGHS exhibits a broader dispersion along these axes. In this particular case, we can infer that for an instance that falls outside the approximate range of $180,000 \leq var\_fat \leq 240,000$ and $25,000 \leq var\_protein \leq 39,000$, it is more likely to be solved using HiGHS. However, it is important to consider other features as well to obtain more precise predictions.

The presence or absence of remain features were discussed to make the necessary changes for the next iteration. By repeating this process, a lot of the initial features were removed progressively. Giving as a result the selected features to train the Machine Learning model: **n_ingredients, median_protein, var_protein, median_carbo, var_carbo, median_fat, var_fat, budget, variety**, as observed in the Correlation Matrix (Fig. 1).

4.5   Evaluating Model Precision

The training of the model was made using a Random Forest Classifier configured with a $n\_estimators$ value of 100 and a k-fold cross validation with a "k" value of 7, the selected features (Sect. 4.4) and labels (Sect. 4.3). The confusion matrix with the test group and a feature importance, were plot to analyze the results. The model was able to predict the algorithms that solve the problem more efficiently with an accuracy of 68.07%.

In the confusion matrix (Fig. 3), the vertical axis represents the actual values and the horizontal, the values predicted by the model. For HiGHS, 515 instances were predicted correctly, and 174 were wrongly given to COIN-BC; and for COIN-BC, 423 were predicted correctly while 266 were wrongly given to HiGHS.

While in the Feature Importance graph (Fig. 4), can be observed that the most influential features during the classification were "n_ingredients" and "req_min_cal", which can be analyzed in further feature selections to improve the model accuracy.

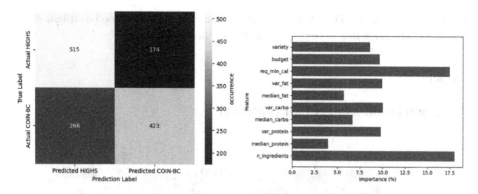

Fig. 3. Confusion matrix for the test group.   **Fig. 4.** Feature importance in prediction.

Finally, the results obtained are presented in a Classification Report (Table 2). This report provides an assessment of the model's performance by evaluating four key metrics. Precision, which represents the accuracy of positive predictions made by the model, was 0.66 for COIN-BC and 0.71 for HiGHS. Recall, which quantifies the model's ability to correctly identify all relevant positive instances, was 0.75 for COIN-BC and 0.61 for HiGHS. F1-score, a harmonic mean of precision and recall, was 0.70 for COIN-BC and 0.66 for HiGHS. Lastly, support, representing the number of instances of each class in the dataset, was 689 for both COIN-BC and HiGHS.

Table 2. Classification report for the test group.

	Precision	Recall	f1-score	Support
$COIN - BC/largest - indomain\_max$	0.66	0.75	0.70	689
$HiGHS/largest - indomain\_max$	0.71	0.61	0.66	689

5   Conclusions and Future Work

The existence of patterns that allow to predict the best solver to solve an instance has been evidenced and justifies the exploration of the Machine Learning approach to improve the precision even more. For this study, we applied our method using two solving algorithms, but allowing integration with additional solvers as they emerge, which holds significant importance for future experimentation and evaluation. The outcomes indicate potential for further improvement through tuning using feature selection algorithms for instance.

Given that the Diet Problem is an NP-Complete Problem, known for it's computationally intensive nature, this method offers a solution. Trough Machine Learning we were able to significantly reduce the computational time required to solve it. This approach may have the potential to optimize the NP-Complete problems solvable at a larger scale. In the case of the Diet Problem, enabling the optimization of food distribution in real-world scenarios that were previously deemed infeasible.

Appendix

A   Correlation Matrix (All Features)

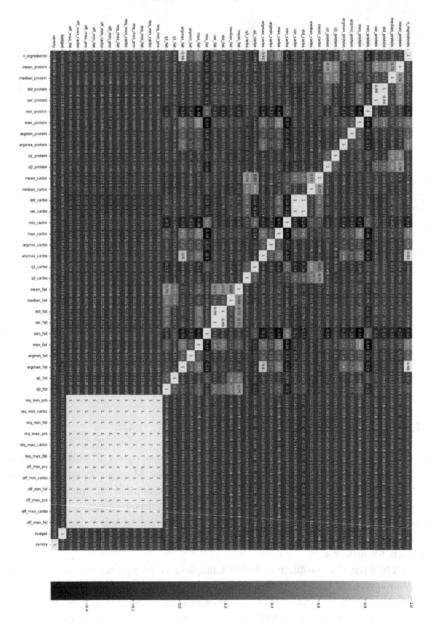

B   Candidate Features

- **n ingredients:** Quantity of products.
- **mean protein:** The mean protein value between between the products.
- **median protein:** The median protein value between between the products.
- **std protein:** The standard deviation protein value between between the products.
- **var protein:** The variance protein value between between the products.
- **min protein:** The minimum protein value between between the products.
- **max protein:** The maximum protein value between between the products.
- **argmin protein:** The position of the minimum protein value between between the products.
- **argmax protein:** The position of the maximum protein value between between the products.
- **q1 protein:** The first quartile protein value between between the products.
- **q3 protein:** The third quartile protein value between between the products.
- **mean carbo:** The mean carbohydrate value between between the products.
- **median carbo:** The median carbohydrate value between between the products.
- **std carbo:** The standard carbohydrate value between between the products.
- **var carbo:** The variance carbohydrate value between between the products.
- **min carbo:** The minimum carbohydrate value between between the products.
- **max carbo:** The maximum carbohydrate value between between the products.
- **argmin carbo:** The position of the minimum carbohydrate value between between the products.
- **argmax carbo:** The position of the maximum carbohydrate value between between the products.
- **q1 carbo:** The first quartile carbohydrate value between between the products.
- **q3 carbo:** The third quartile carbohydrate value between between the products.
- **mean fat:** The mean fat value between between the products.
- **median fat:** The median fat value between between the products.
- **std fat:** The standard fat value between between the products.
- **var fat:** The variance fat value between between the products.
- **min fat:** The minimum fat value between between the products.
- **max fat:** The maximum fat value between between the products.
- **argmin fat:** The position of the minimum fat value between between the products.
- **argmax fat:** The position of the maximum fat value between between the products.
- **q1 fat:** The first quartile fat value between between the products.
- **q3 fat:** The third quartile carbohydrate value between between the products.
- **req min pro:** The minimum requirement of proteins.
- **req min carbo:** The minimum requirement of carbohydrates.
- **req min fat:** The minimum requirement of fats.
- **req max pro:** The maximum requirement of proteins.
- **req max carbo:** The maximum requirement of carbohydrates.
- **req max fat:** The maximum requirement of fats.
- **off min pro:** The minimum offset of proteins.
- **off min carbo:** The minimum offset of carbohydrates.
- **off min fat:** The minimum offset of fats.

- **off_max_pro:** The maximum requirement of proteins.
- **off_max_carbo:** The maximum requirement of carbohydrates.
- **off_max_fat:** The maximum requirement of fats.
- **budget:** The maximum budget.
- **variety:** The maximum variety.

References

1. Dash, M., Liu, H.: Feature selection for classification. Intell. Data Anal. **1**(1–4), 131–156 (1997)
2. Dekker, J.: Introduction to minizinc. https://www.minizinc.org/doc-2.7.2/en/intro.html
3. Dorado, J.J., Maradiago, S.J.: Menus. https://github.com/SJMC29/MENuS
4. Huberman, B.A., Lukose, R.M., Hogg, T.: An economics approach to hard computational problems. Science **275**(5296), 51–54 (1997). https://doi.org/10.1126/science.275.5296.51
5. ICBF: Resolución número 003803 de 2016 del ministerio de salud y protección social (2016)
6. Martos-Barrachina, F., Delgado-Antequera, L., Hernández, M., Caballero, R.: An extensive search algorithm to find feasible healthy menus for humans. Oper. Res. **22**, 1–37 (2022)
7. Murphy, K.P.: Machine Learning: A Probabilistic Perspective. MIT Press, Cambridge (2012)
8. Rossi, F., Van Beek, P., Walsh, T.: Handbook of Constraint Programming. Elsevier, Amsterdam (2006)
9. Scikit learn developers: 1.11. ensemble methods. Accessed May 2023. https://scikit-learn.org/stable/modules/ensemble.html#random-forests (2007-2023)
10. Scikit Learn developers: 3.1. cross-validation: evaluating estimator performance. Accessed May 2023. https://scikit-learn.org/stable/modules/cross_validation.html# (2007-2023)
11. Stigler, G.J.: The cost of subsistence. J. Farm Econ. **27**(2), 303–314 (1945)
12. Tang, J., Alelyani, S., Liu, H.: Feature selection for classification: a review. Data Classif. Algorithms Appl. 37 (2014)

Assessing ChatGPT's Proficiency in CS1-Level Problem Solving

Mario Sánchez$^{(\boxtimes)}$![ORCID] and Andrea Herrera ![ORCID]

Universidad de los Andes, Bogotá, Colombia
{mar-san1,a-herrer}@uniandes.edu.co

Abstract. ChatGPT is an advanced large language model (LLM) capable of generating code to solve specific problems when presented with carefully designed prompts, among other capabilities. The existence of ChatGPT raises signifi-cant questions regarding teaching practices and evaluations within the dis-cipline. If ChatGPT can effectively solve exercises assigned to students, it prompts a reevaluation of the skills and knowledge that we teach and eval-uate. The objective of this paper is to assess the proficiency of ChatGPT in solving exercises commonly encountered in a CS1 course. This serves as an initial step in exploring the implications of ChatGPT for computer science education. By examining ChatGPT's performance and comparing it with real students, we aim to gain insights into its capabilities and limitations. Our evaluation encompasses a comprehensive examination of 125 problems specifically designed for CS1-level learners. The experiment revealed that ChatGPT successfully solved approximately 60% of the provided prob-lems. Subsequently, we conducted a detailed analysis of the characteristics of the problems that ChatGPT could not solve, aiming to gain a deeper understanding of the nuances that make them challenging for LLMs. This study contributes to the ongoing discourse surrounding the integration of AI-based tools, such as ChatGPT, in computer science education, and high-lights the need for a reevaluation of educational objectives and methods employed in traditional educational institutions.

Keywords: CS1 · Large language model · Computer science education · Generative AI

1 Introduction

In recent years, the field known as Artificial Intelligence in Education (AIED), which focuses on leveraging AI technologies for educational purposes, has experienced a surge of interest among researchers, practitioners, and educators. The ultimate goal of the field is to improve the effectiveness of educational practices by means of AI-powered tools [1]. Much like previous technological advancements introduced in the education sector, "learning how to embrace new technologies in teaching is not easy" [2] and presents both unique challenges and promising opportunities. Over time, curricula and teaching practices should adapt and

M. Tabares et al. (Eds.): CCC 2023, CCIS 1924, pp. 71–81, 2024.
https://doi.org/10.1007/978-3-031-47372-2_7

incorporate these new technologies to enable the development of even more advanced competences [2]. For example, AI-based tools are being used today in science curricula to improve the assessment - feedback loop that has typically been too long and not specific enough [3].

Among all of the available technologies that fall within the scope of AIED, Natu-ral Language Processing (NLP), Large Language Models (LLMs), and tools based on them such as OpenAI's ChatGPT [4,5] are creating the greater disruptions. It is no secret that students all over the world have been extensively using ChatGPT since it was released as a public (and free) service at the end of 2022, a reality that has ignited considerable controversy in the educational sphere, even prompting calls for prohibitions [6]. Similar to other advances from the past, ChatGPT makes it possible for a machine to perform activities that were previously restricted to humans, such as writ-ing a paragraph or essay about a given topic, with proper structure, internal coherence, and advanced use of the language to pass as written by humans. Given that these characteristics are typically central to the teaching and assessment processes [2], there exists a widespread apprehension that students may excessively depend on this tool, which markedly eases information acquisition, thereby engaging less with course materials, and failing to develop skills to investigate, synthetize, and critically ana-lyze information to come to their own conclusions and solutions [6,7]. Ultimately, overreliance on AI-based tools and models may led to increased laziness, less creativi-ty, less appreciation of human-generated content, and diminished communication abilities [4,6,7]. Rather than adopting reactionary measures, such as outright bans on these technologies, what is required is a strategy with educational systems and curricula to adopt these technologies and use them to enable students to understand and solve even more advanced problems than they do today [2,6].

Among ChatGPT's most touted capabilities is its ability to interact with code [4]. Specifically, it can generate code based on user prompts [8], identify inefficiencies in code to recommend improvements and optimize algorithms [9], and help developers to identify and resolve errors faster than with traditional debugging tools [10]. The abilities that humans require to perform this kind of activities are precisely a subset of the abilities typically targeted in a CS-1 course [11], i.e., an introductory course to programming. Consequently, the advent of ChatGPT has given rise to the same con-cerns regarding AIED in these courses, as we discussed earlier.

Given that the AIED field is relatively new, there are still large uncertainties and avenues for research. The open problems that we need to solve are varied and will probably require the collaborative efforts of several disciplines such as computer-science and psychology. In this paper, our intent is to contribute to the discourse by examining a very specific problem we have encountered firsthand: is it possible to write programming exercises for a CS-1 course that are solvable by students but are not easily solved by ChatGPT? Our motivation for this inquiry stems from the ob-servation that our students in a large CS-1 course have been resorting to ChatGPT for assistance, in contravention of course rules and arguably against their best interests. Since exercises in this course are mainly a formative tool to practice and strengthen abilities, delegating this work to ChatGPT is counterproductive.

The rest of this paper is organized as follows. Section 2 presents the context for our experiment, which is fully described Sect. 3. In this experiment we evaluated ChatGPT's capabilities with 125 exercises from our CS-1 course and compared its results with actual students' performance. Notably, all of our experiments were per-formed in Spanish, the language of instruction of the course. Next, Sect. 4 presents the analysis of the experiment's results and tries to understand what are the common characteristics among the 48 problems that Chat-GPT failed to solve. Finally, Sect. 5 concludes the paper and discusses potential avenues for research.

2   Experimental Context: A CS-1 Course

This research was conducted in the context of a large CS1 course at the Universidad de los Andes in Colombia. This course teaches basic programming concepts using Python and serves approximately 1000 students per semester from different programs and schools (Engineering, Sciences, Economics, Design) in groups of at most 24 students. The course is taught in Spanish, and it is divided into four modules: (1) discovering the world of programming, (2) making decisions, (3) repeating actions and handling one-dimensional data structures, and (4) solving problems with arrays and libraries [12].

A key characteristic of this course is the usage of Senecode, an automated grading tool to support deliberate practice [13]. When using Senecode, a student gets the de-scription of a problem that he must solve by writing a Python function with a specif-ic signature (function name and parameters). After he submits a possible solution, the tool runs it using predefined inputs and compares the produced output with the known correct answers. For several problems, Senecode is also capable of generating synthetic inputs and outputs to use during this evaluation phase which concludes when the student receives feedback on his submission. Instead of rendering a binary verdict of 'correct' or 'incorrect', this platform aims to provide constructive feedback that could assist students in refining their solutions, thereby supporting their educational process.

There are currently 125 problems in the platform classified by course module, with different degrees of difficulty: problem authors assign an intended difficulty (a number from 0 to 50) but students may perceive difficulty in a different way. Figure 1 shows, for each problem, the assigned difficulty compared to the percentage of submissions that have been successful, and the percentage of students that have tried to solve a problem and have been able to do it after one or many attempts. The latter may be considered the real difficulties of the problems since they are grounded on student behavior. The figure shows that 1) the assigned and the real difficulty typically do not match; 2) that there are "hard" problems where most submissions are wrong; 3) and that for the majority of problems, most students eventually solve the problems that they attempt.

The final characteristic of the Senecode platform is its ability to reject submissions that employ language features that are above the course level at the

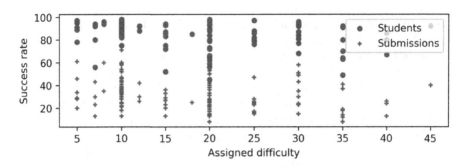

Fig. 1. Assigned difficulty vs. Student success rate and submission success rate, for each problem.

module. For example, problems intended to reinforce conditionals -in the second module of the course- are configured to disallow the usage of loops and lists. Another example is a module 1 problem where tree numbers have to be sorted without using conditional statements. These restrictions are automatically enforced and are clearly announced as part of problem statements. Finally, some constructs that are not studied on the course, such as lambdas and list comprehensions, are also disallowed.

3   Experimental Design and Results

It is not surprising that students are already using ChatGPT to help them when solving code problems. Regardless of the ethical considerations and the fact that it does not make sense to use external help to solve problems designed for training, this generates interesting questions for instructors and problem designers. For this paper, we have summarized these concerns into one research question:

How can we design problems so that
ChatGPT will not be able to naively solve them.   (RQ.1)

We use the "naively" qualifier because we expect students to be using simple prompts based on the problem statements - even just copy-pasted text - instead of very elaborated reinterpretations. After all, if students can write precise prompts, they are probably capable of solving every CS1 problem and do not need ChatGPT help at all.

To answer this question, we planned an experiment based on asking ChatGPT to solve each problem in the Senecode platform and comparing its results with those of actual students. For this purpose, we created an automated pipeline that i) gets each problem statement from Senecode, ii) generates a complete prompt, iii) uses OpenAI's API to query GPT 3.5-turbo model in a new session per problem, iv) gets the response and extracts the meaningful answer (a Python function), v) and submits the solution to Senecode so that it can be automatically graded. After this pipeline was run for each problem, we first used Python scripts to analyze the results and compare them with actual students, and then performed a manual analysis - problem by problem - to try to understand the characteristics of those that remained unsolved by ChatGPT.

For illustration purposes, we now present an example of a prompt used for one of the simplest problems and the solution that ChatGPT offered for this problem. Since the original experiment used a prompt completely written in Spanish, ChatGPT provided a solution also written in Spanish. The following is a translation as close to the original as possible.

Problem Prompt. I need a Python function to help me solve the following problem.

"Create a function that receives the cost in pesos of a restaurant bill, and then calculates the associated VAT tax and the tip for the waiter. The VAT rate is 19%, and the tip in the restaurant is 10% of the bill value (without tax).

The function must return a string showing the VAT, tip and total as follows: "'X,Y,Z'", where **X** is the VAT, **Y** the tip and **Z** the total.

Do not forget to approximate your result to the nearest integer.

Note: The approximation must be done only on the return string (not before)"

The function to solve the problem must be in Python, must be named calculate_vat_tip_total_bill and must comply with the following restrictions:

The function must receive only the following parameter:
 * bill_cost (parameter of type 'int'): cost of the restaurant bill, without tax or tip.

The return of the function must be of type 'str'. The function returns a string with the vat, tip and total bill, separated by commas.
 In addition, the function must respect the following restrictions:

* It should not use the 'if' primitive to solve this problem.
* It should not use the 'for' primitive to solve this problem.
* It should not use the 'while' primitive to solve this problem.

ChatGPT's Solution. The following is the solution that ChatGPT proposed for the above prompt.

```
1 def calculate_ vat_ tip_total_bill bill_cost: int) -> str:
2     vat = int (round (bill_cost * 0.19))
```

```
3     tip = int(round(bill_cost * 0.1))
4     total = bill_cost + vat + tip
5     return "{},{},{}".format(vat, tip, total)
```

As shown in this example, problem statements frequently have some context and are not direct questions: they require some level of interpretation to get to the correct answer. Also, some of the problems are known problems that are typically found in any introduction to programming book, but most are somehow original. Every prompt used for the experiment was structured in the same way to be as clear as possible. Before the whole experiment was run, we tested several prompt structures, and we selected the one that got the best results. In ChatGPT's answer we see that it has understood the general request and has provided a function with the right signature. However, in this case it has provided a faulty solution for the problem: it does not consider that rounding must be done only in the return string (not before) and thus in some cases it provides a wrong answer.

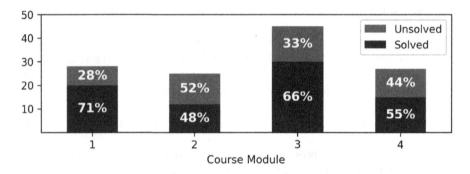

Fig. 2. Number and percentage of problems solved by ChatGPT per course module.

After running the whole experiment, we found that ChatGPT was able to solve only 62% of the problems, which came as a surprise since we were expecting a number close to 90%. Figure 2 shows the number of problems successfully solved by ChatGPT for each of the four modules in the course.

4 Analysis and Discussion

In order to try to answer our research question (RQ1: How can we design problems so that ChatGPT will not be able to naively solve them) we have to analyze the results obtained in the experiment, from a number of perspectives.

Figure 2 already showed that the course module is not a definitive factor. For example, we initially expected problems from module 2, which do not require loops and linear data structures, to be easier than problems in module 3 but that was not the case. ChatGPT was unable to solve 52% of problems in module 2 and 33% of problems in module 3. This suggest that the content of the problems, at least in the context of a CS-1 course, is not a factor that makes a problem easier of harder for ChatGPT. It is also worth noting that ChatGPT did not solve all the problems of each module: it should be possible, in principle, to write additional problems for each module that are "unsolvable".

Our second analysis considered the difficulty of the problems. Figure 3 shows the behavior of ChatGPT in each problem compared to their assigned difficulty, the student success rate, and the submission success rate: each dot in the left side of the diagram represents a problem that ChatGPT solved while dots in the right side are represent those that remained unsolved. What we can see from the first diagram is that ChatGPT success in each problem does not appear to be related to the assigned difficulty. The second diagram shows that ChatGPT was able to solve both problems that are hard and easy for students; moreover, all the problems that ChatGPT failed to solve also have a success rate among students that is less than 70%. Finally, the submission success rate appears to be related to ChatGPT effectiveness. This means that problems where students typically struggle and have to make more submissions to get to the correct answer, are also harder for ChatGPT.

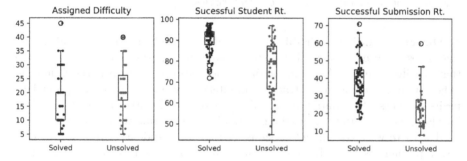

Fig. 3. ChatGPT results compared to a) assigned difficulty, b) student success rate, and c) submission success rate.

These results led us into a problem-by-problem analysis of the problem statements to understand what makes a problem hard to solve for ChatGPT (and for students!). The first analysis considered the length of the prompts, measured by the number of words. As shown in Sect. 3, the length of a prompt depends on the amount of information on the problem statement, in the function description, and in the restrictions. We found a correlation that was the contrary to the one we were expecting: problems with longer prompts are more likely to be solved than problems with shorter prompts. Our interpretation of this phenomenon considers two aspects. First, that giving ChatGPT more information about a problem steers him into the right direction. Secondly, that prompts for these problems are not long enough to make it loose attention and start forgetting the initial parts of each one. The lesson learned from this is that problem statements should be succinct, but not too much, in order to confuse ChatGPT (Fig. 4).

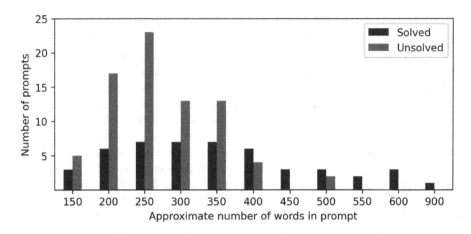

Fig. 4. ChatGPT results compared to the number of words in the prompts.

Next, we performed a qualitative analysis of each problem statement and classified them according to four characteristics.

1. Direct or Indirect Problem. An indirect problem is understood as one that gives a context or describes a scenario and then poses a problem to solve in that specific scenario. An example of a short indirect problem is the following: "The computing department tracks computer usage in one of the computer labs for its students. Basic data is collected on the date and start time of each session, how long the computer was used measured in minutes, and who was the student. Find if there were concurrent sessions by the same student.". An example of a direct problem is the following: "Write a function that receives a string as a parameter and removes all the vowels (lowercase or uppercase) in it".

2. Typical Programming Problem. Typical problems are those problems that are commonly studied in CS1 and are found in books, training materials, videos, etc., without major variations. The following is a typical problem: "Write a function that searches within a number (received by parameter) what is the largest digit appearing in it". On the contrary, the following is a non-typical problem "Create a function that calculates the body mass index BMI of a person with the formula $BMI = weight/height^2$, where the weight is in kilograms and the height is in meters. Note that the weight and height that your function receives will be given in pounds and inches respectively".

3. Problem with Format Requirements. While some problems ask for a single and simple return, such as in the BMI example, there are some problems that ask a specific format for the output data. For example, "The return of the function must be of type 'str'. The function returns a string indicating the person's age in years, months, and days as integers separated by single blank spaces".

4. Problem with Rounding Requirements. The fourth characteristic is related to the previous one and focuses on specific issues with rounding operations, including the number of decimal places in the answer and when rounding should be done. For example, "The function returns the angle (in degrees) between the hands of the clock according to the hour and minute given as parameter, which must have a single decimal digit". The problem presented in Sect. 3 also exhibits this characteristic.

After classifying the 124 problems in the experiment with respect to these four characteristics, we obtained the results shown in Tables 1 and 2. Table 1 shows how many problems in the data set had each characteristic, and how many of those problems remained unsolved for ChatGPT. These results show that only the third characteristic proved to be a consistent challenge for ChatGPT: in 51% of the problems with specific formatting requirements, ChatGPT failed to provide a correct answer. The indirect and rounding characteristics followed with 42% and 40% of unsolved attempts.

Table 1. ChatGPT results compared to single features.

Feature	Indirect	Typical	Format	Rounding
#Problems	79	66	41	20
Unsolved	42%	33%	51%	40%
Solved	58%	67%	49%	60%

Table 2 shows the results of the analysis by combining two of the four defined characteristics. These results show that indirect problems requiring formatting represent a challenge for ChatGPT, which fails in 53% of the cases. The problems requiring both formatting and rounding shows promising results because ChatGPT failed in 100% of these problems, but unfortunately only 3 problems in the problem set meet this combination of characteristics. We do not report any combination of more than two characteristics because the problem set did not have any problems with this combination of characteristics.

Table 2. ChatGPT results compared to combined features.

Feature	Indirect + Format	Indirect + Rounding	Typical + Format	Typical + Format	Format + Rounding
#Problems	30	6	19	9	3
Unsolved	53%	17%	47%	22%	40%
Solved	47%	83%	53%	78%	0%

Another result in Table 2 that is worth studying is the 47% of success found in the 'Typical + Format' column: a possible interpretation is that a strategy for making typical problems harder is to add formatting requirements (and get from 42% to 47%). This is an important consideration given that typical problems must be studied in CS1.

Finally, we also analyzed the impact on the success rate of ChatGPT of the restrictions in problems which disallow certain language constructs. Initially, close to 38% of ChatGPT's solutions were rejected because they did not respect or meet restrictions such as not using loops or lists in some problems. We lifted the restrictions and identified a minimal increase in the percentage of unsolved problems (from 38% to 35%). This showed that those restrictions are not the defining factor that makes a problem easy or difficult for ChatGPT to solve. This is interesting especially because empirical observations tell us that they make the problems considerably harder for those students that already know the language structures that are forbidden.

5   Conclusions

ChatGPT is already changing things in many contexts including software development and education, and it is here to stay. Educators and curricula need to adapt, learn how to use it to their benefit, and introduce changes in courses and evaluation methods to take advantage of this technology instead of seeing it just as a cutting-corner mechanism. Since it is impossible to control what students do and, it is probably impossible to discover when a solution was created by ChatGPT, we ought to learn how to design exercises that are not solvable - to a certain degree - with this kind of technologies.

With the experiment reported in this paper, we showed that in the context of a CS1 course, ChatGPT is not infallible. Even in the limited scope of the 124 problems in the Senecode platform, we found that especially problems with special formatting restrictions tend to be harder for ChatGPT. This information should be useful for us to write new problems in the future, but we believe that it is also applicable to any CS1 course.

There are several limitations in the experiments that we report in this paper that we expect to address in subsequent experiments. In particular, we would like to see the behavior of more advanced models, like GPT-4, which was not available via an API when this report was written. Another possible evaluation is to analyze the difference between several of OpenAI's models (ChatGPT, GPT-3, GPT-4) since there are slight differences in their training methods and tuning, and also with other companies' models such as Bard from Google.

Anther future experiment is to assess the impact of language. All of our prompts were prepared in Spanish, and the generated Python functions had function names and parameters in Spanish as well. Even though restricted experiments seem to imply that ChatGPT has a comparable behavior in Spanish and English, it would be interesting to have a better confirmation. Another avenue for research is the fact that ChatGPT does not always produce the same answer for the same prompt. In our experiment we only asked for one solution for each problem, but maybe asking for several could lead to different and possibly better answers. In fact, this is part of the strategy used by DeepMind's AlphaCode to succeed in programming competitions [14].

Finally, one of the goals of Senecode is to give students feedback for wrong submissions and guide them to the right answer without giving away the solution. Using ChatGPT we could assess the value of the feedback and improve it to better help the students.

References

1. Zhang, K., Begum, A.: AI technologies for education: recent research & future directions. Comput. Educ. Artif. Intell. **2**, 1–11 (2021)
2. Joyner, D.: ChatGPT in education: partner or pariah? XRDS **29**(3), 48–51 (2023)
3. Zhai, X.: ChatGPT for next generation science learning. XRDS **29**(3), 42–46 (2023)
4. Pratim Ray, P.: ChatGPT: a comprehensive review on background, applications, key challenges, bias, ethics, limitations and future scope. Internet Things Cyber-Phys. Syst. **3**, 121–154 (2023)
5. Assaraf, N.: Online ChatGPT - Optimizing Language Models for Dialogue. Accessed 2 June 2023. https://online-chatgpt.com/
6. ChatGPT for good? On opportunities and challenges of large language models for education. Learn. Individ. Differ. **103**, 1–9 (2023)
7. Hang Choi, E., Lee, J.J., Ho, M., Kwok, J., Lok, K.: Chatting or cheating? The impacts of ChatGPT and other artificial intelligence language models on nurse education. Nurse Educ. Today **125**, 1–3 (2023)
8. Kashefi, A., Mukerji, T.: ChatGPT for Programming Numerical Methods, arXiv pre-print arXiv:2303.12093. Accessed 2 June 2023
9. Biswas S.: Role of ChatGPT in computer programming.: ChatGPT in computer programming. Mesopotamian J. Comput. Sci. **2023**, 8–16 (2023)
10. Surameery, N.M.S., Shakor, M.Y.: Use chat GPT to solve programming bugs. Int. J. Inf. Technol. Comput. Eng. (IJITC) **1**, 17–22 (2023)
11. Dale, N.: Content and emphasis in CS1: SIGCSE Bull. **37**(4), 69–73 (2005)
12. Buitrago, F., Sanchez, M., Pérez, V., Hernandez, C., Hernandez, M.: A systematic approach for curriculum redesign of introductory courses in engineering: a programming course case study. Kybernetes **1**(1), 1–10 (2022)
13. Sanchez, M., Salazar, P.: A feedback-oriented platform for deliberate programming practice. In: ITiCSE 2020: Proceedings of the 2020 ACM Conference on Innovation and Technology in Computer Science Education, pp. 531–532 (2020)
14. Yujia, L., et al.: Competition-level code generation with alphacode. Science **378**(6624), 1092–1097 (2022)

Clean Architecture: Impact on Performance and Maintainability of Native Android Projects

Javier Alfonso Santiago-Salazar🆔 and Dewar Rico-Bautista[✉]🆔

Universidad Francisco de Paula Santander Ocaña, Sede Algodonal Vía Acolsure,
546551 Ocaña, Colombia
{jasantiagos,dwricob}@ufpso.edu.co

Abstract. In software development, following an architecture is extremely essential for any project. Clean Architecture, since 2017, has become popular among the Native Android development community. It helps to improve the efficiency of the development process by establishing a clear separation of concerns, achieving modular, scalable, and maintainable code. Its advantages and how it can improve the efficiency of development projects in the Android ecosystem are shown. It examined the challenges faced by Android developers and how Clean Architecture moving from its original version to a shorter version that revolves around native Android development can solve them. The main objective is to introduce the adaptation of the original Clean Architecture model to the current state of native Android development, all oriented towards an application called "InstaFlix", by creating a shorter and more coupled format. The developer will follow best practices and promote the use of presentation patterns such as Model-View-ViewModel (MVVM) or Model View Presenter (MVP), as well as encourage dependency injection. In short, it makes it easier for many developers to work simultaneously on different parts of the system. This separation also generated a noticeable improvement in the code base, as changes can be made to specific components without affecting the rest of the system; focusing on modularity and maintainability, making it clear that it is valuable for any Android developer who wants to create high-quality software.

Keywords: Android · Clean Architecture · Maintainability · Software development

1 Introduction

Clean Architecture is a software design approach proposed by Robert C. Martin, also known as "Uncle Bob" which is based on solid design principles and promotes the creation of robust, scalable, and maintainable systems, thanks to this since 2017, it has become popular among the Native Android development community, experiencing impressive growth and has become a widely adopted approach by both established companies and startups [1]. The importance of clean

© The Author(s), under exclusive license to Springer Nature Switzerland AG 2024
M. Tabares et al. (Eds.): CCC 2023, CCIS 1924, pp. 82–90, 2024.
https://doi.org/10.1007/978-3-031-47372-2_8

architecture lies in its ability to positively impact the performance and maintainability of Android projects by providing an organized and modular structure that promotes good development practices [2,3].

Another outstanding feature of Clean Architecture is its focus on SOLID (Single Responsibility, Open-Closed, Liskov Substitution, Interface Segregation and Dependency Inversion) principles, which promote a robust and flexible object-oriented design. By following these principles, greater cohesion and less coupling between system components is achieved, making the code easier to understand and maintain over the long term [4,5].

Chaos is common when it comes to software development, the larger the size of a project the more complex is its organization, but this is solved thanks to the application of Clean Architecture, which can have a significant impact on both medium and large Android projects [6,7]. For established companies, adopting this architecture can lead to cleaner, more structured, and easily maintainable code, reducing the costs associated with software maintenance and evolution [8]. For startups, Clean Architecture provides the advantage of starting with a solid and scalable foundation, allowing them to adapt quickly as the project grows and faces new challenges [3,9].

The developed application is called "InstaFlix" presented as a catalog of movies and TV shows, which was developed using an agile SCRUM methodology [10], and applying a direct adaptation with certain changes of the original model of Clean Architecture optimizing it to Android development and thus improving many net aspects of the development and performance of the application itself [2,11].

This article is organized as follows: Section 1 gives a brief introduction to what the article shows. Section 2 presents the research methodology, and describes what has been developed and its characteristics, as well as what is currently proposed. Section 3 shows us the denoted results of the application of the above-mentioned in the article. Finally, Sect. 4 shows the conclusions.

2 Methodology

In the development of the example application called "InstaFlix", which is an application that represents a catalog of popular movies and TV shows for Android devices which directly consumes the API of TheMovieDb in order to display the updated catalog and get all the relevant information from it, For the development of the application the agile Scrum methodology was used. Scrum is a collaborative framework based on iterative and incremental delivery of software, allowing continuous adaptation as feedback is obtained from the customer and the development team [12,13].

To start the project, a planning session was held to define the scope of the first sprint, which would be the unit of time in which the development of the application would be divided [14,15]. During this session, the key features, and functionalities of "InstaFlix" were identified and prioritized. These were grouped in the "Product Back-log", which is an ordered list of the elements to be developed.

Once the Product Backlog was defined, the tasks were divided into "User Stories", which represent the needs or requirements of the end user. Each user story was described in clear terms and an estimated level of effort was assigned for its implementation. These user stories were converted into smaller, more manageable tasks, which formed the "Sprint Backlog" for the first sprint.

During the daily development, short and focused meetings called "Daily Scrums" were held, but these had a marked difference since, being a project carried out by only one person, the Daily Scrums were held to emphasize and organize the development carried out the previous day and what was going to be done the day of the meeting. In addition, possible obstacles or impediments that could affect the progress of the project were reviewed and actions were taken to resolve them.

The scope of the project focused in terms of time was 30 days, developed by a single person and divided into 2 sprints, each with 2 weeks of development, the user stories were detailed and broken down into two epics each epic with 10 user stories.

The application of Clean Architecture in "InstaFlix" was fundamental to maintaining a modular and decoupled structure. Clean Architecture made it possible to clearly separate the different layers and components of the application, such as the user interface, business logic, and data access [1]. This provided a clear structure and facilitated the parallel development of different parts of the system.

Each sprint focused on developing a specific set of functionalities, with a focus on meeting the user stories selected for that sprint. During development, Clean Architecture principles were applied to ensure layer independence and reuse of existing code. This allowed for agile development and the ability to perform unit and integration testing effectively [16].

In summary, the Scrum methodology enabled agile and effective management of the "InstaFlix" project. The application of Clean Architecture ensured a modular and decoupled code, which facilitated the iterative development and future maintenance of the application.

3   Results

Layers: are units of common logic, normally Some layers communicate with others through the concept of boundaries, and this allows for limiting the visibility and that the innermost layers have no knowledge of the outermost layers so that if an outer layer changes that inner layer does not need to be modified. This isolation ensures that the independence in each of the layers is strong enough so that if there are important structural changes on the outside, the inside is not affected.

Most internal layers do not know the external ones. Still, there must be interactions from inside to outside, for example: The layer of use cases must be able to communicate with a database and that layer where the database is located is external and the UseCase layer is more internal than the one containing the database but it must be able to make a request and thus paint UI, for this to work it is necessary to invert the dependencies, that is to apply the fifth SOLID principle, see Fig. 1.

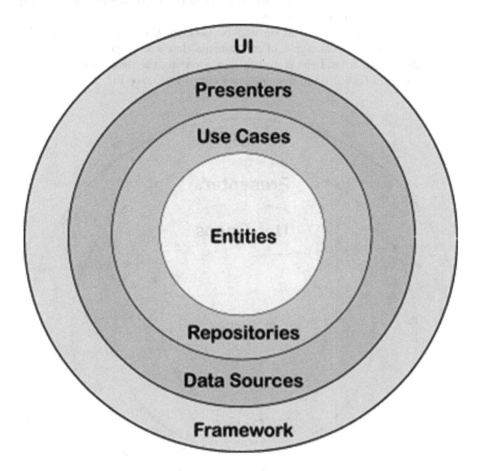

Fig. 1. Propose Clean Architecture model as a starting point Source: Author.

The borders: are the connection points between the different layers, when there is a direct dependency they can be concrete classes, it is not necessary to create interfaces of absolutely everything since this will only complicate the code, therefore if the de-pendency is direct and external layer has to communicate with a more internal one, this can be achieved automatically without the need to create an abstract connection but, if the dependency is inverted there is more remedy than to create an interface to communicate.

Making several changes in this architecture will end up optimizing it and the first of them is to join the framework and UI layer, so they will be in the same layer but they will not really be the same layer, they will only be within the same module, since in Android it is possible to create different types of modules and in this way we ensure that these two layers are in the same module of type App, and so it will be an application layer in which everything related to communication to the outside will be stored, whether painting in the UI or storing in database or sending information to a server etc.

The second change to be made will be between the repositories and the data sources which are two types of components that work together so it is not worthwhile enough to add the complexity of reversing the dependencies in this case, so they will be united in a single layer called Data, see Fig. 2.

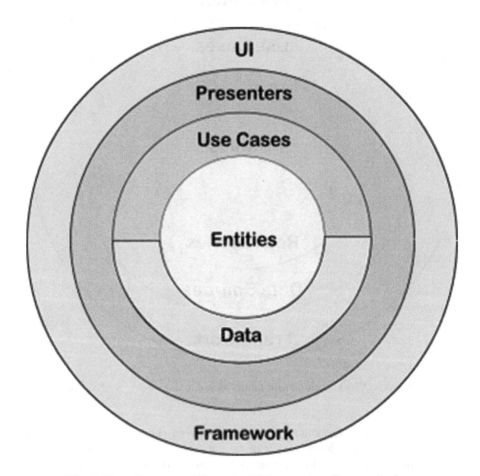

Fig. 2. Data Sources and Repositories integration Source: Author.

The third change to be made is between the presenters and viewmodels, but these are so tightly coupled to the UI it doesn't make much sense to keep a separate layer, so they will be integrated into a layer to called the presentation layer, instead of having two independent ones, see Fig. 3.

The integration of UI and presenters improves the readability and comprehension of the code by creating a direct connection between the user interface and the presentation logic. This makes it easier to understand the data flow and interaction logic between the UI elements and the underlying logic. By having this clearer connection, the code becomes more readable and easier to understand, which in turn facilitates the maintenance and evolution of the project, also facilitates the separation of responsibilities, and allows the user interface to focus solely on data presentation and user interaction, see Fig. 4.

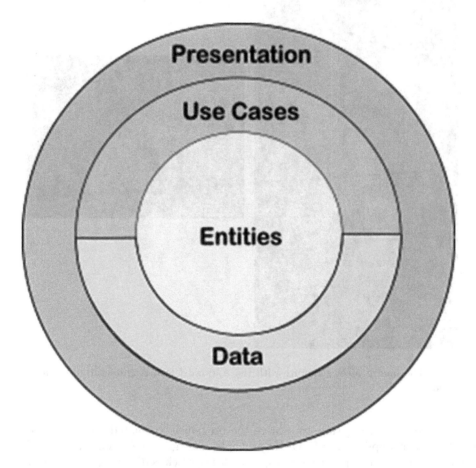

Fig. 3. Presenters, ViewModels and UI integration Source: Author.

The presenters take care of the presentation logic and coordinate the interaction between the UI and the rest of the system. This allows a clear separation of responsibilities, which makes the code more modular and easier to maintain and test.

The benefits of InstaFlix after making changes to the structure of the project thanks to the original application and the changes made in Clean Architecture,

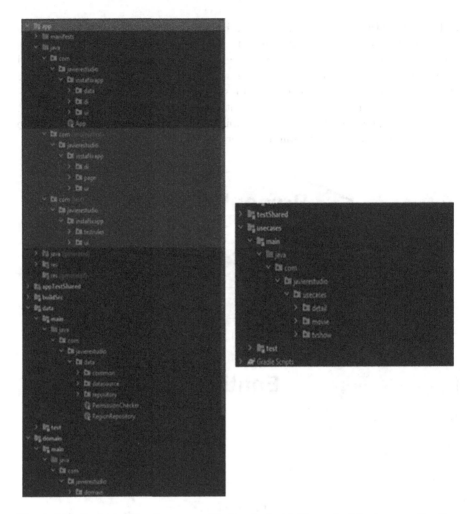

Fig. 4. The final project structure with the Android Clean Architecture application: Author.

greatly improved the time to achieve the previously evaluated scope and have an excellent application of SOLID principles and great cohesion and low coupling, with a clear separation of responsibilities which is directly reflected in the performance of the application.

4   Conclusions

The agile Scrum methodology, applied in conjunction with Clean Architecture, also plays a key role in the development process. The planning and execution of sprints, daily follow-up meetings, and periodic reviews with the customer enable agile and collaborative project management. This facilitates continuous adaptation, iterative and incremental delivery of the software, and early feedback, resulting in more efficient and user-driven development.

Something that is possible to evaluate InstaFlix is to make a further abstraction at the repository level and add using the SOLID principle of inversion of dependencies an interface of the repository itself, in turn improve the use of some dependencies to third-party libraries such as Glide, which currently allows the upload of images communicating directly from the Internet, and review the possibility of changing the classic design of views by Jeckpack Compose. In summary, Clean Architecture positively impacts the performance and maintainability of native Android projects. Its adoption provides a clear and modular structure, facilitates the separation of responsibilities, improves code reuse, and optimizes system performance. Combined with the agile Scrum methodology, it provides a comprehensive and effective approach to developing high-quality native Android applications. By following these principles, development teams can create robust, scalable, and easy-to-maintain applications adapted to changing market needs.

References

1. Rachovski, T., Hadzhikoleva, S., Hadzhikolev, E., Lengerov, A.: Using clean architecture principles to improve the design and implementation of the mobiles online platform. In: Shakya, S., Du, K.L., Haoxiang, W. (eds.) Sustainable Expert Systems. LNNS, vol. 351, pp. 11–19. Springer, Cham (2022). https://doi.org/10.1007/978-981-16-7657-4_2
2. Nugroho, Y.N., Kusumo, D.S., Alibasa, M.J.: Clean architecture implementation impacts on maintainability aspect for backend system code base. In: 2022 10th International Conference on Information and Communication Technology (ICoICT) pp 134–139. IEEE (2022)
3. Bukovcan, M., Blazevic, D., Nenadic, K., Stevic, M.: Clean architecture of client-side software development for smart furniture control. In: 2022 11th Mediterranean Conference on Embedded Computing (MECO), pp. 1–4. IEEE (2022)
4. Bennett, K.H., Rajlich, V.T., Wilde, N.: Software evolution and the staged model of the software lifecycle, pp 1–54 (2002)
5. de Dieu, M.J., Liang, P., Shahin, M., Khan, A.A.: Characterizing architecture related posts and their usefulness in stack overflow. J. Syst. Softw. **198**, 111608 (2023)
6. Hawick, K.A., James, H.A.: Simulating a computational grid with net-worked animat agents. In: ACSW Frontiers 2006: Proceedings of the 2006 Australasian Workshops on Grid Computing and E-research, pp. 63–70 (2006)
7. Boukhary, S., Colmenares, E.: A clean approach to flutter development through the flutter clean architecture package. In: 2019 International Conference on Computational Science and Computational Intelligence (CSCI), pp 1115–1120. IEEE (2019)
8. Stolle, R., Rossak, W., Kirova, V.: A component-driven architecture for internet-based, directly reactive information systems. In: Proceedings Seventh IEEE International Conference and Workshop on the Engineering of Computer Based Systems (ECBS 2000), pp 129–137 IEEE Comput. Soc (2000)

9. Nugroho, Y.N., Kusumo, D.S., Alibasa, M.J.: Clean architecture implementation impacts on maintainability aspect for backend system code base. In: 2022 10th International Conference on Information and Communication Technology (ICoICT), pp 134–139. IEEE (2022)
10. Arango, E.C., Loaiza, O.L.: SCRUM framework extended with clean architecture practices for software maintainability. In: Silhavy, R. (ed.) CSOC 2021. LNNS, vol. 230, pp. 667–681. Springer, Cham (2021). https://doi.org/10.1007/978-3-030-77442-4_56
11. Oliveira Rocha, H.F.: Defining an event-driven microservice and its boundaries. In: Practical Event-Driven Microservices Architecture, pp. 85–131. Apress, Berkeley (2022). https://doi.org/10.1007/978-1-4842-7468-2_3
12. Singh,, M.: U-SCRUM: an agile methodology for promoting usability. In: Agile 2008 Conference, pp. 555–560. IEEE (2008)
13. Cervone, H.F.: Understanding agile project management methods using scrum. OCLC Syst. Serv. Int. Digital Libr. Perspect. **27**, 18–22 (2011)
14. Rover, D., Ullerich, C., Scheel, R., Wegter, J., Whipple, C.: Advantages of agile methodologies for software and product development in a capstone design project. In: 2014 IEEE Frontiers in Education Conference (FIE) Proceedings, pp 1–9. IEEE (2014)
15. Francese, R., Gravino, C., Risi, M., Scanniello, G., Tortora, G.: Using project-based-learning in a mobile application development course-an experience report. J. Vis. Lang. Comput. **31**, 196–205 (2015)
16. Bass, J.M.: Agile software engineering skills (2023). https://doi.org/10.1007/978-3-031-05469-3

Evaluation of AI Techniques to Implement Proactive Container Auto-scaling Strategies

Bryan Leonardo Figueredo González and Mariela J. Curiel H.$^{(\boxtimes)}$

Pontificia Universidad Javeriana, Bogotá, Colombia
{bryan.figueredog,mcuriel}@javeriana.edu.co

Abstract. This paper evaluates techniques for improving the use of cloud computing resources through autoscaling. Autoscaling, also referred to as auto-scaling or automatic scaling, is a cloud computing technique for dynamically allocating computational resources. Autoscaling can be reactive (responding to resource needs as they arise) or proactive (anticipating future demands). Our study proposes the use of AI-based models to predict the creation of new computational entities under varying load conditions. The proposed methodology included data cleaning, correlation analysis to select relevant features, and the evaluation of several supervised and unsupervised machine learning models. The results shown that machine learning techniques can be used to anticipate and optimize the capacity of computing systems.

Keywords: Elasticity · Proactive Autoscaling · Machine Learning

1 Introduction

Elasticity is the ability of a system to dynamically adapt to load variations, increasing or decreasing resources to meet performance and efficiency demands. There are several platforms, both in the public cloud and on-premises, that provide autoscaling functionality to implement elasticity. However, in some cases (e.g. Kubernetes) their approach is based on a reactive algorithm that can have difficulty anticipating and handling rapid and extreme changes in load.

Rather than simply reacting to load changes after they occur, our approach aims to use the predictive capability of AI models to forecast load variations and proactively adapt system resources. The approach has the potential to improve the efficiency, performance and responsiveness under highly variable loading conditions. This paper will evaluate the use of supervised machine learning models such as logistic regression, decision trees and neural networks, as well as the unsupervised K-means strategy. This paper is structured as follows: Sects. 2 and 3 present the background and related works. Subsequently, in Sect. 4 we present the methodology used. Then in Sects. 5 and 6 we present the data collection and preparation process. Section 7 presents the results obtained. Section 8 shows the preliminary conclusions of the work.

M. Tabares et al. (Eds.): CCC 2023, CCIS 1924, pp. 91–96, 2024.
https://doi.org/10.1007/978-3-031-47372-2_9

2   Background

Before starting, it is important to introduce the concepts related to research.

As previously mentioned, **elasticity** is the ability of certain types of systems to automatically create or eliminate resources in order to adapt to varying load conditions. One of the ways to implement elasticity is by means of autoscaling or automatic scaling. There are two fundamental types of autoscaling. In **reactive autoscaling**, the system monitors current workload traffic or resource usage; when certain thresholds in performance metrics are reached, the system will then calculate and determine a suitable scaling decision. **Proactive autoscaling** uses sophisticated techniques to predict future resource demands. Based on these predictions the autoscaler decides to scale up or down according to a predetermined forecast.

The following is a brief description of the models evaluated in this work:

Logistic regression [3] is a statistical technique that aims to produce, from a set of observations, a model that allows the prediction of values taken by a categorical variable, often binary, from a series of continuous and/or binary explanatory variables.

Decision trees [7] are supervised learning models that predict output as a function of successive decisions made on inputs. Each node in the tree represents a decision, which makes the trees easy to understand and interpret. The Gradient Boosting algorithm [1] builds predictive models as an ensemble of weaker models, usually decision trees. Gradient Boosting combine several weak models to create a strong model. *XGBoost* is a specific implementation of Gradient Boosting that has been optimized to be highly efficient and flexible. Finally, **Neural Networks** [2] are deep learning models that mimic the way the human brain works. They are particularly useful for tasks that involve learning from large amounts of high-dimensional data, such as images or text.

The **K-means algorithm** [4] is one of the most widely used unsupervised learning algorithms for partitioning a given data set into K groups. The "means" in the name refers to the centroids of the groups, which are imaginary or real points representing the center of the groups.

3   Related Work

In the literature, there are several works that have addressed the proactive self-scaling in containers through AI techniques. In [8], for example, proactive autoscaling using a LSTM (recurrent neural network) is proposed. The authors describe a methodology similar to the one presented in this paper by collecting a data set coming from cloud-native applications. The data set is used to train a learning-based forecasting model. The model is used to effectively predict the future resource demand for the application. Authors of [5] propose artificial neural networks (ANN) for proactive autoscaling and [6] use an extreme learning machine (ELM) based workload prediction model, whose learning time is very low. The workload is predicted more accurately.

4   Methodology

The methodology used in this work was based on CRISP-DM (Cross Industry Standard Process for Data Mining). We add some steps to build and tune the AI models: model architecture selection, hyperparameter tuning, data augmentation, and cross-validation. The steps are shown in Fig. 1.

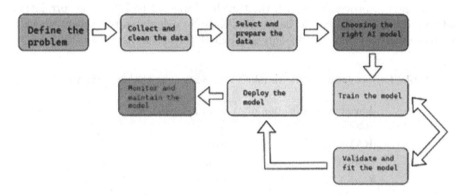

Fig. 1. Implementation phases of CRISP-DM methodology for IA (Image authored by the authors)

5   Data Generation

In order to obtain the data to train the models, we developed and deployed three services on a machine with a Windows 11 operating system, Intel Pentium i7 hardware, 16 GB of RAM 4 cores, and 8 logical processors.

The services, implemented in Spring Boot and under a Rest API, are described as follows: a) Create-token is responsible for generating a token with a parametric controlled validity to allow authentication of a user with the correct credentials in a given period of time. b) generateRAMMemoryConsumption is a code that gradually increases its RAM memory usage, emulating a scenario where a service requires more and more resources as it processes more data. c) calculoAltoConsumoProcesador generates a high CPU usage, performing mathematical operations to calculate prime numbers in a specific range.

The metrics obtained for each service were CPU and memory usage. The load was generated using JMeter, and it wa gradually increased to simulate different levels of demand. More than 30,000 observations were collected.

6   Data Preparation

Once the data had been collected, the relevant features had to be selected and prepared to be compatible with the AI models. First, a cleaning process was performed to remove any incorrect, incomplete, null, inaccurate or irrelevant data. Then, data transformation and normalization processes were performed. Finally, a new feature (variable) called "new_vm" was created, which is a binary representation of whether or not a new virtual machine or container needs to be created. This feature was generated using a threshold defined on CPU and RAM usage. If CPU or RAM usage exceeded this threshold, then "new_vm" was set to 1, indicating that a new computing entity was needed. Otherwise, it was set to 0. In the pre-processing stage, the threshold was set to 74%. The correlation between different features in the data set was also calculated to identify whether there are features that are strongly associated with each other (see Table 1).

Table 1. Correlation of the variables with respect to the new_vm variable

Variables (Utilization of resources)	Correlation with new_vm
RAM	0.616374
Core 0	0.650212
Core 1	0.676897
Core 2	0.639347
Core 3	0.667906
Core 4	0.671855
Core 5	0.650212
Core 6	0.673821
Core 7	0.675053
Avg. CPU Utilization	0.676279

According to the results in Table 1, all the characteristics related to processor and memory usage show a moderate to strong positive correlation with 'new_vm', implying that when these parameters increase, the need for a new computing entity (virtual machine or container) also tends to increase.

The last step was to split the data into training and test sets. For the exercise, a 70/30 split was used, where 70% of the data was used to train the models and 30% to test them.

7   Results

A summary of the results of the unsupervised techniques is shown in Table 2. Details of each technique are discussed below the table.

Logistic Regression: With an accuracy of 87%, this model provided a good basis. However, its performance may not be sufficient for critical applications where prediction accuracy is of paramount importance. The main advantage of this model is its simplicity and ease of interpretation.

Table 2. Summary of unsupervised techniques

Model	Precision (True)	Recall (True)	F1 Score (True)	Precision (False)	Recall (False)	F1 Score (False)	Accuracy	AUC
Logistic Regression	0.83	0.86	0.85	0.91	0.89	0.90	0.88	0.96
Decision tree	0.96	0.96	0.96	0.98	0.98	0.98	0.97	0.97
Gradient Boosting	0.96	0.97	0.96	0.98	0.97	0.98	0.97	0.97
Neural Network	0.98	0.92	0.95	0.95	0.99	0.97	0.96	0.96

Decision Tree: With 97% accuracy, this model outperformed logistic regression. It can be used as a proactive solution because of its training speed and clear graphical representation of decisions, which can be useful in understanding which factors are most important in the autoscaling decision. It was the second best ranked model in terms of FN (False Negatives), however, its initial depth suggested that over fitting may have occurred in the training data, which could affect its performance with new data.

Gradient Boosting: Like the decision tree, this model achieved an accuracy of 97%, which suggest that it is capable of making very accurate predictions. An advantage of Gradient Boosting is that it can capture complex interactions between features, which could be useful given the nature of the data. It was the model that stood out with respect to the False Negatives and its training time makes it a good choice for further use.

Neural Network: Although it had a slightly lower accuracy of about 96%, this model showed good performance. We believe that further adjustments could be made to optimize its performance, such as modifying the hyperparameters or changing the architecture. Neural networks are especially powerful in capturing nonlinear interactions and complex patterns in data. A disadvantage, in a practical implementation, is that if the model is required to constantly learn and retrain itself with new data, the time it takes to train may affect its usability.

With respect to the application of the K-means algorithm we can comment that although its use is not to obtain predictions, its silhouette coefficients of 0.53 and WCSS of 1996, indicate that it makes a good segmentation of the data. This technique is useful for exploring the underlying structure of the data and detecting patterns. It can be used when clear labels are not available or when seeking to understand the underlying relationships and structures between variables.

8 Conclusions

The results of the applied models shown good performance, with some of them achieving an accuracy of up to 97%. These results suggest that it is feasible to predict the need for new computing entities using the available monitoring data. Although there are other ways to address this autoscaling problem, such as with the use of expert systems, the results obtained and previous work, lead us to believe that machine learning techniques are suitable for further investigation. These techniques will be applied in variable load scenarios, especially in cloud environments; in these scenarios expert systems can become difficult to maintain and scale. Machine learning models can handle large volumes of data in an efficient, scalable manner.

As future work, the evaluated models can be integrated into a container orchestration system such as Kubernetes to predict to predict the need for new resources and to proactively scale up. In this way, one could have a proactive system instead of a reactive one, meaning that the system could adapt to resource needs before a decrease in performance occurs.

References

1. Chen, T., Guestrin, C.: Xgboost: a scalable tree boosting system. In: Proceedings of the 22nd ACM SIGKDD International Conference on Knowledge Discovery and Data Mining, pp. 785–794 (2016)
2. Goodfellow, I., Bengio, Y., Courville, A.: Deep Learning. MIT press, Cambridge (2016)
3. Hosmer, D.W., Jr., Lemeshow, S., Sturdivant, R.X.: Applied Logistic Regression, vol. 398. John Wiley & Sons, Hoboken (2013)
4. Jain, A.K.: Data clustering: 50 years beyond k-means. Pattern Recogn. Lett. **31**(8), 651–666 (2010)
5. Kumar, J., Singh, A.K.: Workload prediction in cloud using artificial neural network and adaptive differential evolution. Futur. Gener. Comput. Syst. **81**, 41–52 (2018)
6. Kumar, J., Singh, A.K.: Decomposition based cloud resource demand prediction using extreme learning machines. J. Netw. Syst. Manage. **28**, 1775–1793 (2020)
7. Maimon, O.Z., Rokach, L.: Data Mining with Decision Trees: Theory and Applications, vol. 81. World scientific, Singapore (2014)
8. Marie-Magdelaine, N., Ahmed, T.: Proactive autoscaling for cloud-native applications using machine learning. In: GLOBECOM 2020–2020 IEEE Global Communications Conference, pp. 1–7. IEEE (2020)

Teaching Strategy for Enabling Technologies of Industry 4.0 to High School Students

Duby Castellanos-Cárdenas$^{(\boxtimes)}$ and María Clara Gómez-Álvarez

Universidad de Medellín, Medellín, Colombia
{dcastellanos,mcgomez}@udemedellin.edu.co

Abstract. Industry 4.0 enabling technologies are impacting several sectors of the economy by automating organizational processes. As a result, the demand for professionals with the necessary skills to face the challenges imposed by the new industrial trends has increased. This represents a challenge for technological and university institutions as they are at the forefront of the training and educational transformation processes. While there are various governmental strategies to provide training in technological topics, the most active stakeholders in implementing such strategies are higher education institutions, where the shortage of students in the foundational careers that support I4.0 technologies is particularly noticeable. For this reason, universities, as well as elementary and high schools, are consolidating strategies that could enhance the motivation of young people to choose technology-based careers.

This paper presents an educational experience in Education 4.0 focused on enabling technologies for I4.0 oriented to high school students and led by The University of Medellín. Implementing this educational experience enabled the participants to devise solutions to problems real-world challenges using the Internet of Things. Among the benefits of this strategy, it does not require prior training in computational thinking or electronics fundamentals. Additionally, it integrates didactic strategies such as co-creation, gamification, and project-based learning, while allowing students to build a basic prototype within a relatively short period.

Keywords: Educational Experience · Industry 4.0 · Enabling Technologies · Gamification · High School

1 Introduction

Industry 4.0 (I4.0) can be defined as a trend toward the digitalization and automation of the organization's business process, especially the manufacturing environments [1,2]. It allows organizations to shorten development periods, facilitate client customization products (more flexibility), and improve resource use (efficiency). I4.0 is achieved by incorporating Enabling Technologies (ET)

M. Tabares et al. (Eds.): CCC 2023, CCIS 1924, pp. 97–108, 2024.
https://doi.org/10.1007/978-3-031-47372-2_10

such as embedded systems, industrial robots, 3D printing, Internet of Things (IoT), cloud computing, and big data, among others. Enterprises are experiencing an incremental demand for professionals with the necessary skills to face the requirements imposed by this new industrial trend [2].

This fact constitutes a challenge for universities and technological institutions responsible for training these professionals, prompting them to modify their curricula and didactic strategies to promote the technical and social skills expected of technology experts [3]. In this context, some Colombian government strategies exist, such as offering free online courses in programming, big data, and artificial intelligence through a program called "Misión TIC 2022". However, due to the persistent deficit of professionals in these areas, it is necessary to promote integration between universities and high school institutions to provide early information about ET and motivate students to pursue STEM (Science, Technology, Engineering, Mathematics) careers [4].

In this regard, there are proposals, such as an outreach program to introduce high school students to basic concepts of robotics, the IoT, and programming through collaborative work and a mobile robotic arm [5]. In Brazil, an approach integrating I4.0 and vocational education in schools is highlighted. This approach utilizes hands-on practice activities, free online applications, and debates to discuss social problems and I4.0 technologies as alternative solutions [6].

Regarding teaching IoT to high school students, there are initiatives to promote computational thinking abilities, such as decomposition, pattern recognition, and abstraction through IoT projects focused on environmental variable measures, smart and human cities, and open data concepts [7]. Additionally, there are educational platforms specifically designed for teaching IoT concepts to school students, such as the "IoT Maker Lab" which provides the necessary elements for students to construct IoT online prototypes [8].

This paper presents a strategy that enables high school students to make a first approach to learning an ET of I4.0, which can serve as a vocational orientation process. The University of Medellín leads the strategy to motivate young people to participate in ICT (Information and Communication Technology) programs. Such a University provides an interesting educational experience through two fundamental pillars: (1) Full-time professors dedicated to guiding the learning process of young students. These experienced educators play a pivotal role in leading the educational experience, ensuring that students receive the highest quality of instruction and mentorship. (2) The University also places a strong emphasis on robust physical infrastructure, thoughtfully designed to enhance the learning environment. From laboratories to cutting-edge equipment and well-equipped auditoriums, every aspect is meticulously arranged to support a comprehensive educational experience.

The strategy includes two components: (1) a Technological component and (2) a Pedagogical component. The technological component involves the software and hardware that students will use for developing practical projects based on ET. The pedagogical component is based on project-based learning (PBL), gamification, and co-creation techniques to enhance motivation and commitment among high school students. Applying this strategy allowed the participants to develop IoT technology-based solutions to problems in their environment.

The paper structure is the following: Sect. 2 describes previous works about the teaching of Industry 4.0 IoT Technology for school students; Sect. 3 presents the proposed strategy and its components; Sect. 4 shows a case study oriented to an IoT course for high school students based on the proposed strategy and the preliminary results in the implementation of the strategy. Finally, Sect. 5 presents the conclusions and future work lines of this research.

2   Background

This section presents some proposals related to teaching I4.0 ET for high school students, their components, main elements, and results obtained.

Verner et al. [5] proposed an outreach program for introducing the basic concepts of robotics, IoT, and programming to high school students. The program aimed to teach ET and promote collaboration among school students. It included two modules: (1) robotics, where the participants program a mobile robotic arm using the platform ThingWorx; and (2) programming, where the students constructed a TurtleBot Waffle robot. As a result of this proposal, the students understood the fundamental concepts.

Moreover, In Brazil, there has been an experiment of integrating Industry 4.0 technologies into vocational education programs for high schools that have traditionally focused on humanist formation [6]. This experience included interdisciplinary teaching activities to discuss the relationship between I4.0 technologies (especially IoT, data mining, and cloud computing), education, production systems, and a final evaluation questionnaire. The didactic strategies included hands-on practice activities, free online applications, and debates. As a result, it highlights the increase in motivation levels among students by incorporating sociological issues related to applying I4.0 technologies in the educational experience.

In the same line, Chou et al. [9] conducted a research to understand industry participants' opinions on the incorporation of I4.0 ET in technical and vocational education in Taiwan. This study resulted in the introduction of new courses associated with extensive data analysis, cloud computing, and IoT, among others. Additionally, it initiated close cooperation between industry and schools to establish practical I4.0 classrooms.

Furthermore, Verner et al. participated in a study highlighting the importance of incorporating I4.0 concepts in school education to prepare students for the knowledge society and industry demands, especially in STEM education [4]. This implies the need to train teachers to acquire knowledge of I4.0 technologies and teaching skills associated with these concepts. The study collected data through questionnaires, reflections, and reports from the participants (teachers and high school students), revealing the essential need to train teachers in technical and teaching skills to address the challenges of Education 4.0 in high schools.

About IoT technology, Uspabayeva et al. [10] present a proposal where they evaluated 83 high school students' perception of IoT incorporation in their education in Kazakhstan after a 4-week IoT online training. After the training, the results showed a positive change in their perception of IoT applications in education and other economic sectors. However, it is also necessary to prepare school infrastructure and reform curricula to incorporate IoT teaching in school education. In fact, in high school, IoT can be used to teach computational thinking, as described by Schneider, Bernardini, and Boscarioli [7]. They explained a pedagogical practice for promoting computational thinking abilities such as decomposition, pattern recognition, and abstraction through IoT projects focused on environmental variable measures, smart and human cities, and open data concepts. The goal was to encourage students to reflect on city problems and data protection by applying IoT technology to address social issues.

Moreover, Rodriguez-Calderón and Belmonte-Izquierdo proposed an educational platform called "IoT Maker Lab" oriented to IoT teaching in high schools with the possibility of configuration for different courses [8]. This platform provided the elements needed for developing IoT applications, allowing the construction of prototypes based on I4.0 technology. This platform has shown potential in supporting multiple courses and generating motivation among high school students regarding I4.0 ET through practical teaching activities.

3   Strategy Proposal

I4.0 is supported by nine ET responsible for facilitating the digital transformation process and leading the way to consolidate smart factories [11]. The Industrial Internet of Things utilizes intelligent devices with extensive connectivity to make autonomous decisions [12]. It enables centralized integration of all machines and devices in the network, allowing real-time information to be collected and accessed from anywhere [11,12].

In addition, technologies like Cloud Computing enable the storage of data generated by thousands of devices [13]. Big Data Analytics enables the extraction of relevant information to support accurate decision-making [11]. In this context, cybersecurity systems must be developed to protect confidential information for companies and all stakeholders involved in digital transformation [13,14]. Simulation using computational tools for developing planning and exploration models to optimize decision-making, design, and operate complex and intelligent production systems [15]. System integration facilitates communication and coordination between employees at the same level and between management and floor workers [11,16].

Augmented reality enhances users' perception of reality by integrating artificial information with the environment [16]. Additive manufacturing, including rapid prototyping tools like 3D printing, enables companies to meet the challenges posed by the demand for complex and customized products at reasonable costs [16]. Autonomous robots also play a significant role in the new production trends, as they can reconfigure themselves to shift from mass production to customized production [16].

The proposed educational strategy consists of two components: technological and pedagogical. It was designed generically to apply to emerging technologies (ETs). The target audience for this strategy is high school students who do not require prior knowledge of computational thinking, electronic fundamentals, networking, and other related topics. Figure 1 shows the elements of educational strategy.

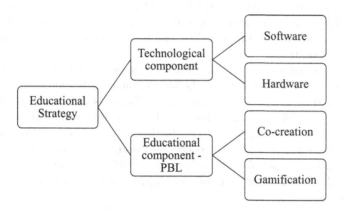

Fig. 1. Proposed strategy diagram

3.1 Technological Component

The technological component comprises the software and hardware elements, and both must be selected according to the requirements imposed by the ET. Software tools must be chosen considering the target public, in this instance, high school students. In this scenario, the programming blocks become an attractive alternative because they are used with early students and even for developing STEM skills with high school students [17, 18].

Regarding the hardware component, there is a marked trend toward using Open-Source Hardware (OSH) because it offers accessible costs, broad compatibility with electronic components caused by an active community of manufacturers who provide facilities for programming, and full access to tutorials and information about codifying and electronic circuits implementation [19, 20]. Some of the most widely used OSH are Arduino, Raspberry Pi, NodeMCU, Spark-Fun, etc. We can find multiple editors for microcontroller programming based on blocks, especially for Arduino; some examples are Arduinoblocks, Blockly-Duino, Tuniot, S4A, and Thinkercad. These are online and free access, and even sometimes offer the possibility of simulating with basic electronic components.

The selection of software and hardware elements can be made based on a technology assessment model for I4.0, such as the one proposed by Mon and Del Georgio [21], in which, based on three components: software, hardware, and infrastructure, an assessment of the maturity level of these technologies is generated.

3.2   Pedagogical Component

Regarding the educational part, the unifying thread is Project-Based Learning (PBL). PBL successful approach to strengthening STEM (Science, Technology, Engineering, Mathematics) proficiencies and encouraging multi-disciplinary knowledge [22,23] besides enables students to take a proactive role in the learning process and creates an ideal learning environment [23,24]. Additionally, PBL is the most important learning strategy used to teach enabling technologies [25–27]; it is used for teaching interpersonal skills and solutions to real-world problems [28]. The PBL strategy is supported by two fundamental axes: (1) Gamification and (2) Collaborative learning.

Gamification refers to applying game design elements to non-game contexts [29]. This is a growing trend where the human factor is fundamental in terms of motivation and commitment in participants [29], as is the case of teaching and learning processes. About the scope of such a strategy, we include gamification activities seeking to promote in students the acquiring and reinforcing of soft skills such as creativity, effective communication, teamwork, problem-solving, and leadership as proposed by Zepeda et al. in [30]. In our strategy, the teacher can choose the gamification techniques according to their goals and specific soft skills to promote.

Collaborative Learning (CL) is an approach teachers use to facilitate learning and improve students' performance [31]. CL involves students participating and interacting in a work team to resolve problems and manage their relations and responsibilities [32]. In this context, co-creation techniques can enrich the collaborative learning environment and allow students to express themselves openly and obtain more meaningful experiences [32].

The following section presents a detailed description of the proposed strategy' implementation methodology.

3.3   Implementation Methodology for the Proposed Strategy

It is necessary to consider strategy aspects, such as the number of sessions and their duration, the number of students, and the availability of economic and technological resources. These elements can influence the selection of gamification and co-creation techniques to be used. Initially, this proposal was designed to be carried out over two weeks and 4 h per day; but the duration can be adjusted based on the groups' needs. Figure 2 shows the methodology proposed for the strategy implementation. The proposed methodology can be summarized as follows:

1. Define the ET, which will be the focus of the strategy: It is possible to include the study from two different ET due to the close relationship between ET.
2. Select the hardware and software components according to the ET and available resources: the hardware component imposes the software tools to use, so it is essential to make an election simultaneously.

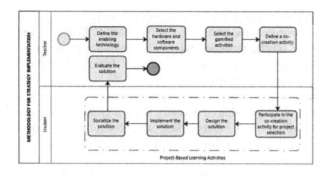

Fig. 2. Methodology for strategy implementation

3. Define the gamified activities based on the targeted skills: In each session, choose a game that aligns with the skill to develop. It is convenient to begin the session with this activity as it can serve as an icebreaker.
4. Develop a co-creation activity where each team collaboratively defines the problem to be addressed and establishes the projects' aim: it is advisable to suggest topics related to students' interests. However, at this stage, students need to have some background in ET to define achievable objectives.
5. Utilize PBL for the designing and developing of solutions: every session should be carefully planned, considering the available time and the activity schedule. Due to time constraints, it may be necessary to combine the teaching of TE topics, practical activities, and the execution of project tasks.
6. Socialize and validate the proposed solution: Despite being the final stage, it can become the most important for the student. The evaluation of the prototype must be carried out in the light of a rubric known and previously defined by the students. To further a motivating factor, the teachers and families of students can participate in the socialization process.

As a result, the following section presents a case study in which the strategy was implemented for IoT technology, involving the participation of high school students. The University of Medellín provided the physical infrastructure, technological devices, and professors.

4   Case Study: IoT

The following section provides a comprehensive description of the strategy's implementation and the results achieved during its application.

4.1   Case Study Description

The proposed strategy was applied to 14 high school students from 6 different educational institutions. The classes were held over two weeks with 4-hour sections each, for 40 h. The selected ET was IoT, so the course focused on topics related to operating electronic components and programming microcontrollers. The chosen hardware component was the NodeMCU ESP8266 microcontroller, which allows easy Internet connectivity. The students then utilized the Tuniot Platform to develop programming blocks and downloaded their code to the microcontroller using the Arduino IDE.

The skills targeted for improvement were creativity, effective communication, teamwork, and problem-solving. There are several games to enhance these skills, such as marshmallow tower, storytelling with technological vocabulary, copy-cats, and tangram. Figure 3-a illustrates the marshmallow tower activity one of the teams carried out.

During the co-creation activity, the teacher distributed sticky notes to each student, featuring a diverse range of places of interest and public locations in a random manner. The students were grouped into teams, where they shared and discussed the notes, aiming to associate a specific public with a suitable place. Their objective was to delve into the potential problems the identified public might encounter within that location. Subsequently, the proposed issues were collaboratively organized on a billboard, and the students were collectively selected. The activity generated innovative ideas and a precise definition of the project's goal. Figure 3-b shows the evidence of co-creation activity.

(a) Marshmallow tower   (b) Project idea generation

Fig. 3. Gamification and Co-creation activities

Next, the prototype was developed following the PBL activities. Each team created a schedule of activities, and as they learned about the microcontroller, sensors, and actuators, they implemented in the prototype what they learned. Figure 4-a illustrates the construction process of the smart parking prototype.

4.2   Preliminary Results

The projects were evalued during a socialization event, where parents, teachers, and friends had the opportunity to participate. Each team had its stand and project presentation poster. The project teams were evaluated by professors from the University of Medellín engineering faculty, who used a rubric to assess the contextualization and description of the addressed problem, the presentation of the proposed solution and its added value, and the technical functionality and aesthetics of the prototype. Additionally, the projects were published on social media such as Facebook and Instagram. The teams with the highest evaluations, both by the teachers and on social media, were awarded in a closing ceremony where the work developed by the students was recognized, and they received a participation certificate. Figure 4-b the prototype along with the student team, referred to as the "Patient Care Project," during the socialization event.

(a) Smart parking project   (b) Patient care project

Fig. 4. Construction and socialization of the prototype

5   Conclusions

This strategy constitutes a proposal of articulation between the universities and high school institutions to face the challenges imposed by Industry 4.0 regarding human resource training. Such a strategy incorporated two important axes for enriching the teaching and learning process: (1) game elements and (2) collaborative activities to promote teamwork in problem-solving.

The study case allowed not only the introduction of students to the fundamental concepts of IoT technology but also the interaction among students from different schools to solve problems of their environment. The preliminary results showed that project-based work to solve everyday problems by applying an ET generates student commitment and motivation. Another motivating factor for the students to tackle the project prototype is the fact that their teachers, family, and friends will participate in the socialization event for the exhibition of the products constructed by the teams.

The students could construct a prototype and rapidly apply the theoretical and practical concepts they had learned. As a result, the young participants actively engaged and, in some instances, developed an interest in pursuing careers in STEM fields.

As a future work lines, we identify: (1) Apply the strategy to other enabling technologies; (2) incorporate other gamification and co-creation techniques additionally from those used in the case study presented, (3) the design of case studies that combine different technologies looking for robust prototypes, (4) design and implement assessment metrics of the strategy from a didactic point of view, and (5) the inclusion of engineering program students in the sessions, such as a mentorship program, to assist the lead teacher.

References

1. Brettel, M., Friederichsen, N., Keller, M.: How virtualization, decentralization and network building change the manufacturing landscape: an industry 4.0 perspective. search.ebscohost.com (2017). https://publications.waset.org/9997144/how-virtualization-decentralization-and-network-building-change-the-manufacturing-landscape-an-industry-40-perspective
2. Oesterreich, T.D., Teuteberg, F.: Understanding the implications of digitisation and automation in the context of Industry 4.0: a triangulation approach and elements of a research agenda for the construction industry. Comput. Ind. **83**, 121–139 (2016)
3. Sánchez-Dams, R., Baron-Salazar, A., Gómez-Álvarez, M.C.: An extension of the SEMAT kernel for representing teaching and learning practices about embedded systems. In: Proceedings - 2016 4th International Conference in Software Engineering Research and Innovation, CONISOFT 2016, pp. 39–46 (2016)
4. Verner, I., Perez, H., Cuperman, D., Polishuk, A., Greenholts, M., Rosen, U.: Enriching teacher training for industry 4.0 through interaction with a high school engineering project. In: Auer, M.E., Pachatz, W., Ruutmann, T. (eds.) ICL 2022. Lecture Notes in Networks and Systems, vol. 633, pp. 542–552. Springer, Cham (2023). https://doi.org/10.1007/978-3-031-26876-2_52
5. Verner, I., Cuperman, D., Romm, T., Reitman, M., Chong, S.K., Gong, Z.: Intelligent robotics in high school: an educational paradigm for the industry 4.0 era. Adv. Intell. Syst. Comput. **916**, 824–832 (2020)
6. Calaon, M., Vieira, C., Gouveia, R.C., Dias, A.L.: Interdisciplinary teaching activities for high school integrated to vocational education promoting reflections on industry 4.0 technologies and their implication in society. J. Tech. Educ. Train. **14**, 75–89 (2022). https://publisher.uthm.edu.my/ojs/index.php/JTET/article/view/10967
7. Schneider, G., Bernardini, F., Boscarioli, C.: Teaching CT through Internet of Things in high school: possibilities and reflections. In: Proceedings - Frontiers in Education Conference, FIE 2020-October (2020)
8. Rodríguez-Calderon, R., Belmonte-Izquierdo, R.: Educational platform for the development of projects using Internet of Things. Revista Iberoamericana Tecnologías del Aprendizaje **16**, 276–282 (2021)
9. Chou, C.M., Shen, C.H., chi Hsiao, H., Shen, T.C.: Industry 4.0 manpower and its teaching connotation in technical and vocational education: adjust 107 curriculum reform. Int. J. Psychol. Educ. Stud. **5**, 9–14 (2018)
10. Uspabayeva, A., Sattarova, A., Mirza, N., Kubeeva, M., Abdualievich, Z.K., Rysbayeva, G.: Evaluation of high school students' new trends in education: internet of things. Int. J. Emerg. Technol. Learn. **17**, 159–175 (2022)

11. Parvanda, R., Kala, P.: Trends, opportunities, and challenges in the integration of the additive manufacturing with industry 4.0. Prog. Addit. Manuf. **8**, 1–28 (2022). https://link-springer-com.udea.lookproxy.com/article/10.1007/s40964-022-00351-1
12. Cilardo, A., Cinque, M., Simone, L.D., Mazzocca, N.: Virtualization over multiprocessor systems-on-chip: an enabling paradigm for the industrial internet of things. Computer **55**, 35–47 (2022)
13. Sharifzadeh, M., Malekpour, H., Shoja, E.: Cloud computing and its impact on industry 4.0. Industry 4.0 vision for the supply of energy and materials: enabling technologies and emerging applications, pp. 99–120 (2022)
14. de Azambuja, A.J.G., Plesker, C., Schützer, K., Anderl, R., Schleich, B., Almeida, V.R.: Artificial intelligence-based cyber security in the context of industry 4.0-a survey. Electronics **12** (2023). https://www.mdpi.com/2079-9292/12/8/1920
15. de Paula Ferreira, W., Armellini, F., Santa-Eulalia, L.A.D.: Simulation in industry 4.0: a state-of-the-art review. Comput. Ind. Eng. **149**, 106868 (2020). https://doi.org/10.1016/j.cie.2020.106868
16. Alcácer, V., Cruz-Machado, V.: Scanning the industry 4.0: a literature review on technologies for manufacturing systems. Eng. Sci. Technol. Int. J. **22**, 899–919 (2019)
17. Dúo-Terrón, P.: Analysis of scratch software in scientific production for 20 years: programming in education to develop computational thinking and STEAM disciplines. Educ. Sci. **13** (2023). https://www.mdpi.com/2227-7102/13/4/404
18. Pellas, N., Tzafilkou, K.: The influence of absorption and need for cognition on students' learning outcomes in educational robot-supported projects. Educ. Sci. **13** (2023). https://www.mdpi.com/2227-7102/13/4/379
19. Abekiri, N., Rachdy, A., Ajaamoum, M., Nassiri, B., Elmahni, L., OubailL, Y.: Platform for hands-on remote labs based on the ESP32 and NOD-red. Sci. African **19** (2023). https://www.sciencedirect.com/science/article/pii/S2468227622004069
20. Álvarez Ariza, J., Galvis, C.N.: RaspyControl lab: a fully open-source and real-time remote laboratory for education in automatic control systems using Raspberry Pi and Python. HardwareX **13**, e00396 (2023). https://www.sciencedirect.com/science/article/pii/S2468067223000032
21. Mon, A., Giorgio, H.D.: Modelo de evaluación de Tecnologías de la Información y la Comunicación para la Industria 4.0 (2019)
22. Lin, X., et al.: Applying project-based learning in artificial intelligence and marine discipline: an evaluation study on a robotic sailboat platform. IET Cyber-Syst. Rob. **4**, 86–96 (2022). https://ietresearch.onlinelibrary.wiley.com/doi/abs/10.1049/csy2.12050
23. He, P., Chen, I.C., Touitou, I., Bartz, K., Schneider, B., Krajcik, J.: Predicting student science achievement using post-unit assessment performances in a coherent high school chemistry project-based learning system. J. Res. Sci. Teach. **60**, 724–760 (2023). https://onlinelibrary.wiley.com/doi/abs/10.1002/tea.21815
24. Tikhonova, E., Raitskaya, L.: Education 4.0: the concept, skills, and research. J. Lang. Educ. **9**, 5–11 (2023). https://jle.hse.ru/article/view/17001
25. Darmawansah, D., Hwang, G.J., Chen, M.R.A., Liang, J.C.: Trends and research foci of robotics-based STEM education: a systematic review from diverse angles based on the technology-based learning model. Int. J. STEM Educ. **10**, 12 (2023). https://doi.org/10.1186/s40594-023-00400-3
26. Zhu, Z., et al.: LearnIoTVR: an end-to-end virtual reality environment providing authentic learning experiences for internet of things. Association for Computing Machinery (2023). https://doi.org/10.1145/3544548.3581396

27. Ekong, J., Chauhan, V., Osedeme, J., Niknam, S.A., Nguyen, R.: A framework for Industry 4.0 workforce training through project-based and experiential learning approaches (2022). https://peer.asee.org/40637

28. Ghannam, R., Chan, C.: Teaching undergraduate students to think like real-world systems engineers: a technology-based hybrid learning approach. Syst. Eng. https://incose.onlinelibrary.wiley.com/doi/abs/10.1002/sys.21683

29. Gasca-Hurtado, G.P., Gómez-Alvarez, M.C., Muñoz, M., Mejía, J.: Toward an assessment framework for gamified environments. In: Stolfa, J., Stolfa, S., O'Connor, R.V., Messnarz, R. (eds.) EuroSPI 2017. CCIS, vol. 748, pp. 281–293. Springer, Cham (2017). https://doi.org/10.1007/978-3-319-64218-5_23

30. Hurtado, M., Cortés Ruiz, J.A., Espinosa, E.: Estrategias para el desarrollo de habilidades blandas a partir del aprendizaje basado en proyectos y gamificación. RIDE Revista Iberoamericana para la Investigación y el Desarrollo Educativo **13** (2022)

31. Qureshi, M.A., Khaskheli, A., Qureshi, J.A., Raza, S.A., Yousufi, S.Q.: Factors affecting students' learning performance through collaborative learning and engagement. Interact. Learn. Environ. **31**(4), 2371–2391 (2023)

32. Lee, S.M.: The relationships between higher order thinking skills, cognitive density, and social presence in online learning. Internet High. Educ. **21**, 41–52 (2014)

Automatic Translation of Text and Audio to Colombian Sign Language

Santiago Fernández Becerra⬤, Fabián Andrés Olarte Vargas⬤,
Johan Mateo Rosero Quenguan⬤, Andrés Felipe Vásquez Rendón⬤,
and Andrea Rueda-Olarte⁽✉⁾⬤

Pontificia Universidad Javeriana, Bogotá, Colombia
{sa.fernandez,olarte_fabian,roseroq-j,af.vasquezr,
rueda-andrea}@javeriana.edu.co

Abstract. The communication gap between deaf and hearing people remains a significant issue today, as the language used by both parts creates barriers affecting multiple aspects on people's lifes. To address this, we propose a system for translation of text and audio into Colombian Sign Language using an accessible and user-friendly mobile application to facilitate communication between both parties. For this prototype, 76 phrases and words that represent signs were selected for the system. Pre-recorded videos of a sign language interpreter were employed to perform translations based on the previously established vocabulary. The service works via video concatenation based on the client's text or audio request, using a Whisper AI model for audio transcription. In the context of an undergraduate thesis project, a mobile application prototype that translate text and audio into Colombian Sign Language was successfully developed. This project contributes to bridging the communication gap between deaf individuals and the hearing community.

Keywords: Automatic translation · Colombian sign language · Speech to text · Sign interpreter

1 Introduction

By the year 2020, in Colombia there were 1'319,049 people (2.6% of the population) who had a disability, where 470,637 of them have disabilities with permanent hearing and speech impairments (mute, deaf and deaf-mute) [1]. Although it is a small percentage of the population, it is a minority that faces several problems due to their condition. One of the problems is the difficulty of access to different services provided by the State, such as participation in recreational activities or paperwork, due to the communication barriers that still exist. Another is related to working conditions, since deaf people are, in most cases, employed in activities that require low qualification [2]. Around the world, means have been sought by which to solve this problem for sign language, proposing complex learning models [3], various interfaces [4] and use of sensors [5], among

© The Author(s), under exclusive license to Springer Nature Switzerland AG 2024
M. Tabares et al. (Eds.): CCC 2023, CCIS 1924, pp. 109–114, 2024.
https://doi.org/10.1007/978-3-031-47372-2_11

others. Although the translation is bidirectional in these solutions, the use of these tools in daily life is still not easy to access in terms of the technologies required for their correct operation. On the other hand, in Colombia there are currently no solutions that allow to streamline communication between hearing and deaf people. For this reason, this paper presents a proposal that seeks to eliminate this communication gap, through a system of translation of text or audio to Colombian sign language, which is developed as a mobile application that hopes to improve the interaction between both population groups.

2   Methodology

The methodology used for this project was a combination of two existing agile frameworks: Disciplines Agile Delivery (DAD) y SCRUM. Additionally, an iterative model was developed, consisting of the following phases: characterization, desing, development, validation and release.

Characterization Phase. This phase consists in the search and selection of letters, words, and phrases to translate to Colombian Sign Language, chosen based on their frequency of use in basic communication. For this phase a subdictionary of words was created, which includes common basic words and phrases used by people. Furthermore, this list contains all the letters of the Spanish alphabet, except for "ñ", double "l", double "r" and accented words.

2.1   Design Phase

In this section we will provide a general overview of the interaction with the system. First, the user utilizes the mobile application, developed in React Native, which communicates with Firebase authentication services during registration and login. Likewise, the application communicates with AWS services for all the translations and an self hosted virtual machine for audio to text transcription. In AWS we use API Gateway for routing the request and Lambda functions for partition and assembly processes, which consume S3 storage. In our self hosted virtual machine, a Docker container is deployed, containing a server for the transcription requests (Fig. 1).

2.2   Implementation Phase

In this section we will provide evidence to the development process of the project components. In addition to this, we present the tools used and the approach taken for implementing the mobile application. Below, we provide the most relevant aspects of frontend and backend development.

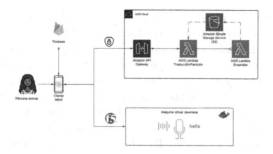

Fig. 1. High level architecture diagram

Frontend Development. The development of the software component was carried out using React Native for the frontend. The application was built following a component-based architecture, where each component is responsible for carrying out a defined action within the application. To achieve an effective interaction between the components, hooks were used, which allow to execute actions depending on the change of state of each component. This functionality was essential to adapt the behavior of the components according to their state. The components were divided into two main categories: logic components and presentation components. The logic components were in charge of handling the logic corresponding to the collection of information from the user through inputs. For example, a versatile input was implemented in the translation screen that allows the user to enter text or audio, providing greater convenience and flexibility in their choice of format. In addition, a component was developed to make requests to the backend component, sending the information collected by the aforementioned component and waiting for the response in the form of a video containing the translation, to later show it to the user. In the presentation components, the user's information was displayed. This information was obtained from a logic component in charge of collecting data from the database and sent to these components for presentation to the end user. Regarding user management, the Firebase authentication service was integrated, which provides a reliable tool to authenticate users. In addition, Firebase's real-time database service was used to store user information.

Backend Development. For the development of the backend, as mentioned in previous sections, three AWS cloud services were used: AWS S3 service is used for the storage of the different videos. Mainly, pre-recorded videos are previously stored, which are the basis for the formation of different phrases or new words. These new phrases or words will also be stored in this service, in order to increase the base of known words or phrases in the system and along with this, the speed of response to future requests. As for the AWS Lambda service, two lambda functions were created. The first function handles the entire translation system of the application, this means that all words and phrases that are requested by the user will be processed in this Lambda function. To achieve this, there are two flows; the first one in which the phrase or word is already in S3 and the link is obtained to access that resource for a limited time. The second case is in which the phrase or word is not found in S3, at that time the phrase or word is partitioned in order to obtain the necessary keys of the videos corresponding to the request made by the user. Once these keys are obtained, the second lambda function is called. After the execution of this second function is finished, a value is returned which allows to obtain the link of the new video. The second function contains all the necessary logic to download, cut and join the videos corresponding to the user's request. To achieve this, use is made of the temporary memory of the AWS Lambda functions, in which the videos associated with the phrase or word of the user are stored and with the help of the 'ffmpeg' library, the processing is done to cut the videos so that the transitions between videos look more natural for the union of these in a single video. Once the new video is obtained in temporary memory, it is stored in S3 with the same name of the phrase or word requested by the user. Although communication between AWS cloud services is done internally using the ARN of each service created, communication with the user cannot be done through this means, which is why we use the AWS API Gateway service, which provides a public link that allows users to make their requests.

2.3 Testing Phase

In this phase we planned the way we would verify the functionality and quality of the mobile application. It's worth to mention that all tests presented below were successful.

Frontend Unit Test. The tests made with the Jest library verified the functionality of all elements in the application. We ensured the creation and modificability of fields in each component, as well as the elements on screen and function calls. Also, we evaluated the navigation between components.

Backend Testing. This tests were implemented using the AWS cloud integrated test tools and Postman to ensure the quality and proper functionality of the backend component. The lambda functions were evaluated in different scenarios, and main test cases were configured at Speech to Text. These tests covered the union and storage of new videos, sending the links according to the presence of words and phrases in the system, the manage of terms not stored and partitioning phrases based on their context.

End to End Testing. This tests were implemented using the Detox library to ensure the functionality of the application. This tool, based on Jest, allows end-to-end testing in a mobile application environment, simulating real interactions such as taps, swipes and text inputs. The tests focused on general interactions, login and registration, translation service, history and favorites services.

Load Testing. To ensure the concurrency of the application's service, the JMeter tool was used to simulate the presence of 50 to 150 concurrent users within the platform. These tests were designed considering the limitations and capabilities of the free tier of the AWS cloud provider used in this project. The tests focused on verifying the functionality of the translation system with new or previously recorded words and phrases in the storage system.

3   Results

All the mentioned phases of the project resulted in a mobile application that is easy to access and use, which we named toLSC (LSC for the Colombian Sign Language acronym in Spanish). This application allows unidirectional translation of text and audio into Colombian Sign Language. The usage logic of the application consists of several screens. First, the login or registration screens allows the user to set their credentials for the system. After accessing the system the user find the main translation screen, where users can enter text or record an audio file, limited to a maximum of five words in either case. Subsequently, the video display component presents the video generated for the corresponding translation request. The application provides a translation history where the user can easily view the request they have made through their account and save favorite words or phrases. Finally, there is also a settings screen where the user can access basic profile information and log out. To fully visualize the application functionalities and interactions, you can access the following link: https://bit.ly/tolscdemo (Fig. 2).

4   Conclusions and Future Work

Regarding the work done, we believe that the objectives set in this project have been achieved. We have successfully developed a mobile application prototype that allows the translation of text and audio to Colombian Sign Language. As outlined in the problem statement, we focused on key features of the final product, such as user-friendly components for all indivuduals, quick access to primary translation functions, the inclusion of a history module to improve interaction and the ability to save favorite words or phrases to enhance the usage. In terms of future work, we propose expanding the translation database for Colombian Sign Language, which currently is limited to 76 expressions. Furthermore, we suggest developing machine learning models that use visual examples from sign language interpreters to establish precise movements based on the context of the user requests. To ensure the project's success, collaboration with specialized sign language entities like the National Institute for the Deaf (INSOR) and universities for development are recommended. Additionally, we see a potential for implementing bidirectional translation to enhance the functionalities developed on the mobile application developed in this project.

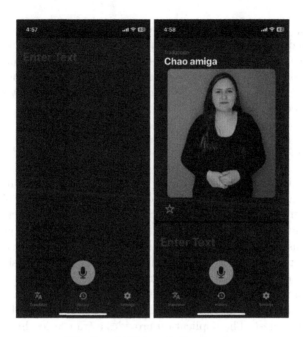

Fig. 2. toLSC translation service

References

1. César, C.A.S.: Boletines Poblacionales: Personas con Discapacidad -PCD1 Oficina de Promoción Social. p. 15 (2020)
2. INSOR. Plan estratégico de tecnologías de información-PETI-2018-2022.pdf. https://www2.sgc.gov.co/ControlYRendicion/planes-presupuesto-gestion/ Indicadores/Plan%20estrat%C3%A9gico%20de%20tecnolog%C3%ADas%20de %20informaci%C3%B3n%E2%80%93PETI-2018%E2%80%932022.pdf
3. López-Ludeña, V., San-Segundo, R., Morcillo, C.G., López, J.C., Muñoz, J.M.P.: Increasing adaptability of a speech into sign language translation system. Expert Syst. Appl. **40**(4), 1312–1322 (2013)
4. Glauert, J.R., Elliott, R., Cox, S.J., Tryggvason, J., Sheard, M.: Vanessa—a system for communication between deaf and hearing people. Technol. Disabil. **18**(4), 207–216 (2006)
5. Wang, F., Sun, S., Liu, Y.: A bi-directional interactive system of sign language and visual speech based on portable devices. In: Proceedings of the IEEE International Conference on Robotics and Biomimetics ROBIO 2019, pp. 1071–1076 (2019)

Movement in Video Classification Using Structured Data: Workout Videos Application

Jonathan Múnera[✉] and Marta Silvia Tabares

Grupo GIDITIC/Universidad EAFIT, Medellín, Colombia
jd.skratchy@gmail.com

Abstract. Nowadays, several video movement classification methodologies are based on reading and processing each frame using image classification algorithms. However, it is rare to find approaches using angle distribution over time. This paper proposes video movement classification based on the exercise states calculated from each frame's angles. Different video classification approaches and their respective variables and models were analyzed to achieve this, using unstructured data: images. Besides, structure data as angles from critical joints Armpits, legs, elbows, hips, and torso inclination were calculated directly from workout videos, allowing the implementation of classification models such as the KNN and Decision Trees. The result shows these techniques can achieve similar accuracy, close to 95%, concerning Neural Networks algorithms, the primary model used in the previously mentioned approaches. Finally, it was possible to conclude that using structured data for movement classification models allows for lower performance costs and computing resources than using unstructured data without compromising the quality of the model.

Keywords: Machine Learning · computer vision · KNN · mediapipe · supervised classification · video classification · deep learning · tensorflow · neural network · workout · fitness · exercise · signal

1 Introduction

Fitness industry relies on videos to instruct their users how to perform better on their workouts, this also helps people train from home when schedules do not allow to go to the gym. This video classes or video workouts have multiple exercises to focus user efforts on multiple sections of their body, hence, a long video with different movement is created. This gives rise to the necessity of tagging these videos with each of their movements and identify the time where each one is performed, this is achieved manually by a person doing the job, which is inefficient and slow. Consequently, machine learning algorithms can help with this task, making it faster and easier. This task contains two different efforts to fulfill, the first one, identifying the changes in the exercises so each movement can be classified individually, and the second one, movement classification. For the first task it will be used an algorithm called ruptures [1] which allows to detect the signal breaks on the movement thus identifying exercises changes. The second task, which is this paper's focus, represents a movement classification problem,

M. Tabares et al. (Eds.): CCC 2023, CCIS 1924, pp. 115–127, 2024.
https://doi.org/10.1007/978-3-031-47372-2_12

which can be approached by many means, the most common methods include using sequential neural networks [2] and recurrent neural networks [3] to capture the sequence of poses in each video frame, this is a great method when you have the computational resources and abundant training data. This research evaluates a niche of exercises that are trained manually which means there is not plenty of data samples, making the use of said methods harder. To achieve the main goal, then, the data is prepared in a different format; to process the poses in each video frame as mentioned before, the input data would be unstructured, images coming from the video; in this new proposed format of data it is calculated the angles in the body from each frame, this way the data gets a structured format allowing the use of a wide range of machine learning algorithms with high precision and lower computational cost.

2 Literature Review

The main focus of this paper is to present an effective way to make video training and classification extracting structured data from the videos instead of processing them as they come: a collection of images. For this reason this section is only reviewing literature based on video training and classification and doesn't express any concerns regarding to the change point in the signal.

In [4], it is proposed a way to identify actions performed by people. using fixed cameras on rooms to capture the movement and the person in frame as well as capturing a called ego-view to create better samples for the model. However, this is more focused on detecting an specific action rather that a set of movements, and this can be better segregated from one action to another based on the camera location and object detection. Multiple cameras are detecting multiple inputs at the same time, one first person view combined with at least one third person view to allow having a holistic view on the action. This is then combined with object detection, and camera placement to have a better understanding on what the person is doing. Finally, for the classification model it is used a **Convolutional 3D-ResNet model** as in [5], using unstructured data as input for the model, processing the images in each frame. It is also used an athomic actions recognition allowing the model to predict better the final action based on those athomic ones, so the result would be a combination of these individual actions as well as what is being captured from the cameras. From this commented research it is possible to use its object recognition technic, based on the fact that some exercises include equipment so that may help better classification, however, this could be a future work, since the current scope is only focused on exercises with no equipment required.

The article *Piano Skills Assessment* [6] uses an 3DCNN to classify little video clips, which means its goal is not only to detect an action or specific instance in time, but to classify input video data. Its experiment consists in assess a pianist skill level based on their performance using aural and video input. Aural does not concern to this paper, so the video input is the one being analyzed. **3D convolutional neural networks** can be specially useful for the purpose of video classification, so instead of classifying frame per frame, its input can be directly short video clips that allow to adquire more information for the model. However, work in this paper are trying to detect movement and poses on a video, so that methodology helps for an instance in which the comparison between this CNN and the method proposed here is being conducted.

Hierarchical video frame sequence representation [7], presents an interesting way of processing videos, this is done by using each frame as a node and their respective relations between these nodes as edges for them. This relation is weightened by each frame similarity vector, which means that similar shots or frames, would be closely connected between them. This hierarchical approach helps understand videos as a whole action, so it could be an interesting approach on exercise video classification if same movements are strongly connected to each other.

Yoga pose detection is one of the many applications in image and video recognition when it comes to workouts, and the used technic in this cases get closer to the one in this paper. As implemented by Gupta and Jangid in [8], they are using **Human Pose Estimation** in their work, helping them extract structured data from the videos. They proceed to calculate the angles using the inverse cosine function based on the dot product as shown in (1) which have been copied exactly as it appears in their paper. This equation allows to calculate the angles in 2 dimensions making it clear that the person in the video is standing in front of the camera and ignoring depth in **z axis**.

$$\theta = \cos^{-1} \left(\frac{X_{PQ}*X_{QR} + Y_{PQ}*Y_{QR}}{\sqrt{X_{PQ^2} + Y_{PQ^2}} \sqrt{X_{QR}^2 + Y_{QR}^2}} \right) \tag{1}$$

where,

$$X_{PQ} = x_2 - x_1$$
$$Y_{PQ} = y_2 - y_1$$
$$X_{QR} = x_3 - x_2$$
$$Y_{QR} = y_3 - y_2$$

It is important to notice that this [8] article is focused on pose detection or classification which means that they only need to classify the pose on one time, which reduces the complexity of the movement. Yoga has this particularity in which their poses are very static, so classifying them can be based on the angles for each frame, if they change, the pose change. For the purpose of this paper, the movement or change in the angles doesn't necessarily means change in the exercise, on the contrary, movement allows to identify the exercise, which adds a layer of complexity for this model.

3   Methodology

3.1   Proposed Method

Movement in video classification has being mostly approached by processing frames as images and then finding a relationship between them so the video is understood as a collection of images in sequence or with a correlation between them. This is highly useful when we are labeling what is happening on the videos or to identify an action in it. It gets harder when it is needed to determine the specific action between a set of multiple ones, for example, classifying a person doing exercise is a relatively easy task, but to label which exercise are they doing is more complex. This paper proposes this exercise labeling based on the angles distribution on each frame in time, different set of angles would represent different exercises and, since exercises are repetitive movements, it is understandable that the dataset will have a recognizable pattern among the angles distribution, allowing to detect peaks and valleys in the signal. This extreme points are exercise states and since all of the exercises would have a range of angles distribution, these states are helpful to differentiate them apart. After that having multiple up and down states combining them creates more data samples, this is, all up states mixed with all down states, obtaining not only more records on the dataset but better training data. These record combination (up and down states) are used to train multiple ML models, allowing to classify the movement in video not only based on the image, but rather on the actual movement.

3.2 Angles Calculation

For this task the use of the mediapipe library [9] is implemented, this library allows users to detect 32 body landmarks as shown on Fig. 1. With these landmarks it is possible to calculate the angles [10] made up of vectors created with the limbs that comforms important joints for the exercises, these joints -as shown in Fig. 2 - being armpits, knees, hip and elbows.

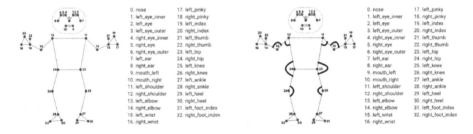

Fig. 1. Mediapipe body Landmarks   **Fig. 2.** Calculated angles

Since the landmarks are in a 3D space, angles between the joints are calculated on the vectors created by the limbs. For example, the left arm vector is created between the points (in a 3D space) **11** and **12** in Fig. 1, so calculating the left armpit angle would imply calculate this vector as well as the vector created by landmarks **11** and **23**. These vectors are created using the mutual joint (in this case **11**) as the starting point, so vectors are created as shown in Eq. (2). Where **11** corresponds to the left shoulder landmark, **12** to the left elbow landmark and **23** to the left hip landmark, all of them with their respective 3D coordinates.

$$LeftArmVector = (LE_x - LS_x, LE_y - LS_y, LE_z - LS_z)$$

$$LeftTorsoVector = (LH_x - LS_x, LH_y - LS_y, LH_z - LS_z) \tag{2}$$

Where,

$$LE = Left\_Elbow$$
$$LS = Left\_Shoulder$$
$$LH = Left\_Hip$$

This process is repeated for every joint of interest shown in Fig. 2 so we can obtain the necessary angle distribution for the following sections. Once the vectors needed for every joint angle are calculated it is then calculated each angle. This is done based on the dot product which states what is shown in Eq. (3) for the vectors **a** and **b**. So clearing for the angle it is obtained a good equation to calculate the angles between these limb vectors, obtaining the eight needed angles for this work.

$$a.b = |a||b|\cos\theta$$

$$\theta = \arccos\left(\frac{a.b}{|a||b|}\right) \tag{3}$$

This angles creates a distribution in time for the movement. For better understanding, this movement is transformed into a single variable created based on the sum of the average of the angles on each side of the body as explained on Eq. (4). This aggregation is created over each processed frame of the video, so a vector is obtained.

$$\left(\frac{LAA_i + RAA_i}{2}\right) + \left(\frac{LEA_i + REA_i}{2}\right) + \left(\frac{LHA_i + RHA_i}{2}\right) + \left(\frac{LKA_i + RKA_i}{2}\right) \tag{4}$$

where,

$$LAA = leftArmpitAngles$$
$$RAA = rightArmpitAngles$$
$$LEA = leftElbowAngles$$
$$REA = rightElbowAngles$$
$$LHA = leftHipAngles$$
$$RHA = rightHipAngles$$
$$LKA = leftKneeAngles$$
$$RKA = rightKneeAngles$$

This new vector expresses a wave of the body movement as shown on Fig. 3, where x axis is time in seconds and y axis is the angles aggregation. In this figure we can see how some segments of the signal show a periodical pattern, this is due to the person in video, the trainer, doing repetitive movements, in this case exercises, so we can start to separate these signals and analyze each movement individually. This particular example consist of a 20 min workout doing multiple exercises.

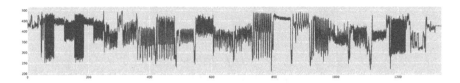

Fig. 3. Workout Motion Wave

3.3 Movement Segregation

Figure 3 shows the wave of a compilation of multiple exercises, and visually can be differentiated because of the changes in the signal intensity and frequency, so for the next step it is needed to detect this changes automatically and to separate the exercises using a ruptures [1] algorithm for off-line change point detection. Off-line methodology is used based on the fact that all of the frames have already been processed. Online change point detection could be a possible next implementation for reducing processing time detecting changes on the signal at the same time the frames are being processed. This algorithm helps users obtain the points where the signal switch from one pattern to another as shown in Fig. 4, some exercises need to be manually separated from each other, but this is minimal compared to the number of exercises performed in this workout. This exercise segregation allows to start the classification process.

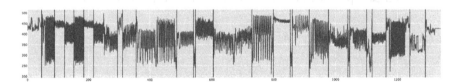

Fig. 4. Ruptures algorithm applied over the workout signal

3.4 Exercise States

After the change point identification its needed to detect the exercises states, this is done with the help of another library for the peak and valley detection, this is the peakdetect [11] library and, with some tuning, allows to detect the maximum and minimum values for each segment, as shown on Fig. 5. This signal represents the first exercise being done by the trainer, in this case, corresponds from the second 58 to the 87, the first random signal received, second 0 to 57, is the introduction to the workout, so it is ignored. States are used for training data due to the fact that exercises in this case are made up of two main positions, up and down, so these allows to identify the exercise with fewer data than using the whole movement pattern.

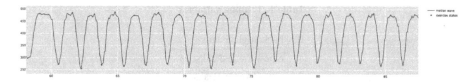

Fig. 5. Exercise States

The next step after obtained these states is to create model training data labeling this exercise based on previous knowledge and expertise, this is done via manual tagging or either obtaining video metadata to correctly label this signal. This training dataset is the input for the machine learning algorithms to be tested. The dataset is not created based on the angles aggregation, but on the individual angles present in each state of the exercise, this means that for every state -either up or down- we obtain the angle distribution at that time, creating 17 dimensional vectors -being each of the 8 joints times both states- and adding one last variable being the person's body inclination. This last metric is calculated based on a new artificial vector created on the center of the torso, this vector represents the torso position over the 3 dimensions -x,y,z- so its respective coordinates are obtained and evaluated, if **y** coordinate is greater than the other two, the person is standing based on a simple definition stipulated, if not, they are lying and is a boolean feature added to the dataset.

3.5   Exercise Classification

3.5.1   Creating More Samples in Dataset
The input dataset from peak detection will contain as much samples as repetitions being done by the trainer, this is, if the trainer did 10 squat repetitions, 15 push-ups and 10 burpees, the dataset will contain the angle distribution for state up and down for each repetition of each exercise, so it would be 10 samples with label squat, 15 with label push-ups and 10 with label burpees. For this particular example, the dataset contains around 15 samples of each exercise and a total of 5 exercises, which is too few samples for a proper model training. Artificial data is created based on those samples we already have, since the dataset contains up and down states, it is combined every down state of an exercise with every up state of the same exercise, obtaining, from 15 repetitions, 225 records to train the model per exercise. So the final training dataset contains the columns shown in Table 1 and the label would be only the exercise name for each case.

3.6   Model Training

Before the last fix on the dataset -cross join every down state with every up state- the validation accuracy of every model tested didn't get over 83%, which re-afirm the fact that good models train over good datasets.

Table 1. Training variables

0	backAnglesPeaks
1	elbowAnglesPeaks
2	armpitAnglesPeaks
3	legsAnglesPeaks
4	backAngles2Peaks
5	elbowAngles2Peaks
6	armpitAngles2Peaks
7	legsAngles2Peaks
8	slopePeaks
9	backAnglesValleys
10	elbowAnglesValleys
11	armpitAnglesValleys
12	legsAnglesValleys
13	backAngles2Valleys
14	elbowAngles2Valleys
15	armpitAngles2Valleys
16	legsAngles2Valleys
17	slopeValleys

First model tested was a **KNN classifier** [12]. This was due to the first conception of having an 8 dimensional array of angles converted into 16 dimensions when joining both states -up and down-, so having the dataset across multiple dimensions gave the idea of classifying with an algorithm suitable for this task, keeping in mind that exercises would fall around the same space when distributed over the 17 dimensions, here is where KNN looked useful. For this particular training the following parameters in Table 2 where used.

Table 2. Parameters used for the KNN algorithm

Parameter	Value
algorithm	'auto'
leaf_size	15
metric	'manhattan'
n_neighbors	1
weights	'uniform'

The manhattan parameter for the distance metric was the most impactful one, making the model improve significatively, and the fact that using only one neighbor to compare produced the best results means that the classes are very well separated from each other, which is good in this cases. Using a 70-30 data split for training and validation KNN gives results above the 98% of accuracy testing it multiple times and performing cross_validation, these are very good numbers in terms of a machine learning model.

Some of the most popular machine learning algorithms used due to their reliability are tree classification models, these being **Decision Tree** [13], and the ensemble models **Extra Tree** [14] and **Random Forest** [15], all of these algorithms comming from the **scikit-learn** [16,17] library. All of these tree based algorithms got similar accuracy, with a little more variation between iterations, varying from 93% to 98% of accuracy, practicing the same methods of evaluation as with the **KNN classifier**. Parameters for each of these algorithms are found in Table 3.

Table 3. Tree based algorithm parameters

Algorithm	Parameter	Value
decissionTreeClassifier	criterion	'entropy'
	max_depth	6
	max_leaf_nodes	58
	min_samples_split	2
extraTreeClassifier	max_leaf_nodes	33
	min_samples_split	2
	n_estimators	90
RandomForestClassifier	max_depth	5
	min_samples_leaf	1
	min_samples_split	2
	n_estimators	300

The last algorithm tested is the **Sequential Neural Network (SNN)** [2], using directly the **Keras** [18] library from **Tensorflow** [19]. The model is constructed as shown in Table 4 and is using dense layers for training, and dropout and normalization layers to avoid overfitting.

Table 4. SNN Parameters

Model: "sequential"		
Layer (type)	Output Shape	Param #
dense (Dense)	(None, 512)	9728
batch_normalization (BatchNormalization)	(None, 512)	2048
dropout (Dropout)	(None, 512)	0
dense_1 (Dense)	(None, 256)	131328
batch_normalization_1 (BatchNormalization)	(None, 256)	1024
dropout_1 (Dropout)	(None, 256)	0
dense_2 (Dense)	(None, 128)	32896
batch_normalization_2 (BatchNormalization)	(None, 128)	512
dropout_2 (Dropout)	(None, 128)	0
dense_3 (Dense)	(None, 64)	8256
batch_normalization_3 (BatchNormalization)	(None, 64)	256
dense_4 (Dense)	(None, 32)	2080
dense_5 (Dense)	(None, 5)	165
Total params: 188,293		
Trainable params: 186,373		
Non-trainable params: 1,920		

For model compilation the used values are shown on Table 5. Since **categorical_crossentropy** is used it is needed to transform the labels vector **y**, so first of all convert the label vector to numbers –0 to 4 being 5 different classes/exercises-, and then using the **one hot encoding** methodology [20] vector **y** should look like Fig. 6, where each column represents each class an its respective boolean indicates whether or not the label corresponds to this class.

y
1
2
0
3
4
4
1
0
2

➡

0	1	2	3	4
0	1	0	0	0
0	0	1	0	0
1	0	0	0	0
0	0	0	1	0
0	0	0	0	1
0	0	0	0	1
0	1	0	0	0
1	0	0	0	0
0	0	1	0	0

Fig. 6. One hot encoding y label

Table 5. Compilation parameters for the SNN

Parameter	Value
loss	'categorical_crossentropy'
optimizer	'nadam'
metrics	['categorical_accuracy']

The training for this model was made using 20% data for testing, and 80% for training, iterating over 100 epochs, the results can be seen on Fig. 7, where it can be seen that the training as well as validation get to very high values, ensuring that the model is not overfitting the data.

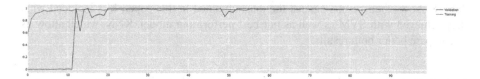

Fig. 7. SNN accuracy over the epochs

Table 6 shows the final comparison between the tested models and shows how high the accuracy reach. This shows that with the implemented methodology in this paper, several models can be implemented achieving very goo results and we can classify movement in videos not only with unstructured data and convolutional neural networks, but with any vector supported model.

Table 6. Model Accuracy Comparison

Model	Min_accuracy	Max_accuracy
KNN	98.2%	100%
Decision Tree	65.8%	93%
Random Forest	86.4%	100%
Extra Tree	95.2%	100%
SNN	75.8%	100%

4 Discussion and Conclusion

Compared to [4], it can be appreciated that their methods present very good results for the use of Neural Network configurations, They use the precision as their main metric so we can use the average precision as well for a better comparison, as shown in Table 7, the average precision of our model looks better once it reaches the stabilization point after the 20 first training epochs of the model. For comparison purposes, we added the full average precision as well so we can have the full view.

Table 7. Model Accuracy Comparison vs Hierarchical

Model	Average_Precision	Average_loss
SNN	98.9%	0.054
SNN without stabilization	82.6%	0.37
Hierarchical + average graph pooling	84.1%	4.01
Hierarchical + self-attention graph pooling	84.5%	3.98

The Hierarchical model uses image video classification with their own methodology to achieve their goal, however, in this paper it is used bodymarks recognition so it is only logical to compare with the Yoga pose estimation research [8]. They achieve the best results using a SVM, in this paper we did not tested that model, however they are also using RandomForest algorithm, which allow us to have a very good validation start line. Table 8 shows their results against the ones obtained in this paper. It is included what they achieved with SVM as well as our best performing model, KNN, which allow us to compare better both results.

Table 8. Model Accuracy Comparison vs Yoga. This paper's results are expressed as average, while yoga research results are as reported on their results

Model	Average_Accuracy
KNN	99.6%
Our RandomForest	96.8%
Yoga RandomForest	96.47%
Yoga SVM	97.64%

It is seen that classifying videos can be well performed with structured data based on relevant information extracted from the video, unlike "normal" video classification in which we process every frame as a picture, processing every frame as a collection of structured data can be helpful to implement not only neural networks -which is the main algorithm for image/video processing- but classical classification algorithms. It is proved once more that achieving a well trained and useful model can only be done by preprocessing the training dataset, making cleanse and adding the right features, even restructuring the whole dataset. With these methodology, we were able to perform faster and accurate video classification to improve the speed of content delivery. Next steps will be to test this trained models over new exercises and collect more data for the existing ones, as well as testing to another trainers, and normalize and standardize the body length for more consistent data. In general terms this work turned out to be a success given the fact that we can classify the videos using a wide variety of classification algorithms available, making it easier and faster for users that are not familiarized with neural networks. Recurrent neural networks [3] are very helpful for classification in videos due to their ability to preserve information over the layers, however, they were not necessary in this case because of the way the data was prepared, making a mix with the multiple states of the exercise repetitions.

References

1. Truong, C., Oudre, L., Vayatis, N.: Selective review of offline change point detection methods. Sig. Process. **167**, 107299 (2020)
2. Denoyer, L., Gallinari, P.: Deep sequential neural network. CoRR, abs/1410.0510 (2014)
3. Schmidhuber, J., Hochreiter, S.: Long short-term memory (1997)

4. Rai, N., et al.: Home action genome: cooperative compositional action understanding (2021)
5. Hara, K., Kataoka, H., Satoh, Y.: Can spatiotemporal 3D CNNs retrace the history of 2D CNNs and ImageNet? In: 2018 IEEE/CVF Conference on Computer Vision and Pattern Recognition, pp. 6546–6555 (2018)
6. Morris, B., Parmar, P., Reddy, J.: Piano skills assessment (2021)
7. Rai, N., et al.: Hierarchical video frame sequence representation with deep convolutional graph network (2019)
8. Gupta, A., Jangid, A.: Yoga pose detection and validation. In: 2021 International Symposium of Asian Control Association on Intelligent Robotics and Industrial Automation (IRIA), pp. 319–324 (2021)
9. Lugaresi, C., et al.: MediaPipe: a framework for perceiving and processing reality. In: Third Workshop on Computer Vision for AR/VR at IEEE Computer Vision and Pattern Recognition (CVPR) 2019 (2019)
10. Andrilli, S., Hecker, D.: Chapter 1 - vectors and matrices. In: Andrilli, S., Hecker, D. (eds.) Elementary Linear Algebra, 5th edn., pp. 1–83. Academic Press, Boston (2016)
11. avhn. Simple peak detection library for python (2022)
12. Cunningham, P., Delany, S.: k-nearest neighbour classifiers. Mult. Classif. Syst. **54**, 04 (2007)
13. Fürnkranz, J.: Decision Tree. In: Sammut, C., Webb, G.I. (eds.) Encyclopedia of Machine Learning, pp. 263–267. Springer, Boston (2010). https://doi.org/10.1007/978-0-387-30164-8_204
14. Simm, J., de Abril, I.M., Sugiyama, M.: Tree-based ensemble multi-task learning method for classification and regression (2014)
15. Breiman, L.: Random forests. Mach. Learn. **45**(1), 5–32 (2001)
16. Buitinck, L., et al.: API design for machine learning software: experiences from the scikit-learn project. In: ECML PKDD Workshop: Languages for Data Mining and Machine Learning, pp. 108–122 (2013)
17. Pedregosa, F., et al.: Scikit-learn: machine learning in python. J. Mach. Learn. Res. **12**, 2825–2830 (2011)
18. Chollet, F., et al.: Keras (2015)
19. Abadi, M., et al.: TensorFlow: large-scale machine learning on heterogeneous systems (2015). https://tensorflow.org/
20. Hancock, J.T., Khoshgoftaar, T.M.: Survey on categorical data for neural networks. J. Big Data **7**(1), 1–41 (2020). https://doi.org/10.1186/s40537-020-00305-w

Planning Navigation Routes in Unknown Environments

Laura Rodriguez$^{(\boxtimes)}$, Fernando De la Rosa , and Nicolás Cardozo

Systems and Computing Engineering Department, Universidad de los Andes, Bogotá,
Colombia
{la.rodriguez,fde,n.cardozo}@uniandes.edu.co

Abstract. Self-driving robots have to fulfill many different operations,
as coordinating the motors' traction, camera movement, or actuator arms
mechanics, as well as more high-level operations like driving to different
places. Autonomous navigation is of utmost importance for exploration
robots, which must drive around exploring areas with unknown terrain
conditions, as for example is the case of mars rovers and other space
exploration vehicles. Given that the environment is unknown, planning
a specific route and driving plan is challenging or even inappropriate
due to blocking obstacles in the terrain. To overcome such problems
we propose an adaptable plan for driving robots in different situations.
Our solutions mixes both global and dynamic planning algorithms to
take advantage of available information, if it exist beforehand, and to
overcome unknown obstacles if they appear, while still moving towards
the goal. In particular, we apply our algorithm to the movement of robots
between posts in environments with partial information, as it is the case
of space mission competitions. We evaluate our solution in a simulated
environment taking into account the effectiveness in fulfilling a mission
in the shortest time, using the shortest possible path. Our results show
that of the A* algorithm with diagonals in combination with the ABEO
algorithm offer the best combination reaching the goal in most cases, in
optimal (planning + execution) time.

Keywords: Mobile robotics · Autonomous driving · Dynamic planning

1 Introduction

Autonomous navigation is one of the goals in space missions, as promoted by the
University Rover Challenge (URC)[1] or the European Rover Challenge (ERC)
competitions.[2] In these missions, a rover robot is required to navigate given
GNSS-only waypoints through posts across an easy and moderate terrain. Teams
may visit locations in any order, but must declare when they are attempting an
objective out of order. Teams are provided with a high-accuracy coordinate at
the start gate as a reference. Each post has a marker displaying a black and
white ARUCO tag using the 4×4_50 tag library as shown in Fig. 1.

---

[1] https://urc.marssociety.org.
[2] https://roverchallenge.eu/.

© The Author(s), under exclusive license to Springer Nature Switzerland AG 2024
M. Tabares et al. (Eds.): CCC 2023, CCIS 1924, pp. 128–140, 2024.
https://doi.org/10.1007/978-3-031-47372-2_13

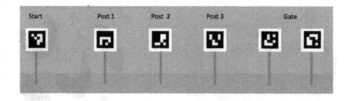

Fig. 1. ARUCOS to visit in a competition.

One problem in navigation competitions is that teams have partial or unknown information about the terrain in which the competition takes place. This means that it is not possible to predefine a route to successfully reach the desired posts, as unknown obstacles (*e.g.,* rocks, steep hills, craters) may be in the way.

The contribution of this paper consists of the exploration of a combination of planning algorithms that allow a rover to autonomously navigate between ARUCO waypoints sorting unknown obstacles. Our solution (Sect. 2) uses a global planning algorithm with the available information to sketch the shortest route between waypoints. Then, at run time, we use ABEO, a bio-inspired algorithm to avoid obstacles and continue towards the goal. Our evaluation of the combination of global and dynamic planning (Sect. 3) proves effective in finding an optimal route with respect to the execution time (*i.e.,* route planning and navigation between the points) using an improvement of the A* algorithm we posit by drawing diagonals between the points in the route. Moreover, our algorithm is also effective in reaching the goal in spite of possible obstacles in the planned route, thanks to the ABEO algorithm.

2 Route Planning for Unknown Environments

We posit a solution to the problem of autonomous navigation in unknown environments, in two parts: (1) a global or static planning, to define a potential route using available map information, and (2) a dynamic planning to sort out obstacles (*e.g.,* rocks, steep hills, craters) unknown during the planning phase.

2.1 Global Planning

In known environments it is possible to plan a route between two points avoiding all obstacles, as explained in the following. In our case, the robot only has partial information about the environment. Nonetheless, it is possible to plan an initial route. Take for example the environment in Fig. 2a. The rover may produce an approximated map as the one shown in Fig. 2b, where the most visible obstacles on the map are marked in black. From this image it is possible to plan a route, globally, given the initial and destination waypoints.

We explore three different algorithms to define a route globally, based on classic shortest-path and computational geometry. We present the reasoning behind each of the algorithms now, presenting the results later, in Sect. 3.

(a) Original Terrain   (b) Image Transformation

Fig. 2. View of the terrain and the identification of obstacles for the robot

A*. The A* algorithm [4] is a heuristic-based search algorithm to find the shortest path between two points in a graph. If we represent the map as a graph, where each pixel corresponds to a node and the edges between nodes correspond to the robot's movements (*e.g.,* up, down, left, and right), we can use A* to plan a route between the given initial and end waypoints. The objective used for the heuristics is to find a path between waypoints that takes the shortest time, and/or the shortest distance.

A* with Diagonals. Starting from the A* algorithm, we implement an extension using diagonals to cut corners between the points used to surround obstacles. The diagonals are drawn by taking rays from the points in the route and projecting them in the direction of the destination. If we intersect the route, then this is updated with the diagonal. This extension of A*, should reduce the distance between waypoints.

Convex Hull. The Convex hull [6] is an algorithm to calculate the smallest convex polygon that encloses all the points in a set. We use the convex hull to enclose each of the obstacles in the map in its convex hull. Then we use the A* algorithm to better avoid obstacles. This extension should give a shorter distance, as we are stepping away from obstacles' irregularities.

2.2   Dynamic Planning

As mentioned before, having an initial route may not be sufficient in unknown environments as obstacles may appear in the route. To overcome this problem we evaluate three algorithms designed for obstacle avoidance.

The Bubble Rebound Algorithm. This algorithm detects obstacles within the robot's *sensitivity bubble*. The area covered by the sensitivity bubble depends on the robot's sensors, speed, and geometry, among other characteristics. Upon detecting an obstacle, the robot *bounces* in a direction that has the least obstacle density and continues its movement in this direction until the target becomes visible or the robot encounters a new obstacle [8].

Figure 3a shows the sensitivity bubble at work, as a semi-ring (only 180°) equidistant from the robot's center. The bubble defines a protection field, where, if a sensor detects an obstacle in a direction (*e.g.*, ray −3), it bounces the robot to the area with the lowest obstacle density (*e.g.*, rays −2, −1, and 1), as represented in the distribution in Fig. 3b, where higher bars mean less density.

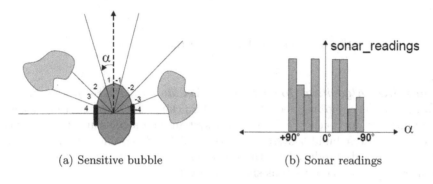

(a) Sensitive bubble   (b) Sonar readings

Fig. 3. Sensitive bubble (taken from [8])

The flow chart in Fig. 4 shows the algorithm's process. The algorithm continuously tries to move towards the objective, once an obstacle is found, the movement direction is adjusted until the robot surrounds the obstacle.

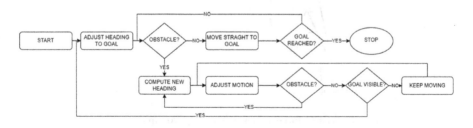

Fig. 4. Flow chart Bubble rebound algorithm [8]

Obstacle-Dependent Gaussian Potential Field (ODG-PF). The idea behind this method is that, after receiving distance data from the range sensors, the robot considers the objects within a given threshold as obstacles. To avoid obstacles, these are made larger with respect to the size of the vehicle, building a Gaussian (repulsive) potential field. Next, we calculate the attractive field from the yaw angle information of an Inertial Measurement Unit (IMU). The total field is a combination of the two fields. We choose the angle with the minimum value of the total field [1]. Figure 5 describes the process to define the Gaussian field around the robot and choose the minimum angle for the robot's direction.

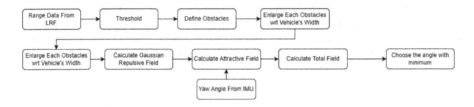

Fig. 5. Algorithm flowchart for the ODG-PF [1]

Bioinspired Algorithm for Obstacle Avoidance (ABEO). The ABEO algorithm [7] is a bio-inspired algorithm mimicking the behavior from nature combining two approaches: a force vector system, and a contour following. The force vector system builds a system of forces, which is determined by the repulsive forces F_r (in red) produced by the obstacles, and the attractive force F_a (in green) received by the target, as shown in Fig. 6.

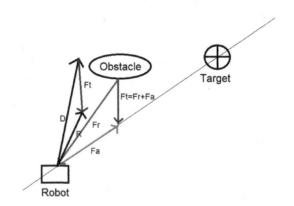

Fig. 6. ABEO force vector system approximation [7]

One of the most significant advantages of this approach, is that the robot gradually moves away from obstacles, and deviates its trajectory in short steps, so its movements are smooth. Additionally, the low complexity in computing and implementing the F_r and F_a vectors is an advantage of the algorithm. This computation entails basic linear algebra vector operations.

2.3 Implementation

The development of the route planing in unknown environments is built on top of: (1) the Robot Operating System (ROS), to communicate with the robot's sensors and actuators, and (2) Gazebo, used as a simulation environment to test the different algorithms.

We first use Jupyter notebook to implement and test algorithms, to then deploy them into the robot.

ROS. ROS consists of a set of software libraries and tools to build robot applications. The main functionality of ROS is to communicate robot systems. ROS defines the components, interfaces, and tools to build robots. The connection between tools and components is done through topics and messages [2].

We use two main topics in the project. One topic is used to publish the initial and final coordinates for the robot. The second topic is used to publish the route to follow. The architecture of our solution using ROS is shown in Fig. 7.

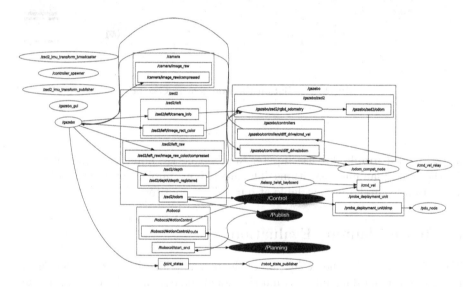

Fig. 7. ROS nodes' graph and associated topics

In Fig. 7 three main nodes (in black) publish information: the planning node (`Planning` is in charge of planning the route given its coordinates), the publish coordinates node (`/Publish`) is in charge of publishing the initial and final coordinates, and the control node (`/Control`) is in charge of sending signals to the robot's wheels, so that it moves. These nodes, in turn, subscribe and publish different information to different topics. For example, the `/zed2/odom` topic is in charge of receiving and publishing the information about the odometry (position) of the robot; the `/Robocol/start_end` topic is in charge of receiving and publishing the information of the initial and final waypoints for the planning, and the /Robocol/MotionControl/route topic is in charge of connecting the planning nodes and control of the rover.

Gazebo. Gazebo is an open source robotic simulator, which provides an opportunity to simulate different environments with a complete toolbox of development libraries and cloud services. In this project, we use the Gazebo environment from the ERC competition as the platform to run our experiments on autonomous navigation. This simulation environment loads the information of the rover and the ARUCOS to mark each of the way-points, and the information about the terrain conditions. Figure 8 captures images from the simulation environment used in this project.

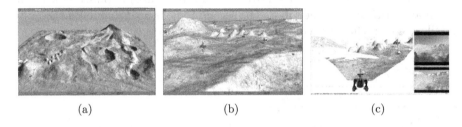

| (a) | (b) | (c) |

Fig. 8. Simulation Environment in Gazebo

Jupyter Notebook. We use Jupyter Notebook as the implementation platform for the route planning algorithms. The algorithms' implementation, results and simulation examples are available at our online repository.[3]

3   Route Planning Evaluation

This section presents the evaluation of the planning algorithms described in the previous section, taking into account the global and dynamic planning algorithms individually. Our experiments are run in a ASUS - ROG Zephyrus machine with 16GB of RAM and a AMD Ryzen 9 processor, using Python version 3.8.10 with the roslib, rospy, cv2, numpy, cv_bridge, matplotlib, rospkg, pynput libraries. Additionally, video recordings of the simulation for the different algorithms are available online.[4]

---

[3] Repository: https://anonymous.4open.science/r/Navigation_Planning-C3D9.
[4] Simulation videos: https://tinyurl.com/Simvid52.

3.1 Global Planning Results

To evaluate the effectiveness of global planning algorithms we measure three variables: (1) the time that the algorithm takes to finish the planning, (2) the number of coordinates that it sends to the control node to start moving the rover, and (3) the total distance in the planned route. The evaluation scenario for the three algorithms consists of 6 waypoints visited in order.

Table 1. A* Results.

Waypoint	Time (ms)	Number of Coordinates	Total Distance (m)
W1	**3.1178**	9	12.68857754
W2	**6.0641**	26	21.65640783
W3	**9.9446**	15	16.94107435
W4	**3.5518**	20	**20.29778313**
W5	**4.0237**	25	21.9544984
W6	**10.0512**	24	29.84962311

Table 1 shows the results for the global planning using the A* algorithm, which we use as a baseline for the comparison with the other two implementations. A* shows the best planning time performance. However, we observe that A* generates multiple coordinates between waypoints, as these are the points in which the robot turns to avoid obstacles. Finally, the last column presents the total distance traveled by the robot in between waypoints.

Table 2. A* with Diagonals Results.

Waypoint	Time (ms)	Number of Coordinates	Total Distance (m)
W1	4.0906	**7**	**9.38083152**
W2	11.9102	**17**	**12.32882801**
W3	21.9023	24	**15.23154621**
W4	4.2370	**6**	21.72556098
W5	8.2526	**18**	**19.89974874**
W6	18.8678	**20**	**14.83239697**

Table 2 shows the results for our extension of the A* algorithm using diagonals. In the table we see that this algorithm has a better performance with respect to the distance traveled and the number of points visited than the baseline A* algorithm. The gained performance in the distance (0.10× to 0.76× shorter routes) comes at the cost of having to plan the route for longer, as we now need to project the diagonals in the route, and therefore take longer in planning the route; a slowdown factor of 0.16× to 0.55×. The advantage of this algorithm is that in an unknown environment, a shorter planning route is an advantage because the rover may encounter fewer unknown obstacles.

Table 3. Convex Hull Results.

Waypoint	Time (ms)	Number of Coordinates	Total Distance (m)
W1	5.3812	11	13.6898965
W2	11.9906	30	21.98456783
W3	17.0895	27	18.5643461
W4	5.0672	25	25.2873613
W5	6.3678	30	23.95444345
W6	25.9430	27	34.1131986

The convex hull algorithm has the worst performance results across the three metrics, shown in Table 3. This can be explained as to calculate the route, we first calculate the convex hull, and then use A* (or A* with diagonals) to plan the route. Moreover, as we use either A* or A* with diagonals to plan the route, the distance covered would be at best that of the original algorithm, disproving our hypothesis that we generate less intermediate points traveling a shorter distance.

Figure 9 shows the route planned for the 6 way-points using each of the aforementioned global algorithms.

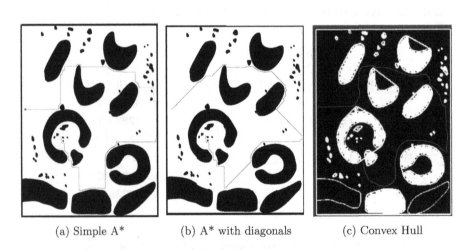

(a) Simple A*   (b) A* with diagonals   (c) Convex Hull

Fig. 9. Comparison of the planed routes

3.2   Dynamic Planning Results

For dynamic planning we concentrate on the evaluation of the ABEO algorithm by means of a simulation placing unknown obstacles in the path between way-points, as shown in Fig. 10. The initial simulation environment tests the algorithm in 10 × 10 and 20 × 20 grids, before testing them on the Gazebo. We focus on the ABEO algorithm, as this is the algorithm that presents the best opportunities to sort obstacles with a lower computational cost. In our evaluation we focus on the success of the robot to avoid obstacles placed in the route between waypoints. To do this, we run ABEO 60 times starting randomly from any of the yellow numbered points in the Fig. 10, to reach the green square in the middle. All blue squares are obstacles unknown to the robot. The result of this simulation is that all executions successfully reach the objective without crashing into any of the obstacles.

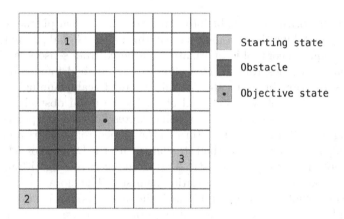

Fig. 10. Jupyter Notebook simulation environment

Once tested, we used ABEO on the Gazebo simulator (Fig. 11), where we observed that the robot can indeed reach the destination in most cases. Inaccuracies in reaching the goal are due to terrain conditions that cause the robot to tip over, or get stuck in a hill because the motor has insufficient power to climb, these factors are not related to the algorithm's performance but to the robot's specification and the environment conditions.

4   Related Work

There exist different route planning algorithms for autonomous navigation, as the ones already discussed in the previous sections. In this section we present further algorithms relevant to route planning in unknown environments, and put them in perspective of our work.

Fig. 11. Video of the ABEO simulation

Planning algorithms are split into two categories, global planning and local planning [1], matching the division we use in this paper. Global planning refers to plans that require geographic information, gathered from sensors, and a global localization of vehicles/robots. This allows us to set a defined route and see the robot's position in every step of said route. Local planning is based on relative positioning (of the robot and obstacles) to avoid obstacles effectively. In our work, this division is used to define routes between waypoints globally, and sorting obstacles locally (to return to the planed route afterwards). Global planning algorithms are off-the-shelf standards with the Dijkstra or A* algorithm as a base, optimized with an heuristic. This is similar to our algorithm, where we use A* with diagonals as an optimization heuristic. Therefore, the results using other variants, should be comparable with the ones we obtained.

Local planing algorithms have a larger variability, as we now discuss. A bio-inspired algorithm for local planning and emergence is that of ant colony behavior [5]. Route planning using ant colony algorithms is based on the probabilistic states of transition and a strategy based on the pheromones of the ants, which are used to follow a functional route planning algorithm. The behavior of ant colony algorithms is similar to the approach taken by us. However, the implementation of ABEO is simpler as we do not require to encode pheromones, which would require a sensor signaling in the robot.

A second category of algorithms consists of field-boundary definition algorithms, in which a boundary field is build around the robot/obstacle to avoid collisions. Dynamically, the robot is pushed away from high density boundary detection (*i.e.*, obstacles). Exemplars of these algorithms are the bubble rebound algorithm [8], and ODG-PF [1], discussed previously.

Finally, genetic algorithms are also used for obstacle avoidance. Here, a genetic search technique is used for a faster execution to find a way of avoiding an obstacle [3]. This algorithm presents a strategy called *survival of fitness* to determine the best solution over a set of competing potential solutions. The alternative of genetic algorithms adds the complexity of defining the fitness function and population to generate the potential solutions, but is an interesting possibility to study further.

5 Conclusion and Future Work

Route planning in unknown environments is a challenging task, as autonomous vehicles/robots may find a variety of obstacles blocking their path, and possibly get stuck. Unfortunately, these situations are common in rover space missions or disaster area exploration, where no defined satellite images are available to plan a route avoiding all obstacles. To tackle the complexity of moving through unknown environments, in this work, we use a combination of global and dynamic planning to route robots. We use global planning optimizing the route that the robot should follow, taking into account the trade off between the routing algorithm's execution time and total distance traveled. Our experiments show that while the A* algorithm with diagonals is between $0.16\times$ and $0.55\times$ slower than the A* baseline in calculating the route, the distance traveled by the robot is between $0.10\times$ to $0.76\times$ shorter (in most cases). Therefore, we conclude that it is better to use the A* with diagonals algorithm for the global planning, as this is the algorithm that optimizes time overall. Now, since we know obstacles may appear at run time, the robot uses the ABEO dynamic planning algorithm to sort obstacles in the way. Our evaluation shows that in a small simplified simulation environment, the robot is always able to avoid unknown obstacles and reach its destination. However, we note that in the simulated environment, the robot does not always reach its goal, due to terrain conditions and the physical capabilities of the robot, which are not included in the simulation.

As future work, we foresee the further evaluation of dynamic planning algorithms to be able to identify the optimal algorithm for the fastest route, with the highest success rate. Finally, we require a real-world experimental environment to work with our rover and make tests to fine tune the algorithms.

Acknowledgment. Laura Rodriguez acknowledges the support of a UniAndes-DeepMind Scholarship 2023

References

1. Cho, J.H., Pae, D.S., Lim, M.T., Kang, T.K.: A real-time obstacle avoidance method for autonomous vehicles using an obstacle-dependent gaussian potential field. J. Adv. Transp. 1–16 (1: school of Electrical Engineering. Korea University, Seoul, Republic of Korea (2018)
2. Garage, W.: Ros robot operating system. https://www.ros.org/ (12 2007). Stanford Artificial Intelligence Laboratory Open Robotics
3. Han, W.G., Baek, S.M., Kuc, T.Y.: Genetic algorithm based path planning and dynamic obstacle avoidance of mobile robots. In: International Conference on Systems, Man, and Cybernetics. Computational Cybernetics and Simulation, vol. 3, pp. 2747–2751 (1997). Intelligent Control and Dynamic Simulation Lab

4. Hart, P.E., Nilsson, N.J., Raphael, B.: A formal basis for the heuristic determination of minimum cost paths. IEEE Trans. Syst. Sci. Cybern. **4**(2), 100–107 (1968)
5. Meng, X., Zhu, X.: Autonomous obstacle avoidance path planning for grasping manipulator based on elite smoothing ant colony algorithm. Symmetry **14**(9), 1–20 (2022)
6. Sklansky, J.: Finding the convex hull of a simple polygon. Pattern Recogn. Lett. **1**(2), 79–83 (1982)
7. Susa Rincon, J.L., Ramos, D.: (ABEO) - Algoritmo Bioinspirado de Evasión de Obstáculos. Tecnura **13**(25), 36–47 (2009)
8. Susnea, I., Minzu, V., Vasiliu, G.: Simple, real-time obstacle avoidance algorithm for mobile robots. In: International Conference on Computational Intelligence, Man-machine Systems and Cybernetics. World Scientific, Engineering Academy e Society, pp. 24–29. WESEAS 2009 (2009)

Integration of Cyber-Physical System and Digital Twin for Controlling a Robotic Manipulator: An Industry 4.0 Approach

Oscar Loyola[1]([⊠]), Benjamín Suarez[2]([⊠]), César Sandoval[3]([⊠]), and Eduardo Carrillo[4]([⊠])

[1] Engineering Department, Universidad Autónoma de Chile, Av. Pedro de Valdivia 425, Santiago, Chile
oscar.loyola@uautonoma.cl
[2] Fundación Instituto Profesional Duoc UC, Santiago, Chile
ben.suarez@duocuc.cl
[3] Engineering, Architecture and Design Department, Universidad San Sebastián, Bellavista 7, Santiago, Chile
cesar.sandoval@uss.cl
[4] Technical and Technological Studies Department, Universidad Autonóma de Bucaramanga, Bucaramanga, Colombia
eduardo.carrillo@unab.edu.co

Abstract. This paper considers the integration and application of a Cyber-Physical System (CPS) and a digital twin to control a three-degree-of-freedom (3DoF) robotic manipulator. Here, framed in Industry 4.0, we consider robots as interconnected components within a broader network. Supported by current literature, we contribute to advancing interlinked systems that mirror the physical dynamics of equipment and facilitate their remote visualization–a cornerstone in the architecture of Internet of Things (IoT) robotics. Our strategy is rooted in three core stages: modeling, simulation, and implementation, and aims to seamlessly integrate the constituent elements of a robotic agent within an Internet of Robotic Things (IoRT) environment. At this nascent stage, the system has undergone testing at the prototype level, with ambitions to scale it for deployment in industrial settings. Preliminary results demonstrate the efficacy of the system in simulating and controlling the robotic manipulator, highlighting the potential of this integrated approach in practical applications. Our findings are pivotal to these concepts' evolution and roll-out, bolstering understanding of the nexus between CPS, digital twins, and robotics within Industry 4.0.

Keywords: Cyber-Physical Systems · Industry 4.0 · Robots · Robot Internet of Things

M. Tabares et al. (Eds.): CCC 2023, CCIS 1924, pp. 141–152, 2024.
https://doi.org/10.1007/978-3-031-47372-2_14

1 Introduction

In the age of digitalization and connectivity, Industry 4.0 has dramatically revolutionized manufacturing and production through the employment of cyber-physical systems (CPS), the Internet of Things (IoT), and digital twins. The confluence of these technologies has paved the way for the burgeoning field of the Internet of Robotic Things (IoRT). However, despite substantial advancements, there are still hurdles to seamlessly integrating these constituents into a holistic system. The present study aims to bridge this gap by delving into the application of a CPS and a digital twin for the governance of a three-degree-of-freedom (3DoF) robotic manipulator.

Our investigative approach adopts a comprehensive methodology, beginning with the mathematical modeling of the kinematics of the robotic manipulator, followed by simulation to anticipate system behaviour across various scenarios in conjunction with designing its digital twin. Ultimately, we instituted and assessed the system remotely in a regulated environment. This method enabled us to gauge the efficacy of the system whilst identifying and resolving potential issues.

The insights garnered from this research underline that integrating the CPS and digital twin in steering the robotic manipulator yields significant enhancements for tool users, whether they are local or remote. This conclusion reinforces the viability of our proposition and accentuates the potential of these technologies in the progression of Industry 4.0.

We surmise that the successful deployment of our proposal represents a notable advance in support for Industry 4.0. The findings furnish a robust foundation for subsequent investigations, facilitating the exploration of more intricate and scalable applications of these concepts, thus bringing an innovative perspective to robot control in an IoRT setting.

The paper is structured with Sect. 2 dedicated to a literature review, exploring the various global implications of IoRT. This section concludes with a brief bibliometric study which underscores the value of fostering these research themes in Latin America. Section 3 highlights the methodology employed, encompassing the kinematic analysis performed on the robot, its simulation, and ultimately the implementation of the system. Section 4 examines the results garnered from the research conducted, and Sect. 5 articulates the conclusions drawn.

2 Literature Review

The concept of the Internet of Robotic Things (IoRT) has been coined in recent years as an extension of Internet of Things (IoT) systems. Recent work [17] has established that this new concept seeks to extend the use of intelligent things in different fields. One major challenge of this emerging line of research is the development of algorithms which allow the execution of "intelligent" actions through the information the devices obtain from the network in which they operate. It is also essential to define that terminology, such as cyber-physical systems [11] and [9] It gains more preponderance by providing these agents with the particularity that their interaction would not only be at the physical level of inputs and outputs but also has a facet in the world, which would enhance the decision-making capacity that could be provided in networks of agents that exchange information among themselves.

According to [20], Internet of Things (IoT) networks enable technology elements for the Internet of Robotic Things (IoRT). These networks make it possible to leverage more complex control structures, which consider the interaction of various actors in the system. This implies that these heterogeneous and distributed networks' interaction can lead to significant performance improvement. In robotics, the unique characteristics and inherent capabilities of each component of these networks can help physically simplify on-board robots. [4], while simultaneously enriching their characteristics through the information provided by each agent. This includes sensory data, control commands, status updates, and real-time feedback. Implementing IoT networks in IoRT enables robots to operate in more intelligent and adaptive environments [8].

Considering the anteroom proposed in the literature and according to the definition by [14] and [1], the structure of an IoRT-type system can be stratified according to layers, as shown in Fig. 1. Under this consideration, a scheme will be proposed that allows the interaction of the system at the aforementioned levels along with its subsequent physical implementation for behavioral testing, providing the possibility of operation for non-remote users.

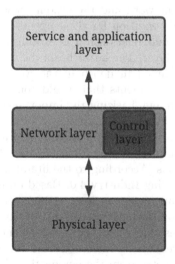

Fig. 1. Layers in a system that is described as IoRT, [14]

This collection of elements thus defines the existence of three interconnected layers in the application of IoRT. The first is the physical layer, which refers to the robotic agent and its unique characteristics. The second layer is a combined network and control layer in which both elements require each other in a continuous symbiosis, with the network acting as a hub for interaction and control actions due to the interaction of devices exchanging information. Here, devices are understood not only as robots but also as sensors that provide additional information to the system. Finally, the third layer is a services and applications layer, where robots' interactions with the environment can be observed.

These elements define the existence of three interconnected layers on the Internet of Robotics. This conceptual framework creates macro-networks for information exchange, a concept coined as the Web of Robotics Things (WRT) [13], which seeks the integration of architectures that allow real-world elements to become part of the World Wide Web.

In this study, multiple application areas are suggested, taking advantage of distributed networks that provide robots with a greater degree of autonomy and allow them to interact with their environment and with each other in more sophisticated ways. This can improve efficiency and open up new possibilities in diverse applications, from manufacturing and logistics to healthcare and agriculture. For example, [12] applied this concept to solutions in agriculture, while the work of [18] applies it to autonomous vehicles for the deployment of wireless sensor networks. Additionally, in the medical field, [5] eds a system for dispensing drugs through a web-based system. In all cases, the robots can adapt and respond to unexpected environmental changes, providing unprecedented resilience and flexibility in automation operations.

Considering the above, there is an inherent integration between the agents that form an IoRT-type network and the system in which they operate. This integration is an essential condition for these agents' existence since, as shown in the layer model, a formal relationship is established between the network layer and the application layer. The latter hosts the services that these systems can provide. This is examined in depth in the work of [19], where a model of interaction between the elements that would comprise a system with these characteristics is proposed, emphasizing the importance of this interrelation for the effective functioning of the IoRT system.

Up to this point, the IoRT strategies are vast and multiple applications can be observed; however, one underexplored facet is their linking with elements of recreation of robotic actions. According to the literature, the concept of Digital is an essential point regarding Industry 4.0. Based on the points from [15] and [16] these and other technologies, such as artificial intelligence in robots [2], are elements which are transformed into means for the growth of Industry 4.0. Finally, other technologies that allow the development of digital elements are virtual and augmented reality. [7] indicated that this demonstrated advances for the manufacturing industry from the perspective of multi-level environment visualization, highlighting the linkage between the virtual and cyber worlds.

In the literature analysis, [3] provides some applications that cross the use of digital with robots [21]. It is desired to improve efficiency and energy awareness in smart manufacturing through crucial solutions such as real-time monitoring or simulation techniques. For this reason, it is interesting to conduct a study on the bibliographic references that involve the topics addressed in this work. We can note this in Fig. 2, which presents the relationships between the fields of IoT and systems; however, the robot concept is isolated. This indicates that according to the WoS database with the search criteria "TC = Internet of Robotics things* AND Digital Twins*) AND WC = (Industry 4.0)" of the keywords used, the IoRT concept is a space that allows research on the mutual interaction of its constituent elements.

Fig. 2. Graph of studied topics according to WoS database.

Most importantly, these studies benefit from a dense global collaboration network, as illustrated in Fig. 3. This graph highlights the limited interaction between Latin America and the significant powers working in these critical areas to develop innovative solutions. There is an opportunity of significant interest here to promote and strengthen the interconnection of Latin American research with these global innovation centers. This interconnection could foster the development of solutions adapted to the specific needs and characteristics of the region, while contributing to the diversity and richness of the global body of knowledge in these essential areas.

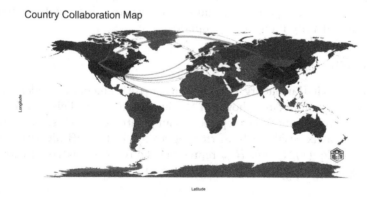

Fig. 3. World map of collaboration according to WoS database.

In response to the challenges presented, and in line with our research objectives, we present a significant and novel contribution to the Internet of Robotic Things (IoRT) field. Our proposal focuses on integrating three degrees of freedom (3DoF) robots that can be remotely operated and visualized through a digital twin which replicates its movements, thus coordinating with its physical performance.

While there is abundant literature defining concepts and theorizing about IoRT-type systems, there is little research that presents practical solutions to the challenges and effectively integrates the different layers of the analysis framework. This is what makes our work stand out, since we are not only developing theories and models but also carrying out a concrete and actual application that will demonstrate their value in real situations. This practical and application-focused approach can catalyze future developments in this field, thus contributing to the progress of Industry 4.0.

3   Methods

In the development of this research, a strategy based on three fundamental stages (modeling, simulation, and implementation) is adopted to integrate the constituent elements of a robotic agent in an IoRT environment.

It starts with modeling, where a mathematical and physical model of the robotic agent is built, covering all fundamental characteristics and behaviors. An equivalent digital twin is also generated to represent the robotic agent in virtual space. The second stage, simulation, uses the model to predict system behavior in various situations. This process is essential to identify and resolve potential problems before real-world implementation.

Finally, in the implementation stage, the system is applied to the robotic manipulator in a controlled environment. During this phase, the behavior of the system is monitored, and data is collected for further analysis.

The experiment was designed to evaluate the effectiveness of integrating the cyber-physical system and the digital twin in managing the robotic manipulator. Through the tests performed, data were collected to evaluate system performance and identify improvement opportunities.

3.1   Modeling and Simulation

Using the Denavit-Hartenberg (DH) algorithm [10] a kinematic model was built for the robotic manipulator shown in the image provided. This algorithm is a standard method in robotics to represent manipulator kinematics. The canonical form of the matrix resulting from the application of the DH algorithm is presented in the Eq. (1), where: $R_{z,\theta}$ represents the rotation matrix, q coordinate vector of the form $[x_i \ y_i \ z_i]^T$ and n the link to be analyzed.

$$T_0^n = \begin{bmatrix} R_{z,\theta} & q \\ 0^T & 1 \end{bmatrix} \tag{1}$$

Based on the above, the manipulator under study is described through the following set of matrices evaluated for each link. The kinematics obtained can be seen in Eqs. (2), (3) and (4), where $c\theta_i$ represents the function $\cos\theta_i$ and $s\theta_i$ shall be the function $\sin\theta_i$. The indicated models allow us to determine the positions of the links, and use simulations to determine the working volume of the robot, as shown in the following figure Fig. 4.

$$T_1 = \begin{pmatrix} c\theta_1 & 0 & s\theta_2 & 0 \\ s\theta_1 & 0 & -c\theta_2 & 0 \\ 0 & 1 & 0 & l_1 \\ 0 & 0 & 0 & 1 \end{pmatrix} \tag{2}$$

$$T_2 = \begin{pmatrix} c\theta_1 c\theta_2 & -c\theta_1 s\theta_2 & s\theta_1 & l_2 c\theta_1 c\theta_2 \\ c\theta_2 s\theta_1 & -s\theta_1 s\theta_2 & -c\theta_2 & l_2 c\theta_2 s\theta_1 \\ s\theta_2 & c\theta_1 & 0 & l_1 + l_2 s\theta_1 \\ 0 & 0 & 0 & 1 \end{pmatrix} \tag{3}$$

$$T_3 = \begin{pmatrix} c(\theta_2 + \theta_3)c\theta_1 & -s(\theta_2 + \theta_3)c\theta_1 & s\theta_1 & c\theta_1(l_3 c(\theta_2 + \theta_3) + l_2 c\theta_2) \\ c(\theta_2 + \theta_3)s\theta_1 & -s(\theta_2 + \theta_3)s\theta_1 & -c\theta_1 & s\theta_1(l_3 c(\theta_2 + \theta_3) + l_2 c\theta_2) \\ s(\theta_2 + \theta_3) & c(\theta_2 + \theta_3) & 0 & l_1 + l_2 s(\theta_2 + \theta_3) + l_2 s\theta_2 \\ 0 & 0 & 0 & 1 \end{pmatrix} \tag{4}$$

The importance of this graph lies in the determination and understanding of the singularities of the system, thus avoiding the generation of mechanical stresses when the system reaches maximum angular points. For this case, we use the Jacobian matrix, described by $\begin{bmatrix} \dot{x} \\ \dot{y} \\ \dot{z} \\ \omega_x \\ \omega_y \\ \omega_z \end{bmatrix} = J_{6xn} \begin{bmatrix} \dot{q}_1 \\ \dot{q}_2 \\ \vdots \\ \dot{q}_n \end{bmatrix}$, where $\dot{q}_n$ represents the linear and angular velocities of each link. On the other hand, n is the number of links which each equipment unit has. In order to clarify the model explanation, a rotational type link can be described as shown in Eq. (5).

$$J = \begin{bmatrix} J_v \\ J_\omega \end{bmatrix} = \begin{bmatrix} R^0_{i-1} \begin{bmatrix} 0 \\ 0 \\ 1 \end{bmatrix} \times (q^0_n - q^0_{i-1}) \\ R^0_{i-1} \begin{bmatrix} 0 \\ 0 \\ 1 \end{bmatrix} \end{bmatrix} \tag{5}$$

From the above, we can conclude that the angular values taken by θ_2 y θ_3 are critical to the system according to the determinant of $det(J_{6x3})$. This behavior can be better appreciated when the aforementioned angles take the

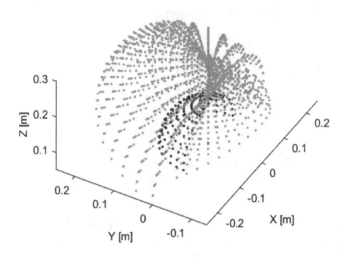

Fig. 4. Behavior of the robotic manipulator in different displacement positions.

same value for the evaluated case 180°. This situation appears in Fig. 5, and this behavior is essential during system implementation to avoid equipment damage. Generalization of the associated elements in the particular case under analysis appears in Eq. (6).

$$J = \begin{bmatrix} J_v \\ J_\omega \end{bmatrix} = \begin{bmatrix} R_0^0 \begin{bmatrix} 0 \\ 0 \\ 1 \end{bmatrix} \times (q_3^0 - q_0^0) & R_1^0 \begin{bmatrix} 0 \\ 0 \\ 1 \end{bmatrix} \times (q_3^0 - q_1^0) & R_2^0 \begin{bmatrix} 0 \\ 0 \\ 1 \end{bmatrix} \times (q_3^0 - q_2^0) \\ R_0^0 \begin{bmatrix} 0 \\ 0 \\ 1 \end{bmatrix} & R_1^0 \begin{bmatrix} 0 \\ 0 \\ 1 \end{bmatrix} & R_2^0 \begin{bmatrix} 0 \\ 0 \\ 1 \end{bmatrix} \end{bmatrix} \tag{6}$$

3.2   Implementation

The digital twin is created using Unreal Engine [6] because it establishes communication with hardware through a serial communication plugin. For its precise design, the range of movement is established based on the analysis obtained from the simulation to emulate the behavior of the physical object. The environmental visualization appears in Fig. 6.

The system integration follows a layered architecture proposed by [1] and [19]. The application of the different elements comprising the model strata has

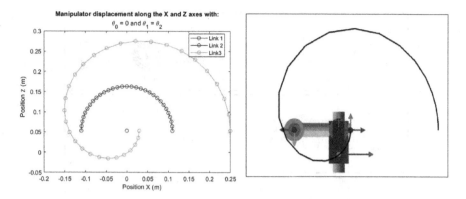

Fig. 5. Singularities when the angular values of links 2 and 3 are equal.

Fig. 6. 3 DoF digital robot model.

been developed, as shown in Fig. 7. This application of the model includes two supervision elements based on a virtual twin. One operates parallel to the robot at one location, while the other can be observed and controlled remotely. This action allows remote communication and control, and observation of the device. Data is stored in a database via direct communication between the cyber-physical device (NodeMCU) and the database.

4 Results and Discussion

Our main findings, their novelty and our contribution to existing knowledge is summarized below:

– Design of the digital twin in Unreal Engine: Unreal Engine was used as the design environment for the digital twin due to its characteristics and features to establish communication with hardware through a serial communication plugin. This choice provided a robust and versatile platform for developing the digital twin.

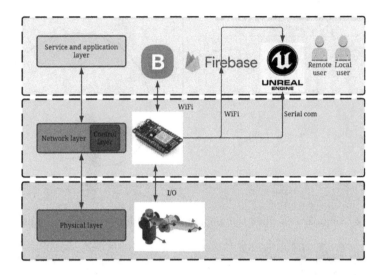

Fig. 7. Proposal for applying an IoRT system according to what is established in the literature.

- The motion ranges and behavior of the digital twin: The motion ranges of the digital twin were established based on the analysis and simulations performed. It was possible to emulate the behavior of the physical element accurately, which allowed us to have a digital twin that accurately represented the natural behavior.
- Layer architecture and supervision elements: System integration followed a layered architecture proposed in the literature. Considering the models proposed by the literature, the necessary elements for implementing the system were added. Two supervision elements based on the virtual twin structure were developed.

The application possibilities of the system in more demanding environments will depend on scalability. However, integrating multiple tools is an advance that could be enhanced in industrial scenarios.

5 Conclusion

We demonstrated the potential of integrating cyber-physical systems and digital twins to control robotic manipulators. The developed digital twins and the implemented layered architecture provide a solid basis for managing and optimizing automated systems in the context of Industry 4.0. The results contribute to advancing and understanding the interconnection between cyber-physical systems, digital twins, and robotics, laying a foundation for future developments and applications in the field. As a future work, we propose the integration of industrial robots and creation of control algorithms that perform better in the physical element and with its digital twin.

References

1. Afanasyev, I., et al.: Towards the internet of robotic things: analysis, architecture, components and challenges. In: 2019 12th International Conference on Developments in eSystems Engineering (DeSE), pp. 3–8. IEEE (2019). https://doi.org/10.1109/DeSE.2019.00011
2. Andò, B., et al.: An introduction to patterns for the internet of robotic things in the ambient assisted living scenario. Robotics 10(2), 56 (2021)
3. Aria, M., Cuccurullo, C.: bibliometrix: an R-tool for comprehensive science mapping analysis. J. Inform. 11(4), 959–975 (2017)
4. Bacciu, D., Rocco, M.D., Dragone, M., Gallicchio, C., Micheli, A., Saffiotti, A.: An ambient intelligence approach for learning in smart robotic environments. Comput. Intell. 35(4), 1060–1087 (2019). https://doi.org/10.1111/coin.12233
5. Cao, H., Huang, X., Zhuang, J., Xu, J., Shao, Z.: CIoT-robot cloud and IoT assisted indoor robot for medicine delivery. In: Proceedings of the 2018 Joint International Advanced Engineering and Technology Research Conference (JIAET 2018). Atlantis Press (2018). https://doi.org/10.2991/jiaet-18.2018.14
6. Games, E.: Unreal Engine (2019). https://www.unrealengine.com. Version 5
7. Geng, R., Li, M., Hu, Z., Han, Z., Zheng, R.: Digital twin in smart manufacturing: remote control and virtual machining using VR and AR technologies. Struct. Multidiscip. Optim. 65(11), 321 (2022). https://doi.org/10.1007/s00158-022-03426-3
8. Gómez, A.V., de la Puente, P., Losada, D.R., Hernando, M., Segundo, P.S.: Arquitectura de integración basada en servicios web para sistemas heterogéneos y distribuidos: aplicación a robots móviles interactivos. Rev. Iberoamericana de Automática e Informática Ind. 10(1), 85–95 (2013)
9. Harrison, R., Vera, D., Ahmad, B.: Engineering methods and tools for cyber-physical automation systems. Proc. IEEE 104(5), 973–985 (2016). https://doi.org/10.1109/JPROC.2015.2510665
10. Hartenberg, R., Danavit, J.: Kinematic Synthesis of Linkages. McGraw-Hill, New York (1964)
11. Jazdi, N.: Cyber physical systems in the context of Industry 4.0. In: 2014 IEEE International Conference on Automation, Quality and Testing, Robotics, pp. 1–4. IEEE (2014). https://doi.org/10.1109/AQTR.2014.6857843
12. Ju, C., Son, H.I.: Modeling and control of heterogeneous agricultural field robots based on Ramadge-Wonham theory. IEEE Robot. Automa. Lett. 5(1), 48–55 (2020). https://doi.org/10.1109/LRA.2019.2941178
13. Kamilaris, A., Botteghi, N.: The penetration of internet of things in robotics: towards a web of robotic things (2020)
14. Khalid, S.: Internet of robotic things: a review. J. Appl. Sci. Technol. Trends 2(03), 78–90 (2021). https://doi.org/10.38094/jastt203104
15. Malik, A., Rajaguru, P., Azzawi, R.: Smart manufacturing with artificial intelligence and digital twin: a brief review. In: 2022 8th International Conference on Information Technology Trends (ITT), pp. 177–182. IEEE (2022). https://doi.org/10.1109/ITT56123.2022.9863938
16. Radanliev, P., De Roure, D., Nicolescu, R., Huth, M., Santos, O.: Digital twins: artificial intelligence and the IoT cyber-physical systems in Industry 4.0. Int. J. Intell. Robot. Appl. 6(1), 171–185 (2022). https://doi.org/10.1007/s41315-021-00180-5
17. Ray, P.P.: Internet of robotic things: concept, technologies, and challenges. IEEE Access 4, 9489–9500 (2016). https://doi.org/10.1109/access.2017.2647747

18. Romeo, L., et al.: Automated deployment of IoT networks in outdoor scenarios using an unmanned ground vehicle. In: 2020 IEEE International Conference on Industrial Technology (ICIT), pp. 369–374. IEEE (2 2020). https://doi.org/10.1109/ICIT45562.2020.9067099

19. Romeo, L., Petitti, A., Marani, R., Milella, A.: Internet of robotic things in smart domains: applications and challenges. Sensors **20**(12), 3355 (2020)

20. Simoens, P., Dragone, M., Saffiotti, A.: The internet of robotic things. Int. J. Adv. Robot. Syst. **15**(1), 172988141875942 (2018). https://doi.org/10.1177/1729881418759424

21. Stan, L., Nicolescu, A.F., Pup, C., Jiga, G.: Digital twin and web services for robotic deburring in intelligent manufacturing. J. Intell. Manuf. 1–17 (2022)

Declarative Visual Programming with Invariant, Pre- and Post-conditions for Lattice Approximation of 3D Models

Oscar Ruiz-Salguero[1]([✉])[ID], Carolina Builes-Roldan[1], Juan Lalinde-Pulido[2][ID], and Carlos Echeverri-Cartagena[3]

[1] CAD CAM CAE Laboratory, U. EAFIT, Medellín, Colombia
{oruiz,cbuilesr}@eafit.edu.co
[2] High Performance Computing Facility APOLO, U. EAFIT, Medellín, Colombia
jlalinde@eafit.edu.co
[3] Machine Tool Laboratory, U. EAFIT, Medellín, Colombia
cechever@eafit.edu.co
http://www1.eafit.edu.co/cadcamcae

Abstract. In the context of Visual Programing for Product Design, the endowment of the Designer with programing tools to boost productivity is central. However, Product (and Architectural) Design are usually taught without programing courses. This manuscript reports the results of Lattice DesignVisual Programming by a Product Designer with no previous exposure to programing but provided with the intuitive concepts of Pre-, Post-condition and Invariant logical first-order predicates for imperative programing. The scenario of application is the population of 3D domains (i.e. solid models) with lattice individuals of the type zero-curvature Truss (colloquially called 1.5D and 2.5D) structural elements. Result show that, although Pre-, Post-condition and Invariant are devised for imperative programing, they provide a solid and successful structure for visual programming (e.g. Grasshopper) for Designers with no mathematical or programming background. Regarding the specific Additive Manufacturing scope, the manuscript depicts the population of the target domain with lattice individuals which, in this case, undergo a rigid transformation before docked in the target domain. The lattice design presented allows for the grading of the lattice geometry. Future work addresses the programing of non-rigid transformations (non-affine, non-conformal, etc.) which dock the lattice individual into the target solid domain. Regarding the endowment of non-programmer Product Designer with visual programing and pre-, post- and invariant conditions, the performance results are very positive. However, as with any work team, experts must be recruited to help with highly specialized topics (e.g. computational mechanics, differential geometry, discrete mathematics, etc.).

Keywords: visual programming · predicate-based programming · lattice families · truss · frame

Supported by U. EAFIT and Carolina Builes-Roldan.

M. Tabares et al. (Eds.): CCC 2023, CCIS 1924, pp. 153–172, 2024.
https://doi.org/10.1007/978-3-031-47372-2_15

Glossary

2-manifold	a surface point set locally isomorphic to a flat disk (i.e. without self-intersections)
1-manifold	a curve point set locally isomorphic to a straight wire (i.e. without self-intersections)
BODY Ω	a solid, or subset of $\mathbb{R}^3$, which is compact (bounded and containing its boundary)
$\partial\Omega$	Boundary Representation (B-Rep or skin $\partial\Omega$) of solid Ω
M	the (2-manifold) triangular B-Rep of a solid Ω. Also called a closed triangular mesh
$S(u, w)$	a 2-manifold parametric surface in $\mathbb{R}^3$. That is, $S : [0, 1] \times [0, 1] \to \mathbb{R}^3$
$C(u)$	a 1-manifold parametric curve in $\mathbb{R}^3$. That is, $C : [0, 1] \to \mathbb{R}^3$
FACE F	a connected subset of a parametric Surface (FACE $F \subset S$)
EDGE E	a connected subset of a parametric Curve (EDGE $E \subset C$)
VERTEX v	an element of the border of an EDGE, or an endpoint of an EDGE E: $\partial E = \{v_0, v_f\}$
[FACE + thickness]	Finite Element Analysis approximation (for the sake of computing savings) of a 3D thin solid plate as a 2D FACE added with thickness information, colloquially called 2.5D element
[EDGE + area]	Finite Element Analysis approximation (for the sake of computing savings) of a 3D slender solid rod as a 1D EDGE added with area information, colloquially called 1.5D element
VoXel	Volumetric piXel or 3D rectangular prism whose dimensions correspond to the resolution of a 3D Scanner (e.g. computer tomograph, magnetic resonator, ultrasound probe, etc.)
Lattice	in Additive Manufacturing, the smallest topological structure that is repeated (possibly with geometrical gradients) to fill a solid domain Ω. Scale-wise, size(VoXel) $\ll$ size(Lattice)
I, O, NIO	qualifiers of a lattice with respect to a solid domain Ω (inside, outside, neither inside nor outside)
pre-condition	1-st order logic predicate describing the status of program execution *before* an instruction sequence is executed
post-condition	1-st order logic predicate describing the status of program execution *after* an instruction sequence is executed
invariant	1-st order logic predicate describing the status of program execution *before any and each iteration* in a (**for** or **while**) loop is executed
CBP	Contract-based Programming, in which formal logic predicates are used to specify the input, output, and intermediate checkpoints of a software piece, with machine-driven checks assessing the compliance of the code with the specified ontracts
EUP	End User Programming
VPL	Visual Programming Language

1   Introduction

Research Target. This manuscript presents a development executed on Visual programming tools (i.e. Grasshopper^{TM}) which (a) defines lattice individuals based on the limbs of types 1.5D [EDGE + area] and 2.5D [FACE + thickness] due to their lower computing consumption, (b) executes the approximation of a BODY (i.e. 3D region) by an enumeration of the given lattice individuals, tuned by using the usual thresholds in Exhaustive Enumerations. This development is executed by a Designer who does not have previous training in programming but is equipped with intuitive knowledge of the Pre-condition, Invariant and post-condition formalisms for programming [7].

Although it is not within our target, it is worth to remark the potential of Declarative, Dataflow or Flow-based Programming environments (e.g. Grasshopper^{TM}) in parallelization, fault-tollerance and scalability. Ref. [15] is a soft introduction to these topics.

Programming for Non-programmers. Visual Programming is built as a tool for practitioners and experts in topics other than from the programming aspect. This tool which would allow them to build/assemble applications based on icons of pre-defined pre-compiled functions. Visual programming and in particular Grasshopper^{TM} is a good starting tool for non-programmers to create scenario-driven, generative designs. However, it presents limitations in more complex scenarios. One of these scenarios is *parametric* design, which Grasshopper underlying kernel (Rhinoceros^{TM}) does not support.

Computer-Aided Design and Manufacturing. Lattice-based objects present advantages in lower material spending and weight and their realization by Additive Manufacturing (AM) offers internal cavities which traditional Removal Manufacturing does not offer. On the other hand, usual 3D solid modeling Boundary Representation (B-Rep) of lattices represents explosive amounts of data, and the same is valid for 3D Finite Element Analyses (FEA). However, if a lattice design has slender limbs (e.g. plates or rods), the more economical representation by Trusses or Frames is possible. In this case, Kinematic or Position constraints are enforced among the pieces. As a result, the number of topological, geometrical and finite elements is lowered.

Geometry Scope. The present work addresses lattice limbs whose medial axes or skeletons have zero curvature. The plates have constant thickness. The rods, however, may have changing cross section. This manuscript is concerned neither with supporting structures *during* the additive manufacture nor with the computational mechanics of the lattices.

Section 1 reviews the state of art of Topologic and Geometric Modeling for lattices. Due to the special subject of this manuscript (Visual programming for Lattice Modeling and Object approximation), Sect. 3 discusses the Methodology used and simultaneously presents the results of the modeling. Section 4 concludes the manuscript and indicates aspects for future work.

2   Literature Review

2.1   Lattice Families and Properties

Refs. [2] and [14] evaluate strategies (solid, intersected, graded, scaled, uniform) to map Solid Isotropic Material Penalisation (SIMP) material densities for a cantilever load case into lattice structures. 3D Solid Finite Element simulations are carried out with a wall (i.e. Schwarz) lattice model and not with truss or frame structures. AM *degradee* patterns are employed according to the support structures, surface areas, processing times, and other criteria. The softwares used are Magics (Materialise Magics. Materialise N.V., Leuven, Belgium, 2014.), Autofab (Autofab Software, Marcam Engineering, 2011), MSC Nastran, Grasshopper - Rhino for complex designs of lattices (no library names specified). No test is given to measure the discrepancy, resiliency, processing effort, and in-process support requirements.

Ref. [2] generates a MATLAB VoXel Representation of a lattice set that approximates the interior of a 3D body. The lattices have their own internal design. It presents the union of the body interior lattice structure with a thick version of the 3D body skin (i.e. B-Rep), discussing the grading of the lattice individuals. This manuscript produces a double discretization of the 3D Body lattice representation by VoXels: (i) a VoxXel set builds a lattice and (ii) a lattice set builds a 3D Body. No Finite Element computation is presented in this manuscript.

Ref. [8] proposes a Programed Periodic Lattice Editor (PLE), based on a set of parameters and lattice topologies, to fill a given 3D solid region $\Omega \subset \mathbb{R}^3$. This user-driven SW addresses honeycomb, octahedral, octet, and other lattice individual types. A given lattice is modeled as a set of spherical nodes and rods (i.e. truss representation). It considers limited, "steady" gradients in the 3 axis. To reduce data size, it establishes that the output of PLE is a Constructive Solid Geometry (CSG) instruction sequence to build the full lattice domain $\tilde{\Omega}$ and not the B-Rep of it. However, this decision only postpones the expense of Structural Analysis, which requires large number of finite elements. The PLE supports an $\mathbb{R}^3$ warping library, supporting cylindrical-, curve- and surface-driven gradings for the lattice geometries. Readers interested in the industrial application of Grasshooper for 3D printing may want to seek Ref. [6].

IntraLattice [10] is a software running on Grasshopper, whose functionality is the generation of graded lattice sets filling up a solid region $\Omega \subset \mathbb{R}^3$, with and without the boundary or skin of Ω, $\partial\Omega$. *IntraLattice* is able to (a) apply non-affine deformations upon the domain Ω, along its constitutive lattices to achieve smooth shapes, (b) generate a triangular B-rep of the lattice-made Ω domain and (c) post-process the B-Rep for actual Additive Manufacturing.

As application of the [FACE+thickness] and [EDGE+area] abstractions in the Computational Mechanics of Lattices area, Ref. [18] presents a process sequence for additive manufacturing of deformed lattices with links of circular cross sections, and gradient-driven geometry along the structure. Ref. [18] informs the articulation of a non-linear Cosserat stress-deformation iso-geometric solver [19] onto *IntraLattice* [10] to estimate the mechanical behavior of the $\tilde{\Omega}$ lattice set. Refs. [11] and [19] model the lattice set as a frame or truss structure, with torque being transmitted at the limb junctions. Ref. [11] executes a linear finite element analysis, while Ref. [19] performs a non-linear one.

2.2   Text vs. Visual Programming. Grasshopper

This section gives the reader a context to appraise the contributions of this manuscript from the point of view of computer programming education.

Ref. [9] compares 3 systems for Visual Computing applied to CAD (e.g. Grasshopper, used also in our implementation). The paradigms present in Visual Computing are *node-based* and *list-based*. This Ref. concludes that *Node-based* Visual programming (e.g. Houdini) presents theses advantages: (a)- combines iteration and encapsulation, (b)- supports both forward- and reverse- order modeling methods, (c)- has implicit iterative process, and, (d)- allows to define more complex processes. On the other hand, *List-based* Visual Programming (e.g. Grasshopper - Rhino, Generative Components CG -Microstation) presents higher difficulty, specially originated in : (1)- non-available or limited encapsulation, (2)- non-available iteration.

Ref. [3] compares the capacity of architects to program Computer Aided Architecture Design tools with script vs. visual programming. Both *Scripting* (e.g. Visual Basic AutoCAD -VBA) and *Visual* (e.g. Grasshopper - Rhino) tools use dialects internal to the host CAD software which are interpreted (as opposed to *compiled*). Beginner designers performed better with Visual Programming. These designers were able to streamline many repetitive and cumbersome tasks of the CAD user tasks. Both groups encountered problems (larger with Visual Programming) when devising complex programs in which fundamental concepts of algorithmic were needed.

Ref. [12] discusses common characteristics of *flow-based programming* FBP languages: (a) Input/Output black-box components in graph-like topology, (b) a manager of the information flow in the graph, (c) Graphic User Interface, (d) documentation and tutorials, (e) hands-on education. In FBP, the program flow is dictated by the characteristics of the instantaneous data, and is it not hard-wired (i.e. written) as a programming code. The clarification is relevant because this is the type of programming that was used for the present experiment.

Ref. [1] discusses End-user Programming (EUP) in which non-programmer users create applications for their particular work domains. Visual Programming Languages (VPLs) are one variety of EUPs. VPLs sub-divide into form-, flow- and rule-based programming. This particular reference addresses Robot Programming, by using a Flow-based Programming in which: (a) box icons represent functions or actions, and connectors represent data. (b) no flow control tokens (`while, for, repeat`) are available. (c) boxes are SIMO (Single Input Multi Output) functions, (d) semantics are located in the boxes and not in the connectors.

2.3 Pre-condition, Post-condition, Invariant. Contract-Based Programming

Ref. [13] discusses (a) operational, (b) denotational, and (c) axiomatic semantics. This reference addresses the semantics of an existing piece of code (*code* → *semantics*), in contrast with the intuitive or automated generation of a code to satisfy a semantical specification. In our work we informally use *axiomatic semantics*. Axiomatic semantics maps the variable states into logical predicates and the instructions into premises. Premises transform the states as proven by predicate logics. We work in the direction *semantics* → *code*. We do not apply formal logic predicate calculus, due to the assumption that the practitioner is neither a programmer nor a mathematician.

Ref. [7] dissects Pre-condition, Post-condition and Invariant of a Loop:

```
1 Pre: <initial program variables status>
2 WHILE <C: boolean condition for loop execution>
3 Inv: <invariant status of variables during Loop>
4 . . . keep the Invariant True while progress towards termination
5 . . .
6 ENDWHILE
7 Post:  <final program variables status>
```

They are predicates before, after or during a loop execution (Pre-, Post- and Invariant respectively). These are 1st-order logic predicates (**not instructions**). They are True when the program execution hits the corresponding lines (1,3,7). The Pre-condition (line 1) and Post-condition (line 7) describe the values of the *relevant* variables before and after the loop, respectively. The Invariant (line 3) pictures a typical un-finished state of variables when the loop is executing. One value of the invariant is that $\text{Inv} \wedge (\neg C) = \text{Post}$. Therefore, the instructions in the loop (lines 4,5) must work towards $(\neg C)$ while keeping Inv being true. This last consideration dictates the instruction of the loop (lines 4,5).

Pre-, Post-conditions and Invariant are to be sketched, written or added by either the programmer or a program-by-contract editor. An informal process allows for the sketching of them and the programmer endeavoring to implement the sketch. An automated process includes typing the logic predicates and using an automated code-producer that adheres to them

Ref. [17] discusses the capabilities of ADA-2012 for Contract-baset Programming (CBP). In CPB, software piece specification is conducted by evaluating logic predicates about the computer status before and after the execution of the piece. CBP is supported by Pre- and Post-conditions to ensure Input/Output compliance with specifications. Code Contracts are independent of language and compiler. However, by applying ADA-2021, it is possible to also assess the compliance of object types and static/dynamic predicates.

Ref. [4] reports *Clousot*, a tool for Code Contract Checking. *Clousot* does: (1) check Pre- and Post-condition, (2) check common runtime errors, (3) infer Invariants., (4) allow for tuning of checking cost vs. precision, (5) allow domain refinement (pre-condition), (6) back-propagate conditions to determine software pieces, (7) infer precondition and postcondition inference from a given software piece, among other correctness tests and/or syntheses.

Ref. [16] addresses the absence of programming loops in Grasshopper and possible (cumbersome) repairs for this deficiency. For the present purposes, the important point is that, in absence of loop instructions, the application of Pre-condition, Post-condition and Invariant is apparently impossible. Yet, our project shows that the non-programmer Product Designer was able to enforce those logical predicates in Grasshopper and to obtain the correct voxel enumeration for the 3D region (i.e. solid).

2.4 Conclusions of the Literature Review

The examined literature shows the existence of commercial or quasi-commercial visual-computing generative software for lattice-based object (a) design and (b) mechanical simulation.

Regarding (a) above, the goal of this manuscript is to report the perfor-mance of a non-programmer product designer in programming generative geom-etry visual programming applications. This non-programmer designer is only equipped with intuitive notions of pre-conditions, post-conditions and invari-ants. It is well known that these notions are the mathematical kernel [7] of *imperative programming* and automated *imperative* code generation. Yet, the test reported in this manuscript pertains to the domain of visual programming (i.e. Grasshopper) and the capacity of this non-programmer product designer to compose a Grasshopper program for the approximation of a 3D object by lattice individuals of diverse topology and geometry.

Regarding (b) above, the current state-of-art is the following: computa-tional mechanics computations based on B-Reps of lattice structures is simply intractable, due to the massive size of the geometric or finite element models. As alternative, it is true that the truss/frame (also called [FACE+thickness] or [EDGE + area]) simplification of lattice structures indeed lowers the compu-tational burden of stress - strain predictions for the lattice-based objects. This geometrical simplification allows the computations to finish (which is a consid-erable milestone). However, the mechanical soundness of this computation is at this time open for much clarification and improvement. These computational mechanics predictions are not, in any case, the goal of this manuscript.

To the best of our knowledge, no previous manuscripts report this special set of circumstances: (a) no programming experience, (b) use of imperative pro-gramming Pre-, Post-conditions and Invariant mathematical formulation, and (c) visual programming. We show that mathematical foundations of *imperative* programming are quite effective in helping a non-programmer designer to write a plug-in even if using visual programming Grasshopper.

The particular domain of application for the above features is the population of a given domain (or region) $\Omega \subset \mathbb{R}^3$ with lattice individuals of diverse topolo-gies and graded geometries. For the sake of computational resource savings in subsequent computational mechanics simulations, the [EDGE + area] (1.5D) and [FACE + thickness] (2.5D) truss formalism will be used.

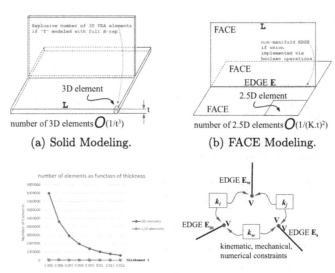

(a) Solid Modeling.

(b) FACE Modeling.

(c) Number of 3D vs 2.5D (d) Kinematic Constraints on
(FACE + thickness) elements VERTEXs.
in slender T shape.

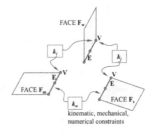

(e) Kinematic Constraints on
EDGEs.

Fig. 1. Slender Shape Modeling. Order $O(n)$ of number of Finite Elements for the cases: Solid (3D) vs. FACE (2.5D) modeling. Savings by using 2.5D elements when $t \to 0$. Kinematic (or other) constraints as alternatives to Full B-Reps, while avoiding non-manifold topology.

3   Methodology

3.1   Modeling of Slender Members

Construction of [EDGE + area] and [FACE + thickness] Limbs in Lattices. Slender members have a thin dimension (thickness, radius, or other) which is much smaller than the other member dimensions L. Full 3D B-Rep models decompose in a Topology Hierarchy such as BODYs, LUPMs, SHELLs, FACEs, LOOPs, EDGEs, VERTEXes, embedded in Geometries (e.g. Curves $C(u)$, Surfaces $S(u,w)$) in $\mathbb{R}^3$. The fact that $t/L \ll 1$ (Fig. 1(a)) causes the

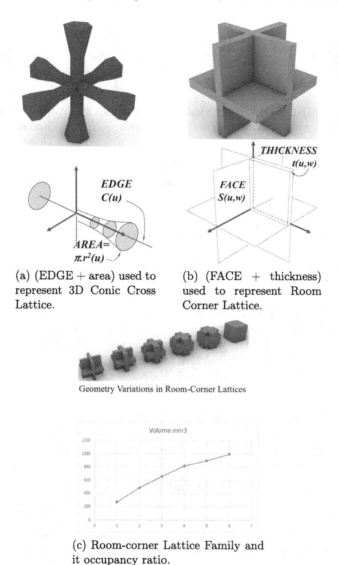

(a) (EDGE + area) used to represent 3D Conic Cross Lattice.

(b) (FACE + thickness) used to represent Room Corner Lattice.

Geometry Variations in Room-Corner Lattices

(c) Room-corner Lattice Family and it occupancy ratio.

Fig. 2. Representation of 3D Conic Cross and Room Corner lattice individuals by using [EDGE + area] and [FACE + thickness] limbs, respectively.

number of finite elements to be very large ($O(1/t^3) \rightarrow \infty$ as $t \rightarrow 0$, Fig. 1(c)). When members are slender, their medial axes (a.k.a. skeletons) are 1-dimensional (set of curves) or 2-dimensional (set of surfaces). This manuscript addresses such cases. We do not address cases in which the medial axis is a mixture of 1- and 2-dimensional sets.

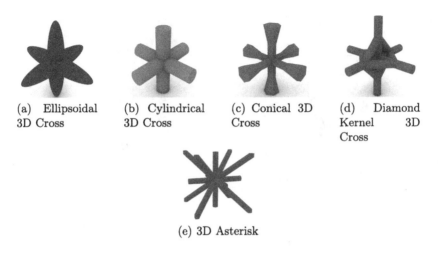

(a) Ellipsoidal 3D Cross	(b) Cylindrical 3D Cross	(c) Conical 3D Cross	(d) Diamond Kernel 3D Cross

(e) 3D Asterisk

Fig. 3. [EDGE + area] (i.e. 1.5D) limb based Lattice Individuals.

[FACE + thickness] or 2.5D Limbs. The case in Fig. 1(b) shows subdivision in larger (and fewer) 2D tiles equipped with a thickness t. They are colloquially called *2.5D Finite* or [FACE + thickness] Elements. The number of 2.5D elements is in the order $O(1/t^2)$ (red trend, Fig. 1(c)), thus requiring less elements than full B-Rep 3D models, which are in the order $O(1/t^3)$ (both measures when $t \to 0$).

[EDGE + area] or 1.5D Limbs. Similarly, slender members whose medial axis is 1-dimensional look like wires (Fig. 1(d)), equipped with a cross section or area. They are colloquially called 1.5D or [EDGE + area] elements. Examples of the modeled [EDGE + area] limb-based lattice individuals appear in Fig. 3.

Manifold Enforcement in 1.5D and 2.5D Elements. [FACE + thickness] or [EDGE + area] finite elements do not admit boolean operations since the result might be non-manifold (Fig. 1(b)). Since manifold conditions are *sine qua non* ones, kinematic constraints K_i are enforced among 1.5D and 2.5D elements (Figs. 1(d), 1(e)), thus replacing the non-manifold prone boolean operations. In this manner, the solidarity among structural members in trusses or frames is ensured, without resorting to define a boolean union of their struts or plates.

Figure 2(a) shows lattice individuals whose medial axis are 1-dimensional, showing the particular case of a 3D cross built by 6 conic rods. The EDGE is the medial axis $C(u)$ of the rod. The local rod cross section or area $\pi.r^2(u)$ is dependent on the parameter u parameterizing the rod medial axis.

Figure 2(b) represents analogous situation, this time applied to lattices built with thin walls. The medial axis of the Room Corner lattice individual is a 2-dimensional set. Therefore, the simplification applicable here is the [FACE + thickness] modeling. The Room Corner lattice individual admits representation by 12 [FACE + thickness] elements. Each element contains a FACE $S(u, w)$ and a thickness map $t(u, w)$. Figure 2(c) shows Room-corner lattice individuals. It also displays diverse lattice individuals of this type, achieved by varying wall thickness and their proportion of occupied 3D space.

3.2   Lattice Family Creation via Visual-Programming

The visual code appearing in this manuscript is not polished or optimized. It appears exactly as the designer produced it, counting with no previous programming experience.

This section will discuss as example the Diamond lattice family. Figure 4 displays a partial view of the Grasshopper circuit for their construction. These lattice individuals *are not* full B-Reps, but instead a collection of 8 faces. The basic strategy is:

(a) Lattice Coordinates Order.

(b) Lattice Coordinates Retrieval.

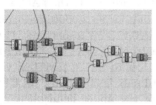

(c) FACE creation and Pyramid Reflection.

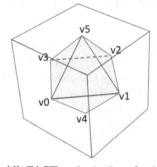

(d) FACEs v0-v1-v5 and v0-v5-v3 in upper pyramid.

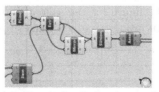

(e) Circuit for Reflection and FACE Boolean Union.

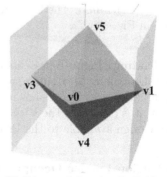

(f) Diamond Lattice Individual.

Fig. 4. Grasshopper Circuits for Diamond Family Lattice.

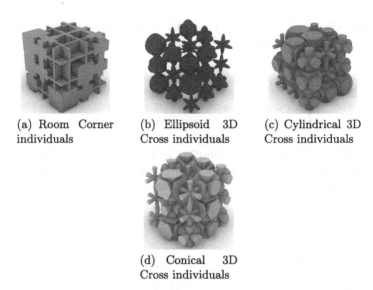

(a) Room Corner individuals

(b) Ellipsoid 3D Cross individuals

(c) Cylindrical 3D Cross individuals

(d) Conical 3D Cross individuals

Fig. 5. Rectangular prismatic 3D region filled with $N_x \times N_y \times N_z$ lattices. Individuals with Constant Topology and Diverse Geometry.

(1) Create a Cube (B-Rep) which will circumscribe the diamond. (2) Explode the Cube into FACEs, EDGEs, VERTEXes. (3) Interrogate the FACEs for their geometric center. (4) Classify the FACE centroids as per z-coordinate, obtaining 3 bins with 1, 1 and 4 vertices ({v5},{v4},{v3,v0,v1,v2}, respectively (Figs. 4(a) and 4(f)). (5) Choose the bin with 4 FACE centroids ({v0,v1,v2,v3} in Figs. 4(d) and 4(b). Construct segments from these vertices to the cusp vertex, v5, of the pyramid (i.e. bin with 1 vertex, whose z coordinate is maximal). (6) Create (by extrusion, Fig. 4(c)) the triangular FACEs of the upper hemisphere by using the geometric centers of cube FACEs (e.g. FACE [v0,v1,v5] in Fig. 4(d)). (7) Reflect the upper pyramid (Figs. 4(c) and 4(d)) with respect to plane z=1/2.H to obtain the lower pyramid. The finished FACE-based Diamond lattice individual is displayed in Fig. 4(f).

Pattern Grading. Figure 5 presents a case in which the *topology* of the lattice individual is kept along the domain, while their *geometry* is modified. This effect may be gradual or drastic (as shown in the figure for the sake of illustration). In any event, it is clear that the Visual Computing paradigm makes this form of Generative Design available to the Product Designer.

3.3   3D Region Lattice Occupancy

Figure 6(a) displays the generic workflow for the construction of the Lattice enumeration that fills a given B 3D domain representing a solid, with boundary representation M (2-manifold mesh).

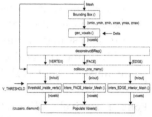

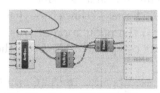

(a) Workflow to determine Lattice occupancy in a 3D domain.

(b) Grading of VERTEXes of a given lattice as Inside (I) or Outside (O) a given mesh M.

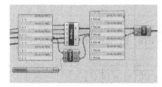

(c) Grading of Lattices according to the threshold number of I VERTEXes (vertices Inside Mesh M).

Fig. 6. VERTEX-based Threshold for Lattice Inclusion in a 3D Region bounded by a manifold mesh **M**.

The following adjectives are used [5,20] for a given lattice: **I**=lattice is inside M, **O**=lattice is outside M, **NIO**=lattice is neither inside or outside M.

3.4 Application of Pre-, Post-condition and Invariants in Imperative and Declarative Programming

It is not possible to directly define an axiomatic semantics, as it is based on states and instructions, for declarative programming languages. Because of this reason, we have resorted to a 2-step process to reach a declarative visual program from Pre-, Post-condition and Invariant: (i) from Pre-, Post-condition and Invariant to an Imperative Program, and (ii) from an Imperative Program to a Declarative Visual Program.

It is not intention of this manuscript to discuss grammars, theorem-proving engines or code-generators that automatically execute translations (i) and (ii) above. We do not aspire to such an endeavor, and it would defeat the informal mental processes (i) and (ii) that our non-programmer Product Designer executes.

From Pre, Post, Inv to Imperative Programming. Algorithm 1 exemplifies how the Pre-, Post-condition and Invariant is applied for the population and approximation of a solid region *Omega* by using lattice individuals. Pre-,

Post-condition and Invariants (lines 7, 19 and 9) are not instructions. Instead, they are comments that describe the status of the code execution at particular checkpoints. The set C (lines 5, 8, 16 and 17) of already estimated cells measures how advanced the population of $\widetilde{B}$ is. Growing C to equal the grid G (line 16) clearly means completion. However, the invariant must be kept (**IF** decision in line 10).

As expressed before, $\text{Inv} \wedge \neg (C \neq G) \Rightarrow \text{Post}$. Effectively, $(\widetilde{B} \approx (\Omega \cap C)) \wedge (C = G) \Rightarrow (\widetilde{B} \approx (\Omega \cap G))$. In this manner, $\widetilde{B}$ approximates the solid Ω immersed in grid G. Notice that c_{ijk} is an empty cell of the grid, while l_{ijk} is a lattice individual (e.g. in Fig. 3) populating the space c_{ijk}.

Algorithm 1. Generic Pre- and Post-condition and Invariant for Approximation of B-Rep Ω.

```
 1: procedure [B̃]=PopulateGrid(Ω,G)
 2:              ▷ c_ijk:grid cell, l_ijk:lattice individual in cell c_ijk, C:set of cells c_ijk,
 3:                          ▷ G: axis-aligned grid containing solid Ω, made of cells c_ijk
 4:      B̃ = {}
 5:      C = {}
 6:      c_ijk = first(G)
 7:                                                        ▷ Pre: solid Ω ⊆ grid G
 8:      while (C ≠ G) do
 9:                                                        ▷ Inv: B̃ ≈ Ω ∩ C
10:          if ( (Ω ∩ c_ijk) ≈ c_ijk ) then
11:              l_ijk = RigidTransform(BasicLattice)    ▷ e.g. Lattices in Fig. 3
12:          else
13:              l_ijk = Φ
14:          end if
15:          B̃ = B̃ ∪ l_ijk
16:          C = C ∪ c_ijk
17:          c_ijk = successor(c_ijk, G) )
18:      end while
19:                                                        ▷ Post: B̃ ≈ Ω ∩ G
20: end procedure
```

From Imperative to Declarative Programming. Figure 7 presents the translation of Algorithm 1 to a generic equivalent of Grasshopper. For the sake of generality, this section uses generic feature names instead of Grasshopper names. In declarative visual programming, no FOR or WHILE iterations are available. Instead, iterators provides access to list elements (in this case, cells c_{ijk} of a grid G). A generic fuzzy lattice - in - solid inclusion diagnose is applied to each cel c_{ijk}. If a certain threshold number of elements FACE, EDGE or VERTEX of the lattice individual are inside Ω, the lattice c_{ijk} is considered INSIDE. This decision is implemented with the romboid icon gate that corresponds to line 10 of Algorithm 1. If the lattice c_{ijk} is considered to be Inside Ω, a rigid transformation is computed and applied to move the basic lattice individual (e.g. Fig. 3) to the position of lattice c_{ijk}, thus producing the lattice individual l_{ijk}. This lattice filling is added to the result set $\tilde{B}$ via a set-ADD operation. It must be pointed out that in declarative visual programming the *overall steady state* of the gate network is contains the result of the computation. The *transient states* are by definition unstable. Also, no specific instruction can be used for checkpoint, as in imperative programming, since individual instructions do not exist.

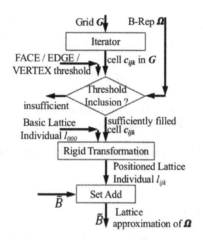

Fig. 7. Generic Declarative Equivalent of Algorithm 1

4   Results

The workflow of Fig. 6(a): (1) identifies a rectangular prismatic Bounding Box enclosing M and orthogonally oriented w.r.t. World axes. (2) builds a 3D regular lattice grid within the Bounding Box, (3) for each cubic lattice, its FACE, EDGE and VERTEX sets are extracted (BRep deconstruction), (4) for the particular topology e.g. VERTEX, the number of VERTEXes inside and outside the mesh M is identified (Fig. 6(b)), (5) a Threshold value is used (Fig. 6(c)) to decide whether the **NIO** lattices are graded as **I** (e.g. a lattice is considered I if more than Threshold=5 of its VERTEXes are inside M), (6) once the lattice is graded as **I**, a rigid transformation is applied on a generic copy of that particular lattice individual (e.g. diamond, 3D cross, room corner, etc.) to populate the region enclosed by mesh M with the lattice individuals graded as **I** (i.e. inside M). Results for the *Whale* dataset of this lattice enumeration process are displayed in Figs. 8 and 9.

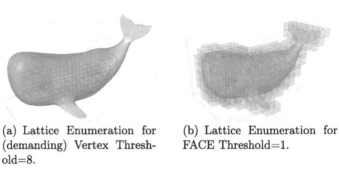

(a) Lattice Enumeration for (demanding) Vertex Threshold=8.

(b) Lattice Enumeration for FACE Threshold=1.

(c) Lattice Enumeration for FACE Threshold=5.

Fig. 8. Whale data set. Threshold number of Topologies (EDGE or FACE) needed to declare a lattice as **I** (Inside)

4.1 Lattice Enumeration

Figure 9 shows diverse lattice populations of the Whale dataset. This particular figure displays actual FACE sets building the lattice individuales of all cells. No [FACE + thickness] or [EDGE + area] simplifications are executed.

Figure 10 depicts results of the visual computing circuits applied to approximate the Cat dataset with lattice individuals of the type Asterisk. Figure 10(a) shows the 2-manifold Triangular Boundary Representation (i.e. mesh M), or skin, enclosing a solid body B. Figure 10(b) displays the immersion of the B-Rep M into an orthogonal cubic grid. Figure 10(c) shows an approximation of the Cat M with [EDGE + area] type limbs (type 3D Asterisk). An over-estimation of B is achieved if a lattice receives an I (Inside) grade when one of its six VERTEXes is Inside mesh M. A more sensible grading of a lattice as **I** occurs if a large portion its VERTEXes are inside M.

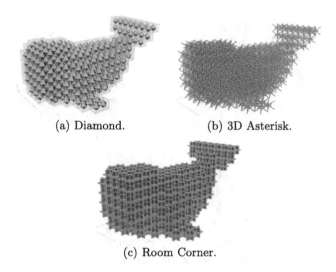

(a) Diamond.   (b) 3D Asterisk.

(c) Room Corner.

Fig. 9. Results of assorted Lattice individuals occupancy of the Whale 3D model.

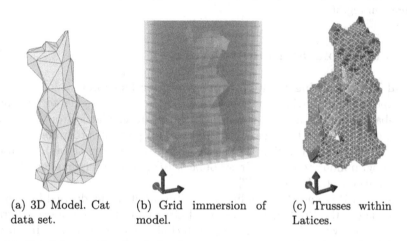

(a) 3D Model. Cat   (b) Grid immersion of   (c) Trusses within
data set.   model.   Latices.

Fig. 10. Cat data set. Results of visual programming processing: immersion of model in grid, lattice approximation and inner lattice trusses.

4.2 Material Realization

Figure 11 presents an Additive Manufacturing realization of two individuals of the family Conical 3D Cross (Fig. 3(c)). In this material incarnation, the section radius is decreasing along the limb axis curve. In Fig. 3(c), the section radius grows along the limb axis curve. They obviously belong to the same lattice family. However, it must be emphasized that the *kernel of this manuscript is not the material realization of the lattice family,* but instead the successful application of Contract-Based Programming (Pre-condition, Post-condition, Invariants) in Flow-based Programming by a non-programmer Designer and the 1.5D and 2.5D truss - frame modeling strategies.

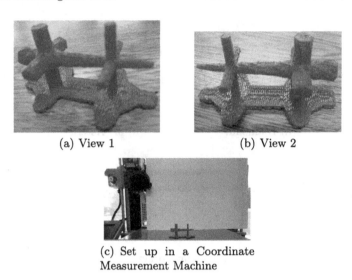

(a) View 1   (b) View 2

(c) Set up in a Coordinate
Measurement Machine

Fig. 11. Additive manufacturing realization of two Conical 3D Cross lattice individuals of family in Fig. 3(c).

5   Conclusions and Future Work

Visual Programming for a Non-programmer Designer

The experiment of having a non-programmer Product Designer to program a lattice-based filling of a 3D region using a set of suitable lattice topologies with varying geometry had these circumstances: (a) no previous programming training, (b) independent learning (i.e. absence of programming tutors), (c) use of visual programming tools (i.e. Grasshopper), (d) informal seminars on Pre- and Post-conditions and Invariants [7].

In spite of Pre- and Post-conditions and Invariants being devised for *imperative* languages, the Product Designer used Grasshopper, a *flow-based* programming language, with high proficiency and technically correct results. It must be noticed however, that it was not intention of the present research to compete against professional lattice-based design tools.

Therefore, this work shows the power of the Visual programming paradigm and tools for the particular domain of lattice-based geometric modeling. In particular, the change of paradigm from iteration-based imperative programming towards flow-based programming (e.g. in Grasshopper) does not impede the novice visual programmer to enforce code correctness and pre- and post-condition clauses.

Region Population with Lattice Individuals

Several families of slender-limb lattice individuals have been modeled. They include(a) rods modeled as [EDGE + area] (a.k.a. 1.5D) elements and (b) plates modeled as [FACE + thickness] (a.k.a. 2.5D) elements.

The approximation of domain Ω by lattices is tuned (as usual in enumerations) by considering inclusion thresholds above which a *partially* included lattice is declared to be *full*.

A reduced Additive Manufacture of (two) lattice individuals of the family Conical 3D Cross is presented to illustrate how they spatially and kinematically relate to each other. However, it most be noticed that the manufacture of the approximation to the 3D region Ω via lattices is not the purpose of this manuscript.

We do not seek to equate informal seminars on pre-, post-conditions and invariants for a non-programmer Product Designer with the complex, very long and formal process that formal logic represents for even trained programmers. All what we can aspire is that an informal treatment, allows the non-programmer Product Designer to be proficient vis-a-vis development of declarative visual programs and correction of his/her run results.

Future work is required in the application of non-affine geometric transformations to the lattice individuals before their docking in the target 3D region. This extension would permit lattices whose geometry contains straight-to-curve deformations, dictated by the functionality of the Additive Manufacturing.

Acknowledgments. The authors wish to thank U. EAFIT, Colombia for the funding and academic space for this investigation, channeled through its CAD CAM CAE Laboratory. Special thanks are presented to M.A. Carolina Builes-Roldan for funding an important portion of the project.

Conflicts of Interest. The Authors declare that they have no conflict of interest in the publication of this manuscript.

References

1. Alexandrova, S., Tatlock, Z., Cakmak, M.: RoboFlow: a flow-based visual programming language for mobile manipulation tasks. In: 2015 IEEE International Conference on Robotics and Automation (ICRA), pp. 5537–5544 (2015). https://doi.org/10.1109/ICRA.2015.7139973
2. Aremu, A., et al.: A voxel-based method of constructing and skinning conformal and functionally graded lattice structures suitable for additive manufacturing. Addit. Manuf. **13**, 1–13 (2017)
3. Celani, G., Vaz, C.E.V.: CAD scripting and visual programming languages for implementing computational design concepts: a comparison from a pedagogical point of view. Int. J. Architectural Comput. **10**(1), 121–137 (2012). https://doi.org/10.1260/1478-0771.10.1.121. ISSN 1478-0771
4. Fähndrich, M., Logozzo, F.: Static contract checking with abstract interpretation. In: Beckert, B., Marché, C. (eds.) FoVeOOS 2010. LNCS, vol. 6528, pp. 10–30. Springer, Heidelberg (2011). https://doi.org/10.1007/978-3-642-18070-5_2
5. Garcia, M.J., Henao, M.A., Ruiz, O.E.: Fixed grid finite element analysis for 3D structural problems. Int. J. Comput. Methods **02**(04), 569–586 (2005). https://doi.org/10.1142/S0219876205000582

6. Garcia-Cuevas, D., Pugliese, G.: Advanced 3D Printing with Grasshopper: Clay and FDM. Independent (2020). iSBN 979-8635379011

7. Gries, D.: The Science of Programming. Springer, New York (1981). iSBN 978-0-387-90641-6, eISBN 978-1-4612-5983-1. Chapter Developing Loops from Invariants and Bounds

8. Gupta, A., Kurzeja, K., Rossignac, J., Allen, G., Kumar, P.S., Musuvathy, S.: Programmed-lattice editor and accelerated processing of parametric program-representations of steady lattices. Comput. Aided Des. **113**, 35–47 (2019)

9. Janssen, P., Chen, K.: Visual dataflow modelling: a comparison of three systems. In: Design Futures 2011 - Proceedings of the 14th International Conference on Computer Aided Architectural Design Futures, Liee, Belgium, pp. 801–816 (2011)

10. Kurtz, A., Tang, Y., Zhao, F.: Intra lattice (2015). http://intralattice.com, generative Lattice Design with Grasshopper. McGill Additive Design and Manufacturing Laboratory - ADML

11. Montoya-Zapata, D., Cortes, C., Ruiz-Salguero, O.: Fe-simulations with a simplified model for open-cell porous materials: a kelvin cell approach. J. Comput. Methods Sci. Eng. 1–12 (2019, in press). https://doi.org/10.3233/JCM-193669. Published online: 27 May 2019

12. Morrison, J.P.: Flow-Based Programming: A New Approach to Application Development, 2nd edn. CreateSpace Independent Publishing Platform (2010). ISBN-10: 1451542321, ISBN-13: 978–1451542325

13. Nielson, H., Flemming, N.: Semantics with Applications: An Appetizer. Undergraduate Topics in Computer Science (UTiCS) Series. Springer, London (2007). iSBN-13: 978-1-84628-691-9, e-ISBN-13: 978-1-84628-692-6

14. Panesar, A., Abdi, M., Hickman, D., Ashcroft, I.: Strategies for functionally graded lattice structures derived using topology optimisation for additive manufacturing. Addit. Manuf. **19**, 81–94 (2018). https://doi.org/10.1016/j.addma.2017.11.008

15. Schwarzkopf, M.: The remarkable utility of dataflow computing (2020). https://www.sigops.org/2020/the-remarkable-utility-of-dataflow-computing/, ACM - SIGOPS. Special Interest Group in Operating Systems

16. Sebestyen, A.: Loops in grasshopper. In: Bricks are Landing. Algorithmic Design of a Brick Pavilion, pp. 15–24. T.U. Wien (2019). iSBN 978-3-9504464-1-82

17. Wang, B., Gao, H., Cheng, J.: Contract-based programming for future computing with Ada 2012. In: 2016 International Conference on Advanced Cloud and Big Data (CBD), pp. 322–327 (2016). https://doi.org/10.1109/CBD.2016.062

18. Weeger, O., Boddeti, N., Yeung, S.K., Kaijima, S., Dunn, M.: Digital design and nonlinear simulation for additive manufacturing of soft lattice structures. Addit. Manuf. **25**, 39–49 (2019). https://doi.org/10.1016/j.addma.2018.11.003. https://www.sciencedirect.com/science/article/pii/S2214860417303962

19. Weeger, O., Yeung, S.K., Dunn, M.L.: Isogeometric collocation methods for Cosserat rods and rod structures. Comput. Methods Appl. Mech. Eng. **316**, 100–122 (2017). https://doi.org/10.1016/j.cma.2016.05.009. https://www.sciencedirect.com/science/article/pii/S004578251630336X, special Issue on Isogeometric Analysis: Progress and Challenges

20. Xie, Y.M., Steven, G.: A simple evolutionary procedure for structural optimization. Comput. Struct. **49**(5), 885–896 (1993)

Using Open Data for Training Deep Learning Models: A Waste Identification Case Study

Juan Carlos Arbeláez[1(✉)], Paola Vallejo[1], Marta Silvia Tabares[1],
Jose Aguilar[1,2,3], David Ríos Zapata[1], Elizabeth Rendón Vélez[1],
and Santiago Ruiz-Arenas[1]

[1] Universidad EAFIT, Medellín, Colombia
{jarbel16,pvallej3,mtabares,jlaguilarc,drioszap,erendonv,
sruizare}@eafit.edu.co, aguilar@ula.ve
[2] Universidad de Los Andes, Merida, Venezuela
[3] IMDEA Network Institute, Madrid, Spain
jose.aguilar@imdea.org

Abstract. One of the main challenges of building commercial solutions with Supervised Deep Learning is the acquisition of large custom-labeled datasets. These large datasets usually fit neither commercial industries' production times nor budgets. The case study presents how to use Open Data with different features, distributions, and incomplete labels for training a tailored Deep Learning multi-label model for identifying waste materials, type of packaging, and product brand. We propose an architecture with a CBAM attention module, and a focal loss, for integrating multiple labels with incomplete data and unknown labels, and a novel training pipeline for exploiting specific target-domain features that allows training with multiple source domains. As a result, the proposed approach reached an average F1-macro-score of 86% trained only with 13% tailored data, which is 15% higher than a traditional approach. In conclusion, using pre-trained models and highly available labeled datasets reduces model development costs. However, it is still required to have target data that allows the model to learn specific target domain features.

Keywords: Deep Learning · Transfer Learning · Waste Identification · Solid Waste Management

1 Introduction

Deep Learning (DL) models are made of multiple layers of nonlinear functions that automatically learn features from raw inputs. This property of the DL models allows us to reduce the costs and time of feature engineering compared to developing Machine Learning (ML) models [1]. However, for the model to learn the mapping function between the raw inputs and the desired outputs and

M. Tabares et al. (Eds.): CCC 2023, CCIS 1924, pp. 173–187, 2024.
https://doi.org/10.1007/978-3-031-47372-2_16

at the same time achieve good generalization, it is required to feed them with a large amount of labeled data (for supervised learning). The prevalence of large datasets is one of the main reasons for the success of DL models, especially the Convolutional Neuronal Networks (CNN) that have dominated the state-of-art in the later years in computer vision problems such as object detection, image classification, or semantic segmentation [16]. Nevertheless, gathering the required amount of labeled data for building strong solutions is impossible in many cases. This could be due to many reasons, for example, high costs of data labeling when experts' knowledge is required, for instance, in medical fields. Another case is when the observations (input data) are difficult to obtain in the case that rarely occurs, or there are privacy concerns for acquiring the data. For commercial solutions, the time required to assemble large datasets usually does not fit the market times or tight budgets used in the industry.

Particularly, one of the biggest challenges of the development of computer vision applications is the amount of data required [8]. Different methods are used to train DL models with scarce data: (i) Transfer Learning that aims to use knowledge of a source model trained on different but related domain and task [23]; (ii) Data augmentation that applies a set of transformations (i.e. Affine or point operators) to each sample of the training dataset to generate new ones [7]; (iii) Synthetically generated data that uses simulations to create new data (in the case of computer vision tasks, renders or animations are used for training the model [13]); and (iv) Few-shot learning that aims to train a model with fewer samples but generalize to unfamiliar samples [6]. In all of the presented methods, the main challenge is the discrepancy between the domains (source and target), where the feature space or label space is different or has different distributions.

Open Data (OD) refers to data that can be published and reused without price or permission barriers [12]. In the later years, the availability of large OD online has increased through platforms such as Kaggle or Roboflow that allows users to share labeled datasets. Although it is possible for academic purposes to use them for bench-marking, they can not be used directly for industrial or commercial purposes as they differ from the target domain and task. For instance, they have different labels, or the images are related but in different contexts. This article presents an approach for using OD from multiple domains and labels to train a supervised image multi-label model (Sect. 3). The approach is composed of three elements: a training pipeline (Sect. 3.1), an attention module (Sect. 3.2), and a Focal loss with incomplete data (Sect. 3.3). We validated the proposed approach in a case study of waste identification (Sect. 2), where the model is trained to predict the material, type of packaging, and product brand of waste in an image (Sect. 4). The proposed approach reached an average F1-macro-score of 86% on the target dataset and 85.8% evaluated in the source domains (Sect. 4.3). Section 5 present the research conclusions.

Figure 1 shows a random sample from the source (also includes 12.5% of target domain images) dataset with the three categories of labels. The label of the material, the type of packaging, and the product brand occupy the first, second, and third positions, respectively.

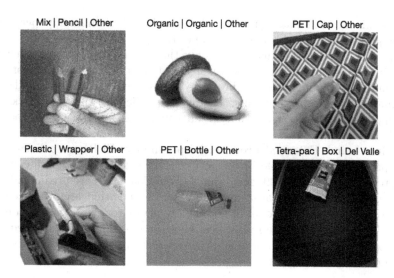

Fig. 1. Random sample from the source (also includes 13% of target domain images) dataset with the three categories of labels. The label of the material, the type of packaging, and the product brand occupy the first, second, and third positions, respectively. Section 6 describes the datasets used and the link where they are available.

2 Waste Identification Challenge

The world's cities generate 1.5 billion tonnes of solid waste per year, and it is expected to increase to 2.2 billion tonnes by 2025 [4]. Therefore Solid Waste Management (SWM) is a global issue that affects every individual and government. At least 21% of municipal waste is not managed correctly, directly impacting public health and the environment [4]. Performing the correct waste separation increases the material recovery rate and reduces environmental impacts and economic expense [2]. Nevertheless, performing the waste separation is difficult as it is affected by multiple factors such as physical, human behaviors, knowledge, and policies, among others [14].

ML models are frequently used for waste classification and location in waste management systems. The CNNs are commonly used to perform these tasks [15,17,19,22] but two main barriers are typically mentioned: (i) The size of the datasets: given that the visual appearance of waste can vary a lot due to high deformations, dirt, and material degradation, it is required to have many samples of the same type of object that includes multiple variations. (ii) Location tailored: brands, products, objects' appearance, and even recycling categories vary from place to place, such that training datasets need to be custom for a specific location. These reasons prevent the reuse of datasets for different places.

In the proposed case study, a DL model is trained using datasets from different locations with different products, contexts, brands, and labels. The predictive function takes an image of a waste and outputs three categories of predictions (Fig. 1 shows a random sample from the source):

1. Material: one of 12 classes: plastic, PET, cardboard, aluminum, paper, Tetra-pac, glass, steel, paper towel, mix, paper receipt, and organic.
2. Type of packaging: because of not only the material but the recycling process and type of the object gives insights about the recycling category. For instance, aluminum cans can be reused to contain food again, unlike aluminum used on other products. The model predicts 12 classes of packaging: wrapper, container, box, can, bottle, foil, cap, pencil, cutlery, organic, battery, and masks.
3. Product brand: Extended Producer Responsibility (EPR) are policies where the producer is responsible for the post-consumer stage of product life, including recycling [10]. Thus 39 local brands (from Colombia) are predicted by the model, and one additional to include "other" brands that are not taken into account but allow the model to not classify mandatory in one of the defined brands. Particularly, brand identification is the most local-tailored prediction category compared to material and type of packaging that share more similar features in different places.

The source dataset labels are composed of three categories: the material, the type of packaging, and the product brand occupy the first, second, and third positions, respectively.

3   Our Open Data Approach to Train Deep Learning Models

The presented approach aims to improve the performance of a model on a target domain that contains fewer samples (or none) required to learn a predictive function with samples of other domains. This problem is formally defined under the term of Transfer Learning [20] where a *Domain* $\mathcal{D}$ is described by two parts, a feature space $\mathcal{X}$ and a marginal probability distribution $P(\mathbf{X})$ where $\mathbf{X} = \{x_1, \ldots, x_n\}$. The feature space $\mathcal{X}$ comprises all possible features, and $\mathbf{X}$ is a particular set of the domain with n number of instances. For a domain $D = \{\mathcal{X}, P(\mathbf{X})\}$. A *task* $\mathcal{T}$ is defined by two components as well, a label space $\mathcal{Y}$ and a predictive function $f(\cdot)$ trained from the feature-label x_i, y_i where $x_i \in \mathbf{X}$ and $y_i \in \mathbf{Y}$. $\mathbf{Y} = \{y_1, \ldots, y_n\}$ are the corresponding labels of the particular learning sample set $\mathbf{X}$, and the function $f(\cdot)$ is the predictive function that can be seen as $P(y|x)$, the probability of y given a feature x. In a general case, we have two domains with their related tasks, the *source domain* $\mathcal{D}^S = \{\mathcal{X}^S, P(\mathbf{X^S})\}$ and its respective task $\mathcal{T}^S = \{\mathcal{Y}^S, P(\mathbf{Y^S}|\mathbf{X^S})\}$. Similarly, the *target domain* $\mathcal{D}^T = \{\mathcal{X}^T, P(\mathbf{X^T})\}$ with $\mathcal{T}^T = \{\mathcal{Y}^T, P(\mathbf{Y^T}|\mathbf{X^T})\}$. Therefore, TL is defined in this context as the process of improving the target predictive function $P(\mathbf{Y^T}|\mathbf{X^T})$ using information from $\mathcal{D}^S$ and $\mathcal{T}^S$ with the condition that $\mathcal{D}^S \neq \mathcal{D}^T$ or $\mathcal{T}^S \neq \mathcal{T}^T$.

For our case, we have a source composed of multiple domains, each one with its related task: $\mathbf{D^S} = \left[(\mathcal{D}^S, \mathcal{T}^S)_1, \ldots, (\mathcal{D}^S, \mathcal{T}^S)_n\right]$ for improving one target predictive function in the domain $\mathcal{D}^T = \{\mathcal{X}^T, P(\mathbf{X^T})\}$.

The proposed approach comprises three elements: a training pipeline, an attention module placed in the head of a pre-trained *feature extractor*, and a

Focal loss for incomplete data. The approach is defined for a multi-label task where the labels can be grouped into categories that are not mutually exclusive. The same approach can be used for traditional multi-label or classification problems.

3.1 Training Pipeline

The pipeline is performed in three stages. The first is to prepare the datasets, then model training, and the last is the model evaluation.

Data preparation. After gathering the source datasets, the first step is performing a *label mapping*. In the *label mapping*, each class of the target categories (i.e., material or brand) is labeled encoded (each class is represented by a consecutive integer number starting by zero), and an additional class *"Unknown"* represented by -1 is added. The mapping is performed as follows: if the class is in the set of target classes, then assign it the corresponding label (y_i). Otherwise, it is assigned to *"Unknown"*:

$$y_i = \begin{cases} y_i^T, & \text{if } y_i^S \in \mathcal{Y}^S \\ -1, & \text{otherwise} \end{cases}$$

The *label mapping* allows easy processing of all the samples of the source datasets without the need to manually relabel, and at the same time, at the training time, to detect if a sample has an *"unknown"* label (if its value is less than 0). Later, the labels are one-hot encoded by category; each category label is represented by a K dimensional vector corresponding with length of the number of classes of the category, and one element is equal 1 that corresponds to the position of the label encoded and the rest remains 0. The final label is a vector of the concatenated one-hot encoded categories of $\mathbb{R}^{\sum K_i}$. Figure 2 shows an example of the encoded label process for each image, where each category generates a one-hot encoded vector concatenated to produce the final label. If the label is *"Unknown"*, a zero vector of K dimension is generated.

Model training. The model training is performed with Adam [9], a stochastic gradient-based optimization. The train split is composed of all source datasets randomly shuffled where a training sample is a pair feature, label (x_i, y_i). The training is performed in two steps:

1. Attention training: The parameters of the attention module described in Sect. 3.2 are tuned first, the rest of the model parameters are frozen (not updated during backpropagation), and the attention module is only trained with the target dataset on one prediction category (i.e., brand or material). The category selection is based on the one that can provide more local or domain-tailored information (i.e., the brand category).

2. Prediction training: After the attention module is trained, the layers in charge of the final prediction are trained. Both the attention module and the *feature extractor* are frozen during this step, and the model is trained with the source datasets.

178   J. C. Arbeláez et al.

The proposed pipeline intends that the *feature extractor* is already pre-trained in a general dataset (ImageNet) and "knows" to extract features from images. The attention module is trained to weigh features relevant to the tailored dataset for the target task. Therefore, step 2 (Prediction Training) later pays more attention to these features during the training of the final prediction layers. The model is trained using backpropagation with the loss presented in Sect. 3.3.

Model evaluation. To evaluate the model with highly unbalanced datasets with missing labels, a non-zero average macro F1-score is used as a performance metric. The F1-score is the harmonic mean between the precision and recall, thus penalizing if the model's prediction is biased to a majoritarian class. The average macro F1-score is calculated by each class and averaged by the prediction categories. Given that some datasets could not be present in some classes, it is not considered in the average.

Fig. 2. Example of the encoded label process for each image. For each category is generated a one-hot encode vector that is concatenated to produce the final label.

3.2 Attention Module

The model architecture is composed of a *feature extractor*, an attention module, and a custom head for performing the predictions (Fig. 3).

The *Feature extractor* is a CNN model pre-trained on ImageNet where the prediction head is removed and is only used in the last convolution layer output. For the feature extraction, any state-of-art model could be used, such as VGG16 [18], MobileNet [5], or ResNet50 [3]. For example, ResNet50 (achieved the highest score) produces a *feature map* of $(7,7,2048)$ dimensions (red in Fig. 3). Resnet50 is a CNN architecture that uses skipped connections to fix the gradient-vanish problem related to backpropagation on deep models. The *feature map* is passed by a CBAM Attention module [21] that is composed of channel (green on Fig. 3) and spatial (yellow on Fig. 3) modules.

(i) The attention module produces a channel attention map (M_c) using the *feature map* (F) channels inter-relationship, such that each channel can be considered a feature detector. The channel attention emphasizes what is meaningful in an input image. In the channel module, the spatial dimension is squeezed by adding two pooling operations over the channel dimension that produces an average (F_{avg}^c) and max (F_{max}^s) pooled features and passed by the same Fully Connected (FC) network:

$$M_c(F) = \sigma(FC(F_{avg}^c + FC(F_{max}^c)))$$

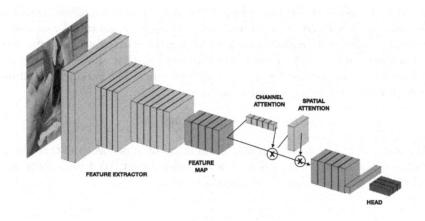

Fig. 3. Model architecture composed of a Feature extractor (in blue) that produces a feature map (red). The feature map is passed by a CBAM Attention with spacial (yellow) and channel (green) modules, and finally, fully connected layers for the prediction for each category. (Color figure online)

(ii) The spatial attention module produces a map (M_s) using the features' relationship. It determines the relevant information of the feature map (F) and encodes where to emphasize or decrease its contribution to the prediction. The spatial attention module is calculated by performing a *Sigmoid activation* (σ) of the convolution ($f^{n \times n}$) over the concatenated a max (F_{max}^s) and average pooled-features (F_{avg}) of the *feature map*.

$$M_s(F) = \sigma \left(f^{n \times n}(F_{avg}^s; F_{max}^s) \right)$$

Each one of the attention maps multiplies the *feature map*; the channel attention vector multiplies each channel of the map and the spatial each feature (Fig. 3). The attention module (spatial and channel) are trained only on one prediction category with the target dataset. Later, their weights are frozen, and the rest of the model is trained for all the categories.

3.3 Focal Loss for Incomplete Data

The Focal Loss [11] is used for training models with highly unbalanced datasets. For instance, on object detection usually there is more background than foreground objects, which causes the model to be biased for the amount of one class. For dealing with dataset unbalance, there are other techniques, such as dataset sampling, which can be performed by oversampling the classes with fewer observations, or undersampling the majoritarian classes. Another technique commonly used is to add a weight to each sample depending on its class that defines their contribution to the loss during training (Weighted loss). However, both of these techniques usually do not work well when there are large differences between the classes (i.e., Brands distribution in Fig. 6) because training is inefficient and the model tends to over-fit given that a small set of samples are continually repeated.

Focal Loss (FL) is intended to work when there is an extreme class unbalance by adding a term $(1 - p)^\gamma$ to the Cross-Entropy loss that allows reducing the contribution of easy samples focus on the difficult ones. The parameter γ adjust how much easy samples are weighted down:

$$FL(p_i) = -(1 - p_i)^\gamma \log(p_i)$$

For our case, the multi-label problem can be decomposed as a multiple classification problem, given that each category is independent. We have a composed loss L of each categories loss L_c weighted by factor:

$$L = \sum_1^c W_c L_c$$

Each category loss is computed using the Focal Loss, and each sample (i) is only considered if the label of its category is known. Given that the "unknown" labels are set to a zero-vector and the Cross-Entropy loss is computed by multiplying the log of the predictions by its true probability (t_i), the loss for each category is computed as follows:

$$L_c = -\frac{1}{n_c} \sum_i^n (1 - p_i^c)^\gamma \log(p_i^c) t_i^c$$

Each category loss is normalized by the number of known samples (n_c), where p_i^c is the model prediction of the sample i regarding the category c and t_i^c is the true label of the sample regarding the same category.

4   Definition of a Multi-label Deep Learning Model Using Our Open Data Approach

4.1   Dataset Acquisition and Preparation

In our case study, we train a predictive function that takes an image of waste and outputs three categories of predictions: its material, type of packaging, and product brand (Sect. 2). For the acquisition of the target data, a photography device (A in Fig. 4) was designed to control environment variables such as lighting or background, and perform an efficient data collection. The photography device is composed of 5 elements (B in Fig. 4).

1. Chasis in an aluminum profile that allows configuring the components in multiple positions; 2. Profile unions; 3. Multiple cameras that can be positioned with a support that allows to place them in any position and rotation; 4. Configurable lighting ring of three colors (natural, warm, and cold) and ten light intensities; 5. Background panels that can be changed to use different colors.

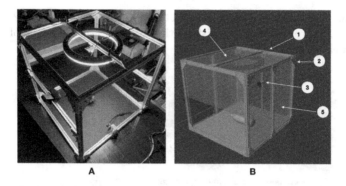

Fig. 4. (A) Photography device used for the target dataset acquisition. The photo shows three cameras and a lighting ring. **(B)** Photography device design, composed of five main parts: Chasis in aluminum profile, profile unions, multiple cameras, lighting ring, Background panels

The target dataset comprises 624 products commonly consumed in Universidad EAFIT - Colombia. An ID is assigned to each product, labeled according to the three categories to predict (material, type of packaging, and product brand). Generic products are also included for products that are not possible to know any labels. For each product, multiple photos are taken with three deformations: (0) No deformation is applied to the product, (1) Mild deformation: the product is opened for consumption and has some deformation, and (2) Severe deformation is applied to the packaging. Additionally to the photos taken with the device, 191 photos of products in different contexts were taken. Figure 5 shows random samples from the target dataset.

Fig. 5. Random sample images from the target dataset, taken with the photography device and with random context

The target dataset is composed of 11.207 images, from which 25% is used for testing. Figure 6 shows the distribution of the target dataset of the three prediction categories.

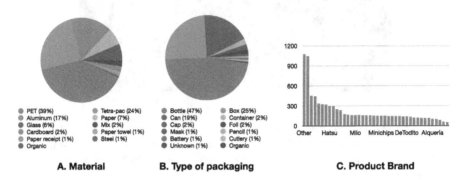

● PET (39%)	● Tetra-pac (24%)
● Aluminum (17%)	● Paper (7%)
● Glass (6%)	● Mix (2%)
● Cardboard (2%)	● Paper towel (1%)
● Paper receipt (1%)	● Steel (1%)
● Organic	

● Bottle (47%)	● Box (25%)
● Can (19%)	● Container (2%)
● Cap (2%)	● Foil (2%)
● Mask (1%)	● Pencil (1%)
● Battery (1%)	● Cutlery (1%)
● Unknown (1%)	● Organic

A. Material   **B. Type of packaging**   **C. Product Brand**

Fig. 6. Class distribution of target dataset of the 3 distribution categories

The source dataset has been created from 34 online datasets and contains 75.101 images, from which 20% is used for testing. In the next link are available the sources, the class contribution to the source dataset, and its respective references: Open Data waste datasets.

4.2 Model Training

The training dataset split comprises the source and target training splits. First, the attention module (Sect. 3.2) is trained for brand prediction as it contains more target-tailored information. After the attention module is trained, the rest of the model (type of packaging and material) is trained, freezing the weights of the attention module. Finally, the model training is performed with Adam [9] with the loss function described in Sect. 3.3. All the models were trained for 18 Epochs in total, ten epochs for the attention module and eight epochs with Early-stopping for the rest of the prediction heads(material and type of packaging).

Five models were trained, four of them using the proposed approach with different *feature extractors*: **(i) OpenData-VGG6** using VGG16 [18] as feature extractor, **(ii) OpenData-MOBIL** using MobileNet [5] as feature extractor, **(iii) OpenData-RESN** using ResNet50 [3] as feature extractor, and one **OpenData-NoFL** with ResNet50 as feature extractor and trained without Focal Loss; **(iv) BASE**, the traditional approach where a ResNet pre-trained model is fine-tuned with Cross Entropy loss.

Figure 7 shows the training curves of the highest performance model (OpenData-RESN). There is a larger difference between validation and training split in the brand category training because it is more difficult to make generalizations as it contains more categories and many of them look very similar in general (the package) but with some details different (the logo of the brand). This is less the case in material and packaging type training, where, for example, for the packaging type, the object shape characteristics are more universal.

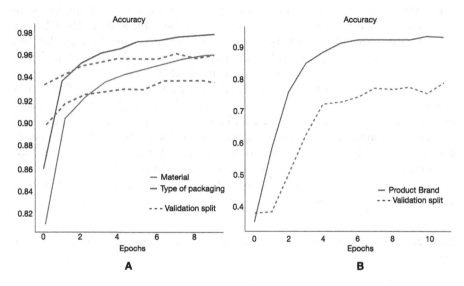

Fig. 7. Training curves of the highest performance model (OpenData-RESN). In **A**, the training of material and type of packaging model, and in **B**, Brand and attention module training. In dashed, the performance of the model in the validation split (5% of training dataset).

The data pre-processing was the same for each of the models evaluated, the images were loaded and converted from RGB to BGR, then each color channel was zero-centered for the ImageNet dataset without pixel intensity scaling. After the data pre-processing, feature extraction was performed using a pre-trained CNN model directly from the images without performing features selection. Hyperparameter selection was manually performed on the cross-validation split (5% of training split), and the samples of each split remained the same in all the experiments (Table 1).

Table 1. Training hyperparameters used in all the experiments.

Hyperparameter	Value
Learning Rate	0.003
Epochs	10, 8
Batch size	500
Radom seed	1

4.3 Model Evaluation

Table 2 summarizes the performance of the evaluated models. In blue is the performance over the source dataset, and in green is the performance over the target dataset. The metric used is the non-zero average macro-F1-score. The non-zero means that classes without samples will not be considered in the F1-score computation to avoid division by zero. Given the unbalanced target dataset, the F1-score is used as the evaluation metric as it penalizes lower precision and recall. The proposed approach OpenData-ResN achieved the highest result with ResNet50 as the feature extractor. Although the average macro F1-score is almost similar between the sources and the target datasets (1%), there is a major difference in two categories: material (-15 on target) and brand (+23 on target) The difference in the material performance may be due to the prediction depends of specific visual features that can be miss leading, for instance, packages that may look like other material (plastic as aluminum). On the other hand, in source datasets, many samples are labeled as "other" that may look very similar to a brand in the target dataset.

Table 2. Models performance evaluation results. The metric used is the macro F1-score (Sect. 3.1)

MODEL	Source Dataset				Target Dataset			
	F1 MAT	F1 TYPE	F1 BRAND	F1 AVG	F1 MAT	F1 TYPE	F1 BRAND	F1 AVG
OpenData-RESN	0,94	0,96	0,65	0,85	0,79	0,90	0,88	0,86
OpenData-NoFL	0,94	0,95	0,65	0,85	0,74	0,84	0,88	0,82
OpenData-MOBIL	0,93	0,94	0,68	0,85	0,73	0,83	0,85	0,80
OpenData-VGG16	0,93	0,94	0,66	0,84	0,72	0,81	0,88	0,80
BASE	0,75	0,78	0,84	0,79	0,75	0,78	0,59	0,71

Figure 8 shows the confusion matrices of material and type of packaging of OpenData-RESN in the target dataset. Worth noting that the target dataset is extremely unbalanced (Fig. 6). Additionally, there is one class (organic) that does not have evaluation samples, thus, it is not taken into account to calculate the evaluation metric (non-zero average macro-F1 score) due to zero division in the recall computation. Also, most of the miss classification occurs in the classes with more samples ("easy classes"), and the reason for this could be the use of the Focal loss and that the model can learn the difficult classes due to it being trained in a larger domain.

In order to evaluate the effect of the Focal loss, two brand classifiers were trained with and without Focal Loss, achieving 84% with Focal loss and 59% trained with Cross-Entropy loss.

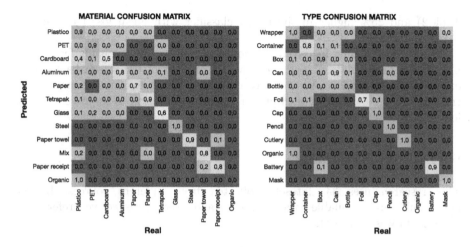

Fig. 8. Normalized confusion matrices by prediction of materials (left) and type of packaging (right) of the highest performance model (OpenData-RESN) on the target dataset.

5 Conclusions

This article presents a TL approach for using multiple source datasets from different domains with incomplete labels (Sect. 3) with three main elements: a training pipeline, an attention module, and a focal loss for missing labels. The approach was validated in a case study for waste identification using an image-based multi-label model with three categories: material, type of packaging, and product brand (Sect. 4).

The proposed approach performs better than the standard form of training custom models (15% increase in average macro F1-score, see Table 2) in the target domain. At the same time, the model trained with the proposed approach has a similar performance considering all the domains (85% average macro F1-score). The model was not biased toward the classes with more samples, given that the dataset was highly unbalanced (Fig. 6) and was able to differentiate the classes in both domains (Table 2).

The selection of the *feature extractor* has little impact on the performance regarding (1% in all the domains and 6% with the target). These differences could be due to the size of the feature map of each of the evaluated architectures.

The difference in the performance of the model regarding the prediction categories (11% between material and type of packaging) could be due to some categories using mode "generalizable" image features, for instance, the type of packaging is related to the shape of the object that is the same in different contexts opposite to the brand or the material that depends uniquely of the object appearance.

The inclusion of the Focal Loss has a positive impact on the performance of the models, 4% higher in the OpenData models on the target dataset (see

Table 2) and 25% higher in the brand classifier with Focal loss (see the last paragraph of Sect. 4.3).

Future work should focus on techniques and algorithms for using fewer samples of the target dataset and reducing the impact of the image background on inter-domain models. Additionally, exploring different electromagnetic spectra and lighting conditions with proper camera calibration to improve material identification.

6   Dataset Statement

This research uses 34 datasets collected from different sources. In the next link are available the sources and their respective references: Open Data waste datasets.

References

1. Arnold, L., Rebecchi, S., Chevallier, S., Paugam-Moisy, H.: An introduction to deep learning. In: European Symposium on Artificial Neural Networks (ESANN) (2011)
2. Chen, G., et al.: Environmental, energy, and economic analysis of integrated treatment of municipal solid waste and sewage sludge: a case study in China. Sci. Total Environ. **647**, 1433–1443 (2019)
3. He, K., Zhang, X., Ren, S., Sun, J.: Deep residual learning for image recognition. In: Proceedings of the IEEE Conference on Computer Vision and Pattern Recognition, pp. 770–778 (2016)
4. Hoornweg, D., Bhada-Tata, P.: What a waste: a global review of solid waste management (2012)
5. Howard, A.G., et al.: MobileNets: efficient convolutional neural networks for mobile vision applications. arXiv preprint arXiv:1704.04861 (2017)
6. Jadon, S.: An overview of deep learning architectures in few-shot learning domain. arXiv preprint arXiv:2008.06365 (2020)
7. Kaur, P., Khehra, B.S., Mavi, E.B.S.: Data augmentation for object detection: a review. In: 2021 IEEE International Midwest Symposium on Circuits and Systems (MWSCAS), pp. 537–543. IEEE (2021)
8. Khan, A.A., Laghari, A.A., Awan, S.A.: Machine learning in computer vision: a review. EAI Endorsed Trans. Scalable Inf. Syst. **8**(32), e4 (2021)
9. Kingma, D.P., Ba, J.: Adam: a method for stochastic optimization. arXiv preprint arXiv:1412.6980 (2014)
10. Leal Filho, W., et al.: An overview of the problems posed by plastic products and the role of extended producer responsibility in Europe. J. Clean. Prod. **214**, 550–558 (2019)
11. Lin, T.Y., Goyal, P., Girshick, R., He, K., Dollár, P.: Focal loss for dense object detection. In: Proceedings of the IEEE International Conference on Computer Vision, pp. 2980–2988 (2017)
12. Murray-Rust, P.: Open data in science. Nat. Precedings, p. 1 (2008)
13. Nikolenko, S.I.: Synthetic data for deep learning. arXiv preprint arXiv:1909.11512 (2019)

14. Oluwadipe, S., Garelick, H., McCarthy, S., Purchase, D.: A critical review of household recycling barriers in the United Kingdom. Waste Manag. Res. **40**(7), 905–918 (2022)
15. Panwar, H., et al.: AquaVision: automating the detection of waste in water bodies using deep transfer learning. Case Stud. Chem. Environ. Eng. **2**, 100026 (2020)
16. Patel, R., Patel, S.: A comprehensive study of applying convolutional neural network for computer vision. Int. J. Adv. Sci. Technol. **6**(6), 2161–2174 (2020)
17. Qin, L.W., et al.: Precision measurement for industry 4.0 standards towards solid waste classification through enhanced imaging sensors and deep learning model. Wirel. Commun. Mob. Comput. **2021**, 1–10 (2021)
18. Simonyan, K., Zisserman, A.: Very deep convolutional networks for large-scale image recognition. arXiv preprint arXiv:1409.1556 (2014)
19. Singh, S., Gautam, J., Rawat, S., Gupta, V., Kumar, G., Verma, L.P.: Evaluation of transfer learning based deep learning architectures for waste classification. In: 2021 4th International Symposium on Advanced Electrical and Communication Technologies (ISAECT), pp. 01–07. IEEE (2021)
20. Weiss, K., Khoshgoftaar, T.M., Wang, D.: A survey of transfer learning. J. Big data **3**(1), 1–40 (2016)
21. Woo, S., Park, J., Lee, J.Y., Kweon, I.S.: CBAM: convolutional block attention module. In: Proceedings of the European Conference on Computer Vision (ECCV), pp. 3–19 (2018)
22. Xie, S., Girshick, R., Dollár, P., Tu, Z., He, K.: Aggregated residual transformations for deep neural networks. In: Proceedings of the IEEE Conference on Computer Vision and Pattern Recognition, pp. 1492–1500 (2017)
23. Zhuang, F., et al.: A comprehensive survey on transfer learning. Proc. IEEE **109**(1), 43–76 (2020)

Instructional Strategies for Performance Improvement in Algebra: A Systematic Mapping

Shirley Tatiana Garcia-Carrascal🆔, Laura Daniela Sepulveda-Vega🆔, and Dewar Rico-Bautista(✉)🆔

Universidad Francisco de Paula Santander Ocaña, Sede Algodonal Vía Acolsure, Ocaña 546551, Colombia
{stgarciac,ldsepulvedav,dwricob}@ufpso.edu.co

Abstract. Mathematics, specifically in the field of Algebra, becomes complicated for students to understand and this is reflected in their low academic grades. Additionally, in the results of reports of the international program for the evaluation of students in which Colombia is located with a lower score than the OECD average. This problem generates stress and anxiety, which can affect their ability to concentrate and retain information. The social and affective environment can also be an important factor in the learning of algebra. The methodology used for the selection of documents was systematic mapping. A total of 138 documents were found and, applying inclusion and exclusion criteria, 40 of these were selected. The most relevant current trends were found, which are the use of educational software and strategies such as gamification. It is important to find effective didactic tools that have the capacity to teach algebra in an effective way to students.

Keywords: Algebra · Didactic strategies · Gamification · Systematic mapping · Performance

1 Introduction

In Colombia, students in eighth grade face a new subject, this is Algebra and it is perceived as a subject that brings with it several difficulties such as problems with learning and this is reflected in their low academic grades [1], since the student has to explore terms, variables, and values that are unknown and brings with it mathematical anxiety [2,3], which limits him/her in the learning process.

An exact amount of 9000 students from Colombia participate in the Program for International Student Assessment (PISA) test, it is of vital importance to highlight that this program has been created to provide information that will allow countries that are part of the OECD to adopt strategies or make decisions that are necessary to improve educational levels, the tests are based on problem-solving with the use of realistic situations. The results, according to the PISA report, Colombia ranks below the average of all other countries belonging to the

© The Author(s), under exclusive license to Springer Nature Switzerland AG 2024
M. Tabares et al. (Eds.): CCC 2023, CCIS 1924, pp. 188–198, 2024.
https://doi.org/10.1007/978-3-031-47372-2_17

OECD with a mathematics score of 391, about 35% of students in Colombia reached Level 2 or higher in mathematics (OECD average: 76.

It is important to mention that, according to the digital bulletin of the Saber 11 tests, access to information technologies such as the Internet and computers in both the academic and family environment brings with it positive and significant aspects to the results of the PISA tests [4,5]. The average for students with internet access was higher compared to students who did not have these tools; taking the specific case of the Pacific region and comparing the results of students who have or do not have access to the internet and new technologies, it was observed that students who do not have internet access scored 211 and those students who do not have access to computers scored 186.

In the national report on the results of the 3rd, 5th, 9th, and 11th grade 2022 application it is stated that the proportion of students in the highest level of performance is quite low, with a percentage of less than 6%, the national average of the saber tests rose to 400 points; it is worth specifying that the score scale is from 100 to 700 points [2,6,7].

The tests carried out show that people belonging to a high socioeconomic level tend to obtain better results in Mathematics, it can be affirmed that one of the causes of the deficiency in the subject of mathematics is due to the socioeconomic level of the student, since he/she does not have the necessary tools to strengthen his/her knowledge [8,9]. The current methodology presented by schools in Colombia is traditional and it is necessary to update these methods and strategies aligned with technology to increase the academic performance of students in this subject [10–14].

This is why another cause of low performance lies in the lack of innovative academic proposals in teaching that awaken and encourage the interest of students through different methodologies that contribute to enhancing motivation [15], Educational organizations require teaching strategies that promote a cognitive commitment in the acquisition of new knowledge, highlighting as a first instance the resolution of mathematical problems due to the low competencies that students present in mathematics [16,17]. Currently, there is research available by different authors, where strategies and teaching methodologies applied in mathematics and its branches are observed [4,18], but there is no explicit document in which the techniques used effectively are reflected, in order to facilitate the work of future researchers on this topic, a systematic mapping is made in which all research on the use of strategies, methodologies and techniques aligned to technology to improve academic performance in the subject of algebra is reflected [5,19–21].

It should be considered that the main objective of the strategies is to help all students acquire knowledge in a more effective way, to develop skills in relation to critical thinking, and to achieve motivation for class participation [22]. It is necessary to emphasize that to meet the challenge of increasing students' academic performance, it is the duty of teachers to take the lead and implement these new learning strategies [1,6,23,24].

This document has the following structure: Sect. 2 provides the methodology used to carry out the proposed systematic mapping. Section 3 shows the results obtained and finally, Sect. 4 presents the conclusions of the research carried out.

2   Methodology

In this review, the methodology proposed by Revelo [11] was used. The series of steps to carry out the proposed systematic mapping are detailed below [25].

2.1   Design Research Questions

The objective of the systematic mapping is to find the strategies and techniques used aligned to technology to improve academic performance in the subject of algebra. The following review questions were formulated:

- What are the most relevant trends you have employed as a didactic strategy for teaching/learning Algebra?
- What gamification technologies have been used in teaching in areas such as algebra and mathematics?

2.2   Perform a Detailed Search for Documents Based on the Keywords Already Defined

Table 1 shows the keywords and their synonyms. Boolean operators were used to concatenate them and generate the search equation, as shown below:

- *(algebra OR math OR education) AND (e-learning OR teaching) AND (application OR app)*

Table 1. Key words and related terms.

Keywords	Related terms
algebra	math, education
e-learning	teaching
application	app
teaching strategies	active learning

Electronic databases such as ACM Digital Library, Science Direct, Scopus, and IEEE Xplore were used for the literature search. The results can be seen in Table 2.

Table 2. Numbers of documents found.

Database	Quantity
ACM Digital Library	30
ScienceDirect	18
Scopus	43
IEEE Xplore	47
Total	138

2.3 Perform Exclusion and Inclusion of Documents According to the Established Criteria

The following were the inclusion criteria:

- A defined period of 6 years (2017–2023).
- Articles whose abstract is consistent with the subject matter.
- Articles related to education or directly to the subject of Algebra or mathematics.

The following were the exclusion criteria:

- Articles in languages other than English or Spanish.
- Articles published in a period greater than 6 years.
- Articles whose abstract is not related to the subject matter addressed.
- Incomplete and in some cases duplicated articles.

2.4 Select Documents with Relevant Information on the Subject

After the application of the criteria of the previous section, the correct selection of articles is made, it is necessary to carefully read each title and summary of this, and in some cases, the conclusions, to verify that the information is related to the topic addressed and thus record each of the related articles in a document, see Table 3.

Table 3. Numbers of selected documents.

Database	Quantity
ACM Digital Library	12
ScienceDirect	5
Scopus	7
IEEE Xplore	16
Total	40

2.5   Conduct a Thorough and In-Depth Analysis of the Documents Included in the Systematic Mapping

The analysis carried out was aimed at answering the review questions posed in Sect. 2.1, each selected article was subjected to an exhaustive review where the data and mapping of the study were extracted. The documents were analyzed and classified to extract those with greater relevance and usefulness based on the information.

3   Results

This section shows the results obtained from the proposed systematic mapping, the main objective of which is to obtain an overview of the best methodologies and strategies used aligned with technology for the teaching/learning process of the algebra subject and thus improve students' academic performance. The series of steps presented in Sect. 2.1, Sect. 2.2, Sect. 2.3, and Sect. 2.4 were carried out. In the following, based on the analysis and study, the most relevant results that will answer the review questions are presented.

3.1   What are the Most Relevant Trends You Have Employed as a Didactic Strategy for Teaching/Learning Algebra?

Table 4 shows the most relevant trends and approaches that were found as a strategy for teaching/learning algebra in classrooms.

The motivation of students is one of the main requirements to acquire the necessary knowledge, which is why the best methodologies should be used focusing and focusing on the convenient ones according to the needs of the class [3, 21]. Although gamification is seen as a tool that brings great benefits, it is not the only methodology with which to improve academic performance in the subject of algebra, all current trends should be known to provide students with better learning experiences [3]. It is important to mention that, as studied in the article, it has been shown that gamification increases user engagement, especially in learning/training-related contexts that have a certain amount of daily routine work [36].

3.2   What Gamification Technologies Have Been Used in Teaching in Areas Such as Algebra and Mathematics?

Moodle learning management system (LMS) is one of the technologies mostly used in teaching/learning processes in education, according to Lampropoulos [37], this provides interaction between different traditional teaching techniques and digital learning resources, many of the educational institutions have employed LMS and recommend using it due to its various advantages, it allows creativity to teachers to develop specific course material so that dynamic and entertaining techniques are used on the platform in a way that integrates gamification elements to enhance the student experience and increase motivation such as points, rankings, rewards or any other type of motivator to recognize student achievements and progress.

Table 4. Educational trends and approaches that are being used successfully to improve algebra learning.

Trends	Brief definition
Problem-Based Learning (PBL)	It is an educational approach where students work in teams to solve real-life problems, exchange ideas, and can solve problems or achieve a common goal (Problem-Solving) [26]
Online Learning	Students work with the support of technology through online tools. Seeing the possibility of disrupting traditional teaching/learning methodologies and processes for the benefit of students [27,28]
Augmented and Virtual Reality	Augmented reality shows virtual elements in the environment and virtual reality shows a simulated digital world, both technologies help to learn in a more fun and interesting way [5]
Gamification	Gamification [29], is inspired by game theory/game design to be used in a different domain from it, in this case, to enhance the learner's own motivation and engagement towards learning [24,30,31]
Computational thinking	More than an approach, it is a skill that helps to approach complex problems in a structured way and to find efficient and effective solutions [32–34]. It develops logical and computational skills in the student while strengthening the understanding of mathematical concepts [35]

- In the article [21], the authors explored the peer pressure theory mentioned earlier by SLK Carden and SA Fowler by doing so through gamification. The following gamification elements were introduced to the experimental group consisting of 229 final year computer science students: points, badges, rewards, levels, ranks, and leaderboards. They were also provided with initial information about the gamification environment. The results of applying this experiment indicate that student performance in the gamified environment was statistically better than performance in traditional classrooms. Gamification improves students' grades over time. The authors confirmed through their experimental study that gamification can be used to improve students' academic performance.

- Intelligent tutoring based on a concept-effect relationship (CER) model is a concept map-oriented approach gamification technology that provides learners with personalized learning guidance. This system initiates by identifying the learning sequence relationships between concepts, each prerequisite concept affects the learning of the following higher level (more complex) concepts. The system uses TIRT which is the test item relationship table to establish the degree of association between test items and related concepts, this table has values that indicate the importance of each test item for each concept and is used to calculate the error rate of each student [14].

- In the article [21], they implement gamification for the theoretical sessions of a course consisting of 41 students. Two types of games are performed, games at the beginning of classes to remember the concepts of the previous day and games during the theoretical classes, this using a technological tool called Wooclap, which allows students to participate in games during class, with real-time interactions that provide feedback.

- In the practical sessions, the Discovery Learning instructional model was used, using the didactic strategy WebQuest, all this to get students to learn or improve their research skills and find solutions to the problems presented on their own. The results of this experiment confirm that the use of gamification and discovery learning improve academic results since the average grade of the group has increased by 0.84 points compared to the previous course and the total number of failures has decreased by 15.55%, in addition to the fact that students were more motivated in class because they have fun, they feel positive and this makes them pay more attention in class [3].

- Gamified learning platforms such as Kahoot! and Quizizz which are effective tools for interactive learning and formative assessment, are popular and well received with excellent student learning responses increasing student performance with moderate to large positive effect, teachers can use such platforms to make the learning process more engaging and entertaining [2].

- The project [21], authors design ALGEBrigth, which is a Game-Based Learning (GBL) mobile application, easy to understand and use, available at any time and is intended for beginner students in algebra, with the added value that they can customize the character they play with and has the built-in instructor/teacher module to monitor student participation and achievement. The goal of the game is not only to evaluate the student but to inform the user where he/she made the mistake each time he/she answers the question wrong.

- The study [38] developed an interactive mathematics learning application using Augmented Reality technology, together with tools such as Unity and Vuforia, which offers students to improve their interest in studying by exploring mathematical concepts in 3D in a motivating and practical way.

- PolyMath application software can be delivered to many students who learn at their own pace, encouraging learning. Through experimentation and curious observations, students acquire useful information about the mathematical topic at hand [38].

In the review of the articles it is evident that in most cases the use of gamification in school classrooms is proposed using different technologies for its correct implementation, in some cases didactic tools such as mobile applications, web applications, or learning platforms are used [17,28], a part of the documents investigated use applications that are available to the general public and the other part of the documents use applications that have been properly developed [1,26,27].

All this is in order to motivate students to learn mathematical topics, in general, these reacted positively, seeing an improvement in the performance of tests or exercises, It is worth mentioning that not all the proposed tools were implemented, also gamification improves learning skills and personal development and autonomy of the student; although there are more advantages and benefits of using the gamification strategy, it is important to recognize that it also includes some disadvantages such as possible dependence on technology, limited access to mobile devices, which can generate inequality in this form of learning, it can also be a possible distraction, and to implement this strategy has high cost in the development of applications and their maintenance [39–41].

4 Conclusions

Technology used as a teaching/learning strategy in the educational system is booming due to its effectiveness; academic performance is a research topic of relevance due to the benefits it brings specifically in the improvement of study in the subject of algebra because this is one of the most difficult subjects in the learning process.

In the era of technology, it is necessary that teachers opt for different teaching methods and innovation, it is unpredictable that the new use of strategies that respond adequately to the educational processes and that in this way can promote effective learning of students. This is why the gamification technique is used to create an environment that promotes motivation.

It is deduced that thanks to systematic mapping, it is possible to provide the research and educational community with a holistic view of the research on strategies and techniques to improve skills and academic performance in the subject of mathematics and its branches. We found 40 antecedents, of which about 80% used technology as a didactic tool for teaching mathematics, and also used various techniques of gamification, which suggests that the use of gamification as a strategy for learning is an effective technique, using gamification principles such as the pedagogical principle, rewards and achievements, feedback and monitoring.

References

1. Li, Q., Yin, X., Yin, W., Dong, X., Li, Q.: Evaluation of gamification techniques in learning abilities for higher school students using FAHP and EDAS methods. Soft. Comput. (2023). https://doi.org/10.1007/s00500-023-08179-9

2. Huesca, G., Campos, G., Larre, M., Pérez-Lezama, C.: Implementation of a mixed strategy of gamification and flipped learning in undergraduate basic programming courses. Educ. Sci. (Basel) **13**, 474 (2023)
3. Guo, N., Chen, J.: Application of learning motivation theory in mathematics teaching in primary schools. In: 2021 2nd Asia-Pacific Conference on Image Processing, Electronics and Computers, pp. 626–629. ACM, New York (2021)
4. Kaldarova, B., et al.: Applying game-based learning to a primary school class in computer science terminology learning. Front. Educ. (Lausanne) (2023). https://doi.org/10.3389/feduc.2023.1100275
5. Gamage, S.H.P.W., Ayres, J.R., Behrend, M.B.: A systematic review on trends in using moodle for teaching and learning. Int. J. STEM Educ. **9**(1), 1–24 (2022). https://doi.org/10.1186/s40594-021-00323-x
6. Klock, A.C.T., Ogawa, A.N., Gasparini, I., Pimenta, M.S.: Does gamification matter? In: Proceedings of the 33rd Annual ACM Symposium on Applied Computing, pp. 2006–2012. ACM, New York (2018)
7. Ahmad, A., Zeshan, F., Khan, M.S., Marriam, R., Ali, A., Samreen, A.: The impact of gamification on learning outcomes of computer science majors. ACM Trans. Comput. Educ. **20**, 1–25 (2020)
8. Rodrigues, L.F., Oliveira, A., Rodrigues, H.: Main gamification concepts: a systematic mapping study. Heliyon **5**, e01993 (2019)
9. Wang, Y., Qiao, Y., Wang, X.: Effects of gamified learning platforms on students' learning outcomes: a meta-analysis taking Kahoot and Quizizz as examples. In: Proceedings of the 13th International Conference on Education Technology and Computers, pp. 105–110. ACM, New York (2021)
10. Peixoto, M., Silva, C.: A gamification requirements catalog for educational software. In: Proceedings of the Symposium on Applied Computing, pp. 1108–1113. ACM, New York (2017)
11. Revelo Sánchez, O., Collazos Ordoñez, C.A., Jiménez Toledo, J.A.: La gamificación como estrategia didáctica para la enseñanza/aprendizaje de la programación: un mapeo sistemático de literatura. Lámpsakos, pp. 31–46 (2018)
12. Jurado-Castro, J.M., Vargas-Molina, S., Gómez-Urquiza, J.L., Benítez-Porres, J.: Effectiveness of real-time classroom interactive competition on academic performance: a systematic review and meta-analysis. PeerJ Comput. Sci. **9**, e1310 (2023)
13. Hosseini, C., Humlung, O., Fagerstrøm, A., Haddara, M.: An experimental study on the effects of gamification on task performance. Procedia Comput. Sci. **196**, 999–1006 (2022)
14. Tan, C.W., Ling, L., Yu, P.-D., Hang, C.N., Wong, M.F.: Mathematics gamification in mobile app software for personalized learning at scale. In: 2020 IEEE Integrated STEM Education Conference (ISEC), pp. 1–5. IEEE (2020)
15. Prieto Andreu, J.M.: Revisión sistemática sobre la evaluación de propuestas de gamificación en siete disciplinas educativas. Teoría Educ. Rev. Interuniversitaria **34**, 189–214 (2021)
16. Klock, A.C.T., Gasparini, I., Pimenta, M.S., Hamari, J.: Tailored gamification: a review of literature. Int. J. Hum Comput Stud. **144**, 102495 (2020)
17. Çubukçu, Ç., Wang, B., Goodman, L., Mangina, E.: Gamification for teaching Java. In: Proceedings of the 10th EAI International Conference on Simulation Tools and Techniques, pp. 120–130. ACM, New York (2017)
18. Pastushenko, O.: Gamification in assignments. In: Extended Abstracts of the Annual Symposium on Computer-Human Interaction in Play Companion Extended Abstracts, pp. 47–53. ACM, New York (2019)

19. Vale, I., Barbosa, A.: Active learning strategies for an effective mathematics teaching and learning. Eur. J. Sci. Math. Educ. **11**, 573–588 (2023)
20. Safitri, M., Suryani, N., Budiyono, G.N., Sukarmin, G.N.: Integrated mathematics teaching material of computer-supported collaborative learning (CSCL). In: ICLIQE 2021: Proceeding of The 5th International Conference on Learning Innovation and Quality Education, pp. 1–7. ACM, New York (2021)
21. de Castro, J.H.C.C., Divino, R.J.Z., Cambe, W.J., Lati, B.T., Fabito, B.S., Jamis, M.N.: ALGEbright: design of an avatar customization game-based learning for algebra. In: 2019 IEEE Student Conference on Research and Development (SCOReD), pp. 49–52. IEEE (2019)
22. Zhan, Z., He, L., Tong, Y., Liang, X., Guo, S., Lan, X.: The effectiveness of gamification in programming education: evidence from a meta-analysis. Comput. Educ.: Artif. Intell. **3**, 100096 (2022)
23. Pacheco-Velazquez, E.: Using gamification to develop self-directed learning. In: Proceedings of the 2020 International Conference on Education Development and Studies, pp. 1–5. ACM, New York (2020)
24. Murad, D.F., Dwi Wijanarko, B., Leandros, R., Akrama, Ramadhan, F.I., Ade Putra Siregar, Y.: Interaction design of mathematics learning applications for elementary school students. In: 2021 3rd International Symposium on Material and Electrical Engineering Conference (ISMEE), pp. 37–41. IEEE (2021)
25. Aldalur, I., Perez, A.: Gamification and discovery learning: motivating and involving students in the learning process. Heliyon **9**, e13135 (2023)
26. Chugh, R., Turnbull, D.: Gamification in education: a citation network analysis using CitNetExplorer. Contemp. Educ. Technol. **15**, ep405 (2023)
27. Aryasa, K., Fabrianes, J.C., Irwan, A.M., Sy, H., Paulus, Y.T., Irmayana, A.: The use of game puzzle application for presenting arithmetic problems. In: 2021 3rd International Conference on Cybernetics and Intelligent System (ICORIS), pp. 1–4. IEEE (2021)
28. Cukierman, U.R., et al.: A student-centered approach to learning mathematics and physics in engineering freshmen courses. In: 2018 World Engineering Education Forum - Global Engineering Deans Council (WEEF-GEDC), pp. 1–5. IEEE (2018)
29. Rico-Bautista, D., Hernandez, L.L., Suárez, A.: La gamificación y arquitectura funcional: Estrategia práctica en el proceso de enseñanza/aprendizaje usando la tecnología. Rev. Ingenio UFPSO (2017)
30. Loyola, C.J.O., De Luna, L.R., Diloy, M., Rivera, V.: Systematic mapping: a study of gamified education tool for teaching basic mathematics in flexible learning option (FLO). In: Proceedings of the 6th International Conference on Digital Technology in Education, pp. 52–59. ACM, New York (2022)
31. Mera, C., Ruiz-Cagigas, G., Navarro-Guzmán, J.I., Aragón-Mendizábal, E., Delgado, C., Aguilar-Villagrán, M.: APP designed for early math training. Magnitudes comparison. In: Proceedings of the 5th International Conference on Technological Ecosystems for Enhancing Multiculturality, pp. 1–8. ACM, New York (2017)
32. Rico-Bautista, N.A., Rico-Bautista, D.W., Arévalo-Pérez, N.: Construction of an amusement park using STEAM and LEGO education to participate in the science fair. J. Phys: Conf. Ser. (2021). https://doi.org/10.1088/1742-6596/1981/1/012019
33. Rueda-Rueda, J.S., Rico-Bautista, D., Flórez-Solano, É.: Education in ICT: teaching to use, teaching to protect oneself and teaching to create [Educación en TIC: Enseñar a usar, enseñar a protegerse y enseñar a crear tecnología]. RISTI - Revi. Iberica Sist. Tecnol. Inform. **2019**, 252–264 (2019)

34. Rico-Bautista, N.A., Rico-Bautista, D.W., Medina-Cárdenas, Y.C., Arévalo-Pérez, N.: Case studies: learning strategy incorporating Lego education in the seventh-grade math course at the school. J. Phys: Conf. Ser. (2020). https://doi.org/10.1088/1742-6596/1674/1/012014

35. Dahalan, F., Alias, N., Shaharom, M.S.N.: Gamification and game based learning for vocational education and training: a systematic literature review. Educ. Inf. Technol. (Dordr) (2023). https://doi.org/10.1007/s10639-022-11548-w

36. Tondello, G.F., Nacke, L.E.: Gamification. In: Extended Abstracts of the 2018 CHI Conference on Human Factors in Computing Systems, pp. 1–4. ACM, New York (2018)

37. Lampropoulos, G., Keramopoulos, E., Diamantaras, K., Evangelidis, G.: Augmented reality and gamification in education: a systematic literature review of research, applications, and empirical studies. Appl. Sci. **12**, 6809 (2022)

38. Chao, W.-H., Yang, C.-Y., Chang, R.-C.: A study of the interactive mathematics mobile application development. In: 2018 1st IEEE International Conference on Knowledge Innovation and Invention (ICKII), pp 248–249. IEEE (2018)

39. Çiftçi, A., Topçu, M.S.: Improving early childhood pre-service teachers' computational thinking skills through the unplugged computational thinking integrated STEM approach. Think Skills Creat. **49**, 101337 (2023)

40. Trenholm, S., Peschke, J.: Teaching undergraduate mathematics fully online: a review from the perspective of communities of practice. Int. J. Educ. Technol. High. Educ. **17**(1), 1–18 (2020). https://doi.org/10.1186/s41239-020-00215-0

41. Rehman, N., Zhang, W., Mahmood, A., Fareed, M.Z., Batool, S.: Fostering twenty-first century skills among primary school students through math project-based learning. Humanit. Soc. Sci. Commun. **10**, 424 (2023)

Model for Fruit Tree Classification Through Aerial Images

Valentina Escobar Gómez[(✉)], Diego Gustavo Guevara Bernal,
and Javier Francisco López Parra

Faculty of Engineering, Master's Degree in Artificial Intelligence, Pontificia
Universidad Javeriana, Bogotá, Colombia
{valentina.escobar,d_guevara,jlopez}@javeriana.edu.co
{valentina.escobar,d_guevara,jlopez}@javeriana.edu.co

Abstract. Manual measurements and visual inspection of trees are
common practices among farmers, which incur labor costs and time-
consuming operations to obtain information about the state of their crops
at a specific moment. Considering that an approximately 1-hectare (ha)
plot of land can have up to 1100 planted trees [1], this becomes a challenging task, and human error in such cases tends to be high. To address
these issues, the emphasis is placed on the use of Convolutional Neural
Networks (CNNs); however, CNNs alone are not robust enough to detect
complex features in any given problem. Therefore, this article proposes a
model that supports agricultural activities in organizing their tasks. The
main procedure of the model is the classification of fruit trees (mango,
citrus, and banana) using aerial images captured by a drone (UAV) in the
Colombian context. The technique employed in this procedure is known
as Mask R-CNN, which enables automatic segmentation of fruit trees.

Keywords: Artificial Intelligence · fruit trees · aerial images · deep
learning · classification · agriculture · resources · production ·
investigation · crop · support · monitoring · features

1 Introduction

In recent years, there has been exponential growth in food production worldwide,
and it is projected that agricultural production will increase by 14% within the
next 10 years. By 2031, it is expected that 18% of global food exports will come
from Latin America [2].

The production of fruit crops is an important sector in Colombia's economy.
Processes have been improving and new proposals have been introduced in the
agricultural sector, addressing topics such as precision agriculture. Precision agriculture is described as a set of advanced technologies including sensors, GPS,
drones, and Geographic Information Systems (GIS) [3] to gather information
about crops and their surroundings, efficiently applying it to their management.

M. Tabares et al. (Eds.): CCC 2023, CCIS 1924, pp. 199–214, 2024.
https://doi.org/10.1007/978-3-031-47372-2_18

While collected data allows for a detailed description of the structural and morphological characteristics of trees, in practice, this data is still collected manually, especially in rural areas of Colombia, which are often difficult to access and lack the necessary resources to acquire all the technologies required for smart farming [4].

For this reason, an intuitive and accessible model is needed, where resources used are specific and data collection is straightforward. The suggestion is to use Artificial Intelligence (AI) paradigms as the technical foundation along with low-cost technologies. Artificial Intelligence (AI) is defined as the ability of machines and computational systems to imitate human intelligence and perform tasks such as learning, pattern recognition, and decision-making, among others [5]. Specifically, machine learning is a technique that allows machines to learn from data and improve their performance in specific tasks [6], such as image classification, which is commonly used in agriculture to analyze the condition of crops and detect early signs of diseases, pests, or overall plantation conditions before they become major issues.

Unmanned Aerial Vehicles (UAVs), including drones, enable flights over large land areas and capture high-resolution images containing a wealth of data [7]. The demand for drones has increased due to their numerous applications and uses, including crop monitoring by taking photographs of tree canopies or videos [8].

One of the challenges when detecting trees through aerial images is the delineation and recognition of fruit trees in irregular terrains (as it is common to find large territories with mountainous topography in South America [9]). Additionally, many of these trees are planted in a disorganized manner, causing them to grow too close to other trees, making it difficult to detect each individual considering that only the canopies are used in this approach.

Taking into account the challenges of working with irregular terrains, this paper presents a model that considers and analyzes different variables (topography, lighting, space) to classify trees by type. This model can serve as a source for future research and as a support tool for monitoring the condition of trees in rural areas of Colombia, considering the increasing use of technology in the country and the widespread interest in crop management in South America [10].

Subsequent sections will present the case study, materials, methods, and the overall procedure carried out to apply the proposed model, based on the technical foundation of Mask R-CNN. The results of adopting this type of neural network to the geographical conditions of the case will also be discussed.

2   Model

This section presents the general model for fruit tree classification (see Fig. 1).

2.1   Inputs

Initially, the terrain conditions are studied to define the variables to consider for executing the flight plan. An unmanned aerial vehicle (UAV) with a stabilizer-equipped camera capable of capturing photos in 4K resolution (4000 × 2250) is required. This high resolution allows for more explicit object recognition from an aerial perspective without being affected by device movement. Additionally, the UAV must have a GPS module and be able to integrate with a flight planning application (such as DJI Pilot [11], Dronelink [12], etc.) to adjust parameters such as altitude, speed, and area, which are necessary for executing flights in specific terrain conditions.

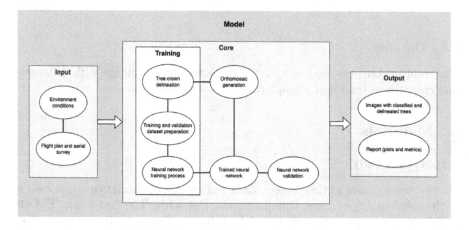

Fig. 1. Model for fruit tree classification. It consists of three main elements that constitute the inputs, the model core and the outputs.

The images captured by the UAV should be in the sRGB color space and properly georeferenced, taking into account ideal lighting conditions that are usually present around noon when the solar elevation angle is highest in areas located at mid-latitudes and in the tropics [13]. A solar elevation angle below 75° is not acceptable for capturing desired detail in photographs. Regarding terrain conditions with steep slopes or variable relief, it is ideal to fly at different altitudes [14] to capture details of taller or shorter trees as appropriate. Multiple flights at a single altitude should be sufficient in flat or regular terrains.

2.2   Model Core

Once the study and flight plan is completed and the images are obtained as the primary input, orthomosaics are generated. These orthomosaics are used for manually delineating the tree crowns, which serve as inputs for training the neural network. During the labeling process, individual trees are selected, and their corresponding type is defined (for this research, only mango, citrus, and banana trees are recognized). The labeled data is then used to create training and validation datasets.

Table 1. Flight plan parameters

Farm	Height	Duration (mm:ss)	Speed	Distance	Images
A	30m	22:10	14 km/h	4.4 km	504
	50m	10:44	24 km/h	2.8 km	184
	75m	07:20	31 km/h	2.0 km	86
B	25m	10:04	12 km/h	1.8 km	229
	30m	10:01	12 km/h	1.7 km	238

2.3 Outputs

The resulting outputs are two-fold: the respective terrain image with delineated and categorized trees and a graphical report with performance metrics.

3 Materials

3.1 Case Study

For the development of this project, data was recollected from two farms located in the municipality of Tena, Cundinamarca, Colombia. The first farm, "El Otro Lado", has an approximate area of 5 hectares. Additionally, it is characterized by irregular terrain, and some crops within the farm are not planted in rows or mix different types of trees, which can make crown segmentation challenging. The other farm under study, "El Paraíso", has an area of around 1.6 hectares. The terrain there is less irregular; however, there is a steeper slope, which results in more variations in the details obtained in the aerial photographs. This farm will be used solely to evaluate the finalized model.

3.2 Data Acquisition

The images were acquired using the DJI Mini 2 drone [15] and Dronelink application to automate flight plans [12] (see Fig. 2-a). These flights were typically conducted between 10:00 AM and 3:00 PM at three different altitudes, with a horizontal and vertical overlap ranging from 70% to 75%. It was established that the larger farm would be used to train the model while the second farm would be used to test its performance. Table 1 presents some average metrics of the flight plans per farm.

The flight plans were carried out in January, June, July, September, and December, mainly during 2022 and the beginning of 2023. On the same day, different altitudes were flown over each farm to capture greater detail of the tree crowns due to the differences in terrain relief and slope. A total of 8,438 georeferenced RGB images were obtained with a resolution of 4K (4000 × 2250), which were subsequently used to generate orthomosaics with the help of the open-source WebODM tool [16].

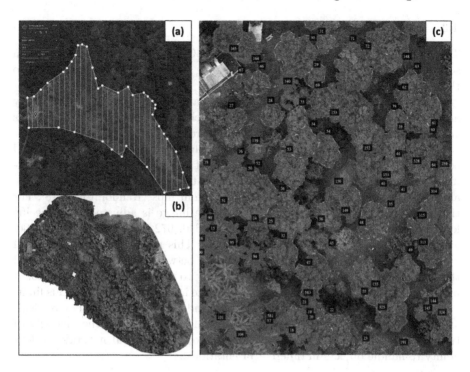

Fig. 2. (a) Example of a flight plan at 30 m from the study site; (b) orthomosaic generated from aerial images, and (c) examples of manually labeled fruit trees of different types highlighted in red. (Color figure online)

4   Methods

4.1   Orthomosaic Generation

As a first step, orthomosaics (see Fig. 2-b) were generated with WebODM [16] (an open-source software) to obtain a complete farm map in a single image. The process involves image processing, mosaic creation and finally the geometrically corrected and georreferenced image.

4.2   Crown Delineation Using Orthomosaics

Applications that allow for automatic crown delineation are scarce and often need help to accurately capture the boundary of each tree for input into a deep learning algorithm, especially when the trees are not planted in rows. Therefore, the crowns were manually delineated using the open-source program VGG Image Annotator (see Fig. 2-c) [17]. This was based on the knowledge of tree distribution in the farms and the separation between them. This tool does not require installation or setup, making it easy to resume the labeling work from any device. Twenty-two thousand five hundred sixty crowns were manually delineated and distributed as follows: 11,502 mango trees, 6,609 plantain trees, and 4,449 citrus trees.

4.3 Data Processing

The corresponding labels were exported in JSON format from the annotation software and underwent code processing using Python to adapt the format to the expected input for the neural network.

Analysis and processing of the data were carried out to ensure label quality and consistency, as well as to address specific challenges in the context, such as variability in the shape and size of fruit tree crowns.

Preprocessing stages were conducted, including contrast adjustment and color correction to enhance relevant details of the fruit tree crowns and minimize noise or inconsistencies in the images. Data augmentation techniques were also applied, such as image resizing and random flips (RandomFlip) [18]. For the resizing technique, the shorter side of the image is adjusted to a specific length. The values used for this purpose are 640, 672, 704, 736, 768, and 800, which define the final size of the shorter side. This means that the image will be resized so that the shorter side has a length between 640 and 800 pixels, and the longer side will be adjusted proportionally to maintain the aspect ratio. A maximum size of 1,333 pixels is set to ensure the images do not exceed this limit.

In the case of the random flip technique, random flips (horizontal or vertical) are applied to the images during training. This helps increase the diversity of training data in imbalanced classes and improves the neural network model's ability to handle objects in different orientations.

4.4 Data Partitioning

The data was divided into training (80%) and testing (20%). The distribution of labels per class is as follows: (a) mango training 9202; (b) citrus training 3559; (c) banana training 5287; (d) mango testing 2300; (e) citrus testing 890 and (f) banana testing 1322.

The data partitioning was done manually by selecting the majority of orthomosaics with ideal lighting conditions for the training set and a minority with less favorable conditions. The reverse process was applied for the test set. Out of 27 orthomosaics, 22 were selected for training and 5 for testing. Notably, orthomosaics from all three heights were distributed in each dataset.

4.5 Detectron 2 Framework

Detectron 2 [19] is an open-source deep learning framework that Facebook AI Research (FAIR) developed for object detection and instance segmentation tasks. This tool has a flexible architecture that allows customization and expansion of various components, such as backbone networks and feature extractors for research purposes. Considering the large amount of data received for the particular case study, scalability was necessary, which is achieved by using distributed training strategies and data parallelism (scaling across multiple GPUs) in Detectron. Mask R-CNN serves as the backbone along with ResNet for this investigation.

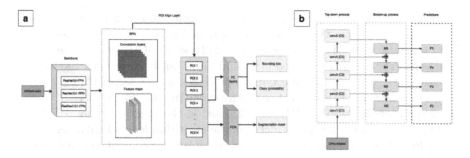

Fig. 3. (a) Operation of Detectron 2 with Mask R-CNN and ResNet-50-FPN as the base. ROI = Region of Interest, RPN = Region Proposal Network, FPN = Feature Pyramid Network, FC = Fully Connected Layer, FCN = Fully Convolutional Network. (b) Backbone Structure showing the interaction between the ResNet/ResNeXt network (green dashed line) and the Feature Pyramid Network (FPN) (orange dashed line), finally displaying the predictions (blue dashed line). (Color figure online)

4.6 Mask R-CNN

Mask R-CNN [20], like Detectron 2, is developed by Facebook (FAIR), and it is a powerful architecture for semantic and instance segmentation. It is necessary to grasp the underlying technique of the algorithm, called R-CNN. The Region-based Convolutional Neural Network (R-CNN [21]) is an approach that involves detecting objects by enclosing them in a square region (bounding box) and evaluating them independently (in each region) using convolutional neural networks to determine their class. Mask R-CNN is a more intuitive version of R-CNN, focusing on instance segmentation. This approach generates three outputs, first, the bounding box, then the label, and finally, the segmentation mask by predicting the region of interest [20].

4.7 Base Structure (Backbone)

The input orthomosaic passes through a neural network, which serves as the base structure in the process (see Fig. 3-a). This structure varies depending on training speed, performance, and computational resource limitations. The Mask R-CNN architecture consists of a bottom-up and a top-down process (see Fig. 3-b). The bottom-up approach performs convolutions and generates feature maps using ResNet [22] and ResNeXt [23] as neural networks. These networks consist of multiple layers called ResBlocks or BottleneckBlocks, which use convolutions and batch normalization to extract features from the input image. In this case, ResNet50, ResNet101, and ResNeXt101 were used. ResNeXts generally yield better results than ResNets because they utilize multiple parallel convolutions. However, this increases the training time significantly. The top-down process refers to the Feature Pyramid Network (FPN), which has four modules (M5, M4, M3, M2), where the spatial dimensions double in size from one module to another [24]. The M5 module has higher semantic information and lower spatial dimensions, while the lower modules have higher spatial dimensions and lower semantic value. The module stops at M2 instead of M1 because the spatial dimensions at that point are too large and significantly slow down the training process. These bottom-up and top-down processes are connected through lateral connections, ensuring spatial coherence from one module to another, ultimately obtaining a prediction (P5, P4, P3, P2) used in the Region Proposal Network (RPN). As convolutional layers increase, the algorithm learns increasingly complex information but risks overfitting and requires more computational resources for objects of different sizes.

4.8   Residual Neural Network (ResNet)

The neural network used in this case is ResNet [22]. This deep neural network architecture utilizes residual connections or skip connections to address the problem of gradient vanishing in intense networks [25]. Skip connections allow information to flow directly from earlier to later layers, preventing the gradient from vanishing during backpropagation [26]. The additional layers added to the network should not worsen the network's behavior, as instead of learning a complete representation from the input to the expected output, it learns from the differences or residuals between the input and the desired outcome, gradually improving the network's accuracy. In ResNet, residual blocks are used, which consist of multiple convolutional layers followed by skip connections that enable the flow of information. ResNeXt [23] is a variant of ResNet that introduces the concept of cardinality to improve the accuracy of residual neural networks further. It expands the original ResNet architecture with a grouped convolution operation that divides the input channels into multiple groups.

4.9   Region Proposal Network, ROI Align Layer and FCN

The outputs from the backbone (P2, P3, P4, P5) are the feature maps used in the Region Proposal Network (RPN) to generate anchor boxes. Each high-probability region generates anchor boxes with different aspect ratios (e.g., 1:1, 2:2, 1:2) and scales (e.g., 0.5, 1, 2). The Region of Interest (ROI) passes through the ROI Align layer, where bilinear interpolation is performed, preserving spatial information without quantization. The Fully Convolutional Network (FCN) takes the compact representation of the proposed regions and applies a linear transformation followed by an activation function (ReLU). The output is used for region classification, where each neuron represents a specific class and represents the probability that the region belongs to that class.

4.10   Outputs

The first output is the segmentation mask, a binary classification involving a single classifier per class using a one-vs-all strategy, so each ROI considers only one object at a time. Regression and the L1 loss function are used to obtain the bounding box coordinates for the calculation of the bounding box. The four coordinates "x1", "x2", "y1", and "y2" are employed, and the L1 loss is calculated for each coordinate to minimize the difference between the model's predictions and the actual box values. Object classification results from processing in the last layer of the Detectron model (FCN layer). The object region (defined by the bounding box) is fed into the network, and a probability of belonging to each class is obtained. The class with the highest probability is the object's classification label.

5 Experimentation

5.1 Definition and Configuration of Hyperparameters

Based on the base structures mentioned in Sect. 4, Subsect. 4.7, for the classification of tree crowns present in the orthomosaic, the size and aspect ratio of the bounding boxes that the model can predict were taken into account, in addition to conventional parameters such as the number of iterations and batch size of images to analyze. Parameters were also set for the neural network to discard predictions with a score lower than 50% and filter out segments or masks with more significant overlap than 10%.

These parameters were manually defined with the aim of adapting the different backbones to the complexity of the problem. This involved an initial exploration of the networks trained with a relatively low number of iterations, between 500 and 1,000, and observing the prediction results. It is worth noting that the weights of the pre-trained network available in the framework were used for each experiment.

In these initial observations, the need to limit the size of the bounding boxes was identified since the model's testing process generated predictions encompassing multiple trees of the same type. Furthermore, bounding boxes and masks were observed to be contained within larger areas or partially labeled on numerous surrounding trees. As a result, the allowed overlap between these boxes was adjusted. On the other hand, an image batch size of 2 was established since a larger number demanded more graphic memory resources than available on the machine. An ROI batch size of 256 was also set as a representative sample of the number of labels present per image. A larger selection would have required more computational resources, similar to the image batch size.

5.2 Experimental Procedure

The experimentation was limited due to the available computational resources for this task. Therefore, a conservative approach was taken at the beginning of this task. For the execution of the experiments following are the technical specifications:

- CPU: AMD Ryzen 9 5900HX @ 3.3 GHz with eight cores and two logical processors each.

- RAM: 32 GB @ 3200 MHz.
- GPU: NVIDIA GeForce RTX 3080 Laptop with 16 GB dedicated memory.

Exploratory experiments were carried out to analyze the behavior of the neural networks with the weights provided by the framework. This was done to define the values of the hyperparameters that came closest to solving the problem. Most of this experimentation phase was carried out with the ResNet50-FPN backbone since it was the least complex, allowing for multiple configurations with few iterations to analyze the behavior of metrics and predictions on the validation orthomosaics. Subsequently, experiments with a higher number of iterations were performed to evaluate if there was an improvement in the classification results. During this stage, predictions with bounding boxes and masks containing multiple trees of the predicted type were detected. A subscription to Colab Pro+ service was acquired, along with additional computing units to access a graphics card with more memory. This was done in order to run experiments with several iterations.

5.3 Evaluation Metrics

The precision analysis is essential when measuring the effectiveness of a deep learning model because it defines how well the model performs when receiving new data. In classification tasks, the concepts of false positives (FP) and false negatives (FN) are introduced, referring to elements that were classified incorrectly, as well as true positives (TP) and true negatives (TN), which refer to cases that were classified correctly [27].

Considering that this work focuses on instance segmentation, two metrics called precision (Eq. 1) and recall (Eq. 2) are highlighted, which, in turn, use the variables presented in the previous paragraph.

$$\text{Precision} = \frac{TP}{TP + FP} \tag{1}$$

$$\text{Recall} = \frac{TP}{TP + FN} \tag{2}$$

Instance segmentation in Detectron is evaluated using COCO (Common Objects in Context) metrics, where the concept of Intersection over Union (IoU) of bounding boxes is introduced. In object detection, IoU measures the area of overlap between the predicted bounding box B_p and the ground truth bounding box B_gt, divided by the union area between them [28] (see Eq. 3).

$$J(B_{p,B_{gt}}) = \text{IOU} = \frac{\text{area}(B_p \cap B_{gt})}{\text{area}(B_p \cup B_{gt})} \tag{3}$$

A low IoU captures more objects than a high IoU so the optimal point may vary depending on the problem [28]. When comparing the IoU with a given threshold value l, the detection of a tree is considered correct or incorrect. If IoU $\geq$ l, then the detection is considered accurate. If IoU $<$ l, then it is erroneous

[28]. Once the concept is understood, the following metrics specifically used in Detectron are listed:

5.4 Average Precision (AP)

It is a weighted average of precision at different confidence thresholds or limits for a specific class (see Eq. 4). It calculates the area under the precision-recall curve. This metric uses the average value of 10 IoU thresholds ranging from 0.5 to 0.95 with steps of 0.05. The closer the value is to 1, the better the model [22].

$$AP = \sum_{k=0}^{n-1} [\text{Recall}(k) - \text{Recall}(k+1)] \cdot \text{Precisions}(k) \qquad (4)$$

where Recall(n) = 0, Precisions(n) = 1, and n represents the limits.

There are multiple variations of AP, such as AP_50 and AP_75, which represent the calculation of average precision using a maximum IoU threshold of 0.5 and 0.75, respectively. These precisions are calculated both for segmentation masks and bounding boxes. Average precision across classes (AP_area) is also commonly calculated, corresponding to an average of the AP values across multiple classes [29].

$$\text{mAP} = \frac{1}{n} \sum_{k=1}^{n} \text{AP}_k \qquad (5)$$

where APk is the AP of class k, and n is the number of classes.

5.5 Average Recall (AR)

Average recall measures the object retrieval rate at different confidence thresholds or limits. It represents the model's ability to correctly detect true objects relative to the dataset's total number of true objects. The IoU thresholds used are the same as those used for the AP metric (see Eq. 6) [28].

$$AR = \frac{\sum_{k=1}^{n} Recall(k)}{n} \qquad (6)$$

6 Results Analysis

Backbone configurations and hyperparameters that yielded the best results in the experimentation phase are shown in Table 2. The number of iterations plays a fundamental role in model fitting, as those with the highest number of iterations achieved the best results. However, the average precision across the three categories could be much higher.

In this analysis, it was found that the limitation imposed on the size of bounding boxes led to the models not classifying trees that exceeded the allowed values or only classifying branches of such trees, as seen in Fig. 4.

Table 2. Best results

Parameters	E22	E18	E17
Iterations	250,000	30,000	30,000
Batch Size	256	256	256
Neural Network	ResNeXt101	ResNeXt101	ResNet101
Learning Rate	0.0005	0.005	0.005
Anchor Box Size	32, 64, 128, 256	32, 64, 128	32, 64, 128
Anchor Box Aspect Ratio	1.0, 2.0	0.5, 1.0	0.5, 1.0
IoU Thresholds	0.5, 0.6, 0.7	0.5, 0.6, 0.7	0.5, 0.6, 0.7
Memory Consumption (MB)	29,689	10,763	9,921
Total Time	122:43:36	07:55:25	07:55:25
B.B. Precision Mango	9.818%	8.138%	6.256%
Segmentation Precision Mango	11.064%	7.085%	5.347%
B.B. Precision Banana	6.727%	2.017%	2.516%
Segmentation Precision Banana	3.659%	0.441%	0.689%
B.B. Precision Citrus	9.833%	0.642%	1.034%
Segmentation Precision Citrus	12.535%	0.906%	1.331%

On the other hand, in experiments where these limiting parameters were not included, the resulting boxes and masks encompassed multiple instances of the predicted tree type achieving better percentages in segmentation and bounding box precisions.

Regarding banana plants, which have the lowest average precision in most experiments, it can be observed that the predicted masks by the models fail to define the leaf endings. This difficulty arises because these plants have a completely irregular shape and are often closely grouped.

As for citrus cultivation, which is distributed in clearly defined rows, the model correctly classified multiple instances of this type, despite being in one of the steepest areas of the terrain within the farm.

The relationship between the number of iterations and the average precision of bounding boxes is not linear. Increasing the number of iterations from 30,000 to 250,000 did not result in the same proportional increase in precision as increasing from 30,000 to 20,000 iterations. This suggests that beyond 250,000 iterations, other hyperparameters become more important for improving results.

The average segmentation precision showed a similar behavior to bounding boxes. However, in one experiment (22), the precision for the citrus class was higher than for mangoes.

The precision of bounding boxes and segmentation for banana plants needs improvement compared to other types, even in the last experiment. The precision of bounding box predictions for bananas was almost twice as high as segmentation precision.

Fig. 4. Crop of prediction made by E18 where two mango trees are not classified due to exceeding the expected size.

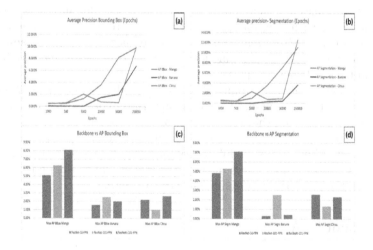

Fig. 5. Metrics of the training process.

In Fig. 5, the precision behavior for mangoes was consistent with the theory on ResNet and ResNeXt, where each subsequent backbone model outperformed the previous one. However, ResNet101-FPN performed better for bananas in both bounding box and segmentation outputs.

For citrus, the precision behavior differed between the ResNet50-FPN and ResNeXt-101-FPN models. The former had better performance for bounding boxes, while the latter was better for segmentation.

Finally, model validation was performed in Farm B, where multiple trees were classified with confidence levels between 60% and 100%. The tree classifications are correct, but the same issues identified in the experimentation persist, such as partial delineation of some trees or even trees not identified in the field.

7   Conclusions

Based on the conducted project and its results, it is concluded that the proposed model fulfills the objective of classifying multiple instances of the selected tree types. However, the accuracy percentages in various experiments were low, and it was not possible to recognize some trees in the images. The main reasons were related to the training phase, where, firstly, the complexity of the problem demanded a high computational cost. Additionally, the variability in shapes and sizes of tree canopies, as well as the distribution of crops, added difficulty to both the labeling process and the segmentation and classification carried out by the model.

For the training, it was necessary to adapt the experimental parameters (anchor box size, number of epochs, among others) so that the computer could handle the variables and successfully classify the trees. This success was evident when validating with new data, where the model recognized instances of the three types of trees with a high confidence percentage. However, the adaptation of hyperparameters affected the model's accuracy, considering the variability in shapes and sizes of tree canopies.

The scalability and adaptability of Artificial Intelligence solutions are demonstrated by developing a model for tree monitoring under diverse conditions in Detectron2, a framework that allows choosing multiple base structures and facilitates the experimental phase due to its flexibility in adjusting hyperparameters. Although Detectron2 is a powerful library for computer vision tasks, one should consider its steep learning curve, memory or storage constraints for the chosen model, and the preprocessing of inputs prior to training.

A   Appendix A

In Table 3 of Appendix A, the experimental results of the models' evaluation with their different configurations.

Table 3. Experimental Configurations

No.	Neural Network	Iterations	Learning Rate	Batch size	Anchor box size	Ratio Aspect Anchor
1	ResNet101	500	0.001	256	*	*
2	ResNet50	500	0.001	256	*	*
3	ResNeXt101	500	0.001	256	*	*
4	ResNet101	1000	0.001	256	*	*
5	ResNet50	1000	0.001	256	*	*
6	ResNeXt101	1000	0.001	256	*	*
7	ResNet101	5000	0.0005	256	32, 64, 128	1.0, 2.0
8	ResNet50	5000	0.0005	256	32, 64, 128	1.0, 2.0
9	ResNeXt101	5000	0.0005	256	32, 64, 128	1.0, 2.0
10	ResNet50	20000	0.0005	256	*	*
11	ResNet101	20000	0.0005	256	*	*
12	ResNeXt101	20000	0.0005	256	*	*
13	ResNet50	20000	0.0005	256	32, 64, 128	1.0, 2.0
14	ResNet101	20000	0.0005	256	32, 64, 128	1.0, 2.0
15	ResNeXt101	20000	0.0005	256	32, 64, 128	1.0, 2.0
16	ResNet50	30000	0.005	256	32, 64, 128	0.5, 1.0
17	ResNet101	30000	0.005	256	32, 64, 128	0.5, 1.0
18	ResNeXt101	30000	0.005	256	32, 64, 128	0.5, 1.0
19	ResNet50	30000	0.0005	256	32, 64, 128	1.0, 2.0
20	ResNet101	30000	0.0005	256	32, 64, 128	1.0, 2.0
21	ResNeXt101	30000	0.0005	256	32, 64, 128	1.0, 2.0
22	ResNeXt101	250000	0.0005	256	32, 64, 128	1.0, 2.0

References

1. Corporaciones Autónomas Regionales. Guía técnica cultura del árbol (2020). https://www.car.gov.co/uploads/files/5acbd3e842e9b.pdf
2. PepsiCo. Bloomberg Línea (2023). https://www.bloomberglinea.com/2023/01/23/claves-para-regenerar-la-agricultura-latinoamericana-en-2023/
3. Cropin Cloud. Precision Agriculture for Productivity (2023). https://www.cropin.com/precision-agriculture
4. González, N.G.: AgroNegocios (2022). https://www.agronegocios.co/agricultura/segun-minagricultura-cerca-de-15-del-sector-agro-utiliza-tecnologia-de-ultima-generacion-3299246
5. Norvig, P., Russell, S.: Artificial Intelligence: A Modern Approach. Stanford University (2009)
6. Multiple Contributors. Microsoft (2023). https://learn.microsoft.com/en-us/azure/machine-learning/concept-automated-ml?view=azureml-api-2
7. Yang, X., Pei, X.: ScienceDirect (2022). urlhttps://www.sciencedirect.com/topics/engineering/unmanned-aerial-vehicle
8. Thales. Asociación Colombiana de Ingenieros de Sistemas (2022). https://acis.org.co/portal/content/mercado-de-drones-en-colombia-sigue-creciendo-y-demanda-mayor-seguridad

9. topographic-map. Mapa Topográfico de Suramérica (2020). https://es-hn. topographic-map.com/map4xj4s/Am%C3%A9rica-del-Sur/?center=-20.2622 %2C-14.45801&zoom=4

10. Sotomayor, O., Ramírez, E., Martínez, H.: Economic Commission for Latin America and the Caribbean (2021). https://repositorio.cepal.org/bitstream/handle/ 11362/46965/4/S2100283_es.pdf

11. DJI. DJI Pilot (2023). https://www.dji.com/downloads/djiapp/dji-pilot

12. Dronelink. Dronelink (2023). https://www.dronelink.com/

13. Weber State University. The Sun and the Seasons (2011). https://physics.weber. edu/schroeder/ua/sunandseasons.html

14. Kozmus Trajkovski, K., Grigillo, D., Petrovič, D.: Optimization of UAV Flight Missions in Steep Terrain. MDPI (2020). https://www.mdpi.com/2072-4292/12/ 8/1293

15. DJI. DJI Mini 2 Specifications (2023). https://www.dji.com/mini-2/specs

16. WebODM. WebODM - Drone Image Processing (2023). https://webodm.net/

17. Dutta, A., Gupta, A., Zisserman, A.: VGG Image Annotator (VIA) (2023). https:// www.robots.ox.ac.uk/vgg/software/via/

18. Keras. Keras - RandomFlip layer (2023). https://keras.io/api/layers/ preprocessing_layers/image_augmentation/random_flip/

19. Meta. Detectron2 (2023). https://ai.facebook.com/tools/detectron2/

20. Meta. Mask R-CNN (2023). https://github.com/matterport/Mask_RCNN

21. Girshick, R., Donahue, J., Darrell, T., Malik, J.: R-CNN: region-based convolutional neural networks (2023). https://github.com/rbgirshick/rcnn

22. He, K., Zhang, X., Ren, S., Sun, J.: Deep residual learning for image recognition. IEEE Xplore **45**, 770–778 (2016)

23. Xie, S., Girshick, R., Dollár, P., Tu, Z., He, K.: Aggregated residual transformations for deep neural networks, pp. 5987–5995. IEEE (2017)

24. Lin, T.Y., Dollár, P., Girshick, R., He, K., Hariharan, B., Belongie, S.: Feature pyramid networks for object detection, vol. 2, pp. 936–944. IEEE (2016)

25. Wang, C.-F.: Medium - the vanishing gradient problem (2019). https:// towardsdatascience.com/the-vanishing-gradient-problem-69bf08b15484

26. Solai, P.: Medium - convolutions and backpropagations (2018). https://pavisj. medium.com/convolutions-and-backpropagations-46026a8f5d2c

27. Carvalho, O.L.F.D., et al.: Instance segmentation for large, multi-channel remote sensing imagery using mask-RCNN and a mosaicking approach. Remote Sens. **13**(39), 10 (2020)

28. Padilla, R., Netto, S.L., Da Silva, E.A: A survey on performance metrics for object-detection algorithms, vol. 1, p. 2. IEEE (2020) ¡error l="305" c="Invalid command: paragraph not started." /¿

29. Wei, S., et al.: Precise and robust ship detection for high-resolution SAR imagery based on HR-SDNet, vol. 12. IEEE (2020)

Change Point Detection for Time Dependent Counts Using Extended MDL and Genetic Algorithms

Sergio Barajas-Oviedo[1]📷, Biviana Marcela Suárez-Sierra[2]([✉])📷,
and Lilia Leticia Ramírez-Ramírez[1]📷

[1] Centro de Investigación en Matemáticas, Guanajuato, Guanajuato, Mexico
{sergio.barajas,leticia.ramirez}@cimat.mx
[2] Universidad EAFIT, Medellín, Antioquia, Colombia
bmsuarezs@eafit.edu.co

Abstract. This article introduces an extension for change point detection based on the *Minimum Description Length* (MDL) methodology. Unlike traditional approaches, this proposal accommodates observations that are not necessarily independent or identically distributed. Specifically, we consider a scenario where the counting process comprises observations from a Non-homogeneous Poisson process (NHPP) with a potentially non-linear time-dependent rate. The analysis can be applied to the counts for events such as the number of times that an environmental variable exceeded a threshold. The change point identification allows extracting relevant information on the trends for the observations within each segment and the events that may trigger the changes. The proposed MDL framework allows us to estimate the number and location of change points and incorporates a penalization mechanism to mitigate bias towards single regimen models. The methodology addressed the problem as a bilevel optimization problem. The first problem involves optimizing the parameters of NHPP given the change points and has continuous nature. The second one consists of optimizing the change points assignation from all possible options and is combinatorial. Due to the complexity of this parametric space, we use a genetic algorithm associated with a generational spread metric to ensure minimal change between iterations. We introduce a statistical hypothesis t-test as a stopping criterion. Experimental results using synthetic data demonstrate that the proposed method offers more precise estimates for both the number and localization of change points compared to more traditional approaches.

Keywords: Change point detection · Evolutionary algorithm ·
Non-parametric Bayesian · Non-homogeneous Poisson Process · Bilevel
Optimization

1 Introduction

Identifying change points in time series is paramount for several analysis that helps understanding the underlying dynamic or performing some practically cap-

M. Tabares et al. (Eds.): CCC 2023, CCIS 1924, pp. 215–229, 2024.
https://doi.org/10.1007/978-3-031-47372-2_19

ital tasks as forecasting. A prime example of the latter is on the scenario of cybersecurity, where the focus lies in monitoring the instances of breaching a pre-defined threshold for data transfer volume over a network. This study employs a cutting-edge model for identifying the number of change point and their values in a time series of counts, such as the threshold breaches as a function of time.

The literature consistently emphasizes a fundamental flaw in many models designed to detect change points in time series. These models tend to assume equal and independent distribution of the data points within a segment, which fundamentally contradicts their inherent nature. As eloquently discussed in [9], this research endeavor ingeniously sidesteps the aforementioned assumption by considering a flexible family of non-homogeneous Poisson processes.

This investigation leverages a genetic algorithm to ascertain the optimal solution for the time series groupings (segments) in the overall observation time interval. A possible grouping is ingeniously represented as individuals (also referred to in the literature as chromosomes, creatures, or organisms) consisting of binary vectors, with a value of one indicating the time when we have a change point and zero otherwise. The evolutionary principles of selection, mutation, mating, evaluation, and replacement are deftly applied, drawing inspiration from the realms of probability, Bayesian computational methods, and information theory.

Pre-specifying the number of generations originated by the algorithm can lead to unnecessary evaluation of the objective function, [14]. In this study, a judicious stopping criterion is established, underpinned by a simple yet effective decision rule involving a t statistic. Moreover, this research achieves a higher rate of accurately pinpointing the number and location of change points, employing the same principle as in [14], which relies on counting the exceedances to a threshold value instead of using the measurements per se. Additionally, the algorithm provides insights into the composition of the intensity function parameters governing the Non-Homogeneous Poisson process (NHPP), shedding light on the non-linear tendencies inherent in the observational emission patterns.

In this work we assume that the NHPP has a decaying and non-linear intensity described by a Weibull distribution, however, the methodology can easily be extended to broader cases that can include some other possible families of intensities. The decision to adopt the Weibull distribution as the intensity function is primarily based on the interpretative potential of the Weibull's shape parameter and the wealth of experience gained from prior seminal works such as [1-3], and [13].

Through computation experiments, we observe that this approach exhibits superior efficacy in identifying change points, particularly when confronted with extreme data scenarios.

2   Non-homogeneous Poisson Process

A Non-Homogeneous Poisson process (NHPP) extends the ordinary Poisson process allowing the average rate can vary with time. Many applications that generate counts (random points) are more faithfully modeled with such NHPP with the cost of losing the practically convenient property of stationary increments.

NHPPs are an excellent tool for modeling counting processes of the number of occurrences at time t due to their easy interpretability. In particular, the focus of this study is to count the number of times a threshold is exceeded, with each occurrence referred to as an "exceedance". Therefore, this process generates a new series of count observations that records, per unit of time, the number of exceedance up to t, denoted as $N(t)$.

We consider the stochastic process $N(t)$ as an NHPP, where the increments $N(t+s) - N(t)$ follow a Poisson distribution with a parameter $(m(t+s) - m(t))$ that depends on time t. This condition allows for the change points identification without assuming that the observations are equally distributed. Therefore, the probability that starting at time t, the time to the next exceedance is greater than a length of time s is denoted as $G(t; s)$. In other words, the probability of no exceedances occurring in the interval $(t, t + s]$ is given by

$$G(t; s) = P(N(t + s) - N(t) = 0) = \exp\left\{-[m(t + s) - m(t)]\right\}.$$

Then, the probability that starting at time t, the time to the next exceedance is less than s is given by

$$F(t; s) = 1 - G(t; s) = 1 - \exp\left\{-[m(t + s) - m(t)]\right\}.$$

The probability density function of the interval to the next exceedance is denoted as

$$f(t; s) = \lambda(t + s) \exp\left\{-[m(t + s) - m(t)]\right\},$$

where $\lambda(t)$ is the intensity function that characterizes an NHPP and relates to the process parameters as

$$m(t_{i+1}) - m(t_i) = \int_{t_i}^{t_{i+1}} \lambda(u)du. \tag{1}$$

According to [5], for time-dependent Poisson processes, the intervals between successive events are independently distributed. The probability, starting at t_i, that the next exceedance occurs in the interval $(t_{i+1}, t_{i+1} + \Delta t]$ is given by

$$\lambda(t_{i+1}) \exp\left\{-[m(t_{i+1}) - m(t_i)]\right\} \Delta t + o(\Delta t) \tag{2}$$

If a series of successive exceedances is observed in the time interval $(0, T]$, occurring at $\mathbf{D} = \{t_1, t_2, \ldots, t_n\}$, the likelihood function, which will be part of the objective function in the genetic algorithm, is expressed as

$$\left[\prod_{i=1}^{n} \lambda(t_i) \exp\left\{-[m(t_i) - m(t_{i-1})]\right\}\right] \exp\left\{-[m(T) - m(t_n)]\right\}, \tag{3}$$

with $t_0 = 0$. The last element in (3) is the survival probability $G(t_n; (T - t_n))$ since the interval $(t_n, T]$ do not register any exceedance.

Since $m(0) = 0$ and $m(T) = \int_0^n \lambda(u)du$, we can simplify the previous likelihood to

$$L(\mathbf{D}|\phi) \propto \left\{ \prod_{i=1}^{n} \lambda(t_i) \right\} \exp\left\{-m(T)\right\}.$$

The parameter ϕ specify the model and it is present in the intensity $\lambda(t)$ and cumulative mean, $m(t)$. Hence we can explicitly express this fact using the following expression for the likelihood

$$L(\mathbf{D}|\phi) \propto \left\{ \prod_{i=1}^{n} \lambda(t_i \mid \phi) \right\} \exp\left\{-m(T \mid \phi)\right\}. \tag{4}$$

The estimation of parameters ϕ is one of the main objectives of this study. However, there is another key characteristic we want to infer and this is the point where we can have regimen changes (hence different ϕ values). These points are called change points and we denoted them as $\boldsymbol{\tau} = \{\tau_1, \tau_2, \ldots, \tau_J\}$, $J \in \mathbb{N}$, where $0 \leq \tau_i \leq T$ for $i = 1, \ldots, J$.

The overall likelihood based on the observations $\mathbf{D}$ during the period of time $(0, T]$ of a NHPP with known change points $\boldsymbol{\tau}$ corresponds to

$$L(\mathbf{D}|\phi, \boldsymbol{\tau}) \propto \left[\prod_{i=1}^{N_{\tau_1}} \lambda(t_i \mid \phi_1) \right] \exp\left\{-m(\tau_1|\phi_1)\right\}$$

$$\times \left[\prod_{j=2}^{J} \left(\prod_{i=N_{\tau_{j-1}}+1}^{N_{\tau_j}} \lambda(t_i|\phi_j) \right) \exp\left\{-[m(\tau_j|\phi_j) - m(\tau_{j-1}|\phi_{j-1})]\right\} \right]$$

$$\times \left[\prod_{i=N_{\tau_J}+1}^{n} \lambda(t_i|\phi_{J+1}) \right] \exp\left\{-[m(T|\phi_{J+1}) - m(\tau_J|\phi_J)]\right\}, \tag{5}$$

where N_{τ_i} is the cumulative number of observations up to time τ_i, ϕ_i is the parameter that describes the NHPP during $(\tau_{i-1}, \tau_i]$, $i = 1, \ldots, n$, (with $\tau_0 = 0$), and ϕ_{J+1} describes the NHPP during the last observe regimen in $(\tau_n, T]$. For more details see [13].

If we know the change points number and location, as in (5), we can select the parameter ϕ that characterize the model that better fit the data using the Bayesian paradigm. The log-posterior distribution, that describes the updated information on the parameter ϕ is

$$\ln f(\phi|\mathbf{D}, \boldsymbol{\tau}) \propto \ln(L(\mathbf{D}|\phi, \boldsymbol{\tau})) + \ln(f(\phi|\boldsymbol{\tau})), \tag{6}$$

where $f(\phi|\mathbf{D}, \boldsymbol{\tau})$ is the *posterior* distribution and $L(\mathbf{D}|\phi, \boldsymbol{\tau})$ is the likelihood (5) regarding the parameter ϕ as the variable, and $f(\phi|\boldsymbol{\tau})$ contains the prior information we have on the real value of ϕ for given values of $\boldsymbol{\tau}$.

The expression (6) defines the posterior distribution for the parameters, and we use the value of the parameter that maximizes it. This is called the maximum *a posteriori* or MAP. With the genetic algorithm approach, we compute the MAP among each generation and use them to compute to select the best individuals for the following generation.

Now we proceed to describe the proposed method for the overall model with unknown change points. For this, we require to determine the change points τ before estimating the rest of the parameters involved. That is, the first step is selecting the number and location of the change points. This involves a model selection that will be handled with by the MDL approach.

3   MDL

The Minimum Description Length (MDL) combines Occam's razor and information theory to determine the model that better fits the data. It first appeared on [11], but has been widely explored both theoretically [7] and in many popular applications such as PCA [4].

In the early days of mathematical modeling, simple models, such as linear ones, were the only ones explored to 'fit' the data. Since then, not only richer models are being used but also some different criteria for selecting their parameters have been developed. One of them is rooted in the information theory, which focuses on encoding the data to describe the contained information. From a computational point of view, data is encoded in many ways which include arrays, matrices, and many kinds of structures. However, any kind of representation costs a number of bits in memory space, this number of bits is what we call the code length. Different representations might require a different code length and when encoding data, shorter codes are preferred over longer ones as they take less memory space. For efficiency, one of the main tasks consist in assigning a model that has the shortest code and in the change point detection problem, we need to encode the number and location of the change points, as well as the model to fit the data within each regimen between consecutive change points. The MDL principle is used to give a numeric value to the code length associated with different assignations of the change points.

The MDL code length is divided into two summands.

$$MDL(\tau) = -\ln f(\hat{\phi}|\mathbf{D}, \tau) + P(\tau). \tag{7}$$

The first summand is a term related to the fitted model considering the data and selected change points τ. This term corresponds to the negative of the logarithm of the MAP for ϕ and measures how well the model fits the data on each regimen, given τ. When considering the model associated with the posterior (6), we notice that the length of the parameter $\phi = (\phi_1, ..., \phi_J)$ is fixed if we know the number of change points $|\tau| = J$. However, as τ is also a parameter to fit, the parametric space for ϕ must consider spaces with different dimensions. That is, the number of parameters is not constant. For estimating all parameters ϕ and τ, in the complex parametric space they are defined, we use a non-parametric approach to select τ and then we harness the posterior distribution and MAP to establish a criterion for selecting all the parameters using (7).

Fixing the number of change points, we stablish the number of parameters required, however, we still have to determine where to locate them as the posterior depends on it to be properly defined. The second summand in (7) is meant to control both, the number of change points and their location. It can be seen as a penalization function that increases with the number of parameters that are to be encoded in the model and their location in the selected model. Explicitly, the penalization function takes the form of (8) which is an upgrade from [14].

$$P(\boldsymbol{\tau}^*) = R \sum_{i=1}^{j^*+1} \frac{\ln\left(\tau_i^* - \tau_{i-1}^*\right)}{2} + \ln\left(j^* + 1\right) + \sum_{i=2}^{j^*} \ln(\tau_i^*), \qquad (8)$$

where $\boldsymbol{\tau}^* = (\tau_1^*, \ldots, \tau_{j^*}^*)$ is a set of possible change points with j^* different elements, and R is the number of parameters the model has on each regimen.

In [14], the term $\ln(j^*+1)$ was $\ln(j^*)$. So when there is no change point, gave a value of $-\infty$ which made the single regimen model automatically win over any other change point configuration. Because of this, this the single regimen had to be explicitly excluded. Now with $\ln(j^*+1)$ we can naturally incorporate this case. This means that the single regimen model can also be incorporated and compared against any other one models with multiple change points.

Let us notice that for evaluating (7) we need to calculate $\hat{\phi}$ for a given value of the vector $\boldsymbol{\tau}^*$. This procedure for the MDL classifies as a bi-level optimization problem, where a problem is embedded within another. We refer to the embedded and outer problems as inner and outer optimization, respectively. In this case, the optimization for the MAP, $\hat{\phi}$, is the inner problem and the MDL approach corresponds to the outer optimization problem. For a more mathematical description of this kind of problem, the reader can refer to [8].

It is worth noting that the discrete nature of the location and number of change points makes this optimization problem harder to solve using continuous techniques such as gradient descent or the Newton Method, and in some cases, these techniques may be completely inapplicable. Consequently, a genetic algorithm proves to be a valuable tool for effectively exploring the parametric space.

4   Genetic Algorithm Details

The genetic algorithm is one of the so-called bio-inspired optimization algorithms based on evolution theory that aims to find the optimal value of a function. In our case, to identify the change point and parameters that better describe the data we use, we minimize (7).

The basic elements and tasks are done on the proposed genetic algorithm are:

Individual. We codify each individual as a logical vector of the length of the observed times. "True" means that the corresponding time is a change point, and "False", otherwise. Though the beginning and end of the scope of time are not properly change points, the coding should start and finish with "True" to define at least one regimen. The algorithm in [14] is considered to directly enlist the proposed ordered times as change points, but this new individual encoding is more convenient in terms of memory space and genetic operators.

The scope of time. We consider the data that we want to estimate its change points as equidistant and discrete observations for exceedances in equal and non-overlapping units of time. Then the scope of time is equal to the length of data observations.

Parameter estimation. Typical genetic algorithms do not include this step. Once an individual is defined, the change points are given and (6) can be optimized to find the MAP. The optimization can be done using any preferred method being *Nelder-Mead* our selected choice. The values for the parameters are part of the coding of an individual and are attached to the logical vector once they are estimated.

A population. Consists of a fixed number of individuals and remains constant for different generations. This number is denoted by n.

Fitness function. Once the parameter estimation is done, we can compute the MDL (7). This plays the role of the fitness function that induces a ranking for the individuals a generation. Based on this ranking, for each generation, we order the individuals to have an increasing ranking.

Individual Generator. The first generation is generated with random individuals. Each logical value in each individual is assigned the same distribution where "True" is drawn as the "Success" in a distribution Bernoulli($\alpha = 0.06$). In consequence, the number of change points in each individual has a binomial distribution with an average of six percent.

Parents selection. In genetic algorithms, reproduction is simulated to generate new individuals. For this task, a pair of parents are selected with replacement with a weighted probability according to their rank. That is if i is the rank of i-th individual in the current population, it is selected with probability $i/\sum_{j=1}^{n} j$.

Crossover operator. The child will inherit all the change points from both parents. Then we keep each of these change points with probability 0.5.

Corrector operator. In practice, it is inadequate to consider change points to be right next to each other. This operator prevents this from happening. In this scenario, one of the consecutive change points is randomly discarded. This excludes the first and last elements in the individual that must remain "True".

Mutation operator. Each of the new individuals is submitted to the mutation operator, where each change points is assigned a value of $-1, 0$ or 1 with probabilities $0.4, 0.3$ and 0.3 respectively. Then, the change points are modified accordingly by moving them one place to the left if the -1 value was assigned, unchanged if the 0 value is selected, and one place to the right if the 1 value is selected. This modification excludes the first and last elements of each individual.

Evolutionary algorithms start by setting an initial population of individuals. Since its selection involves some randomness, in an early stage, these individuals have a huge spread on the feasible space (see example in Fig. 1a) with respect to the best individual (red dot). This spreading is useful as it promotes the exploration of the search space. However, as generations pass, this spreading reduces considerably (Fig. 1b). While the typical genetic algorithm relies on a fixed number of iterations, an alternative is proposed that takes advantage of this behavior.

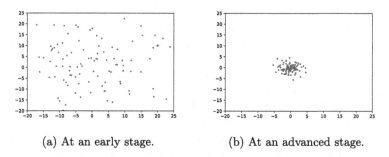

(a) At an early stage.   (b) At an advanced stage.

Fig. 1. Individuals in $\mathbb{R}^2$ at different generations of the genetic algorithm (Color figure online)

We define the *Average Generational Spread* (AGS) as a measure of the dispersion of individuals in a generation. It is formally defined as:

$$\text{AGS}(k) = \frac{1}{n} \sum_{i=1}^{n} \|\boldsymbol{x}_i^{(k)} - \boldsymbol{x}^{*(k)}\|^2 \tag{9}$$

where $\boldsymbol{x}^{*(k)}$ is the individual with the best value according to the fitness function MDL in the k-th generation, and $\boldsymbol{x}_i^{(k)}$ is the i-th individual in k-th generation. The individual codified as a logical vector makes the AGS function be evaluated very quickly using bit operations.

The AGS metric decreases rapidly in the first stages of the genetic algorithm and more slowly in the latter stages. See Fig. 2. To exploit this phenomenon, we propose using linear regression for the AGS values and the last K generations, where K is a fixed number. The idea is to determine an approximate value for the AGS slope ψ for these last K generations. As a linear model is adjusted via linear regression, it can be determined, with a given significance, if there is evidence that the slope is still decreasing.

It can be seen in Fig. 2, that the values for the AGS have some noise due to the randomness induced by the genetic algorithm. For this reason, a statistical test is ideal for the task. Even more, as AGS is defined as an average, this suggests that it will tend to have a normal distribution. A classical t-test is used to evaluate the null hypothesis $H_0 : \psi \leq 0$ versus $H_1 : \psi > 0$. If we reject H_0 we proceed to obtain the next K generations, and we stop otherwise.

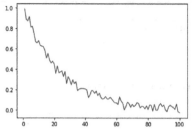

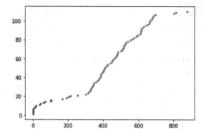

Fig. 2. AGS value through generations.

Fig. 3. Simulated Non-Homogeneous Poisson Process.

Algorithms 1 and 2 present the overall proposed method.

5   Simulated Experiment

We evaluated the proposed algorithm using simulated data for which we know the number and location of its change points.

We generated a non-homogeneous Poisson process that simulates the cumulative counts of events with change points on times 299 and 699 with a scope of time of 1000. In contrast with some popular time series, the simulated times between counting increments are not equally distributed, which is one of the difficulties that our algorithm has to handle.

Figure 3 shows the simulated data. On the x-axis the time at which an event occurred and on the y-axis the cumulative counting process of these. It is shown in blue, orange, and green the three regimens induced by the change points. All three regimens are simulated with a Weibull rate function with parameters $[\alpha, \beta]$ equal to $[0.4, 0.1]$, $[0.8, 1.0]$, and $[0.4, 0.1]$ for each regimen, respectively.

Now, to compute the MDL, and more precisely, the posterior density, we require to define the prior for the parameters involved. To do this we consider $\alpha \sim \text{Gamma}(1, 2)$ and $\beta \sim \text{Gamma}(3, 1.2)$, and an initial guess for parameter estimation we use $\alpha = 0.1$ and $\beta = 0.5$ for each regimen.

To assess the algorithm stability we ran it 100 times setting $K = 10$ and a significance level of 0.05. This allows us to see if it is able to produce results that are consistently close to the true values.

We recorded the fitted number of change points, their location, and the number of generations spent to produce the output.

As for the number of change points, the algorithm was able to identify the true number of change points every single time. Regarding their positions, Figs. 4a and 4b show the histograms for the fitted times for the first and second change points. Both reported values are centered around the true values (lines in red). Mean values and variances are 295.01, 43.65 for the first change point, and 706.82, 151.11 for the second change point. Figure 4c depicts both histograms and makes evident how consistent the produced fitted values are in the 100 algorithm executions, as they present a very low deviation from the true values.

Algorithm 1. Genetic Algorithm

Require: A set of times where exceedances occurred.
Ensure: The individual that minimizes MDL.
  Initialization Process.
  for $i = 1 : n$ **do**
    Generate the i-th logical vector using **Individual Generator**
    Apply **Corrector Operator** to last logical vector.
    Estimate the parameters for this logical vector to form the i-th individual x_i
    $F_i \leftarrow MDL(x_i)$
    Order individuals in crescent order according to F_i
  end for
  Evaluate the AGS metric.
  while Stopping criterion not fulfilled **do**
    Iteration Process.
    for $i = 1 : n$ **do**
      Choose two parents using **Parents Selection.**
      Generate child i using **Crossover Operator** and the previous two parents.
      Apply **Mutation Operator** to last child.
      Estimate its parameters.
      Evaluate its MDL.
      Add the last child to the current population.
    end for
    Choose the half of the population with the highest MDL value to pass to next generation.
    Evaluate AGS for the new generation.
    Determine Stopping criterion using the AGS metric for the last K generations.
  end while
    return The Best individual of the last generation.

Algorithm 2. Stopping criterion

Require: The AGS metric for the last K generations.
Ensure: A value True or False meaning to stop the algorithm or to continue, respectively.
  if AGS array does not have K values. **then return** False
  else AGS array have K values.
    Do the t-test for testing $H_0 : \psi < 0$ versus $H_1 : \psi \geq 0$.
    if There is evidence against H_0 **then return** False
    else return True
    end if
  end if

Regarding the algorithm efficiency, we plot the histograms for the number of generations before stopping. The algorithm was allowed to run a maximum of 100 generations, however, as we can see in Fig. 5a, most of the time it stopped before reaching 100 generations, and an important number of times it stopped close to the 20th generation.

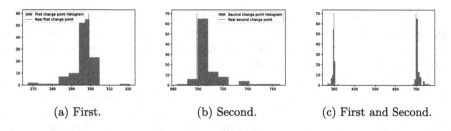

(a) First.   (b) Second.   (c) First and Second.

Fig. 4. Histogram for the first and second reported change points. (Color figure online)

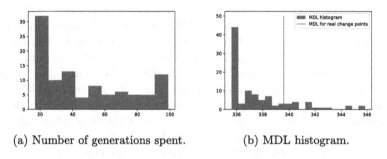

(a) Number of generations spent.   (b) MDL histogram.

Fig. 5. Resulting number of generations spend and MDL histograms.

Figure 5b shows the histogram of the MDL values reported for the best individual in each of the 100 executions (between 332 and 346). With a red line, we mark the MDL value for an individual having the real values for the change points. It can be observed that our algorithm, achieves acceptable MDL values that are equal or lower than the MDL value at the real change points.

5.1 Comparison with Other Algorithms

The comparison of our method has been done with other four algorithms: (1) *MDL2023*, (2) *Changepoint*, (3) *Prophet* and (4) *bcp*.

MDL2023 is the version described in [14] and uses the same parameters (maximum number of generations, prior distribution, likelihood function, population size) as in our method. **Changepoint**, is a method that comes from the library *changepoint* in R, [10]. This library adjusts a Gaussian distribution to each regimen and, using a probability test determines the location of change points. For doing the fitting there are three options, (a) to detect a change in the mean, (b) to detect a change in variance, and (c) to detect a change in mean and variance. We report the results for these three options. **Prophet** corresponds to Facebook's *prophet* algorithm, which is available for both Python and R, [15]. This method decomposes time series into three components

$$y(t) = g(t) + s(t) + h(t) + \varepsilon, \tag{10}$$

with $g(t)$ as the trend component, $s(t)$ as the seasonal component, and $h(t)$ as a special day component that considers events, like Easters, that occur every year, but not on the same day. The term ε is an error with distribution $N(0, \sigma^2)$. More features about the algorithm are detailed in [15].

Prophet is mainly focused on forecasting and the user can specify the known change points. However, when the change points information is not provided, it runs an algorithm to detect them. We considered four different options for change point detection, the first one runs the default settings. This suggests 25 change points and then uses the trend parameters to decide if these change points are significant or not. For the second option, the number of change points to be detected is given, but we do not specify their position. For this case, we select a number of 500 change points evenly distributed during the observation period. The algorithm establishes which ones are significant. For the fourth option, we set the threshold to a high value to keep more significant change points.

Finally, the fourth competing algorithm is Bayesian Change point, (***bcp***), [6]. This method is implemented in an R library that fits a Gaussian likelihood to data and assigns a prior density to the location of change points by assuming that whether a time is a change point or not depends on a subjacent Markov process. The output is a list of probabilities for each time to be a change point so we have to give a threshold to discriminate what we consider to be a change point.

We use the previous simulated NHPP data, depicted in Fig. 3, as the input for all the methods and we compare the results in terms of the number and location of the produced change points. The first algorithm, *MDL2023*, does not have a stopping criterion so the best individual at the last generation is reported.

For comparing the performance of *MDL2023* and our proposed genetic algorithms, we ran each algorithm a hundred times. The reason to consider this is that the algorithms can return different results: number of change points and their respective locations. After that, we use all returned change points, for each method, to estimate their density. In a good identification scenario, we would expect a density with values mainly distributed around 299 and 699 (the true change points) and if the methods were similar we expected to have same density high around these values. With this density, we intend to visualize in a single plot, both fitting criteria (number and position) but we can also compare each of the method's consistency.

Figure 6a shows the density obtained from *MDL2023*. This method frequently returned more change points than two, and their positions are pretty dispersed. Figure 6b shows the estimated density returned by our algorithm which is much more stable and consistently close to the real position values.

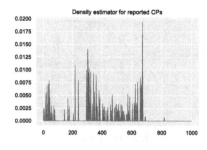 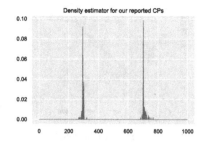

(a) Density of CPs in *MDL2023*.   (b) Density of CPs with our algorithm.

Fig. 6. Density of change point reported.

As the algorithms *Changepoint*, *Prophet* and *bcp* provide only one possible output, we only required to run them once to evaluate its results, however, some options were explored to compare their performance against our method.

To apply *Changepoint*, we detrend the series by taking the first-order differences. Its first option (mean) did not report any change point at all. The second option (variance) detected only the change point at 699 which is the true position for one change point. The third option (mean and variance) returns a change point in 816 when the true position of the second change point is 699.

Prophet tends to return many more change points. The first option considered (default parameter values with 25 initial change points) 21 were returned (Fig. 7a). From this 21 there are a pair that are close to the real values of 299 and 699. For the second option, we specify two change points but they are not even close to their real position (Fig. 7b). For the third option, a total of 175 change points are returned (Fig. 7c). By default, the threshold parameter is set to 0.01. In the fourth option, we set again 500 change points, but a threshold of 0.15. The number of change points is reduced to sixteen, but only the value of 699 is caught between the reported change points (Fig. 7d).

For the case of *bcp*, the method reports 185 change points when setting a threshold of 0.9 for the probability of a time to be a change point.

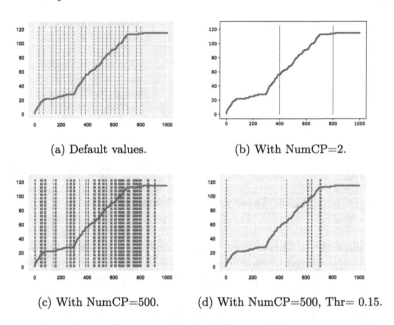

(a) Default values.   (b) With NumCP=2.

(c) With NumCP=500.   (d) With NumCP=500, Thr= 0.15.

Fig. 7. Resulting change points with *Prophet* using different parameter values: Number of change points (NumCP) and Threshold value (Thr).

5.2   Conclusions and Future Work

One of the important features of the presented algorithm is that it can be used for observations that are similar to NHPP with Weibull rates. This proposal can be extended to other important types of parametric NHPP models, that share the attributes of not having increments that are identically distributed. Our method shows to be capable to identify the correct number of change points and provide good estimates for the change points positions.

On the other hand, the proposed stopping criterion allows the method to be highly efficient without sacrificing its precision. Compared to other competing methods, the results based on the simulated data show that our proposal can be very efficient, consistent, and can closely detect true change points (number and location).

Though the algorithm is giving good results, there still are many features that can be improved.

1. Starting point for parameter estimation. We used the same starting point for each individual to be optimized, however, the estimated parameters for the parents could provide a better initial estimate for the parameters of the child.
2. Hyper-parameters for the prior distribution. Justifying the parameters of prior distributions is always something to have in mind as they could lead to bias in the estimation. This usually is proposed using previous information, but a cross-validation technique could be applied.

3. Other penalization terms. Current penalization comes from [12] and information theory. The penalization used in this paper has made a little upgrade, but this can be improved by penalizing too short or too long regimes or promoting the exploration of other specific and desired properties of the data.
4. Prior distribution for τ. MDL can be interpreted from a Bayesian perspective as to give a prior distribution to τ. MDL could be modified using another criterion rather than information theory to give a more informed penalization term.

References

1. Achcar, J., Fernandez-Bremauntz, A., Rodrigues, E., Tzintzun, G.: Estimating the number of ozone peaks in Mexico City using a non-homogeneous Poisson model. Environmetrics **19**, 469–485 (2008). https://doi.org/10.1002/env.890
2. Achcar, J., Rodrigues, E., Paulino, C., Soares, P.: Non-homogeneous Poisson processes with a change-point: an application to ozone exceedances in México City. Environ. Ecol. Stat. **17**, 521–541 (2010). https://doi.org/10.1007/s10651-009-0114-3
3. Adams, R.P., MacKay, D.J.: Bayesian online changepoint detection. arXiv preprint arXiv:0710.3742 (2007)
4. Bruni, V., Cardinali, M.L., Vitulano, D.: A short review on minimum description length: an application to dimension reduction in PCA. Entropy **24**(2), 269 (2022)
5. Cox, D.R., Lewis, P.A.: The Statistical Analysis of Series of Events. Springer, Heidelberg (1966)
6. Erdman, C., Emerson, J.W.: bcp: an R package for performing a Bayesian analysis of change point problems. J. Stat. Softw. **23**, 1–13 (2008)
7. Grünwald, P., Roos, T.: Minimum description length revisited. Int. J. Math. Ind. **11**(01), 1930001 (2019)
8. Gupta, A., Mańdziuk, J., Ong, Y.S.: Evolutionary multitasking in bi-level optimization. Complex Intell. Syst. **1**, 83–95 (2015)
9. Hallgren, K.L., Heard, N.A., Adams, N.M.: Changepoint detection in non-exchangeable data (2021). https://doi.org/10.1007/s11222-022-10176-1, http://arxiv.org/abs/2111.05054
10. Killick, R., Eckley, I.: Changepoint: an R package for changepoint analysis. J. Stat. Softw. **58**(3), 1–19 (2014)
11. Rissanen, J.: Modeling by shortest data description. Automatica **14**(5), 465–471 (1978)
12. Rissanen, J.: Information and Complexity in Statistical Modeling, vol. 152. Springer, Heidelberg (2007)
13. Rodrigues, E.R., Achcar, J.A.: Modeling the time between ozone exceedances. In: Applications of Discrete-Time Markov Chains and Poisson Processes to Air Pollution Modeling and Studies, pp. 65–78 (2013)
14. Sierra, B.M.S., Coen, A., Taimal, C.A.: Genetic algorithm with a Bayesian approach for the detection of multiple points of change of time series of counting exceedances of specific thresholds (2023)
15. Taylor, S.J., Letham, B.: Forecasting at scale. Am. Stat. **72**(1), 37–45 (2018)

An Exploration of Genetic Algorithms Operators for the Detection of Multiple Change-Points of Exceedances Using Non-homogeneous Poisson Processes and Bayesian Methods

Carlos A. Taimal$^{(\boxtimes)}$, Biviana Marcela Suárez-Sierra ,
and Juan Carlos Rivera

Universidad EAFIT, Medellín 050022, Colombia
`cataimaly@eafit.edu.co`

Abstract. In this paper it is presented an exploration of different strategies to generate solutions in a genetic algorithm for the detection of multiple change-points in univariate time series. The purpose is to find which combination of these is the optimal one while modelling times where there is an exceedance from a given threshold through Non Homogeneous Poisson Processes. Likewise, elements from information theory are taken to define a parsimonious model such that the explained phenomenon has a low memory usage and an optimal quantity of parameters which are estimated through a Bayesian approach. These elements define the objective function. Thus and after evaluating different operators it is found that the optimal strategy to generate and to combine new solutions is through a random keys initialization, selection of the parents through the ranks and Boltzmann tournament method or through a roulette strategy and using a fixed low mutation rate such that the diversity component is supplied through a neighborhood exploration while keeping the fitness of the solutions close to the real value.

Keywords: Genetic algorithm · Multiple Change-point detection · Non-homogeneous Poisson Process · Minimum Description Length · Bayesian Statistics

1 Introduction

In the time series and signal processing literature a common problem is to find the times where a system experiences abrupt changes. Such times are known as change-points and the abrupt changes can be variations in the parameters of the fitted model to the observed measures or resume measures (statistics); these include but are not limited to the mean of the data, its variance and standard deviation, the parameters of a time series process, the coefficients of a linear regression, to name a few [3,36].

© The Author(s), under exclusive license to Springer Nature Switzerland AG 2024
M. Tabares et al. (Eds.): CCC 2023, CCIS 1924, pp. 230–258, 2024.
https://doi.org/10.1007/978-3-031-47372-2_20

To decide what times are points of change, it is proceeded in a sequential manner defining a set of candidate change-points and then through an algorithm of three components establishing whether these constitute such kind of times or not. Those components are: an objective function that measures the quality of the segments delimited by the change-points; some of these functions include maximum likelihood ones, probability density functions, piece-wise linear regressions, time series models and in general, any function that captures the similarity notion among the data. The second component is a penalty that allows for a low complexity model and finally, the third component is the method to explore the solution space according to initially defined conditions and it is named "search method".

While search methods as those based on dynamic programming have been documented to have linear complexity time ($\mathcal{O}(T)$), these suppose objective functions with a linear behavior as well [19] and likewise there are complex scenarios where such performance is not always reached [33]. On the other side, some methods require previous knowledge in regards of the distribution of the data as the normal distribution [27] or do require to know beforehand the generating process which in turn defines the objective function [21]. Thus, it is necessary on the one hand, a method to model the presence of a change-point and on the other one, a method to locate them. For the first problem we propose modelling through Non Homogeneous Poisson Processes (NHPP) the times where does exist a deviation from a given threshold, in this case, the arithmetic mean. On the other side, in order to evaluate the solution space in an intelligent manner, it is proposed the use of a genetic algorithm, which through evolutionary principles, omit infeasible solutions or ones that are not efficient according to some criteria. Furthermore, given the low availability of genetic algorithms literature [6, 9, 16–18, 21, 28, 37] in contrast to other documented methods [2, 36], it becomes attractive to use and explore heuristic-based methods such as the genetic algorithms.

The rest of the paper proceeds as follows. The next section presents a description of the problem and the methods used to approach it. The third section presents the performance metrics to assess the quality of the solutions, the next one presents an experiment on different explored strategies and operators and the last section presents some conclusions in regards of the work and future developments.

2   Description of the Problem

2.1   Change-Point Detection Algorithms

Consider a time series $y = \{y_t\}_{t=1}^{T}$ as a sequence of observations from a sequence of independent and identically distributed (*iid*) random variables $\{Y_t\}_{t=1}^{T}$ with $t = \{1, 2, \ldots, T\}$ the set of times where such random variables were measured. A subset $\mathcal{T} = \{\tau_1, \tau_2, \ldots\} \subset t$ will be referred as a set of time indexes.

Now, consider an abrupt change in a parameter of y or a summary measure such as the mean, variance, standard deviation or correlation, then the time were such change happens is known as a change-point, and a set of J change-points is then $\mathcal{T} = \{\tau_1, \tau_2, \ldots, \tau_J\}, \tau_1 < \tau_2 < \ldots, \tau_J,\ J \leq T$ using the index notation $\tau_1, \tau_2, \ldots, \tau_J, \tau_1 < \tau_2 < \ldots < \tau_J$. Such indexes will also be configured as parameters in the model of interest [36]

Then the general change-point detection problem can be formulated as one of optimization [36] with three components: a quantitative criterion $V(\tau, y)$ that depends on the observed data y, a penalty or constraint on the parameters of the assumed model and an optimization or search method to locate the change-points and estimate the parameters. The choice of $V(\cdot, \cdot)$ depends on the problem and includes but is not limited to distance-based functions, probability density functions, nonparametric density estimators and in general, any function that captures similarity or discrepancies between observations.

Assuming $V(\cdot, \cdot)$ for the whole time series is the sum of its evaluation in each segment, from now on referred as regime, delimited by two change-points $\tau_j,\ \tau_{j+1}, \tau_j < \tau_{j+1} \forall\ j = 0, 1, \ldots, J$, we have,

$$V(\tau, y) := \sum_{j=0}^{J} V(y_{t_j} \ldots y_{t_{j+1}})$$

that is, $V(y_{t_j}, y_{t_{j+1}})$ measures the goodness of fit of the model to the observations in the interval (t_j, t_{j+1}) with $\tau_0 = 1$, the first time of the series and $\tau_{J+1} = T$ the last one. Thus the best segmentation is the set of indexes τ that optimize $V(\tau, y)$. If the number of change-points, J is unknown, a penalty $\text{pen}(\tau)$ is introduced and we have the discrete optimization problem,

$$\min_{\tau} V(\tau, y) + \text{pen}(\tau). \tag{1}$$

Otherwise (1) becomes $\min_{|\tau| = J} V(\tau, y)$, with $|\tau|$ the cardinality or numbers of elements in τ. Thus we have defined so far, two of the three components proposed by [36]. The third one is the method used to solve (1) known as "*of search*" that includes dynamic programming, binary segmentation, sliding windows and any other approximate method that manages to explore the solution space while being computationally effective and correctly balancing between goodness of fit and parsimony.

As stated by [21], there are 2^T possible combinations of the total of change-points and their locations making an exhaustive evaluation an impractical and computationally expensive task. Thus it is attractive to use a metaheuristic making an intelligent search through the solution space, while discarding the infeasible solutions as per evolutionary and probabilistic principles, overcoming limitations from exhaustive methods and those that are not rigorous enough in regards of the search of optimal solutions.

In the following section we will introduce the quantitative criterion $V(\cdot, \cdot)$ based on nonhomogeneous Poisson processes (NHPP) as well as the penalty that are defined as a whole on the basis of the informative principle of *Minimum Description Length*.

2.2   Time Series of Measures and of Exceedances

The series y will be now known as TS_1 or series of measures. A threshold $Thresh \in \mathbb{R}$ will be defined. The times t where $y_t \geq Thresh$ will be determined. Thus, the series of exceedances will be defined as in (1).

Definition 1 (Series of Exceedances).
The series of exceedances is defined as the set of instants where y_t overshoots a given threshold $Thresh$. That is,

$$TS_2 = \{t : y_t \geq Thresh,\ t \in \{1, 2, \ldots, T\}\}$$

Then TS_2 can be modelled using a Non Homogeneous Poisson Process (NHPP), furthermore, in the presence of the J change-points $\mathcal{T}$, such the times that segment TS_2 segment TS_1 as well, this without distribution assumptions for y or a specific model.

2.3   Non Homogeneous Poisson Processes

A counting process $\{N(t), t \geq 0\}$ is said non stationary Poisson or non homogeneous Poisson with intensity function $\lambda(t), t \geq 0$ if [32],

1. $N(0) = 0$
2. $\{N(t), t \geq 0\}$ has independent increments
3. $P(N(t + h) - N(t) \geq 2) = o(t)$
4. $P(N(t + h) - N(t) = 1) = \lambda(t)h + o(h)$

Making,

$$m(t) = \int_0^t \lambda(s) \tag{2}$$

It can be shown that,

$$P(N(t + s) - N(t) = n) = exp\{-[m(t + s) - m(t)]\}[m(t + s) - m(t)]^n / n!, n \geq 0 \tag{3}$$

That is, $N(t+s) - N(t) \sim Poisson(m(t+s) - m(t))$. $\lambda(t)$, known as function of intensity can be assumed as any of (4).

$$
\begin{aligned}
\lambda^{(W)}(t \mid \theta) &= (\alpha/\beta)(t/\beta)^{\alpha-1}, & \alpha, \beta &> 0 \\
\lambda^{(MO)}(t \mid \theta) &= \frac{\beta}{t+\alpha}, & \alpha, \beta &> 0 \\
\lambda^{(GO)}(t \mid \theta) &= \alpha\beta \exp(-\beta t), & \alpha, \beta &> 0 \\
\lambda^{(GGO)}(t \mid \theta) &= \alpha\beta\gamma t^{\gamma-1} \exp(-\beta t^{\gamma}), & \alpha, \beta, \gamma &> 0.
\end{aligned}
\tag{4}
$$

Such that the superindex on the left side corresponds to the first letter of the name of the distribution used as follows, Weibull (W) [25,29], Musa-Okumoto

(MO) [26], Goel-Okumoto (GO) and a generalization of the Goel-Okumoto model (GGO) [11]. For each of the previous functions the Mean Cumulative Function, $m(t \mid \theta)$, is defined as:

$$
\begin{aligned}
m^{(W)}(t \mid \theta) &= (t/\beta)^{\alpha}, & \alpha, \beta > 0 \\
m^{(MO)}(t \mid \theta) &= \beta \log\left(1 + \tfrac{t}{\alpha}\right), & \alpha, \beta > 0 \\
m^{(GO)}(t \mid \theta) &= \alpha[1 - \exp(-\beta t)], & \alpha, \beta > 0 \\
m^{(GGO)}(t \mid \theta) &= \alpha[1 - \exp(-\beta t^{\gamma})], & \alpha, \beta, \gamma > 0.
\end{aligned} \tag{5}
$$

Thus from the definition of a NHPP the objective function, $V(\mathcal{T}, y)$ can be defined. Besides the previously stated, using the informative principle *Minimum Description Length* the penalty $P_{\tau}(\theta)$ will also be derived.

Objective Function and Penalty: *Bayesian Minimum Description Length*. The *Minimum Description Length* (MDL) is an informative principle that formalizes that of the Ockham's razor [30]. The purpose is to find the most parsimonious model or the one with the least complexity given by its *bits* representation. The general expression of the *MDL* is given by,

$$
MDL = -\log_2(L_{opt}) + P_{\tau}(\theta) \tag{6}
$$

Without loss of generality, $\log_2$ is replaced by the natural logarithm or of base e [21]. L_{opt}, which corresponds to the maximum likelihood function evaluated in the estimators found through such method, is replaced by the posterior distribution function evaluated in the Maxmimum A Posteriori (MAP) estimators. Then,

$$
\begin{aligned}
Bayesian - MDL &= -ln(f(\theta|\mathbf{D})) + P_{\tau}(\theta) \\
&= -ln(f(\mathbf{D}|\theta) \times f(\theta)) + P_{\tau}(\theta) \\
&= -[lnf(\mathbf{D}|\theta) + lnf(\theta)] + P_{\tau}(\theta) \\
&= P_{\tau}(\theta) - lnf(\mathbf{D}|\theta) - lnf(\theta)
\end{aligned} \tag{7}
$$

$P_{\tau}(\theta)$ in (7) is the penalty term. The formulation of the MDL establishes that the parameters are bounded according to their nature as follows [6]: a real-valued parameter whose estimation is made with k observations needs $\frac{1}{2}\log_2 k$ *bits* to be codified. Estimating each parameter regime-wise, $\tau_j - \tau_{j-1}$ realizations are needed, that is, $\frac{1}{2}\log_2 \tau_j - \tau_{j-1}$ *bits* are used to represent $\theta \in \mathbb{R}$. On the other hand, to codify an integer parameter I there are needed $\log_2 I$ *bits* always that an upper bound is not provided; in the case of the change-points, $\tau_1 < \tau_2 < \ldots < \tau_J$, thus, every $\tau_j, j = 1, 2, \ldots, J$ must be represented with $\log_2 \tau_{j+1}$ *bits*. Finally, $J \leq T$, that is, there can be many change-points as realizations exist, thus this parameter is not bounded and $\log_2 J$ *bits* are required to represent it.

Replacing $\log_2$ by natural logarithm, again, without loss of generality and under the additivity property of the penalty, $P_{\tau}(\theta)$ becomes,

$$P_\tau(\theta) = R \sum_{j=1}^{J+1} \frac{ln(\tau_j - \tau_{j-1})}{2} + ln(J) + \sum_{j=2}^{J+1} ln(\tau_j) \qquad (8)$$

With R in (8) the cardinality of the vector of real parameters. On the other hand, $f(\theta)$ is the joint prior distribution for the assumed intensity function. For a $Weibull(\alpha, \beta)$ intensity and mean cumulative function,

$$\log f(\alpha, \beta, \tau_j) \propto (\phi_{12} - 1) \log \alpha - \phi_{11}\alpha + (\phi_{22} - 1) \log \beta - \phi_{21}\beta - \log(T - 1) \quad (9)$$

Assuming $\alpha \sim Gamma(\phi_{11}, \phi_{12})$, $\beta \sim Gamma(\phi_{21}, \phi_{22})$ and $\tau_j \sim Unif(1, T)$, $\forall, j = 1, 2, \ldots, J$ [20]. The joint prior distribution for other intensity functions are presented in [34].

Finally and using again a $Weibull(\alpha, \beta)$ intensity and Mean cumulative function for the piece-wise exceedances, (7) becomes,

$$\ln P_\tau(\theta) - \ln f_\tau(D \mid \theta) - \ln f_\tau(\theta)$$

$$= 2 \sum_{i=1}^{J+1} \frac{\ln(\tau_i - \tau_{i-1})}{2} + \ln(J) + \sum_{i=2}^{J} \ln(\tau_i)$$

$$- \sum_{j=1}^{J+1} \left(\frac{\tau_{j-1}^{\alpha_j} - \tau_j^{\alpha_j}}{\beta_j^{\alpha_j}} + (N_{\tau_j} - N_{\tau_{j-1}}) (\ln(\alpha_j) - \alpha_j \ln(\beta_j)) (\alpha_j - 1) \sum_{i=N_{\tau_{j-1}}+1}^{N_{\tau_j}} \ln(d_i) \right)$$

$$- \sum_{j=1}^{J+1} ((\phi_{12} - 1) \ln \alpha_j - \phi_{11}\alpha_j + (\phi_{22} - 1) \ln \beta_j - \phi_{21}\beta_j) + J \, ln(T - 1) \qquad (10)$$

where N_{τ_j} is the number of exceedances before the $j - th$ change-point, $j = 1, 2, \ldots, J$, and d_i is the $i - th$ is the time where an exceedance in the $j - th$ regime occurs. Next, (10) will be optimized using a genetic algorithm described in the following section. The details of $\ln f_\tau(D \mid \theta)$ and $\ln f_\tau(\theta)$ are given in the Appendix A.2.

2.4   Genetic Algorithms

Just as [21] provided the approach to define the BMDL along with [6], the first work is also used to define the search method, the genetic algorithm.

A genetic algorithm is a family of methods formalized by John Holland for adaptive systems [7] whose use has become widespread to optimization problems where an exact solution is not feasible and are in turn part of the family of metaheuristics. In a genetic algorithm the solutions are specified as a tuple of symbols or numbers known as *chromosomes* such that a set of k chromosomes generated in the same iteration are known as a *Population*; the first iteration is known as the *initial population*. In each iteration, from now, *generation* after the initial one, new solutions are created choosing two from the previous generation as per evolutionary principles and then they are combined and transformed through functions named *genetic operators* or *operators* for short. For each new generation created and according to the strategy defined by the researcher, the previous one is replaced completely or partially resulting in a new population. This process is repeated as many times while a stopping criterion is not reached or satisfied, which is usually running the algorithm for a number of r generations or until the solutions do not improve or are not genetically diverse.

In our problem, the chromosomes will be defined as $(J, \tau_1, \tau_2, \ldots, \tau_J)$ with the first component or *allele* being the number of change-points and the next ones their locations. We can now define the genetic algorithm to use and the modifications that will be made using as starting point [21].

2.5 Initial Genetic Algorithm

In [21] the initial population of the genetic algorithm is created by sampling a random uniform variable $Unif(0,1)$, T times and storing those values in a vector $(u_1, u_2, \ldots, u_T)$. Each sample is associated to every time of the series y, such that if the relationship $u_t \leq 0.06$ $t = 1, 2, \ldots, T$ is satisfied (0.06 is roughly the proportion of change-points in ecological time series [21]) the $t - th$ time is taken as a possible change-point and stored in a tuple with structure $(J, \tau_1, \tau_2, \ldots, \tau_J)$ resulting in a chromosome where J is the number of times satisfying the condition. This procedure is repeated $k - 1$ times until completing a population of size k and each chromosome is saved in a matrix P_0 of size $k \times T$. Since $J \leq T$, the $T - (J + 1)$ remaining alleles of each solution are completed with zeroes so the solutions have the same size and can be treated more properly.

From the initial population, each individual is evaluated in (10) thus obtaining the so called fitness values that then are sorted decreasingly (worst to best), while also saving the corresponding index of the individual in the population matrix. On the other hand, the position each individual holds according to its fitness value are named "ranks" and are denoted as S_j, $j = 1, 2, \ldots, k$; for example, if in P_0 with $k = 50$ individuals the eighth one was the worst according to its fitness value, then its rank is 1, that is, $S_8 = 1$ meanwhile if 32nd solution in P_0 obtained the lowest score, $S_{32} = 50$. This is illustrated in the Table 1.

Table 1. $BMDL$ scores sorted from worst to best

Individual	BMDL Score
8	−1810.06
1	−1999.08
⋮	⋮
5	−3107.67
32	−3109.89

Then for each of the ranks the proportional probability is established, $S_i / \sum_{j=1}^{k} S_j$. With these ranks it is proceeded to create new solutions through a mating or recombination process. A random number $u \sim Unif(0, k/\sum_{j=1}^{k} j)$ is generated and if $u \in (S_{i-1}/\sum_{j=1}^{k} j, S_i/\sum_{j=1}^{k} j]$ the $i - th$ chromosome is taken from P_0 as the mother. With the $k - 1$ remaining solutions the father is selected analogously while seeking not to use the same chromosome as parents, if they are the same the process is repeated from scratch. With the chromosomes of the parents selected, let's suppose, $(J_1, \eta_1, \eta_2, \ldots, \eta_{J_1})$ and $(J_2, \delta_1, \delta_2, \ldots, \delta_{J_2})$, the child is created joining the alleles of them, $Child''' = (J_1 + J_2, \tau_1, \tau_2, \ldots, \tau_{J_1+J_2})$ while also removing potential duplicates such that, $Child'' = (J'', \tau_1, \tau_2, \ldots, \tau_{J''})$, $J'' \leq J_1 + J_2$.

Next, for each allele in $Child''$ a fair coin is thrown and if a success is observed, this is preserved, otherwise this is removed such that the chromosome of the child can be of a lesser length than those of the parents and after once again, removing duplicates we have $Child' = (J', \tau_1, \tau_2, \ldots, \tau_{J'})$, $J' \leq J_1 + J_2$.

Finally a coin with probability of success 3% is thrown. If a success is observed, the current child is mutated as follows. For each of the J' alleles of the child $(\tau_1, \tau_2, \ldots, \tau_{J'})$ a "three-sided dice" with values $(-1, 0, 1)$ and probabilities $(0.3, 0.4, 0.3)$ is thrown. If for one allele the dice returns -1, the corresponding time becomes the previous one, if the dice returns 1 the associated time increases one unit and if the dice returns 0 the associated time remains the same. The mutated alleles are stored and after removing once again duplicates, they are stored in the tuple $Child = (J, \tau_1, \tau_2, \ldots, \tau_J)$, $J \leq J_1 + J_2 \leq T$.

The previous process is repeated $k - 1$ times until completing a new generation of k individuals all with different chromosomes and the process is repeated for r generations. Thus the genetic algorithm is one with operators of crossover and mutation and with strategies for creating an initial population and replacing it in each generation. The modifications we intend to apply are the following, the initial population will be generated through random keys, the parents will be selected using ranks while also introducing a tournament step with a modified Boltzmann procedure, the mutation rate will be calibrated to find the optimal one and three strategies will be tested to replace the population in each generation. Each one of these strategies is described in detail in the next section.

2.6   Proposed Algorithm

Population Initialization Through Random Keys. To create the initial Population, k solutions are randomly generated adopting the Random Keys representation [13]. Each Random Key solution (RK) is composed by $T + 1$ pseudo-random numbers (*i.e.*, $RK = (rk_0, rk_1, \ldots, rk_{T-1}, rk_T)$ with $rk_j \sim U(0, 1)$, $j = 0, 2, \ldots, T$. For each solution, the number of candidate change-points is obtained by multiplying the first random key value (rk_0) by T and rounded to the closer integer value, that is, $J = \lceil rk_0 \times T \rceil$.

Then, random keys values rk_1 to rk_T are used to determine the candidate moments where an abrupt change could happen in y. Random keys values rk_1

to rk_T are sorted non-decreasingly, so that the indices corresponding to the J minimum rk are the candidate change-points.

For instance, for $RK = (0.37, 0.87, 0.21, 0.55, 0.38, 0.67)$ with $T = 5$ then $J = \lceil 0.37 \times T \rceil = 2$ and the candidate change-points are times 2 and 4 that corresponds to the $J = 2$ random keys with the smallest values. Then we have the chromosome $(2, 2, 4)$, that is two change-points in times 2 and 4. This procedure is repeated $k - 1$ times until completing the initial population P_0 of size k and the children in the next generations are created as described in the following section.

This method is contrasted with the one proposed by [21] to create an initial population. First, the number of change-points is selected as a realization from a binomial distribution, that is, $J \sim Binom(N - 2, p = 0.06)$. $p = 0.06$ is chosen as per [21]. Now with J^*, the number of change-points to generate is chosen as a realization from said distribution.

Next, we generate $N - 2$ realizations from a distribution $Unif(0, 1)$ and these are stored in an array $Chromosome'$; $Chromosome'$ is sorted increasingly and its values stored in $Chromosome''$ such that the values of $Chromosome'$ in the first J^* positions of $Chromosome''$ are the values that will compose the chromosome, $Chromosome$. Additionally to the possible times of change, $Chromosome$ must include the first time of the series, 1, the last one, T and the number of change-points, J. Thus, the general structure of a solution is given as follows,

$$(J, 1, \tau_1, \tau_2, \ldots, \tau_J, T)$$

Selection Strategy: Boltzmann Tournament with Ranks. We start by using the method in Sect. 2.5 to assign ranks to the solutions according to their fitness values such that the best one has rank $S_j = 50$ and the worst, $S_{j'} = 1$, $j \neq j' \in \{1, 2, \ldots, k\}$. While this strategy avoids possible selection biases that favours the best solutions, adjacent solutions to the ones selected for mating are discarded such the exploration of the solution space could be not optimal in regards of this procedure. Thus through a tournament selection two solutions are compared and the best one according to a given criterion is used for the mating process; then the process is repeated again to select possible candidates for the other parent and finally with two different parents a child is created as in Sect. 2.5).

The here proposed tournament is a modification of the Boltzmann procedure presented in [5] and instead of allowing a tournament between a few of parents, all of them are selected in such way to create the children. Let's suppose there is a parent with a fitness value $BMDL_{Old}$ and then let's suppose a neighbor solution with fitness value $BMDL_{New}$; subsequently, each one is evaluated in the function (11),

$$P_{Boltzmann}(BMDL_j) = \frac{e^{-BMDL_j/T}}{\sum_j^k e^{-BMDL_j/T}} \tag{11}$$

whose probability distribution is approximately the Boltzmann one, thus the name, and T is a temperature parameter similar to the one used in (*Simulated Annealing*) [12]. Then if $P_{Boltzmann}(BMDL_{New}) < P_{Boltzmann}(BMDL_{Old})$, the solution associated to $BMDL_{New}$ is chosen for mating, otherwise the "old" solution associated to $BMDL_{Old}$ is kept, such that (11) defines a rejection probability.

The problem that arises is defining the neighbor(s) of a solution. For this we can use the ranks Table 1); if the chromosome associated to $BMDL_{Old}$ is located in the first position, its neighbor will be the solution with rank 2 or the second worst. If the solution with fitness value $BMDL_{Old}$ has a rank k or is located in the last position in the ranks table, then its neighbor solution will be the one with rank $k - 1$ or the second best.

For instance, in Table 1 the neighbor solution to the chromosome 8 is the chromosome 1 in the population matrix while the neighbor solution to chromosome 32 is chromosome 5. Now if $BMDL_{Old}$ is located around the center in the ranks table, a neighborhood is defined as the two previous solutions and the two following ones if it has two neighbors in both directions, otherwise it will have only one neighbor above and one neighbor below (see Table 2).

Table 2. Neighbors of a central solution

Index	BMDL
⋮	⋮
$i - 2$	-2099.55
$i - 1$	-2105.13
i	-2105.67
$i + 1$	-2222.89
$i + 2$	-2291.11
⋮	⋮

Then a neighbor from the set of two or four is randomly selected and compared to the previous solution using (11). Thus through the ranks method the best solutions are not privileged and with the tournament procedure, solutions with an "average" behavior are explored and given the chance of improving. We will set the temperature parameter as $T = 27$, close to the maximum average in Medellín, Colombia (26 °C–28 °C) [15].

This method is compared with two other strategies to select the parents, the roulette method and the Stochastic Universal Sampling (SUS).

- **Roulette method:** Let's suppose we have for each chromosome of the initial population a value of the objective function, $BMDL_i, i = 1, 2, \ldots, k$. Then, we proceed to sum all the objective function values, multiplied by -1,

$BMDL_{sum} = \sum_{i=1}^{k} -BMDL_i$ and each $-BMDL_i$ is divided by $BMDL_{sum}$; according to the proportion of $BMDL_{sum}$ every $BMDL_j$ represents, we assign an area in the roulette represented as Fig. 1.

Thus, it is appreciated how a better solution has a larger area in the roulette. We "spin" the roulette to generate a value $R^* \in (0,1)$ and if $R^* \leq \sum_{j=1}^{i} -BMDL_j/BMDL_{sum}$ the $i-th$ chromosome is selected as the father. This procedure is repeated once again to select the mother. If the associated chromosome to the father is identical to the one of the mother, the process is repeated [4]. Once selected the mother and father we proceed to mating them and/or crossing them.

- **Stochastic Universal Sampling (SUS):**
  In this method, we have to define a roulette with the values of the objective function as in the case of the roulette method. In contrast with such strategy, in the interval $(0,1)$ ancillary partitions must be made, all with length $1/k$ in order to select the parents. The roulette is "spun" once and two "pointers" are defined (or more according to the problem). We stored the position where such pointers fall; then the parents are chosen such that the original roulette contains the pointers in the ancillary roulette [4].

  For example in Fig. 2 a roulette with 5 areas or divisions of the same length, $1/5$ is spun and five pointers are defined. The first pointer fell in the area of the first chromosome, the second one in the area of the third chromosome, the pointers three and four fell in the area of chromosome 4 and the fith pointer fell in the area of the fifth chromosome. Thus the selected chromosomes for mating are the $1, 3, 4, 4, 5$.

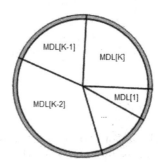

Fig. 1. Graphical representation of the roulette method. Adapted from [4].

Replacement Strategy. Two strategies are proposed to update the population in each generation. Such strategies define which individuals survive from one generation to the other. Both are known as elitists and privilege the best solutions, yet the first one considers diversity criteria to keep the exploratory nature of the algorithm. These are described in detail as follows.

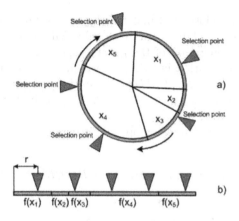

Fig. 2. Taken from [4].

- **Total replacement:** the so called classical procedure. Here the k individuals of each previous generation are replaced by k children created after mating the parents.
- **Steady state:** In the steady state approach instead of creating k new individuals, k^*, $k^* \leq k$ are generated using the procedure described in Sect. 2.6 and then the worst k^* solutions are replaced [22,23].
  [23] suggest k^* should be the two worst solutions while [22] points out that k^* should be a random number between 1 y k. We propose defining k^* as follows. A pseudo-random number $u \sim Unif(0,1)$ is sampled and then we take k^* as the integer part of $k \times u$, that is, $k^* = \lceil k \times u \rceil$. Thus we randomly replaced a proportion of bad solutions in each generation favoring the election of the best ones through an elitist approach [23].

Mutation. For the mutation rate two strategies are tested. The first one consists in mutating the 3% of the solutions in each generation as proposed in [21] and the second one consists in taking a random proportion of individuals to mutate in each population, that is, denoting the proportion of individuals to mutate as $p_m \sim Unif(0,1)$ we select randomly $\lceil k \times p_m \rceil$ to mutate.

Once found the best way to mutate the individuals if the fixed mutation rate proves to give the best results, new rates in the interval $(0, 0.1)$ are tested, 0.03, 0.05, 0.05 and 0.1. Such rates are chosen in order to guarantee diversity without transforming the genetic algorithm into a random search [14].

3 Performance Metrics

To define whether a solution is better than the others, we use as performance metrics the runtime of the algorithm in seconds, the times the algorithm detected the real number of change-points, that is, J, the average value of the Bayesian-MDL and the average percentage change of all the generations, defined as follows.

Let's consider the global optimal for the fitness function which is known beforehand as we use simulated data. Such value will be denoted as $BMDL_{Opt}$. Now, be the $j - th$ generation of the genetic algorithm under evaluation, $j = 1, 2, \ldots, r$ each of them with k individuals evaluated in the fitness function thus having $BMDL_1, BMDL_2, \ldots, BMDL_k$. From these we take the minimum that will be denoted as $BMDL_{min,j} \; \forall \; j = 1, 2, \ldots, r$ such that we have r fitness values.

The percentage change from the optimal is defined as,

$$BMDL_{AvgPerc,j} = [(BMDL_{min,j} - BMDL_{Opt})/BMDL_{Opt}] \times 100, \; \forall \; j, j = 1, 2, \ldots, r$$

And the average percentage change is thus,

$$\bar{BMDL}_{AvgPerc} = \frac{1}{r} \sum_{j=1}^{r} BMDL_{AvgPerc,j}$$

Finally we have the best chromosome from the overall generations, that is, the one associated with the minimum value for the fitness function in all generations. For example, let's suppose we have $r = 50$ and then, fifty minima observations of the $BMDL$, $BMDL_{min,1}, BMDL_{min,2}, BMDL_{min,50}$, then we proceed to take the overall minima, denoted as $BMDL_{min}^{*}$ as the minima of all $BMDL_{min,j}, j = \{1, 2, \ldots, 50\}$, that is,

$$BMDL_{min}^{*} = min\{BMDL_{min,1}, BMDL_{min,2} \ldots, BMDL_{min,50}\}$$

and the optimal chromosome is the one whose evaluation in the fitness function returns $BMDL_{min}^{*}$.

4   Implementation and Results

The different versions of the algorithm are tested in three simulated datasets all with $log - normal(\mu, \sigma)$ distribution that were the same used in [35]. If a random variable $X \sim log - normal(\mu, \sigma)$, then its probability density function is given by expression (12).

$$f(x) = \begin{cases} \frac{1}{x\sigma\sqrt{2\pi}} exp\left(- \frac{(ln(x)-\mu)^2}{2\sigma^2} \right), & x > 0 \\ 0, & x < 0. \end{cases} \tag{12}$$

On the other hand, we assumed three settings for the locations of the change-points as given in Table 3 and as we have a piecewise density function (12) the parameters for each subseries or regime are given in Table 4 and graphically in the Fig. 3.

Table 3. Different Change-points simulations considered

Number of Change-points	Locations	*Bayesian-MDL*
1	$\tau_1 = 825$	830.86
2	$\tau_1 = 365, \tau_2 = 730$	726.59
3	$\tau_1 = 548, \tau_2 = 823, \tau_3 = 973$	597.73

On the other side, as prior distributions for the parameters of the Weibull intensity function we set $\alpha \sim Gamma(\phi_{11}, \phi_{12})$ and $\beta \sim Gamma(\phi_{21}, \phi_{22})$ and the change-points $\tau_j \sim U(1, T), \forall j = 1, 2, \ldots, J$ [20]. The number of generations (r) and their sizes (k) are fixed beforehand as suggested by [8], $r = 1000$, $k = 200$, while the other genetic operators and parameters are varied as previously exposed.

4.1   Initial Population

We compare two methods to initialize the genetic algorithm creating with each one an initial population of size $r = 200$ with one individual, that is, $k = 1$. In the first place, the method proposed by [21], which is similar to sampling $T - 2$ realizations (omitting the first and last time) from a random variable with a $Bernoulli(p = 0.06)$ distribution is compared to the random keys one. To assess the best strategy the runtime was measured, as well as the average value of the BMDL for all generations and the most commonly detected number of change-points, J. Additionaly on the BMDL values for each type of population, the nonparametric comparison test of Wilcoxon [38], was used and its p-value was also computed; its hypotheses are given in (13). The results of this experiments are given in Fig. 4.

Table 4. Settings for the time series regimes for different number of change-points

Number of Change-points	Number of regimes	Regime distribution
1	2	$log-normal(\mu = 3.5, \sigma = 0.32)$, $log-normal(\mu = 4.0, \sigma = 0.32)$
2	3	$log-normal(\mu = 3.5, \sigma = 0.32)$, $log-normal(\mu = 4.0, \sigma = 0.32)$, $log-normal(\mu = 4.5, \sigma = 0.32)$
3	4	$log-normal(\mu = 3.5, \sigma = 0.32)$, $log-normal(\mu = 4.0, \sigma = 0.32)$, $log-normal(\mu = 4.5, \sigma = 0.32)$, $log-normal(\mu = 5.0, \sigma = 0.32)$

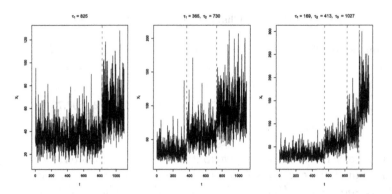

Fig. 3. Simulation settings

Thus, each method in each setting creates an initial population in under 10 s such that each chromosome is created in under one second. Now the value of the Bayesian-MDL was large in regards of the real one which is consequent with the estimated number of change-points, J that was over 60 for all the cases.

On the other hand, the generated BMDL in each population were compared using the Wilcoxon test such that its p-value were over 50% (50.18%, 51.35% and 95.14%) and under a significance level of 5%, we can conclude the populations generated by both methods do not differ statistically. Thus we can proceed with any of the methods to initialize the genetic algorithm. We will use with the random keys as its definition is probabilistic based and to explore other alternatives in the change-points detection problem. The results are given in Fig. 4.

$$H_0 : \textit{The samples are independent and identically distributed}$$
$$\textit{vs.} \tag{13}$$
$$H_a : \textit{The samples are not independent and identically distributed}$$

4.2   Parents Selection Method

Now, after the initial solutions were created through the random keys method, we proceed to create the new populations through a mating process. In order to select the parents to mate we compare three strategies: the roulette method, the selection through the *SUS* method and the selection using both the ranks method and the Boltzmann tournament. The results are given in Fig. 5.

Again a genetic algorithm with $r = 1000$ generations and $k = 200$ individuals each was used. It was measured the runtime in seconds, the average value of the BMDL for each selection method in every setting, the average percentage change, the most commonly number of detected change-points and the optimal chromosome.

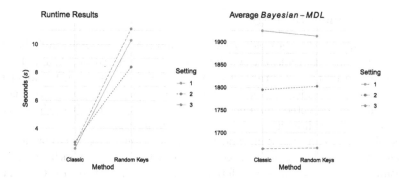

Fig. 4. Results for the two initialization strategies

The runtime in the roulette and SUS method was lower than that of the ranks-Boltzmann for one and two change-points. For three change-points the runtime was lower when using the ranks-Boltzmann selection method.

The average *Bayesian-MDL* was closer to the real value for the SUS when there are three change-points. When there are one and two change-points the ranks-Boltzmann method is closer to the optimal Bayesian-MDL value.

Finally the lower average percentual difference is achieved with the Roulette and ranks-Boltzmann method. Thus these are the methods preferred for two change-points and one and three change-points, respectively.

According to the results and the different criteria, to detect 1 and 3 change-points the best method was the combination of ranks and Boltzmann tournament. On the other side, the best method to select the parents in the case of two change-points was the roulette one, the simpler one.

While the roulette method succeeded at approximating the optimal change-points when $J = 2$, in the three cases the ranks-Boltzmann tournament method is the one that found the real number of change-points the most number of times (88.1%, 91.9% and 81.1% for each setting).

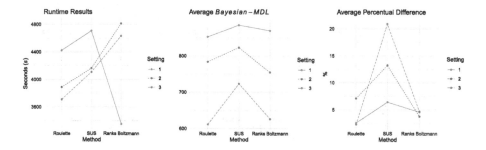

Fig. 5. Results for the parent selection strategies

4.3 Replacement Strategy

Here we compared the classical approach (complete population) and the elitist one (steady state) to replace the solutions in each generation. Again the same criteria were used to assess the performance of each variation of the algorithm, the runtime in seconds, the mean BMDL, the average percentage change, the most commonly detected number of change-points and the best chromosome. The results for the three first metrics are shown in Fig. 6.

Usually the steady state method has a lower runtime as it is not necessary to create k new solutions in each generation of the genetic algorithm. Thus in a runtime context the highest difference happens when there are two change-points with the steady state representing a reduction of 10% in comparison to the replacement of the whole population. When there is one change-point the maximum reduction in a runtime context is close to 5% and where there are three change-points there is no significative difference between one method and the other.

On the other hand, the average value of the objective function does not vary between one method or another, while for two and three change-points using the steady state method seems to generate solutions closer to the original according to the *Bayesian-MDL*. Likewise the average percentage difference supports the hypothesis that the steady state replacement method generates better solutions. Nevertheless for one and two change-points the complete replacement detects more frequently the real value of J in the 1000 generations (91.2% and 61.5% respectively) and furthermore, and furthermore, using such method the best chromosome in the whole population is closer to the real one: (1, 1, 826, 1096), (2, 1, 295, 736,1096) and (2, 1, 579, 841, 1096) for 1, 2 and 3 change-points. Thus, in order to keep the evolutionary features of the algorithm and as per the quality of the solutions, a total replacement strategy in each generations is kept. Now, the best way to mutate the individuals is explored.

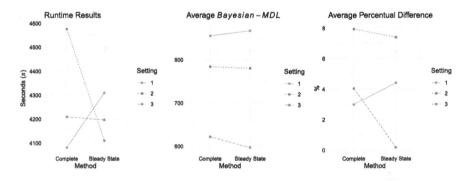

Fig. 6. Results for the replacement strategies

4.4 Mutation

Assessing the Best Strategy to Mutate the Individuals. After choosing the best strategy to replace the individuals in each generation, a total replacement, it is proceeded to evaluate the best way to mutate the individuals. The fixed mutation rate proposed by [21], $p_m = 3\%$ was used and contrasted to a random one, $p_m \in (0,1) \times 100$. The results of these tests shown in Fig. 7.

For the three settings we have then that choosing the number of individuals to mutate in a random manner does not change the results in a significantly. Nevertheless to guarantee that the algorithm continues to be a genetic one, a fixed mutation rate is kept. Different rates of mutations are explored in the next subsection.

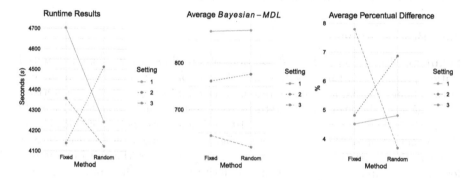

Fig. 7. Results for the mutation strategies

Selecting the Best Mutation Rate. Finally we explore different mutation rates. As previously mentioned, their values are restricted to the $(0, 0.1)$ interval such that the algorithm keeps its evolutionary features and does not becomes a random search algorithm [14]. The results of such experiment are given in Fig. 8.

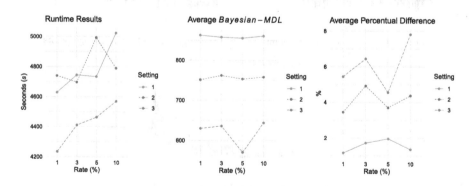

Fig. 8. Results for the mutation rates

Thus, in all cases it is appreciated that the genetic algorithm has the best results with low mutation rates $p_m = \{1\%, 3\%\}$. This can be appreciated in the runtime and the average percentage difference of the Bayesian-MDL from the real optimum such that as the value of p_m approaches 10% the quality of the solutions gets worse. When using a mutation rate $p_m = 1\%$, the proportion of times the genetic algorithm detected the real value of J was 91.8% and 91.70% for 1 and 2 change-points and while using a mutation rate $p_m = 3\%$ the proportion of times the genetic algorithm detected $J = 3$ for three change-points was 67.1%. On the other hand, the best chromosome in all 1000 generations was, using $p_m = 1\%$ (1, 1, 806, 1096), (2, 1, 346, 736, 1096) and (2, 1, 528, 822, 1096). Thus, keeping a low mutation rate provides the better results for this genetic algorithm such that the exploration procedure is accomplished using the neighborhood rejection procedure through the ranks-Boltzmann tournament.

4.5   Best Solutions

Segmentations. Thus, the best solutions obtained using a random keys initialization procedure, a ranks-Boltzmann selection or the roulette one in the case of two change-points, a fixed low rate mutation and the previous characteristics of the genetic algorithm in [21] returns the chromosomes: (1, 1, 806, 1096), (2, 1, 346, 736, 1096) and (2, 1, 528, 822, 1096). Using these points of change, then the segmentation of the original series Fig. 3 is the one shown in Fig. 9. Such segmentation is precise for the first two settings while in the third one it is so for times 548 and 823 but given the similarity between values of a regime and another it is not possible to find the change close to time 973.

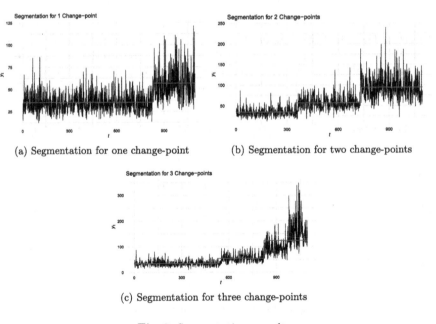

(a) Segmentation for one change-point   (b) Segmentation for two change-points

(c) Segmentation for three change-points

Fig. 9. Segmentations results

Estimated Intensity Functions. Finally, the estimated intensity functions are shown in Fig. 10. In the three cases such function captures the presence of the change-points given in the emissions of exceedances. The speed of generation of exceedances is approximately similar for two and three change-points which is greater in comparison to the the first case, the presence of one change-point. The estimated parameters are given in Table 5.

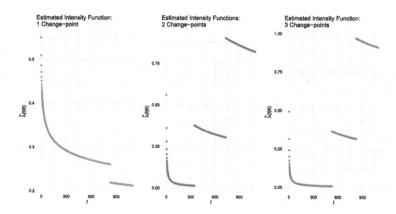

Fig. 10. Estimated Intensity Functions

Table 5. Parameter estimation for the Weibull Intensity Function

Setting	Regime	$\hat{\alpha}$	$\hat{\beta}$
1	1–830	0.89	1.72
	831–1096	0.75	1.72
2	1–345	0.37	0.31
	346–735	0.71	0.24
	736–1096	0.76	0.09
3	1–527	0.35	0.38
	528–821	0.67	0.12
	822–1096	0.78	0.11

5 Conclusions

The use of genetics algorithms to detect change-points was explored in a systematic manner.

A set of modifications were proposed to the genetic algorithm found in [21] with a focus in the mating strategy that combines a tournament selection with the linear ranks.

The concept of neighborhood was presented in the context of change-points solutions. While the use of the genetic algorithms was used given its previous documentation in literature, other metaheuristics such as Iterable Neighborhood Search or Variable Neighborhood search could be approached given this new definition of a neighbor solution [10].

For this specific problem it was found that a no completely elitist genetic algorithm was the best at optimizing the Bayesian Minimum Description Length criteria. A lower mutation rate was required as the exploration and diversity of the algorithm is supplied by the neighborhood search using the ranks-Boltzmann procedure.

While the calibration of the values of operators was done sequentially it could be done from a Design of Experiments approach [24].

There is still chance to explore strategies for an automated stopping and as well possible combinations of this family of algorithms with statistical strategies such as Markov Chains [16].

Finally with the obtained results, we proceed to define the best algorithm as one with the following features,

- **Initialization method:** Random keys
- **Parent selection method:** Ranks with a modified Boltzmann tournament or a Roulette method
- **Crossover method:** uniform like
- **Replacement strategy:** classic approach, the whole population in every previous generation was replaced by a new one
- **Mutation method:** Fixing the number of individuals to mutate at $p_m = 1\%$ of the whole population in all settings
- **Mutation strategy:** "three-sided dice" with values $(-1, 0, 1)$ and probabilities $(0.3, 0.4, 03)$.

A   Appendix

A.1   Tables for Implementation Results

(See Tables 6, 7, 8, 9 and 10).

Table 6. Results for Population Initialization

Setting	Initialization Method	Runtime (seconds)	Runtime per chromosome (seconds)	Mean Bayesian-MDL (Coefficient of Variation %)	More common number of Change-points (Frequency %)	Wilcoxon Test p-value
1 Change-point	Classic	2.59	0.012	1295 (6.18%)	66	50.18%
	Random Keys	10.29	0.051	1913 (6.73%)	66	
2 Change-points	Classic	3.04	0.015	1795 (6.56%)	67	51.35%
	Random Keys	8.39	0.042	1802.80 (6.75%)	62	
3 Change-points	Classic	2.86	0.014	1665 (7.65%)	66	95.14%
	Random Keys	11.11	0.05	1667 (7.56%)	64	

Table 7. Results for the Parents Selection Strategy

Setting	Selection Method	Runtime (s)	Runtime per generation (s)	Mean Bayesian-MDL (Coefficient of Variation %)	Average Percentage Difference	More common number of Change-points (Frecuency %)	Best Chromosome
1 Change-point	Roulette	4422.18	4.42	852.3 (9.67%)	2.58	1 (79.3%)	(1, 1, 830, 1096)
	SUS	4707.61	4.70	884.3 (9.28%)	6.43	1 (83.1%)	(1, 1, 803, 1096)
	Boltzmann Ranks	3352.9	3.35	868.9 (9.02%)	4.58	1 (88.1%)	(1, 1, 829, 1096)
2 Change-points	Roulette	3887.35	3.88	783.99 (9.3%)	7.09	1(54.2%)	(2, 1, 245, 721, 1096)
	SUS	4165.39	4.16	822.65 (9.33%)	13.22	1 (54.2%)	(2, 1, 345, 721, 1096)
	Boltzmann Ranks	4812.66	4.81	753.92 (12.34%)	3.76	2(91.9%)	(2, 1, 384, 768, 1096)
3 Change-points	Roulette	3709	3.71	611.42 (12.29%)	2.29	1 (65.20%)	(2, 1, 546, 823, 1096)
	SUS	4110.07	4.11	722.61 (11.14%)	20.89	1 (61.40%)	(1, 1, 558, 1096)
	Boltzmann Ranks	4632.34	4.63	625.74 (11.97%)	4.68	2 (81.11)	(2, 1, 548, 815, 1096)

Table 8. Results for the Population Replacement Strategy

Setting	Replacement strategy	Runtime (s)	Runtime per generation (s)	Mean Bayesian-MDL (Coefficient of Variation %)	Average Percentage Difference	More common number of Change-points (Frecuency %)	Best Chromosome
1 Change-point	Complete	4081.31	4.08	855.89 (9.25%)	3.01	1 (91.2%)	(1, 1, 826, 1096)
	Steady State	4309.57	4.31	867.62 (13.08%)	4.42	1 (85.1%)	(12, 1, 11, 17, 152, 170, 237, 483, 530, 550, 598, 801, 851, 1083, 1096)
2 Change-points	Complete	4576.42	4.57	784.36 (9.54%)	7.95	2 (61.5%)	(2, 1, 295, 736, 1096)
	Steady State	4110.56	4.11	780.4227 (12.22%)	7.409	2 (52.1%)	(4, 1, 5, 317, 583, 722, 1096)
3 Change-points	Complete	4209.59	4.21	622.02 (12.83%)	4.06	2 (47.70%)	(2, 1, 579, 841, 1096)
	Steady State	4196.48	4.19	596.61 (29.75%)	0.18	2 (63.1%)	(2, 1, 473, 804, 1096)

Table 9. Results for the Mutation Strategy

Setting	Mutation Strategy	Runtime (s)	Runtime per generation (s)	Mean Bayesian-MDL (Coefficient of Variation %)	Average Percentage Difference	More common number of Change-points (Frecuency %)	Best Chromosome
1 Change-point	Fixed rate	4704.42	4.70	868.47 (8.84%)	4.52	1 (92.2%)	(1, 1, 806, 1096)
	Random rate	4242.42	4.24	870.95 (8.76%)	4.82	1 (84.4%)	(1, 1, 820, 1096)
2 Change-points	Fixed rate	4138.14	4.14	761.59 (9.76%)	4.82	1 (84.4%)	(1, 1, 820, 1096)
	Random rate	4511.95	4.51	776.57 (9.64%)	6.88	2 (83.30%)	(2, 1, 350, 709, 1096)
3 Change-points	Fixed rate	4358.36	4.35	644.41 (11.98%)	7.80	2 (64.90%)	(2, 1, 524, 814, 1096)
	Random rate	4123.28	4.12	619.84 (12.77%)	3.70	1 (69.90%)	(2, 1, 547, 848, 1096)

Table 10. Results for Different Mutation Rates

Setting	Mutation Rate	Runtime (s)	Runtime per generation (s)	Mean Bayesian-MDL (Coefficient of Variation %)	Average Percentage Difference	More common number of Change-points (Frecuency %)	Best Chromosome
1 Change-point	1%	4629.61	4.63	862.46 (9.27%)	1.16	1 (91.8%)	(1, 1, 831, 1096)
	3%	4744,17	4.74	857.53 (9,33%)	1.72	1 (78.7%)	(1, 1, 840, 1096)
	5%	4734.19	4.73	855.43 (9.56%)	1.96	1 (77.8%)	(1, 1, 831, 1096)
	10%	5024.11	5.024	860.74 (9.88%)	1.36	1 (88.1%)	(1, 1, 825, 1096)
2 Change-points	1%	4740.11	4.74	751.64 (10.00%)	3.45	2 (91.7%)	(2, 1, 346, 736, 1096)
	3%	4696.7	4.70	762.39 (13.83%)	4.92	1 (70.6%)	(1, 1, 834, 1096)
	5%	4993.08	4.99	753.56 (14,42%)	3.71	2 (89.3%)	(2, 1, 334, 757, 1096)
	10%	4789.69	4.79	758.36 (10,45%)	4.38	2 (72.4%)	(2, 1, 268, 756, 1096)
3 Change-points	1%	4234.94	4.23	630.24 (11.51%)	5.44	2(52.4%)	(2, 1, 528, 822, 1096)
	3%	4410.8	4.41	636.27 (11,78%)	6.45	2 (67.1%)	(2, 1, 838, 973, 1096)
	5%	4463.17	4.46	570.48 (32.11%)	4.56	2 (78.3%)	(1, 1, 906, 1096)
	10%	4569.4	4.5694	644,48 (14,90%)	7.82	2 (48.1%)	(1, 1, 906, 1096)

A.2   Derivation of the Bayesian Minimum Description Length

Remember the change-points vector $T = \{\tau, \tau_2, \ldots, \tau_J\}$ and define the regimes or segments as $y_t, t \in (\tau_j, \tau_{j+1}), j = 0, 1, 2, \ldots, J$ such that $\tau_0 = 1$ y $\tau_{J+1} = T$, that can be can be attributed to the entrance of public policies by government agencies, macroeconomic policies from an economic/financial standpoint or to some stimuli in a neuroscience context. Thus, assuming that the values from TS_2 between two change-points can be modelled as a NHPP, the following intensity functions are given,

$$\lambda(t \mid \theta) = \begin{cases} \lambda(t \mid \theta_1), & 0 \leq t < \tau_1, \\ \lambda(t \mid \theta_j), & \tau_{j-1} \leq t < \tau_j, j = 2, 3, \cdots, J, \\ \lambda(t \mid \theta_{J+1}). & \tau_J \leq t \leq T, \end{cases} \tag{14}$$

with θ_j the vector of parameters between the change-points τ_{j-1} and τ_j, $j = 2, \ldots, J$ and θ_1 y θ_{J+1} the parameter vector before and after the first change-point and the last change-point, respectively. With n exceedances the mean cumulative functions are (see, for example, [31]),

$$
m(t \mid \theta) = \begin{cases}
m(t \mid \theta_1), & 0 \le t < \tau_1, \\
m(\tau_1 \mid \theta_1) + m(t \mid \theta_2) - m(\tau_1 \mid \theta_2), & \tau_1 \le t < \tau_2, \\
m(t \mid \theta_{j+1}) - m(\tau_j \mid \theta_{j+1}) & \\
+ \sum_{i=2}^{j}[m(\tau_i \mid \theta_i) - m(\tau_{i-1} \mid \theta_i)] & \\
+ m(\tau_1 \mid \theta_1), & \tau_j \le t < \tau_{j+1}, j = 2, 3, \cdots, J,
\end{cases}
\tag{15}
$$

(15) is defined as such because $m(t \mid \theta_1)$ represents the average number of exceedances for the given threshold before the first change-point. $m(\tau_1 \mid \theta_1) + m(t \mid \theta_2) - m(\tau_1 \mid \theta_2)$ is the average number of exceedances from the standard between the first change-point τ_1 and the second one, τ_2 given that the vector of parameters θ_2 is known and so on.

Be $D = \{d_1, \ldots, d_n\}$, con d_k the time where the $k - th$ events occurs (for example, the $k - th$ time where the maximum environmental standard is over-shot), $k = 1, 2, \ldots, n$. Then the maximum likelihood function for the exceedances is given by the expression (16), where N_{τ_i} represents the number of such event before the change-point τ_j, $j = 1, 2, \ldots, J$ (see [1,39]).

$$
L(\mathbf{D} \mid \phi) \propto \left[\prod_{i=1}^{N_{\tau_1}} \lambda(d_i \mid \theta_1) \right] e^{-m(\tau_1 \mid \theta_1)}
$$

$$
\times \prod_{j=2}^{J} \left(e^{-[m(\tau_j \mid \theta_j) - m(\tau_{j-1} \mid \theta_j)]} \prod_{i=N_{\tau_{j-1}}+1}^{N_{\tau_j}} \lambda(d_i \mid \theta_j) \right)
$$

$$
\times e^{-[m(T \mid \theta_{J+1}) - m(\tau_J \mid \theta_{J+1})]} \prod_{i=N_{\tau_J}+1}^{n} \lambda(d_i \mid \theta_{J+1}),
\tag{16}
$$

Considering τ_0, $N_{\tau_0} = 0$ y $m(0|\theta) = 0$, the expression (16) is simplified as follows,

$$
L(\mathbf{D} \mid \phi) \propto \prod_{j=1}^{J+1} \left(e^{-[m(\tau_j|\theta_j) - m(\tau_{j-1}|\theta_j)]} \prod_{i=N_{\tau_{J-1}}+1}^{N_{\tau_j}} \lambda(d_i \mid \theta_j) \right)
\tag{17}
$$

and after applying logarithm to (17),

$$
\log L(D \mid \phi) = \left(\sum_{j=1}^{J+1} m(\tau_{j-1} \mid \theta_j) - m(\tau_j \mid \theta_j) \right)
$$

$$
+ \left(\sum_{j=1}^{J+1} \sum_{i=N_{\tau_{j-1}}+1}^{N_{\tau_j}} \log \lambda(d_i \mid \theta_j) \right)
$$

$$
= \sum_{j=1}^{J+1} \left(m(\tau_{j-1} \mid \theta_j) - m(\tau_j \mid \theta_j) + \sum_{i=N_{\tau_{j-1}}+1}^{N_{\tau_j}} \log \lambda(d_i \mid \theta_j) \right)
\tag{18}
$$

On the other hand, the Bayesian update rule states that,

$$f(\theta|\mathbf{D}) \propto L(\mathbf{D}|\theta) \times f(\theta) \tag{19}$$

Taking logarithm on (19),

$$log f(\theta|\mathbf{D}) \propto log L(\mathbf{D}|\theta) + log f(\theta) \tag{20}$$

where $\log L(\mathbf{D}|\theta)$ corresponds to (18). It is now necessary to establish the joint prior distribution $f(\theta)$. The procedure for the first three cases is defined in (5) where $f(\theta) = f(\alpha, \beta, \tau_j)$, $j = 1, 2, \ldots, J$ while for the last one where $f(\theta) = f(\alpha, \beta, \gamma, \tau_j)$, $j = 1, 2, \ldots, J$, the reader is referred to [34].

Prior Distributions
Assuming $\alpha \sim Gamma(\phi_{11}, \phi_{12})$ then,

$$f(\alpha) = \frac{\phi_{11}^{\phi_{22}}}{\Gamma(\phi_{12})} \alpha^{\phi_{12}-1} e^{-\phi_{11}\alpha} \tag{21}$$

Taking logarithm on (21),

$$
\begin{aligned}
\log f(\alpha) &= \log \left(\frac{\phi_{11}^{\phi_{22}}}{\Gamma(\phi_{12})} \alpha^{\phi_{12}-1} e^{-\phi_{11}\alpha} \right) \\
&= \phi_{12} \log \phi_{11} - \log \Gamma(\phi_{12}) + (\phi_{12} - 1) \log(\alpha) - \phi_{11}\alpha \qquad (22) \\
&\propto (\phi_{12} - 1) \log \alpha - \phi_{11}\alpha
\end{aligned}
$$

Analogously and under the assumption $\beta \sim Gamma(\phi_{21}, \phi_{22})$ then,

$$\log f(\beta) \propto (\phi_{22} - 1) \log \beta - \phi_{21}\beta. \tag{23}$$

On the other hand, assuming each instant of the series can be of change y, $\tau_j \sim Unif(1, T)$, $j = 1, 2, \ldots, J$ [20]. And then,

$$f(\tau_j) = \frac{1}{1 - T} \; \forall j = 1, 2, \ldots, J \tag{24}$$

and after taking logarithm on (24),

$$\log f(\tau_j) = - \log(T - 1) \; \forall j = 1, 2, \ldots, J \tag{25}$$

Finally under the assumption of independence between the distributions of parameters, $f(\theta)$ is constructed as follows,

$$\log f(\alpha, \beta, \tau_j) \propto (\phi_{12} - 1) \log \alpha - \phi_{11}\alpha + (\phi_{21} - 1) \log \beta - \phi_{21}\beta - \log(T - 1) \tag{26}$$

Log Verosimilitud

Then, replacing the intensity function $\lambda^{(W)}(t \mid \theta)$ and the mean cumulative function $m^{(W)}(t \mid \theta)$ from (4) and (5), respectively in (18),

$$
\begin{aligned}
\log L(D \mid \phi) &= \sum_{j=1}^{J+1} \left(m(\tau_{j-1} \mid \theta_j) - m(\tau_j \mid \theta_j) + \sum_{i=N_{\tau_{j-1}}+1}^{N_{\tau_j}} \log \lambda(d_i \mid \theta_j) \right) \\
&= \sum_{j=1}^{J+1} \left(\left(\frac{\tau_{j-1}}{\beta_j} \right)^{\alpha_j} - \left(\frac{\tau_j}{\beta_j} \right)^{\alpha_j} \right. \\
&\quad \left. + \sum_{i=N_{\tau_{j-1}}+1}^{N_{\tau_j}} \log \left(\frac{\alpha_j}{\beta_j} \left(\frac{d_i}{\beta_j} \right)^{\alpha_j-1} \right) \right) \\
&= \sum_{j=1}^{J+1} \left(\frac{\tau_{j-1}^{\alpha_j} - \tau_j^{\alpha_j}}{\beta_j^{\alpha_j}} + (N_{\tau_j} - N_{\tau_{j-1}}) \left(\log(\alpha_j) - \alpha_j \log(\beta_j) \right) \right. \\
&\quad \left. + (\alpha_j - 1) \sum_{i=N_{\tau_{j-1}}+1}^{N_{\tau_j}} \log(d_i) \right)
\end{aligned}
$$

And this function is the one replaced in (10).

References

1. Achcar, J., Rodrigues, E., Tzintzun, G.: Using non-homogeneous Poisson models with multiple change-points to estimate the number of ozone exceedances in Mexico City. Environ. Ecol. Stat. **22** (2011). https://doi.org/10.1002/env.1029
2. Aminikhanghahi, S., Cook, D.J.: A survey of methods for time series change point detection. Knowl. Inf. Syst. **51**, 339–367 (2017). https://doi.org/10.1007/s10115-016-0987-z, http://link.springer.com/10.1007/s10115-016-0987-z
3. Basseville, M., Nikiforov, I.V.: Detection of Abrupt Changes - Theory and Application. Prentice Hall, Englewood Cliffs (1993). http://people.irisa.fr/Michele.Basseville/kniga/
4. Busoniu, L.: Optimization: lecture notes. Technical University of Cluj-Napoca (2018). http://busoniu.net/teaching/opt18en/ln5_ga.pdf
5. Chambers, L.: The Practical Handbook of Genetic Algorithms. New Frontiers, Practical Handbook of Genetic Algorithms, vol. 2, 1 edn. CRC-Press (1995)
6. Davis, R.A., Lee, T.C.M., Rodriguez-Yam, G.A.: Structural break estimation for nonstationary time series models. J. Am. Stat. Assoc. **101**(473), 223–239 (2006). https://doi.org/10.1198/016214505000000745, https://www-stat.ucdavis.edu/~tcmlee/PDFfiles/2006jasa.pdf
7. De Jong, K.A.: Genetic algorithms are not function optimizers. In: Whitley, L.D. (ed.) Foundations of Genetic Algorithms, Foundations of Genetic Algorithms, vol. 2, pp. 5–17. Elsevier (1993). https://doi.org/10.1016/B978-0-08-094832-4.50006-4

8. De Jong, K.A., Spears, W.M.: An analysis of the interacting roles of population size and crossover in genetic algorithms. In: Schwefel, H.-P., Männer, R. (eds.) PPSN 1990. LNCS, vol. 496, pp. 38–47. Springer, Heidelberg (1991). https://doi.org/10.1007/BFb0029729
9. Doerr, B., Fischer, P., Hilbert, A., Witt, C.: Detecting structural breaks in time series via genetic algorithms. Soft. Comput. **21**(16), 4707–4720 (2016). https://doi.org/10.1007/s00500-016-2079-0
10. Gendreau, M., Potvin, J.: Handbook of Metaheuristics. International Series in Operations Research & Management Science. Springer, Heidelberg (2018). https://doi.org/10.1007/978-3-319-91086-4
11. Goel, A.L., Okumoto, K.: An analysis of recurrent software errors in a real-time control system. In: Proceedings of the 1978 Annual Conference, ACM 1978, pp. 496–501. ACM, New York (1978). http://doi.acm.org/10.1145/800127.804160
12. Goldberg, D.E.: A note on Boltzmann tournament selection for genetic algorithms and population-oriented simulated annealing. Complex Syst. **4**, 445–460 (1990)
13. Gonçalves, J., Resende, M.: Biased random-key genetic algorithms for combinatorial optimization. J. Heurist. **17**, 487–525 (2011)
14. Hassanat, A., Almohammadi, K., Alkafaween, E., Abunawas, E., Hammouri, A., Prasath, V.B.S.: Choosing mutation and crossover ratios for genetic algorithms-a review with a new dynamic approach. Information **10**(12) (2019). https://doi.org/10.3390/info10120390, https://www.mdpi.com/2078-2489/10/12/390
15. IDEAM: Cárácterísticas Climatológicas De Ciudades Principales Y Municipios Turísticos. Instituto de Hidrología, Meteorología y Estudios Ambientales (nd). https://tinyurl.com/6fme7xzw
16. Jann, A.: Multiple change-point detection with a genetic algorithm. Soft. Comput. **4**(2), 68–75 (2000). https://doi.org/10.1007/s005000000049
17. Khan, N., McClean, S., Zhang, S., Nugent, C.: Using genetic algorithms for optimal change point detection in activity monitoring. In: 2016 IEEE 29th International Symposium on Computer-Based Medical Systems (CBMS), pp. 318–323. IEEE (2016). https://doi.org/10.1109/CBMS.2016.27
18. Khan, N., McClean, S., Zhang, S., Nugent, C.: Identification of multiregime periodic autotregressive models by genetic algorithms. In: International Conference of Time Series and Forecasting (ITISE 2018), vol. 3, pp. 396–407 (2018). https://doi.org/10.1109/CBMS.2016.27
19. Killick, R., Fearnhead, P., Eckley, I.A.: Optimal detection of changepoints with a linear computational cost. J. Am. Stat. Assoc. **107**(500), 1590–1598 (2012). https://doi.org/10.1080/01621459.2012.737745
20. Koop, G., Potter, S.M.: Prior elicitation in multiple change-point models. Int. Econ. Rev. **50**(3), 751–772 (2009). https://doi.org/10.1111/j.1468-2354.2009.00547.x
21. Li, S., Lund, R.: Multiple changepoint detection via genetic algorithms. J. Clim. **25**(2), 674–686 (2012). https://doi.org/10.1175/2011JCLI4055.1
22. Lobo, F.: Evolutionary computation: lecture Notes. Universidade do Algarve (2019). https://www.fernandolobo.info/ec1920/lectures/GAs-2.pdf
23. Luke, S.: Essentials of Metaheuristics. Lulu, 2nd edn. (2013). http://cs.gmu.edu/~sean/book/metaheuristics/
24. Mosayebi, M., Sodhi, M.: Tuning genetic algorithm parameters using design of experiments. In: Proceedings of the 2020 Genetic and Evolutionary Computation Conference Companion, GECCO 2020, pp. 1937–1944. Association for Computing Machinery, New York (2020). https://doi.org/10.1145/3377929.3398136

25. Mudholkar, G.S., Srivastava, D.K., Freimer, M.: The exponentiated weibull family: a reanalysis of the bus-motor-failure data. Technometrics **37**(4), 436–445 (1995). https://doi.org/10.1080/00401706.1995.10484376

26. Musa, J.D., Okumoto, K.: A logarithmic Poisson execution time model for software reliability measurement. In: Proceedings of the 7th International Conference on Software Engineering, ICSE 1984, pp. 230–238. IEEE Press, Piscataway (1984). http://dl.acm.org/citation.cfm?id=800054.801975

27. Page, E.S.: Continuous inspection schemes. Biometrika **41**(1–2), 100–115 (1954). https://doi.org/10.1093/biomet/41.1-2.100

28. Polushina, T., Sofronov, G.: Change-point detection in biological sequences via genetic algorithm. In: 2011 IEEE Congress of Evolutionary Computation (CEC), vol. 3, pp. 1966–1971. IEEE (2011). https://doi.org/10.1109/cec.2011.5949856

29. Ramirez, C., Esteban, J., Achcar, J.A.: Bayesian inference for nonhomogeneous Poisson processes in software reliability models assuming nonmonotonic intensity functions. Comput. Stat. Data Anal. **32**(2), 147–159 (1999). https://doi.org/10.1016/S0167-9473(99)00028-6

30. Rissanen, J.: Modeling by shortest data description. Automatica **14**(5), 465–471 (1978). https://doi.org/10.1016/0005-1098(78)90005-5

31. Rodrigues, E.R., Achcar, J.A.: Applications of Discrete-time Markov Chains and Poisson Processes to Air Pollution Modeling and Studies (2013). https://doi.org/10.1007/978-1-4614-4645-3

32. Ross, S.M.: Stochastic Processes, 2nd edn. Wiley, Hoboken (1995)

33. Schröder, A.L.M.M.: Methods for change-point detection with additional interpretability. Ph.D. thesis, London School of Economics and Political Sciences, London, UK (2016)

34. Suárez-Sierra, B., Coen, A., Taimal, C.: Genetic algorithm with a Bayesian approach for the detection of multiple points of change of time series of counting exceedances of specific thresholds. Arxiv preprint (2023). https://doi.org/10.48550/arXiv.2210.14807

35. Suárez-Sierra, B.M., Coen, A., Taimal, C.A.: Genetic algorithm with a Bayesian approach for the detection of multiple points of change of time series of counting exceedances of specific thresholds. Arxiv preprint (2023). https://doi.org/10.48550/arXiv.2210.14807

36. Truong, C., Oudre, L., Vayatis, N.: Selective review of offline change point detection methods. Signal Process. **167**, 107299 (2020). https://doi.org/10.1016/j.sigpro.2019.107299

37. Ursu, E., Turkman, K.F.: Periodic autoregressive model identification using genetic algorithms. J. Time Ser. Anal. **33**(3), 398–405 (2012). https://doi.org/10.1111/j.1467-9892.2011.00772.x

38. Wilcoxon, F.: Individual comparisons by ranking methods. Biomet. Bull. **1**(6), 80–83 (1945)

39. Yang, B.Y., Fan, S., Thiering, E.: Ambient air pollution and diabetes: a systematic review and meta-analysis. Environ. Res. **180** (2020). https://doi.org/10.1016/j.envres.2019.108817

Synthetic Hyperspectral Data for Avocado Maturity Classification

Froylan Jimenez Sanchez[1]([✉]), Marta Silvia Tabares[1], and Jose Aguilar[1,2,3]

[1] Universidad EAFIT, Medellín, Colombia
{fjjimenezs,mtabares,jlaguilarc}@eafit.edu.co, aguilar@ula.ve
[2] Universidad de Los Andes, Merida, Venezuela
[3] IMDEA Network Institute, Madrid, Spain
jose.aguilar@imdea.org

Abstract. The classification of avocado maturity is a challenging task due to the subtle changes in color and texture that occur during ripening and before that. Hyperspectral imaging is a promising technique for this task, as it can provide a more detailed analysis of the fruit's spectral signature compared with multi-spectral data. However, the acquisition of hyperspectral data can be time-consuming and expensive. In this study, we propose a method for generating synthetic hyperspectral data of avocados. The synthetic data is generated using a generative adversarial network (GAN), which is trained on a small dataset of real hyperspectral im-ages. The generated data is then used to train a neural network for avocado maturity classification. The results show that the neural network trained on synthetic data achieves comparable accuracy to a neural network trained on real data. Additionally, synthetic data is much cheaper and faster to generate than get real data. This makes it a promising alternative for avocado maturity classification.

Keywords: hyperspectral imaging · classification models · machine learning · Avocado maturity

1 Introduction

Fruit ripeness is an important factor for the fruit industry and final consumers. For fruits like bananas, ripeness can be easily determined by their color. However, for fruits like avocados, mangos, and others, ripeness is not as easy to determine. The fruit industry typically uses destructive methods to determine ripeness, which means that only a small sample of fruit can be tested. This can lead to inaccurate results and wasted fruit.

In this study, we investigated the use of generated hyperspectral imaging data and deep neural networks to predict the ripeness of avocados. Hyperspectral imaging is a technique that uses a sensor to record the reflectance of a surface at multiple wavelengths. This allows for the creation of a spectral signature for each surface, which can be used to identify and characterize different materials.

M. Tabares et al. (Eds.): CCC 2023, CCIS 1924, pp. 259–270, 2024.
https://doi.org/10.1007/978-3-031-47372-2_21

Deep neural networks are a type of machine learning algorithm that can be used to learn complex relationships between input and output data. In this study, we used a deep neural network to learn the relationship between the spectral signatures of avocados and their ripeness level. The following are some of the key findings of this study:

- Synthetic hyperspectral data can be generated using a GAN and can be used to train neural networks for avocado maturity classification.
- The neural network trained with synthetic data achieves comparable accuracy to a neural network trained with real data.
- Synthetic data is much cheaper and faster to generate than real data.

These findings suggest that synthetic hyperspectral data is a promising alternative for avocado maturity classification. Our results showed that generated hyperspectral imaging and deep neural networks can be used to accurately predict the ripeness level of avocados, at a lower cost. This could be a valuable tool for the fruit industry, as it could help to ensure that fruit is sold at its peak ripeness.

This paper is structured as follows. Sections 2 and 3 describes the related works and background. Section 4 presents our approach for generating synthetic hyperspectral data, and Sect. 5 experiments with this data. Finally, Sect. 6 presents the conclusions and future works.

2   Related Works

Previous studies have explored the use of hyperspectral imaging to predict fruit ripeness. [10] and [9] assessed the ripeness of avocados using hyperspectral imaging, while Zhu et al. [14] predicted the firmness and soluble solids content of kiwis using hyperspectral recordings. These studies employed non-neural network approaches. However, our focus is on deep learning techniques, which differ from the approaches used in these works.

The combination of hyperspectral data and deep learning has been extensively studied in remote sensing. Chen et al. [1] introduced deep learning to hyperspectral remote sensing, and in [5], a convolutional neural network outperformed support vector machine (SVM) approaches in classifying hyperspectral remote sensing data. Makantasis et al. [8] utilized contextual deep learning for feature mining, and Ma et al. [7] presented the HTD-Net framework, which focuses on target detection using hyperspectral data, and incorporates an autoencoder to improve prediction reliability.

Nevertheless, remote sensing applications differ significantly from fruit classification tasks, making direct comparisons challenging. Guo et al. [4] demonstrated the prediction capability of a simple neural network for tomato moisture content. Gao et al. [3] successfully predicted strawberry ripeness using hyperspectral imaging and a pre-trained AlexNet, a deep convolutional neural network. Our work shares similarities with these studies; however, we concentrate on one fruit, avocados, which have been validated for prediction using hyperspectral data.

The literature on hyperspectral imaging (HSI) data augmentation is somewhat limited. Deep learning techniques have been used as HSI segmentation methods, utilizing as simple augmentation techniques, such as mirroring training samples, to enhance classification performance. For example, Zhang et al. [13] computed the per-spectral-band standard deviation for each class in the training set, and augmented samples were generated from a zero-mean multivariate normal distribution $\mathcal{N}(0, ad)$, where d represents a diagonal matrix with the standard deviations of all classes along its main diagonal, and a is a hyper-parameter controlling the scale factor. This straightforward augmentation technique demonstrated the potential to improve generalization.

Lin et al. [6] employed spectral information to synthesize new samples through pixel-block augmentation. In [11], two data-generation approaches were utilized: (i) Gaussian smoothing filtering and (ii) label-based augmentation. The latter technique resembles labeling and assumes that near HSI pixels should share the same id. The label of a pixel propagates to its neighbors, generating additional examples that are inserted into the training set. However, this method may introduce mislabeled samples.

In contrast to the aforementioned works, our study employs a broader range of models and a large publicly available dataset. We also investigate whether hyperspectral data is necessary for this task, or if color images alone suffice, a validation that previous works overlooked.

3   Background

3.1   Generative Adversarial Networks and Hyperspectral Imaging

Generative adversarial networks (GANs) are machine learning models that use two neural networks to generate and distinguish between real and fake data. In Fig. 1, a diagram illustrating the classic process of creating new samples using a GAN network can be observed. In this case, a random noise vector is initially used, and the path outlined in the mentioned figure is followed. GANs model unknown data distributions based on provided samples and consist of a generator and discriminator. The generator generates data samples that follow the underlying data distribution, and are indistinguishable from the original data according to the discriminator, leading to a competitive relationship between the two.

GANs have garnered attention in the field of data augmentation due to their ability to introduce invariance to affine and appearance variations. In a recent study, Zhu et al. [14] employed a conditioned GAN to ensure that synthesized HSI examples from random distributions belong to specified classes.

With respect to *hyperspectral images*, refers to a high-dimensional image that captures spectral information across a broad range of contiguous bands. Unlike conventional multispectral or color images, hyperspectral images provide a comprehensive spectral representation, offering detailed insight into the optical

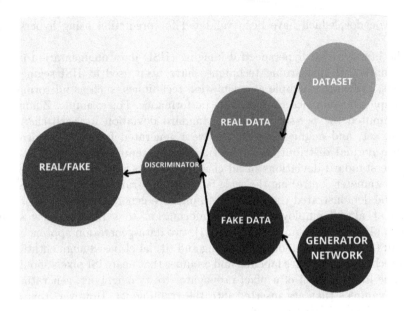

Fig. 1. Workflow of a GAN.

properties of materials and their interaction with light. Each pixel in a hyperspectral image contains a spectrum that encompasses reflectance or emission values at numerous narrow and closely spaced wavelengths. This rich spectral information facilitates advanced analysis techniques, such as machine learning algorithms, to unveil intricate patterns, discriminate between various materials, and extract valuable knowledge.

The hyperspectral sensors work with a wider range of bands of the electromagnetic spectrum. They usually are between 350–2500 nm, whereby the layers are different bands of the spectrum, keeping the information in a hypercube [2]. Hyperspectral sensors are the evolution of multispectral sensors (i.e., 3–10 bands). Figure 2 shows the comparison between them. Hyperspectral data augmentation serves as a valuable method for enhancing the generalization capabilities of deep neural networks in remote-sensing applications. Its primary objective is to generate synthetic samples during inference, specifically, for each incoming example, in order to address the potential uncertainty inherent in deep models. Notably, this augmentation technique hyperspectral data analysis) offers advantages over offline augmentation methods, and it does not introduce additional training times. Thus, it allows significantly improving the accuracy of classification tasks.

3.2 Avocado Ripening and Nutrition Facts

Avocados are climacteric fruits, which means that they continue to ripen after they are harvested. The ripening process is a complex chemical reaction that

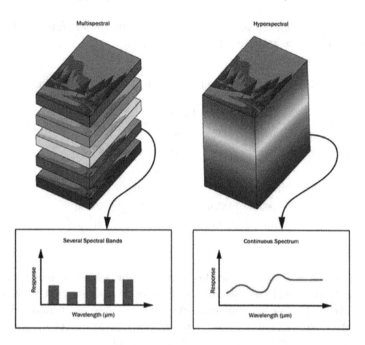

Fig. 2. Comparison between multispectral and hyperspectral images and measurement

involves the breakdown of cell walls, the hydrolysis of starch into sugar, the breakdown of chlorophyll, and the synthesis of other pigments.

The ripeness of avocados can be measured by a number of indicators, including:

- Soluble solids content (SSC): This is a measure of the sweetness of the fruit.
- Fruit flesh firmness: This is a measure of the softness of the fruit.
- Starch content: This is a measure of the amount of starch in the fruit.

The SSC and fruit flesh firmness are the most commonly used indicators of avocado ripeness. These measurements are destructive, which means that they damage the fruit. Other methods of measuring avocado ripeness, such as hyperspectral imaging, are non-destructive and can be used to measure the ripeness of avocados without damaging them.

Avocados are a fruit with a critical ripening process. The time window between unripe and overripe is small. This means that it is important to be able to accurately predict the ripeness of the fruit so that they can be consumed at their peak flavor and nutritional value.

Avocados are not only delicious but also pack a powerful nutritional punch, making them an excellent addition to any diet. Just half of an avocado, weighing around 100 g, provides a variety of essential nutrients that promote overall health and well-being. With 160 cal, 2 g of protein, 8.5 g of carbohydrates, and 14.7 g of healthy fats, as we can see in Table 1, avocados offer a satisfying and nutrient-dense option for those seeking a balanced diet.

Table 1. Nutritional contribution of 100 g of avocado hass

Avocado Nutrition Facts			
Calories	160	Fat	14.7 g
Sodium	7 mg	Carbohydrates	8.5 g
Fiber	6.7 g	Sugars	0.7 g
Protein	2 g	Magnesium	29 mg
Potassium	485 mg	Vitamin C	10 mg
Vitamin E	2.1 mg	Vitamin K	21 mcg

One standout feature of avocados is their impressive micronutrient profile. They are rich in several key vitamins and minerals that support various bodily functions. Avocados are an abundant source of magnesium, a mineral essential for over 300 enzymatic reactions in the body, aiding in energy production, muscle function, and maintaining a healthy immune system.

4   Our Approach

In our approach, we propose the use of GANs to generate hyperspectral imaging data, and then, this data is used to predict the ripeness of avocados. Thus, our GAN is used as an HSI augmentation method. This section presents our approach.

4.1   Dataset

The dataset used in this study was sourced from [12] where the authors detailed the process of data acquisition. The primary focus of this article was to classify various fruits according to the ripening degree, including avocados, by utilizing a neural network.

The dataset contains 1038 recordings of avocados, covering the ripening process from unripe to overripe for avocado fruits. Only 180 avocado recordings are labeled by indicator measurements due to the destructive nature of the labeling process. The data set was recorded in two separate measurement series and was divided into a training set, validation set, and test set. The measurement setup includes an object holder, a linear actuator, a light source, and two different cameras. Background extraction was used to improve the quality of the recorded data, and categories were defined for the labels to classify the fruit's firmness,

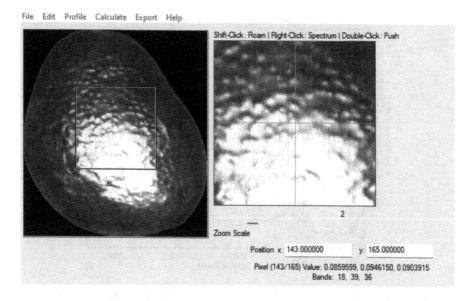

Fig. 3. A preview of a hyperspectral sample collapsed into a 3-channel image

sweetness, and overall ripeness level. A more complete description of the dataset is made in [12].

In Fig. 3, a preview of an avocado from the dataset can be observed. The image is visualized in GLIMPS software, and is collapsed into only three selected channels (18, 39, 36). When other channels are utilized, the image undergoes changes. This approach is employed to gain a better understanding of how a hyperspectral picture functions.

4.2 Data Preparation

Background extraction was used to exclude the background with a simple pixel-based neural network that was trained to differentiate between background and fruit. The smallest possible rectangle around the fruit was extracted from the recordings to remove most of the background. The intensity of the remaining background was forced to zero to improve the results. Categories were defined for the labels, and the goal was to classify whether the fruit is unripe, ripe, or overripe. The complexity was reduced to three classes for ripeness level.

In Fig. 4, a spectral plot of a sample with background removal is depicted. The x-axis represents the number of bands (in this case, 224 bands), and illustrates the significance of specific channels for this particular sample.

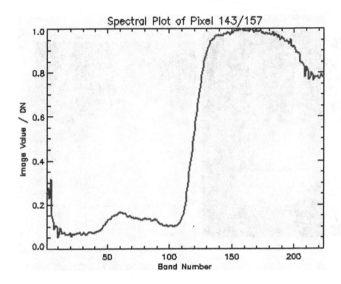

Fig. 4. Spectral plot for the Gaussian correction in the training dataset

4.3 Our HSI Augmentation Method Based on GAN

In this study, a GAN was employed to generate new images of hyperspectral data for avocado fruits. The original dataset used for training the GAN consisted of hyperspectral images captured by a camera equipped with 224 bands [12] defined in the previous section.

Figure 5 describes the procedure to generate new HSI using GANs. It is defined by four steps:

- Analyze Raw data: it identifies the most important bands of the spectrum. With this information, we can visualize the spectral profile, segment the image accordingly, and apply the Savitzky-Golay filter to smooth the image.
- Convert to mat data: It consists of assigning a header and a pointer to each sample, which contains every value of the cuboid element. The header includes the size and basic information, while the pointer stores each value of the channel.
- Merge the data: This step involves selecting only the most relevant channels based on spectral profile analysis and merging those channels for the training phase.
- Define the training dataset: The training dataset is comprised of real examples for the discriminator and random noise applied to the pointers of a subset of samples from the original dataset for the generator.

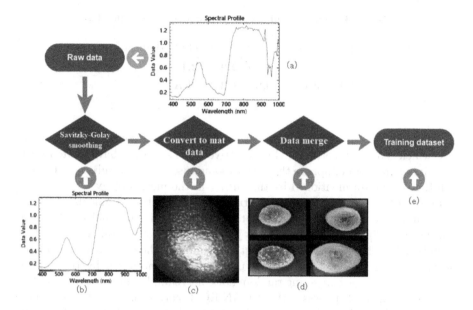

Fig. 5. Process for Generating Synthetic Data.

5   Experimental Results

With the data generated, to test their quality, classification models were developed with different machine learning techniques. Thus, the performance of the generated data was evaluated by comparing it when is used to augment original data described in [12]. The objective was to assess the quality and effectiveness of the generated data for classification tasks related to avocado fruits.

Table 2. Comparative of metrics for this experiment.

Category	Ripeness without GAN RGB			Ripeness without GAN FULL			Ripeness with GAN Modified		
	Accuracy	F1-Score	Recall	Accuracy	F1-Score	Recall	Accuracy	F1-Score	Recall
SVM	0.82	0.83	0.85	0.84	0.80	0.79	0.81	0.80	0.84
KNN	0.78	0.80	0.81	0.75	0.76	0.80	0.80	0.84	0.85
ResNet-18	0.90	0.85	0.86	0.67	0.70	0.65	0.89	0.86	0.91
HS-CNN	0.89	0.89	0.90	0.90	0.85	0.88	0.91	0.92	0.95

We evaluated four models on the given dataset: a Support Vector Machine (SVM), a k-nearest neighbor classifier (kNN), a ResNet-18 (a convolutional neural network architecture with identity shortcut connections and 18 layers), and a Hyperspectral Convolutional Neural Network (HS-CNN). In the last case, we modified the first layer of the ResNet-18 network to accommodate the hyperspectral images as input.

Table 3. Time of training for different settings of inputs.

Time in days	RGB	FULL	GAN Modified
GAN	**1.39**	**2.9**	**2.1**
Without GAN	**0.5**	**1.2**	**N.A**

Table 3 shows the actual time spent on different input configurations for this task, which is a good metric for this objective when scientists have limited setup for training and could improve the time in some cases. These results are obtained with the same data mentioned by the author in the methodology.

In Table 2, we can observe the metrics for the mentioned models. The first two columns represent the results with the data in its original condition as provided by [12]. Both columns employ the same experimental setup used by the author [12]. For this case of the first two columns, the metrics are calculated considering synthetic data generated using methods proposed by the author. These methods involve injecting random noise into samples and applying random cuts. For instance, "Ripeness without GAN RGB" corresponds to the case where the data is collapsed into three channels, serving as the input for each algorithm. In the second case, "Ripeness without GAN FULL", all channels of the dataset are utilized for calculating every metric. Notably, the HS-CNN outperformed the others due to its ability to consider the importance of each channel without applying reduction techniques.

Particularly, for the last column, we observed improvements by utilizing the HS-CNN proposed by the author and the generated data suggested in this article. This result was obtained using a neural network with only 32K parameters, where the first layer was reduced to only 25 channels, the ReLU activation function was used, and an average pooling of 4×4 was employed. The average pooling layer proves to be a better option for handling hyperspectral data in this type of problem. The key difference between this setup and the one proposed by [12] is the significance of reducing the number of channels of the synthetic data to the ones that exhibit greater variation in terms of the spectral profile.

These preliminary results highlight an opportunity in the field of creating synthetic hyperspectral data for classification problems. The experimental results demonstrated that the GAN-generated hyperspectral images achieved comparable performance to the original data augmented with traditional methods. The quality metrics were found to be in line with or even surpass those obtained using augmented data from previous approaches. Thus, these findings suggest that the GAN-generated hyperspectral data can serve as a viable alternative to traditional data augmentation techniques for avocado classification.

6 Conclusions

In this study, we conducted research on the classification of avocados and the assessment of their ripeness using convolutional neural networks, applied to hyperspectral data and synthetic data generated via GAN Technique. We focused on using a dataset of ripening avocados, along with the details of the data acquisition process, which are augmented using the GAN technique.

Overall, the experimental results highlight the potential of GANs in generating high-quality hyperspectral data for avocado classification, showcasing their effectiveness in comparison to traditional data augmentation methods described in previous research. Also, the results of our research demonstrated the effectiveness of the HS-CNN classifier network in accurately predicting the ripeness of avocados.

In a future work will be defined the initial vector for the GAN by following the probability distribution of the dataset. This idea has the potential to improve the generation of synthetic data, although it comes with a significant time cost. Another suggestion is to introduce noise during the synthetic data generation from the real data to try to generate data close to real, but in its neighborhood space. The evolution of these algorithms presents a promising opportunity to explore these proposed approaches in the near future.

References

1. Chen, Y., Lin, Z., Zhao, X., Wang, G., Gu, Y.: Deep learning-based classification of hyperspectral data. IEEE J. Sel. Top. Appl. Earth Observ. Remote Sens. **7**, 2094–2107 (2014)
2. Fahey, T., et al.: Active and passive electro-optical sensors for health assessment in food crops. Sens. (Switz.) **21**(1), 1–40 (2021)
3. Gao, Z., et al.: Real-time hyperspectral imaging for the in-field estimation of strawberry ripeness with deep learning. Null (2020)
4. Guo, J., et al.: Network decoupling: from regular to depthwise separable convolutions. arXiv Computer Vision and Pattern Recognition (2018)
5. Ioffe, S., Szegedy, C.: Batch normalization: accelerating deep network training by reducing internal covariate shift. arXiv Learning (2015)
6. Lin, T.-Y., Goyal, P., Girshick, R., He, K., Dollar, P.: Focal loss for dense object detection. arXiv Computer Vision and Pattern Recognition (2017)
7. Ma, X., Wang, H., Geng, J., Wang, H.: Hyperspectral image classification via contextual deep learning. Eur. J. Image Video Process. **1–12**, 2015 (2015)
8. Makantasis, K., Karantzalos, K., Doulamis, A., Doulamis, N.: Deep supervised learning for hyperspectral data classification through convolutional neural networks. Null (2015)
9. Olarewaju, O.O., Bertling, I., Magwaza, L.S.: Non-destructive evaluation of avocado fruit maturity using near infrared spectroscopy and PLS regression models. Sci. Horticult. **199**, 229–236 (2016)
10. Pinto, J., Rueda-Chacon, H., Arguello, H.: Classification of Hass avocado (persea americana mill) in terms of its ripening via hyperspectral images. Null (2019)
11. Sundararajan, M., Taly, A., Yan, Q.: Axiomatic attribution for deep networks. arXiv Learning (2017)
12. Varga, L.A., Makowski, J., Zell, A.: Measuring the ripeness of fruit with hyperspectral imaging and deep learning. In: 2021 International Joint Conference on Neural Networks (IJCNN), pp. 1–8. IEEE (2021)

Fuzzy Model for Risk Characterization in Avocado Crops for Index Insurance Configuration

Juan Pablo Jiménez Benjumea⬤, Laura Isabel López Giraldo$^{(\boxtimes)}$⬤,
Juan Alejandro Peña Palacio⬤, and Tomas Ramirez-Guerrero⬤

Universidad EAFIT, Medellín, Ant, Colombia
{jjimen20,lilopezg,japena,teramirezg}@eafit.edu.co

Abstract. Climate change has caused strong variations in agroclimatic parameters such as precipitation, temperature, and relative humidity, accelerating the phytosanitary conditions associated with agricultural crops, mainly in insect pests, since these generate an alteration in their life cycle and an increase in their population. This causes significant economic damage to important crops such as the Hass avocado, which has had a growing development and demand in national and international markets, which has generated significant income for small and medium-sized farmers and exporters of this fruit in the country. To mitigate the impacts of climate change on agricultural production, it is possible to implement digital agriculture technologies. These technologies allow estimating the incidence of climate variations on crops through the monitoring of agroclimatic and phytosanitary variables that affect fruit growth. Therefore, a variable dispersion model with fuzzy characterization is proposed that seeks to establish a correlation between rainfall and the aggregate distribution of losses in the Hass avocado crop. In order to analyze and validate the proposed model, the random variables related to phytosanitary risk were taken and characterized. Subsequently, the frequency and severity random variables were modeled as linguistic random variables using fuzzy logic concepts. The results indicate that rainfall is the key variable to correlate in the search for an index insurance model based on agricultural risk, as well as in the characterization of qualitative and quantitative risks, promoting the improvement of financial and environmental sustainability by reducing agricultural losses through better crop management.

Keywords: Phytosanitary · Agroclimatic · Fuzzy Logic · Productivity · Insurance · Indexing

1 Introduction

Precipitation is a component that, if not measured or studied, can significantly affect the avocado crop; 90% of the water requirement is obtained from rainwater, and only 10% is supplied by irrigation, which increases the vulnerability

© The Author(s), under exclusive license to Springer Nature Switzerland AG 2024
M. Tabares et al. (Eds.): CCC 2023, CCIS 1924, pp. 271–284, 2024.
https://doi.org/10.1007/978-3-031-47372-2_22

of the sector due to the alteration of precipitation regimes as a result of climate change [1]. Climate change has caused strong variations in agroclimatic parameters such as precipitation, temperature and relative humidity, accelerating the phytosanitary conditions associated with agricultural crops, mainly in insect pests as they generate an alteration in their life cycle and an increase in the population, reducing the effectiveness of control methods and decreasing the presence of natural control organisms. In addition, the appearance of new pests and the increase of weeds that can become potential foci for new pests is observed. This causes significant economic damage to important crops such as Hass avocado, which has had a growing development and demand in national and international markets, which has generated significant income for small and medium farmers and exporters of this fruit in the country [2–5].

Phytosanitary risk management provides an ideal opportunity to improve and rigorously evaluate the efficiency of current integrated pest and disease management (IPPM). In addition, it allows the articulation of new strategies in phytosanitary management provided by precision agriculture, with the objective of improving the environmental and financial sustainability of production systems. The use of digitized tools plays a fundamental role in the efficient management of agricultural activities, fostering an innovative interaction between man and machine. These tools make it possible to optimize activities such as pest monitoring in the field, through the use of heat maps with geographic information systems (GIS), spectral and satellite images [6]. Likewise, unmanned aerial vehicles (UAVs) are used to carry out spraying and fertilization [7], and Internet of Things (IoT) networks are designed for monitoring and differentiated management of crop units using environmental variables [8].

The agricultural sector in Colombia is a little studied environment in relation to the quantification of data and quantitative measurements of agricultural production, being a little digitized sector [9]. In recent years, avocado cultivation, specifically the Hass variety, has experienced a significant expansion in Colombia. This is due to its high yield in production and its late ripening capacity compared to other varieties. The Hass variety is highly valued for its nutritional potential and has desirable morphological characteristics, such as a resistant skin, adequate size and long storage capacity. These qualities make Hass avocado a highly attractive product for the Colombian export market [10].

During the period between January and April 2022, Colombia has positioned itself as the second largest supplier of avocados in Latin America, with exports reaching approximately 876,754 tons. These shipments were mainly destined to countries such as the Netherlands (56%), the United Kingdom (12%), Spain (9%), the United States (5%), Belgium (4%) and France (4%), among others, with smaller shares [11]. Globally, it is estimated that there are around 407,000 hectares dedicated to avocado cultivation, which translates into a total production of 4,000,000 tons. Colombia contributes with 14.2% of the planted hectares, equivalent to a total of 312,615 tons [12]. These figures demonstrate the relevance of avocado as an income generator for small and medium farmers in the country.

The use of fuzzy logic modeling in agriculture, in general, offers a series of significant benefits that contribute to improving the efficiency and sustainability of agricultural production. One of the key advantages is its capacity to handle uncertainty and imprecision present in agricultural and environmental data, where factors such as weather, diseases, and pests can vary significantly. Fuzzy logic allows considering these fluctuations and making informed decisions in risk management. Furthermore, it is highly adaptable to different agricultural and climatic conditions, optimizing the use of agricultural resources by assessing and characterizing risks. Farmers can focus on and use resources such as water, fertilizers, and pesticides more efficiently, benefiting both production and the environment [13].

2   Literature Review

Climate variability is of great importance in fruit growing, especially in avocado cultivation, as pointed out by Caldana [14]. This variability has a significant impact on the physiological development of plants and is essential for agricultural planning, resource conservation and sustainable production management. Fabio et al. [15] commented that agroclimatic zoning is a valuable tool in decision making and agricultural planning, as it provides information on climate-related risks.

Moreover, it is important to recognize that climate change is a reality [16,17] and agriculture faces the challenge not only of defining adaptation strategies, but also of implementing them and monitoring their results. It is necessary to analyze not only the consequences of climate change, but also the causes of vulnerability and make decisions to address them. Risk analysis makes it possible to assess the probability of future losses by analyzing future scenarios.

In 2009, the US Office of the Comptroller of the Currency (OCC) mentioned several researchers who were studying operational risks quantitatively. As a result of this study on operational risk, an article titled "Operational Risk – Modeling the Extreme" was published. One of its findings is precisely the Loss Distribution Approach (LDA), which combines LDA methods with Extreme Value Theory (EVT) to address operational risk [18].

In the journal of the University of Medellín, an article by Franco et al. [19] was published on the quantification of operational risks. This article can be seen as a continuation of Mora's work [20], addressing the problem of estimating high quantiles for operational risk and conducting a review of the most important literature on these methods according to Basel for risk quantification. On the other hand, in the Sustainability journal of 2022, volume 14, page 6668, the authors Peña, A.; Tejada, J.C.; González-Ruiz, J.D.; Góngora, M. [21] discuss the sustainability of agricultural crops affected by phytosanitary events, focusing on financial risks.

The focus on index insurance configuration is a way to address these financial risks associated with avocado crops. By using a Fuzzy Model for Risk Characterization, the mentioned researchers have developed a methodology that allows for a more accurate and detailed assessment of the inherent risks in agricultural crops. The use of fuzzy logic in the model takes into account the uncertainty and imprecision present in agricultural and environmental data, leading to greater accuracy in predictions and risk assessments. In summary, the Fuzzy Model for Risk Characterization in Avocado Crop for Index Insurance Configuration is a valuable contribution in the field of sustainable agriculture and risk management. Its comprehensive approach opens up new possibilities to protect and strengthen avocado crop production and, ultimately, promote a more resilient and sustainable agricultural development.

Author Wenner [22] emphasizes that agriculture is a risky economic activity, subject to climatic, biological, and geological impacts. Traditional risk management strategies and emergency relief have not been sufficiently effective in preventing serious economic losses or enabling rapid recovery. In developing countries, producers are exposed to the vagaries of weather and have little access to formal agricultural insurance to transfer risks. Despite this, agricultural insurance has re-emerged as a necessity to improve competitiveness in integrated markets and address technological, economic, and educational asymmetries.

In Latin America, actions have focused on reactive and emergency responses to adverse climatic events, which is insufficient. A comprehensive risk management strategy is required that includes prevention, mitigation, and risk transfer, with the participation of the public and private sectors in coordination and mutual agreement [23].

In addition, it is essential to recognize the importance of collecting and measuring climatic data on a crop as an essential tool to prevent economic losses. Accurate monitoring of climatic conditions, such as temperature, humidity, precipitation, and solar radiation, allows farmers to make informed decisions and anticipate potential adverse climatic impacts.

The collection and measurement of climate data also plays a crucial role in agricultural risk management. Real-time and historical weather data allows assessing the risks associated with extreme events, such as droughts, floods, or frosts. This information helps farmers make proactive decisions to minimize the impact of these events, protect their crops and minimize expected economic losses. In addition, access to reliable and up-to-date weather data is essential for agricultural insurance. Weather-based agricultural insurance provides a way to transfer the risk of economic losses associated with adverse weather events. Farmers can use the collected weather data to demonstrate the occurrence of damaging weather conditions and thus claim compensation for the losses suffered [22].

3   Methodology

3.1   Case Study

The research project focuses on the Hass avocado production system, one of the main fruit trees exported nationally. To guarantee quality and meet export standards, it is necessary to effectively manage and control agricultural practices. However, this system is affected by insect pests that affect yields and fruit quality during harvest. Two of the most relevant insect pests are the chinch bug (Monalonion velezangeli) and the marceño beetle (Phyllophaga obsoleta Blanchard), especially problematic in the eastern region of Antioquia. We selected a crop located in the northwestern part of Colombia, which has been affected by the aforementioned pests during the months of highest rainfall. This makes it an ideal case to identify the maximum levels of risk that characterize an index-based insurance, and where there is a loss of productivity in the fruit export process. For the analysis and validation of the proposed model, the first step was to collect and characterize the random variables for climate risk and phytosanitary risks. At this point, the data are expected to have a significance ($<5\%$) according to the quadratic error and the sample size. Subsequently, we proceed with the fuzzy modeling of the frequency and severity random variables as linguistic random variables. Here it is expected that the aggregate distribution of losses will present positive skewness coefficients, similar to those obtained by Peña et al. (2020) in the characterization of this type of distributions. Subsequently, we proceeded to establish the correlation between the losses of the aggregate loss distribution and precipitation according to the case study. Based on the structure of these variables, a modified Monte Carlo method will be used to model the aggregate loss distribution, taking into account the fuzzy representation of random variables [24, 25].

3.2   Study Area

The research will be carried out in an agricultural production unit dedicated to the avocado production system. For the characterization of agroclimatic and phytosanitary events, an area of 2 hectares of Hass avocado crop will be taken as a reference, with a total density of 450 trees of 4 years of age. A sample of thirty trees was select-ed to analyze their behavior over time.

3.3   Climate Parameters

The meteorological station was installed in May 2022 and, starting from June of the same year, it has been generating daily data seven days a week, recorded in 15-minute intervals throughout the day. For the study case, data from the station have been used from June 2022 up to the current date, calculating a monthly average of these data. However, it is important to note that this research has a limitation in the amount of data obtained. To overcome this limitation, an estimation of additional data was conducted, ta-king into account previous years, from 2018 to projecting until the year 2025. The additional data was collected with the same frequency as the meteorological station located in the study area. The aim of this estimation was to obtain a larger amount of data and reduce the mean squared error that may arise due to a low frequency in statistical measurements. For the analysis, priority has been given to the precipitation variable, due to its recognized influence on crop productivity results and the incidence of the mentioned pest insects. This choice is supported by relevant bibliographical references [26–28], which back the importance of considering precipitation as a determining factor in crop development and pest incidence. These bibliographical references provide solid foundations to support the selection of the variable and the approach adopted in the research.

3.4   Characterization of Phytosanitary Events

To characterize phytosanitary events, periodic visits are made to the production unit to identify the agronomic risks associated with the insect pests in the study.

3.5   Fuzzy Characterization of Losses on Agricultural Crops

The Aggregate Loss Distribution in avocado cultivation is a model used to analyze and quantify the economic losses associated with adverse events that affect crop productivity in the study area. This model takes into account different factors, such as the frequency and intensity of weather events and the incidence of pests, which are the main factors that can affect the quality and yield of avocado trees. In this model, data is collected on relevant variables such as precipitation, temperature, relative humidity, and other climatic factors, as well as the presence and severity of pests. These data are used to construct a probability distribution that represents the possible economic losses that can occur in the crop. The development of the LDA model requires having an appropriate database to characterize the random variables, including those of linguistic nature. It is essential to perform an analysis of the loss distribution considering two fundamental elements of the model: frequency, which represents the number of crop units affected by risk events in a given period, and severity, which indicates the average loss suffered by each crop unit affected by a risk event. The specific aggregate loss distribution for avocado cultivation is obtained through a convolution with Monte Carlo simulations. This convolution is the resulting process of combining the discrete frequency distribution with the continuous severity distribution. By using this method, a more comprehensive and realistic view of the potential losses that could occur in the avocado cultivation system is achieved. Furthermore, to assess losses from events, the OPVaR percentile (Operational Value at Risk) is used. This value is estimated based on established parameters and represents a statistical measure indicating the level of expected and unexpected losses. It is a valuable tool for calculating potential losses associated with events, allowing for better planning and risk management for the agricultural producer. It is important to highlight that this model is based on historical data and assumptions about the relationships between different factors that influence losses. Moreover, its accuracy and reliability depend on the quality and quantity of available data, as well as the suitability of the probability distribution used.

3.6 Characterization of Quantitative and Qualitative Risks. Risk Map

In this process, the K-Means method is used to group data into categories, classifying objects into groups according to their characteristics. The classification algorithm aims to minimize the sum of distances between each object and the centroid of its group or cluster, commonly by using the quadratic distance. The K-Means method consists of several steps. First, the number of clusters is selected and the centroids are set in the data space, which can be randomized. Second, the objects are assigned to the centroids, assigning each object to the nearest centroid. Finally, the centroid position of each group is updated, taking as the new centroid the average position of the objects belonging to that group. This approach is based on relevant literature references [29–31] and is widely used in various clustering and data analysis applications. It allows the identification of patterns and structures within the data, which facilitates the understanding and analysis of complex data sets.

4 Results

In this case study, information collected by the meteorological and hydrological station in the study area was used. However, there was a limitation in the frequency of the available data, since the station began to record information in June 2022. At the beginning of the investigation, a quadratic error of more than 12% was detected in the calculations performed. Despite this drawback, it was possible to significantly reduce this error by incorporating additional data estimates from 2018 and projecting up to 2025. This made it possible to obtain a greater amount of data and reduce the quadratic error to 4.94%. The distribution obtained follows a normal pattern, based on a correlation of 0.86 between rainfall and the aggregate distribution of losses. This distribution shows a long tail, indicating that catastrophic losses are less likely due to the asymptotic shape of the distribution. In the sample of thirty (30) crop units selected, a total of 42 losses are expected in both crops, and farmers should consider this in their economic estimates. It is important to note that the distributions analyzed should have a long tail. If this is not the case, there may be a crop problem or a phytosanitary event that is affecting the crop units. This is confirmed by the co-efficient of skewness, which must be positive to indicate a long-tailed distribution. In this particular case, the coefficient is 1.59, which means that catastrophic losses are less frequent due to the asymptotic shape of the distribution. The mean helps us identify the upper limit of expected losses, meaning those that fall below this limit are considered as expected losses.In the specific case we are analyzing, thirty-nine (39) expected losses have been identified, with an estimated value of COP $ 1,625,725. It is important to note that, in the avocado crop studied, only one case has been identified that could generate a catastrophic loss. To complement this analysis of expected losses, it is essential to take into account the phytosanitary management practices that the farmer must follow in order to achieve adequate pest control and optimal crop management (see Table 1).

Table 1. Characterization of Losses.

Data measures analyzed	Value	Quantity
Medium	$1,625,725	39
Percentile 99.99% (Op-var)	$7,869,317	1
Expected losses	$2,606,727	38

This analysis shows that there are 7 crop units that could be affected, which indicates a low frequency. However, if this figure increases to 39 affected crop units (see Table 2), the frequency becomes very high and the event can cause significant losses for farmers. For this reason, it is necessary to carry out an exhaustive analysis of the events affecting the crop, with the aim of developing plans and actions to help mitigate losses in those crop units that fail to reach the expected forty (40) kilograms of production per month. We will now proceed to model the risks associated with severity, using the same method used previously (see Table 3).

Table 2. Frequency Characterization Cluster

Cluster	Frequency				Events	Expert	Oscillation
Min	LI	1	LS	5		Minimum	
1	$3.16	39712.626	171.572798	0	7	Low	170.572798
2	39712.626	171.572798	191992.38	0	6	Medium	152279.754
3	171.572798	191992.38	97097.2261	0	26	High	96925.6533
4	191992.38	97097.2261	564885.417	0	39	Very High	−191978.38
Max	14			78	Maximum		

Table 3. Severity Characterization Cluster.

Labels	Min	Clusters		$2,000.00	# Data	Labels
1	$3.16060	$39,255.63	$0	$0	8	Slight
2	$39,255.63	$ -	$ -	$ -	$0	Moderate
3	$ -	$ -	$ -	-	0	Severe
4	$ -	$ -	$564,885.42	$1.00	0	Catastrophic
			Max			

During the identification of the risks associated with the crop, a total of 26 types of risk were identified, including operational, financial and phytosanitary risks. It is important to note that phytosanitary risks are those that entail the greatest economic loss. In addition, the current risks associated with the presence of insect pests, specifically the marceño cockroach and the monalonion, were monitored. Within the framework of the Integrated Pest Management Plan (IPM), four key strategies were established: cultural, physical/mechanical, biological and chemical. These strategies are fundamental to efficiently manage crops and prevent the spread of pests. Agronomic risks were divided according to each IPM strategy mentioned above. So far, 14 risks related to the presence of insect pests have been identified, some of which significantly affect the increase of economically important insect populations (see Fig. 1).

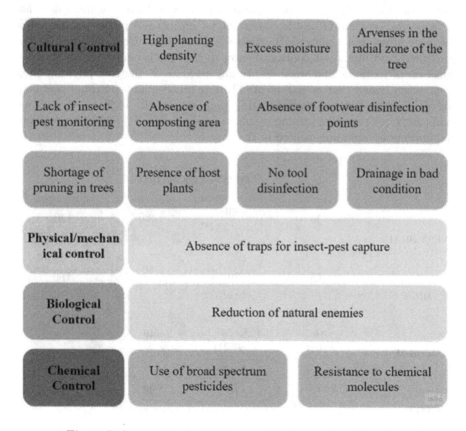

Fig. 1. Risks associated with increased incidence of pest insects.

The effects are the result of agroclimatic events caused by precipitation, as well as the presence of phytosanitary events within the crop. In the characterization of the risks identified, the following are highlighted (see Fig. 2):

High Frequency and Severe Impact: - Excessive atmospheric precipitation: causes yield reduction, plant detriment, loss of flowers, decrease of oxygen in the soil and creates a favorable environment for the marceño beetle during rainy seasons. In addition, it can cause plant death; -Interest rate risk: This risk is generated by fluctuations in interest rates, which affects the sale of fruit for export; -Operational- Phytosanitary Risk: the lack of adequate integrated management of pests and of the plant in general results in the production of fruit that does not meet the qualities required for export, which lowers its value. During the harvest, the farm was able to market only 2.9 tons, which represents a yield of less than 40%.

Very High Frequency and Moderate Impact: - Biological contamination during the pruning and harvesting process: adequate decontamination of cutting tools is not performed between each unit of treated crop. Pruning that is not carried out can lead to excessive vegetative growth of the plants and a decrease in fruit size, creating favorable conditions for an increase in the population of the pest insect pests marceño beetle and chinch bug;- Contamination of the cultivated land: Adequate control of entry to the crop is omitted, including disinfection of footwear and weed or pruning residues at the tree planting site;- Lack of integrated pest management: There is no adequate control of pest control action thresholds or early identification of pests. In addition, there is no monitoring or prevention programs (planting of trap plants) and no traps (light and chromatic) are implemented in the crop.

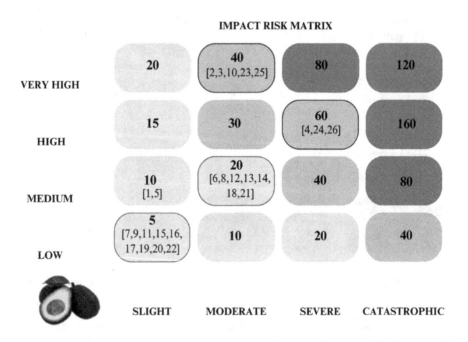

Fig. 2. Risk Matrix

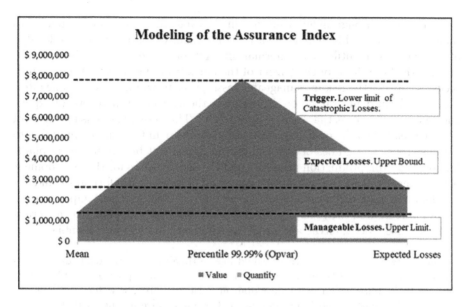

Fig. 3. Modeling of the Assurance Index

Physical-mechanical damage to the fruit (1), biological contamination in the fruit cutting process (2), contamination of cultivated land (3), excess atmospheric precipitation (4), deficit of atmospheric precipitation (5), low temperatures (6), high temperatures (7), failure to develop a crop fertilization plan (8), failure to carry out proper pruning (9), failure to properly execute IPM (Integrated Pest Management) (10), high planting densities (11), lack of tree grafting (12), lack of crop drainage (13), hail (14), public risk (15), legal risk (16), fire risk (17), worker safety and welfare (18), high winds (19), floods (20), landslides (21), market risk (22), exchange rate risk (23), interest rate risk (24), inflation risk (25) and operational - phytosanitary risk (26) (see Fig. 2).

On the other hand, the results have identified the possibility of a single catastrophic event, with an estimated lower limit of COP \$7,869,317 (Op-var). From there, the insurance index defined by the insurer in the policy constitution is defined (see Fig. 3).

5   Conclusions

This study allowed the quantification of agroclimatic data and variables for an adequate risk management in the Hass avocado crop, contributing to the digitization of the agricultural sector in Colombia. It was possible to identify that the variable that most affects crop yield is rainfall, finding a correlation between rainfall and the aggregate distribution of crop losses. This has made it possible to obtain the expected losses that are not insurable in the insurance sector, the manageable losses that are between the average and the Op-var, and that can be transferred through index insurance in the event that the farmer is unable to manage his risks or his management costs are high. Catastrophic losses, located at the 99.9% percentile of the normal distribution, were also identified. Based on this, the lower limit of the trigger of the index insurance is established, which seeks to transfer the risk in manageable losses, thus providing an economic alternative to the agricultural sector, especially to the avocado crop, in case of experiencing economic losses that cannot be assumed. This research opens new lines of research related to the modeling of digital agriculture in Colombia, applicable to various crops. These lines of research aim to implement best practices in planting, pest control, production processes and the use of drones for the development of intelligent systems that allow the generation of networked information and the development of predictive models in the agricultural sector. These improvements are not only limited to avocado cultivation, but can also be applied to other crops such as coffee, cocoa, citrus and other agricultural products in Colombia.

Acknowledgements. The authors would like to thank the Royal Academy of Engineering, through the Distinguished International Associates program (DIA-2122-3-160), for their contribution to the development of this research, as well as the Ministry of Science, Technology, and Innovation of the Colombia Government for their support through the training program for young researchers, specifically the project with the code BPIN 2022000100080.

References

1. IDEAM - Instituto de Hidrología, Meteorología y Estudios Ambientales. Es-tudio Nacional del Agua 2018 (2018). http://www.ideam.gov.co/web/agua/anexos-estudio-nacional-del-agua-2018
2. Lobell, D.B., Field, C.B., Cahill, K.N., Bonfils, C.: Impacts of future climate change on California perennial crop yields: model projections with climate and crop uncertainties. Agric. For. Meteorol. **141**(2–4), 208–218 (2006)
3. Fischer, G., Cleves-Leguizamo, J.A., Balaguera-López, H.E.: Impacto de la temperatura del suelo sobre las especies frutales bajo escenarios de cambio climático. Revista Colombiana de Ciencias Hortofrutícolas **16**(1), e12769 (2021). https://doi.org/10.17584/rcch.2022v16i1.12769
4. Sommaruga, R., Eldridge, H.M.: Avocado production: water footprint and socioeconomic implications. EuroChoices **20**, 48–53 (2021). https://doi.org/10.1111/1746-692X.12289
5. Liu, J., Dong, Z., Chen, X.: Case study on hyperspectral estimation model of total nitrogen content in soil of Shaanxi province. Earth Environ. Sci. **108**, 042025 (2018)
6. Peña, I., Bonet, D., Manzur, M., Góngora, M., Carffini, F.: Validation of convolutional layers in deep learning models to identify patterns in multispectral images. In: Proceedings of the 14th Conference on Information Systems and Technologies, Coimbra, Portugal (2019)
7. Popovic, T., Nedeljko, L., Pesic, A., Zecevic, Z., Krstajic, B., Djukanovik, S.: Architecting an IoT-enabled platform for precision agriculture and ecological monitoring: a case study. Comput. Electron. Agric. **140**, 255–265 (2017)
8. CORNARE: Zonificación de riesgo por movimientos en masa, inundación y avenidas torrenciales. Atención de áreas afectadas por eventos desastrosos, Rionegro (2012)

9. Cepal, Fao, Iica: Perspectivas de la agricultura y del desarrollo rural en las Américas 2021–2022. IICA, San José de Costa Rica (2021)
10. Corporación Colombiana de Investigación Agropecuaria – Corpoica y Ministerio de Agricultura y Desarrollo Rural - MADR (2013). Atlas: Zonificación de las tierras para el uso potencial del cultivo de aguacate cv. Hass en Colombia
11. Corpohass: Plan Persea. Contundente en la optimización de operaciones logísticas. Edición No. 049 (2022). https://www.corpohass.com/revista
12. Valencia, C.M.: Cadena del aguacate Antioquia Carlos Mario Valencia Enlace Cadena Productiva del Aguacate Secretaría Agricultura y Desarrollo Rural Plan Estratégico Cadena Aguacate (2018)
13. Molina, M.R.: Lógica difusa como herramienta para interpretar datos de producción limpia en el sector agrícola. Idesia **27**(3), 101–105 (2009)
14. Caldana, N.F., et al.: Zonificación del riesgo agroclimático del aguacate (Persea americana) en la cuenca hidrográfica del río Paraná II, Brasil. Agricultura (Suiza) **9**(12) (2019). https://doi.org/10.3390/agricultura9120263
15. Martinez, M.F.E., et al.: Agroclimatic zoning methodology for agricultural production systems in dry Caribbean region of Colombia. Agronomía Colombiana, **34**(3), 374–384 (2016). https://doi.org/10.15446/agron.colomb.v34n3.59672
16. IPCC. Grupo Intergubernamental de Expertos sobre el Cambio Climático. Cambio climático 2007: Informe de síntesis. Ginebra (2007)
17. Stern, N.: The Economics of Climate Change. Cambridge University Press, London (2006)
18. Balta, E., Carillo, S., Embrechts, P., Hamidick, K., Swandon, K.: Operational risk - modeling the extreme. OCC-NISS White Paper (2009)
19. Franco, L.C., Murillo, J.G., et al.: Riesgo Operacional: Reto actual de las entidades financieras. Revista Ingenierías Universidad de Medellín **5**(9), 97–110 (2006)
20. Mora, A.: Consideraciones en la estimación de cuantiles altos en riesgo operativo. Análisis - Revista del Mercado de Valores (1), 181–216 (2010)
21. Peña, A., Tejada, J.C., Gonzalez-Ruiz, J.D., Gongora, M.: Deep learning to improve the sustainability of agricultural crops affected by phytosanitary events: a financial-risk approach. Sustainability **14**, 6668 (2022). https://doi.org/10.3390/su14116668
22. Wenner, M.: Los seguros agrícolas: evolución y perspectivas en América Latina y el Caribe. Publicación del Banco Interamericano de Desarrollo. No de referencia RUR–05–02, Washington (2005)
23. Signorino Barbat, A.: Seguros agrícolas en Latinoamérica. La necesidad de superar asimetrías a través de una adecuada gestión de los riesgos implicados. Revista Ibero-Latinoamericana de Seguros **30**(54), 187–206 (2021). https://doi.org/10.11144/Javeriana.ris54.saln
24. Peña, A., Bonet, I., Lochmuller, C., Chiclana, F., Góngora, M.: Flexible in-verse adaptive fuzzy inference model to identify the evolution of operational value at risk for improving operational risk management. Appl. Soft Comput. **65**, 614–631 (2018)
25. Peña, A., Bonet, I., Lochmuller, C., Patiño, H.A., Chiclana, F., Góngora, M.: A fuzzy credibility model to estimate the Operational Value at Risk using internal and external data of risk events. Knowl.-Based Syst. **159**, 98–109 (2018). https://doi.org/10.1016/j.knosys.2018.07.024
26. Borzenkova, I.I.: Types and characteristics of precipitation. State Hydrological Institute, Russia (2009). https://www.eolss.net/sample-chapters/c07/E2-02-05-02.pdf
27. Melker, A.I., Starovoitov, S.A., Vorobyeva, T.V.: Heat, temperature, entropy (2010). https://www.ipme.ru/e-journals/MPM/no3910/melker4.pdf

28. Tojo Fariña, J.: La ciudad y el medio natural. Akal (Akal, Ed.) (1998). https://core.ac.uk/download/pdf/148688249.pdf

29. Broder, A., Garcia-Pueyo, L., Josifovski, V., Vassilvitskii, S., Venkatesan, S.: Scalable k-means by ranked retrieval. In: Proceedings of the 7th ACM International Conference on Web Search and Data Mining, pp. 233–242. ACM (2014)

30. Celebi, M.E., Kingravi, H.A., Vela, P.A.: A comparative study of efficient initialization methods for the k-means clustering algorithm. Expert Syst. Appl. 40(1), 200–210 (2013)

31. Chiang, M.-C., Tsai, C.-W., Yang, C.-S.: A time-efficient pattern reduction algorithm for k-means clustering. Inf. Sci. 181(4), 716–731 (2011)

Safety Verification of the Raft Leader Election Algorithm Using Athena

Mateo Sanabria$^{(\boxtimes)}$, Leonardo Angel, and Nicolás Cardozo

Systems and Computing Engineering Department, Universidad de los Andes,
Bogotá, Colombia
{m.sanabriaa,l.angels,n.cardozo}@uniandes.edu.co

Abstract. The Raft consensus algorithm is widely recognized for its practicality and comprehensibility in achieving consensus within distributed systems. This paper presents a comprehensive exploration of Raft, making clear key concepts and verifying critical properties. We delve into the fundamental components of Raft, encompassing leader election, log replication, and safety guarantees. Detailed explanations are shown in order to illustrate the interactions between actors during commit phases, leader selection, and other significant stages. The Athena proof system is employed to verify essential properties such as leader completeness, log consistency, and fault tolerance, ensuring the algorithm's resilience in the face of failures. Drawing upon the Athena programming language's actor model implementation, we simulate and validate the behavior of Raft, providing practical insights into its functionality.

Keywords: Raft · Consensus algorithms · Athena · Formal verification

1 Introduction

In distributed computing, the quest for reliable, efficient, and understandable consensus algorithms has become increasingly pertinent. The inherent complexities of concurrent computation combined with the demand for robust and responsive distributed systems underlines the necessity for consensus algorithms. The intrinsic complexities of such systems requires effective means of maintaining consistency, especially under the potentially continuous failure of components.

The Raft consensus algorithm emerges as an effective solution, improving system reliability through its unique mechanisms of leader election, log replication, and safety assurance. Raft is put forward as an understandable and functional consensus algorithm, over other algorithm implementations (*e.g.*, PAXOS) [8]. Nonetheless, verifying its critical properties remains a challenge, given the inherent complexity and non-determinism of the distributed environments in which it operates. The verification of Raft's properties is crucial to ensure system-wide integrity and consistency, especially under unpredictable conditions.

The Raft protocol orchestrates the interaction of actors within a distributed system to ensure that they agree on a sequence of values [8]. Raft accomplishes

M. Tabares et al. (Eds.): CCC 2023, CCIS 1924, pp. 285–296, 2024.
https://doi.org/10.1007/978-3-031-47372-2_23

this through three main features. (1) *Leader election* is used to ensure that a single actor takes charge of managing the system's state at every execution point. (2) *Log replication* guarantees that all actors have identical copies of system commands, enforcing a uniform order of execution. (3) *Safety* mechanisms ensure that all operations preserve system integrity, even in the face of component failures. Property verification for Raft is limited. Existing approaches [4,9] fail to account for the inherent non-deterministic nature of distributed systems, and the difficulty of accurately modeling interactions.

The actor computation model posits a tradeoff for concurrent programming, combining theoretical robustness with practical feasibility [1]. The main concurrent entity in the actor model is *actors*. Actors encapsulate their state, and interaction with other actors through asynchronous message passing.

In this paper, we provide an initial actor-based verified implementation of Raft (Sect. 2), focusing on leader election. We pay special attention to interactions between actors at critical failure points (*e.g.,* the commit phases and leader selection). Our implementation uses the Athena proof system and language [3,7], to be able to prove the leader completeness property. We use Athena as it makes it easier to reason about complex systems, drawing on abstract mathematical structures to provide rigorous proofs expressed in a functional and logic manner. Furthermore, we leverage Athena's actor model implementation as a framework of distributed computing, capturing the subtleties of the system under study, yielding practical insights into Raft's behavior.

An integral part of Athena is its conditional-rewriting subset, which allows users to write executable formal specifications of systems and automatically search for counterexamples. Furthermore, the language has a flexible module system for organizing large-scale proofs and an extensible notation that can simplify notation. It also supports abstract proofs and structured theories providing a flexible way to manage structures and theories. Moreover, Athena enables the creation of proof methods and programs specifications that bear a strong resemblance to parameterized procedures used in regular computation. This relationship highlights numerous similarities between proofs-as-programs [3].

In summary, our work presents the following contributions:

- A full functional implementation of Raft within the Athena actor system.
- A safety and correctness proof of the leader election protocol within Raft.

2   Reasoning About Raft

This section presents the formal (*i.e.,* verified) specification of the Raft algorithm using Athena. Before diving into the implementation of Raft, we present the idea behind the algorithm, and the basic abstractions for its implementation.

For the Raft implementation we focus on human-readable functional proofs. The approach taken here is to build a foundational library for reasoning about Raft using Athena [7], which constitutes a correctness proof by construction.

2.1 The Raft Consensus Algorithm

The Raft consensus algorithm [8] proposes an improvement alternative to the PAXOS algorithm [5,6]. PAXOS is the most common consensus algorithm, serving as a base to further consensus implementations, Raft was specifically designed to be easy to understand. However, both algorithms share the same purpose, which is enabling a set of nodes to function as a cohesive group capable of tolerating failures. To achieve this, the problem can be broken down into three sub-problems: *leader election, log replication,* and safety [4].

Leader election ensures liveness properties by guaranteeing the existence of a leader within the group. Log replication ensures that the leader keeps the log distribution updated throughout the entire group of connected nodes, maintaining safety properties during the process. For example, followers only vote for a candidate whose log is more up-to-date than their own. In this paper we focus on proving correct the leader election protocol.

2.2 Node Definition

Actors fulfill a dual role as units of state encapsulation and concurrency, which makes them highly suitable for distribution, mobility, and adaptivity in open systems [1,2]. Each actor possesses a unique identifier, and communicates with other actors through asynchronous message passing. When an actor receives a message, it can modify its internal state, create new actors with predefined behavior, or send messages to known actors.

Actors' behavior provides a suitable theoretical foundation to reason about the Raft consensus algorithm [8]. This is because actors can represent nodes in a distributed system, modeling remote communication with message passing.

Nodes for the Raft algorithm are specified using the Athena datatype, as shown in Algorithm 1.1. Each element of the datatype can be constructed by applying certain operations known as the constructors of the datatype. The specification of a datatype includes its name, possibly followed by its parameters, and a nonempty sequence of constructor profiles separated by the | symbol.

Raft nodes are defined, in Algorithm 1.1, with two basic constructors: Log and Name. These constructors represent the internal state of the node and its name, respectively. The State datatype consists of the following components: the possible states of a node (NLS - leader, candidate, or follower), the node's internal clock represented by a natural number (CLS), and the information about the node that leaders possess (FLS). Note that the Name datatype is composed of an Alias (representing the specific name of the node) and a natural number (N) representing the node's timeout.

Furthermore, the actor framework offers a configuration that can be viewed as a "soup" of components (actors and messages) with constructors Null, One, and ++ [7]. The main idea behind the actor framework is to express the computation in a distributed system as the transition between configurations, where a transition is generated when an actor is *created, sends* a message, or *receives* a message.

```
1    datatype Alias := Jessie | James | Meowth
2    datatype NLS := Follower | Candidate | Leader
3    datatype Name := (Name Alias N)
4    datatype CLS := (Local N)
5    datatype FLS := (Following Alias N)
6    datatype Log := (State NLS CLS FLS)
7    datatype RAFTLS := (Node Log Name)
```

Algorithm 1.1. Raft node definiton in Athena

Using this framework, a valid configuration with three nodes and no messages is specified in Algorithm 1.2. In this configuration, there are three nodes named `Meowth-20`, `Jessie-15`, and `James-10`; with `Meowth-20` as the current leader, holding a total of three votes, and the other two nodes acting as followers. In this particular example, the candidate state is not displayed. Each node's name is endowed with an integer, defining its time out. Additionally, we show the local state of the three nodes in the configuration.

```
1    (Node
2        (State Follower (Local 2) (Following Jessie 0))
3        (Meowth 20)) ++
4    (Node
5        (State Leader (Local 0) (Following Jessie 3))
6        (Jessie 15)) ++
7    (Node
8        (State Follower (Local 4) (Following Jessie 0))
9        (James 10))
```

Algorithm 1.2. Example Raft configuration for three nodes

2.3   Leader Election

Node local computations are used to express the behavior of nodes in the form of two function definitions. The first function, `ready-to`, is a binary predicate that determines whether the node's local state is prepared to engage in a transition. The second function, `next`, takes the node's current local state and a transition step as input, and produces the new local state that the node will assume when actively participating in the transition.

```
1 declare next: [RAFTLS (Step Alias)] -> RAFTLS
2 declare ready-to: [RAFTLS (Step Alias)] -> Boolean
```

Algorithm 1.3. Local definition domains for the **next** and **ready-to** functions

The two **fun** definitions in Algorithm 1.3 are the basis to manage the behavior of each configuration transition, defining a semantics of the leader election that we can verify. Algorithm 1.3 shows the declarations of the domains for the functions. Note that the second attribute of both functions is the polymorphic datatype (**Step Alias**). In the case of Raft this datatype allows us to have transition steps using nodes' names, for the three possible transition steps: **send**, **receive**, and **create**.

Based on nodes' definition, Fig. 1 presents a general overview of the four transitions required to reach a configuration with an elected leader (Fig. 1d), from a configuration with no leader (Fig. 1a). We now present the steps for leader selection based on actor's behavior, achieved through message passing. To accomplish this, we implement/specify the behavior of nodes using Athena.[1]

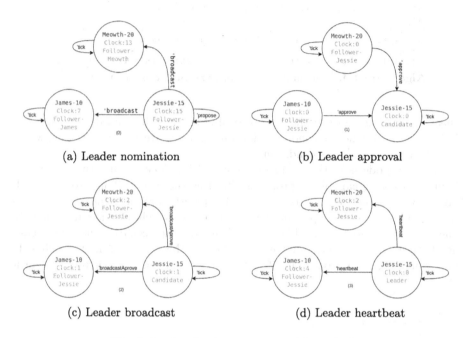

(a) Leader nomination   (b) Leader approval

(c) Leader broadcast   (d) Leader heartbeat

Fig. 1. Leader election process on Athena Raft

The first step in the process is nodes' progress. Nodes progress, independently of each other, by updating their internal clock (Algorithm 1.4). In one step, a node can update its internal state by sending a self-message with the payload ' tick. As a result, the ready-t function needs to specify whether a node is capable of sending or receiving the message. The next function defines the way the node's local state changes when it receives this message.

The behavior definition for Raft's leader election in Athena is made through module definitions, in order to cleanly modularize such functions for different node types; regular nodes (Algorithm 1.4), Follower nodes (Algorithm 1.5), Candidate nodes (Algorithm 1.6), and Leader nodes (Algorithm 1.7).

In Algorithm 1.4, lines 3–4 establish the conditions under which a node becomes ready to send a self 'tick message. Specifically, a node is considered ready to send a tick if its internal clock value is less than the predetermined threshold (specified in the node's name). This readiness condition relies on the

---
[1] The full implementation of our work is available at: undisclosedtokeepanonymity.

```
1 assert ready-to-definition :=
2  (fun [
3  (ls ready-to (send alias alias 'tick)) <==>
4    ((ls=(Node (State nls (Local t0) fls0) (Name alias t1))) & (t0 < t1))
5  (ls ready-to (receive alias alias 'tick)) <==>
6    ((ls=(Node (State nls (Local t0) fls0) (Name alias t1))) & (t0<t1))   ])
7 assert next-definition :=
8  (fun [(next (Node (State nls (Local t0) fls0) (Name alias t1)) (receive
              to fr c)) = [
9    (Node (State nls (Local S t0) fls0) (Name alias t1))
10   when
11   ((t0<t1) & (to=fr) & (to=alias) & (c = 'tick) & (~nls = Leader))
12   (Node (State nls (Local zero) fls0) (Name alias t1))
13   when
14   ((t0<t1) & (to=fr) & (to=alias) & (c='tick) & (nls=Leader)) ] ])
```

Algorithm 1.4. Domain definition for **next** and **ready-to** module Node

specific mapping between the node's local state and the step definition. Similarly, lines 5–6 define the conditions for a node to receive a 'tick message, which aligns with the readiness condition.

When a node is in the **Follower** state and its clock reaches the designated limit, it becomes capable of proposing itself as the leader. This involves sending a **propose** message to itself and subsequently broadcasting the proposal to all nodes in the group. The conditions for this behavior are described in lines 6–9 in Algorithm 1.5. Figure 1a illustrates the scenario where no leader has been established yet. However, the clock of the **Jessie-15** node reaches its limit, enabling it to propose itself as the leader and notify other nodes accordingly.

```
1 assert ready-to-definition :=
2  (fun [
3   ((ls = (Node (State nls (Local t0) fls0) (Name alias t1))) & (t0 < t1))
4   (ls ready-to (send alias alias 'propose)) <==>
5     ((ls=(Node (State Follower (Local t0) fls0) (Name alias t1))) & (t0=t1))
6   (ls ready-to (receive alias alias 'propose)) <==>
7     ((ls=(Node (State Follower (Local t0) fls0) (Name alias t1))) & (t0=t1))
8   (ls ready-to (receive alias alias0 'broadcastAprove)) <==>
9     ((ls = (Node (State Follower (Local t0) fls0) (Name alias t1))) & (t0 < t1)) ])
10 assert next-definition :=
11 (fun
12  [(next (Node (State Follower (Local t0) (Following alias v)) (Name alias0 t1)) (
          receive to fr c)) = [
13   (Node (State Candidate (Local zero) (Following alias (S zero))) (Name alias t1))
14   when
15   ((t0=t1) & (to=fr) & (to=alias0) & (c='propose))
16   (Node (State Follower (Local zero) (Following alias v)) (Name alias0 t1))
17   when
18   ((t0<t1) & (fr=alias) & (to=alias0) & (c='heartbeat) & (~alias=alias0))
19   (Node (State Follower (Local zero) (Following alias1 zero)) (Name alias0 t1))
20   when
21   ((t0<t1)&(fr=alias1)&(to=alias0)&(c='broadcast))] ])
```

Algorithm 1.5. **Follower** module definition for the **next** and **ready-to** behavior

The next step, in Fig. 1b, is for the other nodes to accept the leader; `Jessie-15` in our example. This implies several changes to nodes' local state. For example, nodes `James-10` and `Meowth-20` update their follower information, both now following `Jessie-15` as the leader. Additionally, `Jessie-15` is now in the `Candidate` state, and all the node's local clocks are reset to 0.

The changes in state are defined using the **next-definition** function in Algorithm 1.5. Line 12 defines the pattern to match the appropriate behavior. Specifically, the **next-definition** binary function takes two arguments. (1) The first argument is a node in the `Follower` state with a local clock at `t0`. This node, named `alias0`, is following the node with the name `alias`, with a time limit `t1`. (2) The second parameter is a transition step. Specifically a `receive` step from `fr` directed to the node `to` (both `to` and `fr` are variables representing the node names), and a payload `c` (which is a variable representing the message payload; one of: `'tick`, `'propose`, or `'broadcast`).

Furthermore, lines 13–15 define the local state changes when transitioning from the `Follower` state to the `Candidate` state. During this transition, the state is changed, the local clock is reset to 0 (`zero` in the Athena Peano definition for natural numbers), and the node starts following itself and voting for itself. It's important to note that the message triggering this transition should be sent from the node to itself. Additionally, lines 25–27 define the transition for a node that receives the leader proposal for another node. This step causes the reset of the local clock, the change of the `Following` state, and the voting information.

The fourth step in the process, in Fig. 1, corresponds to the leader election. Election takes place when the candidate node reaches the majority of votes (two in our example configuration) and becomes a leader. The leader first broadcasts its victory, so that no further nominations take place. Figure 1c showcase the `'broadcastApprove` messages send by the candidate `Jessie-15`. Here each clock has updated independently. Lines 5–6 of Algorithm 1.6 show the conditions for a node in the `Follower` and `Candidate` to receive a `'broadcastApprove` message from a `Candidate` node, which can change its state to `Leader` state. This message is key for nodes that did not vote for the winner candidate; this message forces them to follow the new leader.

```
1 assert ready-to-definition :=
2   (fun [
3     (ls ready-to (send alias alias0 'broadcastApprove)) <==>
4       ((ls = (Node (State Candidate (Local t0) (Following alias (S S zero))) (Name
              alias t1)) ) & (t0 < t1) & (~ alias = alias0))
5     (ls ready-to (receive alias alias0 'broadcastApprove)) <==>
6       ((ls = (Node (State Candidate (Local t0) (Following alias v)) (Name alias t1))) &
              (t0<t1) & (alias=alias0) & ((S zero) > v))     ])
7 assert next-definition :=
8   (fun
9   [(next (Node (State Candidate (Local t0) (Following alias v)) (Name alias t1)) (
          receive to fr c)) = [
10      (Node (State Leader (Local zero) (Following alias v)) (Name alias t1))
11      when
12        ((t0<t1) & (to=alias) & (fr=to) & (c='broadcastApprove)) ]    ])
```

Algorithm 1.6. Domain definition for **next** and **ready-to** module Candidate

Once the leader is elected, it takes on the responsibility of instructing the other nodes not to nominate themselves as candidates. This is achieved by the leader continuously sending *heartbeat* messages to the entire group. These messages have the effect of resetting the internal clock of each node, ensuring that no other node reaches its internal clock limit, and avoids proposing itself as a candidate. This behavior is shown in Fig. 1d where the leader node sends the 'heartbeat messages to the follower nodes while every node keeps ticking its own clock. Algorithm 1.7 shows the conditions for the Leader node to send the 'heartbeat messages (*i.e.*, continuously sending messages while available). lines 3–4 define the updated of a follower's local state whenever it receives the hearbeat message, by restarting its internal clock.

```
1 assert ready-to-definition :=
2   (fun [
3   (ls ready-to (send alias alias0 'heartbeat)) <==>
4     ((ls= (Node (State Leader (Local t0) (Following alias v)) (Name alias t1)) ) & (t0<
        t1) & (~alias=alias0)) ])
```

Algorithm 1.7. Domain definition for **next** and **ready-to** module Leader

2.4   Leader Election Structural Properties

The leader election process in Raft relies on two main properties. First, there should be at most one leader in the configuration at any given moment. This property ensures that the system remains in a consistent state and prevents consistency conflicts that may arise from having multiple leaders. Second, a liveness property states that eventually, the system will always have only one leader in the configuration. These properties ensure progress and stability in the leader election process.

Proving these properties can be, however, challenging since leader election is not a trivial process, as it requires a thorough understanding of the algorithm and careful reasoning about its behavior. Therefore, before proving such properties, it is crucial to ensure that the foundational aspects of the leader election process are well-defined and sound. This includes understanding the underlying mechanisms and guarantees provided by the Raft algorithm itself. By establishing a solid foundation, the subsequent verification and proof process can proceed more effectively.

Remember that in our Athena-Raft implementation, the name assigned to each node serves as the limit for its internal clock. When the internal clock of a node reaches its limit, various behavior are triggered within the system. The leader election process relies heavily on the state of the node's clock. Specifically, the state is crucial to ensure that the internal clock of a node never exceeds its specified limit; the safety invariant property for the clock limits. This limitation is essential for maintaining the correctness and integrity of the leader election process. Exceeding the internal clock limit could lead to inconsistencies and unexpected behavior within the system.

Athena's assumption base[2] is originally endowed with the definitions/axioms about the election process, but there is no theorem or any deduction about Raft' behavior. Algorithm 1.8 presents the definition of a judgement to express that after receiving a 'tick message, nodes' safety invariant holds, for nodes in Leader state at lines 5–10 and for nodes in Candidate at lines 11–16. The judgement would be added to the assumption base once it is proven. The functions focus-clock and focus-limit in line 9 and 15 return the current clock value and the limit of the node, respectively.

To include this judgement in the assumption base we need to proved a valid proof for it. Algorithm 1.9 shows Athena's proof (and implementation) for the judgement mentioned above, about Leader nodes. The first proof is based in the behavior that whenever a leader receives a 'tick message it restart its internal clock and zero is the minimum element of the domain N finishing the proof. The proof for Candidate nodes in Algorithm 1.10 is slightly more complex due to the next-definition (Line 9 in Algorithm 1.4) in this case the clock is increased by one unit, however the hypothesis for this theorem is that $t0 < t1$ thus the discrete property for natural numbers, already proved in Athena's natural numbers module, is the key for this proof.

```
 1 define  raftls0 := (Node (State Leader (Local t0) (Following alias0 v)) (
       Name alias1 t1))
 2 define  raftls1 := (next raftls0 (receive alias1 alias1 'tick))
 3 define  raftls2 := (Node (State Candidate (Local t0) (Following alias0 v))
       (Name alias1 t1))
 4 define  raftls3 := (next raftls2 (receive alias1 alias1 'tick))
 5 define safety-name-limit-Leader :=
 6 ( forall t0 t1 v alias0 alias1 .
 7   (t0 < t1)
 8   ==>
 9   (focus-clock raftls1) <= (focus-limit raftls1)
10 )
11 define safety-name-limit-Candidate :=
12 ( forall t0 t1 v alias0 alias1 .
13   (t0 < t1)
14   ==>
15   (focus-clock raftls3) <= (focus-limit raftls3)
16 )
```

Algorithm 1.8. Safety invariant property for the clock limit Leader and Candidate

3 Related Work

The RAFT consensus algorithm has been a significant contribution to the field of distributed systems. It also has been a subject of extensive research. This section presents two related verification approaches for Raft, putting them in perspective with our work. Additionally, we discuss the relevance of the verification of Raft for other related distributed algorithms.

---

[2] Athena's assumption base works as the set of premises held to be true, Athena's system ensures that a sentence is added to the assumption base if and only if it is sound with the current theory.

```
 1 conclude safety-name-limit-Leader
 2    pick-any t0 t1 v alias0 alias1
 3    assume hyp := (t0 < t1)
 4      (!chain<-
 5        [
 6                ((focus-clock (next  (Node (State Leader (Local t0) (Following
                      alias0 v)) (Name alias1 t1)) (receive alias1 alias1 'tick)
                      )) <= (focus-limit (next (Node (State Leader (Local t0) (
                      Following alias0 v)) (Name alias1 t1))  (receive alias1
                      alias1 'tick))))
 7        <==
 8                ((focus-clock (Node (State Leader (Local zero) (Following
                      alias0 v)) (Name alias1 t1)) ) <=
 9                (focus-limit  (Node (State Leader (Local zero) (Following
                      alias0 v)) (Name alias1 t1))) )
10                [Node.next-definition]
11        <==
12                (zero <= t1)
13                [focus-RAFT-definition]
14        <==
15                true
16        ]
17      )
```

Algorithm 1.9. Safety invariant property for the clock limit leader proof

A first approach for verification is based on interactive proof assistants as Coq.

In the Raft consensus protocol it is possible to use a Coq mechanized proof, to verify its safety and correctness. Woos et al. [9] focus on the configuration change property of the protocol by introducing *ghost variables*. Ghost variables are used to reason about the protocol's behavior, specifically preserving safety as its configuration changes.

A second approach for verification exploits the use of solvers, and in particular SAT solvers to reason about algorithms' properties. Bao et al. [4] present a new approach to verifying the safety of the Raft leader election algorithm. The authors use model checking, a technique for verifying finite state concurrent systems, to prove the safety of the leader election algorithm in the Raft protocol. Specifically, the authors use the Promela language and the SPIN model checker to model the algorithm and check its safety properties. They also propose an improved model that reduces the state space and makes the model checking process more efficient.

Both of these approaches provide valuable insights, and a foundational base for the verification of the Raft consensus protocol. However, the focus of the approaches differs from ours. In the first case, our work focuses on the verification of the leader election algorithm, rather than the changes to the configuration. Therefore, these approaches could be complementary.

In the both cases, the approaches highlight the complexity and challenges involved in ensuring the correctness and safety of such protocols. Moreover, as these approaches are mainly developed in external specifications, that may miss the intrinsic complexity of concurrent interactions. Using the Athena executable implementation, we capture such difficulties, by having a fully functional and verified program as part of the same specification.

```
 1 # discrete     := (forall m n . m < n ==> S m <= n)
 2 conclude safety-name-limit-Candidate
 3   pick-any t0 t1 v alias0 alias1
 4   assume hyp := (t0 < t1)
 5     (!chain<-
 6       [
 7                   ((focus-clock (next   (Node (State Candidate (Local t0) (
                     Following alias0 v)) (Name alias1 t1)) (receive alias1
                     alias1 'tick))) <= (focus-limit (next (Node (State
                     Candidate (Local t0) (Following alias0 v)) (Name alias1 t1
                     )) (receive alias1 alias1 'tick))))
 8       <==
 9                   ((focus-clock (Node (State Candidate (Local  S t0) (Following
                     alias0 v)) (Name alias1 t1)) ) <=
10                   (focus-limit  (Node (State Candidate (Local  S t0) (Following
                     alias0 v)) (Name alias1 t1))) )
11                   [Node.next-definition]
12      <==
13                   ((S t0) <= t1)
14                   [focus-RAFT-definition]
15      <==
16                   (t0 < t1)
17                   [N.Less=.discrete]
18      <==
19                   true
20       ]
21   )
```

Algorithm 1.10. Safety invariant property for the clock limit proofs

4   Conclusion and Future Work

Consensus algorithms sit at the core of distributed systems to coordinate the consistent interaction of different agents in the system. To contribute towards this goal, this paper presents the initial development of the first actor-based verification tool for the Raft algorithm, implemented in Athena. Moreover, the advantage of the Athena implementation is that more than a tool for formal verification, it is also an executable implementation of the Raft protocol. our implementation starts from an existing model of actor-based distributed computing to represent Raft node configurations and define the behavior for log replication, and reason about Raft properties, with a specific focus on the leader election process. We extend the actor library to account for the Raft capabilities and to ensure compatibility with the current version of Athena.

This paper serves as the starting point for a comprehensive verification of the Raft algorithm, aligned with the state-of-the-art. Our work is to generate both machine-checkable and human-readable proofs using Athena. Moving forward, we are interested in verifying: (1) All replicated copies of the state machine execute the same commands in the same order. (2) There is at most one leader per term. (3) If two logs contain entries at a particular index and term, then the logs are identical up to and including that index. (4) A successfully elected candidate's log contains every committed entry. (5) The implementation is a linearizable state machine.

Future improvements to the library include definition of actors' IDs. IDs are expressed by relations rather than functions, so that IDs are not unique in the configuration. Using function based IDs would remove such a problem. Furthermore, we still miss the liveness guarantee, which ensures the system effectively process and responds to all client commands, given a sufficiently low failure rate.

References

1. Agha, G.A., Mason, I.A., Smith, S.F., Talcott, C.L.: A foundation for actor computation. J. Funct. Program. **7**(1), 1–72 (1997)
2. Agha, G.A., Thati, P., Ziaei, R., Bowman, H., Derrick, J.: Actors: a model for reasoning about open distributed systems. In: Formal Methods for Distributed Processing: A Survey of Object-Oriented Approaches, pp. 155–176 (2001)
3. Arkoudas, K., Musser, D.: Fundamental Proof Methods in Computer Science: A Computer-Based Approach. MIT Press, Cambridge (2017). ISBN: 9780262035538
4. Bao, Q., Li, B., Hu, T., Cao, D.: Model checking the safety of raft leader election algorithm. In: IEEE International Conference on Software Quality, Reliability and Security, pp. 400–409. IEEE (2022)
5. Lamport, L.: Paxos made simple. ACM SIGACT News (Distrib. Comput. Column) **32**(4), 51–58 (2001)
6. Lamport, L.: The part-time parliament. Trans. Comput. Syst. **16**(2), 133–169 (1998). ISSN: 0734-2071
7. Musser, D.R., Varela, C.A.: Structured reasoning about actor systems. In: Proceedings of the Workshop on Programming Based on Actors, Agents, and Decentralized Control, Indianapolis, Indiana, USA, pp. 37–48. ACM (2013). ISBN: 9781450326025
8. Ongaro, D., Ousterhout, J.: In search of an understandable consensus algorithm (extended version). In: Proceeding of USENIX Annual Technical Conference, USENIX ATC, pp. 19–20 (2014)
9. Woos, D., Wilcox, J.R., Anton, S., Tatlock, Z., Ernst, M.D., Anderson, T.: Planning for change in a formal verification of the raft consensus protocol. In: Proceedings of the Conference on Certified Programs and Proofs, St. Petersburg, FL, USA, pp. 154–165. ACM (2016). ISBN: 9781450341271

Modeling Detecting Plant Diseases in Precision Agriculture: A NDVI Analysis for Early and Accurate Diagnosis

Manuela Larrea-Gomez[1]([⊠]) [iD], Alejandro Peña[1] [iD],
Juan David Martinez-Vargas[1] [iD], Ivan Ochoa[2] [iD],
and Tomas Ramirez-Guerrero[1] [iD]

[1] Universidad EAFIT, Medellín, Colombia
mlarreag1@eafit.edu.co
[2] UNIPALMA de los Llanos S.A., Cumaral, Colombia

Abstract. In precision agriculture, the accurate and timely plant disease identification is crucial. However, the lack of accuracy in current detection systems hampers reducing pesticide and fertilizer usage, causing significant productivity losses. The desired level of precision has not been achieved yet, hindering timely intervention and mitigation strategies. This research presents a novel approach that integrates a Lagrangian Gaussian Puff Dispersion Model (LGPTM) for assessing plant health, with Gaussian bell curve visualization, a tool for visualizing the distribution patterns of these indices in the field of precision agriculture. This integration ameliorates disease detection and monitoring in agricultural contexts, thereby improving disease management practices and enhancing crop health and productivity. The methodology leverages widely adopted libraries to process multispectral images and calculates vegetation index values based on the Normalized Difference Vegetation Index (NDVI). Additionally, the modeling approach employed modular programming. The code structure and execution encompass two main steps: the normalization of the Near-Infrared and Red bands of the multispectral images, and the construction of a three-dimensional Gaussian bell curve to visualize the distribution of vegetation indices using the meshgrid algorithmic technique. The results reveal a significant correlation between variations in the vegetation index and the vertical distribution of the Gaussian curve. Specifically, lower NDVI values indicate a diminished presence of vegetation or plant anomalies, resulting in an increase in the kurtosis of the Gaussian curve. To assess the effectiveness of the approach, Receiver Operating Characteristic analysis was employed, providing conclusive evidence regarding the reliability and performance of the implemented Python model.

Keywords: Precision agriculture · Lagrangian Gaussian Puff Dispersion Model · Plant disease early detection · Multispectral imaging · NDVI Analysis

Supported by Minciencias Colombia.

M. Tabares et al. (Eds.): CCC 2023, CCIS 1924, pp. 297–310, 2024.
https://doi.org/10.1007/978-3-031-47372-2_24

1   Introduction

Plant diseases present a substantial menace to worldwide food security, resulting in crop reductions, quality reduction, and increased production costs [6,15,23]. To address this challenge, precision agriculture techniques have emerged as a promising approach. By leveraging technology to gather data on soil, weather, and crop conditions, precision agriculture enables informed decision-making [15, 23]. In this context, remote sensing based on satellites, airplanes, and drones, captures data from a distance [6,18,23] and plays a crucial role in plant disease detection within precision agriculture. The analysis of the obtained by these sensors make it possible identify changes in leaf characteristics, plant height, canopy density, and plant vigor, which can provide insights into disease presence [6,18].

In addition to remote sensing, precision agriculture techniques enable the collection of data on environmental factors influencing disease development, including soil moisture and temperature [5,12]. These data help identify disease-prone areas and facilitate targeted preventive measures. The integration of precision agriculture techniques holds tremendous potential for enhancing the efficiency and effectiveness of plant disease management. By enabling early detection and timely interventions, precision agriculture reduces crop losses, lowers costs, and contributes to improved yields and global food security [18].

In precision agriculture, the accurate and timely identification of plant diseases is essential for effective disease management and maximizing crop health and productivity [3]. However, current detection systems lack the required level of accuracy, resulting in reduced precision, increased pesticide and fertilizer usage, and significant productivity losses. The existing methods hinder timely intervention and mitigation strategies, which further exacerbate the negative impact of plant diseases on global food security. Current approaches for plant disease detection are not accurate enough and new methods are needed [2].

The aim of this study is to address the limitations of current detection systems and propose a novel approach that integrates a Lagrangian Gaussian Puff Dispersion Model (LGPTM) and Gaussian bell curve visualization. By harnessing multispectral imaging and leveraging the Normalized Difference Vegetation Index (NDVI), this approach aims to enhance disease detection and monitoring in agricultural contexts. The research seeks to develop a reliable and performance-driven Python model that can provide early and accurate diagnosis of plant diseases, enabling farmers to implement targeted preventive measures and optimize resource allocation, thereby enhancing crop health, reducing losses, and contributing to global food security.

2   Overview of Plant Disease Detection: Previous Approaches and Techniques

Airborne imaging systems equipped with multispectral and hyperspectral cameras have been widely employed in agricultural applications, including the identification and spatial analysis of crop diseases. These systems make use of hyper-spectral data and vegetation indices to indirectly monitor plant diseases. However, their ability to distinguish between different diseases on a crop is limited [11].

Conventional methods for evaluating crop health have extensively utilized vegetation indices, including the widely adopted NDVI. Remote sensing spectral imagery has proven its efficacy across diverse applications. For instance, Zhang et al. [24] used NDVI in combination with the Near Infrared (NIR) and red bands to detect crop anomalies in field tomatoes. Seo et al. [19] monitored crop growth and phenology for corn and soybeans using NDVI. Multispectral and hyperspectral images have also been utilized to identify disease symptoms in crops such as grapevines [14] and wheat [8].

Research in the field of disease detection is exploring the promising combination of hyperspectral imaging, machine learning techniques, and image processing. Gómez-Camperos et al. [7] emphasize the effectiveness of hyperspectral images, which capture detailed spectral information, in conjunction with machine learning algorithms for early disease identification. This early detection enables timely implementation of management measures to limit disease spread and reduce crop losses.

Similarly, Zulkifli Bin Husin et al. [9] conducted a comprehensive study utilizing MATLAB for feature extraction and image recognition to assess health of chili plants. They employed various pre-processing techniques, including Fourier filtering, edge detection, and morphological operations, alongside computer vision and LabView Software to enhance their investigation. Furthermore, artificial neural networks have proven to be crucial in disease detection, as demonstrated by Jhuria et al. [10], who utilized image processing techniques, including artificial neural networks, for disease detection and fruit grading. By creating separate databases for training and querying images, they compared color, texture, and morphology as feature vectors, with morphological features yielding superior results.

The continuous evolution of technological tools for disease detection in crops has shown great promise, particularly with the integration of Deep Learning techniques, hyperspectral imaging, and computer vision [13, 20]. These advancements have enabled the timely and accurate identification of diseases in crops, leading to improved management practices and reduced agricultural losses [13, 25].

Despite progress in detection systems, early disease identification remains challenging [20], as symptoms are often already visible in remote sensing images, indicating existing damage [1]. This hinders timely intervention and effective control within the current growing season [21]. Additionally, widespread fungicide use, while reducing yield loss, lacks site specific application and may not address specific diseases with consistent patterns across seasons.

Teledetection techniques are commonly used to estimate disease damage severity, assisting in future management and control strategies [16]. To overcome these limitations, further research is needed to improve early disease detection and implement targeted management approaches [1].

3   Methodology

The proposed approach aims to improve the accuracy and timeliness of plant disease identification in precision agriculture. This study introduces a novel integration of the LGPTM and vegetation index analysis to enhance disease detection
and monitoring in agricultural settings.

3.1   Integration of the Lagrangian Gaussian Puff Dispersion Model (LGPTM)

In the context of simulating the transport and fate of pollutants at different scales
(mesoscale, regional scale, or local scale) from their sources, two main approaches
can be employed: the Eulerian approach and the Lagrangian approach. While
the Eulerian approach focuses on simulating changes in pollutant concentration
across a fixed gridded domain based on numerical or analytical solutions of
governing equations [4], the Lagrangian approach takes a different perspective.

According to Chang [4], the Lagrangian approach is specifically designed to
track emissions from individual point sources, considering a frame of reference
that moves along with the emission along its predicted pathway. By adopting
this model, emissions in both approaches can be represented as plumes, puffs,
or point particles. What distinguishes the Lagrangian approach is its ability
to provide a straightforward delineation of pollutant transport and fate using
models such as the Gaussian dispersion model or the Gaussian plume model.

The Gaussian plume model, denoted by the concentration function C, is
widely used in Lagrangian dispersion models to represent pollutant transport
and dispersion. It characterizes the concentration of a pollutant at point (x, y, z)
downwind of a source, considering the emission rate Q, wind speed at the top
of the stack U, effective plume height H, and dispersion coefficients σ_y and
σ_z which represent the standard deviations of the plume concentration in the
lateral (Y) and vertical (Z) directions, respectively. The previously mentioned
is illustrated in the following equation [22].

$$C(x,y,z,H) = \frac{Q}{2\pi U \sigma_y \sigma_z} \exp\left(-\frac{1}{2}\left(\frac{y}{\sigma_y}\right)^2\right) \left\{ \exp\left(-\frac{1}{2}\left(\frac{z+H}{\sigma_z}\right)^2\right) + \exp\left(-\frac{1}{2}\left(\frac{z-H}{\sigma_z}\right)^2\right) \right\} \quad (1)$$

In a recent study, Peña et al. [17], propose the possibility of applying the
LGPTM model, traditionally used in the study of pollutant dispersion in the
atmosphere, for the identification of plant diseases. Their innovative approach,
called I-LGPTM, introduces two dynamics that allow for a comprehensive understanding of the spatio temporal evolution of diseases in early stages of plant
development. These findings suggest a potential extrapolation of the LGPTM
model to the field of plant disease identification and monitoring, opening new
possibilities for research and application in the agricultural domain. In this sense,
they proposed the following equation [17].

$$Q(x,y) = \frac{1}{(2\pi)^{3/2}\sigma_{xy}^2} \exp\left(-\frac{1}{2}\left(\frac{x_f - x}{\sigma_{xy}}\right)^2 - \frac{1}{2}\left(\frac{y_f - y}{\sigma_{xy}}\right)^2\right) \quad (2)$$

where Q indicates the intensity of the infection at point (x, y). The point (x_f, y_f) represents the location of the center within the dispersion pattern and σ_{xy} refers to the dispersion coefficient. Now, what the current study proposes is a model that utilizes the NDVI as a parameter, enabling valuable information to be derived from variations in vegetation concerning anomalies and potential sources of infection propagation. The LGPTM experiences significant expansion as it incorporates the NDVI effect into the disease intensity function C (x, y), as demonstrated in Eq. (3) derived from the formulation in Eq. (2) below.

$$C(x,y) = \frac{\exp\left(-\frac{1}{2}\left(\frac{ndvi_f - ndvi}{\sigma_{xy}}\right)^2\right)}{(2\pi)^{3/2}\sigma_{xy}^2} \cdot \exp\left(-\frac{1}{2}\left(\frac{x_f - x}{\sigma_{xy}}\right)^2 - \frac{1}{2}\left(\frac{y_f - y}{\sigma_{xy}}\right)^2\right) \quad (3)$$

where C (x, y) represents the intensity of the disease at the point (x, y) within the field of the plant. The term $\exp\left(-\frac{1}{2}\left(\frac{ndvi_f - ndvi}{\sigma_{xy}}\right)^2\right)$ modulates the disease intensity based on the difference between the NDVI at the central point (x_f, y_f) and the NDVI at the current point (x, y). A smaller NDVI difference will result in a higher disease intensity, while a larger difference will lead to a lower disease intensity.

The dispersion coefficient σ_{xy} in Eq. (3) characterize the spreading of the disease in the $X - Y$ plane, within the framework of a Lagrangian dispersion model. This coefficient describes the normalized evolution of the disease in the field, considering the combined effect of wind dispersal and vegetation interactions.

The approach to tackle the aforementioned model involves the introduction of a flowchart that incorporates a modular programming methodology (refer to Fig. 1). This methodology entails the decomposition of the problem into smaller, self-contained modules, each assigned to specific tasks and responsibilities. By embracing the modular programming paradigm, the code structure becomes more organized and adaptable, facilitating streamlined development and maintenance processes. The flowchart serves as a visual representation of the program's logical flow, elucidating the sequence of operations and decision points. This modular approach substantially enhances the efficiency of model development, enabling effective code reuse and fostering facile implementation of future enhancements and modifications.

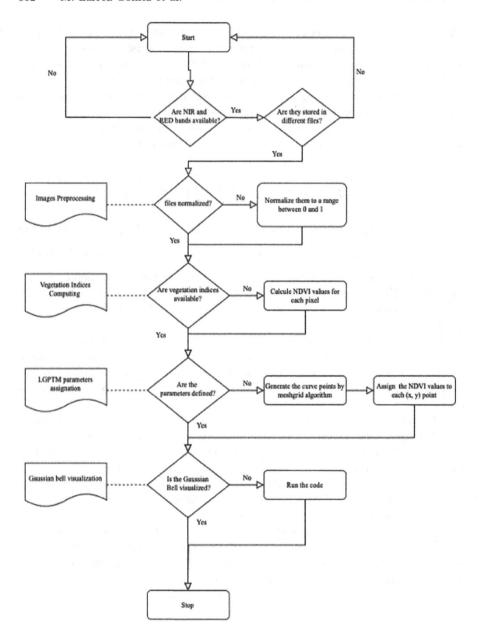

Fig. 1. Python Implementation Flowchart.

3.2   Simulation Study

To validate and evaluate the proposed model, a simulation is conducted using the implemented Python code. This simulation serves as a computational experiment to simulate real-world scenarios and examine the model's performance under various conditions. By leveraging mathematical concepts and computational capabilities, the simulation aims to provide valuable insights and quantitative results that enhance the model's validity and reliability.

Dataset Description. The dataset includes a multispectral image comprising 4 reflectance bands, representing a unit of oil palm crop production (Fig. 2).

Assumptions

1. The multispectral image used in this study focuses solely on the crop unit under evaluation, resulting in a specific point (x, y) at coordinates $(0, 0)$. The image is specifically captured and analyzed to gather information and insights regarding the designated crop unit at its designated location.
2. According to Turner [22], the spread of the plume exhibits a Gaussian distribution in both the horizontal and vertical planes. For this simulation, the dispersion coefficients will be defined in a standard manner. Therefore, the dispersion coefficient is set to $\sigma_{xy} = 1$, allowing for a more meaningful representation of the NDVI values dynamics within the model.

Finally, the NDVI values are computed using the following Eq. 4:

$$NDVI = \frac{NIR - RED}{NIR + RED} \tag{4}$$

4 Results

In accordance with the simulation study design, following the methodology described in Fig. 1, and using the dataset provided, the model generated the following results.

The output of the Python implementation using a LGPTM includes a 3D Gaussian bell visualization representing the NDVI results. The code reads the

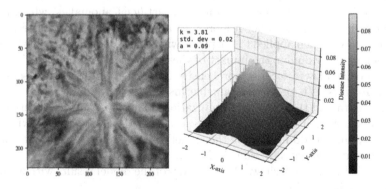

Fig. 2. 3D Gaussian Bell Visualization of LGPTM results for a randomly selected unit of an oil palm crop, with the palm unit displayed on the left.

multispectral image in the red and near-infrared bands and calculates the NDVI values. Subsequently, a meshgrid is created to map the (x, y), and NDVI values. Using these measurements, a 3D Gaussian bell function is constructed, with parameters for the center point and spread in the XY plane (σ_{xy}).

The resulting plot presents the 3D Gaussian bell function, where the x and y axes depict the spatial coordinates, and the z axis illustrates the amplitude of the bell function. Additionally, the plot offers insightful statistical information, including the kurtosis, standard deviation, and amplitude of the bell function. These statistics provide valuable insights into the shape and characteristics of the distribution. These details are displayed through text annotation within the plot, with k representing kurtosis, std.dev indicating standard deviation, and a representing the amplitude.

Regarding the units of Disease Intensity in the Gaussian bell function plot, it is important to clarify that the intensity values are relative and unitless. The Disease Intensity represents the normalized response of the disease in the field based on the differences between the NDVI values at different locations.

This visualization allows for a comprehensive understanding of the spatial distribution and intensity of the NDVI results, facilitating the assessment of vegetation dynamics and health analysis. To demonstrate the model's response to variations in the NDVI within the same image, a function was developed to artificially assign a value of -1 to pixels within a specified radius. This was done with the purpose of simulating anomalies in the vegetation and observing their effects on the model's output.

The choice of assigning a value of -1 as the 'synthetic' NDVI value for the simulated defect was made to represent a scenario where the vegetation exhibits a complete absence of photosynthetic activity. In a real scenario, the NDVI values would not always be exactly -1 if an anomaly or defect is present, as the NDVI index ranges between -1 and 1, with higher positive values indicating healthy and thriving vegetation. Negative NDVI values are typically associated with non-vegetated surfaces, such as water bodies or built-up areas, where there is little to no photosynthetic activity.

By setting the NDVI to -1 in the simulated defect, it allows the model to effectively identify and isolate regions with artificial anomalies, which aids in understanding how the model responds to abnormal vegetation patterns. This modification was then applied to the pixels within the designated radius, enabling us to isolate and examine the impact of these variations on the model's output. This approach allowed for a comprehensive evaluation of the model's sensitivity to changes in NDVI, providing valuable insights into the relationship between the input data and the resulting visualizations. The subsequent section presents the results obtained by systematically adjusting the NDVI values within the specified radius, shedding light on the model's behavior and its ability to capture and represent different variations in NDVI.

Below is Fig. 3 which shows the evolution of the model results with a variable assigned anomaly radius.

The results obtained by the model when inputting images with artificial anomalies reveal an interesting pattern. The generated graphs exhibit a

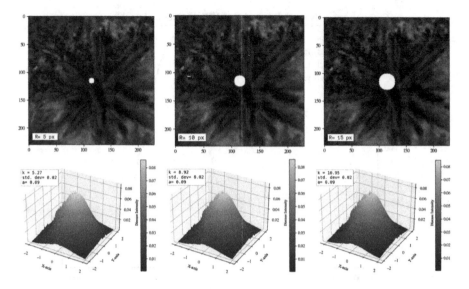

Fig. 3. The Evolution of Model Outputs with Varying Assigned Anomaly-Radius.

noticeable increase in kurtosis, indicating a significant change in the shape of the distribution. This observation suggests that the presence of these artificial anomalies has a substantial impact on the statistical properties of the model's output.

The elevated kurtosis values imply that the distribution becomes more peaked and exhibits heavier tails compared to the original image without anomalies. This change in shape indicates a higher concentration of values around the mean and the presence of more extreme values in the data.

The increase in kurtosis highlights the sensitivity of the model to these artificial anomalies and its ability to capture their influence on the output. This finding emphasizes the importance of considering and accounting for such anomalies when interpreting and analyzing the model's results.

Overall, the results obtained from the images with artificial anomalies provide valuable insights into the model's response to abnormal vegetation patterns. The increased kurtosis serves as a quantitative measure of the deviations introduced by the anomalies and contributes to a deeper understanding of the model's behavior in the presence of these variations. As shown in Fig. 4 which illustrates the Normal distribution of NDVI values for each Anomaly-Radius, the histograms reveal significant changes when artificial anomalies are introduced.

Specifically, for the image without anomalies, the distribution of NDVI values ap-pears relatively symmetric and centered around the mean value. However, with the introduction of artificial anomalies, the distribution exhibits heavier tails, indicating the presence of extreme values that deviate significantly from the mean. This suggests a higher level of variability and a greater range of NDVI values in regions affected by the anomalies.

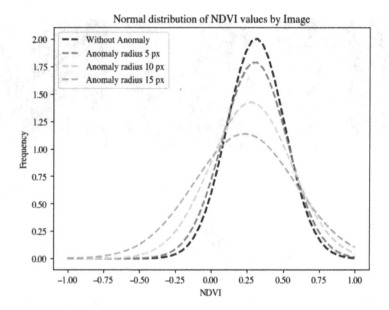

Fig. 4. Normal distribution of NDVI values for each Anomaly-Radius.

Furthermore, the increased dispersion of the NDVI values is evident from the wider spread of the histogram for images with anomalies. This indicates a greater level of heterogeneity in the vegetation patterns within the image. The presence of anomalies introduces additional variability and disrupts the uniformity of the NDVI values across the scene.

4.1 Analysis of the Performance and Precision Model

The evaluation of the Python implementation and the model's performance involved conducting a Receiver Operating Characteristic (ROC) analysis. The objective was to compare the binary response of "Plant with apparent anomaly" versus "Plant without apparent anomaly." The ROC curve provides a graphical representation of the model's ability to distinguish between these two classes at various thresholds.

The results of the ROC analysis (see Fig. 5) yielded an Area Under Curve (AUC) value of 0.73 that suggests that the model exhibits moderate discriminative performance in distinguishing between plants with apparent anomalies and plants without apparent anomalies. The value of 0.73 indicates that the model has a higher probability of assigning a higher score to a randomly chosen "Plant with apparent anomaly" instance compared to a randomly chosen "Plant without apparent anomaly" instance in approximately 73% of cases.

It is important to note that an AUC of 0.73 signifies a reasonably good performance, but there is still room for improvement. Further optimization and

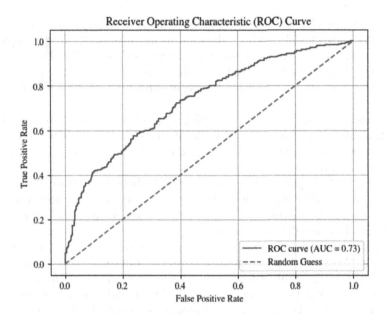

Fig. 5. Normal distribution of NDVI values for each Anomaly-Radius.

fine-tuning of the model could potentially enhance its discriminative power and increase the AUC value.

5   Conclusion

The simulation study conducted in this research validated and evaluated the proposed model through its implementation in Python. The results demonstrated the model's effectiveness in generating 3D Gaussian bell visualizations of the NDVI, providing valuable insights into the spatial distribution and intensity of NDVI values for vegetation dynamics and health analysis. Furthermore, the model demonstrated sensitivity to abnormal vegetation patterns, as evidenced by the variation of statistical parameters like kurtosis in the presence of anomalies.

The dispersion coefficient (σ_{xy}) employed in the model were standardized for this simulation. Further research can delve into optimizing and fine-tuning this coefficient to better represent the normalized evolution of diseases in the field. This could involve incorporating empirical data or calibrating the model with field observations to improve its performance.

This research made certain assumptions, such as focusing on a specific crop unit at a designated location and using standard dispersion coefficients. These simplifications may not fully capture the complexity and variability of real-world agricultural systems. Future research should consider more realistic scenarios and incorporate additional factors, such as crop diversity, environmental variability, and varying disease dynamics.

While the simulation study served as a computational experiment to validate and evaluate the model, further validation using real-world field data is necessary to assess its performance under practical conditions. Collaborating with agricultural experts and collecting field data from diverse crop types and disease scenarios would provide valuable insights and enhance the reliability of the model.

Although the proposed model exhibited promising results, there is room for optimization and fine-tuning. Further improvements in model architecture, parameter selection, and algorithmic enhancements can lead to better performance and accuracy.

While this study primarily focused on NDVI, there are additional vegetation indices that can offer supplementary information about plant health and disease. Exploring the use of alternative indices, could enhance the accuracy and robustness of disease detection models.

Despite the proposed model showing promise in disease identification, its accuracy and efficiency can be improved by integrating advanced machine learning algorithms. These algorithms can learn complex patterns from extensive datasets, enhancing the model's ability to detect and classify diseases accurately. Additionally, the integration of remote sensing technologies in precision agriculture offers new opportunities for disease identification and monitoring. By combining these technologies with the proposed model, we can obtain more detailed and precise information about crop health, enabling proactive disease management strategies.

In conclusion, this research provides a solid foundation for integrating the LGPTM and vegetation index analysis in precision agriculture for disease identification and monitoring. Future research should explore alternative indices, refine dispersion coefficients, integrate advanced machine learning techniques, validate the model with field data, and leverage remote sensing technologies to enhance the accuracy, robustness, and practicality of disease detection models in precision agriculture. Addressing these research directions will contribute to the advancement of precision agriculture and enable more effective disease management strategies for sustainable crop production.

Acknowledgements. The authors would like to thank the Royal Academy of Engineering through the Distinguished International Associates program (DIA-2122-3-160) for their contribution to the development of this research, as well as the Ministry of Science, Technology and Innovation of the Colombian Government for their support through the training program for young researchers, specifically the project with code: BPIN 2022000100080.

References

1. Andrew, J., Eunice, J., Popescu, D.E., Chowdary, M.K., Hemanth, J.: Deep learning-based leaf disease detection in crops using images for agricultural applications. Agronomy **12**, 2395 (2022). https://doi.org/10.3390/AGRONOMY12102395

2. Arsenovic, M., Karanovic, M., Sladojevic, S., Anderla, A., Stefanovic, D.: Solving current limitations of deep learning based approaches for plant disease detection. Symmetry **11**, 939 (2019). https://doi.org/10.3390/SYM11070939
3. Balasundram, S.K., Golhani, K., Shamshiri, R.R., Vadamalai, G.: Precision agriculture technologies for management of plant diseases. In: Ul Haq, I., Ijaz, S. (eds.) Plant Disease Management Strategies for Sustainable Agriculture through Traditional and Modern Approaches. SPCP, vol. 13, pp. 259–278. Springer, Cham (2020). https://doi.org/10.1007/978-3-030-35955-3_13
4. Chang, N.B.: System Dynamics Models and Simulation Analyses. McGraw-Hill Education (2011). https://www.accessengineeringlibrary.com.udea.lookproxy.com/content/book/9780071630054/chapter/chapter11
5. Chen, C.J., Huang, Y.Y., Li, Y.S., Chang, C.Y., Huang, Y.M.: An AIoT based smart agricultural system for pests detection. IEEE Access **8**, 180750–180761 (2020). https://doi.org/10.1109/ACCESS.2020.3024891
6. Devi, M.K.A., Priya, R.: Plant disease identification using the unmanned aerial vehicle images. Turk. J. Comput. Math. Educ. **12**, 2396–2399 (2021)
7. Gómez-Camperos, J.A., Jaramillo, H.Y., Guerrero-Gómez, G.: Digital image processing techniques for detection of pests and diseases in crops: a review. Ingeniería y competitividad **24** (2022). https://doi.org/10.25100/IYC.24I1.10973
8. Huang, W., Lamb, D.W., Niu, Z., Zhang, Y., Liu, L., Wang, J.: Identification of yellow rust in wheat using in-situ spectral reflectance measurements and airborne hyperspectral imaging. Precis. Agric. **8**, 187–197 (2007). https://doi.org/10.1007/S11119-007-9038-9
9. Husin, Z.B., Shakaff, A.Y.B.M., Aziz, A.H.B.A., Farook, R.B.S.M.: Feasibility study on plant chili disease detection using image processing techniques. In: Proceedings of the 3rd International Conference on Intelligent Systems Modelling and Simulation, pp. 291–296 (2012). https://doi.org/10.1109/ISMS.2012.33
10. Jhuria, M., Kumar, A., Borse, R.: Image processing for smart farming: detection of disease and fruit grading. In: Proceedings of the 2013 IEEE Second International Conference on Image Information Processing, pp. 521–526 (2013). https://doi.org/10.1109/ICIIP.2013.6707647
11. Khirade, S.D., Patil, A.B.: Plant disease detection using image processing. In: Proceedings - 1st International Conference on Computing, Communication, Control and Automation, ICCUBEA 2015, pp. 768–771 (2015). https://doi.org/10.1109/ICCUBEA.2015.153
12. Kitpo, N., Inoue, M.: Early rice disease detection and position mapping system using drone and IoT architecture. In: 12th South East Asian Technical University Consortium Symposium. Institute of Electrical and Electronics Engineers Inc. (2018). https://doi.org/10.1109/SEATUC.2018.8788863
13. Li, C., He, M., Cai, Z., Qi, H., Zhang, J., Zhang, C.: Hyperspectral imaging with machine learning approaches for assessing soluble solids content of tribute citru. Foods **12**, 247 (2023). https://doi.org/10.3390/FOODS12020247
14. MacDonald, S.L., Staid, M., Staid, M., Cooper, M.L.: Remote hyperspectral imaging of grapevine leafroll-associated virus 3 in cabernet sauvignon vineyards. Comput. Electron. Agric. **130**, 109–117 (2016). https://doi.org/10.1016/J.COMPAG.2016.10.003
15. Mogili, U.R., Deepak, B.B.: Review on application of drone systems in precision agriculture. Procedia Comput. Sci. **133**, 502–509 (2018). https://doi.org/10.1016/J.PROCS.2018.07.063

16. Neupane, K., Baysal-Gurel, F.: Automatic identification and monitoring of plant diseases using unmanned aerial vehicles: a review. Remote Sens. **13**, 3841 (2021). https://doi.org/10.3390/RS13193841

17. Pena, A., Tejada, J.C., Gonzalez-Ruiz, J.D., Gongora, M.: Deep learning to improve the sustainability of agricultural crops affected by phytosanitary events: a financial-risk approach. Sustainability **14**, 6668 (2022). https://doi.org/10.3390/SU14116668

18. Sandhu, G.K., Kaur, R.: Plant disease detection techniques: a review. In: 2019 International Conference on Automation, Computational and Technology Management, pp. 34–38. Institute of Electrical and Electronics Engineers Inc. (2019). https://doi.org/10.1109/ICACTM.2019.8776827

19. Seo, B., Lee, J., Lee, K.D., Hong, S., Kang, S.: Improving remotely-sensed crop monitoring by NDVI-based crop phenology estimators for corn and soybeans in Iowa and Illinois, USA. Field Crops Res. **238**, 113–128 (2019). https://doi.org/10.1016/J.FCR.2019.03.015

20. Sishodia, R.P., Ray, R.L., Singh, S.K.: Applications of remote sensing in precision agriculture: a review. Remote Sens. **12**(19), 3136 (2020). https://doi.org/10.3390/rs12193136

21. Terentev, A., Dolzhenko, V., Fedotov, A., Eremenko, D.: Current state of hyperspectral remote sensing for early plant disease detection: a review. Sensors **22**, 757 (2022). https://doi.org/10.3390/S22030757

22. Turner, B.: Workbook of Atmospheric Dispersion Estimates - An Introduction to Dispersion Modeling. Environmental Protection Agency (1994)

23. Veroustraete, F.: The rise of the drones in agriculture cronicon agriculture editorial the rise of the drones in agriculture. EC Agric. **2**, 325–327 (2015)

24. Zhang, M., Qin, Z., Liu, X.: Remote sensed spectral imagery to detect late blight in field tomatoes. Precis. Agric. **6**, 489–508 (2005). https://doi.org/10.1007/S11119-005-5640-X

25. Zhang, X., et al.: A deep learning-based approach for automated yellow rust disease detection from high-resolution hyperspectral UAV images. Remote Sens. **11**, 1554 (2019). https://doi.org/10.3390/RS11131554

Towards the Construction of an Emotion Analysis Model in University Students Using Images Taken in Classrooms

Jader Daniel Atehortúa Zapata⬚, Santiago Cano Duque⬚,
Santiago Forero Hincapié⬚, and Emilcy Hernández-Leal[(✉)]⬚

Universidad de Medellín, Cra 87 # 30-65, Medellín, Colombia
ejhernandez@udemedellin.edu.co

Abstract. Data mining is used in various fields, image processing is one of them, a particular application is the identification and classification of emotions expressed by students in the classroom. However, this creates challenges, such as the subjective interpretation of facial expressions and the need for extensive data sets to train and validate the models, for the former it is required to go to other allied research fields, and for the latter, a possibility is glimpsed in the transfer of learning. This work seeks to review and compare different classifiers for the construction of a model that allows the analysis of the emotions of university students from images extracted from recordings of face-to-face classes stored in an educational support platform. For this, the KDD (Knowledge Discovery in Databases) methodology was followed, and experiments were proposed with different configurations of hyperparameters and generation of models from classifiers such as Nearby Neighbors-KNN, Convolutional Neural Networks-CNN, and Random Forest. The performance of each one is contrasted based on precision, recall, F1, Accuracy, and ROC curve. Additionally, an approximation to a learning transfer process was carried out using an open-use data set (taken from the Kaggle repository) for the classification of emotions for the training of the models and validating with the data extracted from the source of the case study. The results support the utility and potential of applying these techniques in scenarios where image-based emotion analysis is required, with CNN being the classifier with the best accuracy and obtaining significant value from knowledge transfer that motivates further deepening of the approach for the treatment of this problem.

Keywords: classification · data mining · educational data · image analysis · transfer learning

1 Introduction

The emotional well-being of students holds significant relevance in the educational context. Recognizing and understanding the emotions experienced by students is not only crucial for their personal development but can also have a direct impact on their academic performance and overall success in the educational environment [2]. However, the task of detecting and assessing students' emotions can be complex and subjective for educators and education professionals. In response to this challenge, image processing supported by artificial intelligence approaches offers a promising tool for objectively and accurately analyzing students' emotions [5]. This has already been tested in virtual education processes, where such analysis can even occur in real-time, enabling early interventions in the educational methodologies and resources employed.

Image processing enables the extraction of key visual features from an image, such as facial expressions, gestures, and body postures, which are closely related to human emotions. By combining computer vision and machine learning techniques, it is possible to develop algorithms capable of identifying and classifying the emotions expressed by students in various educational situations and contexts [1].

This work focuses on exploring the possibility of classifying and analyzing emotions in university students based on images extracted from recordings of in-person classes stored on an educational support platform. It is worth noting that this work represents a preliminary approach to building an emotion analysis model, making it an experimental effort involving classification techniques. At this stage, it does not yet propose a fully implementable tool in the classroom. Additionally, the advantages of transfer learning [13] are examined as a means of domain adaptation, using a validation dataset separate from the model's training dataset. The goal is to fine-tune the pre-trained model to the target data by transferring prior knowledge and adapting to the new data. However, it is important to consider certain factors, such as image quality and the interpretation of emotions, which can be influenced by factors like lighting or the presence of facial obstructions. External factors, such as students' mood or personal situations, may also affect facial emotional expression [8].

Throughout the article, various studies and practical applications that have used image processing to analyze students' emotions in educational settings will be presented in Sect. 2. Section 3 will cover the methodology, including data selection and extraction, as well as the experiment setup. The results and their discussion will be presented in Sect. 4, while the conclusions and future work will conclude the document in Sect. 5.

2   Literature Review

There are several studies that have proven the benefits of image processing for the detection of emotions in educational environments. The state of mind can influence the learning process [7], so having knowledge of the emotions that a student is experiencing in a class can help the teacher to propose methodological strategies and didactic mediations.

In [4], a significant experimental benchmark for research on students' emotion recognition and graphical visualization of facial expressions in a virtual learning environment is successfully proposed. This paper presents an exploration of speech and images by comparing the performance of several deep learning neural network algorithms and an improved long term bidirectional memory convolution neural network algorithm is proposed, which achieves satisfactory performance for the addressed case study.

On the other hand, in [10] a framework that combines a facial expression recognition (FER) algorithm with online course platforms is proposed. Students' faces pictures are taken through the cameras of the devices they use to attend classes and the expressions are analyzed and classified into 8 types of emotions (anger, contempt, disgust, fear, happiness, neutrality, sadness, and surprise). The authors used a course with 27 students conducted on the Tencent Meeting platform and the results obtained show that the model based on Convolutional Neural Networks (CNN), demonstrates robustness in various environments. This suggests that facial expression recognition could be an effective tool for understanding students' emotions during online classes.

As for [9], it reports the analysis of behavior and the search for patterns in the oral presentations of a group of students by applying sequential pattern mining techniques. The analysis allowed segmenting into three different groups according to their body postures, sequential pattern mining provided a complementary perspective for data evaluation and helped to observe the most frequent postural sequences of the students.

Another interesting work is presented in [6], which proposes the integration of two models, one for emotion recognition and the other for attention analysis, to facilitate monitoring during a student's interaction in virtual environments. This integration was carried out on a web platform and the results indicate that the platform could be used by teachers as knowledge mediators, since they could understand the behavior of students in virtual environments, whether synchronous or asynchronous, and take actions to improve the learning experience of students.

In relation to transfer learning, the study [3] proposes a two-phase approach to develop an emotion recognition model and face the challenge of data scarcity in this field. Experimental results evidence a significant improvement in performance when applying the transfer learning strategy through implementation in a Convolutional Neural Network (CNN). This resulted in a remarkable increase in recognition efficiency from 86.38% to 95,89%.

Other works, such as those presented in [12] and [11] also recognize the usefulness and benefits of knowledge transfer in the representation of facial expressions and emotion recognition, being in a process of consolidation of this approach, as well as the libraries, algorithm implementations and tools that support it.

A review of previous studies highlights the importance of understanding students' emotions in educational environments. Existing approaches have demonstrated efficacy in emotion recognition through image processing and facial expression analysis. However, they present limitations in terms of generalization, personalization, and data availability. The approach proposed in this manuscript seeks to overcome these limitations by improving performance and adaptability in a technology-assisted face-to-face educational environment.

3   Methodology

A data mining process was carried out following the traditional steps of a KDD (Knowledge Discovery in Databases) methodology, in which experiments with different hyperparameter configurations and model generation from classifiers such as KNN, CCN and Random Forest were proposed, contrasting the performance of each one based on accuracy, recall and F1 metrics.

By using these classifiers, we seek to perform a comparative analysis to determine whether the Convolutional Neural Network (CNN), being specifically designed for image and video processing, could perform greater efficiency in comparison to the other evaluated models.

Additionally, an approach to a learning transfer process was made by using an open-use dataset for emotion classification to train the models and validating with the data extracted from the case study source.

An applied research is developed with a case study corresponding to the analysis of images obtained in a subject of the Systems Engineering program of the University of Medellin in the semester 2022-2, which includes videos captured in the classroom, from which a relevant set of images were extracted for our research. These videos were obtained from the cameras installed in the classrooms, thus guaranteeing the quality of the data. Regarding data privacy, it is important to note that these classes are uploaded to the u-virtual platform, and due to a previously established agreement at the time of enrollment at the university, they are accessible to the university community. Two strategies were proposed for data collection, one for model training data, which were obtained from a free external repository, and one for test data, which were collected from the group described above as a case study.

Figure 1 shows the general scheme of the steps carried out in the process, where the flow between the data obtained for the training of the models, the collection of the test data, the training process that generates results and the pre-trained model that is subsequently used to perform the transfer with the test data extracted from the real case mentioned above is identified.

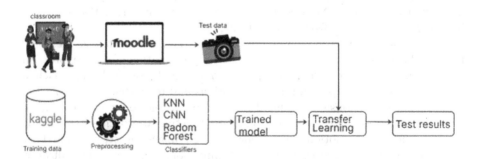

Fig. 1. Scheme of the process carried out.

4   Results

The results at the end of the application of the techniques show that the pre-trained models from a generic dataset of emotions identified in facial expressions demonstrate a medium level of effectiveness in identifying the predominant emotion in students from images of moments extracted from recordings of in-person classes. Together, these results support the utility and potential of applying these techniques in scenarios where image-based emotional analysis is required. Below are the performance metrics obtained for the three implemented models (see Table 1).

Table 1. Evaluation metrics.

Model	F1	Precision	Recall	Accuracy	Accuracy Transfer Learning
Random Forest	0.53	0.54	0.53	0.33	–
KNN	0.32	0.35	0.33	0.325	0.53
CNN	0.55	0.56	0.53	0.56	0.67

On the other hand, the ROC curve is shown in Fig. 2, which illustrates the relationship between the true positive rate and the false positive rate. These curves allow an effective evaluation and comparison of the performance of the models in classification problems. Likewise, the value of the area under the ROC curve will be highlighted, a metric that quantifies the quality of the models in terms of their classification capacity.

In the implementation of the three classification algorithms, it was observed that the CNN model demonstrated superior performance compared to the Random Forest and KNN algorithms. Likewise, after applying Transfer Learning, an improvement in the efficiency of the CNN model was evident. On the other hand, the KNN algorithm also experienced an increase in its efficiency but remained below the CNN. These results suggest that the use of Transfer Learning can enhance the performance of classification models for the processing of emotional images.

These results support the usefulness of the applied techniques and their potential for various applications. For example, in educational settings, the developed models can be used to identify learning situations that generate positive or negative emotions in students, allowing timely intervention to improve the learning experience.

When performing a comparative analysis of the metrics presented in the table (see Table 1) of models, it is clearly highlighted that the CNN model exhibits the greatest efficiency, even when applying transfer learning, reaffirming its position as the most suitable model for the case study. These results coincide with the evidence found in previous studies [8] and [11], where it was also shown that a Convolutional Neural Network (CNN) obtained superior results in efficiency. However, it is important to highlight that, despite these achievements,

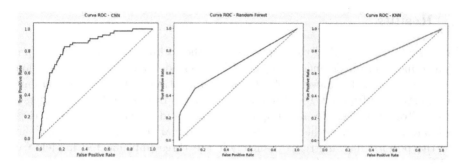

Fig. 2. ROC curve.

we must continue to focus on further improving the efficiency of our case study, considering that the results reported in the literature review exceed 85%.

5   Conclusions

In the processes of classifying educational data, aspects such as the observation of features, that is, exploratory analysis, and the verification of transformation needs are fundamental, as well as the verification of data balance. For this work, the interpretation of emotions present in an image can be subjective and vary among different observers. In image analysis, the consistency and reliability of results can be affected, in addition to the aforementioned factors, by other aspects such as the selection of the partitioning method for the training stage, the definition and execution of experiments, and the strategy for evaluating the results.

The use of transfer learning in image analysis yields favorable results, proving to be an effective way to enhance model performance, especially in situations where there is a limited dataset available or rapid adaptation to new tasks or applications is required. For the experiments outlined in this work, where a comparison of various classification techniques was carried out, it is found that transfer learning is a viable option for training models in problems where obtaining a significant dataset is challenging.

As a future work, the goal is to expand the test dataset taken from the virtual learning environment that supports in-person teaching processes. Additionally, more detailed tracking of a specific subject, along with the visual records, is planned, and these records may be accompanied by sociodemographic characterization data of the student group and the didactic activities carried out at the time of video and image capture. Furthermore, the intention is to incorporate other relevant factors, such as precise emotion interpretation, to achieve more efficient results in the analysis.

References

1. Barrionuevo, C., Ierache, J.S., Sattolo, I.I.: Reconocimiento de emociones a través de expresiones faciales con el empleo de aprendizaje supervisado aplicando regresión logística, pp. 491–500 (2020). http://sedici.unlp.edu.ar/handle/10915/114089

2. Cañero-Pérez, M., Mónaco-Gerónimo, E., Montoya-Castilla, I.: La inteligencia emocional y la empatía como factores predictores del bienestar subjetivo en estudiantes universitarios. EJIHPE: Eur. J. Invest. Health Psychol. Educ. 9(1), 19–29 (2019). ISSN-e: 2254-9625. ISSN: 2174-8144. https://doi.org/10.30552/ejihpe.v9i1.313

3. Hung, J.C., Lin, K.C., Lai, N.X.: Recognizing learning emotion based on convolutional neural networks and transfer learning. Appl. Soft Comput. 84, 105724 (2019). https://doi.org/10.1016/J.ASOC.2019.105724

4. Lu, X.: Deep learning based emotion recognition and visualization of figural representation. Front. Psychol. 12, 818833 (2022). https://doi.org/10.3389/FPSYG.2021.818833

5. Masias, E.J.F., Segovia, J.H.L., Casique, A.G., Díaz, M.E.D.: Análisis de sentimientos con inteligencia artificial para mejorar el proceso enseñanza-aprendizaje en el aula virtual. Publicaciones 53, 185–216 (2023). https://doi.org/10.30827/PUBLICACIONES.V53I2.26825. https://revistaseug.ugr.es/index.php/publicaciones/article/view/26825

6. Piedrahíta-Carvajal, A., Rodríguez-Marín, P.A., Terraza-Arciniegas, D.F., Amaya-Gómez, M., Duque-Muñoz, L., Martínez-Vargas, J.D.: Aplicación web para el análisis de emociones y atención de estudiantes. TecnoLógicas 24, 62–76 (2021). https://doi.org/10.22430/22565337.1821

7. Puertas-Molero, P., Zurita-Ortega, F., Chacón-Cuberos, R., Castro-Sánchez, M., Ramírez-Granizo, I., González-Valero, G.: La inteligencia emocional en el ámbito educativo: un meta-análisis. Anales de Psicología 36, 84–91 (2020). https://doi.org/10.6018/ANALESPS.36.1.345901

8. Saxena, A., Khanna, A., Gupta, D.: Emotion recognition and detection methods: a comprehensive survey. J. Artif. Intell. Syst. 2, 53–79 (2020). https://doi.org/10.33969/AIS.2020.21005. https://iecscience.org/jpapers/46. https://iecscience.org/jpapers/46abstract

9. Vieira, F., et al.: A learning analytics framework to analyze corporal postures in students presentations. Sensors 21, 1525 (2021). https://doi.org/10.3390/S21041525. https://www.mdpi.com/1424-8220/21/4/1525/htm. https://www.mdpi.com/1424-8220/21/4/1525

10. Wang, W., Xu, K., Niu, H., Miao, X.: Emotion recognition of students based on facial expressions in online education based on the perspective of computer simulation. Complexity 2020 (2020). https://doi.org/10.1155/2020/4065207

11. Wu, D., Han, X., Yang, Z., Wang, R.: Exploiting transfer learning for emotion recognition under cloud-edge-client collaborations. J. Sel. Areas Commun. 39, 479–490 (2021). https://doi.org/10.1109/JSAC.2020.3020677

12. Xue, F., Wang, Q., Guo, G.: TransFER: learning relation-aware facial expression representations with transformers, pp. 3601–3610 (2021)

13. Zhuang, F., et al.: A comprehensive survey on transfer learning. Proc. IEEE 109, 43–76 (2021). https://doi.org/10.1109/JPROC.2020.3004555

Cloud-Native Architecture for Distributed Systems that Facilitates Integration with AIOps Platforms

Juan Pablo Ospina Herrera$^{(\boxtimes)}$ and Diego Botia

Maestría en ingeniería, Universidad de Antioquia, Medellín, Colombia
{juan.ospina3,diego.botia}@udea.edu.co

Abstract. DevOps has significantly enhanced application operations through the utilization of containers and CI/CD. It still relies on human intervention in the event of failures in any system component. Many existing solutions are limited to specific issues, such as reacting to server outages and scaling them up. As the complexity of distributed systems continues to grow due to the simultaneous operation of numerous components, even minor unavailability can substantially impact application reliability and result in significant economic consequences for businesses. Therefore, it is imperative that the solutions being developed minimize risks and increasingly automate these operations. In light of these challenges, the emergence of AIOps offers a promising solution using artificial intelligence techniques, including machine learning and big data, to operate and maintain application infrastructures, reduce operational complexity, and automate IT operations processes. Implementing such solutions has been shown to improve system quality and significantly reduce the time it takes to detect errors and recover from them. These advancements mark significant progress in the realm of operations. However, despite these benefits, widespread adoption of AIOps solutions by most companies remains limited due to the challenges associated with implementing them in large projects and the lack of clear integration pathways for emerging solutions. In this paper, we propose a holistic architecture that facilitates the integration of cloud-native distributed systems with these new solutions.

Keywords: Software Architecture · Distributed Systems · AIOps · Cloud-Native

1 Introduction

In distributed environments, maintaining multiple services at the same time is challenging. AIOps seeks to reduce this operational complexity of the systems and automate all operational processes through the application of machine learning algorithms and big data to have services that are capable of managing themselves. Using AIOps, the MTTD (Average time to detect an error) can be

M. Tabares et al. (Eds.): CCC 2023, CCIS 1924, pp. 318–329, 2024.
https://doi.org/10.1007/978-3-031-47372-2_26

reduced from 10 min to 1 min and the MTTR (Average time to repair an error) can be reduced from 60 min to 30 s [1] which shows the great power that we can achieve by implementing this type of technology.

The use of distributed systems implies several complexities such as the fact of using multiple programming languages, libraries, and frameworks, different development teams within the same system, the fact that each architecture carries its own challenges, and that there are multiple clouds that provide different customized services to manage the applications.

Currently, there are specialized solutions that target specific aspects of IT operations management by employing artificial intelligence techniques (particularly within AIOps subcategories). However, there is a lack of clear guidance on effectively harnessing these tools to establish an administration framework based on AIOps. This challenge is especially prominent in the context of distributed systems, where the simultaneous operation of multiple services and the failure of a single component can significantly impact the proper functionality of the system. Consequently, a comprehensive approach is needed to address these complexities and ensure the seamless integration of AIOps principles in managing distributed systems.

Several prior research works have primarily addressed individual tasks or specific subareas within the realm of AIOps [2–4]. The majority of these studies primarily focus on algorithms [1], such as anomaly detection [5–7], clustering analysis [8], failure prediction [9–11], and cost optimization [12]. This motivates the need for a study focused on investigating the main architectures used in case studies of systems managed by AIOps solutions. This research will serve as a foundation for systems to migrate to this type of self-managed administration or new systems that want to take advantage of these powerful solutions.

To build this architecture, 45 articles were analyzed to identify the key patterns, principles, and tools used for integration with AIOps platforms. Next, critical points were identified, and the main patterns for distributed systems were searched to build the proposed architecture, using the C4 model for its presentation. Finally, this new architecture was evaluated through one use case, measuring the MTTD and MTTR times to assess its successful integration with the AIOps platform, along with five specific metrics to evaluate the facility provided by this architecture.

2   Literature Review

Using the IEEE Xplore, Scopus, ACM Digital Library, ScienceDirect, and arXiv databases, an exhaustive search was made for papers that met all the inclusion/exclusion criteria. Different filters were used to discard articles based on their publication date between 2017–2023, English language, free online accessibility, and only science papers or books.

45 papers were selected, of which 39 were discarded, from which the relevant information for our research topic was extracted. We created a comparative table analyzing the relevant aspects and finally, we synthesized the main conclusions of this review.

Table 1. Patterns, principles, and tools used to integrate with AIOps platforms.

Article	Architectural pattern	Cloud-Native	Patterns and principles	Tools
Evolving from Traditional Systems to AIOps: Design, Implementation and Measurements, 2020 [1]	Layered, Microservice	Y	Logging, tracing, Monitoring, Interoperability, DNS, Authority, Approval, REST	ES Cluster, MySQL, Hive, Influxdb, Python, Spring Cloud
A Context Model for Holistic Monitoring and Management of Complex IT Environments, 2020 [13]	Layered	Y	Monitoring, Virtualization	Docker, Kubernetes, OpenStack, AWS, MySQL
An Anomaly Detection Algorithm for Microservice Architecture Based on Robust Principal Component Analysis, 2019 [14]	Microservice, Reactive	Y	Synchronous communication, Middleware, Containerization, Logging, Monitoring	Docker, Oracle
AI-Governance and Levels of Automation for AIOps- supported System Administration, 2019 [15]	N/A	Y	Virtualization, Load balancing, CI/CD, Self-healing, Self-stabilizing	Kubernetes
Ananke: A framework for Cloud-Native Applications smart orchestration, 2020 [16]	Microservice, Serverless, Metal-as-a- service	Y	API gateway, REST, gRPC, Asynchronous communication, Monitoring, Analyzers, Actuators, Shared libraries	Prometheus, OpenShift, Kubernetes, Kafka, DBMS, SPOUT, Raphtory
Managing Distributed Cloud Applications and Infrastructure A Self-Optimising Approach. Chap. 3: Application Optimisation: Workload Prediction and Autonomous Autoscaling of Distributed Cloud Applications, 2020 [17]	Client-server, Cloudlet, Service-oriented, Microservices	Y	API gateway, REST, Load balancing, Autoscaling, Remediation, Virtualization, Monitoring	RECAP

Table 1 presents a comparison of the information found in the selected articles summarizing the patterns, principles, and tools used in each one. There we can see that all the reviewed solutions are focused on the cloud due to the benefits that facilitate the implementation in distributed systems. There are three critical sections that are commonly found in all the papers:

- Monitoring of all system components, relying on existing solutions provided by each cloud provider.
- A middleware in charge of intercepting requests from external clients and between services. Here there are multiple options such as using an API Gateway or a DNS that allows load balancing.
- Apply virtualization strategies for the deployment of components, especially based on containers using technologies such as Docker and Kubernetes as they provide additional advantages to scale each component independently.

After collecting and analyzing the list of patterns for each of these three critical sections, we can detect the similarity that exists among many of them. Developers often face similar problems and come up with similar solutions to solve them. However, some patterns may require more effort to implement than others. Although there are more patterns, the selected ones are those that have been identified as the most useful and effective in those areas, with which architectures for distributed systems can be easily built (Table 2).

In the monitoring section, all patterns must be used, as the more information is collected about the state of the application, the better decisions can be made, especially when working with AIOps platforms where information is the most important. The use of monitoring patterns is crucial in collecting the right data and insights to help identify and resolve issues.

For the middleware patterns, we can select only one and it will be enough. The best pattern may vary, but the API gateway is easy to implement than the service mesh pattern. The asynchronous messaging pattern is only applicable

Table 2. Recommended patterns.

Section	Recommended	Discarded
Monitoring	Health check API, log aggregation, distributed tracing, exception tracking, application metrics, microservices chassis, sidecar	
Middleware	API Gateway, Service Mesh, Asynchronous messaging	Replicated load-balanced services, Ownership election, Adapters
Virtualization	Kubernetes	Virtual machines, Containers

for specific use cases. Replicated load-balanced services, ownership election, and adapters are patterns already implemented in tools like Kubernetes.

The big winner in the virtualization section is Kubernetes. This pattern provides all the advantages of containers and includes the benefits of having an orchestration system. This must be the default solution to use for deploying distributed systems in most cases, it has become the de-facto standard for managing containerized applications in the cloud. It would also be possible to use other self-managed approaches like serverless and get the same benefits, but the use cases for applying it are fewer than Kubernetes.

3   Proposed Architecture

Based on the previous analysis, a general architecture is proposed that is easy to adapt and implement by developers working with distributed systems. For this, the C4 model was used as a tool to create and visualize the different views of the architecture, this because it is a holistic way of diagramming a system from all its levels. The C4 model is focused on a certain perspective of the system [18]. It is based on a hierarchy of four levels: system context, container, component, and code. Each level provides a different level of detail and abstraction.

3.1   System Context Level

At the system context level, there is not much to show as the proposed architecture can be used in any context, so this level may vary depending on the specific business of the application being built. It is important to note that this level defines the boundaries of the system being built and the external systems or users it interacts with. Therefore, it is crucial to understand the business requirements and the stakeholders of the system to determine the appropriate boundaries (Fig. 1).

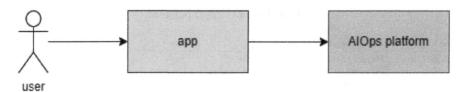

Fig. 1. System context view.

3.2 Container Level

At this level, we applied some patterns such as sidecar and asynchronous messaging. We also have a container dedicated to middleware and represent the monitoring systems.

It is important to highlight that the logging server implements the log aggregation pattern. Similarly, the monitoring server is used to collect all metrics generated using the application metrics pattern. Finally, the alerting server provides the capabilities to implement the exception tracking pattern. All of this observability section collects and sends data to the AIOps platform. These 3 containers were added separately because they can be handled as standalone systems created from scratch or using existing cloud tools that provide these functionalities.

The middleware container is critical and added as a layer between the client and the application backend. It can also intercept requests between backend services that communicate with each other. At this point, the API gateway or service mesh pattern can be used depending on the use case, but for ease of implementation, the recommendation is the former for most applications.

In the backend, multiple containers representing the backend are observed, which is typical in distributed systems. Kubernetes is used to manage these containers, which also implements additional patterns such as health check API, replicated load-balanced services, and ownership election. The adapter pattern can also be implemented at this point or in the middleware through the API gateway. The sidecar pattern can be customized depending on the use case, but Kubernetes provides Envoy Proxy to implement it easily and natively within Kubernetes.

In Fig. 2, the backend communicates with external systems such as databases, third party systems, and message brokers. While these are optional and may not be present in every use case, they are included since it is very common to connect distributed systems with these types of systems. However, for the architecture being proposed, the main focus will be on the backend itself.

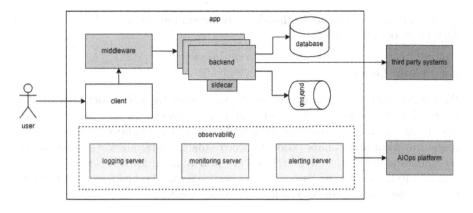

Fig. 2. Container view.

3.3 Component Level

It's not possible to provide specific details on which components to use as it will depend on the specific system, but some generic ones are proposed that can be used in most distributed systems applications (Fig. 3).

In the middleware, we must include security responsibilities. Usually in the API gateway, we can add authentication and authorization concerns, however, it can also communicate with a security component, either internal or external. In addition, an extra layer of security can be added, such as the WAF. This component may be integrated within some API gateways or it may be an external component. Clouds usually provide a ready solution for these security issues.

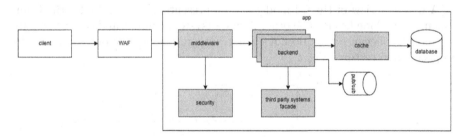

Fig. 3. Component view.

We also have a cache component which is common among distributed systems, since it stores frequently accessed data in memory or a faster storage medium to reduce the response time of read requests. Caching is an effective technique for improving the performance of database-driven applications, as it reduces the number of database queries required to serve requests [19].

Finally, a component widely used in enterprise and cloud-based systems is the facade for third-party systems. It abstracts communication complexity and provides a simpler and more standardized interface with external third-party systems. It is responsible for handling the communication and translation of data formats and protocols.

3.4   Code Level

We cannot propose a generic code-level view with the C4 model because it is designed to be a high-level model that is independent of any particular programming language or implementation. The model is intended to be a tool for communication and collaboration between stakeholders, allowing them to better understand the system's architecture and make informed decisions. So, it depends 100% on the use case. It varies according to the business requirements, the languages, frameworks, and libraries to be used.

4   Validation and Results

As AIOps Platform we will use DevOps Guru which is an AWS service that helps developers and IT teams improve application reliability and performance [20]. It uses ML algorithms to analyze application telemetry data, such as logs, metrics, and events, to identify operational issues, provide root cause analysis, and make recommendations to resolve or prevent incidents. In that case we only configure it to take the logs generated on CloudWatch and generate an alert to create new instances before the error occurs.

We tested the architecture with one use case and model a business that allows users to order food delivery from local restaurants. Although such applications may have multiple functionalities, we will focus on the ability of the user to order food for delivery.

A detailed view of the C4 model will be presented, specifically for the Components and Code levels. The other 2 views (system context and containers) are not modeled because they do not change with respect to the one shown in the proposed architecture (Fig. 4).

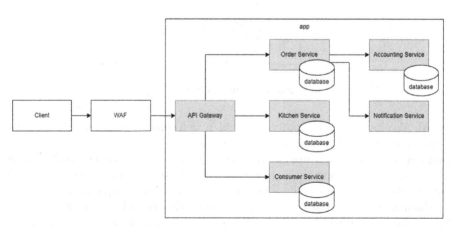

Fig. 4. Component view for the order food delivery application.

It is a typical microservices architecture where each one has its own database and all of them are behind an API gateway that receives all external HTTP requests and redirects them to the corresponding service. All microservices have a similar architecture at the code level, so we are going to diagram the Order service which is the main one for this business model.

An important point to highlight in all microservices is that they have configuration files that allow them to generate logs of the operations they are performing. This configuration class was introduced in each service using the Microservice Chassis pattern, so for the creation of each microservice, we shared the same base code for them. It also includes the configuration to enable a health check endpoint (Fig. 5).

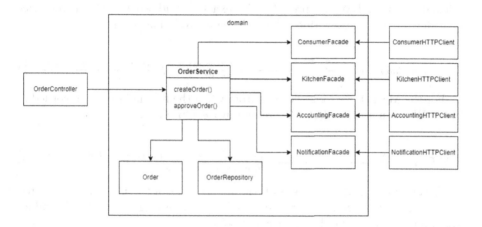

Fig. 5. Code view for the Order service.

This application was deployed in EKS using a t2.nano (512 MiB RAM and 1 vCPU) machine with a single instance for each microservice in the cluster and the opportunity to scale up to 2 instances manually. Load tests using JMeter 5.5 were carried out on the order microservice, simulating 100 concurrent users trying to create new orders for 22 min. For this test, errors were also injected into all microservices every 5 min, so those errors shut down the Java virtual machine, requiring new instances to be created in those cases. DevOps Guru was configured to trigger the alert to EKS and ask it to create a new instance.

The percentage of failed requests was 0.492% of 1159040 requests executed, which is low considering the conditions provided. It is important to note that these results obtained by JMeter reflect the responses of the order microservice, so the behavior of the pods in each microservice should be analyzed separately (Table 3).

Table 3. Microservices results AWS.

Microservice	Number of pods created	Average down-time (seconds)	MTTD (seconds)	MTTR (seconds)
Order	5	34.4	24.5	9.9
Consumer	5	21.5	15.2	6.3
Kitchen	5	23.9	15.8	8.1
Accounting	5	24.3	16.1	8.2
Notification	5	20.3	15.2	5.1

It makes sense that all microservices had 5 pods created as they were shut down 4 times plus the initial pod creation. The average downtime is easy to calculate as Cloud Watch provides the exact second when each microservice went down and the exact time when it became available again.

$$Average\ downtime = \frac{\sum_0^{num\ of\ restarts}(first\ successful\ request - first\ failed\ request)}{number\ of\ restarts} \quad (1)$$

For the MTTD, we took the time from when the first failure was recorded in Cloud Watch until the alert was created in DevOps Guru.

$$MTTD = \frac{\sum_0^{num\ of\ restarts}(time\ insight\ created\ -\ time\ first\ failed\ request)}{number\ of\ restarts} \quad (2)$$

Finally, for the MTTR, we took the moment when the alert was generated and the exact time when the requests started functioning again. All the values were approximated to only one decimal point.

$$MTTR = \frac{\sum_0^{num\ of\ restarts}(time\ first\ successful\ request -\ time\ insight\ created)}{number\ of\ restarts} \quad (3)$$

Considering the benchmark values obtained in the state of the art for MTTD times of less than 1 min and MTTR of less than 30 s, the results obtained in this case are very good, which demonstrates that the AIOps platform works very well integrated with this use case. It is important to mention that Java was used for these microservices, so the time to create a new instance depends on the application's execution.

Now we need to find out if this architecture truly facilitates integration with AIOps platforms. To do this, we will measure the ease in terms of the non-functional requirements of Adaptability and Interoperability [21]. There is no single way to measure these two requirements, however, a time-based approach is proposed that is easy to validate and contrast. For adaptability, the following measures were considered:

Scalability Capability: Scalability can be measured in units of time by the system response time when the workload is increased. For example, the time required to process a request when the number of users is increased. In this case, when a single request is launched, the average response time is 511 milliseconds, when 100 concurrent users are launched the average time is 726 milliseconds, and if 1000 users are launched in parallel the average time is 759 milliseconds. It can be evidenced that the application is not degrading significantly, so it scales correctly. **Robustness of a system:** It measures a system's ability to maintain its operation despite errors or changes in its environment. This metric can be quantified by the frequency and severity of errors and the system's ability to recover from them. Thanks to the results obtained in AWS, we can conclude that the application recovers in less than 10 s, demonstrating its robustness. **Flexibility:** Flexibility can be measured in units of time by the time required to make a change in the system. For example, the time required to add new functionality or to adapt the system to a new environment. See Fig. 6.

For interoperability, the following measures were considered: **Response time:** The response time is the period of time it takes for a system to respond to a request from another system. This time can be a good metric for measuring interoperability in terms of time, especially in real-time applications. In the test performed, the average response time was 738 milliseconds, which aligns with the number of operations to be performed. **Integration time:** Integration time is the period of time it takes to integrate two or more systems to work together. This time can be a good metric to measure interoperability in terms of time. See Fig. 6.

Flexibility and integration time are two metrics that require input from multiple individuals to avoid biases in the results. For this exercise, the evaluation techniques of Experiments and Surveys [22] were combined. This approach involves conducting controlled experiments and then using surveys to obtain the participants perceptions. It is a great option for measuring complex topics that are subjective and do not have a single, exact way of measurement. It is ideal for measuring these two times. In this way, a more comprehensive understanding of the architecture's impact on adaptability and interoperability can be achieved.

An analysis was conducted on a sample of 22 Java developers from Colombia to add integration of the Consumer microservice from scratch with the AIOps platform through the logs to be generated. The code for the microservice was provided to them without the chassis that included the configuration to send the logs to Cloud Watch. With this experiment, we can measure the integration time. After integrating it, they were asked to modify the configuration to also generate logs in a local plain file to measure the flexibility.

The average integration time spent was 44.8 min. This means that for a person adopting the architecture and wishing to integrate with an AIOps platform, the time investment required is less than an hour, which is considered a very good result. The average time spent on flexibility was 24.7 min. This means that for someone using the architecture, it takes less than half an hour to make modifications to it to add new functionality, which is considered a very positive result. Both results show that in a few minutes the architecture can be integrated and made changes (flexible).

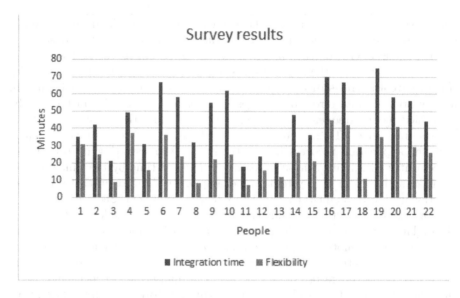

Fig. 6. Survey results for integration time and flexibility.

5 Conclusions

Out of the 16 patterns analyzed, 11 were selected, 7 of which correspond to monitoring patterns. These were used to build the proposed architecture, in which the use of monitoring patterns, middleware, and virtualization. Although the validation with the use case required extensive analysis, the benefits provided by the proposed architecture were successfully evaluated. A low error rate of less than 1% was obtained, and error detection and correction times were below the standards (MTTD of 1 min and MTTR of 30 s). Based on the results of the 5 metrics obtained for the use case, it can be inferred that the architecture implemented in this use case is adaptable and interoperable. As a result, we can conclude the proposed architecture facilitates integration with AIOps platforms.

The proposed architecture provides a clear blueprint for designing, deploying, and managing distributed systems in a way that aligns with AIOps principles and it is easy to adapt for any business problem. It ensures that the various components, such as middleware, monitoring systems, and virtualization, are properly integrated to support AIOps capabilities effectively. By following this architecture, organizations can ensure easier integration between distributed systems and AIOps platforms.

References

1. Shen, S., Zhang, J., Huang, D., Xiao, J.: Evolving from traditional systems to AIOps: design, implementation and measurements (2020)
2. Notaro, P., Cardoso, J., Gerndt, M.: A systematic mapping study in AIOps. In: Hacid, H., et al. (eds.) ICSOC 2020. LNCS, vol. 12632, pp. 110–123. Springer, Cham (2021). https://doi.org/10.1007/978-3-030-76352-7_15
3. Kobbacy, K.A., Vadera, S., Rasmy, M.H.: Ai and or in management of operations: history and trends. J. Oper. Res. Soc. 58 (2007)
4. Mukwevho, M.A., Celik, T.: Toward a smart cloud: a review of fault-tolerance methods in cloud systems. IEEE Trans. Serv. Comput. (2018)
5. Li, L., Hansman, R.J., Palacios, R., Welsch, R.: Anomaly detection via a gaussian mixture model for flight operation and safety monitoring (2016)
6. Farshchi, M., Schneider, J.G., Weber, I., Grundy, J.: Metric selection and anomaly detection for cloud operations using log and metric correlation analysis (2017)
7. Nedelkoski, S., Cardoso, J., Kao, O.: Anomaly detection from system tracing data using multimodal deep learning (2019)
8. Du, M., Versteeg, S., Schneider, J.G., Han, J., Grundy, J.: Interaction traces mining for efficient system responses generation (2015)
9. Salfner, F., Lenk, M., Malek, M.: A survey of online failure prediction methods (2010)
10. Wang, Z., et al.: Failure prediction using machine learning and time series in optical network (2017)
11. Wang, H., Zhang, H.: AIOps prediction for hard drive failures based on stacking ensemble model (2020)
12. Chen, Q., Zheng, Z., Hu, C., Wang, D., Liu, F.: Data-driven task allocation for multi-task transfer learning on the edge (2019)
13. Mormul, M., Stach, C.: A context model for holistic monitoring and management of complex it environments (2020)
14. Levin, A.: An anomaly detection algorithm for microservice architecture based on robust principal component analysis (2019)
15. Gulenko, A., Acker, A., Kao, O., Liu, F.: AI-governance and levels of automation for AIOps-supported system administration (2019)
16. Di Stefano, A., Di Stefano, A., Morana, G.: Ananke: a framework for cloud-native applications smart orchestration (2020)
17. Cardoso, J., Kao, O.: Application optimisation: workload prediction and autonomous autoscaling of distributed cloud applications (2020)
18. Vázquez-Ingelmo, A., García-Holgado, A., García-Peñalvo, F.J.: C4 model in a software engineering subject to ease the comprehension of UML and the software (2020)
19. Noah, P., Seman, S.: Distributed multi-level query cache: the impact on data warehousing. Issues Inf. Syst. (2012)
20. Sawant, N., Sengamedu, S.H.: Learning-based identification of coding best practices from software documentation (2022)
21. Paz, J.A.M., Gomez, M.Y.M., Rosas, S.C.: Análisis sistemático de información de la norma iso 25010 como base para la implementación en un laboratorio de testing de software en la universidad cooperativa de colombia sede popayán (2017)
22. Wohlin, C., Runeson, P., Host, M., Ohlsson, M.C., Regnell, B., Wesslen, A.: Experimentation in Software Engineering. Springer Science & Business Media, Berlin, Heidelberg (2012). https://doi.org/10.1007/978-3-642-29044-2

Comparing Three Agent-Based Models Implementations of Vector-Borne Disease Transmission Dynamics

María Sofía Uribe⬤, Mariajose Franco⬤, Luisa F. Londoño$^{(\boxtimes)}$⬤,
Paula Escudero⬤, Susana Álvarez⬤, and Rafael Mateus⬤

Universidad EAFIT, Medellín, Colombia
{msuribec,mfrancoo,llondo61,pescuder,salvarezz1,rmateusc}@eafit.edu.co

Abstract. Aedes aegypti, the vector responsible for transmitting diseases such as dengue, zika, and chikungunya, poses a significant public health threat in many regions. Understanding the dynamics of Aedes aegypti propagation is crucial for designing effective control and prevention strategies.

Agent-Based Models (ABMs) have emerged as valuable tools for studying complex systems like vector-borne disease dynamics. Hybrid Agent-Based Models (HABMs), a variation of these models that incorporates Ordinary Differential Equations to model mosquitoes and ABMs to model humans, have been proposed by several authors.

This study presents a comparative analysis of three HABMs to model Aedes aegypti propagation dynamics, with a focus on the impact of different modeling frameworks. The first model was built using Repast Simphony, a widely used ABM framework. It incorporates key factors such as mosquito life cycle, environmental conditions, and human-mosquito interactions. To enhance computational performance, the second model is migrated to a high-performance environment using Repast HPC. This migration leverages parallel computing capabilities to simulate larger populations. The third model is migrated to Mesa-Geo, a Python library specifically designed for geospatial agent-based modeling. This migration facilitates the integration of geospatial data into the model.

Preliminary results show that migrating the model to a high performance environment enables more comprehensive analyses and reduces simulation runtime. Moreover, migrating to Mesa-Geo provides enhanced geospatial capabilities, and allows us to analyze the results in a graphical interface, which facilitates communication with decision makers.

The main contributions of this research are: 1) insights into the trade-offs and benefits of using Repast Simphony, Repast HPC, and Mesa-Geo for modeling the transmission of viruses, and 2) a guide to researchers and stakeholders in selecting the most suitable modeling framework based on their specific requirements and available computational resources.

Keywords: Repast Simphony · Repast HPC · Mesa-Geo · HABMs · ABMs · Vector-Borne Diseases

© The Author(s), under exclusive license to Springer Nature Switzerland AG 2024
M. Tabares et al. (Eds.): CCC 2023, CCIS 1924, pp. 330–349, 2024.
https://doi.org/10.1007/978-3-031-47372-2_27

1   Introduction

The Aedes aegypti mosquito is recognized as the main carrier of diseases like Dengue, Chikungunya, and Zika, making it a significant species. The prevalence of these diseases has been on the rise in recent years, causing millions of people around the globe to be affected each year. Transmission of these diseases happens when infected female mosquitoes bite humans, and their presence is closely associated with human habitation. While Dengue, Zika, and Chikungunya impact individuals across various social strata, they exhibit a greater propensity to affect the economically disadvantaged, particularly those residing in suburban regions. Consequently, factors such as climate, social conditions and human behavior play a crucial role in the spread of this mosquito species and the occurrence of the diseases it carries.

This research is specifically driven by the case of Bello, a city in Colombia, which possesses distinctive characteristics that make it an ideal subject for examining the impact of dengue in densely populated urban areas. Bello's proximity to other urban centers and transportation hubs heightens the risk of disease transmission, rendering it a potential epicenter for outbreaks that can propagate to other parts of the country.

Agent-based modeling and simulation (ABMs) is a powerful framework for understanding the dynamics of vector-borne disease transmission and devising effective control and prevention strategies. ABMs captures the complex interactions between individual agents, environmental characteristics, and intervention strategies, considering the heterogeneous characteristics and behaviors of the agents. It also allows the incorporation of spatial and temporal dimensions and their impact on disease transmission.

However, the complexity of ABMs models in this context requires significant computational resources, which can be addressed by employing High-Performance Computing (HPC). HPC provides the computational power to handle large numbers of agents and their interactions, ensuring timely simulations. Furthermore, HPC allows for the scalability of ABMs models, accommodating the increasing complexity and size of an urban area such as Bello. This combination of ABMs and HPC could enable researchers to gain valuable insights into disease dynamics, assess the effectiveness of various strategies, and make informed decisions for control and prevention efforts.

Limited research has been conducted on agent-based models that capture the intricate dynamics of vector-borne disease transmission, particularly in relation to the diverse geospatial characteristics of urban areas. This paper aims to address this gap by presenting an exploratory study that offers a comparative analysis of three distinct agent-based modeling implementations using different programming languages and simulation toolkits. The first implementation employs Python, the second utilizes Repast Simphony (Java), and the third utilizes Repast HPC. The analysis specifically considers factors such as computational capacity, computer memory usage, and implementation characteristics. By evaluating these aspects, this study aims to provide valuable insights into the strengths and limitations of each implementation, creating opportunities for further advancements in agent-based modeling approaches for studying vector-borne diseases dynamics in urban settings.

This paper commences with a comprehensive review of the existing literature regarding the utilization of ABMs in modeling vector-borne diseases within urban areas. Subsequently, it outlines the methodology employed to tackle the research problem. The paper proceeds to present the findings in the results section, followed by the conclusions drawn from the study and an exploration of potential future research directions.

2   Literature Review

The existing literature on the use of agent-based models (ABMs) to simulate the spread of vector-borne diseases has predominantly emphasized the relation between human behavior and disease propagation. However, there is a notable gap in considering other crucial factors, such as geospatial, social, and climate characteristics, within these models. For example, [20] employed agent-based models (ABMs) to investigate the influence of human behavior on the transmission of infectious diseases. The study revealed that even minor alterations in human behaviors can yield significant variations in outcomes, ultimately exerting a profound impact on virus propagation. Similarly, a model to address the propagation of Dengue and Chikungunya outbreaks in Colombia was developed in [6]; however, the model overlooked important factors such as spatial complexity and urban area density, limiting its ability to fully capture the dynamics of disease transmission. Furthermore, [9] implemented an ABMs that focused on simulating mosquito population dynamics at a neighborhood level. The study revealed a notable relation between urban topology, human population density, and adult mosquito flight. To account for the diverse geography of the area, the researchers incorporated distinct values for characteristics like temperature and light into different zones of the spatial representation. In [15], an agent-based simulation framework to analyze and predict mosquito population density and its impact on dengue spread, is proposed. The proposed framework provides visualization and forecasting capabilities to study the epidemiology of a certain region and aid public health departments in emergency preparedness. They identified several expected dengue cases and their direction of spread, which can help in detecting epidemic outbreaks. In a similar manner, [1] developed an agent-based model to investigate the African trypanosomiasis disease dynamics and as a tool for scenario testing at an appropriate spatial scale to allow the design of logistically feasible mitigation strategies. They implemented an agent-based model because this vector-borne disease is prevalent in sparsely populated rural environments, and the traditional compartmentalised models such as SIR don't always capture the spatial and demographic heterogeneity within an area, and the varying exposure to the disease that this can cause. They incorporated spatial data for the Luangwa Valley case study, along with demographic data for its inhabitants.

The literature has also shown that the utilization of hybrid agent-based models incorporating ordinary differential equations offers the advantage of capturing both individual-level interactions and population-level dynamics, enabling a more comprehensive understanding of the propagation of vector-borne diseases. For instance, in a study by [16], a novel hybrid model was proposed for simulating the transmission of mosquito-borne diseases. Instead of explicitly modeling the individual movement of each mosquito agent, the model employed Ordinary Differential Equations (ODEs) to capture the dynamics of mosquito populations. The authors argued that this approach offered a higher level of detail compared to using solely agent-based methods, while also improving computational efficiency.

Moreover, high-performance agent-based models (ABMs) provide a promising approach to study the propagation of vector-borne diseases. Recognizing the need for computational power in analyzing the complex dynamics of disease spread, researchers have started investigating the use of HPC agent-based models or migrated existing models to frameworks that support HPC and parallel simulation. An example of an HPC model in this context is the work by [18], which focuses on assisting decision-making for disease prevention and control. However, to the best of the authors' knowledge, there have been no other High-Performance Computing (HPC) implementations dedicated to modeling the propagation of Aedes aegypti mosquitoes.

Similarly, [11] describe how they converted an existing agent-based model for simulating the population dynamics of the Anopheles gambiae mosquito, one of Africa's most significant malaria vectors, to a parallel model. The initial model was created using AGILESim, a Java application designed exclusively for simulating populations of disease vectors and the migrated model was implemented in OpenCL. The authors' findings suggest that using OpenCL for bigger population sizes is particularly successful, with a speed up of 46 times faster than the Java version of AGiLESim. [19] describe the design, implementation, and parallelization of an epidemiological ABM that is used to model the spread of direct contact infectious illnesses using real-world data. High memory consumption and long execution times are both problems addressed by the authors in this research. To address the memory issue, the authors implement an innovative feature which they name the bitstring approach. This approach consists in using an array of bits instead of using conventional data structures to save the attributes for each agent. To address the high computational demands, the authors develop a parallel version of the model aiming multicore CPUs and GPUs architectures. According to the authors' findings, parallelization and the use of the bitstring technique considerably reduced both computational time and memory consumption. Computation time was reduced by 103.25%, and memory use was reduced by 41%.

In addition, [5] present a case study of how an existing agent-based model of Community Associated Methicillin Resistant Staphylococcus Aureus (CA-MRSA5) transmission in Chicago from 2001 to 2010 was parallelized and distributed to produce a scalable general epidemiological model. The authors

migrated the model from Repast Simphony to Repast HPC. In comparison to
the original approach, the parallelized strategy delivered a 1350% gain in run
time performance.

The literature consistently has highlighted the critical role of human behavior
in shaping the dynamics of disease spread and has exhibited the limitations of
using agent-based models (ABMs) for modeling vector-borne diseases, primarily
related to their computational complexity and the inability to conduct real-scale
experiments, thus limiting our understanding of virus dynamics. Moreover, there
is a gap in incorporating spatial characteristics into these models. Therefore,
by building hybrid models within high-performance computing (HPC) environments we can enhance realism by scaling the geographical representation and
population size, addressing these limitations.

3 Methodology

The transmission dynamics of vector-borne diseases are mostly the same regardless of whether Dengue, Zika, or Chikungunya is being discussed. It occurs from
vector to human and from human to vector. For Zika virus, it can occur from
human to human [3], but we will not consider this way of transmission.

Humans have four states of infection: Susceptible (S) which is when the
human does not have the infection in their body and has not been bitten by
a mosquito recently. Exposed (E) is when an infected mosquito has recently
bitten the human but the virus can not be transmitted yet because it has not
been incubated in the human body. The third stage of infection in the human
is the Infected state (I), which is when the virus is in the human body and can
be transmitted to other mosquitoes. In this state, is important to consider the
infection period, which is the time the virus will be in the human body. When this
time period is reached, the human will pass to the last state which is Recovered
(R). The infection in the mosquito occurs when a susceptible mosquito bites an
infected human. Unlike humans, mosquitoes can be in only 3 states: Susceptible
(S), Exposed (E), and Infected (I) and they never recover because their lifespan
is about 2 to 3 weeks, so it is not the longest enough to live until a recovery
happen. In the model, we will not consider the birth or death of humans, due to
the short simulation time contemplated, but it is considered the birth and death
of mosquitoes because their lifespan is shorter and their reproduction affects the
propagation of these viruses.

Agent-Based Modeling focuses on modeling individuals and the interactions between them and the environment. The behavior of the whole system
is obtained as a result of these interactions [14]. Each individual in the model
is called an agent and it has its own sets of decision and behavior rules. Agents
can be modeled to represent various entities, such as individuals, animals, organizations, or even abstract concepts. They are typically characterized by their
state, which includes variables representing their current conditions, characteristics, or attributes. Agents can perceive and sense their environment, gather
information, make decisions, and take actions based on predefined rules. They

can also interact and communicate with other agents, influencing each other's behavior and potentially leading to emergent properties and complex system-level behaviors. By simulating the actions and interactions of multiple agents, ABMs provides a framework to study the dynamics, patterns, and outcomes of complex systems. It allows researchers to explore how individual agent-level behaviors and interactions can collectively shape the behavior and outcomes of the entire system. ABMs has been widely used in various domains, including social sciences, biology, economics, transportation, and ecology, to gain insights into real-world phenomena and inform decision-making processes.

3.1 Conceptual Model

The model consists of two main components: humans and mosquitoes. Humans are represented as individual agents, whereas mosquitoes are modeled as "clouds of mosquitoes" distributed across the spatial area. The spatial representation is achieved using patches, where each patch holds a cloud of mosquitoes with counts for the number of mosquitoes in each state: susceptible, exposed, and infected. These patches represent static agents characterized by state variables indicating temperature and the number of mosquitoes in each state. Each human agent in the model represents one citizen of Bello, and the spatial representation encompasses the entire territorial area of the city of Bello in Antioquia, spanning 149 square kilometers. This spatial layout is organized as a 2D grid with individual squares, and each square contains a patch. The grid dimensions consist of 32×32 patches.

Each time step of the simulation, also known as a tick, represents one day. The model was run for 365 days. Each day the temperature and the number of mosquitoes in each patch change. Also, each human moves according to the activities that it has assigned, and at the end of the day, each human returns to its house. Each time a human makes a movement, the probability that this human gets infected is calculated and it is determined whether this human gets infected or not in this new place.

The input data for the model consisted of the minimum and maximum temperatures of Bello in 2019, which were used to assign a temperature value to each patch for every day. The model incorporates various parameters, as outlined in Table 1, with values sourced from [16]. To address the inherent parametric uncertainty in individual mosquito models, we adopted the authors' approach, which focuses on addressing heterogeneity in disease spread at the patch level rather than individual mosquito locations.

To determine the temperature of each patch on a given day, a uniform distribution with the minimum and maximum temperatures recorded in Bello during 2019 for that day was employed. To calculate the counts of susceptible, exposed, and infected mosquitoes in each patch at every time step, a system of continuous differential equations is solved using the 4th-order Runge-Kutta numerical method with a time step of $h = 0.1$.

Table 1. Parameters values

Variable	Name	Value
μ_v	Per capita mosquito death rate	$\frac{1}{14}$
ψ_v	Per capita natural emergence rate of mosquitoes	0.3
β_{vh}	Probability of transmission from an infectious human to a susceptible mosquito given that a contact between the two occurs	0.333
β_{hv}	Probability of transmission from an infectious mosquito to a susceptible human given that a contact between the two occurs	0.333
σ_v	Maximum number of bites per mosquito per unit time	0.5
σ_h	Maximum number of bites a human can get per unit time	19
K_v	Carrying capacity of the mosquitoes in the patch	1000

3.2 Mosquitoes Behavior

This section presents the process of calculating the number of susceptible $(S_v{}^k)$, exposed $(E_v{}^k)$, and infected mosquitoes $(I_v{}^k)$ in each patch k over time using a system of differential equations. These equations depend on the number of humans in the patch and the temperature of the patch. The equations used for these systems of differential equations were taken from [16] and [17] and are presented in 1.

$$
\begin{aligned}
\frac{dS_v{}^k}{dt} &= h_v{}^k - \lambda_v{}^k S_v{}^k - \mu_v S_v{}^k \\
\frac{dE_v{}^k}{dt} &= \lambda_v{}^k S_v{}^k - v_v{}^k E_v{}^k - \mu_v E_v{}^k \\
\frac{dI_v{}^k}{dt} &= v_v{}^k E_v{}^k - \mu_v I_v{}^k
\end{aligned}
\tag{1}
$$

The subscript v refers to the mosquito vector, the superscript k refers to the patch, $h_v{}^k$ is the total birth rate of mosquitoes in patch k, $\lambda_v{}^k$ is the per capita rate of infection of mosquitoes in patch k, $v_v{}^k$ is the per capita rate of progression of mosquitoes from exposed state to the infectious state in patch k, and μ_v is the per capita death rate of mosquitoes (parameter).

The equations for calculating the total birth rate in patch k $(h_v{}^k)$, per capita rate of infection of mosquitoes in patch k $(\lambda_v{}^k)$, and per capita rate of progression of mosquitoes from exposed state to the infectious state in patch k $(v_v{}^k)$ are shown in Eq. 2.

$$h_v{}^k = N_v{}^k \left(\psi_v - \frac{r_v * N_v{}^k}{K_v} \right) \qquad r_v = \psi_v - \mu_v$$

$$\lambda_v{}^k = b_v{}^k * \beta_{vh} * \left(\frac{I_h{}^k}{N_h{}^k} \right) \qquad b_v{}^k = \frac{b^k}{N_v{}^k} \qquad (2)$$

$$b^k = \frac{\sigma_v * N_v{}^k * \sigma_h * N_h{}^k}{\sigma_v * N_v{}^k + \sigma_h * N_h{}^k} \qquad N_v{}^k = S_v{}^k + E_v{}^k + I_v{}^k$$

ψ_v refers to the natural per capita-emergence rate of mosquitoes (parameter), r_v is the mosquito population growth rate, K_v is the carrying capacity of the mosquitoes in a patch (parameter), and $N_v{}^k$ is the total number of mosquitoes in the patch k. The subscript h refers to humans, $N_h{}^k$ is the total number of humans in the patch k, β_{vh} is the probability of transmission from an infectious human to a susceptible mosquito given that a contact between the two occurs (parameter), and $b_v{}^k$ is the number of bites per mosquito per unit of time in the patch k. b^k refers to the total number of contacts between humans and mosquitoes (bites) in the patch k, σ_v is the maximum number of bites per mosquito per unit of time (parameter) and σ_h is the number of bites a human can get per unit of time (parameter).

The equation for calculating the per capita rate of progression of mosquitoes from the exposed state to the infectious state in patch k ($v_v{}^k$) is

$$v_v{}^k = \frac{1}{tinc_v{}^k} \qquad (3)$$

where $tinc_v{}^k$ is the incubation time of the virus in the mosquito in patch k. We have made a modification to this equation to establish a dependency for the incubation time on the patch's temperature (T^k), with distinct modeling approaches applied for each of the viruses. For Zika, $tinc_v{}^k = 7 + \frac{0.667-0.378(T^k-26)}{0.299+0.027(T^k-26)}$ [22]; for Chikungunya, $tinc_v{}^k = 4 + e^{5.15-0.123T^k}$ [10]; and for Dengue: $tinc_v{}^k$ follows a uniform distribution, more specifically $U(10, 25)$ if $18 < T^k \leq 21$, $U(7, 10)$ if $21 < T^k \leq 26$ and $U(4, 7)$ if $26 < T^k < 31$

For Zika and Dengue viruses, if the temperature of the patch is less than $15\,°C$, the incubation time of the virus in the mosquitoes is not defined, and the rate of progression of mosquitoes from exposed to infected ($v_v{}^k$) is equal to zero. Similarly, for Chikungunya, if the temperature in the patch is less than $12\,°C$, the mosquito incubation time is not defined in this patch and the rate of progression of mosquitoes from exposed to infected ($v_v{}^k$) is equal to zero. This happens because, at low temperatures, the incubation time of the virus in mosquitoes is really long, so mosquitoes reach life expectancy and die before incubating the virus.

3.3   Human Behavior

This section focuses on representing human behavior within the model. Humans are assigned specific activities to perform during the day, and their movements are determined accordingly. As they move through different patches, certain variables related to infection state, time since a successful mosquito bite, and time since infection are updated.

At the beginning of each day, human individuals start at their respective homes. The first activity is determined by selecting the activity's coordinates from their list, and the humans are then moved to that specific location. As the probability of infection varies in each patch, the variables related to the human's infection state are updated with every movement they make. This updating process helps to determine if the human will get infected in the new location or not. Then, each human is moved to the coordinates of their second activity, and the relevant variables are updated again. Finally, each human returns to its home location, and the variables related to infection state, time since a successful mosquito bite, and time since infection are updated for the last time.

Unlike the mosquito behavior, which is modeled using differential equations to update state variables, the behavior of humans is modeled stochastically using probabilities. This probabilistic approach accounts for the uncertainties and randomness associated with human movement, infection, and recovery processes. In the model, a susceptible human in patch k can transition to the exposed state with a probability of $p_{SEh}{}^k$. Once in the exposed state, a human can become infected with a probability of $p_{EIh}{}^k$, and an infected human can recover with a probability of $p_{IRh}{}^k$. The probability $p_{SEh}{}^k$ is determined by calculating the rate of infection of humans in patch k. On the other hand, both $p_{SEh}{}^k$ and $p_{IRh}{}^k$ are represented by random variables.

The equation for calculating the probability of a human passing from susceptible to exposed in patch k ($p_{SEh}{}^k$) is the following: $p_{SEh}{}^k = 1 - e^{-\lambda_h{}^k}$ where $\lambda_h{}^k$ is the rate of infection of humans in patch k and is defined as

$$\lambda_h{}^k = b_h{}^k * \beta_{hv} * \left(\frac{I_v{}^k}{N_v{}^k} \right) \tag{4}$$

where $I_v{}^k$ is the number of infected mosquitoes in patch k, $N_v{}^k$ is the total number of mosquitoes in patch k, β_{hv} is the probability of transmission from an infectious mosquito to a susceptible human given that a contact between the two occurs (parameter), and $b_h{}^k$ is the number of bites a human receives per unit time in the patch k and is defined in the following way: $b_h{}^k = \frac{b^k}{N_h{}^k}$, where b^k is the total number of contacts between humans and mosquitoes (bites) in the patch k (as defined previously) and $N_h{}^k$ is the total number of humans in patch k.

As stated previously, the probability of a human passing from exposed to infected in patch k ($p_{EIh}{}^k$) is calculated by using a random variable approach. In this case the incubation time of the virus in patch k ($t_{inch}{}^k$) is a random variable that follows a different probability distribution for each virus. For Zika it is $t_{inc_h} \sim Weibull\,(\alpha = 2.69, \beta = 6.70)$ [12]; for Chikungunya it is $t_{inc_h} \sim$ $Lognormal\,(\mu = 1.099,\ \sigma = 0.139)$ [13] and [16]; and for Dengue it is $t_{inc_h} \sim$ $Gamma\,(\alpha =\ 5.5,\ \beta = 1.12)$ [4].

$p_{EI_h}{}^k$ is obtained by calculating the probability that the random variable($t_{inc_h}{}^k$) is exceeded by the time passed since the human received a successful bite (timeSinceSuccessfulBite) which is a state variable of the human. The equation for this probability calculation is described below.

$$p_{EI_h}{}^k = p(t_{inc_h}{}^k \leq timeSinceSuccessfulBite) \tag{5}$$

In this manner, every time a human moves, $p_{EI_h}{}^k$ is calculated in the patch k using the human's state variable timeSinceSuccessfulBite. Knowing this probability, it is then used to determine if the human gets infected or not.

The probability of a human passing from infected to recovered in patch k $(p_{IR_h}{}^k)$ is also calculated by using a random variable approach. In this case, the time of infection of the virus in patch k $(t_{inf_h}{}^k)$ is a random variable that follows a different probability distribution for each virus. For Zika $t_{inf_h} \sim$ $norm\,(\mu = 6, \sigma = 1)$ [7]; for Chikungunya $t_{inf_h} \sim Uniform\,(a = 3, b = 7)$ [16] and for Dengue $t_{inf_h} \sim Uniform\,(a = 2, b = 7)$ [4].

$p_{IR_h}{}^k$ is obtained by calculating the probability that the random variable $(t_{inf_h}{}^k)$ is exceeded by the time passed since the human got infected (timeSinceInfected) which is a state variable of the human. The equation for this probability calculation is presented below.

$$p_{IR_h}{}^k = p(t_{inf_h}{}^k \leq timeSinceInfected) \tag{6}$$

This probability $p_{EI_h}{}^k$ is then used to determine if the human gets recovered or not.

3.4   Computational Implementation

The computational implementations of the conceptual model that we described above, were done using the following two frameworks: Mesa-Geo library, which is an ABMs library implemented in Python, and the Repast Suite. Figure 1 shows the process overview of the model implementation.

Repast Suite is a free and open-source family of agent-based modeling and simulation platforms. It includes Repast Simphony, a Java toolkit that provides a range of features and tools to facilitate the creation, visualization, and analysis of complex systems using agent-based modeling. It also offers Repast HPC, a C++ toolkit that implements the core concepts of Repast Simphony and extends them into a parallel distributed environment.

Mesa-Geo provides a simple and intuitive interface for ABM simulations, making it easier for beginners to get started. As it is built using Python, a widely used and popular programming language known for its simplicity and readability, allows users to leverage the extensive Python ecosystem and easily integrate with other data analysis and visualization tools. It also includes built-in spatial analysis capabilities, allowing users to simulate and analyze geospatial patterns and interactions among agents. It provides tools for handling geographic data and visualizing spatial patterns. One of the disadvantages of Mesa-Geo is that it is primarily designed for small to medium-scale simulations. It may not perform optimally for large-scale simulations with thousands or millions of agents. On the contrary, Repast HPC is specifically designed to handle large-scale agent-based simulations efficiently. It also offers a wide range of advanced features and functionalities, including complex agent behaviors, network modeling, and distributed computing capabilities. However, integrating the geography of a region could be a challenging task that requires more advanced programming knowledge.

4   Results

Results obtained from the conducted simulations provide valuable insights into the dynamics of the transmission of the virus in an urban area. In this section, we present an analysis of the outcomes, highlighting key findings and their implications. The results not only shed light on the effectiveness and performance of the three models implemented but also offer valuable information on the impact on simulation capabilities.

The behavior shown by the three implementations reflects the typical behavior of SEIR models. Figure 2 shows the propagation of Dengue among humans over 100 days in the Python implementation. Figures 3 and 4 show the propagation of Dengue, Zika, and Chikungunya during a calendar year, using Repast Simphony and Repast HPC, respectively. For the Mesa-Geo model, we are not showing the results for the three diseases and overall the year due to the high computing time required to run it. Each virus has a peak, as real disease outbreaks do. After those peaks, no significant spread of the disease occurs and the number of susceptible humans stabilizes, which was also expected since we are not considering reinfection for any disease. Also, it is important to notice that we are simulating the viruses in a separate environment, i.e., agents are not exposed to Dengue, Zika, and Chikungunya at the same time.

4.1   Mesa-Geo Implementation

Mesa-Geo is a Python-based ABM framework providing built-in core components to easily create, visualize, and analyze simulations. It is one of the most used and actively supported ABM libraries, which exploits Python's popularity to provide ease of use and accessibility [2]. The model implemented in Mesa-Geo was initialized with a total number of humans of 1000 and an initial number of infected humans of 10 and the results are shown on Fig. 2.

Mesa-Geo implements a GeoSpace that can host GIS-based GeoAgents, which are similar to usual Agents, except that they have an attribute for its Coordinate Reference System. It allows to directly create arbitrary geometries or import them from a file. Mesa-Geo allows to create GeoAgents from any vector data file, GeoJSON objects or a GeoPandas GeoDataFrame [21].

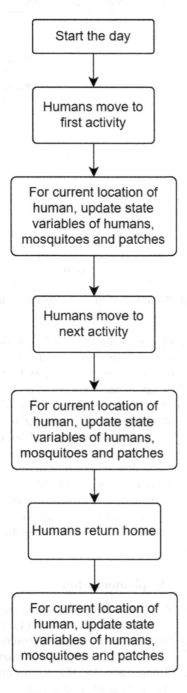

Fig. 1. Process Overview

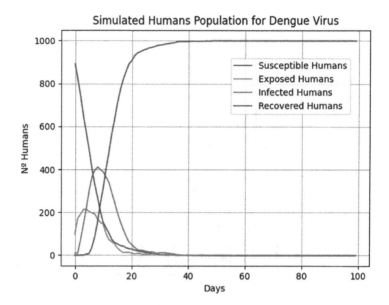

Fig. 2. Results of Python Model for Dengue.

Two key factors impact the performance of this model. In the first place, the model includes the representation of all individuals in the city and their respective states (susceptible, exposed, infected, and recovered) each time they move. This process involves updating the state of each individual, which incurs significant computational overhead. As the number of humans increases, the computational burden grows exponentially, leading to longer execution times. In addition to that, the graphical representation of humans as points on a map exacerbates the computational demands of the model. Visualizing each human's position and state in a city requires rendering graphics or updating a graphical user interface (GUI) in real-time. These graphical operations involve additional calculations and memory management, leading to increased computational complexity. Consequently, the model's runtime is significantly prolonged due to the computational cost of maintaining an up-to-date graphical representation of the city and its inhabitants.

4.2 Repast Simphony Implementation

Repast Simphony is a richly interactive and easy to learn Java-based modeling toolkit that is designed for use on workstations and small computing clusters. It provides automated methods to perform all the common tasks required in an ABMs simulation [2]. The model implemented in Repast Simphony was initialized with a total number of humans of 120571 and an initial number of infected humans of 1000 and the results are shown on Fig. 3.

Events in simulations are driven by a discrete-event scheduler, and each timestep is equivalent to a tick. Ticks do not necessarily represent clock-time but

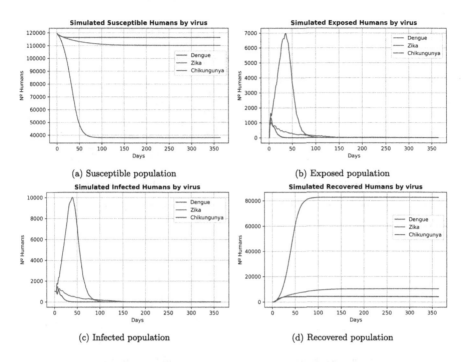

Fig. 3. Results of Repast Simphony model for Dengue, Zika and Chikungunya.

rather the priority of its associated event. A context encapsulates the agents, contexts can have projections that establish relationships within agents. For instance, a grid projection allows agents to move in a matrix-type structure where each agent has a location.

4.3 Repast HPC Implementation

Repast HPC is an expert-focused C++-based distributed agent-based modeling toolkit that is designed for use on large computing clusters and supercomputers. This toolkit enables the execution of massive simulations containing hundreds of thousands of agents of very complex behavior whose execution requires high computational power [2]. The model implemented on Repast HPC framework was initialized with a total number of humans of 120571 and an initial number of infected humans of 1000 and the results are shown on Fig. 4. Because of the model's geography (which was divided in four sectors), the model was designed to be run with four processes.

Repast HPC is object-oriented. An agent's internal state (e.g. its age, wealth, level of hunger, etc.) is easily represented in an object's fields while the agent's behavior (e.g.eating, aging, acquiring and spending wealth, etc.) is modeled using an object's methods. Agent types are implemented as C++ classes [2].

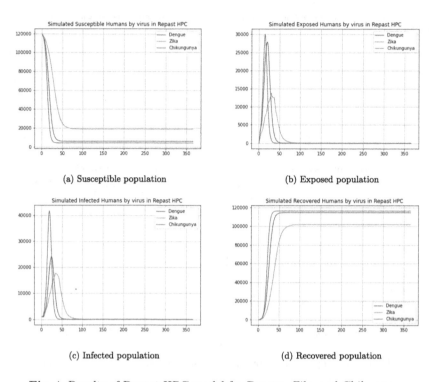

(a) Susceptible population

(b) Exposed population

(c) Infected population

(d) Recovered population

Fig. 4. Results of Repast HPC model for Dengue, Zika and Chikungunya.

This framework also incorporates Message Passing Interface (MPI), an industry-standard for message passing. The implementation of MPI allows sending and receiving messages between processes. This includes performing operations on data in transit and synchronizing information from the agents and the geographical context. In MPI applications, a process can not see the other processes' memory. Each process is responsible for the agents local to that process. When a process contains non-local agents, the copies must be updated with the latest state from the original. Movement from one process to another can be the result of grid movement and may be handled automatically by Repast HPC or, in certain cases, it may require manual synchronization.

The model's definition must allow different processes to run in parallel without sharing all memory. Our model fit this description because the Dengue, Zika, and Chikungunya do not have human-to-human transmission. Each subsection of the grid can make computations to update the number of susceptible, exposed, infected, and recovered humans with the information about the mosquitoes and the temperature in that patch. Thus, the parallelization of the model does not violate any assumptions regarding the behavior of the diseases.

An analysis of memory usage yielded an average 31% decrease in memory use over the Repast Simphony models. The improvement in memory usage is notable, however, part of the improvement may be due to the differences between programming languages. Notably, the Repast Simphony model required an increase in memory allocation to run the model. An analysis of the program revealed that the lack of memory was not due to a memory leak. Thus, it is related with the way Java handles memory and garbage collection causes excessive memory use. Unfortunately, the java memory management scheme is automated and is not subject to change. In contrast, it is possible to improve the results obtained in the Repast HPC models through more customized memory management.

4.4 Comparative Analysis

This section presents a comparative analysis of three different agent-based modeling implementations aimed at studying vector-borne disease dynamics in urban settings. The goal of this analysis is to gain valuable insights into the strengths and limitations of each implementation and its potential applicability in understanding disease dynamics and developing control strategies.

Table 2 provides a comparison of the three distinct agent-based modeling implementations. The comparison considers essential factors such as the programming language used, computer memory usage, and parallelization support. These factors play a critical role in determining the efficiency and scalability of the models. Additionally, we examine the ease of model development and the visualization capabilities, which are crucial for aiding non-experts, such as health decision-makers.

Table 2. Comparative Analysis of the Agent-Based Modeling Implementations.

Aspect	Python	Repast Simphony	Repast HPC
Programming Language	Python	Java	C++
Ease of Model Development	Easy	Moderate	High
Computer Memory Usage	High	High	Moderate
Parallelization Support	Limited	Limited	High
Scalability	Limited	Moderate	High
Visualization Capabilities	Yes	Limited	Limited

Regarding programming language and ease of model development, Java, Python, and C++ are all free and open-source programming languages. Python's syntax is simpler and more concise compared to Java and C++. Java follows a class-based object-oriented approach and has a syntax similar to C and C++. Python stands out in ease of model development due to its straightforward process, whereas Repast Simphony and Repast HPC require a moderate and high level of expertise, especially for non-experienced programmers. Python is an easier language to learn, while Java and C++ require more experience and programming skills. Our aim for the model is to assist health decision makers. We seek to create a user-friendly and intuitive platform that allows non programming experts to use the model effectively, enabling them to gain valuable insights and make informed decisions. To use it on a day-to-day basis, Python could be more approachable due to its simplicity, readability, and extensive libraries and frameworks. Finally, Python has included in the library Mesa-Geo an easy way to visualize the spread of the disease in a graphical interface. Repast Simphony also allows a graphical interface but is not as easy to implement as in Python. Repast HPC does not include a graphical interface.

In terms of computer memory usage, Python and Repast Simphony exhibits relatively high consumption, while Repast HPC require moderate memory usage. The high memory consumption in Python and Repast Simphony can be attributed, on the one hand, to the graphical interface of the library, and on the other hand, to the memory management approach employed by these programming languages, which lack flexibility. Conversely, C++ offers a flexible memory management system that can be customized to meet the requirements of each processor.

The parallelization support aspect examines the capacity to enable multiple processes to be executed simultaneously [8]. Python and Repast Simphony offer limited support, while Repast HPC excels in high parallelization. Additionally, the scalability aspect assess the ability of an implementation to handle larger and more complex simulations. The key advantages of Repast HPC over Repast Simphony or Python-based ABMs are its focus on parallelization, efficient resource utilization, and compatibility with high-performance computing environments. This allows it to handle more extensive and complex simulations, making it a better choice for scalability when dealing with large-scale agent-based models.

All three implementations support the incorporation of spatial and temporal dimensions in the modeling approach, as well as agent heterogeneity and environmental interaction capabilities. Agent heterogeneity is represented by modeling agents with diverse characteristics and behaviors, and environmental interaction examines whether the implementations allow agents to interact with the environment.

Overall, this comparative analysis aids researchers in understanding the different features and performance characteristics of each implementation, enabling them to make informed decisions regarding the choice of agent-based modeling approach for studying vector-borne disease dynamics in urban settings, based on their specific requirements and constraints.

5   Conclusions and Future Research

In this paper, we explored the use of agent-based modeling and simulation (ABMs) to analyze the dynamics of vector-borne disease transmission, specifically focusing on the Aedes aegypti mosquito and its role in spreading diseases such as Dengue, Chikungunya, and Zika. We conducted an exploratory study in the city of Bello, Colombia, which possesses characteristics that make it suitable for examining the impact of dengue in densely populated urban areas. Our study aimed to address the limited research conducted on ABMs models that capture the complex dynamics of vector-borne disease transmission in urban areas. We compared three distinct agent-based modeling implementations using different programming languages and simulation toolkits: Python, Repast Simphony (Java), and Repast HPC. By evaluating factors such as computational capacity, computer memory usage, and implementation characteristics, we aimed to provide valuable insights into the strengths and limitations of each implementation and contribute to the advancement of agent-based modeling approaches for studying vector-borne disease dynamics in urban settings.

The results obtained from the three implementations showed the typical behavior of SEIR models, with each virus exhibiting a peak and the number of susceptible humans stabilizing over time. The Python implementation using Mesa-Geo provided a simple and intuitive interface, while the Repast Simphony implementation offered advanced features and tools for complex agent behaviors. The Repast HPC implementation demonstrated the scalability and efficiency of HPC in handling large-scale simulations.

We encountered computational difficulties while running simulations for the three models on a desktop computer, preventing us from experimenting with the actual population of the city of Bello. Although the HPC model showed satisfactory results in reducing memory usage, our next step is to test the models on a supercomputer since they have been specifically optimized for such devices. Furthermore, as part of our future work, we plan to explore the possibilities of parallelizing the Python model to enhance its performance and speed. By leveraging parallel computing techniques, we can achieve significant improvements in execution time. The substantial decrease in processing time will enable us to conduct numerous experiments, perform a comprehensive sensitivity analysis, estimate parameters, and validate the models. As a result, we will gain a deeper understanding of the transmission dynamics of the virus in an urban area.

In conclusion, our research contributes to bridging the gap in ABMs models for studying vector-borne disease transmission in urban areas. The comparative analysis of different implementations provides insights into their strengths and limitations, paving the way for further advancements in agent-based modeling approaches. By incorporating spatial, social, and climate characteristics and leveraging the computational power of HPC, researchers can gain valuable insights into disease dynamics, assess the effectiveness of control strategies, and make informed decisions for disease prevention and control efforts in urban settings.

References

1. Alderton, S., et al.: A multi-host agent-based model for a zoonotic, vector-borne disease. a case study on trypanosomiasis in eastern province, Zambia. PLoS Negl. Trop. Dis. **10**(12), e0005252 (2016). https://doi.org/10.1371/journal.pntd.0005252
2. Antelmi, A., Cordasco, G., D'Ambrosio, G., De Vinco, D., Spagnuolo, C.: Experimenting with agent-based model simulation tools. Appl. Sci. **13**(1), 13 (2022). https://doi.org/10.3390/app13010013

3. Caminade, C., et al.: Global risk model for vector-borne transmission of zika virus reveals the role of el niño 2015. Proc. Natl. Acad. Sci. **114**(1), 119–124 (2017)

4. Chan, M., Johansson, M.A.: The incubation periods of dengue viruses. PLoS ONE **7**, 1–7 (2012). https://doi.org/10.1371/journal.pone.0050972

5. Collier, N., Ozik, J., Macal, C.M.: Large-scale agent-based modeling with repast HPC: a case study in parallelizing an agent-based model. In: Hunold, S., et al. (eds.) Euro-Par 2015. LNCS, vol. 9523, pp. 454–465. Springer, Cham (2015). https://doi.org/10.1007/978-3-319-27308-2_37

6. España, G., et al.: Exploring scenarios of chikungunya mitigation with a data-driven agent-based model of the 2014–2016 outbreak in Colombia. Sci. Rep. **8**(1), 12201 (2018). https://doi.org/10.1038/s41598-018-30647-8

7. Fontaine, A., de Laval, F., Belleoud, D., Briolant, S., Matheus, S.: Duration of zika viremia in serum. Clin. Infect. Dis. Off. Publ. Infect. Dis. Soc. Am. **67**, 1143–1144 (2018). https://doi.org/10.1093/cid/ciy261

8. Hager, G., Wellein, G.: Introduction to High Performance Computing for Scientists and Engineers. CRC Press, Boca Raton (2010). https://doi.org/10.1201/EBK1439811924

9. Jindal, A., Rao, S.: Agent-based modeling and simulation of mosquito-borne disease transmission. In: Proceedings of the 16th Conference on Autonomous Agents and Multiagent Systems, pp. 426–435 (2017)

10. Kakarla, S.G., et al.: Temperature dependent transmission potential model for chikungunya in India. Sci. Total Environ. **647**, 66–74 (2019). https://doi.org/10.1016/j.scitotenv.2018.07.461

11. Kofler, K., Davis, G., Gesing, S.: SAMPO: an agent-based mosquito point model in OpenCL. In: Proceedings of the 2014 Symposium on Agent Directed Simulation, pp. 1–10 (2014)

12. Krow-Lucal, E.R., Biggerstaff, B.J., Staples, J.E.: Estimated incubation period for zika virus disease. Emerg. Infect. Dis. **23**, 841–844 (2017). https://doi.org/10.3201/eid2305.161715

13. Leung, C.: Estimated incubation period for mosquito-borne disease-related Guillain-Barre syndrome. Clin. Epidemiol. Glob. Health **8**, 244–250 (2020). https://doi.org/10.1016/j.cegh.2019.08.007

14. Macal, C.M., North, M.J.: Agent-based modeling and simulation: abms examples. In: 2008 Winter Simulation Conference, pp. 101–112. IEEE (2008). https://doi.org/10.1109/WSC.2008.4736060

15. Mahmood, I., Jahan, M., Groen, D., Javed, A., Shafait, F.: Correction to: an agent-based simulation of the spread of dengue fever. In: Krzhizhanovskaya, V.V., et al. (eds.) ICCS 2020. LNCS, vol. 12139, pp. C1–C1. Springer, Cham (2020). https://doi.org/10.1007/978-3-030-50420-5_49

16. Manore, C.A., et al.: A network-patch methodology for adapting agent-based models for directly transmitted disease to mosquito-borne disease. J. Biol. Dyn. **9**(1), 52–72 (2015). https://doi.org/10.1080/17513758.2015.1005698

17. Mniszewski, S.M., Manore, C., Bryan, C., Del Valle, S.Y., Roberts, D.: Towards a hybrid agent-based model for mosquito borne disease. In: Summer Computer Simulation Conference: (SCSC 2014): 2014 Summer Simulation Multi-Conference: Monterey, California, USA, 6–10 July 2014. Summer Computer Simulation Conference (2014: Monterey, calif.), vol. 2014. NIH Public Access (2014)

18. Montes de Oca, E.S., Suppi, R., De Giusti, L.C., Naiouf, M.: Green high performance simulation for AMB models of Aedes aegypti. J. Comput. Sci. Technol. **20** (2020). https://doi.org/10.24215/16666038.20.e02

19. Rizzi, R.L., Kaizer, W.L., Rizzi, C.B., Galante, G., Coelho, F.C.: Modeling direct transmission diseases using parallel bitstring agent-based models. IEEE Trans. Comput. Soc. Syst. **5**(4), 1109–1120 (2018). https://doi.org/10.1109/TCSS.2018. 2871625
20. Scheidegger, A.P.G., Banerjee, A.: An agent-based model to investigate behavior impacts on vector-borne disease spread. In: 2017 Winter Simulation Conference (WSC), pp. 2833–2844. IEEE (2017). https://doi.org/10.1109/WSC.2017.8248007
21. Wang, B., Hess, V., Crooks, A.: Mesa-geo: a GIS extension for the mesa agent-based modeling framework in python. In: Proceedings of the 5th ACM SIGSPA-TIAL International Workshop on GeoSpatial Simulation, pp. 1–10. GeoSim '22, Association for Computing Machinery, New York, NY, USA (2022). https://doi. org/10.1145/3557989.3566157
22. Winokur, O.C., Main, B.J., Nicholson, J., Barker, C.M.: Impact of temperature on the extrinsic incubation period of zika virus in aedes aegypti. PLoS Negl. Trop. Dis. **14**, 1–15 (2020). https://doi.org/10.1371/journal.pntd.0008047

Towards a Predictive Model that Supports the Achievement of More Assertive Commercial KPIs Case: Wood Trading Company

Jhon Walter Tavera Rodríguez[✉]

Grupo GIDITIC, Universidad EAFIT, Medellín, Colombia
jtavera1@eafit.edu.co

Abstract. This article presents a predictive model to determine possible causes of commercial results in a company that commercializes products and services for the furniture and wood industry in Colombia. To achieve this, a literature review was carried out to identify analysis strategies and new technologies that could influence the proposed model. Then, using the CRISP-DM methodology, the main variables and indicators that make up the business model and the problems associated with decision-making were identified, with the aim of predicting and optimizing their KPIs, improving performance metrics and achieving an increase in commercial benefits. A case study was carried out with a data set of 99,972 records collected between 2020 and 2023, which facilitated the application of variable selection techniques to identify the most influential in the prediction. The model was developed using algorithms such as decision trees, random forests, and logistic regression. Once the model was trained, it was determined that the random forest regression algorithm with the Out-of-Bag validation method and an R2 of 94.1% provided the best results and delivered the highest sales prediction. In testing, the model showed that it was influenced by variables such as average invoice value, number of invoices, available inventory, and order fulfillment. These findings expand decision-making capacity by defining which variables must be controlled to improve results. In conclusion, The machine learning-based predictive model can identify potential causes of business outcomes and improve the accuracy of decisions at a strategic level in the area of timber trading. However, it is suggested to complement it with other variables to obtain an even more precise diagnosis.

Keywords: Balance Score Card · Fuzzy logic controllers · Machine Learning · Root Cause Analysis · Artificial intelligence

1 Introduction

One of the common problems that companies must solve in their commercial process is to determine with a high degree of certainty what were the causes

M. Tabares et al. (Eds.): CCC 2023, CCIS 1924, pp. 350–366, 2024.
https://doi.org/10.1007/978-3-031-47372-2_28

that affected the results in the key business indicators and thus make strategic decisions that improve said results. In the past, diagnostic analysis was entirely manual, requiring an analyst's skills to identify anomalies, spot patterns, and determine relationships. Especially in the last five years, medium and large companies are facing new opportunities in the markets, which leads them to invest large sums of money in their transformation and improvement. However, this leads them to face aspects such as greater complexity of their business processes, the diversity and volume of information. This means that even the most experienced business analysts cannot guarantee the coherence and consistency required to achieve a good level of so-called "business intelligence" and consequently continue to use traditional decision-making processes or models based on experience. The experience-based decision-making process is influenced by the personality and mental model of each individual who participates in it. In some cases, it can be said that the causality analysis depends on the observer, cognitive abilities and their mental model are limiting in the diagnostic analysis developed by people, which directly impacts the KPI (Key Performance Indicator) thus becoming vulnerable to its result not being correctly understood to optimize resources and achieve a better return on investment (ROI). These types of risks can be mitigated with the application of analytical techniques, chosen from a series of algorithms, to determine the causality of indicator results and identify independent variables that companies can adjust to achieve positive change. This article presents a predictive model to support the achievement of more assertive KPIs - Case: Wood Trading Company presents a predictive model to determine possible causes of commercial results in a company that commercializes products and services for the furniture and wood industry in Colombia. To achieve this, a literature review was carried out to identify analysis strategies and new technologies that could influence the proposed model. The methodology used was CRISP-DM through which the main variables and indicators that make up the business model and the associated problems to make assertive decisions were identified. Likewise, the necessary data from the information systems that could lead to an accurate prediction were identified. The predictive model will make it possible to more accurately identify the causes of the results of corporate indicators of the commercial process, in a more precise and truthful way, to make better decisions and improve the results of the indicators, which will impact benefits for organizations. For this model, the main variables that make up the commercial model were identified. The scope of the work was defined with commercial data between the years 2020 and 2023, in which 9 predictor variables and one dependent variable were identified. The model was made using regression algorithms, decision trees and random forests, and finally the model was evaluated using the confusion matrix, precision, F1 Score, Recall and cross validation. The article is organized into five sections. Section 2 presents a review of the literature associated with diagnostics using Machine Learning. Section 3 presents the methodology used in this research. The development of the model, including the results obtained and the evaluation. Finally, Sect. 4 presents a discussion with the existing literature, the conclusions and some future work.

2   Literature Review

To develop a conceptual understanding of diagnostic data analysis on key performance indicators (KPIs) and the influence of modern techniques such as artificial intelligence with machine learning on the analysis process, a systematic review of the literature was conducted. The process focused on articles that used machine learning in the analysis of performance indicators. Accordingly, searches for published studies and relevant use cases were carried out using online databases. Since approximately 2017, different investigations have been published around how KPIs are influenced by Machine Learning techniques, some of them are:

[5] present a case study to measure the productivity of manufacturing wiring harnesses within the automotive industry, using machine learning algorithms in KPI prediction. The data was provided by the cutting department of an automotive wiring company. In this case study, the dataset consists of 7 variables, 1,917 observations, and 1 objective (OEE value, Overall Equipment Effectiveness), a metric to identify losses, compare progress, and improve the productivity of manufacturing teams (i.e., eliminate waste). The OEE calculation gives managers the possibility to monitor their process and identify the main losses that reduce the effectiveness of the machine. The objective of this article is to develop a model based on machine learning, which is based on historical measurements of the process, capable of predicting the estimated value of OEE. The predicted OEE value will allow managers the ability to assess the effectiveness of the equipment and therefore examine the inputs to the production process to identify and eliminate relative losses. This will form a decision support tool designed for the purpose of helping managers prevent different types of losses and then act and react according to the given situation to improve and maximize production effectiveness. In the case study, they first tested different linear regression models, namely multiple linear regression, polynomial regression, support vector regression (SVR) and decision tree regression optimized support vector regression. Second, set learning techniques are manipulated with tree-based models. Random forest is tested for the data set and XG-Boost for the boost set. Finally, a deep learning predictor is built to generate a robust model with a high level of performance. The result shows that the use of the cross-validation technique with a relevant division of the data provides more reliable, accurate and unbiased predictors. This comparison was made based on the MAE metrics, MAPE and RMSE and confirmed by statistical techniques such as ANOVA and standard deviation tests. Regarding the random forest, XG-Boost is implemented under two configurations, one that uses simple data division (XGB) and another that uses cross validation (XGBCV), this model was accurate, more efficient and reliable than the others. It is worth mentioning that the result of the investigation mentions that the OEE is just a case study that could be generalized to other KPIs, and the experiment could also be carried out in any other industry, ensuring the necessary changes and adaptations.

[8] use statistical and machine learning methods in an experiment to detect anomalies that may occur in internet service servers in a data center. The goal of the project is to ensure the stability of web services, by monitoring various

key performance indicators (KPIs) to judge whether the web service is stable or not. This article divides the problem into two parts. First, time series analysis methods such as Triple Order Exponential Smoothing (Holt-Winters) and the ARIMA model and regression-based machine learning techniques such as Gradient Boosting Regression Trees (GBRT) and Long Short-Term Memory (LSTM) to predict the value at the next point in the time series. After that, they set the anomaly detection rule. Finally, the predicted value is compared with the actual value to determine if the current point is outlier or not. KPI data corresponds to timestamp, value that was saved at 1 min intervals, means that each hour had 60 data points and each day had 1440 data points. They chose a KPI representative of a search engine that shows search page view (PV). This is one of the most widely used indicators for evaluating website traffic, monitoring the trend of change in PV and analyzing the reasons for its change. In the experiment output they used MSE to evaluate a binary classification and precision, recall and F1 score to evaluate the models. In the project report it is concluded that the models perform well in detecting anomalies, especially Gradient Boosting Regression Trees (GBRT), have the highest recovery and the shortest training time. Machine learning is an efficient and promising method for anomaly detection for KPIs. In the conclusions of the experiment they propose to test other methods of machine learning, especially deep neural networks.

[10] explores how to apply machine learning in two different domains; in predictions of defect inflow and accumulation of single product defects at Ericsson AB company and the state level of parameters used in automotive projects at Volvo Car Corporation (VCC). At VCC, the propulsion unit software department is being investigated. The KPI that relates to the parameter calibration status of a project is inspected. A desired result of applying machine learning would involve a prediction about what the average state will look like in the future. These predictions can help the decision maker in the planning process. A special desire in predictions is to find underlying patterns that make the predictions accurate and reliable. Ericsson AB has established a way of incorporating its KPIs into the daily use of the organization. As there are many KPIs to investigate, one stakeholder suggested the defect inflow rate. This is then expanded by also investigating the Defect Accumulation KPI. The linear regression method is applied to different aspects of the Health KPI in VCC. The rolling time frame is applied to the KPIs investigated in the remaining investigation cycles. This thesis investigated a KPI VCC form regarding the status of calibration variables used in hardware components. The first approach was to use linear regression on the data. The second approach was to use a rolling time frame to predict new values given a certain lag. The second stage of this project was the KPIs investigated at Ericsson AB. The two KPIs were Defect Inflow and Defect Accumulation. Here, the approach used in VCC was repeated using the moving time frame. The results of these predictions showed that the best approach to predict a week ahead was to use the previous value as the prediction, as this resulted in the minimum error of 1%. The best result was achieved using a rolling window and the instance-based learning KNN on the defect input stream. The Defect

Entry KPI at Ericsson AB was the KPI that proved to be the best and was improved with predictions.

[9] present a study using KPIs from the perspective of Balance Score Card (BSC) customers to estimate the success of a new web product using machine learning. Specifically, the estimation was achieved by applying an Artificial Neural Networks (ANNs) algorithm using the Python programming language. In more detail, this paper examines the success of an online product (financial services platform) using KPIs and an ANN model to determine if a potential customer is likely to use the platform. Data collection was carried out using a questionnaire. The sample was obtained by snowball sampling (sharing it on social networks), in an effort to be as large and representative as possible. The questionnaire that was created consisted of two (2) groups of questions: 1) demographic questions and 2) questions related to the scope of the platform's services. The purpose of this article is to demonstrate how a start-up company can estimate the KPI responsible for the success of an online platform before it is launched on the market. The estimation is done using AI, using the KPIs derived from the perspective of BSC customers. For the purposes of this study, the potential development of an online platform by a technology company that provides financial services is explored. This research addresses the contribution of Machine Learning in the design of a strategy for optimal decision making. This occurs as a result of the ANN's ability for pattern recognition and its strength to mimic the neural networks of the human brain. This procedure is currently much more efficient thanks to faster computer processing. From the analysis of the data using the ANN, the following results were obtained. Of 122 participants, 48 chose option number five (5), making it the most popular, indicating that they would use a financial services platform to the extent of 5: A lot (with a range of 1: Not at all - 5: A lot). The result of the questionnaires revealed that 7/10 people would use this online platform, indicating that it would be successful. However, using Machine Learning, it was found that with an accuracy of 91.89%, the company's product will be successful. In addition, given that the threshold that would determine whether or not the new product would be built was set at 60%, and the results revealed that 70% of people would use this online platform, it is concluded that the technology firm in this study will continue with new product development. It is also worth noting that the presence of high precision in the Machine Learning model indicates that the development of the new product will have less financial risk compared to not using Machine Learning for this analysis. In conclusion and based on all the findings of this study, the application of Machine Learning in business is very important. For optimal results, Companies should strive to combine accurate interpretation of the results by qualified analysts and proper data management techniques to be applied before building the models, which can help companies improve their production and economic growth. Additionally, automation frees up more time for analysts to focus on other aspects of the business plan, enabling them to make better decisions. It also reduces costs and improves the customer experience.

[7] present a time series anomaly detection method based on correlation analysis and hidden Markov model (HMM) in the field of intelligent operation and maintenance. You can identify abnormal KPIs within a set period from a large number of KPIs in a system and the transfer status between them. Correlation analysis is used to obtain the correlation between abnormal KPIs in the system, which reduces the false alarm rate of anomaly detection. In the field of smart operation and maintenance, KPI anomaly detection for a multi-index system is difficult. In system KPIs, there can be a temporal correlation between two indicators; that is, when one KPI is abnormal, it will cause similar fluctuations in the trends of other KPIs in a short time. Due to the presence of numerous trailing indicators and complex structures in the distributed system, the fluctuations will continue to spread to more KPIs. This causes more KPI anomalies throughout the system, making anomaly detection and root cause analysis very difficult. Without using correlation analysis, it is very difficult for OyM personnel to analyze and infer the correlation between a large number of complex KPI anomalies. In the anomaly detection method discussed in this paper, a 1D-CNN-TCN prediction model is first proposed to predict the KPIs and obtain the residual sequence to detect the possible abnormal KPIs. This model combines the local variable acquisition capability of convolutional neural network (CNN) with the temporally dependent variable acquisition capability of temporal convolutional network (TCN) to improve prediction accuracy. The residual sequence of abnormal KPIs can highlight the abnormal segment in each KPI, so that the correlation analysis is not affected by the original fluctuation of the KPIs and thus the accuracy of the correlation analysis is improved. The experimental results show that the F1 score of the correlation analysis method in this paper is also the best. The HMM parameters are confirmed based on the correlation matrix. After training the HMM, other KPIs that can cause a KPI abnormality are found, reducing the time required for OyM personnel to find a large number of abnormal KPIs. According to the results of the F1 score evaluation, the optimal F1 scores of abnormality detection and time order are 0.94 and 0.90, respectively, indicating that this method has a good effect on abnormality detection. The method in this document can further determine the influence relationship between KPIs by getting abnormal KPIs, which can help to build a fault propagation diagram and help OyM personnel to perform quick troubleshooting. However, the method of this paper still has some limitations, and the specific threshold of the correlation analysis method still needs to be adjusted according to different environments.

[4] investigate an approach to detect anomalies in financial data, using behavior change indicators (BCIs). The application of the BCIs proposed in this study can be described as a KPI time series analysis. From a data science standpoint, tracking financial KPIs is critical to managing activity and changes in KPIs over time. Performance management assessment requires an understanding of the characteristics of changes in KPIs over time. Based on this assumption, three types of BCI have been defined to detect and assess changes in traditional KPIs in time series: absolute change indicators (BCI-A), relative change indicators

(BCI-RE proportion indicators) and delta forex indicators. (D-BCI). Financial KPI thresholds (normative values) help to assess the state of a company's operations during the financial period, allowing the creation of templates (patterns) that the software system uses to perform such an assessment (for example, zone safe zone, risk zone, disaster zone). Another problem is the financial limits (normative values, thresholds) of the BCIs, which must be set separately for each KPI. By setting BCI thresholds, templates can be created. The software system would automatically assess BCI values and the risks of changes in the KPI time series and would detect KPI changes that indicate anomalies in financial data. Examples of raw accounting data (attributes) used in the experiment include a number of variables including: DBID, FinancialYear, Total Equity, Total Liabilities, Total Assets, Non-current Passive, Current Passive, Revenue, OPEX, Other Income, Financial Income, Taxes, Gross Profit, Operating Profit, EBITDA, Net Profit, Gross Margin%, EBITDA%, NetMargin%, ROA YTD, ROE YTD, Cash Position, Cash Ratio, Working Capital, Current Ratio, Acid Test, Debt/Equity Ratio, Debt/Asset Ratio, OPEX%, Intangible Fixed Asset Ratio, AR, AP and inventory. The advantages of using BCI in financial data analysis can be summarized as follows: BCIs provide a quantitative estimate of KPI changes over a defined period. BCIs highlight KPI changes that are almost impossible for a person to see and understand when analyzing KPI values or just their changes. If the BCI exceeds a certain threshold, such a change in the value of a KPI is one of the most important signs of a change in a company's business decisions or processes or human error. It is almost impossible for an individual expert to detect and understand anomalies simply by analyzing the wealth of financial KPI data. Using BCIs to track changes to KPIs helps users see suspicious trends in some KPI changes (indicating potentially suspicious data) and reduces the amount of data that needs to be analyzed.

[2], developed a method to determine and calculate the performance of employees in virtual environments and access the best talent as a form of competitive advantage using machine learning through the use of methodologies such as the Scikit-learn Multi-Output-Regressor function. Due to certain changes in the formulation of virtual leadership styles, such as the trend towards physically dispersed work groups, new research on the role and nature of team leadership in virtual environments has become necessary more challenging than managing people on the site. The total staff of the company considered is currently 51 employees made up of 78% men and 22% women. The department is made up of vertical teams. Each has a team leader and a team leader responsible for giving directives, setting priorities and goals for the team. Several inducer algorithms were discussed in this project, such as linear regression or a support vector regression (SVR) model with a linear kernel models data in a completely different way than an instance-based learner like the k-neighbor algorithm closest (KNN). Scikit-learn implements a function called GridSearchCV, which is short for grid search cross-validation, which can be used to determine the optimal algorithm along with a number of specific hyperparameters. GridSearchCV sets up a grid of each algorithm with all possible combinations of the given parameters

and their respective values, and using cross-validation and R2 scoring, finds the optimal solution.

[6], used machine learning to predict the performance of key indicators for construction projects. The different aspects of the projects are evaluated by key performance indicators (KPIs) that are used to monitor and control construction projects. In the project, a novel framework was proposed to qualitatively measure and predict six important construction project KPIs using the neuro-fuzzy technique. To map the KPIs of three critical stages of the project to the KPIs of the entire project, neurofuzzy models were developed. In the proposed framework, the neuro-fuzzy technique was applied to forecast the KPIs of the entire project automatically from the data. The neuro-fuzzy technique is a combination of artificial neural network (ANN) and fuzzy logic, which is used to solve different research problems in construction management. In this research, the neural network (ANN) model was used to predict the KPIs of the entire project. The input of the prediction models was 18 KPIs, six KPIs for each of the three stages. The results were six KPIs for the entire project. The ANN models were developed, trained, and tested in MATLAB 2016a. Models were developed using three available training algorithms for neural networks: Levenberg-Marquardt (LM), Bayesian regularization (BR), and scaled conjugate gradient (SCG). The performance of the model was evaluated based on the coefficient of determination (R2), the mean absolute error (MAE), the relative absolute error (RAE), the root relative squared error (RRSE), and the mean absolute% error (MAPE) and each amount of error rate. Six KPIs were chosen for the frequency of their use in the literature; There is cost, time, quality, safety, customer satisfaction, and project team satisfaction. KPIs from three critical project stages (early stage, mid-stage, and late stage) were used to predict project-wide KPIs using two main techniques: artificial neural networks (ANNs) and neuro-fuzzy. In the ANN, the best model was selected by changing the number of neurons in the hidden layer. Neurofuzzy models were developed in two steps; First, the initial FIS models were developed using both subtractive clustering and FCM. In subtractive clustering, the radius of the clustering was optimized to achieve optimal precision without overfitting. Second, optimization of the initial FIS model was performed using ANN. In the neuro-fuzzy technique, 18 different models were developed, six models for each of the three critical stages of the project. The results indicate that the neurofuzzy technique using subtractive clustering performs better and has lower error values compared to the other two methods. Therefore, to predict construction project KPIs, the neuro-fuzzy technique using subtractive clustering is recommended. The proposed framework is designed to be flexible and can be applied to other countries and other types of projects.

[3], elaborates an investigation to establish the bases of a system for the automatic diagnosis of failures in mobile networks using automatic learning. With the knowledge available about the network performance data, the most common problems, and the manual troubleshooting process, the next step was to design an artificial intelligence algorithm that would perform the self-diagnosis. In this thesis, the FLC (Lotfi A. Zadeh. Fuzzy sets. Information and control)

are used as the best option, since they are easily understandable both by human experts (since they use a language close to spoken) and by machines. Fuzzy logic controllers facilitate the automatic generation of diagnostic rules and their integration with existing rules. This solution is also attractive to network operators, as its clarity makes it less confusing than other alternatives, such as Bayesian networks or neural networks. At work, whenever an expert diagnoses a mobile network problem, the expert can report it with minimal effort and store it in the system. The core of this system is a diagnostic algorithm (a Fuzzy Logic Controllers - FLC) that evolves and improves by learning from each new example, until it reaches the point where experts can count on its accuracy for problems more common. Every time a new problem arises, it will be added to the system's database, thus further increasing its power. The goal is to free experts from repetitive tasks, so they can spend their time on challenges that are more rewarding to solve. Therefore, the first objective of this thesis is the collection of a database of real failure cases. For it, A user interface for data collection is designed taking into account ease of use as a priority requirement. Once the collected data is available, it will be analyzed to better understand its properties and obtain the necessary information for the design of data analytics algorithms. Another objective of this thesis is the creation of a mobile network failure model, finding the relationships between network performance and the occurrence of problems. The acquisition of knowledge is done through the application of analytical algorithms on the collected data. A KDD process is designed that extracts the parameters of a fuzzy logic controller and is applied to the collected data base. Finally, this thesis also aims to carry out an analysis of the Big Data aspects of the Self-healing functions, and take them into account when designing the algorithms. The model of network failures obtained in this work constitutes a valuable contribution that helps to understand the relationships between performance measures and modeled failures. Furthermore, the model can be used to generate highly realistic emulated data. The procedure used to extract the model can also be used to model new problems and in different networks. Another contribution of this work is the study of the application of FLCs to diagnosis and the design and implementation of data mining algorithms that adjust a fuzzy logic controller based on a database of diagnostic cases. The extracted fuzzy logic controller (FLC) achieves a high success rate in the diagnosis of the network under test; and the method used to adjust it can be used in other networks. In addition to being useful for diagnosis, the rules are a good source of information about the nature of the observed problems, since they are given in a language close to human.

[11] propose a generic causality learning approach for tracking and monitoring production cycle time. Therefore, a causality analysis of the KPI values is presented, as well as a prioritization of their influencing factors to provide decision support. The purpose of this article is to provide an approach to make predictions and diagnoses in order to detect abnormal situations and identify their causes. For this, Bayesian Networks (BN) are used, which aim to identify the factors that affect the KPI addressed. ANNs are used to solve complex problems

and enable learning and modeling of complex, non-linear relationships between inputs and outputs. To implement the proposed data analysis methodology, the authors have constructed a representative summary data set to validate that the experiments are correct. This dataset respects, in a very flexible way, a certain amount of causality rules that have been previously defined to be compared with the resulting causality links. The use case addresses one KPI: production cycle time. The rest of the data set is made up of variables that may or may not affect the addressed KPI: the day of the week, the time zone, the month, the indoor temperature, the operator's heart rate, their stress level, the default number and the level of training. The objective is to identify, among this data set, the variables that affect the production cycle time and prioritize them. In order to build a realistic and more relevant use case, the authors have ensured that the dataset does not exclusively follow these rules. Basically, this KPI is calculated from two pieces of information: the remaining production time and the number of units produced. Given this, if a deviation is detected, both pieces of information do not give answers either to understand how this happened or to trace the root causes. Use a constraint-based algorithm (Peter and Clarck (PC) algorithm) to define the structure of the BN that will allow causal links to be identified. The PC algorithm is a constraint-based algorithm that starts with a complete undirected graph and removes edges between pairs that are not statistically significantly related by performing conditional independence (CI) tests. The proposal is currently in its early stages of development and many aspects need to be addressed, such as testing and benchmarking of other algorithms and BN structure learning tools.

3 Methodology

The first step in this research methodology was to define the objectives and goals of the project. Subsequently, the CRISP-DM (Cross Industry Standard Process for Data Mining) case study methodology [1] was carried out, which allows us to establish a framework structured to measure and diagnose the causes of the results in business indicators. This gives us support in decision making by identifying relevant actions to improve the value of the KPI. The process includes the identification of the main KPIs of the project through the review of the literature, the knowledge of the business and the opinion of experts, as well as the application of a set of machine learning techniques. The methodology is structured in a hierarchical process, composed of tasks described at different levels of abstraction, ranging from the general to the specific. The process is divided into six phases: Business Understanding, Data Understanding, Data Preparation, Modeling, Evaluation, and Implementation. The activities carried out in each of these phases are described below.

3.1 Business Understanding

The investigation was carried out in a company dedicated to the commercialization of products and services for the furniture and wood industry. The company currently has a nationwide presence and has different operation centers that handle customer orders and services. In addition, it has various lines of business that range from the marketing of raw products such as boards and finished products such as doors, floors, furniture and design services. Currently, the company calculates the results indicators taking into account variables such as quantity delivery compliance, number of orders delivered on time, delivery time in days, number of customers, quantity sales value, number of invoices and number of orders. A group of business experts periodically analyze the causes of their results and have identified that it is not possible to guarantee an accurate diagnosis and accurate decision-making that reflects the correct operation of the company. For this reason, they consider that it is necessary to involve new variables in decision making, such as the average value per invoice and amount of inventory. These new variables are expected to help identify in advance what is causing current misjudgment. Other variables that could be important to consider are: availability of personnel for the process, square meters of the operation centers, location of the operation centers, service level qualification, and marketing and advertising, however, they are in process data collection by the company.

Each of these variables is defined below.

- Compliance delivery in quantities: This characteristic measures a variable that can impact sales and corresponds to the level of compliance in the quantities delivered requested by the customer.
- Orders delivered on time: Corresponds to the number of orders delivered on time, a variable that comes from the company's business intelligence system.
- Delivery time in days: Variable that corresponds to the delivery time of the orders in days.
- Number of customers: Independent variable that corresponds to the number of customers that exist per operation center.
- Quantity sales value: Corresponds to the sum of the quantities sold.
- Number of Invoices: Independent variable that corresponds to the number of invoices issued in the period.
- number of orders: Independent variable that corresponds to the number of orders generated in the period.
- average value per invoice. A variable of the average invoice value was created, at the granularity level of year, month, operation center and product line; This is because the average value is a feature that helps us in the analysis of sales behavior.
- Inventory Quantity: Independent variable that contains the quantities of inventory available at the end of the period (Figs. 1 and 2).

Author	application sector	Predictor Variables	Objetive	Techniques Used
Mazgualdi, Masrour, Hassani, & Khdoudi, 2021	Manufacturing in the automotive industry	Number of orders, days of production, number of losses.	Overall Equipment Effectiveness (OEE)	Random Forest - XGBCV-Boost
Shi, He, & Liu, 2018	Internet Service Companies	Timestamp, website traffic	Internet service stability	Gradient Boosting Regression Trees (GBRT)
THORSTROM, 2017	Manufacture of electronic devices	parameter calibration status, defect input flow rate	Defect flow prediction	KNN learning
Tagkouta, Psycharis, Psarras, Anagnostopoulos, & Salmon, 2023	Companies with online sales	scope of platform services, demographic data.	Estimate the success of a new web product	Artificial Neural Networks (ANNs)
Zijing, and others, 2021	Smart Maintenance	failure propagation, residual sequence of abnormal KPIs	Identify abnormal KPIs	Convolutional Neural Network (CNN)
Lopata, and others, 2022	Financial Process	DBID, FinancialYear, Passive, Revenue, OPEX, Other income, Financial income, Taxes, Gross profit, Operating profit, EBITDA, Net profit, Gross margin%, EBITDA%, NetMargin%, ROA_YTD, ROE_YTD, Cash_Position, Cash_Ratio, Working_Capital, Current_Ratio, Acid_Test, Debt/Equity Ratio, OPEX%.	Detect anomalies in financial data using behavior change indicators (BCI).	Time series analysis,
Paxleal, 2020	Work companies in virtual environments	online leadership styles	employee performance	Scikit-learn Multi-Output-Regressor.
Fanaei, Moselhi, Alkass, & Zangenehmadar, 2018	construction companies	cost, time, quality, safety, customer satisfaction, and project team satisfaction.	Project performance	Artificial Neural Network (ANN) and Fuzzy Logic
Khatib, 2017	Mobile networks	failure occurrence	network performance	Fuzzy Logic Controllers (FLC)
AMZIL, YAHIA, KLEMENT, & ROUCOULES, 2021	production companies	Production day, time zone, month, indoor temperature, operator heart rate, stress level, training level.	production cycle time	Bayesian networks

Fig. 1. Summary of Findings

REGIONAL CENTRO NORT...	7108	AV. 68 (BOGOTÁ)	426	Maderas	13.249	Otros	4794
REGIONAL SUR	6926	CALI CALLE 19	408	Servicios	11.382	Herrajes	2491
REGIONAL NOROCCIDENT...	6857	BUCARAMANGA	398	Puertas De Maderas Y Marc...	9753	Aglomerado	2479
Otro	36.668	Otro	56.327	Otro	23.175	Otro	47.796

Fig. 2. Independent Categorical Variables

3.2 Data Understanding

To achieve the objective set out in the company's need, data was extracted from information systems such as sales, logistics and financial. Data was taken between the month of April 2020 and the month of March 2023, since these met quality elements such as completeness, integrity and availability, required for their analysis. In addition, relevant categorical data was identified in the following data models: commercial, supply, and financial for 13 regions distributed nationwide, 230 operation centers, 14 product groups, and 73 product lines. Based on this information, it was identified that the dependent variable is the value of sales and the variables considered influential correspond to sales in units, compliance with the amounts requested by the client, on-time delivery compliance, order delivery time, number of issued invoices and average value per invoice, etc. These variables were subjected to a cleaning process and their corresponding normalization at the year, month, operation center and product line level. Finally, it was possible to have a data set with 99,972 records and 10 variables, for a total of 999,720 data.

Descriptive data analysis

3.3 Data Preparation

In this phase, new variables are created from those provided by the business. Each of the variables and their calculations are described below average value per invoice. A variable of the average invoice value was created, at the granularity level of year, month, operation center and product line; This is because the average value per invoice is a feature that helps us in the analysis of sales behavior. Compliance delivery in quantities. Corresponds to the percentage of the quantities delivered versus those requested by the client. Order fulfillment: A variable was created that stores the fulfillment of orders, comparing the number of orders delivered on time versus the orders generated (Fig. 3).

A heat map is used to show the correlation matrix between the first group of variables selected for the model, as shown in Fig. 4. The higher the positive

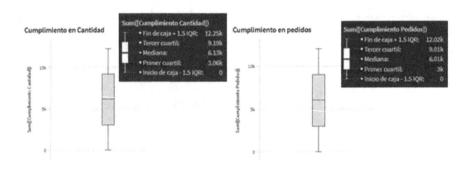

Fig. 3. Independent Variables

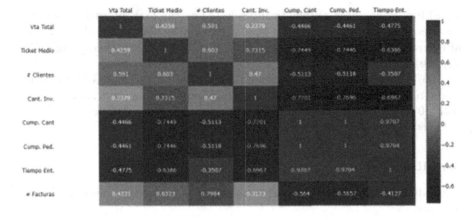

Fig. 4. Correlation Matrix (Color figure online)

Algorithms	variables
• Linear regression • Random forest regression • XGBoost regression • LightGBM regression • CatBoost regression	• Average value of invoices • Inventory Quantity • Number of Clients • Delivery time in days • Number of Invoices • Orders delivered on time • number of orders • Order Fulfillment

Fig. 5. Algorithms and variables selected for each technique

	Arriba	Algoritmo	R2	RMSE	MSE	MAE
☑	♛	Regresión de bosque aleatorio	0.941	19.047.197,266	362.795.723.702.579.250	4,080,836.136
		Regresión CatBoost	0.847	30.641.947,001	938.928.916.008.707.000	4.261.661,994
		Regresión LightGBM	0.743	39.774.551.380	1.582.014.937.463.750.500	4,984,066.516
		Regresión XGBoost	0.901	24.686.214.478	609.409.185.271.831.600	3,966,363.104
		Regresión lineal	0.304	65.406.412.538	4.277.998.801.093.056.000	13.514.461,502

Fig. 6. ROC-AOC of the different models studied

correlation between the variables, the deeper the red color, for conversely, blue signifies a negative correlation.

In the figure it can be seen, in this first group of variables, that quantity delivery compliance has a high correlation with order delivery compliance. Therefore, we only take into account the order delivery fulfillment variable in the model and discard the quantity delivery fulfillment variable (Fig. 5).

3.4   Modeling

Based on the independent variables identified in the previous section, it has been proposed to use a regression model using the random forest regression algorithm. It has been automatically selected as the best alternative based on the Machine Learning component that is part of the Qlik Cloud platform used, after evaluating different algorithms such as CatBoost Regression, LightGBM Regression, XGBoost Regression and Linear Regression.

100% of the data was used to train these models, which represent the inputs. These records were divided into two sets, one representing the training data set with 80% of the records (79,977 records), and the other representing the test data set with 20% of the records (19,995 records).

3.5 Results

Depending on the selected objective, the following algorithms were used in the analysis.

When training the model with the 10 established variables, the best algorithm was the random regression of the forest, with an accuracy of 94.1%.

Figure 6 shows the results of the different algorithms used where the random forest regression stands out with an R2 of 0.941. Machine learning prediction performances are evaluated in terms of Root Mean Square Error (RMSE) as a validation function. The results shown in Fig. 6 indicate that the RMSE ranges from 19,047 to 65,406, which shows a good response to the ML models. As expected, linear regression performed least well because its limitations lie in matching data that is not linear and predicting data that is not within the range of the training sets. CatBoost works best because it reduces any form of overtuning and classifies each attribute precisely. However, it's worth noting that Random Forest Regression outperforms its counterparts. You can appreciate the importance of the variables and their influence on the average ticket variable (Average invoice value), the number of invoices and the quantities sold, as well as the available inventory as shown in Fig. 7.

Fig. 7. Importance of the variables - random forest regression method

4   Discussion, Conclusions and Future Work

This article proposes a model to diagnose the causes of the sales results of a company in Colombia dedicated to the commercialization of products and services for the furniture and wood industry. Many variables, both internal and external, intervene in the identification of these causes, which makes it difficult to carry out a detailed analysis of the results. Diagnostic analysis based on people's experience does not guarantee accurate results and may result in personal criteria influenced by the way they view and contextualize the data, as well as by their knowledge, experience, and judgment of the circumstances surrounding the problem. Our model has shown good performance in detecting the causes of sales results, especially using the random forest regression algorithm, with an accuracy of 94.1% calculated with the cross-validation method. This means that current sales are centered around the average invoice value, which is important information for planning strategies to increase the average invoice value. These strategies can include promotions and cross-selling to improve results. A differentiating factor of this work consisted in the application of theories and methodologies that help to identify the variables that affect sales. The variables that contribute to the efficiency in a commercial process were analyzed using the pentagon model and the value chain in retail companies. This provides the necessary knowledge in the commercial function and allows an efficient response to the demands and challenges of the customer needs satisfaction cycle, thus improving commercial results in this type of business. Therefore, our proposal differs from the models mentioned in the state of the art by grouping variables that are determinant in the results obtained. However, there is still room for improvement in our research by incorporating other exogenous variables into the model. For example, the behavior of the country's construction indicators can be considered, which can generate demand for services and products. In addition, variables such as purchasing power and the effects of market strategies allow the model to be improved.

References

1. Chapman, P., et al.: Wirth: CRISP-DM 1.0: step-by-step data mining guide (2000). https://api.semanticscholar.org/CorpusID:59777418
2. Simi Paxleal, J.: Measuring KPIs of virtual teams in global organization using machine learning. Int. J. Adv. Res. Sci. Commun. Technol. 21–27 (2020). https://doi.org/10.48175/ijarsct-243
3. Khatib, E.J.: Data analytics and knowledge discovery for root cause analysis in LTE self-organizing networks. Ph.D. thesis, Universidad de Málaga (2017)
4. Lopata, A., et al.: Financial data anomaly discovery using behavioral change indicators. Electronics 11(10), 1598 (2022). https://doi.org/10.3390/electronics11101598
5. Mazgualdi, C.E., Masrour, T., Hassani, I.E., Khdoudi, A.: Machine learning for KPIs prediction: a case study of the overall equipment effectiveness within the automotive industry. Soft. Comput. 25(4), 2891–2909 (2020). https://doi.org/10.1007/s00500-020-05348-y

6. Fanaei, S.S., Moselhi, O., Alkass, S.T., Zangenehmadar, Z.: Application of machine learning in predicting key performance indicators for construction projects. Ph.D. thesis, Univ., Montreal, QC, Canada (2018)

7. Shang, Z., Zhang, Y., Zhang, X., Zhao, Y., Cao, Z., Wang, X.: Time series anomaly detection for KPIs based on correlation analysis and HMM. Appl. Sci. **11**(23), 11353 (2021). https://doi.org/10.3390/app112311353

8. Shi, J., He, G., Liu, X.: Anomaly detection for key performance indicators through machine learning. In: 2018 International Conference on Network Infrastructure and Digital Content (IC-NIDC). IEEE (2018). https://doi.org/10.1109/icnidc.2018.8525714

9. Tagkouta, E., Psycharis, P.N., Psarras, A., Anagnostopoulos, T., Salmon, I.: Predicting success for web product through key performance indicators based on balanced scorecard with the use of machine learning. WSEAS Trans. Bus. Econ. **20**, 646–656 (2023). https://doi.org/10.37394/23207.2023.20.59

10. Thorstrom, M.: Applying machine learning to key performance indicators (2017). https://odr.chalmers.se/server/api/core/bitstreams/bee2170c-60ec-4c2e-b3b0-f63ebf1ece00/content

11. Zapata, S.M., Klement, N., Silva, C., Gibaru, O., Lafou, M.: Collective intelligence application in a kitting picking zone of the automotive industry. In: Gerbino, S., Lanzotti, A., Martorelli, M., Mirálbes Buil, R., Rizzi, C., Roucoules, L. (eds.) JCM 2022. LNCS, pp. 410–420. Springer, Cham (2023). https://doi.org/10.1007/978-3-031-15928-2_36

BDI Peasants Model for the WellProdSim Agent-Based Social Simulator

Jairo E. Serrano[1]([✉]) [iD] and Enrique González[2] [iD]

[1] Universidad Tecnológica de Bolívar, Cartagena, Colombia
jserrano@utb.edu.co
[2] Pontificia Universidad Javeriana, Bogotá, Colombia
egonzal@javeriana.edu.co

Abstract. This article describes the design and implementation of BDI agents for the WellProdSim Social Simulator, a system that assesses the productivity and social wellbeing of Peasant Families. A first BDI emotional reasoning model was designed to incorporate personal and social wellbeing components in the agent that represents a Peasant Family. Furthermore, decision-making mechanisms based on variable modulation and fuzzy logic evaluation of human welfare were added. The evaluation aspects include health state, knowledge and skills, food consumption, emotional state and expected productivity. Preliminary results demonstrate a high quality in the proposed model; although, some elements with potential for improvement, in future work, were also identified.

Keywords: Social Simulation · Multi-agent systems · Emotional BDI · Multi-agent simulation · BDI agent · Fuzzy Logic

1 Introduction

WellProdSim is a social simulator based on a multi-agent system (ABSS) that evaluates the productivity and social wellbeing of peasant families, seeking to support decision making in public and private entities that promote the integral development of these families in remote regions of Colombia. This article presents the emotional BDI agent model and the decision-making mechanisms used in the simulation, focusing on the agents that simulate peasant families. The implementation of a contextualized model allows simulating the behavior and complexity of the decisions of peasant families, considering economic, emotional, and social factors, which facilitates a better understanding of rural dynamics and the design of more effective policies for the small-scale agroindustrial sector [1].

For the design of the simulator, it was necessary to establish formal definitions of Peasant Family, productivity, and social wellbeing. The Peasant Family was defined as "a basic multi-functional unit of social organization, crop cultivation and animal husbandry, as a means of subsistence" [2]. Productivity (development) "is both a physical reality and a state of mind in which society has, through some combination of social, economic, and institutional processes,

M. Tabares et al. (Eds.): CCC 2023, CCIS 1924, pp. 367–379, 2024.
https://doi.org/10.1007/978-3-031-47372-2_29

secured the means for obtaining a better life". [3], and social well-being is defined as "the central component of people's overall health" and, in relation to productivity, as "the prosperity of the community and society" [4]. In the context of the social simulator, in order to facilitate the analysis of its productivity and wellbeing, the Peasant Family was modeled as a unit rather than a set of independent individuals.

In addition, the social fabric surrounding the families was taken into account, including norms, customs, and culture that build interactions and common objectives linked to their region. For example, most of the peasant families in the study region do not have adequate technical, organizational, and economic capacity to carry out their productive activities [5], which makes it necessary to maximize efforts to achieve a good productivity level.

In fact, the application of social modeling and simulation tools will help mitigate the uncertainty generated by the particularities of the environment and the variables that influence the success or failure of peasant improvement plans, allowing the testing of different scenarios and intervention strategies before applying them in real life.

The paper is organized as follows: Sect. 2 discusses the basics of social simulation and agent models, as well as related architectures and multi-agent systems; Sect. 3 presents the WellProdSim peasant model, describes the interactions between peasants and discusses the decision making model based on modulating variables using fuzzy logic; and finally, Sects. 4 and 5 present the results and conclusions of the paper.

2 ABSS Literature Review

Social simulation is applied to study and understand the dynamics and behavioral patterns of interacting peasants by modeling both at the microscale, focusing on individual decision-making and behavior, and at the macroscale, representing the social fabric and society at large. As intended in this research work, by analyzing the relationship between these two levels, an understanding of the complex social phenomena is achieved. In this context, social simulation can be defined as "the process of designing a computational model of a system (or process) and conducting experiments to understand its behavior or evaluate operating strategies" [6].

Social simulation is one of the most powerful analytical tools available, with applicability in business, economics, marketing, education, politics, social science, behavioral, transportation, and urban studies, among others [6]. Research on social simulation and its applicability is still ongoing, supported by computational sciences [7]. The possibilities offered by social simulation have been strengthened by working environments with greater computational capacity, in addition to new theories and tools, achieving higher levels of accuracy, better understanding and modeling of the physical world and also of people.

The following subsections present an overview of the applicability of social simulation to various areas and how it complements other implementation techniques.

2.1   Social Simulation Applied

Social simulation, as mentioned above, is a powerful tool for evaluating strategies focused on increasing productivity and social welfare. Socioecological systems (SES) are an example of the application of social simulation, since they jointly model humans in society and their interactions with the environment [8]. This allows understanding the effects and outcomes of human behavior and decisions in relation to the ecology, formalizing them into replicable and configurable models for study.

In this context, agent-based modeling is an interesting approach to develop social simulators. This approach defines an agent as a physical or virtual entity capable of autonomously perceiving and reacting to its environment. Agents must also have the ability to communicate and cooperate with other similar agents, forming a Multi-Agent System (MAS) [9]. Through MAS, it is possible to model and analyze individual decision processes in SES, allowing a better understanding of the social and environmental phenomena at play.

In the context of the productivity and well-being of peasant families, it is crucial to consider environmental and social factors that influence their performance, such as climate [10], soil fertility [11], pest control [12], supply chain and market trends [13], as well as communication with neighbors and efficient ways of production [14]. MAS have been successfully used in various models that facilitate policy decision making in this area.

Agent-based social simulation has been successfully applied in the measurement of social welfare in various scenarios, such as the study of agent behavior in everyday situations [9], decision making in the design of business plans in shopping centers [15], the study of the entrepreneurial capacity of peasants dispossessed of their land [16]. and the evaluation of the integration of laws and public policies for rural development in Europe [17].

In order to achieve a well-founded implementation of the social simulator, it became essential to deepen in the concepts and architectures of the Agent-Based Models (ABM) that act as the basis for the multiagent system with which WellProdSim was developed. The next subsection will explore in more detail the characteristics, components, and architectures that allow the construction of social simulators using agents, providing a solid basis for implementation.

2.2   Agent Based Models and Architectures

The previous subsection explored social simulation and how agent-based models (ABM) can improve the design and development of socioecological systems. Using an ABM oriented approach to implement the behavior and decisions of individuals and peasant communities increases the quality of the results produced by the social simulator [18]. A brief contextualization of the two main types of agent model follows.

Applying a minimalist approach, there are two main types of agent design: reactive and deliberative. Reactive agents only respond to changes in their environment, with a local and time-limited scope. Although useful in certain contexts, such as robotic control, the deliberative approach is more suitable for modeling complex social systems. These agents use symbolic and formal modeling to define behaviors and knowledge, which allows for better decision making, albeit with greater resource consumption.

This project focuses on the BDI (Beliefs, Desires, Intentions) deliberative agent model proposed by Bratman [19]. This approach models intentional agents who make decisions and plan based on a set of beliefs, desires and intentions. Combined with an incipient emotional component, the BDI agent more closely resembles human thinking, improving the accuracy and effectiveness of simulations.

The deliberation process in a BDI [20] agent begins by sensing environmental conditions through sensors. The collected information is processed and stored by the belief updating process. A belief database is used to model the world, skills, agent state, modulating variables, experiences, and rules. Next, desires are detected and evaluated in order to select agent's intentions. Finally, these intentions, that can be seen as dominant goals, perform the mapping that selects an action or set of actions, from the plan library, to be executed.

In the following subsection, a review of the opportunities for improvement of ABS are identified. These opportunities have been taken into account for the design of the WellProdSim.

2.3   ABSS and Opportunities

ABSS have proven to be the ideal and recommended way to understand and address the study of productivity and social wellbeing of peasant families. In this subsection, we will discuss the opportunities for improvement found in some previous ABS developments and how these findings can guide future research in the field of agent-based social simulation.

Based on the literature review and the definition of the conceptual framework, a series of relevant studies have been selected and are presented in Table 1. These studies are compared using six fundamental criteria, which will serve as a basis for identifying opportunities and areas for improvement in the development of social simulators. The criteria include whether the papers make use of a multi-agent system (MAS), whether they use BDI agents with an emotional component, whether the goal of the simulator is to perform an economic analysis, whether the analysis is focused on welfare, whether a model of space is used, and finally, whether the simulator has a time-varying feed-forward.

The results obtained in this analysis were very interesting, because most of the papers reviewed focused on specific and well-defined areas of analysis, each one separately. This fact opens valuable opportunities to develop a social simulator that encompasses a broader spectrum of user characteristics. Currently, there are no options that comprehensively assess individual and community productivity and wellbeing in the context of peasant societies, considering both aspects as fundamental.

In addition, the implementation and optimization of a spatial modeling and a adaptive time model, with variable time progression, presents significant challenges. This situation is largely due to the fact that the reviewed works make

Table 1. Comparison of productivity and wellbeing related work. It has the criterion applied ✓, does not meet the criteria. ✗.

Referenced Previous Work	SMA	eBDI	Prod. Analysis	Well-being Analysis	Space	Variable Time
Bao et al. [16]	✗	✗	✓	✓	✓	✗
Berger et al. [21]	✓	✗	✓	✗	✓	✗
Caron et al. [22]	✗	✗	✓	✗	✗	✗
Grevenitis et al. [23]	✓	✓	✗	✓	✓	✗
Marley et al. [24]	✗	✗	✗	✓	✓	✗
Muto et al. [20]	✓	✓	✓	✗	✓	✗
Ostrom et al. [25]	✗	✗	✓	✓	✗	✗
Potting et al. [12]	✗	✗	✓	✗	✓	✗
Schiavon et al. [9]	✗	✗	✓	✗	✗	✗
Schreinemachers et al. [11]	✓	✗	✓	✓	✓	✗
Valencia et al. [15]	✓	✓	✓	✗	✓	✗
Yuan et al. [26]	✗	✗	✓	✗	✓	✗
Zasada et al. [17]	✗	✗	✓	✗	✗	✗

use of frameworks and libraries previously developed by third parties, without much customization. WellProdSim seeks to overcome these limitations by using BESA, an open and extensible agent library developed within our research group [27], which is one of its main strengths.

The traditional methodologies used for the modeling of multiagent systems do not take into account all the possible features that would allow developing an ABSS in an integral way. Therefore it became practical to include an integrative methodology, which allows flexibility and a holistic view of the whole process, based on design science [28] and integrated with the agent methodology AOPOA [29].

Traditional decision-making mechanisms are often mathematically modeled, which may ignore realistic behavior and characterization. This study uses a more realistic representation of behavior and decision-making processes of peasant families by integrating a BDI emotional engine into a multi-agent system. However, due to the scope of this paper, a more in-depth discussion of emotional BDI implementation will be presented in a separate paper. This will allow for a more comprehensive analysis and evaluation of the emotional BDI engine and its impact on the simulation results. Consistent with the focus of this article, the following section will analyze several opportunities for improvement.

3   Peasant Model Approach

WellProdSim is a social simulator designed to assess both the productivity and social wellbeing of peasant families. The simulator is constructed iteratively, integrating individually developed components of the multi-agent system for consistency and correct interaction. The primary focus is to improve decision-making and planning for small agricultural producers like peasant families, considering their socioeconomic, environmental, and emotional aspects. As the main agent, the Peasant Family's design within WellProdSim aims to accurately represent the behavior, decisions, and interactions of families in rural communities, thus fostering an improved understanding of their specific needs.

To achieve this objective, several key aspects have been considered in the conceptualization and development of this type of agent, such as: the family structure and overall capabilities; the resources and tools to which they have access and how they are used; the decision-making process using the BDI [30] goal oriented approach; the internal emotional model of each family and its influence on the activation and execution of goals controlled by the BDI engine; and the direct and indirect interaction with other agents in the simulation.

The simulation incorporates various types of agents into the WellProdSim system, each with its own distinct goal. The "Peasant Family" agent is designed to represent the focus of peasant families on productivity and wellbeing. The "World" agent constructs a model of the land and environment in which these families carry out their work. The "Bank" agent simulates the financial mechanisms peasant families use, while the "Market" agent replicates the different marketplaces where these families trade their products or purchase inputs. The "Society" agent emulates various factors, including associations, government, and education, that impact the productivity and wellbeing of the Peasant Family. The "Perturbation" agent introduces either positive or negative disturbances to the other agents. Finally, the roles of the "wpsViewer" and "wpsControl" agents are to display the states of the simulation and oversee its management and regulation, respectively.

Considering the previous points, it is possible that some resources used or generated by the agents are limited and the competition for them generates conflicts. Therefore, mechanisms were implemented to manage the interactions between the different agents and avoid possible failures in the simulator, increasing its proximity to reality without neglecting the quality of development. The following subsection introduces the interactions between the simulation agents.

3.1 Multi-agent System Interactions

In WellProdSim, the interactions between the different agents play an important role in the operation and outcome of the simulations. In fact, the dynamics of their interactions is what allows the system to work efficiently and coherently.

To address the interactions in the multi-agent system, it is necessary to identify the relationships established among the agents. In the case of the Peasant Family agent, its interactions with the other agents are what generate productivity and social wellbeing as a result. For example, financial support or resources implemented by the Society agent (government) or the Bank agent can directly affect the agricultural practices of peasant families. While changes in prices by the Market agent directly impact income and indirectly the general wellbeing of the family. The Perturbation agent is necessary to create external events, for instance, to modify the weather conditions, that may affect the normal behavior of the activities of Peasant Family agent.

Remark that the interactions between agents can be collaborative or competitive in nature, depending on the situation and objectives of each agent. In consequence, interactions were analyzed and designed to reflect the reality of the socioeconomic and ecological environment in which the peasant families are located. Figure 1 presents the main agents of WellProdSim in a general scheme, including their interactions. Table 2 addresses the main interactions in more detail.

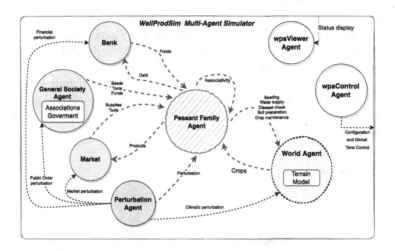

Fig. 1. WellProdSim MAS Interactions

Table 2. WellProdSim Interactions of the Peasant Family agent

Interaction	Agents	Shared Resources
Joint efforts	Peasant Family	Supplies
Seeding	World	Supplies, Tools
Crop care	World	Supplies, Tools
Harvest	World	Supplies, Tools
Land preparation	World	Supplies, Tools
Product sales	Market	Generated Biomass, Money
Provision of supplies	Market	Money
Obtaining profits	Society	Generated Biomass, Supplies, Money
Payment of debts	Society	Money

As expected, the Peasant Family agent, as the main agent of the simulation, has interactions to a greater or lesser extent with all the other agents of the social simulator. The goal model established for this agent will be presented in the next section.

3.2   Peasant's BDI Goal Model

In the previous section, the interactions between agents in the WellProdSim multi-agent system were discussed, highlighting the importance of communication and collaboration for the efficient operation of the simulator. Next, the goal model and the decision making process of the Peasant Family agent will be discussed in more detail.

In the design of the goals model, based on [31], a priority pyramid is used as an instrument to organize and rank at least 35 of the agent's goals according to their importance. The priority pyramid is graphically represented by depicting the most important goals at the top and the less relevant ones at the bottom. Our BDI goal model applied to the priority pyramid focuses on defining: the agent's beliefs about its environment, itself and other agents; the goals and objectives it wishes to achieve, the BDI desires; and the actions it must take to achieve the activated goals, the BDI intentions.

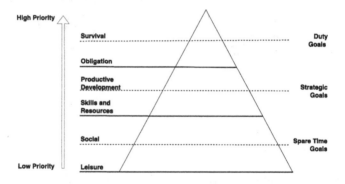

Fig. 2. Priority pyramid

The priority pyramid of the Peasant Family agent, presented in Fig. 2, has three main levels, each one of this levels is divided in to sub-levels. The agent's goals associated to the Duty level are divided into self Survival and Obligation to others. The specific goals included in this level are: DoVitals, DoHealthCare, SeekPurpose, SelfEvaluation, PayDebts and LookForMoney. They are defined as the first level with the highest priority. This means that these goals are fundamental for the well-being of the peasant family and therefore are the first to be given priority over the others.

At the second level of priority, there are the goals related to skills and labor, the Strategic goals. They are divided into Productive Development and Skills and Resources for productive development. Some of the specific goals included in this level are as follows: CheckCrops, PlantCrops, SellCrops, ProcessProducts, HarvestCrops, IrrigateCrops, ManagePests, SpendFamilyTime and ObtainSupplies. It is important to note that these goals do not have the same priority as the Duty goals, but they are important in order to be productive, increase wellbeing, and improve the quality of life of the Peasant Family agent.

Finally, at the third level of priority, there are the Spare Time goals that can be achieved if the peasant family has free time, including Social interactions and Leisure for entertainment. The specific goals included in this level are as follows: Communicate, LookForCollaboration, ProvideCollaboration, FindNews, and EngageInLeisureActivities. These goals have the lowest priority in the pyramid and are only considered when the higher level goals are not activated or have been satisfied.

However, it is important to notice that this list of specific goals is, for sure, incomplete, as human decision-making models are very complex due to the multi-factorial nature of human choices and decisions regarding ecology, contemplating economic aspects, non-economic benefits, social influence, social impact, emotions, uncertainty, knowledge about the environment, spatial location within the ecosystem, among others. Therefore, for practical reasons, only the goals directly related to the main objectives of the simulation, productivity and wellfare, can be included.

Once a better understanding of the interactions in the multi-agent system and the decision-making process of the agents in WellProdSim has been achieved, it is essential to consider the following section where it is explained how the modulating variables influence the behavior of the believes within the states of each of the agents in the simulation.

3.3   Modulating Variables

Modulating variables play an important role in the WellProdSim social simulator. These variables influence the relationship between the independent and dependent variables, adjusting the resulting values in the decision-making process and the behavior of the Peasant Family agent, according to the context.

These modulating variables define the values stored in the agent's beliefs; for instance, to model: Peasant Family Current Emotions, Peasant Family Food Auto Consumption Level, Peasant Family Livestock Affinity, and Peasant Family Collaboration Value, among others. The values of these variables are in the interval $[0,1]$. They are necessary to determine the predominant goals, the BDI intentions, at any instant in time. They change in value as the simulation progresses and alter the agent's beliefs as it interacts with others or its environment. For example, the health of farm animals and collaboration with neighbors may influence the decisions and well-being of the peasant family. As the beliefs change, desires and intentions are also updated and prioritized differently.

To represent the behaviour of peasant families in the simulator, the decision-making mechanism is supported by fuzzy logic rules. These rules, designed on the basis of expert knowledge, allow the agents to reflect human-like reasoning under different levels of uncertainty, thus determining fundamental decisions such as the optimal time to plant crops and the expected duration of the task. This mechanism, based on fuzzy logic, not only allows for adaptability and responsiveness to changes in the environment and the personal circumstances of the agents, but also contributes to a more realistic representation of their behaviour. It also increases the accuracy of the simulation by providing scalability and flexibility in modelling the decision-making processes of different types of agents.

4 Results

In order to validate the goal model of the Peasant Family agent, a set of basic experiments, intended to test the functionality of the priority pyramid, were implemented and performed. Several scenarios representing state variables at different levels were proposed to initialize the Peasant Family agent in the Well-ProdSim simulator.

The state variables are loaded by defining a text file in JSON format containing the initial states of the agent. From there, the agent interacted with the environment and received stimuli that lead it to make decisions and execute actions according to its decision-making process based on our BDI architecture and priority pyramid model presented in Sect. 3.

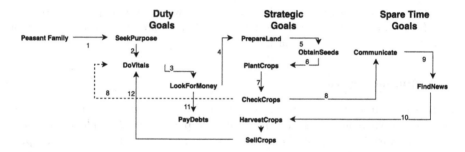

Fig. 3. Common BDI Goals Execution Route

This basic experiment setting was successful in order to verify the parallel behavior for the activation of the goals that potentially will become the intention to be achieved by the execution of agent's actions. In fact, the sequence of actions and decisions taken by the agent resulted coherent with what was expected according to the set of scenarios proposed. These results demonstrate the effectiveness of the proposed approach for simulation of the behavior of the Peasant Family agent.

In the basic experiment, 10 scenarios were created. One such scenario examines if the agent secures all necessary resources for crop sowing. The scenario initializes with the Peasant Family agent missing only seeds for cultivation. The agent performs as anticipated, activating its goals in a sequential manner. Upon starting, the agent sets its goal to cultivate the land, acquires the needed elements, like seeds, and carries out daily vital functions, which require monetary deductions and value adjustments. It recognizes survival needs, pursues food or money, prepares the land, and obtains seeds from Market or Society agents. The agent also interacts with the World agent to monitor crop growth and triggers goals such as neighborhood communication and news seeking. Ultimately, upon crop maturity, it executes the harvesting task and activates the selling products goal. A common execution route is depicted in Fig. 3.

5 Conclusions

This research presents an innovative, integrated methodology for designing and implementing an intelligent agent, specifically the Peasant Family Agent, in the context of social simulators such as WellProdSim. The model effectively integrates the BDI architecture, goal priority pyramid, fuzzy logic, and modulating variables to simulate the agent's decision-making process and behavior in a dynamic and complex environment.

The integrative approach has been successfully demonstrated, with the fusion of the goal pyramid and the BDI architecture proving particularly effective. This integration allows the strategic prioritization and organization of the farmer family's goals in relation to their importance and environmental circumstances, guiding agents towards the most significant goals and promoting coherent and effective decision making.

Furthermore, the implementation of the goal selection module strengthens the adaptability of the agents, enabling them to respond appropriately to environmental changes and interactions with other agents. The inclusion of fuzzy logic and modulating variables in the BDI architecture further enhances this adaptability by capturing and representing uncertainty and variability in the decision process. The adept representation of the dynamic behavior of the peasant family agent under varying conditions attests to the realism and adaptability of the proposed simulation methodology.

Looking ahead, future work aims to enhance the adaptability and realism of the agent by incorporating an emotional component as a complement to BDI reasoning. As the development of WellProdSim continues, it is expected that the proposed techniques and approaches can be applied to other domains and contexts, thereby contributing to advances in the fields of artificial intelligence and social simulation.

Acknowledgements. The author Jairo Enrique Serrano Castañeda thanks MINCIENCIAS, the Pontificia Universidad Javeriana and the Universidad Tenológica de Bolívar for the support received to pursue a doctoral degree within the programme "Becas de la Excelencia Doctoral del Bicentenario (corte 1)".

References

1. Cepal. Agroindustria y Pequeña Agricultura: Vínculos, Potencialidades y Oportunidades Comerciales (1998)
2. Edelman, M., Edelman, M.: Qué es un campesino? Qué son los campesinados? Un breve documento sobre cuestiones de definición. Revista Colombiana de Antropología **58**(1), 153–173 (2022)

3. Todaro, M.P., Smith, S.C.: EconomocDevelopment- Todaro (2012)
4. OMS. Cómo define la OMS la salud? (2020)
5. Aguilera Diaz, M.: Montes de María: Una subregión de economía campesina y empresarial. Banco de la Republica, p. 93 (2013)
6. Shannon, R.E.: Simulation: a survey with research suggestions. AIIE Trans. **7**(3), 289–301 (1975)
7. Silverman, E.: Analysis: frameworks and theories for social simulation. In: Methodological Investigations in Agent-Based Modelling. MS, vol. 13, pp. 107–123. Springer, Cham (2018). https://doi.org/10.1007/978-3-319-72408-9_6
8. Anbari, M.: An uncertain agent-based model for socio-ecological simulation of groundwater use in irrigation: a case study of Lake Urmia Basin, Iran. Agric. Water Manag. **249**, 106796 (2021)
9. Schiavon, E., Taramelli, A., Tornato, A.: Modelling stakeholder perceptions to assess green infrastructures potential in agriculture through fuzzy logic: a tool for participatory governance. Environ. Dev. **40**, 100671 (2021)
10. Zhang, G., Yang, D., Galanis, G., Androulakis, E.: Solar forecasting with hourly updated numerical weather prediction. Renew. Sustain. Energy Rev. **154**, 111768 (2022)
11. Schreinemachers, P., Berger, T., Aune, J.B.: Simulating soil fertility and poverty dynamics in Uganda: a bio-economic multi-agent systems approach. Ecol. Econ. **64**(2), 387–401 (2007)
12. Potting, R.P.J., Perry, J.N., Powell, W.: Insect behavioural ecology and other factors affecting the control efficacy of agro-ecosystem diversification strategies. Ecol. Model. **182**(2), 199–216 (2005)
13. Manasvi, J.K., Matai, R.: Agri-fresh supply chain management: a systematic literature review, pp. 449–457 (2022)
14. Kiesling, E., Günther, M., Stummer, C., Wakolbinger, L.M.: Agent-based simulation of innovation diffusion: a review. Cent. Eur. J. Oper. Res. **20**(2), 183–230 (2012)
15. Valencia, D.S., Serrano, J.E., Gonzalez, E.: SIMALL: emotional bdi model for customer simulation in a mall. In: Gonzalez, E., Curiel, M., Moreno, A., Carrillo-Ramos, A., Paez, R., Florez-Valencia, L. (eds.) Advances in Computing. CCC 2021. CCIS, vol. 1594, pp. 3–18. Springer, Cham (2022). https://doi.org/10.1007/978-3-031-19951-6_1
16. Bao, H., Dong, H., Jia, J., Peng, Y., Li, Q.: Impacts of land expropriation on the entrepreneurial decision-making behavior of land-lost peasants: an agent-based simulation. Habitat Int. **95**, 1 (2020)
17. Zasada, I., et al.: A conceptual model to integrate the regional context in landscape policy, management and contribution to rural development: literature review and European case study evidence. Geoforum **82**, 1–12 (2017)
18. Marvuglia, A., Bayram, A., Baustert, P., Gutiérrez, T.N., Igos, E.: Agent-based modelling to simulate farmers' sustainable decisions: farmers' interaction and resulting green consciousness evolution. J. Clean. Prod. **332**, 129847 (2022)
19. Bratman, M.E., Israel, D.J.,Pollack, M.E.: Pollack. Plans and resource-bounded practical reasoning. Comput. Intell. **4**(3), 349–355 (1988)
20. Muto, T.J., Bolivar, E.B., González, E.: BDI multi-agent based simulation model for social ecological systems. In: De La Prieta, F., et al. (eds.) PAAMS 2020. CCIS, vol. 1233, pp. 279–288. Springer, Cham (2020). https://doi.org/10.1007/978-3-030-51999-5_23

21. Berger, T.: Agent-based spatial models applied to agriculture: a simulation tool for technology diffusion, resource use changes and policy analysis. Agric. Econ. **25**(2–3), 245–260 (2001)

22. Caron-Lormier, G., Bohan, D.A., Dye, R., Hawes, C., Humphry, R.W., Raybould, A.: Modelling an ecosystem: the example of agro-ecosystems. Ecol. Model. **222**(5), 1163–1173 (2011)

23. Grevenitis, K., Sakellariou, I., Kefalas, P.: Emotional agents make a (Bank) run. In: Bassiliades, N., Chalkiadakis, G., de Jonge, D. (eds.) EUMAS/AT -2020. LNCS (LNAI), vol. 12520, pp. 171–187. Springer, Cham (2020). https://doi.org/10.1007/978-3-030-66412-1_12

24. Marley, J., et al.: Does human education reduce conflicts between humans and bears? An agent-based modelling approach. Ecol. Model. **343**, 15–24 (2017)

25. Ostrom, E.: A general framework for analyzing sustainability of social-ecological systems (2009)

26. Yuan, S., Li, X., Du, E.: Effects of farmers' behavioral characteristics on crop choices and responses to water management policies. Agric. Water Manag. **247**, 106693 (2021)

27. González, E., Avila, J., Bustacara, C.: BESA: behavior-oriented, event-driven, social-based agent framework. Communicating Process Architectures (2003)

28. Hevner, A.R., March, S.T., Park, J., Ram, S.: Design science in information systems research. Des. Sci. IS Res. MIS Q. **28**(1), 75 (2004)

29. Miguel, E., Torres, M.: AOPOA-Organizational Approach for Agent Oriented Programming. Technical report (2006)

30. De Silva, L., Meneguzzi, F.R., Logan, B.: BDI agent architectures: a survey. In: IJCAI International Joint Conference on Artificial Intelligence, vol. 2021-Janua, no. Line 3, pp. 4914–4921 (2020)

31. Gonzalez, A., Angel, R., Gonzalez, E.: BDI concurrent architecture orientedto goal management. In: 2013 8th Computing Colombian Conference (8CCC), pp. 1–6. IEEE, August 2013

Discovering Key Aspects to Reduce Employee Turnover Using a Predictive Model

Paula Andrea Cárdenas López$^{(\boxtimes)}$⬨ and Marta Silvia Tabares Betancur⬨

Universidad EAFIT, Medellín, Colombia
paulacardenas_25@hotmail.com

Abstract. High employee turnover is a phenomenon that occurs in different types of companies and often leads to losses that could affect the organization's productive continuity. This situation leads to the understanding, with solid evidence, of the factors that influence employees to leave their jobs and, thus, develop talent retention strategies proactively. This article proposes a predictive model to identify the most relevant factors that could cause employee turnover, specifically in the logistics process of a food and beverage production company. To achieve the objective, the CRISP-DM methodology was applied. Initially, various types of variables were identified, such as demographic, contractual, and payroll-related factors (N = 1517, period: 2017–2022). Then, five machine learning models, namely Logistic Regression, Random Forest, XGBoost, SVM, and AdaBoost, were trained, and optimal hyperparameters were used to improve the models' performance and generalization. The performance evaluation of these models was conducted using classification metrics and the construction of confidence intervals for the accuracy metric through non-parametric Bootstrap. The results obtained demonstrate that the XGBoost and Random Forest models show the highest AUC value, with a result of 99%. This indicates that variables such as work environment, years of service, salary, workplace location, and monthly salary deductions are the most significant factors influencing the evaluated human talent to leave their job. Therefore, it is possible to conclude that the aforementioned two models are accurate and reliable for predicting employee turnover in the logistics process of the analyzed company.

Keywords: Employee turnover · Machine Learning · ROC curve · Non-parametric Bootstrap · Survival analysis

1 Introduction

Voluntary employee turnover is one of the most studied topics in academic literature on organizational management. Aguado [1] presents this challenge as one of the main hurdles for human resources managers in the era of talent competition. Jain and Nayyar [16] explain that employee turnover represents a significant

M. Tabares et al. (Eds.): CCC 2023, CCIS 1924, pp. 380–395, 2024.
https://doi.org/10.1007/978-3-031-47372-2_30

challenge due to its negative impact on productivity, goal achievement, and competitiveness for organizations. For this reason, it is important to understand the reasons that lead employees to leave their positions and, based on that knowledge, redesign their human resources strategies and policies.

Garg et al. [14] propose focusing the prediction on turnover intentions through the use of machine learning models. They suggest a wide range of factors that may be related to the probability of withdrawal, which varies based on employees' location, culture, and job profiles. Sisodia et al. [23] mention that work-related factors such as the number of promotions, salary increase, latest evaluation, tenure in the company, and working hours are fundamental attributes for the classification models used to predict turnover. They also include additional attributes created based on hypotheses, such as employees with promotions but no salary change, employees without promotions in the last 5 years, among others. Liu et al. [21] identified that factors such as age, gender, place of birth, marital status, and family responsibilities are related to the individual and impact turnover. According to the above, most of the data comes from human resource database systems that are not very efficient in prediction and modeling, resulting in less accurate models. Therefore, to achieve more accurate predictions, a machine learning model, specifically XGBoost, is proposed, known for its robustness and ability to significantly improve predictions [16].

However, the previous proposals do not consider external variables such as the unemployment rate, poverty index, and Gini coefficient as relevant factors when understanding employee turnover. In this article, several supervised learning algorithms were applied with the aim of classifying whether an employee will leave the company or not. Additionally, the most important features in the models were identified, which can serve as a basis for decision-makers to improve employee turnover rate. The study also employed the survival analysis technique with the Kaplan-Meier approach to understand how an event is impacted over time.

Several classification models were used, such as Logistic Regression, Random Forest, XGBoost, SVM, and AdaBoost, which were tuned with optimal hyperparameters to improve evaluation metrics. The model performance was assessed using metrics such as accuracy, precision, recall, F1-score, area under the curve (AUC), and 5-fold cross-validation. Additionally, confidence intervals for accuracy were generated using non-parametric Bootstrap.

The CRISP-DM methodology was employed for the development of this study, providing a solid structure for prediction and machine learning projects. Its flexibility allows for iteration and error correction in different phases, addressing challenges in feature extraction, data cleaning, and model performance, seeking continuous improvements at each step. This adaptability is crucial to achieve accurate and reliable results in model development [18].

The document is organized as follows: Sect. 2 presents a brief review of the literature associated with employee turnover. Section 3 presents the development of the proposed model using the CRISP-DM methodology. Section 4 presents the discussion and conclusions.

2   Literature Review

In recent years, organizations have recognized the need to predict employee turnover and identify the key factors that contribute to retaining their workforce in the future. Alaskar et al. [9] have shown that this significantly improves the accuracy of the models. In this study, the most effective model was found to be SVM with SelectKBest feature selection, achieving an accuracy of 97%, followed by Decision Tree with RFE feature selection and an accuracy of 96.2%. Yahía et al. [3], based on the previous approach, found that the Vapnik-Chervonenkis (VC) model achieved the highest accuracy at 99%, followed by Random Forest at 98.3%. The researchers suggest that these types of models should be updated in real-time, as employee characteristics change constantly, thereby impacting the model's results.

On the other hand, Zhao et al. [27] identify that predicting employee turnover has several complexities, including the trade-off between the number of variables and the number of records. In some cases, the Hughes phenomenon, also known as the curse of dimensionality, may arise. In this case, they suggest carefully handling and understanding the dataset to deliver models and results that align with reality.

Srivastava and Eachempati [24] aim to determine the effectiveness of deep learning compared to machine learning using models such as Random Forest and Gradient Boosting. The obtained results are validated using a regression model and a Fuzzy Analytic Hierarchy Process (AHP) that considers the relative importance of the variables. The findings reveal that deep neural networks achieve an accuracy of 91.6%, whereas Random Forest and Gradient Boosting reach 82.5% and 85.4%, respectively.

Cai et al. [5] propose the approach of DBGE (Dynamic Bipartite Graph Embedding) as a method that combines employee data obtained from professional social networks with company information. In this approach, the history of employees' job experiences, including start and end dates, is modeled as a dynamic bipartite graph, which is then used to generate machine learning models. By implementing this approach, the accuracy of the models was improved by 1.5%, with Random Forest being the best-performing model with an accuracy of 89.3%.

Fan et al. [12] propose predicting turnover using unsupervised learning through a hybrid method known as Self-Organizing Map (SOM). This method clusters individual features using backpropagation neural networks, achieving an accuracy of 92%.

3   Development of the Proposed Model

For the development of the model, the CRISP-DM methodology (Cross-Industry Standard Process for Data Mining) [2] is used, specifically for the phases of business understanding, data understanding, data preparation, modeling, and evaluation. The deployment phase is presented as a proposal for future work to put the insights generated by the models into practical use within the organization.

3.1 Business Understanding

The purpose of this article is to address the problem of employee turnover in a logistics process of a food and beverage production company in Colombia, specifically focusing on three workplaces located in the cities of Bello, Bogotá, and Yumbo.

Employee turnover poses various challenges for the organization, including tangible financial costs related to the hiring and training process of new employees, as well as intangible costs associated with the loss of knowledge and skills acquired through experience. Additionally, this turnover can negatively impact productivity and corporate image.

Therefore, the objective of this study is to predict whether an employee will voluntarily leave the company and, at the same time, identify key factors influencing the decision to leave. This will provide a solid and evidence-based foundation for human resources managers to make strategic decisions regarding talent retention, based on data and analysis, enabling them to build an organizational management system with respect to human resources.

3.2 Data Understanding

The dataset comprises information collected from January 2017 to July 2022 and includes data from 1,517 unique employees. Each of these employees is associated with 32 different variables. The classification label 'Turnover' is used to indicate whether an employee leaves the company or not. Table 1 shows the collected variables along with their corresponding descriptions.

Table 1. Description of dataset variables

Variable	Description
Employee Id	Employee identification
Joining Date	Date of joining the company
Leaving Date	Date of leaving the company
Age at retirement	Employee's age at the time of retirement
Gender	Female, Male
Department	Employee's area (General Warehouse, finished goods warehouse, Dispatch, Distribution, Vehicle Maintenance)
City	Workplace location (Bello, Bogotá, Yumbo)
Job position	Job position (Operator, Driver, Warehouse Clerk, distribution Supervisor, among others)
Employment contract type	Contract type (Fixed, Indefinite)
Employment group	Employment group (Direct, Temporary)
Salary	Monthly Income
Marital status	Marital status (Married, Divorced, Separated, Single, Common-law)

(*continued*)

Table 1. (*continued*)

Variable	Description
Children	(0 = No, 1 = Yes)
Years at company	Total years in the company
Promotions	Internal promotions during the employment contract
Salary range structure	Employee's position relative to the salary curve (1 = underpaid below 80%, 2 = paid fairly between 80% and 120%, 3 = overpaid above 120%)
Distance From Home	The Distance From Work To Home
Climate surveys	Factors evaluated in the organizational climate survey (1 = Motivation and recognition, 2 = Learning, 3 = Collaboration, 4 = Commitment and Identity, 5 = Working Conditions, 6 = Job Relationship, 7 = Leadership, 8 = Communication)
Exit Survey	Reasons for retirement marked by the employee at the time of leaving (0 = Work Environment, 1 = Personal or Professional Growth, 2 = Development and Training, 3 = Distance From Work To Home, 4 = Work Flexibility, 5 = Current Job Duties, 6 = Working Hours, Workload and Tools, 7 = Family Reasons, 8 = Not Registered, 9 = Recognition and Appreciation, 10 = Relationship with Managers, 11 = Salary or Benefits)
Workplace accident	An employee voluntarily leaves if they have absences due to work accidents exceeding 3 days. (0 = No, 1 = Yes)
Maternity/paternity leave	An employee voluntarily leaves if they return from a parental leave before 6 months. (0 = No, 1 = Yes)
Absenteeism record	An employee voluntarily leaves if they have a record of absences in the last 3 months before their retirement. (0 = No, 1 = Yes)
Return from vacation	An employee voluntarily leaves if they return from vacation the following month. (0 = No, 1 = Yes)
Sundays and holidays worked	An employee voluntarily leaves if they work more than 3 Sundays and holidays per month, one month before their retirement. (0 = No, 1 = Yes)
Monthly overtime hours limit	An employee voluntarily leaves if they generate more than 48 overtime hours per month. (0 = No, 1 = Yes)
Overtime hours increment	An employee voluntarily leaves if they experience a significant 30% increase in overtime hours. (0 = No, 1 = Yes)
Monthly deductions	Percentage of monthly deductions relative to their income.
Unused vacation days	An employee voluntarily leaves if they have more than two periods of unused vacation. (0 = No, 1 = Yes)
Benefit usage	An employee voluntarily leaves if they have not claimed any benefits from the pact or convention in the last year. (0 = No, 1 = Yes)
Job position tenure	An employee voluntarily leaves if they have remained in the same position for the last 3 years. (0 = No, 1 = Yes)

Additionally, three external variables obtained from DANE related to the labor market are available: unemployment rate [10], monetary poverty, and Gini coefficient [11]. These variables, which experience variations over time, have been integrated into the dataset by assigning to each record the annual unemployment indicator value, uniformly distributed throughout each corresponding retirement year.

It is important to mention that the salary variable was captured considering each individual's salary at the time of their retirement. Additionally, the annual increment adjustment that the company applied was used to bring the salary value of those who retired before 2022 to the current value. In this way, a fair and up-to-date comparison of salaries was ensured for employees who made the decision to retire at different times, allowing for a more accurate and consistent evaluation of their influence on the target variable.

As proposed by Alaskar [9], **Exploratory Data Analysis (EDA)** was employed to identify relevant patterns influencing both employee turnover and the relationships between variables, using graphical techniques and correlation analysis.

During the exploration, it was found that the percentage of employees who voluntarily left was higher compared to those who stayed, with 67% and 33%, respectively. This indicates a class imbalance in the output label, which will be addressed with SMOTE (Synthetic Minority Oversampling TEchnique) in the data preparation step.

Next, some relevant findings are presented:

- The finished product storage process has the largest number of employees, representing 66.5% of the total workforce, followed by the distribution processes with 15%.
- 80% of the employees hold operator positions.
- The marital status of employees shows that 45% are single, while 40% are in a common-law relationship.
- The analysis of distance between home and workplace reveals that employees in Bello have an intermediate distance of 6.42 km. On the other hand, employees in Bogotá have a longer median distance of 10.22 km, while employees in Yumbo have the longest median distance of all, with 12.16 km.
- A total of 40.23% of the retired personnel who have completed the retirement survey or interview have indicated that their main reason for leaving the company is related to long working hours, demanding work schedules, and the physical burden associated with their job. This is in addition to considering both professional and personal growth.

When reviewing the graphical representation of variables to identify outliers in the dataset, it can be observed from Fig. 1 that the median age of retired employees is 28 years, while for active employees, it is 35 years.

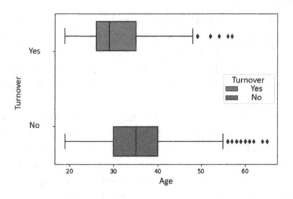

Fig. 1. Boxplot turnover vs age

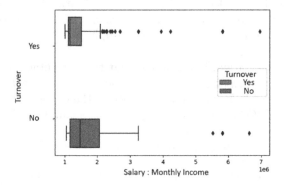

Fig. 2. BoxPlot turnover vs Salary: monthly income

The analysis of Fig. 2 reveals significant differences in salaries between retired and active employees. While the median salary is lower for retired employees (1,161,000), active employees show a higher median (1,471,000) and a wider interquartile range (1,161,000–2,064,000).

In this phase, the statistical technique used to study the time it takes for an event to occur is also included, known as **Survival Analysis**. Survival analysis methods are mainly used to analyze prospective data collected over time, where the time to the occurrence of an event of interest is recorded, allowing for the evaluation of the relationship between explanatory variables and the occurrence of the event, as addressed by Kartsonaki [20].

According to the Kaplan-Meier (KM) or product-limit approach [19], the survival analysis will be applied in this article, as its non-parametric method does not make assumptions about the distribution of the data but rather performs the estimation that best fits the data. The estimation is defined by:

$$\hat{P}(t) = \prod_r \left[\frac{(N-r)}{N-r+1} \right] \tag{1}$$

where N is the number of observations (either censored or not), in ascending order of magnitude $0 \leq t_1' \leq t_2' \leq ... \leq t_N'$, where r assumes those values $t_r' \leq t$, for which t_r' measures the time to event occurrence. This estimation is the distribution that maximizes the likelihood of the observations.

The main objective of this survival analysis is to understand the factors that influence the duration of time that employees remain in the company before leaving. In Fig. 3, it can be observed that employees hired through temporary agencies have a 0.6 probability of surviving for 1 year, while directly hired employees by the company have a 50% probability of lasting for 6 years.

The KM curve in Fig. 4 displays the survival curves by marital status, where it can be seen that Single employees have a survival curve that declines faster over time compared to those who are in a Common-Law Relationship or Married. Therefore, Married employees have a higher probability of survival over time.

3.3 Data Preparation

Preparing the data before carrying out the modeling increases the chances of obtaining accurate results. In this case, a preprocessing phase was executed, which included detecting missing values, outliers, analyzing correlations between features, as well as data transformation and normalization.

It's important to highlight the results of the correlation analysis that reveal significant associations between the following variables:

- There is a strong correlation between the Gini Index and the Monetary Poverty Indicator.
- A notable correlation is observed between the Unemployment Rate and the Monetary Poverty Indicator.
- There is also a significant relationship between Retirement Age and Years Worked.

Some variables mentioned in the data understanding phase, including workplace accidents, maternity leave, absenteeism history, vacation returns, monthly holidays, monthly overtime limit, overtime increase, unused vacations, benefit utilization, and tenure, were generated by constructing new features from existing data. These new features not only enriched the dataset but were also developed with the target variable in mind, which is whether a person decides to retire from the company or not. As a result, these created variables not only enhance our understanding of the data but also directly contribute to the quality and relevance of the subsequent analysis and modeling.

Significant to note is that the dataset exhibited class imbalance in the output label, as only 33% of employees remained in the company. To address this issue, the SMOTE (Synthetic Minority Oversampling TEchnique) technique was implemented, as introduced in the study by Chawla [6]. This technique generates synthetic samples by exploring the feature space instead of the data space, thus overcoming the problem of overfitting. It was the first technique that introduced new samples into the training set to improve the data.

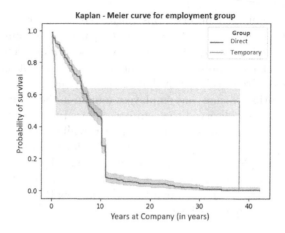

Fig. 3. A Survival Curve Based on Employment Group

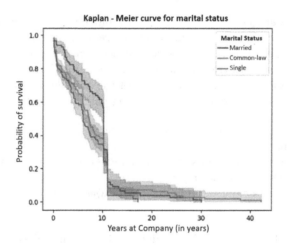

Fig. 4. A Survival Curve Based on Marital Status

3.4   Modeling

In this stage, a set of classification models are executed to predict employee turnover, such as Logistic Regression [17], SVM [15], Random Forest [4], XGBoost [7], and Adaboost [13]. The optimization of each model was carried out using GridSearchCV, aiming to find the optimal combination of hyperparameters that maximizes the model's performance [22]. The best values and combinations of parameters for each model, based on their characteristics, are presented in Table 2:

Table 2. Optimal hyperparameters

Classifiers	Hyperparameters
Logistic Regression	'C': 1.0, 'penalty': 'l1'
Random Forest	'criterion': 'gini', 'max_depth': 22, 'n_estimators': 100
XGBoost	'learning_rate': 0.1, 'max_depth': 15, 'n_estimators': 200
SVM	'C': 10, 'kernel': 'rbf'
AdaBoost	'base_estimator_max_depth': 15, 'learning_rate': 0.1, 'n_estimators': 50

The dataset was partitioned into training and testing sets, where 70% of the total records, equivalent to 1,402, were used for training the models using the **SMOTE** technique. The remaining 30%, corresponding to 456 records, were reserved for the testing phase. This division allowed for a significant portion of data to be used for training the models and properly evaluating their performance on an independent sample during the testing phase.

Additionally, the main features of each model were detected, revealing their contribution in terms of weight or influence on the predictions, using their relative importance. For this purpose, the feature_importances_ function was employed, as mentioned by Liu [21].

Table 3 presents the ten most important features for each model. A high contribution of organizational climate is observed, as well as the variable Absenteeism record, which refers to the hypothesis about the incidence of increased absenteeism 3 months before voluntary departure, among others. These findings highlight the importance of these features in predicting turnover and provide valuable insights into the key factors that influence employees' decision to leave the organization.

Table 3. Top 10 key features by model

Classifiers	Feature Importances
Logistic Regression	Organizational Climate, Expired Vacation Days, Position: 'Operator', Reason for Departure: 'Current Job Responsibilities', Position: 'Sales Driver', City: 'Bello', Employment Group: 'Directs', Employment Group: 'Temporaries', Department: 'Vehicle Maintenance', Tenure in Position
Random Forest	Organizational Climate, Years at Company, Monthly Deductions, Retirement Age, Monthly Sunday Premiums, Distance from Home, Absenteeism Record, Salary, Employment Group: 'Directs', Monthly overtime hours limit
XGBoost	Organizational Climate, Years at Company, Salary, City: 'Bogotá', Monthly Deductions, City: 'Yumbo', Expired Vacation Days, Absenteeism Record, Reason for Departure: 'Development and Training', Children
SVM	Organizational Climate, Tenure in Position, Employment Group: 'Temporaries', Absenteeism Record, Department: 'Distribution', Expired Vacation Days, Monthly overtime hours limit, Position: 'Operator I', Department: 'Finished goods warehouse', Position: 'Sales Driver'
AdaBoost	Organizational Climate, Years at Company, Salary, Monthly Deductions, Expired Vacation Days, City: 'Yumbo', Distance from Home, Absenteeism Record, Position: 'Distribution Analyst', Gender: 'Male'

3.5 Evaluation

To evaluate the performance of each model, appropriate classification metrics such as accuracy, precision, recall, F1-score, and AUC were employed. These metrics provided a comprehensive view of the predictive model's performance, allowing for the assessment of its ability to make accurate predictions and distinguish between positive and negative classes, as proposed by Wang and Zhi [25].

The validation of the model training results was carried out using the test dataset, where XGBoost achieved the highest F1-score of 97.38%, followed by Random Forest with 96.77%. Table 4 presents the evaluation metric results on the test dataset, specifically for the "Turnover" target label.

Table 4. Prediction analysis result

Classifiers	Accuracy	Precision	Recall	F1-score	AUC
Logistic Regression	0.8552	0.8722	0.9130	0.8921	0.9396
Random Forest	0.9556	0.9584	0.9720	0.9677	0.9891
XGBoost	0.9649	0.9520	0.9966	0.9738	0.9880
SVM	0.8793	0.8785	0.9417	0.9090	0.9518
AdaBoost	0.9517	0.9361	0.9932	0.9638	0.9529

In order to assess whether the model could improve its performance, k-fold cross-validation with $k = 5$ was employed. In this step, the dataset was divided into five equal parts, with four parts used for model training and the remaining part as the validation set. This process was repeated five times, each time using a different part as the validation set. Finally, the accuracy results from the five iterations were averaged to obtain a final estimation of the model's performance (Table 5).

XGBoost is the model with the highest average accuracy in the cross-validation, followed by AdaBoost. See Table 6 for details.

Table 5. Cross-validation Results - Accuracy

Classifiers	Accuracy
Logistic Regression	0.8630
Random Forest	0.9550
XGBoost	0.9658
SVM	0.8994
AdaBoost	0.9657

As part of the validation process for the evaluation metrics of the models, the **Non-Parametric Bootstrap** method was used to construct confidence intervals for the accuracy of each model. Wasserman [26] introduces the Bootstrap as a method used to estimate the variance and distribution of a statistic $T_n = g(X_1, ..., X_n)$, also used in constructing confidence intervals. In this case, the interval was constructed using percentile intervals, defined by:

$$C_n = \left(T^*_{(B\alpha/2)}, T^*_{(B(1-\alpha/2))} \right) \tag{2}$$

C_n: the interval is called the confidence interval, with n denoting the sample size, and C signifying that it is an interval.

$(T^*_{(B\alpha/2)}$: It is the $\alpha/2$ percentile of the bootstrap statistics. It represents the value corresponding to the lower limit of the confidence interval.

$T^*_{(B(1-\alpha/2))}$: It is the $(1 - \alpha/2)$ percentile of the bootstrap statistics. It represents the value corresponding to the upper limit of the confidence interval.

By employing this method, 1,000 random Bootstrap samples were generated with a 95% confidence level to calculate the confidence intervals for accuracy. The outcomes reveal that the accuracy estimation for XGBoost is more precise in comparison to the other classifiers mentioned, as its confidence interval is narrower than theirs. Additionally, it can be observed that the confidence intervals of XGBoost, Random Forest, and AdaBoost overlap, indicating that there is no statistically significant difference between the metric estimations. This places XGBoost and Random Forest as the top-performing models. See Table 6.

Table 6. Confidence Intervals of Accuracy with Bootstrap

Classifiers	Accuracy
Logistic Regression	[0.8531, 0.8882]
Random Forest	[0.9298, 0.9583]
XGBoost	[0.9408, 0.9649]
SVM	[0.8377, 0.8750]
AdaBoost	[0.9057, 0.9605]

Lastly, the ROC curve is analyzed to assess the balance between true positives and false positives in the test set. In Fig. 5, it can be observed that XGBoost yields the best results, as it has the highest area under the curve (AUC) with a value of 99%, followed by Random Forest. However, XGBoost is chosen due to its cutoff point being closer to the upper-left vertex of the graph, indicating a high true positive rate (TPR) and a low false positive rate (FPR) [8].

In Fig. 6, the most significant variables in predicting employee turnover with the XGBoost model are shown. It is evident that Leadership, as measured through organizational climate, years at company, and Salary as monthly income are the variables with the highest importance when predicting turnover. This implies that these variables have a positive or negative influence on the decision to leave the company.

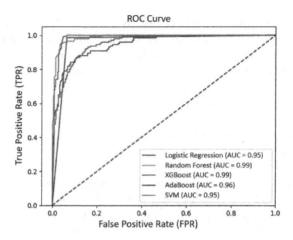

Fig. 5. ROC Curve by model

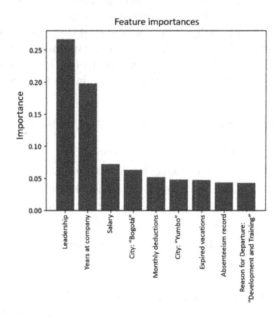

Fig. 6. Weight of variables based on XGBoost

4   Discussion and Conclusions

This article presents a method for predicting whether an employee will leave the company or not, along with the most influential factors in their decision. The method involved the execution of five predictive classification models, namely Logistic Regression, Random Forest, XGBoost, SVM, and AdaBoost. Various important classification metrics were examined to find the best model, and cross-validation and non-parametric confidence intervals were applied using the percentile Bootstrap method.

Based on the findings, it is concluded that the XGBoost model is superior in this type of problem, achieving an accuracy of 96.58% in cross-validation, proving to be efficient and high-performing. Precisely identifying employees with a higher probability of leaving the company is essential for making strategic decisions. By recognizing these potential employees, decision-makers can implement proactive measures, such as retention plans, as early as possible.

An initial focus for these strategies should be on the five most important characteristics identified in all models: work climate, absenteeism record, unused vacation days, years of service, and salary. Additionally, the insights obtained during the exploratory data analysis can serve as valuable inputs for understanding the workforce.

The project also includes a non-parametric survival analysis using the Kaplan Meier approach, which highlights the importance of employee contract type and marital status concerning their tenure in the company. This can further inform and tailor human resource strategies.

In the future, it is expected that this method will be used in all organizations, creating a data-driven decision-making system regarding human resources, enabling the focus on retention strategies and even attracting new talent.

References

1. Aguado, D.: HR Analytics: Teoría y práctica para una analítica de recursos humanos con impacto, vol. 1. ESIC Editorial, primera edición edn. (2018)
2. Ayele, W.: Adapting CRISP-DM for idea mining a data mining process for generating ideas using a textual dataset. Int. J. Adv. Comput. Sci. Appl. **11**, 20–32 (2020). https://doi.org/10.14569/IJACSA.2020.0110603
3. Ben Yahia, N., Jihen, H., Colomo-Palacios, R.: From big data to deep data to support people analytics for employee attrition prediction. IEEE Access **9**, 60447–60458 (2021). https://doi.org/10.1109/ACCESS.2021.3074559
4. Breiman, L.: Random forests. Mach. Learn. **45**, 5–32 (2001). https://doi.org/10.1023/A:1010933404324
5. Cai, X., et al.: DBGE: employee turnover prediction based on dynamic bipartite graph embedding. IEEE Access **8**, 10390–10402 (2020). https://doi.org/10.1109/ACCESS.2020.2965544
6. Chawla, N.V.: Data mining for imbalanced datasets: an overview. In: Maimon, O., Rokach, L. (eds.) Data Mining and Knowledge Discovery Handbook, pp. 875–886. Springer, Boston (2009). https://doi.org/10.1007/978-0-387-09823-4_45
7. Chen, T., Guestrin, C.: XGBoost: a scalable tree boosting system, vol. 13–17-Augu, pp. 785–794 (2016). https://doi.org/10.1145/2939672.2939785
8. Choudhury, P., Allen, R., Endres, M.: Machine learning for pattern discovery in management research. Strateg. Manag. J. **42**, 30–57 (2021). https://doi.org/10.1002/smj.3215
9. Alaskar, L., Crane, M., Alduailij, M.: Employee turnover prediction using machine learning. In: Alfaries, A., Mengash, H., Yasar, A., Shakshuki, E. (eds.) ICC 2019. CCIS, vol. 1097, pp. 301–316. Springer, Cham (2019). https://doi.org/10.1007/978-3-030-36365-9_25

10. DANE: Empleo y desempleo (2022). https://www.dane.gov.co/index.php/estadi sticas-por-tema/mercado-laboral/empleo-y-desempleo
11. DANE: Pobreza monetaria y pobreza monetaria extrema (2022). https://www. dane.gov.co/index.php/estadisticas-por-tema/pobreza-y-condiciones-de-vida/ pobreza-monetaria
12. Fan, C.Y., Fan, P.S., Chan, T.Y., Chang, S.H.: Using hybrid data mining and machine learning clustering analysis to predict the turnover rate for technology professionals. Expert Syst. Appl. **39**, 8844–8851 (2012). https://doi.org/10.1016/ j.eswa.2012.02.005
13. Freund, Y., Schapire, R.E.: A decision-theoretic generalization of on-line learn- ing and an application to boosting. J. Comput. Syst. Sci. **55**(1), 119–139 (1997). https://doi.org/10.1006/jcss.1997.1504. https://www.sciencedirect.com/science/ article/pii/S002200009791504X
14. Garg, S., Sinha, S., Kar, A.K., Mani, M.: A review of machine learning applications in human resource management. Int. J. Product. Perform. Manag. **71**(5), 1590– 1610 (2022)
15. Hastie, T., Tibshirani, R., Friedman, J.: The Elements of Statistical Learning. Springer, New York (2009). https://doi.org/10.1007/978-0-387-84858-7
16. Jain, R., Nayyar, A.: Predicting employee attrition using XGBoost machine learning approach, pp. 113–120 (2018). https://doi.org/10.1109/SYSMART.2018. 8746940
17. James, G., Witten, D., Hastie, T., Tibshirani, R.: An Introduction to Statisti- cal Learning, vol. 103. Springer, New York (2013). https://doi.org/10.1007/978-1- 4614-7138-7
18. Kannengiesser, U., Gero, J.: Modelling the design of models: an example using CRISP-DM. Proc. Des. Soc. **3**, 2705–2714 (2023). https://doi.org/10.1017/pds. 2023.271
19. Kaplan, E.L., Meier, P.: Nonparametric estimation from incomplete observations. J. Am. Stat. Assoc. **53**(282), 457–481 (1958). http://www.jstor.org/stable/2281868
20. Kartsonaki, C.: Survival analysis. Diagnostic Histopathol. **22**(7), 263–270 (2016). https://doi.org/10.1016/j.mpdhp.2016.06.005. https://www.sciencedirect. com/science/article/pii/S1756231716300639, mini-Symposium: Medical Statistics
21. Liu, J., Long, Y., Fang, M., He, R., Wang, T., Chen, G.: Analyzing employee turnover based on job skills, pp. 16–21 (2018). https://doi.org/10.1145/3224207. 3224209
22. Probst, P., Wright, M.N., Boulesteix, A.L.: Hyperparameters and tuning strategies for random forest. Wiley Interdisc. Rev. Data Min. Knowl. Discov. **9**(3), e1301 (2019)
23. Sisodia, D., Vishwakarma, S., Pujahari, A.: Evaluation of machine learning mod- els for employee churn prediction, pp. 1016–1020 (2018). https://doi.org/10.1109/ ICICI.2017.8365293
24. Srivastava, D.P., Eachempati, P.: Intelligent employee retention system for attri- tion rate analysis and churn prediction: an ensemble machine learning and multi- criteria decision-making approach. J. Glob. Inf. Manag. **29**, 1–29 (2021). https:// doi.org/10.4018/JGIM.20211101.oa23
25. Wang, X., Zhi, J.: A machine learning-based analytical framework for employee turnover prediction. J. Manag. Anal. **8**, 351–370 (2021). https://doi.org/10.1080/ 23270012.2021.1961318

26. Wasserman, L.: All of Nonparametric Statistics. Springer, New York (2006). https://doi.org/10.1007/0-387-30623-4
27. Zhao, Y., Hryniewicki, M.K., Cheng, F., Fu, B., Zhu, X.: Employee turnover prediction with machine learning: a reliable approach. In: Arai, K., Kapoor, S., Bhatia, R. (eds.) IntelliSys 2018. AISC, vol. 869, pp. 737–758. Springer, Cham (2019). https://doi.org/10.1007/978-3-030-01057-7_56

Findby: An Application for Accessibility and Inclusive Exploration

David Madrid Restrepo⬡, Mariana Vasquez Escobar⬡,
Diego Alejandro Vanegas González⬡, and Liliana González-Palacio$^{(\boxtimes)}$⬡

EAFIT University, Medellín, Colombia
{dmadridr,mvasqueze,davanegasg,lgonzalez8}@eafit.edu.co

Abstract. Inclusion and accessibility are essential human rights that should be upheld in all aspects of life, including access to both public and private spaces. Unfortunately, in Colombia, the rights of people with disabilities are often marginalized and neglected, with only 7 out of 100 Colombians having disabilities in 2022. Furthermore, despite 36.9% of people with disabilities in Colombia living with reduced mobility, however, the cities remain largely inaccessible for them. This paper introduces Findby, a web application designed for users with reduced mobility, aiming to provide information on the accessibility of places and promote inclusive exploration through challenges and a reward system. The app utilizes user-centered design and leverages technology to improve access to both public and private spaces. Findby's key features include accessibility markers, user-generated content, review comments, ratings, and customized route-based challenges, making the application engaging and user-friendly. Findby has the potential to contribute significantly to improving accessibility and inclusion for individuals with reduced mobility. Future work includes expanding the user community, improving the accuracy of accessibility information, incorporating accessibility information for private spaces, integrating additional features, and expanding globally to promote inclusivity and accessibility worldwide.

Keywords: Accessibility · Reduced mobility · Web application ·
Inclusion · User community · Accessibility bookmarks · Personalized
routes · Inclusive exploration · User-centered design

1 Introduction

1.1 A Subsection Sample

Inclusion and accessibility are fundamental human rights that should be upheld in all aspects of life, including access to public and private spaces. Regrettably, in Colombia, the rights of people with disabilities are violated in approximately

Supported by EAFIT University.

7 out of every 100 cases as of 2022 [1]. This highlights the urgent need to address this issue and ensure equal participation in society for all individuals, regardless of their physical abilities. Notably, 36.9% of people with disabilities in Colombia face reduced mobility, yet the country's cities largely remain inaccessible to them [2]. While several mobile applications on the market provide accessibility information, they were not specifically designed for individuals with reduced mobility; as a result, lack relevant information for this audience. In contrast, Findby stands out due to its user-centered participatory design. It actively involves the community of people with reduced mobility in its development process. In response to this problem, Findby is presented, a web application designed specifically for users with reduced mobility. Its primary objective is to offer comprehensive accessibility information about places and to foster inclusive exploration through challenges and a reward system. This innovative app uses user-centered design and leverages technology to improve access to public and private spaces, thus making life easier for people with reduced mobility. The app also includes custom route-based challenges, encouraging users to explore and discover new accessible places. This promotes social inclusion, encourages individuals to step out of their comfort zones, and broadens their horizons. Findby has the potential to significantly contribute to improving accessibility and inclusion of people with reduced mobility in Colombia. However, future work does not stop here. Additional steps must be taken to expand the user community, ensuring that the app reaches a more significant number of people who would benefit from it. In addition, it is essential to enhance the accuracy of the accessibility information provided by the application. This implies a constant update and verification of the data to ensure that the information is reliable and useful for users. The article is structured as follows: the next section provides the conceptual framework and background information. The methodology is discussed, and the proposed solution is presented afterward. Next, we present the results obtained from the acceptance tests, followed by the conclusions drawn from the findings. Finally, we discuss future work and possible areas for improvement.

2   Background

2.1   Conceptual Framework

There are different types of disabilities, each with its characteristics and challenges: visual, hearing, intellectual, physical, or motor. The solution presented in this report is designed for the latter. Motor disability refers to limitations in mobility or control of the body. It can be caused by spinal cord injuries, birth defects, amputations, or other conditions that affect the musculoskeletal system [2].

The term accessibility refers to the ability of all people, regardless of their physical or mental condition, to access and use the services and environments around them autonomously. Universal accessibility is a condition that guarantees equal opportunities for all, especially for people with disabilities [3].

The Findby app's scope is centered around promoting accessibility and inclusion for people with reduced mobility. The app seeks to leverage technology and user-centered design to improve access to public and private places and to encourage more people to explore these spaces in an inclusive and accessible way.

2.2   Related Work

Several mobile applications on the market provide information on the accessibility of public and private places [4]. Some of the most popular apps are a) Wheelmap: a global map for finding and marking wheelchair-accessible places. Similar to the Findby app; it puts efforts to get as many markers as possible, the difference lies in Wheelmap's mapping events, meanwhile, Findby app utilizes events and rewards to motivate users. b) Access Earth: a travel app that allows users to find accessible accommodations and attractions worldwide. It doesn't encourage users to mark locations. c) AXS Map: a crowdsourced tool that allows users to rate and review the accessibility of various locations. d) AccessNow: an app that lets users find and rate accessible places nearby. It doesn't encourage the users to mark locations. Similar to wheelmap, it encourages users to create Mapathons (mapping marathons) and to participate in them. e) Be My Eyes: a free app that connects blind and low-vision people with sighted volunteers for visual assistance. f) Club2g by MATT: a crowdsourced tool that allows users to rate and review the accessibility of various locations oriented to MATT users in Medellín.

However, many apps are not specifically designed for people with reduced mobility or do not contain detailed and accurate information. In response to this problem, Findby is presented, a web application designed specifically for users with reduced mobility. In addition, the app features an accessibility marker system and customized route-based challenges designed to encourage inclusive exploration of the maps.

3   Method

The development of Findby has been carried out using an agile methodology based on the SCRUM framework. This methodology allows for close collaboration between the development team members and the users of the application, which has allowed for user-centered design and the incorporation of user feedback throughout the development process. The user-centered approach was realized through consistent communication with wheelchair users through chat, periodically presenting them with functional mockups and progress videos of the app, and incorporating the changes they suggested. In the final stages of development, when FindBy had become a functional product, the team presented the Minimum Viable Product to potential end users and experts in the field of disability.

During the development process, the Nesquik team (a group of 6 students of the course integrative project 2 of systems engineering at EAFIT) used four-week sprint cycles to work on the different functionalities of the application. Daily follow-up meetings have been held, where pending tasks have been reviewed, obstacles have been discussed, and work for the next day has been planned. Although the hours of work weren't constant most of the time, the media of hours work per week was of 10 h

The SCRUM framework has allowed the Nesquik team to develop the application iteratively and incrementally, which has allowed it to adjust and improve the application throughout the development process according to the needs of the users and the feedback received.

4 Proposed Solution

After collaborating with the Gobernación de Antioquia (Department of People with Disabilities) and Matt, Nesquik identified the need for a tool that not only inform users about accessible places in Medellín but also kept them engaged with the app. The main distinguishing factor of the Nesquik app compared to other accessibility mapping apps is its focus on gamification and motivation, rather than simply offering the option to use it. To address the challenges faced by people with reduced mobility and promote inclusive exploration, we propose the development of Findby: an open source web application designed specifically for users with reduced mobility. Findby aims to provide information on the accessibility of places and create an inclusive environment through challenges and a reward system. By leveraging user-centered design principles and innovative technologies, Findby offers a comprehensive solution to improve access to public and private spaces. This software is designed with a model-view-controller architecture (see Fig. 1). The view layer is a map with which the user can interact, programmed in HTML, and it is developed in JavaScript. In addition, the presented map is executed with a Google Maps API. This API provides a set of tools and services for working with maps and location data. This includes displaying maps, adding markers, searching for places, and more. The controller layer is in charge of taking the data from the users, their ratings, and the reviews they make. It is programmed in TypeScript and JavaScript. In this layer, the information on the accessible points and their specifications are also created. Finally, in the model layer, user data, points, and reviews are stored in each place, and database systems are used and stored on servers. As an architecture, the user connects through the cell phone to the application, which connects to the servers where the user's information, the map, the ranking, the points of interest, and the treasure hunts are located. All this information is stored in a database server. In terms of technology, Findby is developed using JavaScript, CSS, and a pure HTML architecture. These technologies were chosen for their versatility and widespread use in web development. JavaScript provides the necessary interactivity and functionality, CSS handles visual styling, while HTML structures the content. This architecture ensures a solid foundation for the application's development. The app provides information on the accessibility of these places through a system of accessibility markers. These markers also include information on the location's accessibility level, including details about features

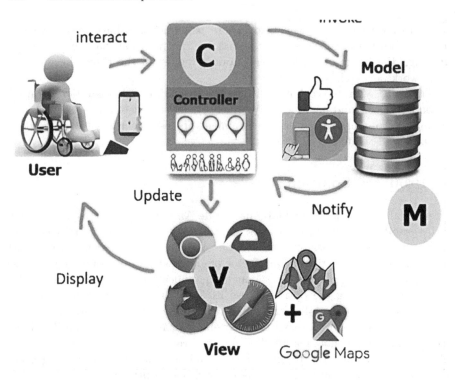

Fig. 1. Findy architecture

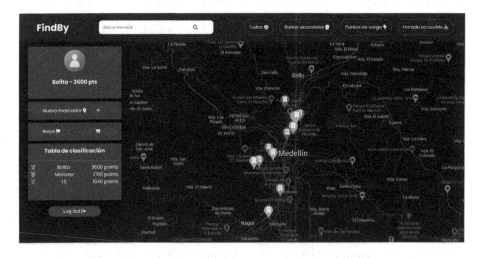

Fig. 2. Map example and accessibility markers

such as ramps, elevators, or accessible restrooms (see Fig. 2). Findby has accessibility markers, which allow users to quickly identify places that are accessible to them. In addition, the app includes user-generated content, which means that people can share their experiences and offer recommendations about the accessibility of different places. This allows other users to make informed decisions and also fosters a collaborative community where people can support each other. The inclusion of accessibility markers allows users to assess the accessibility level of a particular location. These markers are displayed with a color code, representing different accessibility levels as determined by users (green: very accessible, yellow: medium accessible, red: not very accessible). Figure 3 shows the interface to add sites to the map and how the information is recorded. Integration with the Google Maps API is a key feature of Findby. This integration allows the application to display accessibility marker information and create custom routes. By leveraging the power of the Google Maps API, Findby provides users with detailed information about the accessibility of locations, empowering them to plan their routes accordingly and make informed decisions about their mobility. To ensure reliable data storage and efficient data management, Findby utilizes Firebase, a cloud-based solution. Firebase offers a secure platform for storing and retrieving application data, including accessibility markers, user-generated content, and other relevant data points. By leveraging Firebase's capabilities, Findby guarantees a seamless user experience and streamlined data handling.

The availability of customized route-based challenges (see Fig. 4) adds an engaging element to Findby. These challenges motivate users to explore maps inclusively, add an element and unlock rewards or achievements, enhancing their interaction with the application and encouraging the discovery of new accessible places.

5   Results

After the development, acceptance tests were carried out with 2 wheelchair users in the city of Medellín. There wasn't a questionnaire to measure their opinion, instead, the users were asked about their opinion on various aspects of the app. When asked to rate the intuitiveness of the website on a scale of 1 to 10, participants gave it an average rating of 8.75. The layout, buttons, and color scheme were noted as factors that contributed to easy navigation and interaction with the website. Feedback on the aesthetics of the page was mixed. Participants expressed concerns about the disproportionate placement of the magnifying glass icon in the search bar and the potential security implications of automatically setting the password during the login process, and one of the participants mentioned that the pop-ups felt like errors, even if they were only messages of confirmation from the page, because of the different look on these. On the positive side, participants appreciated the responsive design when viewing five-star ratings for locations. However, they found the comments section aesthetics to be somewhat imbalanced. Participants regarded the website as highly useful, particularly in terms of providing precise information about locations that match specific criteria, however, one of the suggestions that was received was that if it were possible to see in the marker for one place, if that place has some kind of "helping item", like a wheelchair. The creation of points on the map was generally deemed to be executed correctly, with no major improvements or concerns

Fig. 3. Interfaces to add sites

raised. They made very valuable suggestions: a) carry out a study on the accessibility filters that we have (charging point, ramp, elevator) if they are types of accessibility (for example, charging point is not an accessibility element); b) it can be dangerous for wheelchair users to use conventional routes where vehicles pass. They suggest that the routing of the challenges be done on bike paths or roads with low traffic flow, to protect users; c) there are accessibility filters that must be met simultaneously. For example, it doesn't help much if a place has an accessible bathroom and a charging point but is located on a second floor where you can only go up by elevator. d) allow the visualization of the map with the accessible points without prior registration.

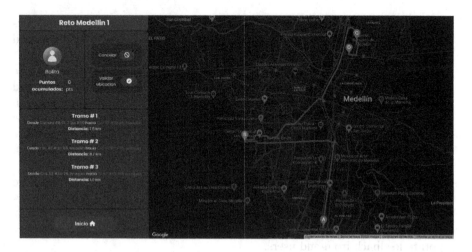

Fig. 4. Customized route-based challenges

6   Conclusions and Future Work

In this paper we presented Findby, an innovative web application that prioritizes accessibility and mobility for individuals with reduced mobility. The application adopts a user-centered design approach, actively involving the community of individuals with reduced mobility in its development. This collaborative process enables continuous feedback and facilitates ongoing improvements. The application's development has been streamlined through the implementation of an agile methodology based on SCRUM. This iterative and incremental approach has allowed for adjustments and enhancements based on user feedback and needs. Findby stands out from other similar applications due to its participatory approach and customized route-based challenges designed to encourage inclusive exploration of maps. The application also includes accessibility markers that allow users to view and add information about the accessibility of different locations, making it a valuable tool for improving accessibility in public spaces. Findby's key features include accessibility bookmarks, user-generated content, review comments, ratings, and custom path-based challenges, making the app engaging and easy to use. In short, Findby represents an important step towards creating more inclusive and accessible environments for people with reduced mobility in Colombia and beyond. This app demonstrates how technology and a user-centered approach can make a difference in the lives of people with disabilities, empowering them to fully enjoy public and private spaces. By continuing to develop and improve Findby, we can move towards a more inclusive society where all individuals have equal opportunity and access. Here are some of the future work areas for the application:

– The Nsquik team should focus on expanding the user community to increase the number of markers and accessibility information available on the application. This could be done through targeted marketing campaigns and collaborations with organizations focused on disability rights and accessibility.

- The accuracy of the accessibility information provided by users needs to be improved to ensure that it is reliable and useful. The Nsquik team could consider implementing a verification process for user-generated information to ensure that it meets certain quality standards.
- Findby currently focuses on public spaces, but the application could be expanded to include accessibility information for private spaces such as offices, stores, and restaurants.
- Findby must consider integrating additional features such as real-time updates on accessibility issues, integration with other accessibility-related services, and the development of a mobile application.
- The most urgent work to be done is to expand acceptance testing and incorporate feedback from end users.

7 Related Links

- Link to FindBy
- User Manual for FindBy
- Wheelmap
- Access Earth
- AXS Map
- AccessNow
- Be My Eyes
- Club2G.

Acknowledgment. Special recognition to the professors of the Integrative Project 2 course (Systems Engineering/Computer Science) to the EAFIT University for its support, to the secretary of inclusion and disability (Gobernación de Antioquia), and the companies Matt and Nebular of the city of Medellín.

References

1. Cortés-Reyes, E., Riveros, L.T., Pineda-Ortiz, G.A.: Clasificación internacional del funcionamiento, la discapacidad y certificación de discapacidad en Colombia. Revista de salud pública **15**, 129–137 (2013)
2. Gharebaghi, A., Mostafavi, M.-A., Chavoshi, S.H., Edwards, G., Fougeyrollas, P.: The role of social factors in the accessibility of urban areas for people with motor disabilities. ISPRS Int. J. Geo Inf. **7**(4), 131 (2018)
3. Altman, B.M.: Definitions, concepts, and measures of disability. Ann. Epidemiol. **24**(1), 2–7 (2014)
4. Garduño-Bonilla, I., de Velasco, E.M., Laureano-Cruces, A.L., et al.: Dispositivo de movilidad urbana para usuarios de sillas de ruedas en la Zona Metropolitana del Valle de México (ZMVM). Revista de Ciencias Tecnológicas **4**(4), 365–387 (2021)

5. Nowak Da Costa, J., Bielski, C.: Towards 'tourism for all' - improving maps for persons with reduced mobility. Int. Arch. Photogrammetry Remote Sens. Spat. Inf. Sci. **XLII-4**, 475–482 (2018). https://doi.org/10.5194/isprs-archives-XLII-4-475-2018
6. Cardoso, P., Domingos, D., Cláudio, A.P.: Indoor navigation systems for reduced mobility users: the w4all case study. Procedia Comput. Sci. **100**, 1200–1207 (2016)
7. da Silva Lima, N., et al.: Mobile application for crowdmapping accessibility places and generation of accessible routes. In: Ahram, T.Z., Falcão, C. (eds.) AHFE 2018. AISC, vol. 794, pp. 934–942. Springer, Cham (2019). https://doi.org/10.1007/978-3-319-94947-5_92

Tracing the Visual Path: Gaze Direction in the 360 Video Experience

Valentina Rozo-Bernal[(✉)] and Pablo Figueroa

Universidad de los Andes, Bogota, Colombia
v.rozob@uniandes.edu.co

Abstract. In traditional storytelling, a kind of predefined structure typically guides the narrative. However, when we move beyond the constraints of a rectangular screen, new possibilities emerge. 360-degree videos offer a unique opportunity to narrate with every element visible to the user in each frame. Nevertheless, some questions arise: What exactly are the end users seeing? Where is their attention directed? This paper deepens into an analysis of the data captured from the position and rotation of the headset worn by viewers while watching 360-degree videos. To accomplish this, two videos created by university students were examined, where gaze information was captured by testing it with a group of participants. Alongside watching the videos, participants provide their feedback on what elements they focused during the video. The findings revealed that participants tend to focus on elements intended to draw their attention. Furthermore, when the camera was stationary, participants found it easier to explore their surroundings, highlighting the value of utilizing the 360-degree format.

Keywords: 360 Videos · Narratives · Gaze Detection · Visual Attention · Focus · Context

1 Introduction

Currently, there are multiple ways of doing videos thanks to the various formats available. A new alternative is the 360 video format, which allows users to explore their surroundings. This experience is called cinematic Virtual Reality (VR) or live-action VR [8]. The 360-degrees camera model used for this study, is known as spherical or equirectangular and is based in the Structured for Motion (SfM) photogrammetry workflow [2]. This means that the workflow of 360-degree videos is similar to the composition of 3D images through the collection of 2D images. In the next figure it is shown the 360-degree video pipeline.

In the Fig. 1 it is displayed the 360-degree video pipeline, and Table 1 provides detailed explanations for each term depicted in the diagram to enhance comprehension.

To provide a clearer understanding of the 360-degree video pipeline in Table 1, are the explanations for each term described in the diagram:

M. Tabares et al. (Eds.): CCC 2023, CCIS 1924, pp. 406–415, 2024.
https://doi.org/10.1007/978-3-031-47372-2_32

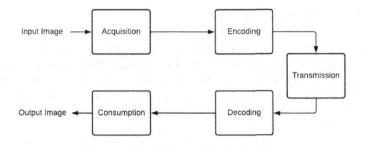

Fig. 1. 360-degree video pipeline

Table 1. Overview of 360-Degree Video Steps

Name	Description
Acquisition	To capture the image through the optical system. This step involves stitching the image. However this step may introduce some distortions within the visual content [1]
Encoding	Reduce redundancy in the signal. Use encoding tools as H.264, H.265, VP9, AVI, depending on the camera [1]
Transmission	It is the process of delivering the video content from the source to the end-user's device [1]
Decoding	Display the geometry and unpack the data into the end-user device [1]
Consumption	Is the final step where the end-user can watch the 360-degree video in a VR environment [1]

In addition to the technical specifications, to create videos in this format there is still room for improvement. For instance, when designing the story, from the script to the storyboard there should exist tools to pre-visualize it in VR, making it so that creators can define the context and focus on the story they are trying to tell.

However, there is not a clear guide to follow when creating content for this format. This raises questions about how to effectively highlight focus and context within the content. So to find some light in this topic, and provide insights into creating content for the 360-degree format, an analysis of gaze direction is conducted.

To achieve this, an app captures gaze direction data while users watched two 360-degree videos. Then the data is extracted and processed, to assess viewers head rotations. The aim of this analysis is to determine if people are utilizing the full 360-degree field of view. This paper is structured as follows. First, there is a brief literature review on how the narratives are applied to 360-degree videos and how this works for traditional storytelling. Then, the methodology to conduct the investigation is explained. Finally, the results and conclusions of the study are presented.

2 Literature Review

There are some examples of studies based on 360 videos in which attention is evaluated, such as, an application designed to minimize distraction among viewers, this investigation contributed to the optimization of adaptive video streaming [13]. Other similar study, is one, which aimed to capture viewing information data to identify popular areas in a 360-degree video, as the researchers believed that users should be guided to achieve a good level of immersion and to reduce the risk of viewers getting lost within the storyline. The objective was to provide insights into guiding viewers and enhancing immersion in 360-degree videos. [9]. Other example, is an investigation in which the researchers extracted a dataset of gaze trajectories from 360-degree videos, this study aims to provide guidance for working with this format and develop a model for predicting eye direction in such videos. One of the findings revealed that people usually have the same view patters, key element to make possible the prediction of gaze direction in 360-degree videos [3].

Finally, talking about capturing attention, there is an investigation that addresses the challenges of transmitting 360-degree videos, and how the attention is influenced by video quality. The study highlights the importance of not only narrative elements but also technical quality in creating a positive viewer experience. Additionally, surprise elements during the transmission were found to be effective in capturing attention, in this way narrative and technical aspects need to be considered when creating a 360-degree video [7].

2.1 Tools in 360-degree Videos

As there are studies to identify and reduce distraction in 360 videos, there are also tools that help to create and adequate narrative to show what is worth watching in this format. For example, there is a Storyboard app to plan and collaborate with other creatives in the process of making videos. This storyboard is presented in a paper in which the researchers propose a workflow and introduce a multi-device storyboard tool to work in virtual reality as well as in traditional formats during the pre-production phase of film-making [4]. Other tool in 360-degree videos was built for evaluating different head predictors in the context of streaming. The primary focus of the study was to compare the performance of various head predictors for 360-degree videos, so it would be easier to pin focus on a given video in this kind of format [11].

As there are tools built for 360-degree videos and investigations which evaluate attention and distraction, there are also, some studies in which the tools are the key to evaluate the areas of interest within such videos. One of this tools is 360RAT a software tool designed to identify areas of interest in this video format. The researchers conducted a experiment in which they observed that individuals tend to focus and highlight regions with minimal object amount in the scene [10].

2.2 Traditional Storytelling

In traditional format videos, there is a structured process that creators can usually follow, there are also different shoots and camera angles, there is also a narrative structure to tell what is off-screen and on-screen. However, in 360-degrees videos following these "instructions" it is quite difficult, first because it is impossible to take some things off screen, there is always something happening, something that the viewer might see when they turn around. Nevertheless, there is something that can be followed and is the narrative structure, always ensuring that the user does not lose track of the storyline. For this purpose there are some guides like the book *The Writer's Journey: Mythic Structure for Writers* in which it is presented a way to structure a story for the characters as well as for the lineal structure once posed by Aristotle [12].

3 Methodology

To investigate the direction of viewers attention, A specific set of steps were followed. First, two 360-degree videos created by a group of students were carefully selected for analysis. The criteria for video selection prioritized those with a clear main plot and rich contextual elements that allowed users to observe the plot from various angles in every frame.

Subsequently, gaze information was collected from a group of students while they watched the selected videos. Additionally, short surveys were conducted with the test viewers to gather further insights. The main goal of this analysis was to determine how frequently the viewers changed their rotation and position during the video, thus revealing patterns of their attention and engagement.

3.1 360 Video Player: A Tool to Capture Gaze Direction

To gather the information about gaze direction from the participants, a 360-degree video player for Oculus Quest 2 was built, it is noted that this headset is the one used for this experiment. To capture the gaze direction, it is used the rotation of the headset in the X, Y and Z axis. The video player was developed in Unity, with a user interface (UI) where eleven 360-degree videos where displayed, as it is shown in Fig. 2, however participants where only allowed to watch two videos during the experiment: one in which there was a stationary camera and other in which the camera was moving in a particular direction.

During the experiment, participants select a video. Once the video start, they have limited control and couldn't fast forward or rewind it. When they finish, they return to the main screen, however as a mechanism to exit the video if participants present motion sickness they may press any button in the controllers to safely return to the initial interface. Data capture begin as soon as the participant start watching the video, the position and rotation are recorded each second to finally be saved in a CSV file. These files are stored with the key name of the video and a random number in order to prevent overwriting of the file. Finally, once the data is captured, the files are stored in the main application files for future analysis.

Fig. 2. 360 Video Player

3.2   Cameras for Capturing 360-degrees Videos

To capture the images, the creators used the Insta360 One X2. This camera is designed to simplify the process of recording videos in the 360-degree format. It has a maximum 5.7k recording resolution and is equipped with movement stabilizer, along with a dual lens. It is important to note that each lens of this camera has a 200-degree field of view. This feature is intended to create a seamless effect where the tripod or selfie stick becomes invisible in the captured images. This effect is achieved by capturing more than 360-degrees of the scene, causing the images to overlap and effectively erase the stick [5].

The Insta360 One X2 offers users the flexibility to record in various formats. However, the chosen mode for this project was the 360-degree mode, with this mode, users can capture video or images and then use the Insta360 App to select their preferred angles and easily edit the video to create final product. Users can also use other editing software, such as Adobe Premiere Pro. In this software, there is a plugin called GoPro GX ReFrame, designed to assist in a process known as reframing. Reframing let users to select the desired viewing angle of the video, transforming it into a flat plane. When editing, users have the possibility to edit based on a specific angle or in the equirectangular view [6]. For this experiment, it is essential to mention that the videos will be exclusively analyzed within a software designed for a virtual reality environment.

3.3   Information from the Creators

The two videos described by it creators follow these main plots:

- Video 1: The video of Fig. 3 show the reality of many people and how they access to benefits from an institution that works to end hunger.
- Video 2: The video of Fig. 4 makes the viewer feel the experience of volunteering at the institution and what this involves.

Taking this into account, the first video emphasizes in the people that access to food, while viewers listen to some interviews about how the beneficiaries of

Fig. 3. Four moments of the first video

Fig. 4. Four moments of the second video

the program access to the resources. This video is narrated from a static camera while people start appearing in the shoot. Thus, the viewer can turn their head 360-degrees to see what is happening all the time. As for the second video, it portrays a day in the life of a volunteer. The narrative is presented in first person to show the viewer as the volunteer. The 360-video makes a tour through the facilities to learn every step they must follow to participate in this initiative. As a result, this video intend to make the viewer turn in every direction as if they were in their first day as volunteer in real life.

3.4 Information from the Viewers

To gather the information from the viewers, there was a test group of 32 students, ages form 19 to 23. The method of the experiment it is as follows; the group was divided in two, the first group, watched the video number one and then the video number two, while the second group watched them in opposite order. Then, they were asked to fill a short survey in which the focus and context of the video were asked. Due motion sickness the data of the 32 participants wasn't collected. As a result, a total of 26 CSV files were extracted for each video, but not all files contained the complete information, the average watched time was 220 s. Despite incomplete data, analysis was conducted on at least the first minute of each video, as this was the minimum duration observed by the participants before experiencing motion sickness.

In order to collect the data an application in Unity for the Oculus Quest 2 was developed, in which the participants could select the video. While they were in this process, every second the position and rotation of the head was captured. It should be noted that, out of the eleven available videos, only two were selected, due the correct use of the 360-degree format, factors such as the position of the camera and the use of additional resources such as voice-overs and on-camera interviews. Finally, the data was extracted from the headsets to continue with the study.

4   Results

As for the results, once the data was analyzed, it was obtained that people tend to look up and down in different positions while watching the first video. In the next plots, for the first video, it is shown that users usually rotate their heads in every direction. The plots from Fig. 5, 6, 7 and Fig. 8 correspond to the data gathered in the CSV files for rotation in x and y axes for video number one and video number two.

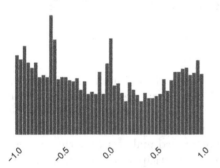

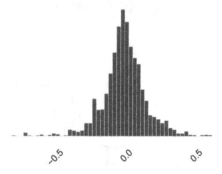

Fig. 5. Rotation in the y-axis for the first video: frequency vs rotation

Fig. 6. Rotation in the x-axis for the first video: frequency vs rotation

On the other hand, the analysis of the same variables in the second video reveals that fewer users tend to look right and left, the most of them remained in the same position in the y axis. In the Fig. 8 there is a smaller range of rotation in x. However, the difference in this axis between the two videos is not significant, as indicated by the similar standard deviation values. For video 1 is 0.1574 and for video 2 is 0.1597 showing that in this axis participants do not explore the most up and down. The major difference is in the y-axis where the standard deviation for the first video is 0.75 while for the second is 0.61.

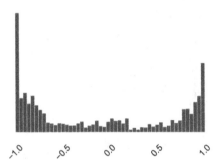

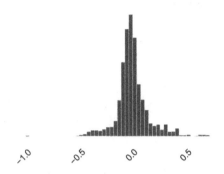

Fig. 7. Rotation in the y-axis for the second video: frequency vs rotation

Fig. 8. Rotation in the x-axis for the second video: frequency vs rotation

The findings indicate that complete control over user attention may not let take the full advantages of utilizing a 360-degree video format. However, when there are elements that control the narrative without being constant and allow viewers explore the scene, there is major sense of enjoyment and better comprehension of the narrative.

In order to compare the rotation in both videos, the plots of the rotation in the x and y axes are displayed below. For better comprehension of the data presented, five CSV files were randomly selected out of the 26 available. In Fig. 9 it can be observed that users tend to look around more frequently in the first video compared to the second video. In the video number two participants tend to stay in the same position for longer duration resulting in minimal rotation.

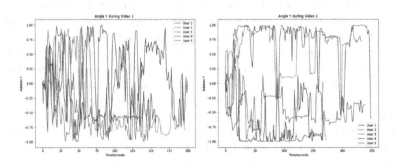

Fig. 9. Rotation in the y-axis for both videos: rotation vs time

In the case of the x-axis in the Fig. 10, it can be observed that participants in the first video exhibit a little higher degree of freedom in their gaze. The plot shows a bit more rotation in this axis, indicating they looked up and down frequently compared to the second video. So, in the second video the rotation angle is smaller than in the first video, suggesting, participants explore a little less vertically.

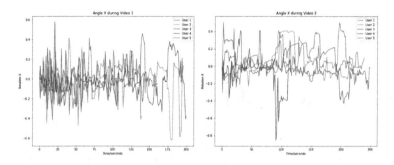

Fig. 10. Rotation in the x-axis for both videos: rotation vs time

5   Conclusions

The observed differences in the previous results can be attributed to the distinct narrative styles employed in the two videos. While the first one is open to explore the scene, the second one is directing the gaze of the viewer to an specific point. Other details that highlight from this is that the only thing trying to catch the attention of the participant in the first video are the audios of interviews, while in the second one has a person in the scene who is talking, so people tend to direct their attention to them. On the other hand, based on the responses from the participants, the surveys indicate that the first video possessed a well-defined storyline, which was crucial for understanding the context. In contrast, feedback from the second video suggests that although context played a significant role, it did not compel the participants to explore their surroundings.

In conclusion, depending on the intention of the creators it is worth the use of a 360-degrees format. The findings from the analyzed data indicate that the participants usually tend to concentrate on what the creator intends them to focus on. In other words, the user feel free to take a look around, but if there is something catching their gaze is easier to just follow that point. Nevertheless, if creators let viewers take a look, giving other elements to focus on as the sound, this could enrich the experience and the use of this format.

For future work, it is recommended that guidelines be developed for using focus and context effectively in a given storyline for this particular format. For the researcher conducting this study, it is worth the use of 360-degree videos if the user is not conditioned to always see the same focus point. While it is essential to guide the viewer's attention, it is not obligatory to do it throughout the entire video. There are some helpers that can prevent the viewer form getting distracted, like sounds or moments of silence and stillness where the viewer is invited to explore the scene.

References

1. De A. Azevedo, R.G., Birkbeck, N., Simone, F.D., Janatra, I., Adsumilli, B., Frossard, P.: Visual distortions in 360-degree videos. IEEE Trans. Circuits Syst. Video Technol. (2019). https://doi.org/10.48550/arXiv.1901.01848
2. Barazzetti, L., Previtali, M., Roncoroni, F.: 3D modeling with 5k 360° videos. Int. Arch. Photogramm. Remote Sens. Spat. Inf. Sci. (2022). https://doi.org/10.5194/isprs-archives-XLVI-2-W1-2022-65-2022
3. Duanmu, F., Mao, Y., Liu, S., Srinivasan, S., Wang, Y.: A subjective study of viewer navigation behaviors when watching 360-degree videos on computers. In: 2018 IEEE International Conference on Multimedia and Expo (ICME) (2018). https://doi.org/10.1109/ICME.2018.8486537
4. Henrikson, R., Araujo, B.D., Chevalier, F., Singh, K., Balakrishnan, R.: Multi-device storyboards for cinematic narratives in VR. In: UIST '16: Proceedings of the 29th Annual Symposium on User Interface Software and Technology (2016). https://doi.org/10.1145/2984511.2984539
5. Insta360: How to use the invisible selfie stick. https://blog.insta360.com/how-to-use-the-invisible-selfie-stick
6. Insta360: Reframe plugin tutorial. https://n9.cl/reframe
7. van Kasteren, A., Brunnström, K., Hedlund, J., Snijders, C.: Quality of experience of 360 video – subjective and eye-tracking assessment of encoding and freezing distortions. Multimed. Tools Appl. **81**(7), 9771–9802 (2022). https://doi.org/10.1007/s11042-022-12065-1
8. Knorr, S., Ozcinar, C., Fearghail, C.O., Smolic, A.: Director's cut - a combined dataset for visual attention analysis in cinematic VR content. In: CVMP '18: Proceedings of the 15th ACM SIGGRAPH European Conference on Visual Media Production (2018). https://doi.org/10.1145/3278471.3278472
9. Mäkelä, V., et al.: What are others looking at? exploring 360° videos on hmds with visual cues about other viewers. In: TVX '19: Proceedings of the 2019 ACM International Conference on Interactive Experiences for TV and Online Video (2019). https://doi.org/10.1145/3317697.3323351
10. Prado, M., et al.: 360RAT: a tool for annotating regions of interest in 360-degree videos. In: WebMedia '22: Proceedings of the Brazilian Symposium on Multimedia and the Web (2022). https://doi.org/10.1145/3539637.3557930
11. Rondón, M.F.R., Sassatelli, L., Aparicio-Pardo, R., Precioso, F.: A unified evaluation framework for head motion prediction methods in 360° videos. In: MMSys '20: Proceedings of the 11th ACM Multimedia Systems Conference (2020). https://doi.org/10.1145/3339825.3394934
12. Vogler, C.: The Writer's Journey: Mythic Structure for Writers (1992)
13. Xue, T., Ali, A.E., Viola, I., Ding, G., Cesar, P.: Designing real-time, continuous QoE score acquisition techniques for hmd-based 360° VR video watching. In: 14th International Conference on Quality of Multimedia Experience (QoMEX) (2022). https://doi.org/10.1109/QoMEX55416.2022.9900914

Using Virtual Reality to Detect Memory Loss: An Exploratory Study

Melissa Lizeth Contreras Rojas$^{(\boxtimes)}$◉ and Pablo Figueroa◉

Universidad de Los Andes, Bogotá, Colombia
{m.contrerasr,pfiguero}@uniandes.edu.co

Abstract. This article presents software that leverages virtual reality (VR) and OpenAI services to assess and detect early cognitive impairments, especially in verbal memory. The Thakira program, created for the Meta Quest 2, presents a natural environment with flying invertebrate animals and an interactive character. Through conversations simulated with artificial intelligence, the three-word recall test (R3P) is carried out on the user. We present the study design to evaluate the effectiveness of our method. This approach could help identify verbal memory impairment in people with neurocognitive disorders and alert them to the need for early professional attention.

Keywords: Virtual Reality · Memory Loss · Cognitive Assessment · Verbal Memory · Early Detection · Artificial Intelligence

1 Introduction

"Currently, more than 55 million people have dementia worldwide, over 60% of whom live in low-and middle-income countries. Every year, there are nearly 10 million new cases" (WHO, 2023) [1]. The various diseases characterized by memory impairment raise the question of whether it is possible to identify them at early stages, which would allow them to be treated or, at least, delay their progression.

Memory is a cognitive function that allows storing, retaining, and retrieving information and past experiences. It is the process by which we encode, store, and recall information for later use. Memory allows us to remember events, concepts, skills, and experiences acquired throughout our lives.

Verbal memory refers to the ability to actively hold in memory words, phrases, or other units of language based on their auditory or phonological representation. For example, when we mentally repeat a telephone number we have been told, we are using our verbal memory to retain and reproduce the specific sounds of the digits. If a person has no verbal memory, he may have difficulty following verbal instructions, remembering conversations, holding information that has been read or written, and expressing himself verbally fluently. They may also have difficulties learning new words or languages, and their ability to understand and communicate effectively would be affected. From this, it can be

M. Tabares et al. (Eds.): CCC 2023, CCIS 1924, pp. 416–425, 2024.
https://doi.org/10.1007/978-3-031-47372-2_33

seen that verbal memory is crucial in a person's daily life. Experiencing difficulties in this aspect affects the health area, and also the personal one. These
difficulties can become more complicated over time and, in some cases, can be
an early indication of serious diseases such as Alzheimer's and other similar
conditions. Early diagnosis of diseases related to memory loss can help with
management, decision-making, and more effective treatment [4].

Virtual reality is a technology that allows the user to enter a virtual world
and experience it as if it were real. It is as if the person is immersed in a video
game or movie, where everything around them looks and feels so real that they
are completely immersed in the virtual experience. By using virtual reality, a
controlled environment can be created, facilitating more accurate assessments
to identify early memory loss, and allowing professionals to determine if more
detailed testing is needed. Several studies have shown that virtual reality is particularly effective in the early diagnosis of diseases such as Alzheimer's, allowing
the study of memory deficits [2]. In turn, research with systematic reviews has
shown that the use of virtual reality resources improves cognition in patients
with neurocognitive disorders [3]. Studies focused on various types of memory,
which include some virtual reality programs, have shown that these types of
tools can improve, control, and treat memory loss [7–10]. Even in severe cases,
they can delay the worst consequences of certain diseases.

2 Objective and Proposal

The central purpose of this study is to establish whether a short-term verbal
memory retention test proves to be more accurate in a controlled environment,
such as a virtual reality scenario, compared to the real-life context. To achieve
this goal, a specific tool has been developed: Thakira. This program, designed
in Unity, was created for the Meta Quest 2.

This software gets its name, "Thakira" from the translation of the word "memory" into Arabic, where its phonetic correspondence is "dhakira". On this basis,
the decision has been made to adopt the variant "Thakira" as a sound adaptation
that faithfully captures the original Arabic pronunciation.

Through the implementation of this program, we seek to explore the fundamental differences between verbal memory tests performed in controlled conditions and everyday life. The creation of Thakira introduces a tangible component
that allows the manipulation and measurement of these contexts in a precise
and detailed manner. This essential approach, based on the intersection between
technology and cognitive psychology, provides an opportunity to broaden our
perception of how environments influence our ability to retain and evoke verbal
information.

3 Previous Work

Articles that use virtual reality to detect cognitive impairment usually simulate
real-life activities, such as fishing, moving objects, shopping, or driving [3, 13–18].

On the other hand, studies that address the detection of diseases with neurocognitive impairment use different assessments or instruments, without resorting to virtual reality [12,19,20]. Usual tests for detecting memory loss include Scenery Picture Memory Test(SPMT), Memory Impairment Screen (MIS), Memory and Executive Screening (MES), Full Object Memory Evaluation (FOME), Mini-Mental State Examination (MMSE), among others [11]. Although the MMSE assessment is unreliable in adequately detecting cognitive impairment, we will focus on testing a specific element of this assessment, known as three-word recall (R3P). Several publications have investigated its efficacy and concluded that it has a high sensitivity, but it is not a reliable diagnostic to rule out cognitive impairment [6,21].

In this regard, according to Allegri and Harris, the prefrontal cortex plays a fundamental role in the regulation of attention and memory required to monitor and adjust the processing of information related to physical actions and fundamental cognitive, emotional, and behavioral functions in humans (p. 452) [5]. With this information in mind, a test was designed that focuses on performing cognitive assessments within a virtual reality environment rather than simulating everyday life activities. This test aims to identify possible cognitive impairments in a controlled context, and to this end, we highlighted distractor items that test the central lobe region of the brain. Specifically, two distraction components have been strategically included. The first distractor consists of the appearance of flying invertebrate animals, designed to be low-level. In addition, another more complex distractor will include, which consists of a speech on a topic of interest to the user, which will end with a question to check if the user paid attention to what the character mentioned. Once the variables of concentration and mental repetition of words have been addressed, we will proceed to ask the user to identify which of the three words he had to memorize, providing him with a set of 10 words to choose from, thus completing the evaluation in the controlled virtual environment. The last stage of the test is based on the need for a more complete and accurate assessment of cognitive ability and memory. By including a broader set of words, we can assess the ability to discriminate and retrieve relevant information in the face of distractions and additional stimuli.

4   Software Architecture

First, a flowchart plan was elaborated for the creation of the Thakira program (see Fig. 1). Within the Unity development environment, models of flying invertebrate animals are built [23], and programmed to perform random flights in a specific area representing the scenario where users can observe them. In addition, adjustments were made to incorporate audio recording functionality through a microphone to record user responses. Animations were also implemented for character movements, including lip-synchronization (see Fig. 2).

Subsequently, a server was created using the Python programming language. This server can receive audio recordings generated by Unity, which contain the voices of the users (see Fig. 3). It then uses the OpenAI service called Whisper to process and convert these recordings into text. The resulting text is sent to the GPT-3.5 Turbo service to obtain an AI-generated response in text format.

Finally, the Google Text-to-Speech API transforms the response text into an audio file. This file is stored in Unity with a corresponding name and played within the program. Throughout this process, the communication between Unity and the server is established through data transfer using the HTTP protocol (see Fig. 4), allowing seamless interaction between the program and the server.

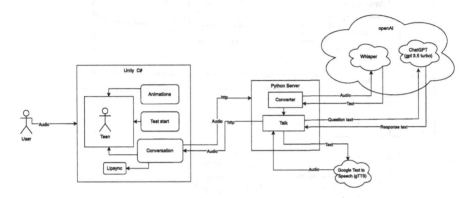

Fig. 1. Thakira program flowchart.

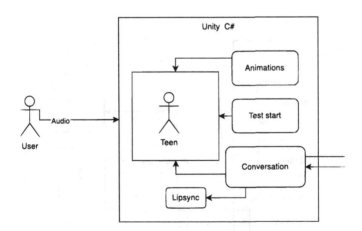

Fig. 2. Program flowchart from Unity.

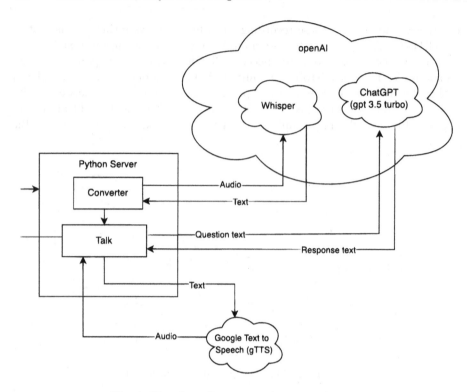

Fig. 3. Flowchart illustrating the server design.

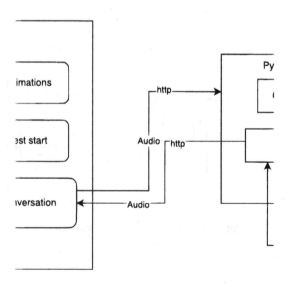

Fig. 4. Connection between the Unity program and the server.

The program includes a natural environment with invertebrate animals flying near and far from the user and an animated character in front of him (see Fig. 5). This character, linked to the OpenAI service, asks the user to memorize three words, asks him a topic he would like to hear about, provides him with information related to the topic, asks a comprehension question, and finally asks him to choose the words he asked to memorize from a set of ten words. He gives feedback on the correctness of the user's answers and, if they are incorrect, the words the person should have remembered mentioned to him[1].

Fig. 5. User view in the Thakira program.

5 Test Design

The test design for a future experiment will be carried out on a population of 50 individuals of various ages. The purpose is to eliminate the influence of age as a study factor and, instead, to detect any possible cognitive impairment. However, the selection process considers whether the individuals have been diagnosed with neurocognitive disorders. The people with a diagnosis will be part of study population A, while those without a diagnosis will be part of study population B. Each population will be composed of 25 people.

Two different tests will be developed. The first will take place in an everyday, informal setting, the person will be asked to memorize three words and, after three hours, will be asked what those words were. The second will run in the virtual environment with the Thakira program, which, unlike the studies conducted

---

[1] A Thakira video can be found at https://youtu.be/oGe_6c2cljY.

with R3P, will ask them to memorize three different words in each session. The aim of this is to follow up on the study population every three months to see if there has been any improvement in their verbal memory. Both tests will be performed with both population A and B subjects.

The final results are determined by calculating the percentage of people in each population who did not retain all the words in the everyday environment, virtual environment, and both environments. It will allow us to assess whether there is any significant difference in verbal memory performance between the two environments and whether either environment is more effective in detecting possible cognitive impairment. The results are expected to identify a possible impairment of verbal memory in 95% of people diagnosed with a neurocognitive disorder.

In addition to calculating the percentage of people who did not retain all the words in each environment, it would also be interesting to analyze and compare the time required for people in each group to remember the words in the different environments. These would provide additional information about the efficiency and speed of verbal memory processing in each context. It is crucial to consider the limitations inherent in this study, as the results are based on the responses provided by the participants, which may be affected by various factors that influence memory, such as personal circumstances and other uncontrolled variables.

6 Future Work

Following the line of tests designed to be carried out in both every day and virtual environments using the Thakira program, the possibility of considering the implementation of a third test, this time in an augmented reality environment, is open. The inclusion of this additional test is intended to examine more comprehensively the impact resulting from the fusion between physical and virtual components on participants' verbal memory.

The choice of augmented reality as the platform for this assessment introduces an intriguing dimension. By combining tangible and intangible elements at the same time, augmented reality promises to provide a highly immersive experience. This synergy, in which real-world attributes merge with virtually generated elements, could potentially influence verbal memory performance favorably.

This innovative approach would engender a context in which participants are immersed in an environment where the boundaries between the real and the virtual are blurred. The resulting experience could foster greater attention and engagement on the part of the study subjects, which in turn could manifest itself in improved retention and recall of verbal information.

Therefore, the incorporation of augmented reality as a third testing scenario adds a layer of depth to the research. Through this foray, it is hoped to broaden the understanding of how different contexts influence human cognition and provide a more complete picture of the effects of the interaction between the physical and the virtual in the sphere of verbal memory.

7 Conclusions

In conclusion, the use of virtual reality as a tool for detecting memory loss shows promise as an innovative approach to cognitive assessment. The present study focuses on verbal memory and seeks to determine whether tests performed in a virtual environment are more effective than tests in an everyday environment in detecting possible cognitive impairment.

To achieve this goal, the Thakira program was developed, which creates a controlled environment where participants must memorize words and then recall them after an auditory activity. The inclusion of distractors and concentration elements in the test allows for a more accurate evaluation of word retention and reproduction capacity. Similarly, the possibility of implementing a third test in an augmented reality environment to evaluate the impact of the combination of virtual and physical elements on verbal memory is proposed.

The final results will be determined by analyzing the percentage of people who did not retain all the words in each environment and the time required to recall the words. Identification of possible impairment in verbal memory in the majority of people diagnosed with neurocognitive disorders could indicate which environment is most effective for detection. Although concrete results are not yet available from this study, preliminary results and theoretical possibilities support the idea that virtual reality could play a significant role in the detection and management of memory loss. While this approach cannot replace a medical diagnosis, it may serve as an early warning to perform prevention or seek professional care. Early detection of memory problems is crucial to monitor their progression and make informed treatment decisions.

On the other hand, this article could lay the groundwork for the development of programs capable of making an accurate diagnosis of cognitive impairment autonomously, reducing the need for the intervention of a professional in the diagnostic process. In this way, the role of the professional would be more focused on treatment and personalized attention for those cases that require specialized intervention and follow-up.

It is relevant to note that, although this study focuses on the field of virtual reality, the trajectory of this concept should not be underestimated. Virtual reality is not as recent a phenomenon as one might think, as its roots date back to 1968 [22]. It is also important to highlight that neurological medicine, another topic addressed in this article, has been the subject of study for several years.

References

1. World Health Organization (WHO). https://www.who.int/news-room/fact-sheets/detail/dementia. Accessed 29 Aug 2023
2. Plancher, G., Tirard, A., Gyselinck, V., Nicolas, S., Piolino, P.: Using virtual reality to characterize episodic memory profiles in amnestic mild cognitive impairment and Alzheimer's disease: Influence of active and passive encoding. Neuropsychologia 50(5), 592–602 (2012). https://doi.org/10.1016/j.neuropsychologia.2011.12.013

3. Oliveira, J., et al.: Virtual reality-based cognitive stimulation on people with mild to moderate dementia due to Alzheimer's disease: a pilot randomized controlled trial. Int. J. Environ. Res. Public Health **18**(10), 5290 (2021). https://doi.org/10.3390/ijerph18105290

4. Jin, R., Pilozzi, A., Huang, X.: Current cognition tests, potential virtual reality applications, and serious games in cognitive assessment and non-pharmacological therapy for neurocognitive disorders. J. Clin. Med. **9**(10), 3287 (2020). https://doi.org/10.3390/jcm9103287

5. Allegri, R.F., Harris, P.: Prefrontal cortex in attentional mechanisms and memory (in Spanish). Rev. Neurol. **32**(05), 449–454 (2001). https://doi.org/10.33588/rn.3205.2000167

6. Fuentes Pérez, M.Á., Belmonte Calderón, L., Monteagudo Caba, P., Muñoz de Escalona Padial, M.A., Vandellós Belmonte, A., Castell Fríguls, E. : The three-word recall: Is it useful in screening for cognitive impairment in the elderly? (in Spanish). Span. J. Geriatr. Gerontol. **42**(3), 167–173 (2007). https://doi.org/10.1016/S0211-139X(07)73543-6

7. Caglio, M., et al.: Virtual navigation for memory rehabilitation in a traumatic brain injured patient. Neurocase Neural Basis Cogn. **18**(2), 123–131 (2012). https://doi.org/10.1080/13554794.2011.568499

8. Moreno, A., Wall, K.J., Thangavelu, K., Craven, L., Ward, E., Dissanayaka, N.N.: A systematic review of the use of virtual reality and its effects on cognition in individuals with neurocognitive disorders. Technol. Innov. Rehabil. Assist. Technol. **1**(2), 61–71 (2019). https://doi.org/10.1016/j.trci.2019.09.016

9. Kim, O., Pang, Y., Kim, J.H.: The effectiveness of virtual reality for people with mild cognitive impairment or dementia: a meta-analysis. BMC Psychiatry **19**, 219 (2019). https://doi.org/10.1186/s12888-019-2180-x

10. Gamito, P., Oliveira, J., Alves, C., Santos, N., Coelho, C., Brito, R.: Virtual reality-based cognitive stimulation to improve cognitive functioning in community elderly: a controlled study. Cyberpsychol. Behav. Soc. Netw. **23**(3), 150–156 (2020). https://doi.org/10.1089/cyber.2019.0271

11. De Roeck, E.E., De Deyn, P.P., Dierckx, E., et al.: Brief cognitive screening instruments for early detection of Alzheimer's disease: a systematic review. Alzheimer's Res. Therapy **11**, 21 (2019). https://doi.org/10.1186/s13195-019-0474-3

12. Chen, N.C., et al.: Learning and error patterns in the chinese verbal learning test in subjects with mild cognitive impairment and normal elderly. Acta Neurologica Taiwanica **20**(2), 114–124 (2011). https://doi.org/10.29819/ANT.201106.0006

13. Pugnetti, L., et al.: Probing memory and executive functions with virtual reality: past and present studies. Cyber Psychol. Behav. **1**(2), 151–161 (1998). https://doi.org/10.1089/cpb.1998.1.151

14. Cho, D.R., Lee, S.H.: Effects of virtual reality immersive training with computerized cognitive training on cognitive function and activities of daily living performance in patients with acute stage stroke: a preliminary randomized controlled trial. Medicine (Baltimore) **99**(20), e20598 (2020). https://doi.org/10.1097/MD.0000000000020598

15. Mrakic-Sposta, S., Di Santo, S.G., Franchini, F., et al.: Effects of combined physical and cognitive virtual reality-based training on cognitive impairment and oxidative stress in MCI patients: a pilot study. Front. Aging Neurosci. **10**(10), 282 (2018). https://doi.org/10.3389/fnagi.2018.00282

16. Faria, A.L., Cameirão, M.S., Couras, J.F., et al.: Combined cognitive-motor rehabilitation in virtual reality improves motor outcomes in chronic stroke - a pilot study. Front. Psychol. **9**, 854 (2018). https://doi.org/10.3389/fpsyg.2018.00854

17. Ettenhofer, M.L., Guise, B., Brandler, B., et al.: Neurocognitive driving rehabilitation in virtual environments (NeuroDRIVE): a pilot clinical trial for chronic traumatic brain injury. NeuroRehabilitation **44**(4), 531–544 (2019). https://doi.org/10.3233/NRE-192718
18. Faria, A.L., Pinho, M.S., Bermúdez i Badia, S.: A comparison of two personalization and adaptive cognitive rehabilitation approaches: a randomized controlled trial with chronic stroke patients. J. Neuroeng. Rehabil. **17**(1), 1–15 (2020). https://doi.org/10.1186/s12984-020-00691-5
19. Breton, A., Casey, D., Arnaoutoglou, N.A.: Cognitive tests for the detection of mild cognitive impairment (MCI), the prodromal stage of dementia: meta-analysis of diagnostic accuracy studies. Int. J. Geriatr. Psychiatry **34**, 233–242 (2019). https://doi.org/10.1002/gps.5016
20. Bruno, D., Gaetane, P., Marie, S.: Early detection of Alzheimer's disease: new diagnostic criteria. Dialogues Clin. Neurosci. **11**(2), 135–139 (2019). https://doi.org/10.31887/DCNS.2009.11.2/bdubois
21. Munro, C., Thompson, L., Smernoff, E.: Three-word recall as a measure of memory. J. Clin. Exp. Neuropsychol. **15**(2), 321329 (1993). https://doi.org/10.1080/01688639308402566
22. Universidad de Los Andes. https://shorturl.at/jIRT1. Accessed 29 Aug 2023
23. Abondano, N., Melendez, N., Carvajal, J.: Butterfly Project (in Spanish). Universidad de Los Andes, 1 June 2022

Author Index

A

Aguilar, Jose 173, 259
Álvarez, Susana 330
Angel, Leonardo 285
Arbeláez, Juan Carlos 173
Atehortúa Zapata, Jader Daniel 311

B

Bairwa, Amit Kumar 1
Barajas-Oviedo, Sergio 215
Botia, Diego 318
Builes-Roldan, Carolina 153

C

Cabrera, Mateo Jesús Cadena 35
Cano Duque, Santiago 311
Cárdenas López, Paula Andrea 380
Cardozo, Nicolás 128, 285
Carrillo, Eduardo 141
Castellanos-Cárdenas, Duby 97
Chaudhary, Shikha 1
Contreras Rojas, Melissa Lizeth 416
Curiel H., Mariela J. 91

D

Díaz Frías, Juan Francisco 57
Dorado Muñoz, Juan José 57
Duque Agudelo, Robinson Andrey 57

E

Echeverri-Cartagena, Carlos 153
Escudero, Paula 330

F

Fernández Becerra, Santiago 109
Figueroa, Pablo 406, 416
Forero Hincapié, Santiago 311
Franco, Mariajose 330

G

Garcia-Carrascal, Shirley Tatiana 188
Gauthier-Umaña, Valérie 45
Gómez, Valentina Escobar 199
Gómez-Álvarez, María Clara 97
González, Bryan Leonardo Figueredo 91
González, Enrique 367
González-Palacio, Liliana 396
Gonzalez-Velez, Juan Carlos 13, 25
Guevara Bernal, Diego Gustavo 199

H

Hernández-Leal, Emilcy 311
Herrera, Andrea 71
Herrera-Ruiz, Veronica 13, 25

J

Jiménez Benjumea, Juan Pablo 271
Joshi, Sandeep 1

L

la Rosa, Fernando De 128
Lalinde-Pulido, Juan 153
Larrea-Gomez, Manuela 297
Llanten, Miguel Angel Llanten 35
Londoño, Luisa F. 330
López Giraldo, Laura Isabel 271
López Parra, Javier Francisco 199
López, Valentina 45
Loyola, Oscar 141

M

Madrid Restrepo, David 396
Maradiago Calderón, Sara Jazmín 57
Martínez, Isabella 45
Martínez-Vargas, Juan David 13, 25, 297
Mateus, Rafael 330
Meza, Brayan Fabian 35
Múnera, Jonathan 115
Muñoz, Juan Diego Eraso 35

O
Obando, Germán   45
Ochoa, Ivan   297
Ojeda, Marta Cecilia Camacho   35
Olarte Vargas, Fabián Andrés   109
Ospina Herrera, Juan Pablo   318

P
Peña Palacio, Juan Alejandro   271
Peña, Alejandro   297
Pérez, Juan F.   45
Perez-Guerra, Jheison   13, 25
Pinta, Johan Manuel Alvarez   35

Q
Quijano, Juan Manuel   35

R
Rambaut, Daniel   45
Ramirez-Guerrero, Tomas   271, 297
Ramírez-Ramírez, Lilia Leticia   215
Rendón Vélez, Elizabeth   173
Rico-Bautista, Dewar   82, 188
Rivera, Juan Carlos   230
Rodriguez, Laura   128
Rosero Quenguan, Johan Mateo   109
Rozo-Bernal, Valentina   406
Rueda-Olarte, Andrea   109
Ruiz-Arenas, Santiago   173
Ruiz-Salguero, Oscar   153

S
Sanabria, Mateo   285
Sanchez, Froylan Jimenez   259
Sánchez, Mario   71
Sandoval, César   141
Santiago-Salazar, Javier Alfonso   82
Sepulveda-Vega, Laura Daniela   188
Serrano, Jairo E.   367
Suarez, Benjamín   141
Suárez-Sierra, Biviana Marcela   215, 230

T
Tabares Betancur, Marta Silvia   380
Tabares, Marta Silvia   115, 173, 259
Taimal, Carlos A.   230
Tavera Rodríguez, Jhon Walter   350
Torres-Madronero, Maria Constanza   13, 25
Trujillo, Nicolas Rodriguez   35

U
Uribe, María Sofía   330

V
Vallejo, Paola   173
Vanegas González, Diego Alejandro   396
Vasquez Escobar, Mariana   396
Vásquez Rendón, Andrés Felipe   109

Z
Zapata, David Ríos   173

Printed in the United States
by Baker & Taylor Publisher Services